MW01069527

Olmec Art and Archaeology

STUDIES IN THE HISTORY OF ART • 58 •

Center for Advanced Study in the Visual Arts

Symposium Papers XXXV

Olmec Art and Archaeology in Mesoamerica

Edited by John E. Clark and Mary E. Pye

National Gallery of Art, Washington

Distributed by Yale University Press,

New Haven and London

This publication was produced by the
National Gallery of Art, Washington

Managing Editor
CAROL LEHMAN ERON

Copy Editor
FRANCES KIANKA

Editorial Assistant
MARIAH SHAY

Designer
PATRICIA INGLIS

Assistant to the Program of Symposia,
Center for Advanced Study in the Visual Arts
KATHLEEN LANE

Distributed by Yale University Press,
New Haven and London

Abstracted and indexed in BHA (Bibliography of the History of Art) and Art Index

Proceedings of the symposium "Olmec Art and Archaeology in Mesoamerica: Social Complexity in the Formative Period," sponsored by the Arthur Vining Davis Foundations, Cotsen Management Corporation, and the Wenner-Gren Foundation for Anthropological Research. The symposium was held 19–21 September 1996 in Washington

The type is Trump Mediæval, composed by Duke & Company, Devon, Pennsylvania

The text paper is 80 pound LOE Dull

Printed by Schneidereith & Sons,
Baltimore, Maryland

ISSN 0091-7338
ISBN 0-300-08522-2

All Spanish translations by Mary E. Pye

Illustrations redrawn by Patrice Moerman:
page 156, fig. 1; page 321, fig. 24a

Frontispiece: Mural painting from Oxtotitlán cave, Guerrero, Mexico, depicting an Olmec king in avian costume on a monster throne. Drawing by Ayax Moreno, courtesy of New World Archaeological Foundation

Contents

Preface

In September 1996 the Center for Advanced Study in the Visual Arts sponsored a symposium devoted to "Olmec Art and Archaeology in Mesoamerica: Social Complexity in the Formative Period." Seventeen papers were delivered at the symposium, as well as a keynote lecture by Beatriz de la Fuente. The symposium emphasized recent research and emerging issues concerning Olmec art and archaeology, and was organized in conjunction with an exhibition of Olmec art at the National Gallery of Art, Washington, held from 30 June 1996 through 20 October 1996. The Center is grateful to John E. Clark and Mary E. Pye for serving as co-editors of this volume. We also wish to thank Mary Pye for developing the symposium, Joanne Pillsbury for providing consultation in its planning, and Barbara L. Stark, David C. Grove, Rebecca González-Lauck, and Ann Cyphers for moderating sessions. Ann Cyphers and Rebecca González-Lauck presented papers at the symposium, but unfortunately were not able to prepare them for publication in this volume. The gathering in Washington was made possible through the generosity of the Arthur Vining Davis Foundations, Cotsen Management Corporation, and the Wenner-Gren Foundation for Anthropological Research.

This volume is number thirty-five in the symposium series within Studies in the History of Art. The series is designed to document scholarly meetings sponsored under the auspices of the Center for Advanced Study, and it is intended to stimulate further research and scholarly debate. A summary of published and forthcoming titles may be found at the end of this volume. The Center for Advanced Study in the Visual Arts was founded in 1979, as part of the National Gallery of Art, to foster study of the history, theory, and criticism of art, architecture, and urbanism through programs of meetings, research, publication, and fellowships.

HENRY A. MILLON
Dean, Center for Advanced Study in the Visual Arts

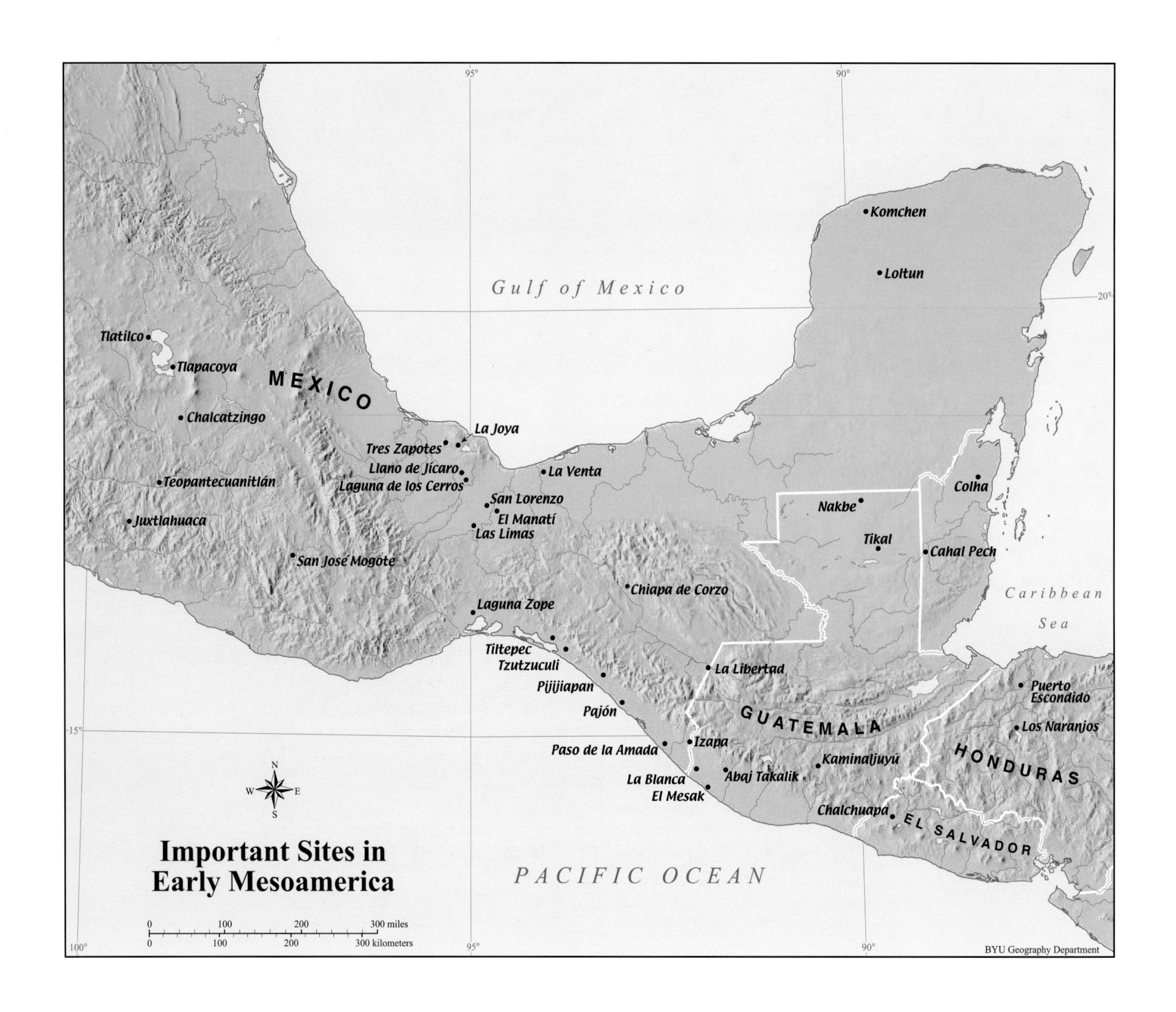
Gulf of Mexico
MEXICO
Tlatilco
Tlapacoya
Chalcatzingo
Teopantecuanitlán
Juxtlahuaca
San José Mogote
La Joya
Tres Zapotes
Llano de Jícaro
Laguna de los Cerros
La Venta
San Lorenzo
El Manatí
Las Limas
Laguna Zope
Chiapa de Corzo
Tiltepec
Tzutzuculi
Pijijiapan
Pajón
Paso de la Amada
Izapa
La Blanca
El Mesak
Abaj Takalik
Kaminaljuyú
Chalchuapa
La Libertad
GUATEMALA
HONDURAS
EL SALVADOR
Komchen
Loltun
Nakbe
Tikal
Colha
Cahal Pech
Puerto Escondido
Los Naranjos
Caribbean Sea
PACIFIC OCEAN
Important Sites in Early Mesoamerica
0 100 200 300 miles
0 100 200 300 kilometers
BYU Geography Department

MARY E. PYE

JOHN E. CLARK
Brigham Young University

Introducing Olmec Archaeology

The emphasis of *Olmec Art of Ancient Mexico,* which opened at the National Gallery of Art, Washington, in June 1996, was on the aesthetic qualities of Olmec art. In contrast to the exhibition, the symposium on which this volume is based focused on recent findings of Olmec settlement patterns, sites, and objects in their archaeological contexts, as well as the visual aspects and anthropological insights such contexts offer concerning the nature of the Olmecs and their neighbors in early Mesoamerica. The fifteen essays in this volume deal with a variety of media and data from sites throughout Mesoamerica. Hence, in this chapter we discuss several issues that we hope will clarify the technical language, theoretical assumptions, and historical background implicit in the following studies.

Mesoamerica is the guiding concept that organizes much of the archaeological research of Middle America. As a spatial concept, "Mesoamerica" is *not* synonymous or coterminous with "Middle America" as defined by geographers. Middle America includes all of Mexico and Central America and is a fixed geographic entity delimited by modern political boundaries. In contrast, Mesoamerica is a flexible anthropological entity whose definition for any given time period depends on (1) certain cultural practices considered Mesoamerican and (2) the contiguous territory occupied by peoples following these practices. This definition begs the question, of course, of just what is meant by "Mesoamerican practices"; these include traits such as the cultivation of chocolate, manufacture of paper, the rubber-ball game, human sacrifice, complex ritual calendars, beliefs in corn deities, and others (see Kirchoff 1943). Mesoamerica, at its greatest extent, just before the Spanish Conquest in the sixteenth century, included central and southern Mexico, Belize, Guatemala, and the western portions of present-day Honduras and El Salvador. Before the Spanish Conquest, peoples of this region shared cultural practices distinct from those of the peoples of the American Southwest, to the north, and from those of Central American peoples in eastern Honduras and El Salvador, Nicaragua, Costa Rica, and Panama, to the south. The best-known peoples of Mesoamerica are the Aztecs and the Maya. The practices and beliefs that constituted their civilizations are what we mean by the Mesoamerican way of life.

It is important to specify the extent of Mesoamerica during particular periods because its spatial boundaries fluctuated over time. As originally defined, Mesoamerica comprised the area occupied by peoples with a certain suite of shared cultural practices. Paul Kirchoff (1943) specified a list of some fifty traits nearly exclusive to Mesoamerica, and many more shared with cultures of adjacent regions, but for our purposes, these can be simplified and summarized as those traits characteristic of social stratification and a particular worldview. As such, Mesoamerica included many different

1. Map of Mesoamerica showing Formative period sites
Jeff Bird, Brigham Young University

Region	Phases (latest to earliest)
Basin of Mexico	Zacatenco; Tetelpan; Manatial; Ayotla; Nevada; Zohapilco
Chalcatzingo	Late Cantera; Early Cantera; Late Barranca; Middle Barranca; Early Barranca; Late Amate; Early Amate
Tehuacan Valley	Early Santa Maria; Late Ajalpan; Early Ajalpan; Purron; Abejas
Oaxaca Valley	Monte Albán Ia; Rosario; Guadalupe; San José; Tierras Largas; Espiridión; Martínez; Blanca
Tres Zapotes	Hueyapan; Tres Zapotes; Early Formative
San Lorenzo	Palangana; Nacaste; San Lorenzo; Chicharras; Bajio; Ojochi
La Venta	Late La Venta; Middle La Venta; Early La Venta; Bari
Chiapa de Corzo	Escalera (Chiapa III); Dili (Chiapa II); Cotorra (Chiapa I)
Pacific Coast SE	Escalón; Late Conchas; Early Conchas; Jocotal; Cuadros; Cherla; Ocos; Locona; Barra; ?; Chantuto B; Chantuto A
Kaminaljuyú	Providencia; Majadas; Las Charcas; Arévalo
Chalchuapa	Kal; Colos; Tok
Copán	Bosque; Uir; Gordon; Plata; Rayo
Belize Valley	Late Jenny Creek; Early Jenny Creek; Cunil
Uaxactún	Late Mamom; Early Mamom; Be

RADIOCARBON YEARS b.c.: 500, 600, 700, 800, 900, 1000, 1100, 1200, 1300, 1400, 1500, 1600, 1700, 1800, 1900, 2000, 2400, 2500, 3000, 3500, 4000

2. Formative chronological phases

ethnic and language groups that shared fundamental beliefs and practices.

Over the last five decades, the original distinction of Mesoamerica as a *cultural area* has become blurred, and most investigators now treat it, in practice, as if it were merely a geographic term specifying the region of the maximal extent of the Mesoamerican way of life. Textbooks perpetuate the fallacy of Mesoamerica as a fixed, geographic territory. The original distinction remains valuable, however, because there was a time, about 1500 B.C., when these cultural practices had not yet been established or disseminated. Along with the "where" of Mesoamerica, we need to consider the "when." How was the Mesoamerican way of life established? How did it evolve? And how did it spread over time?

At the time of the original emergence of the cultural practices of complex society that were to characterize Mesoamerica, the area that could be considered Mesoamerica was less than one-fifth its maximal extent. Not enough research has been conducted to reconstruct the precise limits of early Mesoamerica, but the distribution of the sites shown in figure 1 provides a valuable clue. This map shows the principal sites and regions mentioned in the following essays; all of the sites date to the Early and Middle Formative periods, or about 1800 to 500 B.C.

The basic temporal frame that we use in this volume is presented in figure 2. Mesoamericanists segment time into broad *periods*, such as "Classic" versus "Formative," or into subdivisions within each period, such as Early, Middle, and Late Formative. ("Formative" is also known as "Preclassic" and is used interchangeably with this term.) Most of the essays in this volume are concerned with either the Early Formative (a period from about 1800 to 900 B.C.) or the Middle Formative (about 900 to 500 B.C.). Even finer temporal distinctions within periods, called *phases,* are made by archaeologists. Unlike the period designations, which are pan-Mesoamerican, phases are restricted in space and refer to the regional configurations of archaeological assemblages, generally defined on the basis of changes in ceramic vessels and figurine styles. For example, in a particular region one might divide the Early Formative period into the red pottery phase and the white pottery phase based on an obvious change in artifact styles. The characteristics of the artifact assemblages for each phase are regionally specific and are consequently given regional names. The multiplication of labels is cumbersome but necessary. For the principal regions of Mesoamerica considered by the contributors to this volume, we have listed the various phases in figure 2.

How do archaeologists know how long each phase lasted? They rely on scientific dating methods, principally the analysis of carbon found in association with artifacts. Continuing with our example, imagine that the archaeologist who defined the red pottery phase and the white pottery phase found carbonized wood with many critical archaeological features and artifacts. These samples of carbon would then be submitted for dating. Physicists in the laboratory would then determine, by sophisticated techniques that measure radioactive decay of a heavy carbon isotope (carbon 14), the years of elapsed time since the carbon had been part of a living organism. The laboratory results are given in elapsed time from the base date of A.D. 1950 (the time the technique was established), along with an assessment of the reliability of the date and its margin of error. For example, a typical date could read 2950 ± 100 B.P.; this means that there is 67 percent probability that the carbon sample dates to 2950 years *before present* (B.P., or before 1950), plus or minus 100 years. In other words, there is a 67 percent likelihood that the correct date of the carbon sample falls between 3150 and 2850 B.P. and a 95 percent probability that it falls between 3250 and 2750 B.P. Archaeologists generally only worry about the date in its 67 percent probability range. Converting this radiocarbon date into real time requires that one subtract from it the 1950 base date to derive a calculation in familiar terms. Thus 2950 ± 100 B.P., minus the 1950 of our modern era, yields a date of 1000 ± 100 b.c., or 1100 to 900 b.c.

How reliable are the radiocarbon dates? As noted, an estimate of the reliability of each date is built into the date by the laboratory. There is quite a bit of play for any given date, but with enough dates archaeologists can construct reliable chronological sequences for the defined phases in their regions. Suppose that the archaeologists who identified the red and white pottery phases processed a hundred carbon samples and found that the average results indicated that red pottery dated from 1400 to 1200 b.c. and that white pottery dated between 1200 and 1000 b.c. They could then use these ranges as the probable time and length of the phases. Since all real chronology is regional, one of the vexing problems of archaeology is to correlate the phases of one region to another. Figure 2 is our best current assessment of how the regional phases of the Formative period probably line up.

There is one additional, potential difficulty that needs to be clarified. We have given the calculated date as b.c., meaning *before Christ,* in lower case. Detailed studies of the results of radiocarbon dates from wood of precisely known age (taken from very old trees and dated by counting the annual growth rings) show a predictable divergence between the real age and the calculated age. The older the sample, the greater the divergence of the estimated age from the true age; generally, laboratory results tend to *underestimate* the age of the oldest samples. But the same data that demonstrate the divergence also serve to establish a correction factor for converting analytical ages (b.c.) into real ages (B.C.). Archaeologists generally state whether they are dealing with analytical, "uncorrected" ages (that is, radiocarbon time), b.c., or the adjusted "corrected" ages, B.C. There are advantages and disadvantages for each way of listing time, and both conventions are used in the essays that follow. One additional convention is also used. All assessments of time are "more-or-less" measurements. A typical date for a phase could be "about 1000 to 800 B.C.," or c. 1000–800 B.C.

Olmec and Olmecs: A Problem of Terminology

The notion of what is *Olmec* is still a controversial matter. We discuss the issue at some length in our second essay in this book. The term *Olmec* is an archaeological convention used to label a particular art style (see next section) and the configuration of artifacts generally found in association with it.

The problem, and the reason for some substantive, continuing controversies, is that the term *Olmec* serves too many masters and is thus inherently ambiguous. Ambiguous usage has spawned some fundamental misunderstandings about who the Olmecs were and what they did. The label is used to designate a particular art style, as in the essay by Beatriz de la Fuente in this volume, or a specific group of people who lived in the Gulf lowlands (see the essays by Richard Diehl and Barbara Stark). The Olmec style enjoyed a huge popularity during the earliest years of Mesoamerica as a cultural region. But how can one talk about the movement and adoption of the Olmec art style without implying the movement of Olmec peoples? To avoid confusion, some scholars have suggested that the term *Olmec* be confined in usage to designate the peoples of the Heartland zone (Grove 1989; Flannery and Marcus 1994: 389–390). The implication here is that the term can serve as an ethnic and linguistic marker, much in the manner of terms for other peoples, such as *Maya* or *Zapotec.* We think that such a change in usage would be inappropriate. We suggest, instead, that the term be used to describe peoples who followed a particular suite of cultural practices that included certain forms of visual representations (see Clark and Pye, this volume).

We have phrased the question here in terms of *Olmecs* rather than the more traditional *Olmec.* This modification works well in Spanish translation where Olmec culture is given in the singular *(cultura olmeca),* but the peoples practicing this culture are described in the plural *(los Olmecas).* We also believe that the archaeological record already demonstrates convincingly that there were several contemporaneous Olmec polities or entities for most time periods, so we have opted for the plural to convey the idea of plurality rather than a single, monolithic entity.

Other terminology relates to what archaeologists now agree was the original homeland of the Olmecs: the Gulf lowlands of modern-day Tabasco and southern Veracruz, Mexico. This region is sometimes called the *Heartland* or *Metropolitan Zone,* with outside regions being the *Hinterland.* These terms include not only the geographical reference but also the sites and the people who lived there. The notion of an Olmec Heartland surrounded by a "Hinterland" of other Mesoamerican Formative cultures has been the source of much debate. In this volume, some contributors (for example, Barbara Stark and Stacey Symonds) refer to heartland and hinterland areas, but the terms are restricted in scale and refer to a single site or center and its surrounding population rather than the traditional usage for the whole zone. Richard Diehl suggests using the term *Olman* for the region traditionally designated *Heartland.* This usage would free up the terms *heartland* and *hinterland* for more parochial usage and also remove any stigma involved in designating all areas outside Olmec lands as "hinterland" areas.

Artifact Style

Museums used to be places where archaeology and art resided together. With the demise of large-scale excavation projects funded by the museums of Europe and the United States, and the increase in looting to satisfy art-market demands, archaeologists have tended to avoid museums. Not surprisingly, the study of Pre-Columbian art history has received decreasing attention from the broader field. Pre-Columbian scholars have traditionally been trained as social scientists rather than historians.

Perhaps this distinction is most apparent in attempts to define what *style* is. Art historians define style by referring to the attributes of objects in certain relationships. In this sense, style is used to structure concepts—to provide a framework for description and comparative analysis. But what goes into the making of such a framework? How are the particular defining attributes selected? Meyer Schapiro noted that while the construction of a concept of style is not always done in a logical manner, neither is it arbitrary. He pointed to specific morphological and technological features, but also to the qualitative aspects, noting that it is the strong correlation between the physical forms and their expression that defines a style (Schapiro 1953).

Defining the qualitative aspects of style has always been difficult for archaeologists schooled in a tradition that focuses on the object embedded in a discrete context. Archaeology is "social science," and the "science" aspect encourages quantitative characterization, while the "social" aspect includes a variety of concerns with past usage and meaning. The original meaning(s) of objects for the peoples who made and used them is just one of many variables, and it is often avoided because it cannot be determined precisely or easily. Archaeologist Gordon Ekholm (1959: 81) allowed that "the archaeologist must take cognizance of what we call works of art, but they must be analyzed, of course, in a scientific manner."

The intangible quality of discriminating among the important attributes of objects will perhaps remain the focus of art historians. However, Schapiro (1953: 287) himself highlighted style as "a vehicle of expression within the group, communicating and fixing certain values of religious, social, and moral life through the emotional suggestiveness of forms."[1] Clearly, he felt that context was an important aspect of style; as such, archaeology has much to offer art-historical interpretations. Unfortunately, contextual evidence is often of less interest to art museums. A member of the National Gallery of Art Olmec exhibition team expressed the notion that "the aesthetic qualities of the objects are sufficient to stand alone." Perhaps, but aesthetically beautiful objects abound in the world; context enriches the merely beautiful.

Olmec iconographic studies are also hindered by the lack of context for some objects, particularly jade items, but also some figurines and ceramic vessels. Lacking chronological and contextual evidence for these works, an emphasis on qualitative aspects is inevitable. At times this has led to pressures to assign the most aesthetically impressive objects an "Olmec" pedigree, even though these objects pertain to other archaeologically well-defined styles from the Formative era. Hence, in the National Gallery of Art exhibition *Olmec Art of Ancient Mexico* (1996), ceramic effigy and gourd vessels of the Central Mexican and Puebla regional styles were displayed as "Olmec." If identified outside the exhibition, these vessels would be referred to as Tlatilco, Tlapacoya, or Las Bocas—not Olmec.[2] In fact, ceramic animal effigies and gourd ceramics have a longer tradition along the Pacific Coast of Chiapas and Guatemala than they do in the Gulf Coast region (Clark and Gosser 1995; Lowe 1978).

It is not surprising then that when a single Olmec iconographic motif, such as the flame-eyebrow, is found on what is otherwise a non-Gulf Coast artifact, it is often considered to be an Olmec artifact. The Olmec style and the Gulf Coast Olmec archaeological culture are often conflated, part of the ambiguous definition of Olmec mentioned above. Such conflation obscures the complexity evident throughout the various regions of Mesoamerica and implies a primacy of these attributes to the Gulf Coast (Grove 1993). Some of these attributes may indeed turn out to be Gulf Coast in origin, and ongoing excavations both within and outside the Gulf Coast region will decide the matter, particularly through use of radiocarbon dating to determine where and when certain artifacts and iconography first appeared.

Several good summaries of Olmec research are readily available (de la Fuente 1984; Grove 1992, 1996; Pérez 1994; Sharer 1982) for those desiring more details than space allows here. Olmec artifacts have been known since the first gigantic head was discovered in 1867 at the site now known as Tres Zapotes (see the essay by Christopher Pool in this volume). It was not until the 1920s, however, that a group of artifacts, including jade axes and monolithic sculpture, were recognized as constituting a previously unknown art style. For the next two decades, scholars encountered more of these artifacts and ascribed them to the historic Olmecs who had once occupied the tropical lowlands of the Gulf Coast region. From time to time other possible homelands in the highlands of Mexico were also proposed.

Once it had been identified as a distinct art style, scholars began to find Olmec-style artifacts in the far corners of Mesoamerica. In the 1940s serious archaeological fieldwork at Olmec sites began in earnest, and many more sculptures, jades, and figurines were found in good archaeological contexts. This was still in the era before techniques of absolute dating, so most chronological assessments of sites were done on the basis of comparisons of artifact assemblages between sites and by relying on the principles of stratigraphy and superimposition borrowed from geology and paleontology (that is, the notion that lower strata, or layers, are older than upper layers, all other things being equal). At this time archaeologists had a fair idea of where the Olmecs had lived, but they did not know how old this culture was. Based on the superb quality of their art, some believed that the Olmecs must have lived after the Classic Maya, or after A.D. 900 (Thompson 1941). Others argued that the Olmecs must have preceded the Maya (Caso 1965; Covarrubias 1946).

Subsequent research after the 1950s recovered carbon samples from good contexts, particularly at the site of La Venta, Tabasco, and the antiquity of the Olmecs was established through radiocarbon dating (Drucker, Heizer, and Squier 1959; Berger, Graham, and Heizer 1967). The Olmecs clearly lived long before the Classic Maya. Given the antiquity of the art style, and its pervasiveness in Mesoamerica, Alfonso Caso (1942, 1965), a prominent archaeologist of the time, proposed that the Olmecs were the original *cultura madre* (mother culture) of all subsequent Mesoamerican civilizations. This claim started a controversy that is still very much alive today (see below). By the 1960s, the antiquity of Olmec culture and its spatial distribution had been established. What remained in doubt, and is still in doubt, are the processes that led to the development of this culture and the impact that the Olmecs had on other Mesoamerican peoples, issues addressed by many of the contributors to this volume. Much of current research focuses on processual issues and understanding the Olmec way of life.

Olmec Influence and Political Organization

The debate on the primacy of the Gulf Coast Olmec over their less well known neighbors in the Basin of Mexico (see the essay by Christine Niederberger in this volume), Oaxaca (Flannery 1976; Marcus and Flannery 1996), the Pacific Coast (Demarest 1989), and elsewhere has been intense and ongoing for fifteen years. The debate coalesced in 1983 at a seminar that focused on the issue of Olmec society. At that meeting, scholars came together with the goal of reaching a synthesis for understanding the nature of the Formative era in Mesoamerica (Sharer and Grove 1989; see Diehl, this volume).

Despite expectations, no synthesis was reached; instead, complete disagreement on the nature of Olmec influence led to the development of two positions: (1) the traditional idea that Olmecs transformed all other coeval groups by stimulating developments in social complexity (Coe 1989; Lowe 1989; Tolstoy 1989) and (2) the rival notion that Olmecs were participants, together with other groups, in a broad Mesoamerican community with regional interaction, particularly in the sharing of ideological symbols (Demarest 1989; Grove 1989; Marcus 1989). These counterproposals have split the field of Formative studies between those who believe in the primacy of Olmec society and its influence elsewhere and those who view early civilizational developments as resulting from the joint efforts of many societies of similar complexity, the Olmecs being but one among many.

Many studies have been done since that 1983 seminar. A conference in Mexico reviewed the status of Formative period research throughout Mesoamerica (Carmona Macias 1989). Long-term projects at both San Lorenzo and La Venta in the Gulf Coast have yielded new insights into Olmec society, as seen in the essay by Stacey Symonds in this volume (see also Cyphers 1996). Other sites of the Gulf Coast region are now under study, including work presented in this volume by Ponciano Ortiz and María del Carmen Rodríguez, Susan Gillespie, Philip Arnold, Christopher Pool, and María del Carmen Rodríguez and Ponciano Ortiz. Research continues in other Formative regions, as presented by Christine Niederberger, Richard Lesure, and in our essay. Formative period discussions now take place within a framework of more refined chronologies and increasing quantities and types of evidence.

Few issues have sparked as many scholarly squabbles and tedious, jargonistic distinctions as the question of whether the Olmecs had evolved to the level of a "civilization" or a "state." Of course, answers largely depend on how one defines these sociopolitical entities in the first place and what counts as evidence. As a technical term, "civilization" is inherently ambiguous. For some it means societies centered around "cities" or urban centers; for others it means class societies, or social stratification. Current archaeological discourse restricts "civilization" to a usage synonymous with "primitive state," such as the first civilizations that arose in Mesopotamia, Egypt, the Indus Valley, or China. Did the Olmecs evolve to a level of social complexity similar to early Pharaonic Egypt or Mesopotamia? Did they constitute a true civilization or state?

Some of the authors in this volume present evidence that the Olmecs were the first true civilization in Middle America, and perhaps in the New World. Others argue that the meager evidence better supports the idea that the Olmecs were not so complex. Rather, they argue, the Olmecs were governed by hereditary chiefs (similar to those who governed 19th-century Hawaii) who lacked the coercive force exercised by the rulers of states. In anthropological terms, these less complex entities are known as "chiefdoms." Although most scholars are currently reticent to debate the "chiefdom-versus-state" issue, all tend to have strong views on Olmec sociopolitical complexity and have written their contributions from one or the other of these perspectives. For some scholars the question remains open pending the compilation of more evidence, such as presented in this book.

The following fifteen contributions are organized according to three broad themes. Richard Diehl begins with a discussion of historiographic and thematic issues in Olmec studies, highlighting important areas of study that have been neglected in the past and that are now being addressed by investigators, as well as focusing on areas for future work. The essay by Barbara Stark sets the stage for the section on the archaeology of the Gulf Coast home of the Olmecs by reviewing what is known about the preceding Archaic stage.

Following these works are a series of essays on a variety of Formative period Olmec sites. Stacey Symonds begins with a characterization of the geography and settlement around the site of San Lorenzo. In two essays, Ponciano Ortiz and María del Carmen Rodríguez evaluate the sites of El Manatí and La Merced as "sacred spaces" and examine the artifacts recovered, including wood busts, jade celts, pseudo-celts, rubber balls, and Olmec sculpture, in terms of their possible ritual connections. Susan Gillespie presents an extensive review of the sculptural corpus recovered from the site of Laguna de los Cerros and surrounding areas. Philip Arnold discusses findings from his excavations in the Tuxtla Mountains, an area where the Olmecs obtained their stone for sculpture and grinding implements. Christopher Pool reviews findings from recent work at Tres Zapotes, the site where one of the earliest calendrical Long Count dates carved on a stela has been recovered.

The second section examines Olmec issues at Formative sites outside the Gulf Coast or Olman. Sites in the Basin of Mexico, in particular, Tlapacoya and Tlatilco, have long been known for Olmec-style ceramics and figurines recovered from excavations and looting there over the years. Drawing on her excavations at Tlapacoya and other research, Christine Niederberger reviews the regional importance of these sites and the contexts for the Olmec-style artifacts. Shifting to the Pacific Coast, Richard Lesure examines an Early Formative figurine sequence and chronicles the disappearance of a distinctive Pacific Coast tradition incorporating zoomorphic imagery that is replaced by one with stylized motifs, including fire-serpent and paw-wing motifs associated with Olmecs. In our essay, we highlight findings of sculpture, jades, and ceramics in the Pacific Coast region, demonstrating the complexity of Formative period interaction in Mesoamerica.

The final section treats specific topics in art, iconography, and meaning. Beatriz de la Fuente reviews themes and "schools" of Olmec sculpture. Esther Pasztory discusses the use of realism and portraiture in Olmec art within the broader framework of art history. Iconography is the theme of essays by David Grove and Karl Taube. Grove examines the relationship of serpents, caves, and mountains depicted on monuments from Chalcatzingo, a Formative site in Morelos. Taube focuses on the importance of maize iconography in Formative period Mesoamerica, with a comparative view of subsequent Maya and Aztec cultures and southwestern United States groups such as the Hopi and the Navajo. To varying degrees, and given the limitations of the data, the work of the authors presented here addresses issues of settlement patterns and artifacts in their archaeological contexts, while also considering the visual component of these archaeological remains and the importance of this aspect for understanding the prehistoric past.

NOTES

1. Schapiro was invited to write his seminal article, "Style," for a reader on cultural anthropology.

2. Specifically cats. 27 and 30–32 in The Art Museum 1995 and cats. 54, 57–58, and 61–62 in Benson and de la Fuente 1996. Grove (1996: 108–109) has also highlighted this issue with reference to the use of the site name "Las Bocas" and other names, such as "Tlatilco" and "Olmec," which are used "to provide an air of authenticity."

BIBLIOGRAPHY

The Art Museum

1995 *The Olmec World: Ritual and Rulership* [exh. cat., The Art Museum, Princeton University]. Princeton.

Benson, Elizabeth P., and Beatriz de la Fuente

1996 (Editors) *Olmec Art of Ancient Mexico* [exh. cat., National Gallery of Art]. Washington.

Berger, Rainer, John A. Graham, and Robert F. Heizer

1967 A Reconsideration of the Age of the La Venta Site. *Contributions of the University of California Archaeological Research Facility* 3: 1–24. Berkeley.

Carmona Macias, Martha

1989 (Editor) *El preclásico o formativo: Avances y perspectivas.* Mexico City.

Caso, Alfonso

1942 *Culturas mixtecas y zapotecas.* Mexico City.

1965 Existió un imperio olmeca? *Memoria de El Colegio Nacional* 5(3): 11–60. Mexico City.

Clark, John E., and Dennis Gosser

1995 Reinventing Mesoamerica's First Pottery. In *The Emergence of Pottery: Technology and Innovation in Ancient Society,* ed. William Barnett and John Hoopes, 209–221. Washington.

Coe, Michael D.

1989 The Olmec Heartland: Evolution of Ideology. In *Regional Perspectives on the Olmec,* ed. Robert Sharer and David Grove, 68–82. Cambridge.

Covarrubias, Miguel

1946 El arte olmeca o de La Venta. *Cuadernos Americanos,* año 5, 28(4): 153–179.

Cyphers, Ann C.

1996 Reconstructing Olmec Life at San Lorenzo. In *Olmec Art of Ancient Mexico,* ed. Elizabeth Benson and Beatriz de la Fuente, 61–71 [exh. cat., National Gallery of Art]. Washington.

de la Fuente, Beatriz

1984 *Los hombres de piedra: Escultura olmeca.* 2d ed. Mexico City.

Demarest, Arthur A.

1989 The Olmec and the Rise of Civilization in Eastern Mesoamerica. In *Regional Perspectives on the Olmec,* ed. Robert Sharer and David Grove, 303–344. Cambridge.

Drucker, Philip, Robert F. Heizer, and Robert J. Squier

1959 *Excavations at La Venta, Tabasco, 1955.* Bureau of American Ethnology Bulletin 170. Washington.

Ekholm, Gordon
1959 Art in Archaeology. In *Aspects of Primitive Art,* 70–88. New York.

Flannery, Kent V.
1976 (Editor) *The Early Mesoamerican Village.* Orlando, Fla.

Flannery, Kent V., and Joyce Marcus
1994 *Early Formative Pottery in the Valley of Oaxaca.* Memoirs of the Museum of Anthropology 27. University of Michigan, Ann Arbor.

Grove, David C.
1989 Olmec: What's in a Name? In *Regional Perspectives on the Olmec,* ed. Robert Sharer and David Grove, 8–14. Cambridge.

1992 The Olmec Legacy. *National Geographic Research and Exploration* 8: 148–165.

1993 "Olmec" Horizons in Formative Period Mesoamerica: Diffusion of Social Evolution? In *Latin American Horizons,* ed. Don Rice, 83–111. Washington.

1996 Archaeological Contexts outside of the Gulf Coast. In *Olmec Art of Ancient Mexico,* ed. Elizabeth Benson and Beatriz de la Fuente, 105–116 [exh. cat., National Gallery of Art]. Washington.

Kirchoff, Paul
1943 Mesoamerica. *Acta Americana* 1: 92–107.

Lowe, Gareth W.
1978 Eastern Mesoamerica. In *Chronologies of New World Archaeology,* ed. Robert Taylor and Clement Meighan, 331–393. New York.

1989 The Heartland Olmec: Evolution of Material Culture. In *Regional Perspectives on the Olmec,* ed. Robert Sharer and David Grove, 36–67. Cambridge.

Marcus, Joyce
1989 Zapotec Chiefdoms and the Nature of Formative Religion. In *Regional Perspectives on the Olmec,* ed. Robert Sharer and David Grove, 148–197. Cambridge.

Marcus, Joyce, and Kent V. Flannery
1996 *Zapotec Civilization: How Urban Society Evolved in Mexico's Oaxaca Valley.* London.

Pérez Suárez, Tomás
1994 Breve crónica de la arqueología olmeca. In *Los olmecas en Mesoamérica,* ed. John Clark, 21–30. Mexico City and Madrid.

Schapiro, Meyer
1953 Style. In *Anthropology Today,* ed. Alfred Kroeber, 287–290. Chicago.

Sharer, Robert J.
1982 In the Land of the Olmec. *Journal of Field Archaeology* 9: 253–267.

Sharer, Robert J., and David C. Grove
1989 (Editors) *Regional Perspectives on the Olmec.* Cambridge.

Thompson, J. Eric
1941 *Dating of Certain Inscriptions of Non-Maya Origins.* Washington.

Tolstoy, Paul
1989 Western Mesoamerica and the Olmec. In *Regional Perspectives on the Olmec,* ed. Robert Sharer and David Grove, 275–302. Cambridge.

RICHARD A. DIEHL
University of Alabama, Tuscaloosa

Olmec Archaeology after Regional Perspectives: *An Assessment of Recent Research*

During the sixty years that Olmec studies have existed as a distinct topic, scholars have come together to assess the "state of the art" in Olmec matters on numerous occasions. Three of these conferences led to publications that are classics in the Mesoamerican literature: the 1942 Sociedad Mexicana de Antropología's Round Table, "Mayas y Olmecas"; the 1967 Dumbarton Oaks "Conference on the Olmec" (Benson 1968); and the 1983 School of American Research (SAR) Advanced Seminar, "Regional Perspectives on the Olmec" (Sharer and Grove 1989). A volume of essays in honor of Matthew W. Stirling (Benson 1981) also had a comparable impact, although it did not result from an actual meeting of the contributors. With the exception of the 1942 conference, I have had the good fortune of participating in all of these conferences and thus have a personal appreciation for the role they have played in Olmec studies. Each conference came at a time when there was a backlog of new but only partially published archaeological field data and interpretations of Olmec art, and each left its mark on the field in at least three ways: disseminating new information long before final project publications became available, legitimizing new interpretations, and setting the agendas that guided future investigators.

The SAR seminar is a good case in point. Robert Sharer and David Grove organized the seminar as "a response to the need to reassess the long-standing problem concerned with the role of Gulf Coast Olmec civilization in the origins and evolution of complex societies throughout Pre-Columbian Mesoamerica (Mexico and upper Central America)." They were convinced that the "need for a fresh examination of this problem has become increasingly obvious in recent years due to the availability of an expanding corpus of data with a vital bearing on this issue, produced by a series of new archaeological investigations focused on the Mesoamerican Formative period" (Sharer and Grove 1989: xix).

The seminar and book truly embodied a regional perspective on the Olmecs; the new archaeological investigations that Sharer and Grove allude to occurred in Central America, Chiapas, Oaxaca, Morelos, and the Basin of Mexico, but not in the Olmec homeland. The reason for this apparent oversight is simple; no major fieldwork had been done in the Olmec region since Yale University's Rio Chiquito Project ended in 1968. The three chapters in *Regional Perspectives on the Olmec* devoted to the Gulf Coast included Gareth Lowe's (1989) synthesis of Olmec material culture, Michael Coe's (1989) parallel effort on ideology, and my assessment of what was known about Olmec culture and history (Diehl 1989).

Although *Regional Perspectives* was published in 1989, preliminary versions of chapters were circulated several years earlier, especially among younger archaeologists who were planning new archaeological field projects. While all scholars at the SAR seminar mentioned the need for future investigations, I addressed the

Matthew Stirling with Tres Zapotes Colossal Head 1, 1938
Richard Stewart/National Geographic Society

topic explicitly in the form of nineteen questions to be answered by future research (Diehl 1989: 17–32). These questions focused on six general topics: subsistence (questions 1–3, 5), population (4, 7), sociocultural development (6, 8–10), religion and art (11–13, 16), collapse (17), and relationships with other societies (14–15). Questions 18 (Why did Olmec culture arise where it did?) and 19 (What aspects of the Olmec cultural trajectory were unique?) were so broad as to be almost unanswerable.

Since I first posed these questions, additional archaeological field investigations have been carried out in the Olmec homeland (the region I term *Olman*), and numerous detailed analyses of Olmec art and iconography have appeared. Exhibitions of Olmec art at Princeton's Art Museum in 1995 and the National Gallery of Art in 1996 have brought together unprecedented assemblages of Olmec sculpture and portable art and have provided the venue for two substantial catalogues replete with some of the finest images of Olmec objects ever published (The Art Museum 1995; Benson and de la Fuente 1996). When the results of the conferences held in conjunction with these exhibitions are published in full, they will substantially alter current understandings of the Olmecs and their world. The papers published in this volume, along with the recent compilation of essays edited by John Clark (1994) and essays in the two Olmec exhibition catalogues, synthesize the results of current research. In the following discussion I evaluate the progress that has occurred in Olmec studies since the "Regional Perspectives" seminar. Have we really advanced in our knowledge and understanding of the Olmecs?

Questions of Subsistence

In *Regional Perspectives* I summarized what was known about Olmec subsistence in 1983 and highlighted two major controversies of the day: (1) Were the Olmecs exclusively swidden farmers, or did they employ more intensive techniques of cultivation as well? (2) How important were maize and manioc in Olmec subsistence? I concluded my review of the scanty information on both topics by noting that "we lack solid archaeological data on Olmec land-use patterns, crops, and settlement patterns" (Diehl 1989: 25). The only evidence I could find were the presence of mano and metate fragments, amorphous obsidian chips (then thought to have been used in manioc graters), a small sample of faunal remains at San Lorenzo, and a small Early/Middle Formative planting surface buried beneath volcanic ash in the Tuxtla Mountains. No plant remains had been identified; no palynological investigations had been published; and there were no comparable data from different sites or time periods within a single Olmec polity or at different major centers.

Today we have much more evidence bearing on Olmec subsistence and diet. This new information includes plant and animal remains from La Venta and nearby sites, studies of pollen, phytoliths, and macroremains from San Lorenzo, and more extensive exposure of planting surfaces in the Tuxtlas (Arnold, this volume; Cyphers 1994a, 1996; Rust 1992; Rust and Sharer 1988; Rust and Leyden 1994; Santley 1992). This information has confirmed some traditional ideas while failing to support others. The plant foods the Olmecs consumed turn out to be those always suspected: maize, beans, squash, and nuts of the wild corozo palm. Results of ongoing analyses of macro and micro botanical remains from San Lorenzo, La Venta, and El Manatí should eventually add other cultigens and wild plants to this list. The case for manioc remains unconfirmed (see Stark, this volume). Faunal remains from La Venta and San Lorenzo demonstrate the consumption of white-tailed deer, white-lipped peccary, and domestic dogs. Fish and crocodile bones, clam shells, shark teeth, and turtle remains substantiate earlier ideas about the importance of the region's rich aquatic resources in subsistence strategies (see Arnold, this volume). The distribution of faunal remains also sheds light on status differences within Olmec societies. William Rust (1992) suggests that deer and crocodiles were differentially consumed by elites living in the most important settlements.

While recent research documents what people ate, it fails to address the relative importance of maize or other foods in the diet, or changes in consumption patterns over time. Some investigators believe that maize initially functioned as a special festival food, perhaps brewed into a chicha-like beverage, and that it became a common staple only in later times (Clark and Blake 1994; Clark and Gosser 1995). Archaeologists studying the Mokaya culture in the Soconusco (see Clark and Pye, this volume) have proposed a similar reconstruction based on dietary information from studies of bone chemistry (Blake et al. 1992). Although the validity of the Soconusco interpretations has been challenged (Ambrose and Norr 1992), additional analyses of new samples, and reanalyses of the first samples, uphold the original claim (John Clark, personal communication, 1997). In any case, the human skeletal remains needed for isotope analysis to assess the importance of maize in the diet have not yet been recovered in Olman. Until they are, or until other detailed studies of ancient diets are undertaken, we will not be able to assess the relative importance of maize at any particular time or place in Olmec history (see Arnold, this volume).

The case for maize highlights a broader problem in studies of Olmec subsistence—the need for numerous, large data sets. We cannot really understand the dynamics of Olmec subsistence practices until systematic investigations are carried out at contemporaneous sites and sets of sites occupied at different times. Rust's (1992; Rust and Leyden 1994) investigations of three different levels of La Venta's settlement hierarchy are an initial step in this effort; I hope that other scholars will follow his example in future studies.

Questions of Population, Settlement, and Politics

In my SAR paper I considered data on population history, settlement patterns, and demography as essential foundations for investigating broader issues of sociopolitical development. Question 4 addressed demographic histories of Olman and how these might have affected the transition from egalitarian to complex societies. Question 7 concerned the nature of Olmec settlement patterns and the integration of major and minor communities. Together these questions focused on the nature of Olmec social and political organization, the evolution of complex societies in Olman, the relationships between major Olmec centers, and the demise of Olmec culture.

These questions give rise to others. How many Olmec centers existed, and what were their temporal, political, and social relationships? What factors determined the locations and life spans of Olmec communities of all types? What characteristics of Olmec social and political organization can be detected in the archaeological record? How did the status of individuals and groups relate to control over physical and human resources? All these questions relate to the debate over whether the Olmecs were organized at a chiefdom or state level.

In the SAR seminar I stressed that little progress would be made on the determination of social and political organization "until somebody excavates Olmec houses, burials and temple mounds with preserved superstructures, and conducts detailed settlement pattern surveys" (Diehl 1989: 29). In 1983 we knew virtually nothing about Olmec demography and settlement patterns. Ray Krotser's topographic map of San Lorenzo was the only Olmec site plan in existence (see Coe and Diehl 1980). Systematic regional surveys had not been carried out in Olman proper, although Edward Sisson's (1970, 1976) work in the Chontalpa had shown they were feasible. No villages or special-function sites were known, and no Olmec house had ever been excavated.

How different things are today! Paleoenvironmental research, topographic mapping projects, regional surveys, and excavations at special-purpose sites have yielded exciting new information on many aspects of Olmec settlement and demography (see González 1994, 1996; Cyphers 1994a, 1996; Symonds 1995; Lunagómez 1995; Rust and Leyden 1994; Cobean 1996; Gómez 1989, 1991). Paleoenvironmental studies in the Coatzacoalcos and Tonalá River basins indicate that while modern plant and animal assemblages were present four thousand years ago, river courses and the surrounding landscapes have changed appreciably (Jiménez Salas 1990; Cyphers 1996; Symonds, this volume). Such changes affected the amounts and distribution of first-order agricultural land and other resources, communication routes, the movement of large stones and commercial goods, and perhaps even the fates of centers such as San Lorenzo and La Venta.

Today we possess detailed topographic maps of La Venta, Tres Zapotes, Las Limas, and La Oaxaqueña (see, respectively, González 1988; Pool, this volume; Gómez 1991; Cobean 1996). We also know that Olmec period San Lorenzo extended far beyond the plateau summit (53 hectares) covered by Ray Krotser's map (Cyphers 1996; Symonds, this volume). These recent site maps provide information on the size and extent of major Olmec centers, as well as an idea of how they were organized in the latest phases of their occupation. The true potential of these maps will be realized, however, only when systematic surface collections and test-pit excavations provide chronological controls. Laguna de los Cerros and several other major sites in the Acayucan-Sayula region remain to be mapped. We also lack maps of minor centers, villages, and hamlets—settlement types that vastly outnumber the large Olmec "capitals." Regional surveys in the Tuxtlas (Santley 1992; Santley and Arnold 1996; Arnold, this volume), the middle Coatzacoalcos basin (Lunagómez 1995; Symonds, this volume), and the La Venta hinterland (Rust 1992) have recovered basic information on entire Olmec settlement systems and their major changes over centuries, but maps of individual sites are not yet available.

Finally, we are becoming aware of the range of Olmec activities and the organization of society through the study of specialized activity areas. These include the agricultural field surfaces in the Tuxtlas (Arnold, this volume; Santley 1992), iron-ore workshops and monument recarving stations at San Lorenzo (Cyphers 1996), the Llano del Jícaro monument workshop (Gillespie 1994, this volume), cult shrines at El Manatí and La Merced (Ortiz and Rodríguez 1989, 1994, this volume), and the El Azuzul monument tableau (Cyphers and Botas 1994). Surely this list will grow in the future as we learn more about the vast range of daily activities that made up Olmec life.

The greatest single gap in Olmec settlement studies is the lack of information on residences. Household archaeology has become an integral part of fieldwork everywhere in Mesoamerica except Olman, and it is lamentable that we can still say that no one has excavated a single Olmec house in its entirety, let alone a representative sample of houses. This is arguably the most critical priority for future investigations of the Olmecs. Until we have a large database on Olmec domestic life, we will not truly understand Olmec culture.

Questions of Religion, Ideology, and Art

What were the significant characteristics of Olmec religion, defined in the broadest and most inclusive sense? What is the history of the Olmec art style and how did it change through time? What were the functions and meanings of Olmec "art objects"? Why were green stones so highly valued, and how did this concept of value originate? Religion and ideology served to integrate Olmec culture into an identifiable whole and were the core of the Olmec legacy to later Mesoamerican civilizations. In the absence of writing, the material goods we define as "art" provide the best insights into this realm of Olmec life. When I wrote in 1983, Michael Coe and David Joralemon had published their pioneering studies of Olmec iconography and cosmology (Coe 1968, 1989; Joralemon 1971, 1976, 1981), and Peter Furst (1968, 1981) had written on the possible shamanic foundations of Olmec religion. However, very little was known about other aspects of religion that are preserved in the archaeological record. There was no information on Olmec temples, shrines, household rituals, burial practices, or the functions of the many ritual objects crafted in the Olmec style. Complex A at La Venta was the only ritual setting that had been carefully excavated and reported in detail.

Today the situation is quite different. Field studies have uncovered new monuments and objects, including some in their original-use context. The discovery of sculptural tableaus and sacred shrines where ritual activities were carried out, and confirmation of the hypothesis that stone drains and associated sculpture had ritual functions, all enrich our picture of Olmec religious life.

Near San Lorenzo, the four freestanding sculptures discovered at the secondary center of El Azuzul constitute a tableau and provide rich insights into Olmec beliefs and practices (see Cyphers 1992, 1994b, 1996; Cyphers and Botas 1994). They include two jaguars (of different sizes) and two virtually identical kneeling adult males of the same size, probably twins—images that surely depicted scenes and events later recorded in the sacred Maya book, the *Popul Vuh.* These parallels are so striking that few would deny the Olmec origins of some versions of that Quiche Maya creation epic of the hero twins. The four sculptures also provide strong support for those who maintain that Aztec and Postclassic Maya cosmologies are indeed appropriate models for reconstructing Olmec beliefs. Although I long questioned the wisdom of using these late sources to draw conclusions about Olmec beliefs, recent discoveries, including finds at El Manatí (Ortiz and Rodríguez, this volume) and recent iconographic studies by Karl Taube, Kent Reilly, and others (see Grove 1987a; Joralemon 1996; Reilly 1990, 1991, 1995; Schele 1995; Taube 1995, 1996) have convinced me of their substantial worth.

The sculptural arrangement at El Azuzul also proves that the Olmecs organized their sculpture into ritual displays or assemblages. Many of us have suspected this, but the tableau is the first concrete evidence of the practice. It is not too far-fetched to suggest that such assemblages were ephemeral and may have been rearranged periodically or even during a single ceremony. The El Azuzul arrangement also brings to mind La Venta's famous Offering 4 with its sixteen greenstone figurines and six celts arranged into a ritual scene. Surely these figurines and celts had been used many times in many different ways before coming to rest beneath the floors of Complex A. The same may well have been true of most large Olmec monuments.

At El Manatí and La Merced, wooden busts and greenstone celts placed in formal assemblages analogous to that at El Azuzul (Ortiz and Rodríguez 1989, 1994, this volume; Rodríguez and Ortiz, this volume) were recovered. A basic Olmec concept of sacred places or shrines as loci of repeated ritual activities is implied in these offerings. Also, Cyphers (1992, 1996) has demonstrated the ritual uses of stone drains and associated sculpture at San Lorenzo.

Studies of Olmec objects and art have increased in number, scope, and originality during the past decade. Traditional concerns with iconography, cosmology, the identification of deities, and shamanism remain the primary focus of such studies, but today they are buttressed with more systematic use of ethnographic and ethnohistoric analogies, including detailed comparisons with the rich contents of the *Popul Vuh.* Joralemon (1971, 1996) has refined his earlier reconstruction of the Olmec pantheon based on figures inscribed on the Lord of Las Limas sculpture (see Grove, this volume, fig. 3), whereas Taube's (1995, 1996, this volume) comprehensive studies of the maize and rain deities take our understanding of Olmec religion to new heights.

At the same time, Kent Reilly (1990, 1991, 1995) has presented several studies that interpret Olmec art and architecture in terms of concepts and events mentioned in the *Popul Vuh.* His "Art, Ritual, and Rulership in the Olmec World" (1995), an excellent synthesis of much of the recent thought on Olmec religion, proposes the existence of a "Middle Formative Ceremonial Complex." This complex consists of the archaeological evidence for Olmec ideology, ritual practices, and political structures interpreted through structural analysis of Olmec art and ethnohistoric information. According to Reilly, Olmec art is primarily shamanic in content, reflecting the actual basis of Olmec religion. The Olmec universe consisted of Earth, Sky, and Underworld realms centered on an *axis mundi,* or "world tree." Reilly argues that Olmec rulers served shamanic as well as political functions and that they were seen as representatives of the world tree, the cosmic pivot of the universe. The evidence he adduces includes cave murals in Oxtotitlán, Guerrero, sculpture—including La Venta's Altar 4 and San Martin Pajapan Monument 1—and incised celts, perforators, and other small objects. Many of Reilly's ideas initially struck me as rather far-fetched, but the more I think about them in light of the iconographic evidence, the more reasonable they seem. I particularly appreciate their clear formulation as hypotheses requiring further testing in light of future discoveries.

Olmec art is full of puzzling objects with unknown functions. Archaeologists have created a host of inventive, fanciful names for them: "torches," "knuckle-dusters," "yuguitos," "canoes," "spoons," "perforators," and "mirrors," among others. In some cases we have found examples of the actual objects depicted in Olmec art; other objects are known only from their depictions on sculpture and figurines. Possible uses of these objects have intrigued archaeologists from the very beginning of Olmec studies, and recently there have been numerous attempts to identify their functions. For example, "awls" and "perforators" now are almost universally accepted as bloodletters, and Grove (1987a) believes handheld "torches" and "knuckle-dusters" served the same function. John Carlson's (1981, 1993) exhaustive studies of parabolic iron-ore mirrors have shed considerable light on their manufacture and possible uses to generate smoke or even start fires from a distance. "Spoons" remain as enigmatic as ever. Several figurines and other human portrayals show spoons being worn as chest ornaments, but they have also been interpreted as snuffing tablets, representations of toads or birds, and even paint palettes (see Furst 1968, 1995; Justin Kerr, personal communication, 1994).

Today, as in the past, studies of Olmec religion and art draw heavily on looted or otherwise undocumented objects in museums and private collections. Some archaeologists and art historians believe that looted objects, lacking archaeological context, have no scientific value and that their study merely serves to raise their commercial value and encourages more looting. Others maintain that archaeologists have an obligation to avail themselves of every possible clue to the past, as problematical as their original discovery might be. I hold the latter view for reasons I will develop in a subsequent publication. In any case, a large corpus of Olmec objects lacking archaeological context will always exist, and scholars interested in Olmec art and iconography will continue to study them in the future. What we really need is less polemic and more well-documented objects found in secure archaeological contexts and associations. This should certainly be a field research priority in the future. At the same time, we need a central archive for gathering and housing all information on the entire known corpus of Olmec sculpture and objects. Beatriz de la Fuente's (1973, 1984) catalogues serve this purpose for large sculpture, but nothing like it yet exists for the hundreds of small objects known to exist. The basic data on these materials are scattered through the published literature, personal research notes, and memories that fade with the passage of time.

The Question of Collapse

How, why, and when did Olmec culture collapse, and what do we mean by the concept of collapse in this context? The term *collapse* may be too drastic for the end of Olmec culture (see Pool, this volume). Perhaps in my original SAR essay I should have substituted the phrase "the end of Olmec culture" for the more melodramatic "collapse" then in vogue. William Coe and Robert Stuckenwrath (1964: 34) once compared the "red clay cap" that covers Complex A at La Venta to "a giant red blanket pulled over the site just before the night of its oblivion." At times I consider this an apt image of what we know about the end of Olmec culture in general. The latter half of the first millennium B.C. is the most poorly documented phase of Olmec culture. What we do know is that La Venta attained its climax, San Lorenzo was abandoned for good, Tres Zapotes flourished, the Epi-Olmec writing system came into existence, and Olmec culture changed into something else. What we did not know, and still do not, is how Olmec culture came to an end, when it ended, or why.

The end of Olmec culture can be approached on at least three distinct levels: the decline and abandonment of individual communities, the depopulation of large regions, and/or the transformation of Olmec culture into something we are now calling Epi-Olmec culture. Ongoing investigations at La Venta, San Lorenzo, Tres Zapotes, La Oaxaqueña, and La Joya should ultimately shed light on the histories of those communities. While several authors have speculated about the relationships between late Olmec cultures and their contemporaries in the Soconusco and the Maya Lowlands (see Clark and Pye, this volume), the transformation of Olmec into Epi-Olmec has never been investigated systematically. This would seem to be an especially apt topic for collaborative studies by field archaeologists and students of Olmec art.

Questions of Intersocietal Interaction

What kinds of contacts did Olmec groups maintain with other Mesoamerican societies, and how did these change through time? What roles did external exchange play in the emergence and maintenance of Olmec elites? These questions were the primary concern of the 1983 SAR conference and edited proceedings, as suggested by the title *Regional Perspectives.* I included them on my list because I knew there were many gaps in what we knew about Olmec relationships with the rest of Mesoamerica. Since the seminar, archaeologists have completed considerable research on Formative sites in virtually every region of Mesoamerica. While some of these investigations have directly addressed the issue of Olmec contacts, most have emphasized (correctly, I believe) the understanding of local situations and circumstances. Regions in which there have been major new field projects include the Mazatán region of the Soconusco, adjacent portions of the Chiapas-Guatemalan Pacific coastal plain, Guerrero, especially in and around Teopantecuanitlan, and the Maya Lowlands. Field research slowed considerably in the Central Mexican highlands and the valley of Oaxaca, foci of considerable activity in the 1960s and 1970s, as archaeologists turned their efforts to analyses and publication preparation. Major final publications of the older projects have appeared in recent years, including Flannery and Marcus (1994), Marcus and Flannery (1996), and Kowalewski et al. (1989) on the valley of Oaxaca, Niederberger (1987, this volume) on the Basin of Mexico, and Grove (1984, 1987b) on Chalcatzingo. It is hoped that these publications will encourage the original investigators as well as their students and others to initiate another round of fieldwork in these regions.

Conclusion

What have we learned since the SAR seminar about the Olmec, and how did the conference affect the research agenda? One notable effect previously not discussed is that it formalized and propagated the basic idea that Olmec culture was not Mesoamerica's "mother culture" but rather a *primus inter pares* culture. This school of thought maintains that Formative period cultures outside Olman were the products of local evolutionary processes and were as complex and sophisticated as their "sister" culture, the Gulf Coast Olmec. Although I disagree with its basic premise (see Diehl and Coe 1995), these arguments for peer polities have been an important and positive contribution to continuing discussion. Many of my colleagues also remain unconvinced of the new view, at least to judge from the majority of writings on the topic in recent years (see Clark 1997).

Turning to recent research in Olman, much of it has addressed many questions I raised in 1983. Most research proposals I have seen in the past few years cite my paper as a starting point for the planned investigations. While I am gratified to have had some impact, any personal pleasure is tempered with a good dose of realism. The questions asked were timely in the grand scheme of normal science and certainly would have emerged as major concerns even had I not formulated them. Many people cite my paper but most often as a convenient justification in a grant proposal. Perhaps that is its primary value, as a way to justify funds for new research. If so, I am pleased to have achieved my original goal when I wrote the paper. It is worth emphasizing in this current assessment of recent progress that we are still far from addressing many of the original questions. We may never find all the answers, but that should not deter us from asking more and better questions.

BIBLIOGRAPHY

Ambrose, Stanley T., and Lynette Norr
1992 On Stable Isotopic Data and Prehistoric Subsistence in the Soconusco Region. *Current Anthropology* 33: 401–404.

The Art Museum
1995 *The Olmec World: Ritual and Rulership* [exh. cat., The Art Museum, Princeton University]. Princeton.

Benson, Elizabeth P.
1968 (Editor) *Dumbarton Oaks Conference on the Olmec.* Washington.

1981 *The Olmec and Their Neighbors.* Washington.

Benson, Elizabeth P., and Beatriz de la Fuente
1996 (Editors) *Olmec Art of Ancient Mexico* [exh. cat., National Gallery of Art]. Washington.

Blake, Michael, Brian Chisholm, John Clark, Barbara Voorhies, and Michael Love
1992 Prehistoric Subsistence in the Soconusco Region. *Current Anthropology* 33: 83–94.

Carlson, John
1981 The Olmec Concave Iron-Ore Mirrors: The Aesthetics of a Lithic Technology and the Lord of the Mirror. In *The Olmec and Their Neighbors,* ed. Elizabeth Benson, 117–147. Washington.

1993 The Jade Mirror: An Olmec Concave Jadeite Pendant. In *Precolumbian Jade: New Geological and Cultural Interpretations,* ed. Frederick Lange, 242–250. Salt Lake City.

Clark, John E.
1994 (Editor) *Los olmecas en Mesoamérica.* Mexico City and Madrid.

1997 The Arts of Government in Early Mesoamerica. *Annual Review of Anthropology* 26: 211–234.

Clark, John E., and Michael Blake
1994 The Power of Prestige: Competitive Generosity and the Emergence of Rank Societies in Lowland Mesoamerica. In *Factional Competition and Political Development in the New World,* ed. Elizabeth Brumfiel and John Fox, 17–30. Cambridge.

Clark, John E., and Dennis Gosser
1995 Reinventing Mesoamerica's First Pottery. In *The Emergence of Pottery: Technology and Innovation in Ancient Society,* ed. William Barnett and John Hoopes, 209–221. Washington.

Cobean, Robert
1996 La Oaxaqueña, Veracruz: Un centro olmeca menor en su contexto regional. In *Arqueología mesoamericana: Homenaje a William T. Sanders, Tomo II,*

ed. Alba Guadalupe Mastache, Jeffrey Parsons, Robert Santley, and Mari Serra Puche, 37–61. Mexico City.

Coe, Michael D.
1968 *America's First Civilization: Discovering the Olmec.* New York.

1989 The Olmec Heartland: Evolution of Ideology. In *Regional Perspectives on the Olmec,* ed. Robert Sharer and David Grove, 68–82. Cambridge.

Coe, Michael D., and Richard Diehl
1980 *In the Land of the Olmec,* 2 vols. Austin.

Coe, William, and Robert Stuckenwrath
1964 A Review of La Venta, Tabasco and Its Relevance to the Olmec Problem. *Kroeber Anthropological Papers* 31: 1–43. Berkeley.

Cyphers, Ann
1992 Escenas escultóricas olmecas. *Antropológicas,* new series, 6: 47–52.

1994a San Lorenzo Tenochtitlán. In *Los olmecas en Mesoamérica,* ed. John Clark, 43–68. Mexico City and Madrid.

1994b Three New Olmec Sculptures from Southern Veracruz. *Mexicon* 16: 30–32.

1996 Reconstructing Olmec Life at San Lorenzo. In *Olmec Art of Ancient Mexico,* ed. Elizabeth Benson and Beatriz de la Fuente, 61–71 [exh. cat., National Gallery of Art]. Washington.

Cyphers, Ann, and Fernando Botas
1994 An Olmec Feline Sculpture from El Azuzul, Southern Veracruz. *Proceedings of the American Philosophical Society* 138: 273–283. Philadelphia.

de la Fuente, Beatriz
1973 *Escultura monumental olmeca: Catálogo.* Mexico City.

1984 *Los hombres de piedra: Escultura olmeca,* 2d ed. Mexico City.

Diehl, Richard A.
1989 Olmec Archaeology: What We Know and What We Wish We Knew. In *Regional Perspectives on the Olmec,* ed. Robert Sharer and David Grove, 17–32. Cambridge.

Diehl, Richard A., and Michael D. Coe
1995 Olmec Archaeology. In *The Olmec World: Ritual and Rulership,* 11–26 [exh. cat., The Art Museum, Princeton University]. Princeton.

Flannery, Kent V., and Joyce Marcus
1994 *Early Formative Pottery in the Valley of Oaxaca.* Memoirs of the Museum of Anthropology 27. University of Michigan, Ann Arbor.

Furst, Peter
1968 The Olmec Were-Jaguar Motif in the Light of Ethnographic Reality. In *Dumbarton Oaks Conference on the Olmec,* ed. Elizabeth Benson, 143–178. Washington.

1981 Jaguar Baby or Toad Mother: A New Look at an Old Problem in Olmec Iconography. In *The Olmec and Their Neighbors,* ed. Elizabeth Benson, 149–162. Washington.

1995 Shamanism, Transformation, and Olmec Art. In *The Olmec World: Ritual and Rulership,* 69–81 [exh. cat., The Art Museum, Princeton University]. Princeton.

Gillespie, Susan
1994 Llano del Jícaro: An Olmec Monument Workshop. *Ancient Mesoamerica* 5: 223–242.

Gómez Rueda, Hernando
1989 Nuevas exploraciones en la región olmeca: Una aproximación a los patrones de asentamiento. In *El preclásico o formativo: Avances y perspectivas,* ed. Martha Carmona, 91–100. Mexico City.

1991 Las Limas, Veracruz, y otros asentamientos prehispánicos de la región olmeca. Licenciatura thesis in archaeology, Escuela Nacional de Antropología e Historia, Mexico City.

González Lauck, Rebecca
1988 Proyecto arqueológico La Venta. *Arqueología* 4: 121–165. Mexico City.

1994 La antigua ciudad olmeca en La Venta, Tabasco. In *Los olmecas en Mesoamérica,* ed. John Clark, 93–112. Mexico City and Madrid.

1996 La Venta: An Olmec Capital. In *Olmec Art of Ancient Mexico,* ed. Elizabeth Benson and Beatriz de la Fuente, 73–82 [exh. cat., National Gallery of Art]. Washington.

Grove, David C.
1984 *Chalcatzingo: Excavations on the Olmec Frontier.* London.

1987a "Torches," "Knuckle Dusters," and the Legitimization of Formative Period Rulerships. *Mexicon* 9: 60–65.

1987b (Editor) *Ancient Chalcatzingo.* Austin.

Jiménez Salas, Oscar
1990 Geomorfología de la región de La Venta, Tabasco: Un sistema fluvio-lagunar costero del Cuaternario. *Arqueología,* new series, 3: 5–16. Mexico City.

Joralemon, Peter David
1971 *A Study of Olmec Iconography.* Washington.

1976 The Olmec Dragon: A Study in Pre-Columbian Iconography. In *Origins of Religious Art and Iconography in*

Preclassic Mesoamerica, ed. Henry Nicholson, 27–71. Los Angeles.

1981 The Old Woman and the Child: Themes in the Iconography of Preclassic Mesoamerica. In *The Olmec and Their Neighbors,* ed. Elizabeth Benson, 163–180. Washington.

1996 In Search of the Olmec Cosmos: Reconstructing the World View of Mexico's First Civilization. In *Olmec Art of Ancient Mexico,* ed. Elizabeth Benson and Beatriz de la Fuente, 51–60 [exh. cat., National Gallery of Art]. Washington.

Kowalewski, Stephen, Gary Feinman, Laura Finstein, Richard Blanton, and Linda Nichols

1989 *Monte Albán's Hinterland, Part III: Prehispanic Settlement Patterns in Tlacolula, Etla, and Ocotlan, the Valley of Oaxaca, Mexico.* Memoirs of the Museum of Anthropology 23. University of Michigan, Ann Arbor.

Lowe, Gareth W.

1989 The Heartland Olmec: Evolution of Material Culture. In *Regional Perspectives on the Olmec,* ed. Robert Sharer and David Grove, 36–67. Cambridge.

Lunagómez, Roberto

1995 Patrones de asentamiento en el hinterland interior de San Lorenzo Tenochtitlán, Veracruz. Licenciatura thesis, Department of Anthropology, Universidad Veracruzana, Xalapa.

Marcus, Joyce, and Kent Flannery

1996 *Zapotec Civilization: How Urban Society Evolved in Mexico's Oaxaca Valley.* London.

Niederberger, Christine

1987 *Paléopaysages et archéologie pré-urbaine du Bassin de Mexico,* 2 vols. Études Mésoaméricaines 11. Centre d'Études Mexicaines et Centraméricaines, Mexico City.

Ortiz, Ponciano, and María del Carmen Rodríguez

1989 Proyecto Manatí 1989. *Arqueología,* 2d series, 1: 23–52. Mexico City.

1994 Los espacios sagrados olmecas: El Manatí, un caso especial. In *Los olmecas en Mesoamérica,* ed. John Clark, 69–92. Mexico City and Madrid.

Reilly, F. Kent, III

1990 Cosmos and Rulership: The Function of Olmec Style Symbols in Formative Period Mesoamerica. *Visible Language* 24: 12–37.

1991 Olmec Iconographic Influences on the Symbols of Maya Rulership. In *Sixth Palenque Round Table, 1986,* ed. Merle Greene Robertson and Virginia Fields, 151–166. Norman, Okla., and London.

1995 Art, Ritual and Rulership in the Olmec World. In *The Olmec World: Ritual and Rulership,* 27–46 [exh. cat., The Art Museum, Princeton University]. Princeton.

Rust, William, III

1992 New Ceremonial and Settlement Evidence at La Venta and Its Relation to Preclassic Maya Cultures. In *New Theories on the Ancient Maya,* ed. Elin Damien and Robert Sharer, 123–130. University Museum Monograph 77. University of Pennsylvania, Philadelphia.

Rust, William, III, and Barbara Leyden

1994 Evidence of Maize Use at Early and Middle Preclassic La Venta Olmec Sites. In *Corn and Culture in the Prehistoric New World,* ed. Sissel Johannessen and Christine Hastorf, 181–201. Boulder, Colo.

Rust, William, III, and Robert J. Sharer

1988 Olmec Settlement Data from La Venta, Tabasco. *Science* 242: 102–104.

Santley, Robert

1992 A Consideration of the Olmec Phenomenon in the Tuxtlas: Early Formative Subsistence Pattern, Land Use, and Refuse Disposal at Matacapan, Veracruz, Mexico. In *Gardens in Prehistory: The Archaeology of Settlement Agriculture in Greater Mesoamerica,* ed. Thomas Killion, 150–183. Tuscaloosa, Ala.

Santley, Robert, and Philip Arnold, III

1996 Prehispanic Settlement Patterns in the Tuxtla Mountains, Southern Veracruz, Mexico. *Journal of Field Archaeology* 23: 225–249.

Schele, Linda

1995 The Olmec Mountain and Tree of Creation in Mesoamerican Cosmology. In *The Olmec World: Ritual and Rulership,* 105–119 [exh. cat., The Art Museum, Princeton University]. Princeton.

Sharer, Robert J., and David C. Grove

1989 (Editors) *Regional Perspectives on the Olmec.* Cambridge.

Sisson, Edward

1970 Settlement Patterns and Land Use in the Northwestern Chontalpa, Tabasco, Mexico: A Progress Report. *Cerámica de la Cultura Maya* 6: 40–54. Philadelphia.

1976 Survey and Excavation in the Northwestern Chontalpa, Tabasco, Mexico. Ph.D. dissertation, Department of Anthropology, Harvard University, Cambridge, Mass.

Sociedad Mexicana de Antropología

1942 *Mayas y Olmecas: Segunda reunión de Mesa Redonda sobre problemas antropológicas de México y Centro América, Tuxtla Gutierrez, Chiapas.* Mexico City.

Symonds, Stacey
1995 Settlement Distribution and the Development of Cultural Complexity in the Lower Coatzacoalcos Drainage, Veracruz, Mexico: An Archaeological Survey at San Lorenzo Tenochtitlán. Ph.D. dissertation, Department of Anthropology, Vanderbilt University, Nashville.

Taube, Karl
1995 The Rainmakers: The Olmec and Their Contribution to Mesoamerican Belief and Ritual. In *The Olmec World: Ritual and Rulership,* 83–104 [exh. cat., The Art Museum, Princeton University]. Princeton.

1996 The Olmec Maize God: The Face of Corn in Formative Mesoamerica. *Res: Anthropology and Aesthetics* 29–30: 39–82.

BARBARA L. STARK
Arizona State University, Tempe

Framing the Gulf Olmecs

I use the word *framing* in the title in two distinct senses. For a temporal frame, I first examine processes leading up to the Gulf Olmecs during the Late Archaic period (3500–1800 B.C.). Later I consider the Late Preclassic (600–100 B.C.) and Terminal Preclassic (100 B.C.–A.D. 300) periods. During the Late Preclassic period, cultural traditions began to change from Gulf Olmec stylistic canons, and eventually we no longer designate these societies as *Olmec.* Processes before and after help us understand long-term change, although the Gulf Olmecs must be understood in their own right based on their archaeological record. The second "framework" I consider concerns the theoretical schemes that address how and why complex societies developed. Recent projects give us a chance to rethink some theoretical issues regarding the Gulf Olmecs. In part because of the severe limits to our knowledge of their societies, they have not been a major focus for explanations of social complexity in the archaeological literature, but this situation is changing.

The Bottom of the Frame: The Late Archaic Period

Recently, enough new information has been obtained about the Late Archaic period in the Mesoamerican lowlands, especially in the Gulf and Caribbean areas, so that we can discern a few patterns. The Late Archaic is a period when the lowlands show evidence of occupation and food production at several locations. Increased (or new) occupation in the Late Archaic period may signal population growth that proved important for lowland societies that mobilized public labor, like the Gulf Olmec.

There are reports of remains antedating the Late Archaic period in northern Veracruz (La Conchita [Wilkerson 1975b, 1981, 1988]) and in Belize (various sites [MacNeish and Nelken-Terner 1983; Zeitlin 1984]). For La Conchita we have few details (Stark and Arnold 1997), and for the Belizean sites the material is not as old as first claimed (Kelly 1993). One Clovis point from northern Belize attests to lowland Paleoindians, however (Hester et al. 1981 cited in Kelly 1993).

Most Archaic sites in the Mesoamerican lowlands date to the Late Archaic period. Known sites are few, but pollen evidence for both forest disturbance and cultigens suggests considerable human activity. Since Archaic sites are particularly hard to find in the lowlands because of postdepositional concealment (Stark and Arnold 1997; Voorhies and Kennett 1995), coring sequences with pollen and phytoliths currently play an unusually important role (Pearsall 1995; Piperno 1995; Piperno et al. 1991a, 1991b; Rue 1988). On the basis of these cores, the environmental impact of horticulture is noteworthy, even though food production was almost certainly part of a subsistence mix including wild products, sometimes on a seasonal basis. Shellfish, fish, turtles, and terrestrial animals were used to varying degrees

View of the San Lorenzo area showing tropic vegetation
Photograph: Courtesy of New World Archaeological Foundation

depending on local availability (for example, Voorhies 1976).

Late Archaic sites have been reported from the Gulf and Caribbean lowlands in northern Veracruz, south-central Veracruz, and Belize. These sites plus Matanchén (Mountjoy et al. 1972) and Puerto Marquéz in Guerrero (Brush 1965, 1969: 90) and Tlacuachero in Chiapas (Voorhies 1976) document human use of the Mesoamerican lowlands in the Late Archaic period. Locations on the Pacific side reveal shellfish collecting and use of other estuarine resources, likely on a seasonal basis. The uplifted Pacific Coast is more likely to yield such coastal sites, whereas Gulf lowland discoveries tend to be slightly inland, often in riverine environments and usually deeply buried.

In the Gulf lowlands, Annick Daneels encountered Late Archaic materials at the base of an excavation at Colonia Ejidal along the Cotaxtla River (Daneels and Pastrana 1988). Santa Luisa, near the mouth of the Tecolutla River in northern Veracruz, has produced the most detailed Late Archaic information from the Gulf area (Wilkerson 1972, 1975a, 1975b, 1981). A few other reports indicate Archaic sites, but available data are insufficient to warrant mentioning them here; some may be only aceramic (Stark 1981: 357; Stark and Arnold 1997).

In southern Veracruz a pollen core from Laguna Pompal in the Tuxtla Mountains suggests maize in the Late Archaic period, approximately 2300–1550 B.C. based on uncalibrated accelerator mass spectrometry (AMS) radiocarbon dates from the lowest strata (Goman 1992).[1] The *Zea mays* pollen is accompanied by other signs of forest decline not tied to any volcanic ash layer and, therefore, not ascribable to one of the periodic Tuxtla eruptions. No Archaic sites have been found in the Tuxtlas, however.

Pollen cores from the wetlands of northern Belize indicate maize and manioc before 3000 B.C. and some deforestation about 2500 B.C. (Jones 1994; Pohl et al. 1996). Late Archaic sites, mainly consisting of lithics, include Colha, Ladyville, Pulltrouser, and the Kelly site (Hester et al. 1996; Iceland and Hester 1996; Kelly 1993). Chert artifacts are the principal remains, with some sites producing only a few finds but others suggesting quarrying and knapping at a chert-rich formation (Hester et al. 1996; Iceland and Hester 1996; Kelly 1993).

In the Chiapas lowlands, John Clark (1994b: 140–162, 194–196) detected deeply buried Archaic occupation at the inland site of San Carlos in the Mazatán area. To the northwest, Barbara Voorhies (1996a, 1996b) reports preliminary data from an inland Archaic site called Vuelta Limón,[2] dating perhaps near the close of the Late Archaic period. Phytoliths at Vuelta Limón suggest some forest disturbance and probable cultigens. A pollen record adjacent to the Tlacuachero shell midden indicates forest disturbance by about 2000 B.C., in keeping with the inland data. Voorhies' analysis links her inland site to coastal shell middens left by Chantuto phase inhabitants who pursued a mobile lifeway following a seasonal round (Kennett and Voorhies 1996; Voorhies 1976).

Forest clearing and occasional pollen from cultivars point to food production, but the reasons for this effort are not yet clear. One possibility is that domesticates, especially as their economic value improved, helped reduce risks or resolve problems associated with wild resources. The paucity of concentrated wild carbohydrates in the lowlands may have been an incentive. To me, considerable forest clearance documented by cores in the Tuxtlas, northern Belize, and the Soconusco bespeaks more investment in cultigens, maize among others, than would be required solely for brewing and feasting using maize. Such social uses are the basis for an alternative idea about the early interest in maize cultivation in contrast to maize as a subsistence crop (Bender 1978; Blake, Clark, et al. 1992; Clark and Blake 1994; Hayden 1990, 1992). Brewing and feasting could be expected to have a special social context and to be occasional in contrast to daily subsistence.[3]

The pollen and phytolith records for maize and forest disturbance from Central and South America now antedate most Mesoamerican evidence, although James Schoenwetter (1974) argued from pollen that there was *Zea* cultivation between 8000 and 6000 B.C. in the Oaxaca valley.[4] Consequently, the antiquity and patterning of *Zea* cultivation and domestication in Mesoamerica are problematic because of the apparent dating gap between Latin American macrofossils and microfossils. Microfossils suggest earlier cultivation than do macrofossils, primarily on the basis of forest disturbance in sequences south of Mesoamerica.

So far, the Mesoamerican lowlands do not show evidence of much occupation or cultivation until the Late Archaic period, not long after revised AMS dates for Tehuacan maize (Long et al. 1989). This chronological pattern remains to be explained. Why was adoption of maize and food production (apparently) delayed in the Mesoamerican lowlands compared to other locations to the south in tropical America? Did improvements in the productivity of crop(s) or demographic or environmental changes play a role in making food production a more desirable strategy by the Late Archaic period compared to earlier times?

There are advantages of food production in many lowland areas compared to the highlands: bountiful rainfall and renewable, fertile soils. However, food producers must cut and burn tropical vegetation. Crop productivity would have to be sufficient to warrant the effort. Wild resources, in contrast, are more problematic in the lowlands than in many highland valleys. Despite low rainfall, the latter are relatively well endowed with seasonal wild food plants, such as mesquite and grasses. Concentrated, wild, storable carbohydrates are not plentiful in lowland environments, and tropical forests are not immune to annual swings in resource availability that would affect foragers (Piperno 1989: 538–544). Apart from riverine and especially estuarine aquatic resources, lowland forested environments pose limitations in accessible economic fauna, as well (Stahl 1995). Blake, Clark, et al.'s (1992) view of the lowlands as a "zone of plenty" requires qualification. Except for bountiful aquatic habitats, the lowlands are good for farmers or farmers-collectors, not so good for foragers. Blake, Clark, et al.'s (1992) region of study on the Chiapas coastal plain is particularly rich in seasonal floodlands, especially in the form of old river channels (Clark 1994b: 43–88), but other regions differ and require their own detailed assessment.

Resource limitations may account for the scanty indications of Mesoamerican lowland populations prior to the Late Archaic period when some food production is indicated by pollen and phytoliths. Similarly, the rapid incorporation of some food production could be a response to resource limitations and insecurities, as Piperno (1989) notes.[5] The estuarine, coastal, and riverine associations of Late Archaic sites likely represent populations gravitating to concentrated, accessible aquatic fauna. The proximity of subsequent lowland Preclassic sites to aquatic resources (for example, Clark and Blake 1994: 22; Coe and Diehl 1980, vol. 1; Rust and Sharer 1988; Symonds and Lunagómez 1997) suggests that aquatic fauna continued to be important after sedentary occupation developed. The few faunal analyses bear this out (Blake, Clark, et al. 1992; Clark 1994b: 239–242; Wing 1980).

One implication of growing Late Archaic evidence is a process of population increase in the lowlands. If this process continued, it could have yielded sufficient population to make a more aggregated, "labor exuberant" social form possible, that known for the Gulf Olmecs. Some of this increase may have been due to local growth, but some may reflect a gradual relocation toward the lowlands by some families (or larger groups) attracted to its agricultural potential. A trickling relocation process makes some sense when we recall that Archaic settlement patterns included considerable seasonal mobility until relatively late in some highland valleys (Flannery 1968, 1973; MacNeish 1964).

Another possibility to account for an increasing agricultural population is a shift from hunting and gathering to food production by lowlanders who have remained virtually invisible to us archaeologically because they left ephemeral seasonal forager sites, contrasting with longer-lived residential camps of collectors who also grew some crops (Kennett and Voorhies 1996). In addition to the problem of ephemeral sites, our record for lowland hunter-gatherers prior to c. 6000 B.C. is likely partially obscured by post-Pleistocene sea-level rise affecting coastal and estuarine locations (Kennett and Voorhies 1996: 690).

Another incentive for local population increase has been postulated: the actions and attractions of early leaders engaged in public rituals, feasts, or other social activities. John Clark and Michael Blake (1994: 22–24) argue that competitive early leaders at some locations, such as Mazatán, Chiapas, actively attracted a client population in the Early Preclassic period; they postulate that this process leading to population growth was under way in the Late Archaic period. The argument for the Late Archaic period depends on an interpretation of the feasting functions of the first ceramic containers as substitutes for earlier gourd vessels that have not been preserved. Elsewhere in the lowlands, ceramics contemporaneous with those of the Barra phase (1700–1500 B.C.) either remain unknown or are not as elaborate as those in Mazatán. On the basis of current evidence, lowland agricultural potential is a more widespread factor that may have attracted population than are the actions of aggrandizing leaders during the Late Archaic period.

In sum, Late Archaic remains call attention to the attractions of different regions for early farmers, with the lowlands advantaged. In particular, the southern Gulf lowlands have an edge that may help us understand the later ability of Olmec centers to attract and maintain a noteworthy regional population. Climatological and ethnographic evidence suggests that southern Veracruz has a greater potential than the rest of the state for multiple crops because of the greater frequency of winter rains from *nortes* (Coe 1974; García 1970: 67–125; Stark et al. 1998). Michael Coe (1974) notes the possibility of up to four crops a year, while the Mazatán area, for example, can yield up to three (Clark 1994b: 43–88). Other Gulf assets are the fluvial, estuarine, and alluvial resources to which lowland populations were oriented. The river network of the Coatzacoalcos drainage undoubtedly assisted transportation and communication (Cyphers 1994: 48). The southern Gulf plain is considerably wider than the Pacific coastal plain, affording a bigger "niche." A recent characterization of the southern Gulf lowlands as "comparatively marginal" (Blanton et al. 1996: 8) is an example of how poorly aware the profession has remained about the environmental context of the Gulf Olmecs, despite Coe and Diehl's (1980) efforts.

Nevertheless, an agricultural "land of plenty" idea is insufficient to account for the Gulf Olmecs because early changes pointing to more social differentiation were widespread in Mesoamerica and were not confined to the Gulf Olmec area or to the lowlands. The southern Gulf lowlands were, however, particularly well suited to maintain a large local population and to provide subsistence surpluses on a regular basis. Environmental assets undoubtedly had a positive effect on the long-term successes of Gulf Olmec centers.

Both the Late Archaic and Early Preclassic periods indicate relatively open societies with extensive contacts that may imply accommodation of some mobility or relocation by families, which is crucial for understanding both the increased Late Archaic evidence and the ability of early centers to attract a client population. H. Martin Wobst (1974) has pointed out the role of such contacts in social reproduction for small groups, and many researchers have noted the utility of this kind of social environment in resolving disputes and adjusting to resource imbalances. Late Archaic and Early Preclassic settlements are generally neither large nor dense on the landscape, as I discuss below (see Clark 1991; Hirth 1987: 348–352; Kowalewski et al. 1989: 55–68, 449–494; Sanders et al. 1979: 94–96; Symonds and Lunagómez 1997). Despite the evidence of population growth starting in the Late Archaic period, populations remained generally low except near exceptionally successful centers (Clark and Blake 1994; Feinman 1991), suggesting that political and social factors promoted greater local population concentration (for example, Marcus and Flannery 1996: 88, 106–110).

Trade in obsidian and the spread of cultivars suggest open societies during the Late Archaic period (Zeitlin and Zeitlin 1996). The widely shared ceramic styles in the Early Preclassic period (Clark 1991), traded pottery (Flannery and Marcus 1994: 164–165, 254, 373–384), and the extent of Olmec-style motifs on pottery (Stark 1997b) indicate societies open to nonantagonistic contacts with neighbors. Obsidian procurement at San Lorenzo is striking in the diversity of sources represented (Cobean et al. 1971, 1991). Access to obsidian in nonproducing regions and, in Oaxaca, the diversity of initial procurement patterns among households are other indications of rather fluid, open social networks (Feinman 1991).

If the idea of a relatively open social environment is accepted, then early centers faced prevailing conditions different from most of later prehistory. Neighboring groups did not hem in communities or polities to the same extent. There were many options for dissatisfied or restless community members, and undoubtedly many people did shift their locale. Perhaps the "safety valve" for dissidents was one advantage for early centers that later polities did not enjoy to the same extent (Michael Ohnersorgen, personal communication, 1997). In any case, a series of Gulf Olmec centers thrived for considerable periods, embarking on construction programs of various sorts that demanded public labor, erecting monumental buildings with imported stone, and investing in highly skilled carving of variously sized sculpture, probably by attached specialists, that is, craftspersons supported or commissioned by advantaged patrons (Brumfiel and Earle 1987: 5–6). Exotic materials were obtained from diverse supply zones. Gulf Olmec society overcame the inertia of the "domestic mode of production" (Sahlins 1972) without the social and environmental circumscription that help explain the instability, warfare, and hierarchy of later, especially historic chiefdoms. In these open conditions, what social processes could yield a San Lorenzo and, later, La Venta? This question requires consideration of theoretical models for social change.

A Theoretical Framework for the Gulf Olmecs

This is not the place to attempt a comprehensive review of theoretical models in relation to development of the Gulf Olmecs. Instead, I briefly assess the history of ideas and link recent positions to the Gulf Olmecs. With respect to the Gulf Olmecs, we know so little about their earliest history that evaluation of explanations of what they did should not yet be accorded much weight.

Recently, social variability and competition have become a more prominent theoretical focus in archaeology, both on an intra- and intercommunity basis. In the context of a discussion about political factors within societies, I note below that the Gulf Olmecs created both nonpersonalized communal public monuments and individualizing ones, perhaps one clue to the unusual success of their centers in attracting and maintaining regional populations. Next I sort out some issues surrounding explanations of the Gulf Olmecs that rely on exogenous factors, as opposed to those endogenous to early societies. While none of the exogenous factors is a major "engine" that could be expected to have driven Olmec social change by itself—and some are irrelevant—others may have played a contributing role. Finally, I link the widespread Olmec style and long-distance exchange to a model developed by Mary Helms (1993) that explains the logic of long-distance relationships that involve sacred or prestige goods. It is a logic independent of communal versus individualizing social emphases, and it is partially causal because control of long-distance exchange and scarce valuables can help declare and reinforce the power of individuals (or groups). Helms' perspective also provides insights about the role of the Gulf Olmecs in early Mesoamerica.

Ideas about Complex Society

Because many changes in social institutions and practice are folded into our notion of "the origins of complex society," this development is unlikely to be the result of any single cause or of a universal, yet empirically specific model. Moreover, we know that early complex societies vary among themselves and can be found in highly contrastive environments. "Complex society" is too big an umbrella concept to be more than notionally useful.

One classic approach to breaking down social complexity looked for a developmental pattern. Using contemporary or historical societies, the neoevolutionists defined broad social "types" differing in complexity (Fried 1967; Sahlins 1963; Service 1962). Although enormously influential, the types have proven slippery, often variable to such an extent that scholars have become dissatisfied with them. Persistent problems in accounting for change along the continuum in which the types were arrayed (or for change that was more abrupt and "steplike") has led to further exasperation (for example, Yoffee 1993) and a denial by some scholars that a developmental process was captured by the sequence of classic social types (Sanders and Webster 1978: 282).

Nevertheless, relevant analogues for the Gulf Olmecs have been sought primarily among "chiefdoms," with the expectation that someday we would detect a record of change leading to this kind of social form. Interestingly, no historic chiefdom matches the degree of mobilization of public labor and specialist skills that are indicated by Gulf Olmec "art" and architecture. To me, this divergence is a sign of the distinctive social environment in which Gulf Olmec society operated and a warning that we cannot expect modern analogues to replicate their society very closely.

Growing centralization, differentiation, and hierarchy are terms often used to describe change toward social complexity, but not ones that necessarily instruct us about whether political, economic, or religious/ritual domains undergo key changes. Several researchers have argued, correctly I think, for decomposing social life into domains or variables so that we are better able to register trajectories of change (Blanton et al. 1993: 13–18; Feinman and Neitzel 1984; McGuire 1983; Yoffee 1993). With attention to variability, we should be prepared for differential impacts of exogenous and endogenous factors on societies over time. However, this kind of approach demands a range of data about Gulf Olmec society currently lacking (Diehl 1989; Grove 1997).

Attempts to grapple empirically with variability in complex society demand more attention to modest expressions of social inequality that might help us understand origins. Social inequality has been shown to be relatively widespread (Cashdan 1980; Price and Brown 1985), and the problem has been reconceptualized in terms of the origins of institutionalized social inequality, where transmission of status is heavily influenced by ascribed position. It is particularly the "early innings" of social change that remain unknown for the Gulf Olmecs. At present, we have more fine-grained information from coastal Chiapas and the valley of Oaxaca than from the Gulf lowlands.

Along with a closer empirical look at social inequality, another scholarly change is a stronger emphasis on social dynamics. Among other factors, discoveries in the archaeological record have led to a shift from a focus on "a" or "the" society that undergoes crucial change to a recognition that early complex societies everywhere operated in a regional and interregional social context (see Demarest 1989; Freidel 1978; Renfrew 1986). The social environment of early complex societies had been overlooked in the notion of the "pristine state." An emphasis on the pristine state as a solitary organizational breakthrough was symptomatic of an overreliance on the reality of the classic types and of a deemphasis on variability.

Once plurality is accommodated conceptually, social divisions and competitions, including those among communities, are potentially important, and the political domain can be seen as less a direct consequence of technoeconomic factors and more an independent factor in its own right. Marxist social theory always emphasized change produced by social conflict among classes (see Brumfiel [1992] for a recent summary), and modifications of this theory for classless societies include attention to competition among similar social groups (for example, Brumfiel 1994: 8–9). The so-called "political" approaches (Brumfiel and Earle 1987) that rest on divisions and competition within and among societies are currently the most promising for understanding Gulf Olmec remains.

Currently, one line of reasoning looks for aggrandizing individuals in the earliest steps toward greater social complexity, with an expectation that individual differences and ambitions will lead some people to seek social recognition and power (Bender 1978; Clark and Blake 1994; Hayden 1990, 1992). Individual aggrandizement has a conceptual advantage in its potential to generate genealogical ranking and chiefs (or apical rulers), for which we have considerable ethnohistoric and archaeological evidence, including the Gulf Olmecs.

Less well understood theoretically is a communal (no doubt partly genealogical) emphasis in which cross-cutting institutions mobilize labor and resources without obvious dependence on "aggrandizers" (Blanton et al. 1996; Renfrew 1974). Ritual and mortuary programs are among possible communal foci. By communal institutions I mean not just those that represent the entire community or polity but also those that embody some substantial portion of it, that is, uniting multiple households. These institutions might be outgrowths of ritually focused corporate groups, for example, such as those evident ethnographically and ethnohistorically in the United States in pueblo communities of the Southwest (Adler 1989; Kroeber 1917: 47–50, 183–187), or groups united in their use of mortuary facilities, such as in the American Midwest (Charles 1995; Charles and Buikstra 1983). The early Peruvian record provides some of the most detailed evidence in support of an early communal emphasis. Monumental architecture, ritual, and some long-distance trade are evident in the absence of evidence for hierarchical status differentiation among individuals in the Late Preceramic period in coastal Peru (Burger 1992: 27–55).

Sedentarization of food producers and localization of territories (through population growth and infilling) are examples of factors that might encourage communal institutions that maintain cohesiveness of a localized group. With lessened mobility, relocation as a solution to disputes is reduced by fixed agrarian assets. Social mechanisms that stress cohesive principles can improve cooperation and resolution of disagreements. Institutions that regularize intercommunity relations may become important in moving distant resources to localized populations, in contrast to periods when mobile people moved closer to distant resources or to intermediary groups for exchange (Stark 1981). Below I discuss environmental risks that also may have contributed to communal institutions among the Gulf Olmec.

Gulf Olmec evidence provides clues about both individualizing and communal emphases. Gulf Olmec carvings stressed important individuals, as we can see from the Manatí busts (Ortiz and Rodríguez 1994, this volume; Rodríguez and Ortiz 1997), the colossal heads, and some thrones ("altars"). David Grove and Susan Gillespie (1984) referred to this emphasis as the "cult of the ruler." At San Lorenzo, Ann Cyphers' (1994: 49; 1997) evidence of a large residential structure with partial masonry construction and architectural elaboration provides important evidence of an advantaged household. Later at La Venta, the Mound A-2 stone column tomb, the nearby sandstone coffer/sarcophagus, and a sandstone cist/probable tomb show an exaggerated investment in the burial treatment of high-ranking individuals (Drucker 1952: 22–28; Wedel 1952: 67–73). We cannot yet specify whether shamanistic leaders, senior kinspeople, or headman institutions were the nucleus around which this individualizing focus advanced. Whatever the origins, Gulf Olmec leaders eventually enjoyed a striking differential from commoners in architecture, commemorative monuments, burial, and access to exotic, likely sacred objects.

Other Olmec remains are neither portraiture like the colossal heads nor celebrations of leaders, such as thrones. In the Early Preclassic period, carvings of felines or other animals at San Lorenzo (and nearby sites) and celt offerings at Manatí may show mythicoreligious themes. In the Middle Preclassic period, buried pavements and celt offerings at La Venta likewise do not represent individuals (or not obviously so). Of course, great public endeavors at Gulf Olmec centers may have had known patrons who gained acclaim for their mobilization of ritual efforts. Without more "household archaeology" at Gulf Olmec sites, we cannot trace social patterns that might represent communal institutions.

By way of comparison, Paso de la Amada, Chiapas, has yielded a ballcourt that may represent communal ritual, with some social differentiation in regard to domestic platform size and community sizes (Blake 1991; Clark 1991; Clark and Blake 1994). However, Richard Lesure (1996) found scant evidence between 1400 and 1000 B.C. for differentials in access to exotic items or involvement in feasting among households on platform mounds compared to those that lacked platforms. To date the only iconographic evidence pointing to an early individualizing emphasis in that region are male figurines interpreted by Clark (1994a: 36–40) as possibly depicting leaders or shamans during the Locona and Ocos phases (1500–1350 B.C. and 1350–1200 B.C., respectively). Mazatán burials are too few to reveal much in the way of patterning, although one child was interred with an imported mica mirror in the Locona phase (Clark 1994b: 406) and could indicate ascribed status.

In early valley of Oaxaca phases (Tierras Largas, 1400–1150 B.C., and San José, 1150–850 B.C.), the large village of San José Mogote gradually played a greater role in interregional exchange, and a few households gained prominence in producing ritual objects and centrally procuring obsidian. San José Mogote grew in size and became a center for several surrounding villages (Marcus and Flannery 1996: 76–110). A sequence of early ritual buildings does not display any individualizing traits. It appears that the degree of individualizing emphasis in Gulf Olmec art as well as the scale of ritual endeavors was greater than elsewhere in contemporary Mesoamerica until the Late Preclassic period.

This information suggests—and I think we should expect—variety across Mesoamerica in cultural and social traditions in the Early and Middle Preclassic periods (see Feinman 1991), a point supported by Robert Santley et al. (1997; see Arnold, this volume) through survey in the Tuxtla Mountains. Ethnographically, we also see considerable variation in the mix of leaders' activities and in communal endeavors in "chiefdoms" (Blanton et al. 1996; Earle 1987; Feinman 1991; Feinman and Neitzel 1984; Netting 1972; Spencer 1994).

The Gulf Olmecs seem to have both personalized and nonpersonalized communal monumental efforts strongly represented. While we still need to examine the origins of these emphases, they may be one reason for Gulf Olmec success and longevity in Preclassic

Mesoamerica. Gulf Olmec public monuments and ritual served as a social nexus and attraction for multiple communities, as indicated by the settlement hierarchy that developed in the southern Gulf lowlands around San Lorenzo (Symonds and Lunagómez 1997; see Symonds, this volume). A crucial issue for Gulf Olmec polities was attracting and holding client populations, given generally low population densities and the relatively open social environment especially during the Early Preclassic period. Both communal ritual and competitive leadership that enlisted supportive clients may have maintained social coherence and loyalty.

Olmec iconography in the southern Gulf lowlands addressed fundamental concerns for food producers, such as maize agriculture and rain (Taube 1995, 1996; see Taube, this volume). Karl Taube's thematic approach to Olmec iconography does not hinge upon finding Postclassic period gods in a much different and earlier society. His postulated underlying themes of agriculture and rain have wide Mesoamerican relevance and *could* help account for the distribution of Olmec motifs because both are concerns of food producers in diverse societies. However, much of the Olmec iconographic evidence Taube considers is either Middle Preclassic or else lacking context and firm dating. Complexly incised celts, for example, have not yet been reported from Early Preclassic Manatí, only polished ones and an example carved like a footprint (Ortiz and Rodríguez 1994: 80). It remains to be determined to what extent Taube's interpretations will apply to the Early Preclassic Gulf Olmecs. Early Preclassic Olmec motifs on portable items mainly appear on pottery and show frontal and side views of supernatural creatures without most of the iconographic details Taube considers.

Besides the roles of leaders and of rituals in Gulf Olmec centers, it is necessary to address a wider social context to understand the Gulf Olmecs. The social matrix in which Gulf Olmec societies operated is one key to politically oriented explanations of how their society developed. Before discussing Helms' (1993) model and its potential to account for the distribution of Olmec motifs in a wider context, I weigh the contribution of various exogenous factors to the development of Gulf Olmec society. Helms' (1993) model is useful, but it addresses only part of what we need to explain regarding how Gulf Olmec society became hierarchical.

The Gulf Olmecs and Exogenous Explanations

Politically based explanations of growing social complexity that rest upon a degree of social competition or factionalism are currently the most promising in the Gulf Olmec case, but some exogenous factors may have played a role as well. Several well-known theories propose some crucible outside of society to help account for social change, but most of these theories have a poor fit with the Gulf Olmecs. The technological and social demands of intensified food production, particularly irrigation (Wittfogel 1957), are not compelling in the rainy environment of the southern Gulf lowlands. Environmental heterogeneity involving major contrastive resource zones does not characterize the Gulf lowlands along the Coatzacoalcos and Tonalá Rivers (Sanders and Webster 1978: 290). In the lightly occupied and open social landscape of the Early Preclassic period, demographic pressure (Sanders and Price 1968: 84–97) and social or environmental circumscription leading to warfare and conquest (Carneiro 1970; Coe and Diehl 1980, 2: 147–152) are not convincing explanations for early social change.

Among these theories, demographic pressure on key resources warrants more detailed remarks. Population estimates for the Late Archaic and Early Preclassic periods are unreliable in the lowlands because of the typically small size and numbers of most sites and their susceptibility to disappearance through erosion, disturbance by later human activities, or depositional concealment. In a few places we have enough evidence from survey to identify Early Preclassic settlement patterns, however. Even if these settlement patterns are not sufficiently complete to allow population estimates, we can glean indirect evidence that scarce farmland (especially the fertile levees [Coe and Diehl 1980, 1: 152]) was not as pivotal as has been suggested. In the San Lorenzo area, Early Preclassic settlement dwindled markedly in Middle Preclassic times with the ascendancy of La Venta along the next major drainage to the east (Symonds and Lunagómez 1997). It appears that the Coatzacoalcos did not undergo a substantial resurgence of population until the Postclassic period (Symonds and Lunagómez 1997). Yet the Coatzacoalcos and its tributaries undoubtedly had productive farmlands throughout that time. Cyphers (1994: 66) suggests that volcanic activity, especially uplift, may have disrupted settlement or decreased the attractiveness of the Coatzacoalcos basin near the close of the Early Preclassic period. It remains unclear how profound this possible effect may have been.

In coastal Chiapas, the Mazatán area contained settlement hierarchies during the Early Preclassic period but dropped sharply in occupation during the Middle Preclassic period (Clark and Blake 1994: 23). If population density was so high that it impelled widespread social competition and conflict over land, then we would not predict that the Mazatán region would undergo a decline while neighboring regions such as the Naranjo River drainage gained population (Love 1991: 54–60).

Occasionally, areas form unoccupied or lightly occupied buffer zones between antagonistic polities, but there is no indication yet that the lowland localities that dropped in population during the Middle Preclassic period became buffer zones. Shifts in Preclassic occupation in the southern Gulf lowlands and coastal Chiapas appear to support the idea of social attractions for population in the vicinity of key centers rather than resource-population imbalances that forced social change (Clark 1994b: 216, 478–479).[6]

As noted above, the idea of competition for scarce but more productive levee lands, which are also advantageous in labor investment (Coe and Diehl 1980, 2: 147–152), seems too weak a factor alone to generate social hierarchies when there were many productive locales elsewhere in the southern Gulf lowlands and in Mesoamerica, including levee lands along the Usumacinta-Grijalva, Papaloapan, and other drainages. Nevertheless, the differential use of levee productivity to fund endeavors, including long-distance exchange for prestige items, is promising for understanding the Gulf Olmecs, even if it was not a sufficient precondition for their society.

A process of adjustment to environmental risk is an exogenous consideration that has received little discussion for the Gulf Olmecs. William Sanders and David Webster (1978: 288) downplay it, for example. If favorable agricultural conditions made the southern Gulf region attractive to people, why should we consider risk? Annual floods in the rainy season posed some impediments to travel, hunting, and fishing and made higher elevations likely places of temporary (and permanent) recourse. Good examples are the hills underlain by salt domes where San Lorenzo and La Venta are located. Receding floods brought opportunities in levee planting and backswamp fishing, however. Thus the problems introduced by seasonal floods and rains were compensated by other advantages. The annual flooding and rain imply that Gulf Olmec lifeways must have incorporated flexibility to accommodate seasonal changes. Variations in the extent or severity of flooding or amount of rain are unlikely to have been especially disruptive but may have demanded occasional temporary relocation.

The riverine environment is changeable; sedimentation and channel movement could adversely affect some spots and improve others (Cyphers 1997; Symonds and Lunagómez 1997; von Nagy 1997). The necessity for some flexibility in land access could contribute to the utility of central authority to adjudicate disputes, but the ease of adjustment on a family or community basis (rather than through a higher central authority) depends on the density of settlement, which remains uncertain. The most dramatic changes in the riverine environment (for example, abandonment of a channel) occur at sufficiently long intervals that they are more likely to effect occasional changes in the settlements that are well situated or in the general location of settlement, rather than the nature of regional social organization.

Overall, environmental problems and risks lack the periodicity and impact that might make central leadership a *necessary* response. However, seasonal flooding highlights flood-free elevations and likely contributed to the enduring social and sacred roles of certain promontories, as well as the cooperation that would be useful because of seasonal flooding and landscape change. These environmental factors should not be ignored as a contribution to cross-cutting social institutions in Gulf Olmec society. As indicated above, local factors are not the whole story for early complex societies, and accounting for processes in a larger social field is the next subject.

Long-Distance Exchange and Helms' (1993) Model

The role(s) of exchange seems promising as part of an interactive process involving social factions, intercommunity displays, and competition. Helms (1993) elaborated a general logic for the exaggerated value and special social and ritual uses of objects from distant regions that are rare and unusual.[7] Helms (1993) notes that distant places and times, not easily accessed or apprehended, can have a strong conceptual link to the sacred realm and to primordial or cosmological origins. Exotic, rare items can symbolize the distant and sacred. Finely crafted objects can play a similar role if skills, production, and access are controlled. Because scarce valuables can be subjected to social control or restrictions in access, they can enhance a process of social differentiation. So, too, can finely crafted objects and esoteric knowledge. All three are implied early in the Gulf Olmec record.

Helms' model is pertinent to both the Gulf Olmecs and their neighbors. It is founded upon active manipulation of distant cosmologically and symbolically charged items by any of the "acquisitive" polities involved. In this sense, the process is mutualistic and more balanced than the dynamic described by Rita Kipp and Edward Schortman (1989; Schortman and Urban 1992: 244–245) in which a dominant polity directly or indirectly promotes trade that destabilizes peripheral hierarchical societies; those societies may then undergo political change toward greater central authority. Whether or not Gulf Olmec neighbors were changed by relationships with Gulf centers is a separate issue; we likely will reach different conclusions for different regions (Clark 1997), and especially for the Early versus Middle Preclassic periods.

From the Helmsian perspective, the Gulf Olmecs' efforts to acquire exotic items, such as ilmenite cubes, magnetite mirrors, obsidian blades (Clark 1987), and greenstone, and the assumed integration of these materials into ritual practices and social displays are not a surprising facet of their life. Rather, the question is how they became so successful at it, which we are still far from answering. As we would expect from Helms' model, the Gulf Olmec exchange networks for exotic products are not the only ones that operated during the Preclassic period (see Flannery and Marcus 1994: 373–390; Grove 1987: 436–437). Societies elsewhere display partially distinct patterns in the articles sought, with seashell sought in Oaxaca, for example.

Many uncertainties remain concerning Early Preclassic exchange networks. We do not have source analyses of the celts from Manatí. We are not yet in a position to describe the circulation and consumption (or lack) of exotic materials in the support populations of either San Lorenzo or La Venta, and there remains much to learn about how the Gulf Olmecs of the Early and Middle Preclassic periods may differ from or resemble each other.[8]

Grove (1987: 440–441) particularly has underscored the need to distinguish the conditions and processes of social life in the Middle Preclassic from the Early Preclassic period. He observes that there were more regional centers and perhaps more tightly organized or controlled polities in Mesoamerica during the Middle Preclassic period. Olmec leaders at a center like La Venta had to compete with and more thoroughly cement alliances with distant polities, especially those that could supply desired exotics. The introduction of Gulf Olmec-style stone carving to a number of distant localities remains a challenge for interpretation, but I suspect it is tied to the more systematic efforts to maintain distant alliances in Middle Preclassic times, as Grove has suggested. Procurement of exotic materials continued to be a prominent feature of Gulf Olmec leadership and public ritual through the Middle Preclassic period, likely because of the important linkage between leadership and sacred propositions. Thus Helms' (1993) exposition about the cosmological associations of distant materials seems particularly apt for the Gulf Olmecs. Similarly Gulf Olmec symbols may have been manipulated in the elaboration of central authority in select distant regions.

The Gulf Olmec Role in Mesoamerica and Helms' Model

In assuming that the Gulf Olmecs played a particularly important role in the elaboration and spread of the Olmec style and Olmec symbols, I am building on the perspective first developed by Kent Flannery (1968), who saw them as enjoying a status differential, although he has subsequently revised his opinion (Flannery and Marcus 1994: 373–390). Several scholars now doubt that the Gulf Olmecs had any special role in Early Preclassic Mesoamerica. This position is partly an outgrowth of the recent concern with the wider "peer polity" social environment in early Mesoamerica (diverse views are presented in Grove [1997]; Sharer and Grove [1989]; Flannery and Marcus [1994: 373–390]). Two key points have led to a view that "Olmec" is a mutualistic, interregional development: (1) local variations in the media, details of motifs, and contexts of Early Preclassic Olmec iconography, and (2) its initial synchronicity in many regions, without any region manifesting clear temporal precedence.

The notion of a key role for the Early Preclassic Gulf Olmecs will remain controversial until we understand early variability in social groups across Mesoamerica more clearly than is now the case, but several points lead me to accord the Gulf Olmecs a special role in early Mesoamerica. New dating, the degree of commonality of Olmec symbols and style, and the explanation of long-distance exchange in exotic materials and crafts developed by Helms (1993) are among these considerations.

Radiocarbon dates from Manatí Spring provide some support for the notion that Olmec ritual is earlier in the Gulf lowlands than the San Lorenzo phase, 1150–900 B.C. Initial dates at Manatí are around 1600 B.C., and ceramic cross-dating of the Manatí A phase points to the Barra and Locona phases in Chiapas and to the Bajío, Ojochí, and Chicharras phases at San Lorenzo (Rodríguez and Ortiz 1997; Ortiz and Rodríguez, this volume).

The anomaly of the Manatí sequence is that the abundant offerings are quite different from those at San Lorenzo but overlap in time. Greenstone and other fine-grained stone celts at Manatí are dated coeval with Early Preclassic San Lorenzo but were rare at San Lorenzo. At San Lorenzo, only two celt offerings have been reported, one celt of blue jade observed by Matthew Stirling (Coe and Diehl 1980, 1: 35) and seven serpentine celts found by Coe and Diehl (1980, 1: 100–102) under Monument 21. Early celt offerings at Manatí and San Lorenzo were not unique to the Gulf Olmecs. In the Mazatán area, one house or public building in Mound 6 at Paso de la Amada had an apparently dedicatory celt placed below the floor during the Locona phase (1500–1350 B.C., Blake 1991: 40; Clark 1994b: 412). Later, in the Middle Preclassic period, sizable, systematic celt offerings occur at La Venta, Tabasco, and San Isidro, Chiapas (Lowe 1981). Perhaps public ritual at La Venta eventually incorporated or co-opted practices largely performed at a smaller scale by local communities. Architectural programs were sufficiently different between San Lorenzo and La Venta that it is conceivable that the contexts of ritual offerings shifted dramatically as well.

It is clear that San Lorenzo phase Olmecs were involved in the technology of stone and wood carving, attendant symbolism, and architectural construction efforts to a much greater extent than their contemporaries. I am willing to ascribe to the Gulf Olmecs an important innovative role that provided ritual models, a style in which supernatural and related concepts were expressed, and social institutions that directly *and indirectly* proved profoundly influential in the larger Mesoamerican setting. An important innovative role for the Gulf Olmecs could be accompanied by local reinterpretation and secondary dissemination.

I have argued elsewhere that there was a widespread style in which Olmec iconography was rendered on Early Preclassic pottery; it involved a bold, low-relief or incised presentation, usually occupying most of the vessel sidewall from top to bottom (Stark 1997b). A comparison to Teotihuacán in the Classic period helps put in perspective the widespread occurrence but local reinterpretation of the Olmec style and iconography. During the period A.D. 300–700, selected Teotihuacán ceramic forms became widely appreciated in Mesoamerica, but often were reinterpreted stylistically in local societies. One example is interpretations of the cylinder tripod form among the Maya; Alfred Kidder et al. (1946: fig. 171a–t, fig. 172a–g, and especially figs. 175c and 176a–c) illustrate examples of vessels at Kaminaljuyú that are closer to Teotihuacán stylistic canons and others that are reinterpreted in a Maya style (Kidder et al. 1946: fig. 173). Another example is the sequence of changes in *floreros* at Monte Albán (Caso et al. 1967: 302, 319, 339, 343–344, 352, 368–370, 423–429). Emulation does not rule out assimilation and reinterpretation of styles.[9] At present, Early Preclassic Olmec iconography and style display as much or more commonality among regions than do the Classic period examples mentioned which link to a major center (Teotihuacán) that is a reasonable candidate for stylistic emulation. The major Gulf Olmec centers may have been foci of emulation, as well. With respect to the Early Preclassic period, Clark (1997) notes that San Lorenzo was far larger than contemporary centers elsewhere in Mesoamerica, which lends support to the possibility that it had a special role in the realm of prestige.

Helms (1993) advances Flannery's (1968) perspective by explaining the profound and pervasive fascination with selected exotic or rare items cross-culturally among hierarchical societies. The Gulf Olmec elaboration of public ritual seems likely to have made Gulf centers reference points in terms of status and sacred objects for hierarchically organized people in distant regions. This role for ritual objects suggested by Helms (1993) contrasts with that of William Rathje (1972), who viewed cult elaboration and spread as a by-product of the mobilization and centralization required to obtain nonlocal subsistence resources. Instead, we can see the appreciation of selected rare exotics as a potential interest of all early Mesoamerican communities and the Gulf Olmecs as the people with especially prominent centers who produced commanding symbols of basic and likely widespread cosmological concepts. I suggest these symbols were emulated by early communities elsewhere, especially those at the apex of a social hierarchy.

It is the processes of emulation, adjustment, modification, and incorporation into a local polity that I see as part of a mutualistic process in combination with exchanges of exotic materials. Diachronic research in the valley of Oaxaca, Morelos, and the Basin of Mexico has been especially effective at demonstrating Early and Middle Preclassic variation in regional cultural traditions, with the implication that Olmec iconography does not reflect a pervasive cultural similarity among the Gulf Olmecs and their neighbors, nor an "imprinting" by a "mother culture." It is particularly striking that Early Preclassic Olmec motifs on pottery (earth monster and fire serpent) were employed widely to symbolize two social groups in the valley of Oaxaca (Marcus 1989; Pyne 1976), suggesting that these symbols may have functioned much less restrictively than in the Gulf lowlands (although we cannot yet define their social circulation on Gulf vessels).

Helms' (1993) model does not account for widespread social uses of exotic symbols. One key to Helms' argument is that "acquisition" is an intermittent process involving a poorly known realm, not a regularized process that is part of routine social relations. A fairly widespread use of Olmec symbols in Oaxaca at San José Mogote and satellite villages suggests an inability to restrict access to exotic symbols there, leading to the active use of them in the local genealogical system. However, I suggest that, like the centrally mediated procurement of obsidian, they entered Oaxaca through the central roles of leaders or key families. The Oaxacan system does not violate Helms' model so much as offer a case in which exotic symbols played a different local role because of weakly developed central leadership.

It is particularly important to recognize the active (and varied) role of Olmec symbolism in different regional social systems. Despite the lack of a simple fit between the archaeological evidence and Helms' (1993) model, I suggest that the Gulf Olmecs became the distant foci of emulation, with Olmec iconography sought as symbolic links to cosmologically and genealogically distant sacred realms or time. Perhaps lowland products such as cacao or tropical feathers were sought from Gulf Olmecs as well. Likewise, selected materials from afar were sought by the Gulf Olmecs. In addition to Colin Renfrew's (1986) notion of "peer polities," a crucial role is played by "reference polities" in the process he described as symbolic entrainment (Renfrew 1986: 8). As Helms (1993) notes, some outlying communities may in turn provide this kind of validation to others, yielding a complex multicentric outcome.

In sum, while the fundamental cosmological concepts among different Mesoamerican groups likely overlapped considerably, the particular style and iconographic codes for expressing them likely were inspired by the Gulf Olmecs. Otherwise, I think it is difficult to account for the degree of commonality that existed in abstract Olmec symbols. A series of independent societies sporadically interacting over great distances is unlikely to devise and adopt a consistent abstract symbolic system without a reference site or region. The Gulf Olmec centers operated in a tradition of relatively open societies, as I argued above. This condition surely eased problems among Mesoamerican communities in obtaining access and establishing relations.

The question of when and where Early Preclassic Olmec iconography originated and how it was distributed will remain subject to lively debate because we lack sufficiently well documented and understood examples of these widespread stylistic phenomena. Although I apply a reasoning tied to Helms' (1993) work and accommodate a special role for the Gulf Olmecs, a more important issue than whether the Gulf Olmecs filled this role is the indication of widespread contacts among Early Preclassic societies and a relatively open social environment.

The social and conceptual roles of exotic materials can be fulfilled with scarce, finely crafted, imitative, or labor-intensive articles as well, especially if access to distant exotics is impeded. As mentioned above, by Middle Preclassic times we have signs of more competitive and intensified ties between the Gulf Olmecs and certain distant regions. I suspect that use of local items is more likely to occur with well-institutionalized social hierarchies in which attached specialist labor and access to selected crafts can be controlled effectively. While we may suspect that many portable Olmec objects were such finely crafted objects, we know almost nothing about their contexts of production. However, Late and Terminal Preclassic developments help define a possible process of local craft "substitution" or "elaboration" involving textiles that may have been under way in Middle Preclassic times, as I discuss below.

The Top of the Frame: The Late and Terminal Preclassic Periods

If the Archaic period can give us some clues about the early Gulf Olmecs, what can the Late and Terminal Preclassic periods reveal about the later Gulf Olmecs? My ideas have been developed from data in south-central Veracruz, coupled with Gulf Olmec figural representations. I draw upon studies of pottery, obsidian, and textile-related implements from south-central Veracruz, especially the western side of the lower Papaloapan drainage, where Cerro de las Mesas and La Mojarra are located. The general area is one where Late Preclassic centers were developing, such as Cerro de las Mesas. Terminal Preclassic commemorative stelae bearing writing and Long Count dates at La Mojarra and Tres Zapotes became part of the growing specialized knowledge that helped distinguish and reinforce central authority (Justeson and Kaufman 1993; Miller 1991; Winfield 1988). The proveniences of a statuette from the Tuxtla Mountains and a sherd from Chiapas with the same script as La Mojarra Stela 1 suggest that specialized knowledge may have been widespread among elites in southern Veracruz and Chiapas (Méluzin 1992). However, the Papaloapan drainage is the only region in which the script is closely associated with public monuments. The roots of this writing system likely are represented by the elaboration of esoteric symbols in late Olmec times; for example, there is a vertical row of three glyphlike symbols on La Venta Monument 13 (Drucker 1952: 203).

The Late and Terminal Preclassic are often described as periods of marked regionalization in Mesoamerica in which the foundations were laid for Classic period configurations. I have detected ceramic evidence of stylistic regionalization in the Late Preclassic period for central Veracruz; a set of very finely incised pottery motifs is localized there (Stark 1997b). I suggested that this is a reflection of everyday commoner communication patterns. The extensive style networks of the Early and Middle Preclassic periods were withering as regional polities focused production, distribution, and power within their domains. This likely represents a further outgrowth of the competition that Middle Preclassic Gulf Olmec centers faced. With growing population and hierarchical political change in Mesoamerica, commoners appear to have interacted increasingly with more immediate neighbors who represented centrally organized, sizable local populations, while elites relied somewhat less on strategies involving long-distance exchange of valuables, as I discuss below.

Obsidian distribution networks that had provided San Lorenzo with material from a broad range of sources (Cobean et al. 1971, 1991) may have become more focused at La Venta (Hester, Heizer, and Jack 1971; Hester, Jack, and Heizer 1971). A pattern of narrowing of sources pertains to the Late Preclassic in the Mixtequilla (the area around Cerro de las Mesas), where two residential locations drew mainly upon Pico de Orizaba and Guadalupe Victoria, the two closest sources (about 70 percent of the obsidian [Heller n.d.]), but also used a scattering of obsidian from five other sources (Stark et al. 1992). The Classic period follows with a nearly exclusive reliance upon Zaragoza-Oyameles (Stark et al. 1992). These data may point to a long-term process in which procurement from fewer sources became more reliable in supplying regional needs in the Gulf lowlands. This implies less open exchange relations and more institutionalized or controlled long-distance trade arrangements.

In a study of the history of cotton processing and textiles in the Gulf lowlands, I and my coauthors develop another argument that bears on processes that were under way toward the close of the Olmec era (Stark et al. 1998). Cotton-related spindle whorls attest to a growing emphasis on textiles, perhaps toward the end of the Terminal Preclassic and certainly by the Early Classic period in the Mixtequilla. Similarly, whorls are evident in the Terminal Preclassic period at Balberta on the Pacific Coast of Guatemala (Arroyo 1993). In contrast, earlier implements that might have been related to cotton processing are scarce and equivocal at a Late Preclassic village in the Mixtequilla where test excavations were conducted.

Imagery from figurines suggests that garments (we presume textiles) were not in common use in the Early or Middle Preclassic Olmec periods, nor in the Late Preclassic period. Terminal Preclassic evidence is equivocal on this point. By no later than the Classic period, the situation had changed. Textiles appear frequently on household figurines, and often the textiles are elaborately decorated.

In comparison, carved stone monuments show a different sequence of change. Early Preclassic Gulf Olmec monumental sculpture shows little clothing, with the loincloth most common; occasionally a cape appears. Later in the Middle Preclassic period at La Venta, stelae show increased use of garments and towering headdresses.

Our construal of the evidence is that cotton processing and garments were at a very modest scale in the Early Preclassic period but became more important during the Middle Preclassic for elite consumption, perhaps as sumptuary items. By the Late and Terminal Preclassic periods, feathered regalia also became more pronounced. We suggest that increasing difficulty in the Middle through Terminal Preclassic periods in obtaining and controlling exotic prestige goods led to greater emphasis on local items of limited abundance, perhaps ones tied to highly skilled crafts or esoteric knowledge, as Helms (1993) has suggested. Cotton garments, elaborate headdresses, writing, and calendric (and astronomical) knowledge could have begun to substitute for distant exotics.

Cotton, perhaps after further selective breeding for desirable traits, had a potential to "take off" as a regional specialization. In the Classic period we see a characteristic emphasis on textile garments in imagery from the Gulf lowlands (Stark et al. 1998). Barbara Hall (1997) has suggested that cotton was important in interpolity relations and Classic period political economies on the basis of spindle whorl data. However, southern Veracruz was not as advantaged as south-central Veracruz and the Tuxtlas in cotton production because of the very winter rains that initially made the region especially advantageous for subsistence farming (Stark et al. 1998). Cotton was planted in the winter dry season in the Gulf lowlands, in contrast to the Pacific Coast, where cotton was planted mainly in the drier area near the coast and dependent on summer rains (unless irrigated).

The emphasis on cotton or cotton textiles may have developed in complementary exchange with adjacent highland regions that produced obsidian. The Late and Terminal Preclassic periods tend to reinforce the idea that processes of regionalization and "peer polity" competition or exclusion were important in the decline of Olmec societies in southern Veracruz, in conjunction with a process of economic change involving textile production. With respect to cotton production, the misfortunes of southern Veracruz centers were the opportunities for the growth of Tuxtlas polities like Tres Zapotes and Mixtequilla polities like Cerro de las Mesas.

Conclusion

In the Late Archaic period, increasing human occupation and food production in the lowlands preceded Early Preclassic Gulf Olmec developments. More Late Archaic population may reflect the attraction of the lowlands for food producers. The southern Gulf lowlands were especially advantageous for reliable, productive farming because of winter rains brought by *nortes,* which result in more winter rainfall in southern Veracruz than in central or northern Veracruz (or on the Pacific Coast). Nevertheless, the Late Archaic period and the Early Preclassic alike seem to have had low population densities and small communities compared to later times. Movement of cultigens, widespread ceramic styles, trade in pottery, and obsidian exchange suggest a rather open social environment in these periods.

We are still far from any resolution about how to account for the development of Gulf Olmec society, but techno-demographic-environmental explanations seem weak or inapplicable in the case of the Gulf Olmecs. Seasonal flooding may have enhanced the social roles of promontory settlements and of central authority in adjudicating land access. Control of levee lands may also have enhanced social differences. However, the dynamics of social relations seem more promising than exogenous factors to explain Gulf Olmec society. Social competition expressed by aspiring leaders and ritual-bridging institutions both hold promise in understanding Gulf Olmec social change. Another important factor is the role that long-distance exotic materials and sacred symbols may have played in the elaboration of differentials within communities and among them. Acquisition of exotic sacred items is likely to have been an important strategy for legitimizing Gulf Olmec leaders. The unusually sizable and conceptually elaborate endeavors at Gulf Olmec centers likely made them subject to attention and emulation as reference polities in the Early Preclassic Mesoamerican social landscape.

Gulf Olmec society underwent significant changes in the Middle Preclassic period, with acquisition of different exotic materials at La Venta compared to San Lorenzo and more elite investment in selected distant regions through sculpture (or the expertise to do it). Somewhat greater stylistic localization in ceramics and differential Gulf Olmec involvement with distant regions characterize the Middle Preclassic compared to the Early Preclassic period (Stark 1997b). Greater elaboration of local crafts that had restricted access may have been under way in the southern Gulf lowlands by the Middle Preclassic period. Depictions of garments, I presume textiles, appear on La Venta sculpture, along with towering headdresses. In contrast, ceramic figurines with a wider social distribution typically do not show garments. This pattern may be the inception of more emphasis on cotton and weaving in the lowlands, in the context of attached specialists and elite social displays.

In the Terminal Preclassic period or near its close, spindle whorls in the Mixtequilla indicate more widespread spinning and (presumably) textile production. A regional emphasis on cotton production begins in the central Gulf lowlands. The advantage of the southern Gulf lowlands in food production with winter rains was offset when cotton was at issue because of the necessity of a dry period in the development of bolls. The decline of southern Gulf Olmec centers, or, more correctly, the apparent absence of major successor centers there during the Classic period may partly reflect changing regional economic emphases in the wider Mesoamerican economy.

NOTES

This essay is an outgrowth of diachronic research in the Mixtequilla supported by grants BNS 85-19167 and BNS 87-41867 from the National Science Foundation and grants from the Wenner-Gren Foundation for Anthropological Research. Permission for the investigations was accorded by the Consejo de Arqueología, Instituto Nacional de Antropología e Historia. I appreciate the invitation to participate by the symposium organizers, Joanne Pillsbury and Mary Pye, and I thank John Clark, George Cowgill, Joyce Marcus, Ben Nelson, Michael Ohnersorgen, and Barbara Voorhies for comments that led to improvements in the essay. Their comments do not make them responsible for its deficiencies or peculiarities, and some specifically disagree with points it contains.

1. Coring of Lake Catemaco in the Tuxtla Mountains produced problematic early dates, although possibly the deposits extend into the Preclassic period (Byrne and Horn 1989).

2. Vuelta Limón was previously designated as the Lesher site in Voorhies and Kennett (1995).

3. Subsistence-oriented food production does not preclude a minor dietary role for maize or its use for brewing. Clark (1994b: 226–239) summarizes the evidence from grinding tools, dental patterns, and bone isotope studies (Blake, Chisholm, et al. 1992) that point to modest consumption of maize until perhaps the Conchas phase (850–650 B.C.) in the Mazatán region.

4. AMS dating for the Tehuacan valley reduced archaeologists' perception of the length of time maize was domesticated there (Fritz 1994; Long et al. 1989; Zeitlin and Zeitlin 1996). The earliest Tehuacan maize is closer to 3500 B.C. than 5000 B.C. on the basis of AMS dating of the maize remains. However, suggested dates for cultivated or domesticated *Zea* from pollen and phytoliths elsewhere (for example, Oaxaca [Schoenwetter 1974], Central America [Piperno 1995; Piperno et al. 1991b; Rue 1988]) support the idea of cultivation and possibly domestication as early as 5000 B.C., or earlier. Dolores Piperno (1989) suggests that initial maize domestication may have occurred in the Balsas drainage in West Mexico, home of the closest teosinte relative, with a rapid spread into Central America as well as other parts of Mexico.

5. For example, the coastal plain of Veracruz encompasses such variation in elevation, rainfall, soils, and other environmental factors that there may have been localities better endowed with wild carbohydrate resources than others and, therefore, relatively more favorable for foragers (Gómez-Pompa 1973). Unfortunately, historic and modern disturbance and the difficulty of mapping and measuring wild economic resources handicap efforts to dissect the potential of different areas for mobile hunter-gatherers. There is no indication as yet that gathered plant foods would have been so abundant in most of the Gulf lowlands during an annual cycle that we should discard Piperno's (1989) reservations about reliable calorie resources for tropical lowland hunter-gatherers. One of the possible exceptions is areas with good access to economic species of palm, but in Veracruz, as in Panama, the extent to which palm-rich vegetation types are anthropogenic (through clearing and fire) remains unknown (Gómez-Pompa 1973: 126–127).

6. In other parts of Mesoamerica, such as Oaxaca and the Basin of Mexico, Late Archaic and Early and Middle Preclassic occupations were so light that it is difficult to conceive that the resource base was a limiting factor on population (Clark 1994b; Feinman 1991). Attempts to estimate productivity do not indicate that population approached the agricultural carrying capacity (Feinman and Nicholas 1987; Kowalewski et al. 1989: 462–467; Nicholas 1989; Tolstoy 1982).

7. A quite contrastive view of long-distance exchange was presented by William Rathje (1972) as a spin-off of his arguments advanced for the lowland Maya (Rathje 1971). He looked to locally absent, crucial household resources as a mobilizing incentive that could enhance centralization and differentiation. Unfortunately for his argument, volcanic stones, salt, and obsidian, while not ubiquitous, were either part of the variability of the southern Gulf lowlands (salt at the coastline and hard stones in the Tuxtlas) or problematic as a driving force for social change (people in many regions imported some obsidian but did not undergo the kinds of developments that characterized the Gulf Olmecs). Rathje's (1972) argument constitutes another instance in which failure to characterize adequately the Gulf lowland environment yielded a substantial misunderstanding of what may have transpired.

8. Exchange networks are not the only indication that Gulf Olmec society changed over time. Architectural contrasts between San Lorenzo and La Venta involved the elaboration of artificial mound construction at La Venta. Cyphers (1997) argues that terracing and causeways were monumental constructions at San Lorenzo, not artificial mounds.

9. Another example is Terminal Preclassic and Early Classic scroll styles in the valley of Oaxaca, the Gulf lowlands, and the Basin of Mexico (Stark 1997a). Although scroll-rich designs have greater historical depth in the Gulf and Chiapas lowlands, scroll designs were interpreted differently in each geographic region in the Early Classic period, suggesting a mutualistic process with local reworking of an exogenous style.

BIBLIOGRAPHY

Adler, Michael A.

1989 Ritual Facilities and Social Integration in Nonranked Societies. In *The Architecture of Social Integration in Prehistoric Pueblos,* ed. William Lipe and Michelle Hegemon, 35–52. Cortez, Colo.

Arroyo, Barbara L.

1993 Spindle Whorls from Balberta. In *Balberta Project, the Terminal Formative-Early Classic Transition on the Pacific Coast of Guatemala,* ed. Frederick Bove, Sonia Medrano, Brenda Lou, and Barbara Arroyo, 137–143. Pittsburgh.

Bender, Barbara

1978 Gatherer-Hunter to Farmer: A Social Perspective. *World Archaeology* 10: 204–222.

Blake, Michael

1991 An Emerging Early Formative Chiefdom at Paso de la Amada, Chiapas, Mexico. In *The Formation of Complex Society in Southeastern Mesoamerica,* ed. William Fowler Jr., 27–46. Boca Raton, Fla.

Blake, Michael, John E. Clark, Brian S. Chisholm, and Karen Mudar

1992 Non-agricultural Staples and Agricultural Supplements: Early Formative Subsistence in the Soconusco Region, Mexico. In *Transitions to Agriculture in Prehistory,* ed. Anne Birgitte Gebauer and T. Douglas Price, 133–151. Madison, Wisc.

Blake, Michael, Brian S. Chisholm, John E. Clark, Barbara Voorhies, and Michael Love

1992 Prehistoric Subsistence in the Soconusco Region. *Current Anthropology* 22: 83–94.

Blanton, Richard E., Gary M. Feinman, Stephen Kowalewski, and Peter N. Peregrine

1996 A Dual-Processual Theory for the Evolution of Mesoamerican Civilization. *Current Anthropology* 37: 1–31.

Blanton, Richard E., Stephen Kowalewski, Gary M. Feinman, and Laura M. Finston

1993 *Ancient Mesoamerica: A Comparison of Change in Three Regions,* 2d ed. Cambridge.

Brumfiel, Elizabeth M.

1992 Breaking and Entering the Ecosystem: Gender, Class, and Faction Steal the Show. *American Anthropologist* 94: 554–567.

1994 Factional Competition and Political Development in the New World: An Introduction. In *Factional Competition and Political Development in the New World,* ed. Elizabeth Brumfiel and John Fox, 3–13. Cambridge.

Brumfiel, Elizabeth M., and Timothy K. Earle

1987 Specialization, Exchange, and Complex Societies: An Introduction. In *Specialization, Exchange, and Complex Societies,* ed. Elizabeth Brumfiel and Timothy Earle, 1–9. Cambridge.

Brush, Charles F.

1965 Pox Pottery: Earliest Identified Mexican Ceramic. *Science* 149: 194–195.

1969 A Contribution to the Archaeology of Coastal Guerrero, Mexico. Ph.D. dissertation, Department of Anthropology, Columbia University. University Microfilms, Ann Arbor.

Burger, Richard

1992 *Chavin and the Origins of Andean Civilization.* London.

Byrne, Roger, and Sally P. Horn

1989 Prehistoric Agriculture and Forest Clearance in the Sierra de los Tuxtlas, Veracruz, Mexico. *Palynology* 13: 181–193.

Carneiro, Robert L.

1970 A Theory of the Origin of the State. *Science* 169: 733–738.

Cashdan, Elizabeth A.

1980 Egalitarianism among Hunters and Gatherers. *American Anthropologist* 82: 116–120.

Caso, Alfonso, Ignacio Bernal, and Jorge R. Acosta

1967 *La cerámica de Monte Albán.* Mexico City.

Charles, Douglas K.

1995 Diachronic Regional Social Dynamics: Mortuary Sites in the Illinois Valley. In *Regional Approaches to Mortuary Analysis,* ed. Lane Beck, 77–99. New York.

Charles, Douglas K., and Jane E. Buikstra

1983 Archaic Mortuary Sites in the Central Mississippi Drainage. In *Archaic Hunters and Gatherers in the American Midwest,* ed. James Phillips and James Brown, 117–145. New York.

Clark, John E.

1987 Politics, Prismatic Blades, and Mesoamerican Civilization. In *The Organization of Core Technology,* ed. J. K. Johnson and C. A. Morrow, 259–284. Boulder, Colo.

1991 The Beginnings of Mesoamerica: Apologia for the Soconusco Early Formative. In *The Formation of Complex Society in Southeastern Mesoamerica,* ed. William R. Fowler Jr., 13–16. Boca Raton, Fla.

1994a Antecedentes de la cultura olmeca. In *Los olmecas en Mesoamérica,* ed. John Clark, 30–41. Mexico City and Madrid.

1994b The Development of Formative Rank Societies in the Soconusco, Chiapas,

Mexico. Ph.D. dissertation, Department of Anthropology, University of Michigan, Ann Arbor.

1997 The Arts of Government in Early Mesoamerica. *Annual Review of Anthropology* 26: 211–234.

Clark, John E., and Michael Blake
1994 The Power of Prestige: Competitive Generosity and the Emergence of Rank Societies in Lowland Mesoamerica. In *Factional Competition and Political Development,* ed. Elizabeth Brumfiel and John Fox, 17–30. Cambridge.

Cobean, Robert H., Michael D. Coe, Edward A. Perry, Karl K. Turekian, and Dinkar P. Kharkar
1971 Obsidian Trade at San Lorenzo Tenochtitlán, Mexico. *Science* 174: 666–671.

Cobean, Robert H., James R. Vogt, Michael D. Glascock, and Terrance L. Stocker
1991 High-Precision Trace-Element Characterization of Major Mesoamerican Obsidian Sources and Further Analyses of Artifacts from San Lorenzo Tenochtitlán, Mexico. *Latin American Antiquity* 2: 69–91.

Coe, Michael D.
1974 Photogrammetry and the Ecology of Olmec Civilization. In *Aerial Photography in Anthropological Field Research,* ed. Evon Vogt, 1–13. Cambridge, Mass.

Coe, Michael D., and Richard A. Diehl
1980 *In the Land of the Olmec,* 2 vols. Austin.

Cyphers, Ann
1994 San Lorenzo Tenochtitlán. In *Los olmecas en Mesoamérica,* ed. John Clark, 43–67. Mexico City and Madrid.

1997 Olmec Architecture at San Lorenzo. In *Olmec to Aztec: Settlement Patterns in the Ancient Gulf Lowlands,* ed. Barbara Stark and Philip Arnold, III, 96–114. Tucson, Ariz.

Daneels, Annick, and Alejandro Pastrana
1988 Aprovechamiento de la obsidiana del Pico de Orizaba: El caso de la cuenca baja del Jamapa-Cotaxtla. *Arqueología* 4: 99–120. Mexico City.

Demarest, Arthur A.
1989 The Olmec and the Rise of Civilization in Eastern Mesoamerica. In *Regional Perspectives on the Olmec,* ed. Robert Sharer and David Grove, 303–344. Cambridge.

Diehl, Richard A.
1989 Olmec Archaeology: What We Know and What We Wish We Knew. In *Regional Perspectives on the Olmec,* ed. Robert Sharer and David Grove, 17–32. Cambridge.

Drucker, Philip
1952 *La Venta, Tabasco, a Study of Olmec Ceramics and Art.* Bureau of American Ethnology Bulletin 153. Washington.

Earle, Timothy K.
1987 Chiefdoms in Archaeological and Ethnohistorical Perspective. *Annual Review of Anthropology* 16: 279–308. Palo Alto, Calif.

Feinman, Gary M.
1991 Demography, Surplus, and Inequality: Early Political Formations in Highland Mesoamerica. In *Chiefdoms: Power, Economy, and Ideology,* ed. Timothy Earle, 229–262. Cambridge.

Feinman, Gary M., and Jill Neitzel
1984 Too Many Types: An Overview of Sedentary Prestate Societies in the Americas. In *Archaeological Advances in Method and Theory,* ed. Michael Schiffer, 7: 39–102. Orlando, Fla.

Feinman, Gary M., and Linda M. Nicholas
1987 Labor, Surplus, and Production: A Regional Analysis of Formative Oaxacan Socio-economic Change. In *Coasts, Plains, and Deserts: Essays in Honor of Reynold J. Ruppé,* ed. Sylvia Gaines, 27–50. Tempe, Ariz.

Flannery, Kent V.
1968 The Olmec and the Valley of Oaxaca: A Model for Interregional Interaction in Formative Times. In *Dumbarton Oaks Conference on the Olmec,* ed. Elizabeth Benson, 79–110. Washington.

1973 The Origins of Agriculture. *Annual Review of Anthropology* 2: 271–310. Palo Alto, Calif.

Flannery, Kent V., and Joyce Marcus
1994 *Early Formative Pottery in the Valley of Oaxaca.* Memoirs of the Museum of Anthropology 27. University of Michigan, Ann Arbor.

Freidel, David A.
1978 Maritime Adaptation and the Rise of Maya Civilization: The View from Cerros. In *Prehistoric Coastal Adaptations: The Economy and Ecology of Maritime Middle America,* ed. Barbara Stark and Barbara Voorhies, 239–265. New York.

Fried, Morton
1967 *The Evolution of Political Society.* New York.

Fritz, Gayle J.
1994 Are the First American Farmers Getting Younger? *Current Anthropology* 35: 305–309.

García, Enriqueta
1970 *Los climas del Estado de Veracruz.* Mexico City.

Goman, Michelle
1992 Paleoecological Evidence for Prehistoric Agriculture and Tropical Forest Clearance in the Sierra de los Tuxtlas, Veracruz, Mexico. Master's thesis, Department of Geography, University of California, Berkeley.

Gómez-Pompa, Arturo
1973 Ecology of the Vegetation of Veracruz. In *Vegetation and Vegetational History of Northern Latin America,* ed. Alan Graham, 73–148. Amsterdam.

Grove, David C.
1987 Chalcatzingo in a Broader Perspective. In *Ancient Chalcatzingo,* ed. David Grove, 434–442. Austin.

1997 Olmec Archaeology: A Half Century of Research and Its Accomplishments. *Journal of World Prehistory* 11: 51–101.

Grove, David C., and Susan D. Gillespie
1984 Chalcatzingo's Portrait Figurines and the Cult of the Ruler. *Archaeology* 37(4): 27–33.

Hall, Barbara Ann
1997 Spindle Whorls and Cotton Production at Middle Classic Matacapan and in the Gulf Lowlands. In *Olmec to Aztec: Settlement Patterns in the Ancient Gulf Lowlands,* ed. Barbara Stark and Philip Arnold, III, 115–135. Tucson, Ariz.

Hayden, Brian
1990 Nimrods, Piscators, Pluckers and Planters: The Emergence of Food Production. *Journal of Anthropological Archaeology* 9: 31–69.

1992 Models of Domestication. In *Transitions to Agriculture in Prehistory,* ed. Anne Birgitte Gebauer and T. Douglas Price, 11–19. Madison, Wisc.

Heller, Lynette
n.d. Sources, Technology, Production, Use, and Deposition of Knapped Obsidian. In *Classic Period Mixtequilla, Veracruz, Mexico: Diachronic Insights from Residential Investigations,* ed. Barbara Stark. Albany, N.Y. (in press).

Helms, Mary W.
1993 *Craft and the Kingly Ideal: Art, Trade, and Power.* Austin.

Hester, Thomas R., Robert F. Heizer, and Robert N. Jack
1971 Technology and Geologic Sources of Obsidian Artifacts from Cerro de las Mesas, Veracruz, with Observations on Olmec Trade. *Contributions of the University of California Archaeological Research Facility* 13: 133–141. Berkeley.

Hester, Thomas R., Harry B. Iceland, Dale B. Hudler, and Harry J. Shafer
1996 The Colha Preceramic Project: Preliminary Results from the 1993–1995 Field Seasons. *Mexicon* 18(3): 45–50.

Hester, Thomas R., Robert N. Jack, and Robert F. Heizer
1971 The Obsidian of Tres Zapotes, Veracruz, Mexico. *Contributions of the University of California Archaeological Research Facility* 13: 65–131. Berkeley.

Hester, Thomas R., Thomas C. Kelly, and Giancarlo Ligabue
1981 *A Fluted Paleo-Indian Projectile Point from Belize, Central America.* University of Texas, San Antonio and Centro Studi e Ricerche Ligabue, Venice.

Hirth, Kenneth G.
1987 Formative Period Settlement Patterns in the Rio Amatzinac Valley. In *Ancient Chalcatzingo,* ed. David Grove, 343–367. Austin.

Iceland, Harry B., and Thomas R. Hester
1996 The Colha Preceramic Project: A Status Report. Paper presented at the 61st Annual Meeting of the Society for American Archaeology, New Orleans.

Jones, John G.
1994 Pollen Evidence for Early Settlement and Agriculture in Northern Belize. *Palynology* 18: 205–211.

Justeson, John S., and Terrence Kaufman
1993 A Decipherment of Epi-Olmec Hieroglyphic Writing. *Science* 259: 1703–1711.

Kelly, Thomas C.
1993 Preceramic Projectile Point Typology in Belize. *Ancient Mesoamerica* 4: 205–227.

Kennett, Douglas J., and Barbara Voorhies
1996 Oxygen Isotopic Analysis of Archaeological Shells to Detect Seasonal Use of the Wetlands on the Southern Pacific Coast of Mexico. *Journal of Archaeological Research* 23: 689–704.

Kidder, Alfred V., Jesse D. Jennings, and Edwin M. Shook
1946 *Excavations at Kaminaljuyu, Guatemala.* Washington.

Kipp, Rita S., and Edward M. Schortman
1989 The Political Impact of Trade in Chiefdoms. *American Anthropologist* 91: 370–385.

Kowalewski, Stephen A., Gary M. Feinman, Laura Finstein, Richard E. Blanton, and Linda M. Nicholas
1989 *Monte Albán's Hinterland, Part III: Prehispanic Settlement Patterns in Tlacolula, Etla, and Ocotlan, the Valley of Oaxaca, Mexico.* Memoirs of the Museum

of Anthropology 23. University of Michigan, Ann Arbor.

Kroeber, Alfred
1917 Zuni Kin and Clan. *Anthropological Papers* 18(2): 41–204. American Museum of Natural History, New York.

Lesure, Richard
1996 Egalitarian and Inegalitarian Aspects of the Social Organization of Consumption at Paso de la Amada, 1400–1000 B.C. Paper presented at the 61st Annual Meeting of the Society for American Archaeology, New Orleans.

Long, Austin, B. Benz, D. Donahue, A. Jull, and L. Toolin
1989 First Direct AMS Dates on Early Maize from Tehuacan, Mexico. *Radiocarbon* 31: 1035–1040.

Love, Michael W.
1991 Style and Social Complexity in Formative Mesoamerica. In *The Formation of Complex Society in Southeastern Mesoamerica,* ed. William Fowler Jr., 47–76. Boca Raton, Fla.

Lowe, Gareth W.
1981 Olmec Horizons Defined in Mound 20, San Isidro, Chiapas. In *The Olmec and Their Neighbors,* ed. Elizabeth Benson, 231–255. Washington.

MacNeish, Richard S.
1964 Ancient Mesoamerican Civilization. *Science* 143: 531–537.

MacNeish, Richard S., and Antoinette Nelken-Terner
1983 *Final Annual Report of the Belize Archaic Archaeological Reconnaissance.* Boston.

Marcus, Joyce
1989 Zapotec Chiefdoms and the Nature of Formative Religions. In *Regional Perspectives on the Olmec,* ed. Robert Sharer and David Grove, 148–197. Cambridge.

Marcus, Joyce, and Kent Flannery
1996 *Zapotec Civilization: How Urban Society Evolved in Mexico's Oaxaca Valley.* London.

McGuire, Randall H.
1983 Breaking Down Cultural Complexity: Inequality and Heterogeneity. In *Advances in Archaeological Method and Theory,* vol. 6, ed. Michael Schiffer, 91–142. New York.

Méluzin, Sylvia
1992 The Tuxtla Script: Steps toward Decipherment Based on La Mojarra Stela 1. *Latin American Antiquity* 18: 283–297.

Miller, Mary Ellen
1991 Rethinking the Classic Sculptures of Cerro de las Mesas, Veracruz. In *Settlement Archaeology of Cerro de las Mesas, Veracruz, Mexico,* ed. Barbara Stark, 26–38. Los Angeles.

Mountjoy, Joseph B., Robert E. Taylor, and Lawrence H. Feldman
1972 Matachen Complex: New Radiocarbon Dates on Early Coastal Adaptation in West Mexico. *Science* 175: 1242–1243.

Netting, Robert M.
1972 Sacred Power and Centralization: Aspects of Political Adaptation in Africa. In *Population Growth: Anthropological Implications,* ed. Brian Spooner, 219–244. Cambridge, Mass.

Nicholas, Linda M.
1989 Prehispanic Land Use in Oaxaca. In *Monte Albán's Hinterland, Part III: Prehispanic Settlement Patterns in Tlacolula, Etla, and Ocotlan, the Valley of Oaxaca, Mexico,* ed. Stephen Kowalewski, Gary Feinman, Laura Finstein, Richard Blanton, and Linda Nicholas, 449–505. Memoirs of the Museum of Anthropology 23. University of Michigan, Ann Arbor.

Ortiz, Ponciano, and María del Carmen Rodríguez
1994 Los espacios sagrados olmecas: El Manatí, un caso especial. In *Los olmecas en Mesoamérica,* ed. John Clark, 69–91. Mexico City and Madrid.

Pearsall, Deborah
1995 "Doing" Paleoethnobotany in the Tropical Lowlands: Adaptation and Innovation in Methodology. In *Archaeology in the Lowland American Tropics: Current Analytical Methods and Applications,* ed. Peter Stahl, 113–129. Cambridge.

Piperno, Dolores
1989 Non-affluent Foragers: Resource Availability, Seasonal Shortages, and the Emergence of Agriculture in Panamanian Tropical Forests. In *Foraging and Farming: The Evolution of Plant Exploitation,* ed. David Harris and G. Hillman, 538–554. London.

1995 Plant Microfossils and Their Application in the New World Tropics. In *Archaeology in the Lowland American Tropics: Current Analytical Methods and Applications,* ed. Peter Stahl, 130–153. Cambridge.

Piperno, Dolores, Mark B. Bush, and Paul A. Colinvaux
1991a Paleoecological Perspectives on Human Adaptation in Central Panama. 2. The Holocene. *Geoarchaeology* 6: 227–250.

1991b Paleoecological Perspectives on Human Adaptation in Central Panama. 1. The Pleistocene. *Geoarchaeology* 6: 210–226.

Pohl, Mary D., Kevin O. Pope, John G. Jones, John S.

Jacob, Dolores R. Piperno, Susan D. deFrance, David L. Lentz, John A. Gifford, Marie E. Danforth, and J. Kathryn Josserand
1996 Early Agriculture in the Maya Lowlands. *Latin American Antiquity* 7: 355–372.

Price, T. Douglas, and James A. Brown
1985 (Editors) *Prehistoric Hunter-Gatherers: The Emergence of Cultural Complexity.* New York.

Pyne, Nanette M.
1976 The Fire-Serpent and Were-Jaguar in Formative Oaxaca: A Contingency Table Analysis. In *The Early Mesoamerican Village,* ed. Kent Flannery, 272–282. New York.

Rathje, William L.
1971 The Origin and Development of Lowland Classic Maya Civilization. *American Antiquity* 36: 275–285.

1972 Praise the Gods and Pass the Metates: A Hypothesis of Development of Lowland Rainforest Civilizations in Mesoamerica. In *Contemporary Archaeology: A Guide to Theory and Contributions,* ed. Mark Leone, 365–392. Carbondale, Ill.

Renfrew, Colin
1974 Beyond a Subsistence Economy: The Evolution of Social Organization in Prehistoric Europe. In *Reconstructing Complex Societies: An Archeological Colloquium,* ed. C. Moore, 69–95. Ann Arbor.

1986 Introduction: Peer Polity Interaction and Sociopolitical Change. In *Peer Polity Interaction,* ed. Colin Renfrew and John Cherry, 1–18. Cambridge.

Rodríguez, María del Carmen, and Ponciano Ortiz
1997 Olmec Ritual and Sacred Geography at Manatí. In *Olmec to Aztec: Settlement Patterns in the Ancient Gulf Lowlands,* ed. Barbara Stark and Philip Arnold, III, 68–95. Tucson, Ariz.

Rue, David J.
1988 Archaic Middle American Agriculture and Settlement: Recent Pollen Data from Honduras. *Journal of Field Archaeology* 16: 177–184.

Rust, William, III, and Robert J. Sharer
1988 Olmec Settlement Data from La Venta, Tabasco. *Science* 242: 102–104.

Sahlins, Marshall
1963 Poor Man, Rich Man, Big Man, Chief: Political Types in Melanesia and Polynesia. *Comparative Studies in Society and History* 5: 285–303.

1972 *Stone Age Economics.* Chicago.

Sanders, William T., Jeffrey R. Parsons, and Robert S. Santley
1979 *The Basin of Mexico: Ecological Processes in the Evolution of a Civilization.* New York.

Sanders, William T., and Barbara J. Price
1968 *Mesoamerica: The Evolution of Civilization.* New York.

Sanders, William T., and David Webster
1978 Unilinealism, Multilinealism, and the Evolution of Complex Societies. In *Social Archaeology: Beyond Subsistence and Dating,* ed. Charles Redman, Mary Jane Berman, Edward Curtin, William Langhorne Jr., Nina Versaggi, and Jeffrey Wanser, 249–313. New York.

Santley, Robert S., Philip J. Arnold, III, and Thomas P. Barrett
1997 Formative Period Settlement Patterns in the Tuxtlas Mountains. In *Olmec to Aztec: Settlement Patterns in the Ancient Gulf Lowlands,* ed. Barbara Stark and Philip Arnold, III, 174–205. Tucson, Ariz.

Schoenwetter, James
1974 Pollen Records of Guilá Naquitz Cave. *American Antiquity* 39: 292–303.

Schortman, Edward M., and Patricia A. Urban
1992 Current Trends in Interaction Research. In *Resources, Power, and Interregional Interaction,* ed. Edward Schortman and Patricia Urban, 235–255. New York.

Service, Elman
1962 *Primitive Social Organization: An Evolutionary Perspective,* 2d ed. New York.

Sharer, Robert J., and David C. Grove
1989 (Editors) *Regional Perspectives on the Olmec.* Cambridge.

Spencer, Charles S.
1994 Factional Ascendance, Dimensions of Leadership, and the Development of Centralized Authority. In *Factional Competition and Political Development in the New World,* ed. Elizabeth Brumfiel and John Fox, 31–43. Cambridge.

Stahl, Peter W.
1995 Differential Preservation Histories Affecting the Mammalian Zooarchaeological Record from the Forested Neotropical Lowlands. In *Archaeology in the Lowland American Tropics: Current Analytical Methods and Applications,* ed. Peter Stahl, 154–180. Cambridge.

Stark, Barbara L.
1981 The Rise of Sedentary Life. In *Archaeology,* ed. Jeremy Sabloff, 345–372. Supplement to the Handbook of Middle American Indians, vol. 1. Austin.

1997a Estilos de volutas en el período clásico.

In *Rutas de intercambio en Mesoamérica,* ed. Ellen Rattray. Mexico City.

1997b Gulf Lowland Styles and Political Geography in Ancient Veracruz. In *Olmec to Aztec: Settlement Patterns in the Ancient Gulf Lowlands,* ed. Barbara Stark and Philip Arnold, III, 278–309. Tucson, Ariz.

Stark, Barbara L., and Philip J. Arnold, III
1997 Introduction to the Archaeology of the Gulf Lowlands. In *Olmec to Aztec: Settlement Patterns in the Ancient Gulf Lowlands,* ed. Barbara Stark and Philip Arnold, III, 3–32. Tucson, Ariz.

Stark, Barbara L., Lynette Heller, Michael D. Glascock, J. Michael Elam, and Hector Neff
1992 Obsidian-Artifact Source Analysis for the Mixtequilla Region, South-Central Veracruz, Mexico. *Latin American Antiquity* 3: 221–239.

Stark, Barbara L., Lynette Heller, and Michael Ohnersorgen
1998 People with Cloth: Mesoamerican Economic Change from the Perspective of Cotton in South-Central Veracruz. *Latin American Antiquity* 9: 1–30.

Symonds, Stacey, and Roberto Lunagómez
1997 Settlement System and Population Development at San Lorenzo. In *Olmec to Aztec: Settlement Patterns in the Ancient Gulf Lowlands,* ed. Barbara Stark and Philip Arnold, III, 144–173. Tucson, Ariz.

Taube, Karl A.
1995 The Rainmakers: The Olmec and Their Contributions to Mesoamerican Belief and Ritual. In *The Olmec World: Ritual and Rulership,* 83–104 [exh. cat., The Art Museum, Princeton University]. Princeton.

1996 The Olmec Maize God: The Face of Corn in Formative Mesoamerica. *Res: Anthropology and Aesthetics* 29–30: 39–82.

Tolstoy, Paul
1982 Advances in the Valley of Oaxaca, part 1. *Quarterly Review of Archaeology* 3(3): 1, 8–11.

von Nagy, Christopher
1997 The Geoarchaeology of Settlement in the Grijalva Delta. In *Olmec to Aztec: Settlement Patterns in the Ancient Gulf Lowlands,* ed. Barbara Stark and Philip Arnold, III, 253–277. Tucson, Ariz.

Voorhies, Barbara
1976 *The Chantuto People: An Archaic Period Society of the Chiapas Littoral, Mexico.* Papers of the New World Archaeological Foundation 41. Provo, Utah.

1996a Clamming Up: Shell Mound and Other Archaic Sites of the Soconusco and What They Tell Us. Paper presented at the 61st Annual Meeting of the Society for American Archaeology, New Orleans.

1996b The Transformation from Foraging to Farming in the Lowlands of Mesoamerica. In *The Managed Mosaic: Ancient Maya Agriculture and Resource Use,* ed. Scott Fedick, 17–29. Salt Lake City.

Voorhies, Barbara, and Douglas J. Kennett
1995 Buried Sites on the Soconusco Coastal Plain, Chiapas, Mexico. *Journal of Field Archaeology* 22: 65–79.

Wedel, Waldo R.
1952 Structural Investigations in 1943. In *La Venta, Tabasco, a Study of Olmec Ceramics and Art,* by Philip Drucker, 34–79. Bureau of American Ethnology Bulletin 153. Washington.

Wilkerson, Jeffrey K.
1972 Ethnogenesis of the Huastecs and Totonacs: Early Cultures of North-Central Veracruz at Santa Luisa, Mexico. Ph.D. dissertation, Tulane University. University Microfilms, Ann Arbor.

1975a Pre-agricultural Village Life: The Late Preceramic Period in Veracruz. In *Studies in Ancient Mesoamerica* 2: 111–121. Contributions of the University of California Archaeological Research Facility 27. Berkeley.

1975b Resultados preliminares del estudio de ecología cultural en el norte-central de Veracruz durante 1973. In *Balance y perspectiva de la antropología de Mesoamérica y del centro de México, Arqueología I, XIII Mesa Redonda, 1973,* 339–346. Mexico City.

1981 The Northern Olmec and the Pre-Olmec Frontier on the Gulf Coast. In *The Olmec and Their Neighbors,* ed. Elizabeth Benson, 181–194. Washington.

1988 Cultural Time and Space in Ancient Veracruz. In *Ceremonial Sculpture of Ancient Veracruz,* curated by Marilyn Goldstein, 7–17 [exh. cat., Hillwood Art Gallery, Long Island University]. Brookville, N.Y.

Winfield Capitaine, Fernando
1988 *La Estela 1 de La Mojarra, Veracruz, México.* Washington.

Wing, Elizabeth
1980 Faunal Remains from San Lorenzo. In *In the Land of the Olmec, Vol. 1: The Archaeology of San Lorenzo Tenochtitlán,* ed. Michael Coe and Richard Diehl, 375–386. Austin.

Wittfogel, Karl A.
1957 *Oriental Despotism.* New Haven, Conn.

Wobst, H. Martin
1974 Boundary Conditions for Paleolithic Social Systems: A Simulation Approach. *American Antiquity* 39: 147–178.

Yoffee, Norman
1993 Too Many Chiefs? (or Safe Texts for the 90's). In *Archaeological Theory: Who Sets the Agenda?* ed. Norman Yoffee and Andrew Sherratt, 60–78. Cambridge.

Zeitlin, Judith F., and Robert N. Zeitlin
1996 Rethinking Old Models for the Origin of Food Production in Mesoamerica: Social Interaction and the Development of Agriculture. Paper presented at the 61st Annual Meeting of the Society for American Archaeology, New Orleans.

Zeitlin, Robert N.
1984 A Summary Report on Three Seasons of Field Investigations into the Archaic Period Prehistory of Lowland Belize. *American Anthropologist* 86: 358–369.

STACEY SYMONDS
Universidad Nacional Autónoma de México

The Ancient Landscape at San Lorenzo Tenochtitlán, Veracruz, Mexico: Settlement and Nature

The San Lorenzo Tenochtitlán Project combined regional survey with an in-depth examination of internal and local settlement pattern analysis. Excavations at San Lorenzo and associated sites allowed us to form a more complete picture of settlement types and their incorporation into the regional landscape. Data on the internal and regional patterns of San Lorenzo settlement indicate a highly complex sociopolitical organization with the existence of rulers at the apex of a stratified society. The rulers of the San Lorenzo Olmecs played a central role in integrating a population that transformed the natural environment into both sacred and secular landscapes for the exploitation and glorification of the San Lorenzo polity. In this essay, I describe changes in Olmec landscape and settlement for the Preclassic period (c. 1400–300 B.C.).

The San Lorenzo Tenochtitlán Archaeological Project was designed to investigate settlement patterns at the community and regional levels in response to a perceived need for more intensive and extensive settlement analysis in heartland areas with large centers. Until now, the nature of Olmec local and regional settlement development has been addressed by several projects (see González 1989; Rust and Sharer 1988), but none was conducted at San Lorenzo, the earliest of the Olmec centers. To remedy this obvious gap in data on the Olmecs, the San Lorenzo regional survey undertook a large-scale, intensive regional study aimed at clarifying the regional settlement patterns of the lower Coatzacoalcos basin. This survey was part of the San Lorenzo Archaeological Project, which since 1990 has combined extensive excavations at San Lorenzo and hinterland sites with geomorphological and biological studies of the region.

Several factors dictated the design and goals of the San Lorenzo regional survey. First, we recognized that settlement in the region around San Lorenzo would necessarily have been conditioned by the dynamic riverine environment of the lower Coatzacoalcos drainage. Proximity to the river as a communication and transportation axis may have been a primary consideration for site location in the past. But such sites probably also had to be located above the river's high flood mark, so high ground in this lowland basin would have been another primary settlement consideration. But this same riverine movement affects modern recovery of settlement information because alluvial deposition often reaches up to 3 meters a year.

Given these considerations, the survey sought to define the manner in which the San Lorenzo Olmecs integrated their domestic and monumental settlement contexts into the natural landscape. Analyses of the data were based on the presupposition that settlement and economic activity are intricately intertwined. Settlement development closely follows necessary economic changes that occur in any given area (Blouet 1972). My economic orientation to the study of settlement pattern development correlates with Carol Smith's (1976: 6)

View from El Azuzul of the plain surrounding San Lorenzo
Photograph: Courtesy of New World Archaeological Foundation

claim that "a central place becomes the hub of a region because goods, people, and information flow primarily between it and its less differentiated hinterland." It follows that "*place* within the system is an important economic variable" (Smith 1976: 6).

The San Lorenzo regional survey aimed at identifying settlement patterns and population development through time across the lower Coatzacoalcos drainage. The data obtained from several seasons of full-coverage survey have allowed us to delineate a complex system of regional interaction. This essay delineates the regional settlement for the Preclassic period in the lower Coatzacoalcos and describes the complexity of the settlement system centered around San Lorenzo, a central node in a complex system of intra- and interregional trade and exchange.

Internal Settlement

In the water-rich environment of the lower Coatzacoalcos drainage, the modern selection of settlement location is a prime consideration. Permanent settlement tends to be located on scarce high ground above the flood level. Fresh spring water is located on the elevated lands and is less available in the low areas. Human settlement in the region follows the basic requirements of spring water, high land, and location near river courses. Human settlement in this region had to adapt to surroundings that are generous, life-giving, and sometimes harsh and threatening.

The elevated plateau of San Lorenzo, one of few isolated terrains in the vast lower Coatzacoalcos floodplain, is surrounded by wide floodplains crisscrossed by numerous fluvial courses, tributaries of the meandering Coatzacoalcos River, the Chiquito River directly to the east of the plateau, and the Tatagapa estuary to the west of the plateau. The centrality of this higher ground played an important role in the development of San Lorenzo as a nodal site in the regional network that was to develop across the lower Coatzacoalcos floodplain. How and why did San Lorenzo become the center of Early Preclassic Olmec culture?

One of the most important goals of the regional survey was the definition of San Lorenzo site limits and its inner hinterland. Full-coverage survey by Roberto Lunagómez (1995) determined constant densities of Preclassic materials across the San Lorenzo plateau and down to the 30 meter contour line (fig. 1), resulting in a size estimation for the site of San Lorenzo of 690 hectares rather than the previously estimated 53 hectares (Coe 1981: 119). This revised estimate would make San Lorenzo the largest Early Preclassic site in Mesoamerica (compare Flannery and Marcus 1994). The San Lorenzo plateau may also be considered one of the largest works of monumental architecture in Early Preclassic Mesoamerica; it was modified by deploying enormous human effort in the construction of terraces, filling and cutting operations, and earth removal, thus transforming the natural land into a sacred and quotidian space for the ancient inhabitants (Symonds and Cyphers 1996).

Furthermore, survey and excavations at the site (conducted by Ann Cyphers) demonstrate that San Lorenzo settlement was also complex. The San Lorenzo community contained separate spaces for the elite and ceremonial core, with the most prestigious dwellings located on the highest part of the plateau and less elaborate structures on lower terraces. Dwellings ranged from simple wattle-and-daub constructions with tamped earth floors to more complex structures with rammed mud walls and smoothed bentonite floors. Elegant structures were plastered with hematite-stained sand (Symonds and Cyphers 1996).

In addition to elite residences, separate spaces were created for ceremonial contexts. Monumental sculpture was arranged in layouts designed to transmit symbolic messages (Symonds and Cyphers 1996), possibly related to the position of rulership and its relationship to the cosmos. Finally, evidence of craft specialization can also be seen at San Lorenzo. Deposits of several tons of ilmenite "beads" were concentrated in specific locations at the site. It also appears that types of activities were associated with relative status; middle-range dwellings seem to have engaged in manufacture of greenstone ornaments and obsidian tools, while the more elite residences were associated with the recycling of stone sculpture (Cyphers, personal communication, 1995). San Lorenzo's internal organization alone indicates a highly complex sociopolitical organization centered around the exploitation of "imported" resources within a stratified society.

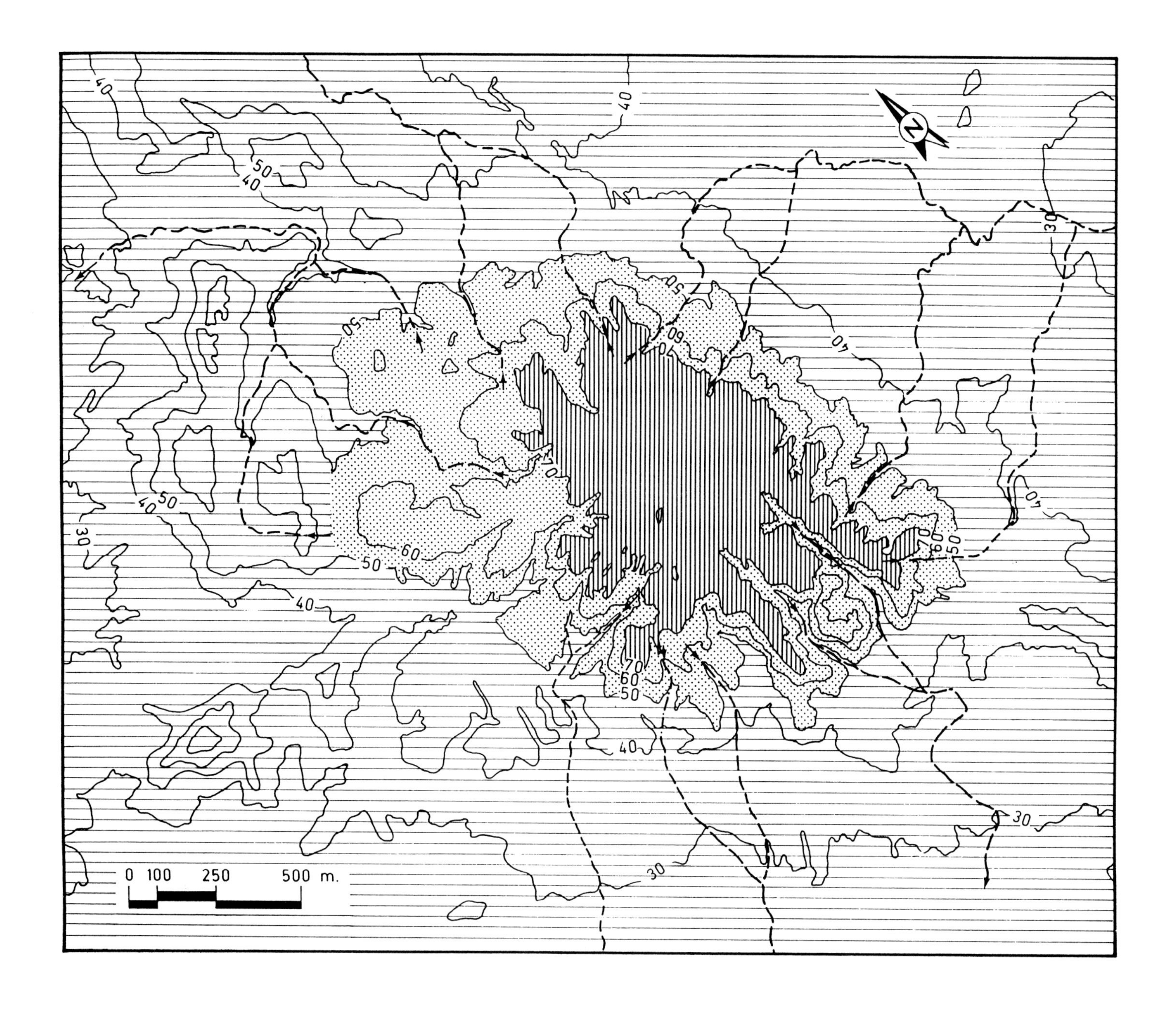

1. San Lorenzo plateau and immediate surroundings, comparing Coe and Diehl's (1980) size estimate (shown with vertical lines) for San Lorenzo with the revised 1995 size estimate
Ann Cyphers

Regional Settlement

Departing from the San Lorenzo plateau as a focal point, the survey extended across the lower Coatzacoalcos River basin in an attempt to determine site development and population density through time and space. The regional survey found that most traces of the earliest settlement in the region have been obscured by thick alluvial deposition (fig. 2). Deep coring at numerous and regular intervals might give a picture of the extent of Ojochí and Bajío phase settlement (see Pye and Clark, this volume, fig. 2 for relative chronological sequence), but this research would have to be complemented by excavations in order to define the nature of such deposits. Nevertheless, excavations at San Lorenzo and some sites in the inner hinterland show that these early layers are quite dense and contiguous with San Lorenzo phase material, implying continuous occupation from these earlier phases into the San Lorenzo A phase.

Excavations at San Lorenzo and associated sites allowed us to form a more complete picture of settlement types and their incorporation into a regional landscape. A preliminary site typology has been established that attempts to distinguish among the different levels of the sociopolitical hierarchy associated with San Lorenzo. These sites also include possible seasonal, functionally differentiated sites for the exploitation of various resources. The criteria used to establish the settlement hierarchy include site size and densities of artifacts, as proposed by others (Blanton et al. 1982; Sanders et al. 1979). My typology is preliminary and will be superseded once excavations have been conducted at each different site type and better data become available for site sizes, functions, and duration.

In the typology, sites were separated into five levels. The first division was based upon the presence or absence of architectural modification (platforms made by modifying natural elevations, or terracing). The second factor was the presence or absence of mounded architecture. The mounds in this type of construction are artificial and not modifications of previously elevated terrain. Final divisions were based upon an analysis of site area (Symonds 1995). The division according to area is important for future analyses, which will include attempts to correct sample biases resulting from differing levels of surface visibility. Sites without architecture (of any visible type) are classified in terms of density of surface artifacts (considering visibility and other factors) and the areal extent of the site.

Early Preclassic settlement provides evidence for seven different site types. The purpose of the typology was to distinguish among different levels of communities within the region and to determine the possible degree of organization and/or administration evident in the settlement pattern. As shown below, the internal complexity found at San Lorenzo was mirrored by a similar level of complexity in the regional settlement, thus reflecting a high degree of complexity in the sociopolitical organization of the lower Coatzacoalcos drainage interaction sphere during the Early Preclassic.

Type 1 sites comprise simple dispersions of artifacts over small areas that do not exceed 5 hectares. These sites are located on elevated terrain. When they are distant from larger sites, Type 1 sites are almost inevitably located along the rivers at points above the flood line, such as the small sites located along Coatzacoalcos to the north of Peña Blanca. Unless associated with other sites, Type 1 sites are not found near important river junctures. Twelve Early Preclassic Type 1 sites were located in the region, eight concentrated in the area contiguous to the San Lorenzo plateau and toward the junctures of the Chiquito, Tatagapa, and El Gato fluvial courses.

Type 2 sites also consist of artifact scatters, but over slightly larger areas and sometimes on naturally elevated platforms. These sites can reach up to 10 hectares in total area. Type 2 sites line smaller fluvial networks, often at midway points between San Lorenzo and important junctures of the Chiquito, Tatagapa, Azuzul, or Coatzacoalcos waterways. A typical Type 2 site can be found at Lomas Cuatas (fig. 3) on the eastern banks of the Chiquito River, to the north of San Antonio. Lomas Cuatas is interesting for its location on elevated mounds in the floodplain of the Chiquito River. In later times (Early Postclassic), these natural elevations were further modified and elaborated for a more complex settlement. In the Early Preclassic, the site represented an important halfway point along the Chiquito between San Lorenzo and the juncture of the Chiquito and Coatzacoalcos Rivers to the north. Seven Type 2 sites were identified for the Early Preclassic.

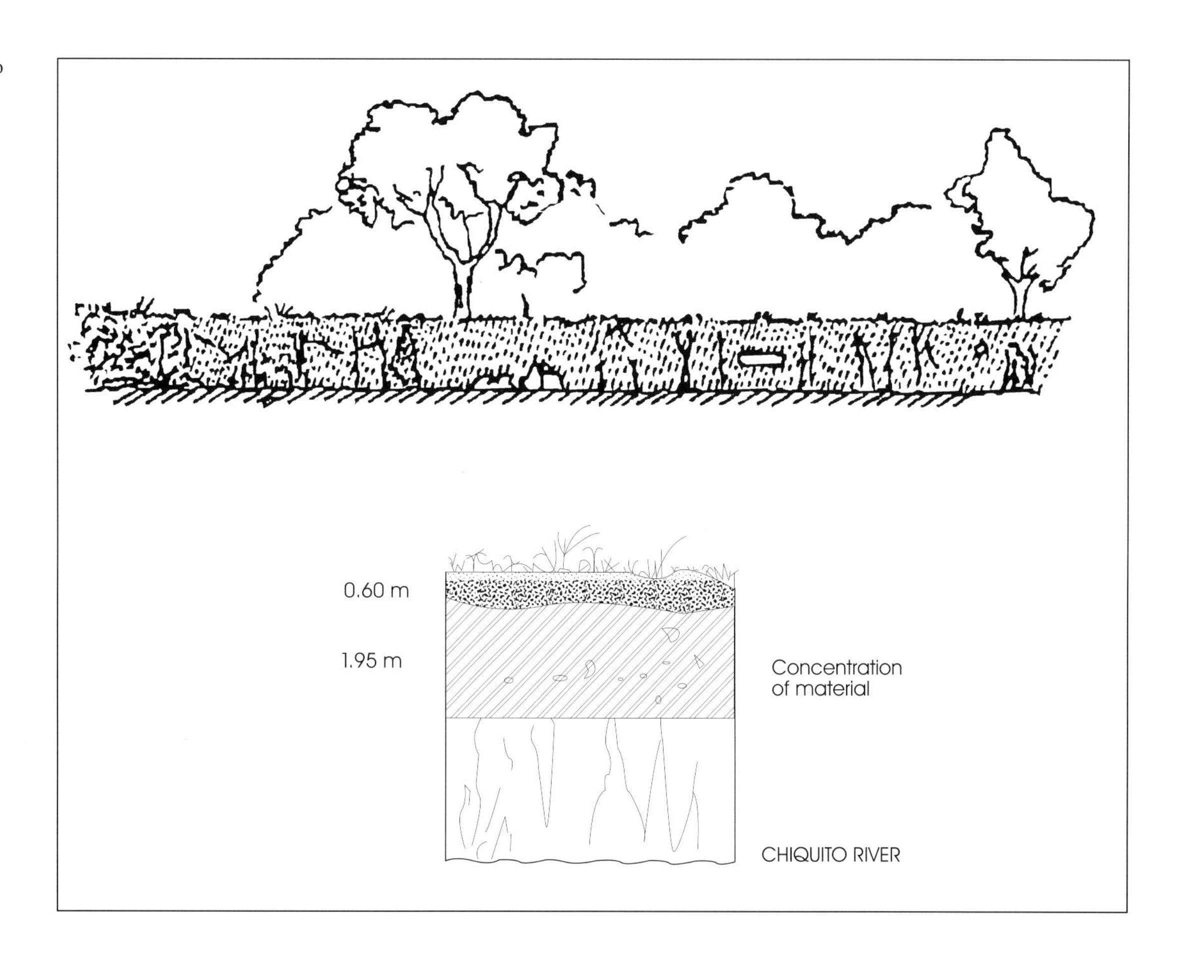

2. Cross section of Chiquito River showing depth of alluvial deposition

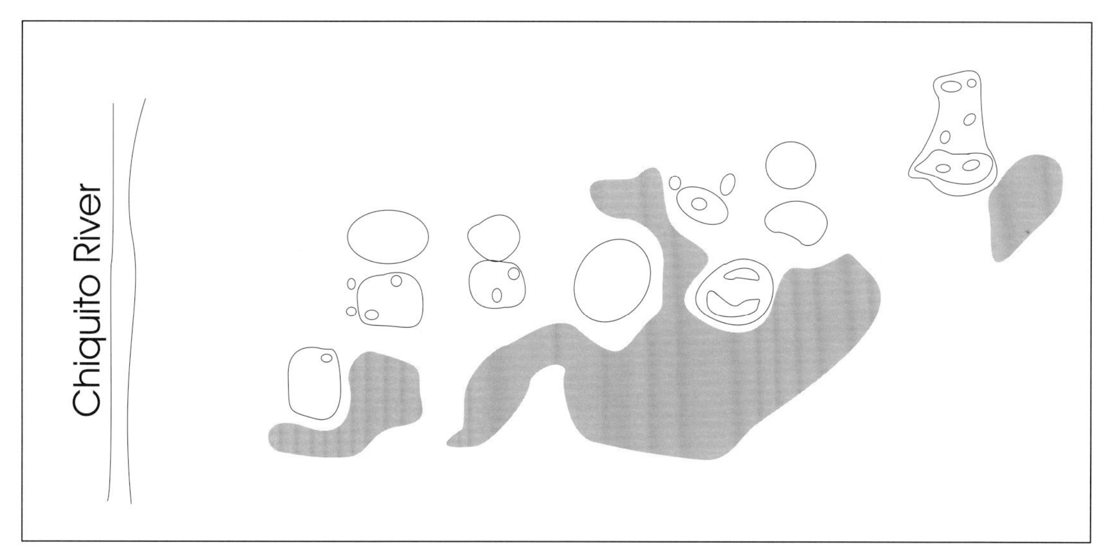

3. Lomas Cuatas site map, Type 2 site (Early Preclassic component), with gray shaded area indicating swampy ground
Drawing by Zachary Nelson

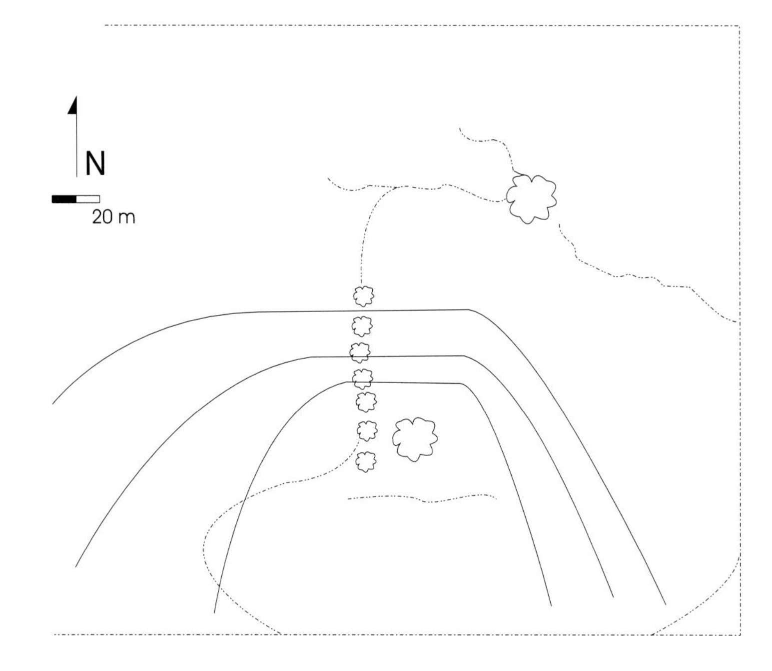

4. Terraced site in Texistepec uplands, Type 3 site
Drawing by Zachary Nelson

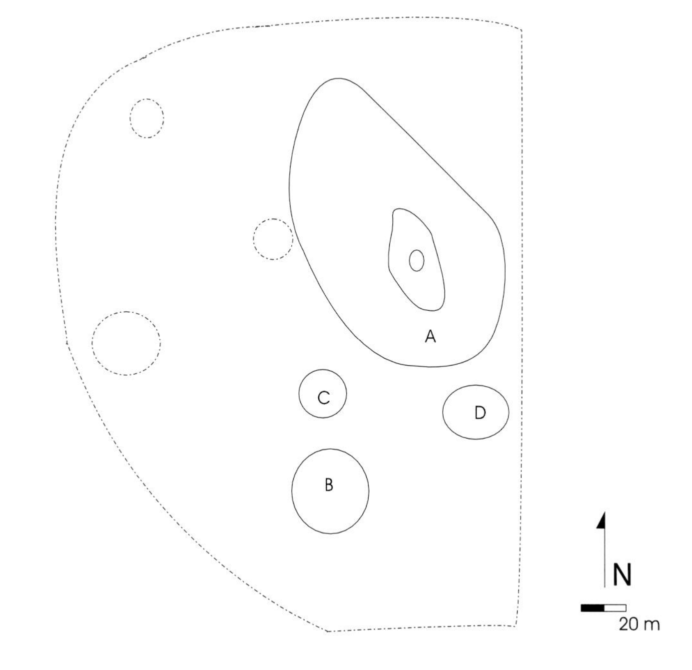

5. Northern plain mound group, Type 4 site
Drawing by Zachary Nelson

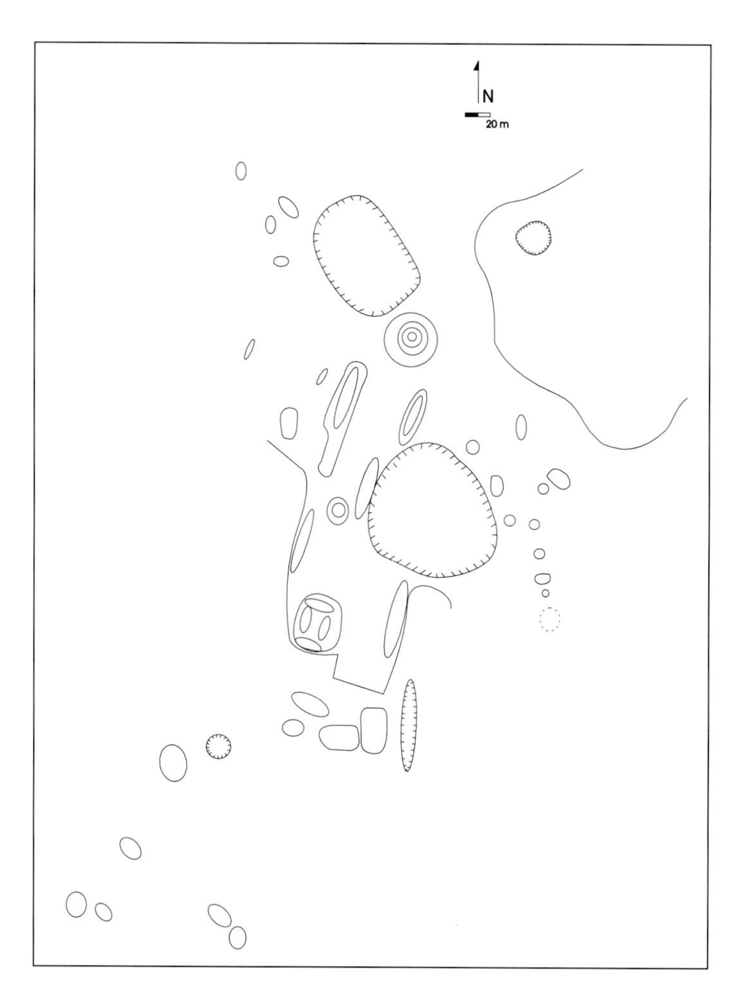

6. Ixtepec, Type 5 site
Drawing by Zachary Nelson

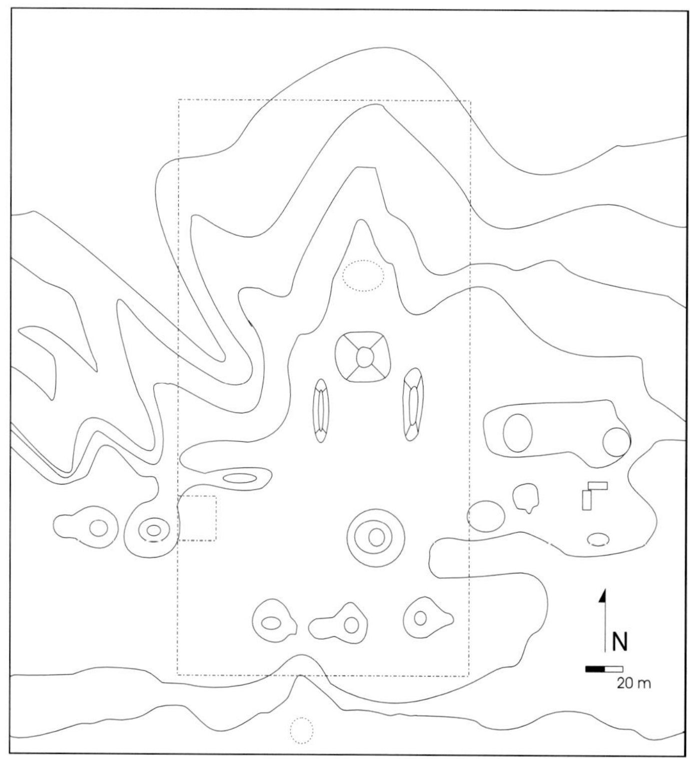

7. Los Pocitos, Type 6 site
(Early Preclassic component)
Drawing by Zachary Nelson

Type 3 sites are notable for the formation of sequential terraces out of and along natural elevations (fig. 4). Type 3 sites are located only on higher ground that lines principal waterways or on smaller pieces of elevated terrain located immediately contiguous to a fluvial route. In the latter case, the terracing is much more rudimentary than on steeper and longer slopes. Type 3 sites are primarily situated between important river junctures and larger sites, creating vital links up and down the fluvial networks.

Type 4 sites exemplify a special construction type created for the exploitation of the vast floodplains that surrounded the San Lorenzo plateau. These sites consist of artificially elevated platforms in terrain that, during the rainy season, falls below the flood line. Such sites, often found in groups, are sometimes organized in plazalike formations (fig. 5). Excavations at one of these sites suggested that they were used for the possible processing of faunal resources (such as varieties of crustaceans) trapped in the floodplains when waters receded at the end of the rainy season. Almost all Type 4 sites are concentrated in the floodplains surrounding the San Lorenzo plateau, although a few can be found in the floodplains of Tacamichapa Island.

Type 5 sites are located above the flood line and contain mounded architecture (fig. 6). These sites can be found at secondary junctures along primary fluvial courses connected to San Lorenzo. Type 5 sites seem to be evenly spaced along a southwest to northeast axis that connected San Lorenzo to the coast and inland to the Isthmus of Tehuantepec. Type 6 sites appear to represent larger, more complex versions of Type 5 sites. These sites are located on elevated terrain at primary junctures or central points throughout the web of connecting waterways. Type 6 sites combine both terracing of natural elevation and mounded architecture (fig. 7). Closer to San Lorenzo, Type 6 sites were more widely dispersed, with some Type 5 sites in between. However, toward the coast, on Tacamichapa Island, these larger sites seem to proliferate along the course of the San Antonio River.

Type 7 is the most complex type of site recorded for the Early Preclassic. This type consists of numerous terraces, mounds, and a wide areal expanse. It represents the most complex type of the typology. San Lorenzo was the Type 7 site for the Preclassic period occupation and was located at the center of the complex web of fluctuating fluvial networks that defined the lower Coatzacoalcos drainage, and was centrally located between the intersections of each waterway.

Settlement Patterns and Spatial Analysis

Determination of the spacing of sites across San Lorenzo's hinterland is crucial to our understanding of the development of settlement at that site and throughout its network. Does this spacing deviate from a random pattern? If so, how can spatial analysis be interpreted in cultural/behavioral terms for the San Lorenzo Olmecs? The Early Preclassic settlement patterns for the San Lorenzo survey region allow us to make several observations about the nature of Olmec sociopolitical organization and regional networks across the lower Coatzacoalcos drainage at that time.

The power of this settlement pattern analysis, however, should not be overestimated. Data collected from the 403 square kilometer area surrounding the site of San Lorenzo do not represent the entire universe of settlement data for this region. Geological factors, coupled with modern agricultural and land use patterns, have combined to bury much of the archaeological remains in the region. With a view of presenting information that will stand the test of time, my settlement study avoids focusing on minor details and favors, instead, a focus on more general trends and patterns.

The primary contribution of the San Lorenzo regional survey is its presentation of an overview of the settlement patterns and population distribution of the lower Coatzacoalcos drainage through time and space. The regional survey describes the site universe around San Lorenzo from the Early Preclassic through the Early Postclassic. Sites were dated from the ceramics recovered in the surface survey. Ceramic diagnostics were determined from excavation data from the San Lorenzo Archaeological Project (Cyphers 1991, 1992, 1993, 1994, and personal communication) and from Michael Coe's and Richard Diehl's (1980) ceramic typology and chronology. (For a complete description of the survey ceramics, see Symonds [1995].) The chronology we used roughly parallels the one defined by Coe and Diehl (1980).

From these data, the settlement history of

8. Early Preclassic settlement
Adapted from Symonds and Lunagómez 1997: 154, fig. 6.3

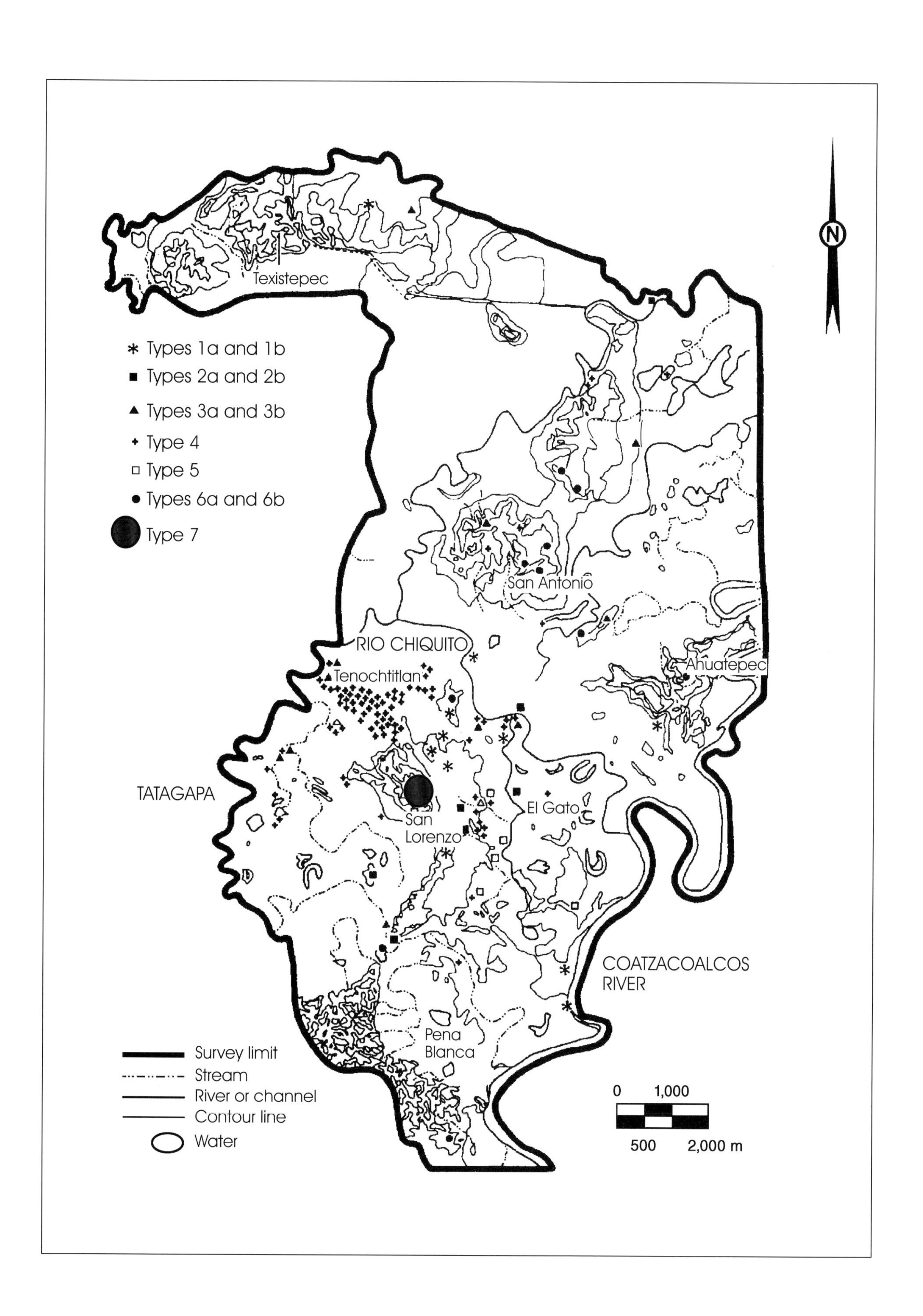

Texistepec
Types 1a and 1b
Types 2a and 2b
Types 3a and 3b
Type 4
Type 5
Types 6a and 6b
Type 7
San Antonio
RIO CHIQUITO
Tenochtitlan
Ahuatepec
TATAGAPA
San
Lorenzo
El Gato
COATZACOALCOS
RIVER
Pena
Blanca
Survey limit
Stream
River or channel
Contour line
Water
0
1,000
500
2,000 m

the lower Coatzacoalcos drainage described by the San Lorenzo regional survey allows us to begin to reconstruct the cultural evolution of the San Lorenzo Olmecs and their earliest manifestations to their apogee as the primary center of a complex civilization.

Early Preclassic

The Early Preclassic San Lorenzo phase settlement of the region was one of the most dense in the history of the lower Coatzacoalcos drainage. The area defined as the inner hinterland, immediately surrounding San Lorenzo, was densely occupied (fig. 8), with all seven site types present and a total of 135 sites recorded for the period. Extrapolation from excavation data (see Cyphers 1991, 1992, 1993, 1994) leads us to believe that this significant population (as indicated by the number of sites) grew fairly rapidly during the Ojochí and Bajío phases (c. 1400–1200 B.C.) at the beginning of the Early Preclassic occupation, so that by the San Lorenzo A phase (c. 1100–1000 B.C.) the population and its organizational characteristics were already in place.

Twenty-nine Early Preclassic sites are currently known for the outer hinterland research area; this contrasts with 106 sites that were recorded for the smaller, 90 square kilometer inner hinterland region immediately contiguous to, and including, the San Lorenzo plateau (Lunagómez 1995). The ancient river courses, defined by the present-day Tatagapa and El Gato estuaries, represented important foci of settlement activity during this early period. Studies of geomorphology (Cyphers and Ortiz 1993) suggest that these two estuaries were once principal river courses. Their proximity to the San Lorenzo plateau would have made them the preferred focus for original settlement of the region. It is important to note that the region circumscribed by these two waterways contained 78 percent of the overall regional settlement during the Early Preclassic. Extending out from San Lorenzo, settlements covered almost all habitable terrain available, marking the Early Preclassic as one of the most important settlement periods for the lower Coatzacoalcos drainage, in terms of both population size and density.

Within this settlement, San Lorenzo was an "island" surrounded by its means of transportation and communication to the outer hinterland and beyond. The Tatagapa, El Gato, Chiquito, and Calzadas Rivers demarcated the zone of immediate control. The plateau of San Lorenzo represents 33 percent of the inner hinterland area. The remaining 67 percent of the area contained 105 sites dispersed toward the major waterways. Sites are clustered in the

9. Colossal head from San Lorenzo, Monument 4, Early Preclassic period, basalt
Museo de Antropología de Xalapa, Universidad Veracruzana

10. Statue of a supernatural being from San Lorenzo, Monument 10, Early Preclassic period, basalt
Museo de Antropología de Xalapa, Universidad Veracruzana

11. Stone monuments from El Azuzul-Loma del Zapote, Early Preclassic period, basalt
Photograph: Courtesy of New World Archaeological Foundation

area immediately contiguous to the San Lorenzo plateau. But this clustered pattern becomes a more organized and regularly spaced organization once one begins to observe the placement of larger sites within the entire survey area. Most of the stone monuments from the region are from San Lorenzo itself (see figs. 9, 10).

Across the expanse of the lower Coatzacoalcos drainage, large sites are located at key nodes in fluvial courses. At the southern confluence, one site that characterizes this pattern is Loma del Zapote, which presents an elevated causeway, monumental architecture, and sculptural art (fig. 11). The El Bajío/Remolino site is located at the northern river juncture. Smaller sites are located along less important transportation and communication routes. Today, as in the past, small sites form an almost continuous line along each of the principal water courses.

The settlement pattern in the outer reaches of the survey region reinforces the implications of the inner hinterland pattern; trade and transportation, and the exploitation of fluvial routes, appear to have been key factors in determining settlement location and importance. Settlement was concentrated along a route toward the Gulf Coast along the San Antonio estuary, a water course that crosses modern-day Tacamichapa Island, and we begin to see settlement along the southern edge of the Texistepec uplands, along a possible ancient fluvial course.

Important sites are primarily located on elevated terrain along the San Antonio network, with the largest sites on its banks and at important junctures. At the possible locale of an ancient juncture of the El Gato estuary with the San Antonio, where Tenochtitlán's elevated terrain would have come nearest to the Tacamichapa elevated terrain, a site called San Antonio dominates the landscape (fig. 12). Here the elevated terrain is modified in the same way as the San Lorenzo plateau, while small islands are created in the floodplains to the site's east, recalling the northern plains mounds at San Lorenzo. On the Texistepec uplands, sites appear on the highest points, areas also least disturbed by modern sulfur mines.

Visually the Early Preclassic settlement can be divided into three distinct settlement clusters or "communities" (fig. 13). The first of these revolved around San Lorenzo itself and the elevated terrain circumscribed by the river courses mentioned above. The second consisted of the lowland, low-order hamlets and the isolated residences that surrounded these primary elevations. The third consisted of a northern component of linearly placed settlements along water courses to the coast, showing a two-tiered site hierarchy, a simplified version of that surrounding the San Lorenzo plateau. Across the lines of these "communities," however, one notes that Type 5 and 6 sites seem to be evenly spaced along the axis of the San Antonio estuary, perhaps in order to exploit and control the flow of resources along this ancient river in the interregional network of the Preclassic, San Lorenzo Olmecs (see Hodder 1972).

Thus the Early Preclassic settlement at San Lorenzo and its hinterland present us with a picture of a large and complex center that was organized to exploit resources efficiently in the area immediately surrounding the site. By this time, San Lorenzo already evidenced a strong presence. San Lorenzo had already established its network of settlements within a well-circumscribed area designed to provide control over resources and access routes. Although San Lorenzo was clearly at the center of all the activity in the inner hinterland, the nature of the settlement hierarchy implies that some of the functions of this center were delegated to lesser centers located at strategic points along the principal waterways. Secondary centers were located at junctures such as that between the Calzadas and El Azuzul estuaries (Las Camelias and Loma del Zapote). These secondary centers have evidence of major ceremonial importance, most easily evident in the monumental sculpture and architecture present at these sites as well as the fine quality of the ceramic material encountered (fig. 11).

San Lorenzo was clearly a central place and hub of regional interaction. The rulers at San Lorenzo were able to establish a complex regional system, with secondary centers as nodes for subsystems nested within the larger system (see Smith 1976: 6). San Lorenzo's location was the critical variable in the network of interaction that allowed for the most efficient control and access to a complex system of communication and transportation mandated by the meandering waterways of the lower Coatzacoalcos drainage.

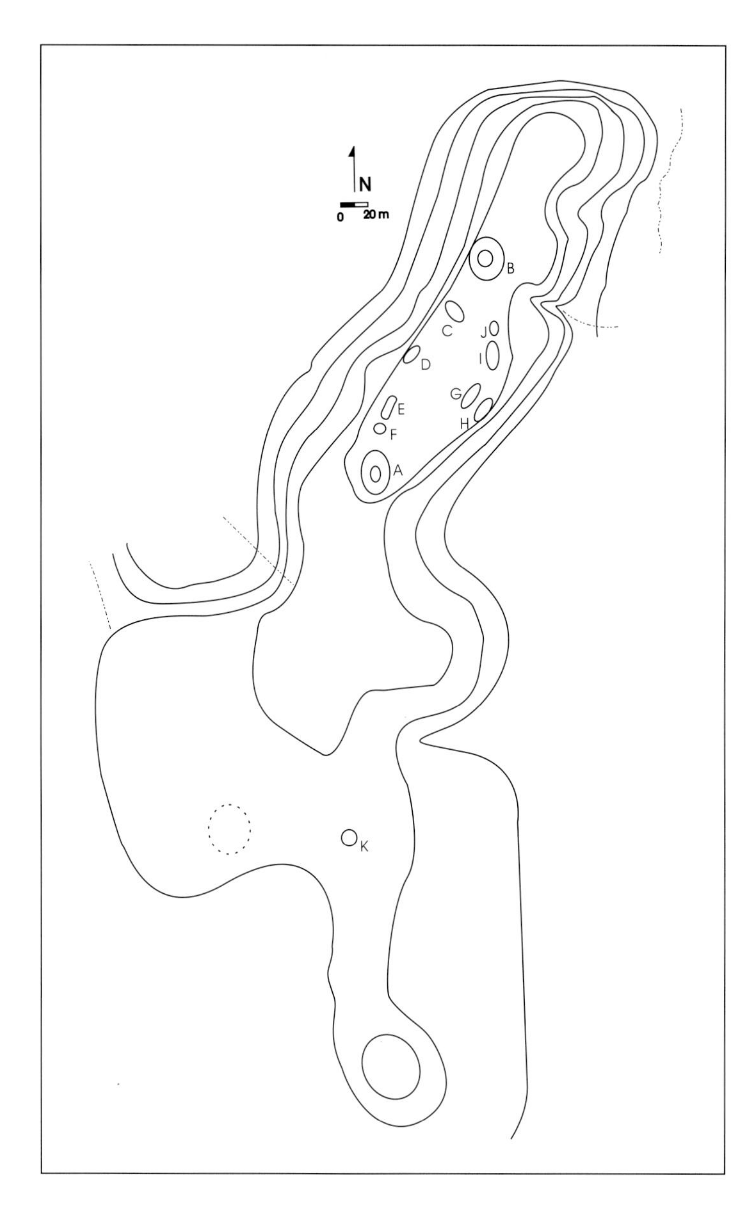

12. San Antonio site map
Drawing by Zachary Nelson

Middle Preclassic

Diagnostics for the Middle Preclassic are often the same as those for the Early Preclassic. In general, most of the utilitarian wares remained the same. For this reason, in the definition of Preclassic occupation, sites with diagnostics common to both Early and Middle Preclassic were assigned only to the latter period, in order to be conservative in the estimation of the number of early sites.

In the Middle Preclassic, new decorative techniques appear, such as the double-line-break, so notorious in Olmec descriptions. Differential firing of gray wares also appears later, as do composite silhouette bowls in this paste type. Indeed, Tigrillo fine gray paste is the most common Middle Preclassic diagnostic. In general, the ceramic assemblage seems to become less complex.

Just as the Middle Preclassic ceramics appear simpler than their Early Preclassic counterparts, the settlement pattern is notable in the reduction in the number of sites in the inner hinterland (fig. 14) and the appearance of new sites at river junctures. Only forty-five sites were recorded for the region immediately contiguous to San Lorenzo (43 percent of the Early Preclassic number). This abandonment of the inner hinterland terrain was coupled with an increase in the number of sites in the outer hinterland that clustered along two transportation networks. Thirty sites were recorded in the outer portion of the survey area. In general, the decrease in site numbers is most evident in the smaller sites. Types 1, 2, and 4 were the first to disappear from the landscape. At the same time, some larger, more complex sites witnessed a reduction in size and possibly importance during the Middle Preclassic.

The Middle Preclassic decrease in the number of small sites across the high floodplains and along the El Gato and Tatagapa Rivers most likely resulted from two events that seem to have been instrumental in shaping the history of the lower Coatzacoalcos drainage basin. The meandering nature of the rivers in this basin cannot be ignored when discussing population development along its banks. Control of transportation and communication routes was invaluable to the rise of San Lorenzo as a major regional center. However, these routes were continually shifting across the landscape, creating new foci and changing resource concentration areas. If, during the Preclassic, the Tatagapa and El Gato Rivers were in the process of shifting, they might have been changing from primary fluvial routes to drier, backswamp regions. Resources may still have been present in these areas, but their importance would have decreased, thereby limiting the need for dense settlement along their banks. Changes in interaction routes and the nature of the routes themselves might easily have fostered shifts in population dispersion in the region. The increase in settlement in the outer hinterland of San Lorenzo at this time dovetails with changing patterns of interaction and settlement in the inner hinterland.

It appears that changes in water courses may have been propitious for the outer reaches of San Lorenzo's hinterland, as other water courses were perhaps forced to fill gaps left in the transportation and communication networks so vital to San Lorenzo's position in the region. Along the San Antonio, an important fluvial course toward the coast, sites appear to have grown in size and complexity at this time. Another, now defunct, fluvial course ran east-west along the southern edge of the Texistepec uplands. Middle Preclassic settlement in this area paralleled the ancient river course south of these uplands. The Middle Preclassic also witnessed the emergence of settlement along the modern course of the Chiquito River. Two second-order sites were located at the center of the western elevated terrain on Tacamichapa Island. Furthermore, Las Lomas de Tacamichapa (at the northern extreme of the island) took on greater importance and size, becoming a second-order site. Smaller sites were scattered toward the river and across the elevated terrain to take advantage of high ground and key positions along the river.

Changes in settlement direction signal possible changes in interaction spheres. For example, the growth of Middle Preclassic settlement along the Texistepec fluvial network may have been instrumental in connecting the lowland sites with inland settlements, such as those located toward and throughout the Tuxtla Mountains. Moreover, as in the case of Early

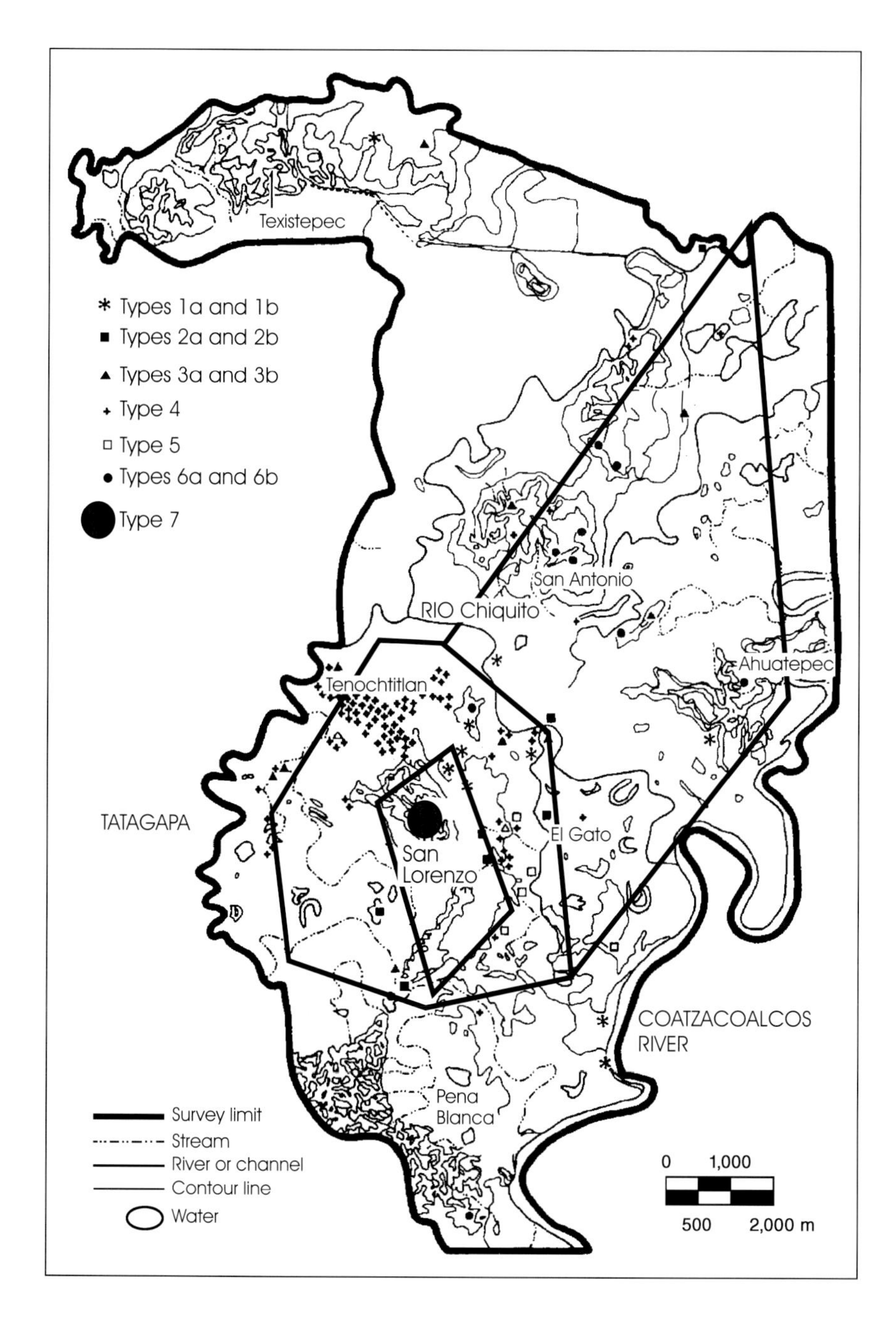

13. Settlement development divisions of survey area

Preclassic San Antonio, the settlements along Texistepec's elevated terrain copied San Lorenzo's site development, with the creation of an elaborate terracing system along the slopes of the uplands, toward the river course (fig. 15). Emerging settlement along different fluvial networks implies that, in the Middle Preclassic, the principal trade routes shifted away from San Lorenzo toward the north and east.

It is important to note that the change in the number and location of sites from the Early to the Middle Preclassic paralleled changes in site types and organizational complexity. The Early Preclassic settlement pattern was comprised of seven different site types, largely concentrated around San Lorenzo, the apex of the site hierarchy. In the Middle Preclassic, however, the number of smaller, less complex sites diminished, and sites around San Lorenzo decreased in size and complexity. To the north, on the other hand, sites continued to become larger and more multifaceted, while those around San Lorenzo seemed to become less so.

During the Middle Preclassic, the settlements around San Lorenzo still formed part of a complex network anchored there. Nevertheless, the network appears to have diminished in size and complexity during this period. This reduction in the inner hinterland implies that San Lorenzo's degree of control and mastery of a system of specialized links in a complex network may have been waning during the latter half of the Preclassic period. It is important to note that complexity at San Lorenzo itself may have been diminishing at this time; primary production there of monumental stone sculpture occurred mostly during the Early Preclassic (Cyphers 1994; personal communication, 1995). As San Lorenzo's interaction system decreased in size and complexity, the degree of centralization of the system also appears to have diminished, with a larger number of secondary centers located in the outer hinterland, a portion of the network whose complexity and size were perhaps at their apogee at this time.

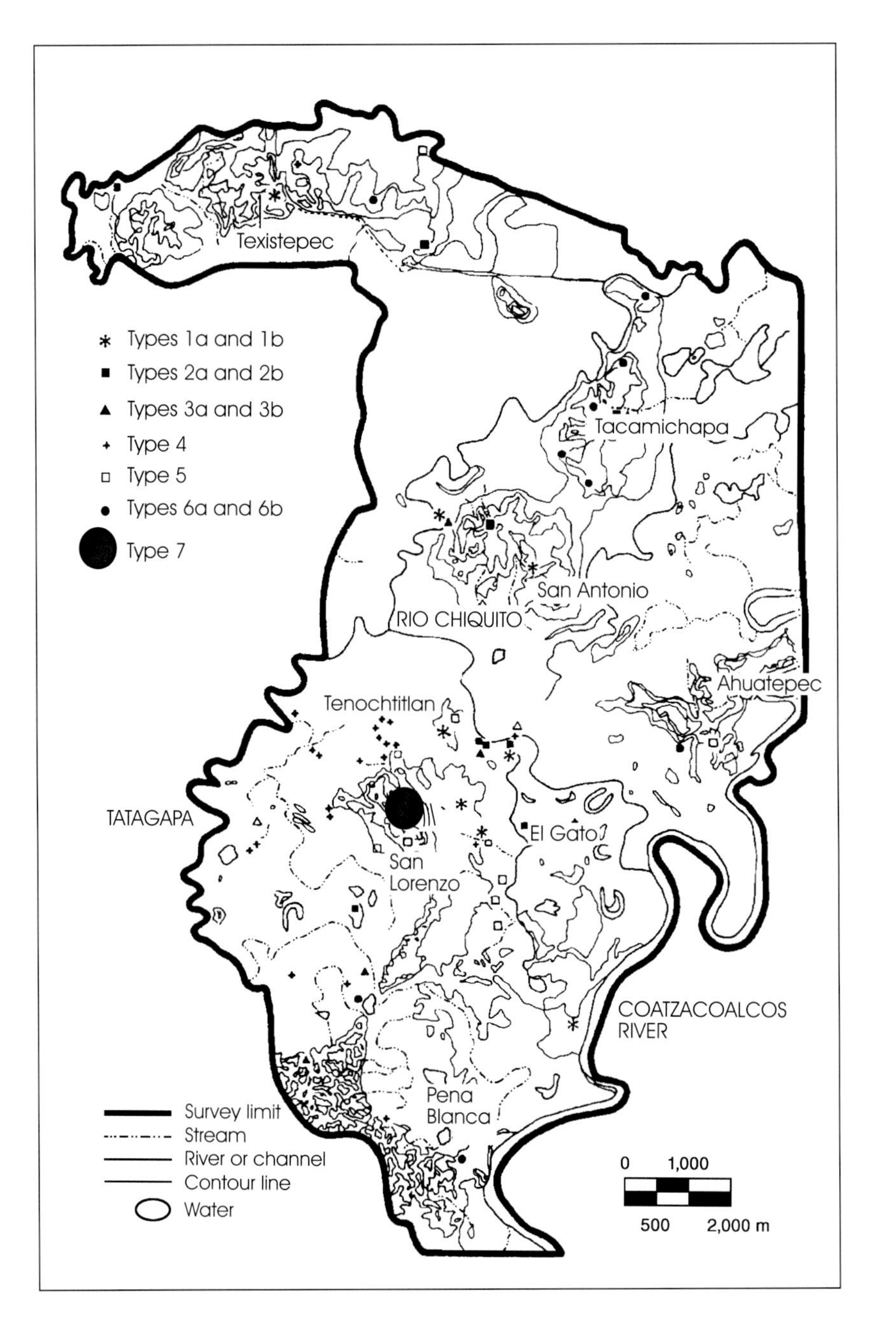

14. Middle Preclassic settlement
Adapted from Symonds and Lunagómez 1997: 159, fig. 6.4

Late Preclassic

Determination of the Late Preclassic settlement pattern in the lower Coatzacoalcos drainage is very difficult because its artifactual diagnostics are poorly known. Recent excavations at San Lorenzo have not revealed evidence for this period, and Coe and Diehl (1980) did not encounter any unmixed strata for this phase, leaving its designation tenuous. Only four sites have been recorded for the Late Preclassic (fig. 16).

Three sites along the course of the San Antonio estuary demonstrate the continued (albeit diminished) importance of this northerly transportation route to the occupation of the region. The access to the coast and sites further north may have been the determining factor in keeping these sites occupied during a period of such drastic depopulation. One site was also recorded in the Texistepec uplands, indicating that perhaps ties to the north were instrumental in the survival of settlements at this time.

The reasons for the dramatic decrease in population and settlement noted in the Late Preclassic remain unresolved. In part, this problem is the result of a lack of excavation data that might shed light on this decline; no Late Preclassic levels are yet available from the region. However, several processes occurred during this period that may have affected settlement and occupation of the lower Coatzacoalcos drainage. First, the river courses of the lower Coatzacoalcos have been shown to be highly active. They change up to 3 meters a year. The process of tectonic uplift, combined with land submersion at sea level, may also have played a significant role in determining the rate and time at which key salt domes arose throughout the region. It is clear that the rivers were vital elements in the determination of the settlement pattern and importance of the region as a whole. Drastic changes in water networks and associated lands would have led to dramatic shifts in population levels and occupational patterns.

15. Texistepec terraces
Drawing by Zachary Nelson

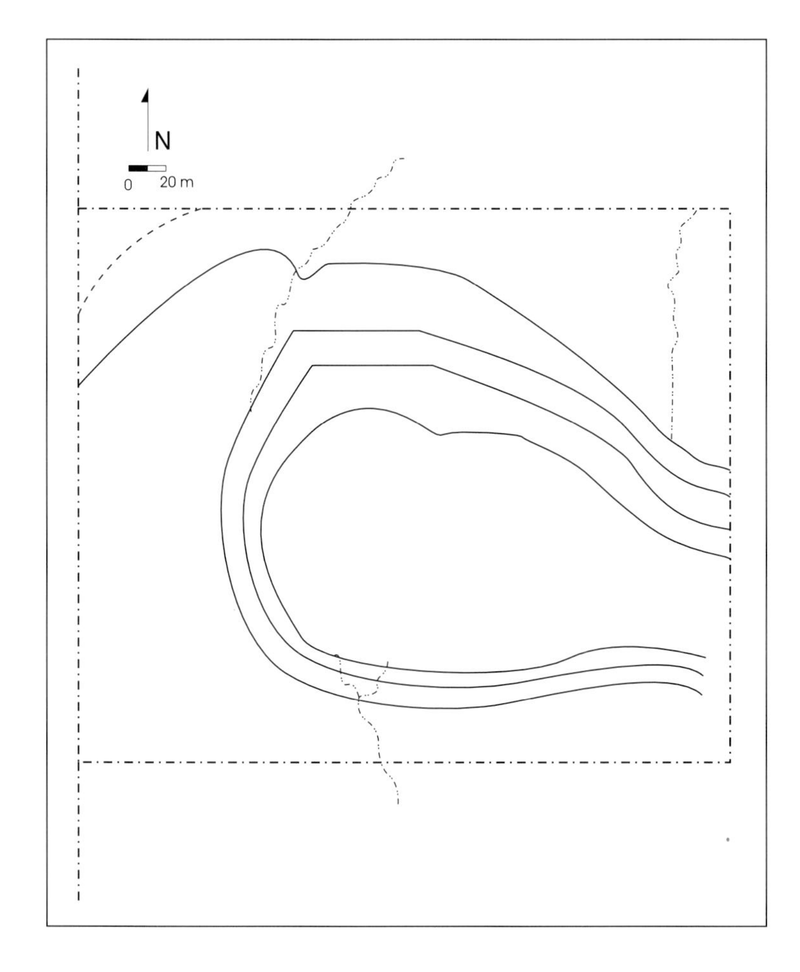

Second, surveys and excavations in the Tuxtlas region have shown a similar decrease in population at the end of the Middle Preclassic and to the beginning stages of the Middle Classic (see Arnold, this volume). Archaeologists in the Tuxtlas posit another volcanic eruption, on the heels of the Middle Preclassic San Martin eruption. They suggest that this later eruption most likely had more severe and extensive effects than the earlier volcanic activity in the region (Santley 1991). Ash layers near Catemaco and associated radiocarbon dates reinforce this conclusion (Santley 1991).

Finally, the Late Preclassic throughout Mesoamerica seems to represent a period of change and disruption of previously established patterns. In Chiapas, the Late Preclassic begins a period of regionalism and increasing significance of Maya incursion and influence (Lowe 1977). The ceramic assemblages from the sites extant in the northern uplands of Texistepec confirm a possible extension of this trend into the lower Coatzacoalcos drainage, with the few ceramics paralleling more southerly, Maya types for this latter period of the Preclassic.

Conclusion

The San Lorenzo Tenochtitlán Archaeological Project combined regional survey with extensive excavations. The settlement patterns inferred from my analysis suggest a high degree of control, not only in the location of population through time but also in the manner in which sites were constructed to conform to a complex and fluctuating environment. The highly complex and well-organized settlement system centered around San Lorenzo during the Early Preclassic indicates the presence of a well-established, hierarchical social order.

In the coastal region where the relatively flat plain is cut by a multitude of rivers and streams, these natural patterns influenced the distribution of human settlement. Riverine patterns and the associated technological developments fomented certain types of political organization and socioeconomic complexity. Human societies adapt to riverine systems without necessarily altering them. As social complexity increases, attempts to modify them may be made. Along the ancient waterways of the San Lorenzo region, reconstructed through geomorphological studies, we note a preference for settlement location and architectural constructions adapted to riverine life.

San Lorenzo's position on elevated land near several river junctures made it an important node in the system because of its high degree of connectivity (fig. 17). The connectivity of locations correlates positively with population concentrations and centralization. San Lorenzo maintained a large number of linkages of varying degrees of importance, as manifested by the size and regularity of population location.

By the Early Preclassic, the Olmecs of San Lorenzo had developed a system of site selection and construction unique to this lowland region and well suited to its exploitation. Local villages were used to control a network of transportation and communication routes that surrounded the San Lorenzo plateau. In addition, these settlements were adapted to exploit resources provided by the environment created in this deltaic basin. A complex system combining strategic site locations and constructions designed to exploit the natural terrain characterized the beginning of San Lorenzo's power in the lower Coatzacoalcos.

As the regional system became more established, San Lorenzo's network was extended along logical transportation lines (see Haggett 1965). The expansion is evident in the relative differences between the inner and outer regions of the survey. By the Early Preclassic, the far reaches of the network were already well established and extended over their own, albeit more simple, system on Tacamichapa Island. As the river courses shifted and spheres of interaction began to change, San Lorenzo's connectivity began to wane, and so, therefore, did its position as a node in a complex regional system. Settlement dispersed in the Middle Preclassic and eventually began to disappear in the Late Preclassic.

Ronald Spores (1972: 177–178) defines a regional center broadly as one that controls an ekistic region. This is a region composed of a geographically delimited area that has "developed a particular system of organized life within these natural boundaries expressed as a system of interrelated human settlements" (Doxiadis 1968: 132). By the Early Preclassic, San Lorenzo controlled a system of linked settlements in a network of functionally interdependent units. These links were comprised of sites specialized "in the macro structural sense in terms of access to local resources, specific local adaptations, part-time occupational specialization, varieties of products, demographic configuration, and probably social ranking" (Spores 1972: 177–178).

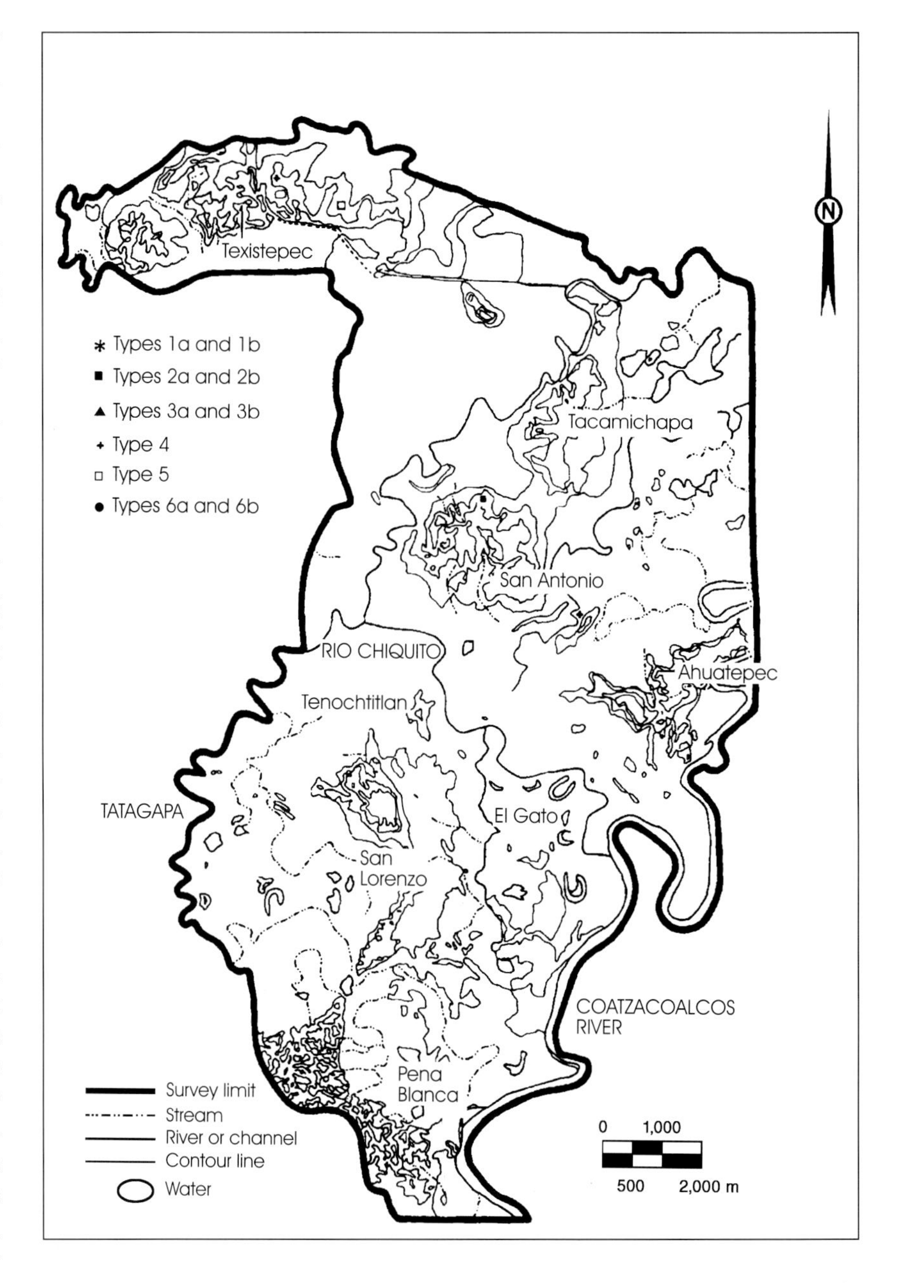

16. Late Preclassic settlement
Adapted from Symonds and Lunagómez 1997: 161, fig. 6.5

San Lorenzo's settlement and settlement development through time demonstrated a high population density, as was clearly indicated in the settlement survey data. This population was organized by an overarching system whose function was to integrate multifaceted components of the settlement system. San Lorenzo controlled a network of regional trade by capitalizing on its position at the center of a complex web of transportation and communication routes. This mediating role provided the San Lorenzo Olmecs with economic control of regional institutions. The elite of San Lorenzo were at the apex of a dendritic, riverine system of settlement organization. The many facets of the settlement system and the fluctuating nature of the environment indicate that the regional organization required the kind of integration provided by a complex and well-developed sociopolitical system. The settlement and excavation data appear to provide evidence that the San Lorenzo Olmecs ruled an incipient state (see Johnson and Earle 1987: 270 for the criteria) whose influence was well established throughout the lower Coatzacoalcos drainage.

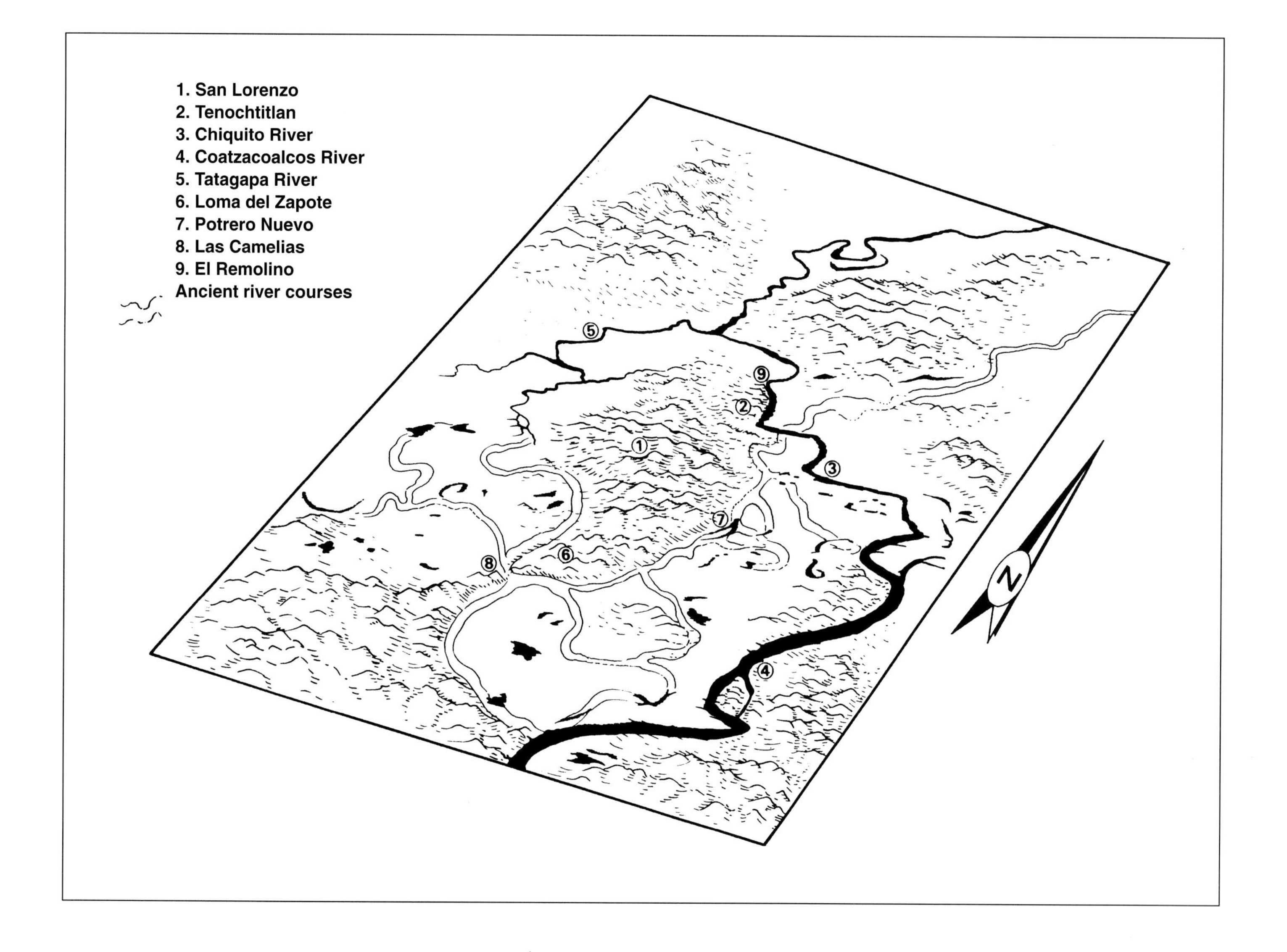

17. Geomorphological model of San Lorenzo region
Ann Cyphers

ACKNOWLEDGMENTS

I wish to thank Zachary Nelson and John Clark for their help with the line art and illustrations.

BIBLIOGRAPHY

Benson, Elizabeth P., and Beatriz de la Fuente
1996 (Editors) *Olmec Art of Ancient Mexico* [exh. cat., National Gallery of Art]. Washington.

Blanton, Richard, Stephen Kowalewski, Gary Feinman, and Jill Appel
1982 *Monte Albán's Hinterland, Part I: The Prehispanic Settlement Patterns of the Central and Southern Parts of the Valley of Oaxaca, Mexico.* Memoirs of the Museum of Anthropology 15. University of Michigan, Ann Arbor.

Blouet, Brian W.
1972 Factors Influencing the Evolution of Settlement Patterns. In *Man, Settlement, and Urbanism,* ed. Peter Ucko, Ruth Tringham, and George Dimbleby, 3–16. London.

Coe, Michael D.
1981 San Lorenzo Tenochtitlán. In *Archaeology,* ed. Jeremy Sabloff, 117–146. Supplement to the Handbook of Middle American Indians, vol. 1. Austin.

Coe, Michael D., and Richard Diehl
1980 *In the Land of the Olmec,* 2 vols. Austin.

Cyphers, Ann
1991 Espacios domésticos olmecas en San Lorenzo Tenochtitlán, Veracruz: Temporada 1991. Report submitted to the Consejo de Arqueología, Instituto Nacional de Antropología e Historia, Mexico City.

1992 Espacios domésticos olmecas en San Lorenzo Tenochtitlán, Veracruz: Temporada 1992. Report submitted to the Consejo de Arqueología, Instituto Nacional de Antropología e Historia, Mexico City.

1993 Espacios domésticos olmecas en San Lorenzo Tenochtitlán, Veracruz: Temporada 1993. Report submitted to the Consejo de Arqueología, Instituto Nacional de Antropología e Historia, Mexico City.

1994 Espacios domésticos olmecas en San Lorenzo Tenochtitlán, Veracruz: Temporada 1994. Report submitted to the Consejo de Arqueología, Instituto Nacional de Antropología e Historia, Mexico City.

Cyphers, Ann, and Mario Arturo Ortiz Perez
1993 Geomorphological Studies of the San Lorenzo Region. Paper presented at the 92nd Annual Meeting of the American Anthropological Association, Washington.

Doxiadis, Constantine A.
1968 *Ekistics: An Introduction to the Science of Human Settlement.* London and New York.

Flannery, Kent V., and Joyce Marcus
1994 *Early Formative Pottery of the Valley of Oaxaca.* Memoirs of the Museum of Anthropology 27. University of Michigan, Ann Arbor.

González Lauck, Rebecca
1989 Recientes investigaciones en La Venta, Tabasco. In *El preclásico o formativo: Avances y perspectivas,* ed. Martha Carmona, 81–89. Mexico City.

Haggett, Peter
1965 *Locational Analysis in Human Geography.* London.

Hodder, Ian
1972 Locational Models in the Study of Romano-British Settlement. In *Models in Archaeology,* ed. David Clarke, 887–909. London.

Johnson, Allen W., and Timothy K. Earle
1987 *The Evolution of Human Societies: From Foraging to Agrarian State.* Stanford, Calif.

Lowe, Gareth W.
1977 The Mixe-Zoque as Competing Neighbors of the Lowland Maya. In *The Origins of Maya Civilization,* ed. Richard Adams, 197–248. Albuquerque, N.M.

Lunagómez, Roberto
1995 Patrones de asentamiento en el hinterland interior de San Lorenzo Tenochtitlán, Veracruz. Licenciatura thesis, Department of Anthropology, Universidad Veracruzana, Xalapa.

Rust, William, III, and Robert J. Sharer
1988 Olmec Settlement Data from La Venta, Tabasco, Mexico. *Science* 242: 102–104.

Sanders, William, Jeffrey Parsons, and Robert Santley
1979 *The Basin of Mexico: Ecological Processes in the Evolution of a Civilization.* New York.

Santley, Robert
1991 Final Field Report: Tuxtlas Region Archaeological Survey, 1991 Field Season. Report submitted to the National Science Foundation, Washington.

Smith, Carol
1976 Regional Economic Systems: Linking Geographic Models and Socioeconomic Problems. In *Regional Analysis. Volume 1: Economic Systems,* ed. Carol Smith, 3–63. New York.

Spores, Ronald
1972 *An Archaeological Survey of the Nochixtlan Valley, Oaxaca.* Vanderbilt University Publications in Anthropology. Nashville.

Symonds, Stacey
1995 Settlement Distribution and the Development of Cultural Complexity in the Lower Coatzacoalcos Drainage, Veracruz, Mexico: An Archaeological Survey at San Lorenzo Tenochtitlán. Ph.D. dissertation, Department of Anthropology, Vanderbilt University, Nashville.

Symonds, Stacey, and Ann Cyphers
1996 Settlement Patterns at San Lorenzo. Paper presented at the 61st Annual Meeting of the Society for American Archaeology, New Orleans.

Symonds, Stacey, and Roberto Lunagómez
1997 Settlement System and Population Development at San Lorenzo. In *Olmec to Aztec: Settlement Patterns in the Ancient Gulf Lowlands,* ed. Barbara L. Stark and Philip J. Arnold III. Tucson.

Nivel:
Elemento: 30
Esculturas: 18-

PONCIANO ORTIZ
Instituto de Antropología, Universidad Veracruzana

MARÍA DEL CARMEN RODRÍGUEZ
Instituto Nacional de Antropología e Historia

The Sacred Hill of El Manatí: A Preliminary Discussion of the Site's Ritual Paraphernalia

Detail of a wood bust from El Manatí
Photograph: Proyecto Manatí

The earliest evidence of ancient Olmec ritual in Mesoamerica dates to about thirty-six hundred years ago and comes from a spring in the Olmec heartland of lowland Veracruz, Mexico. We designate the site El Manatí after the hill, Cerro Manatí, on which the spring is located. Because of special conditions of preservation, we have recovered remarkable artifacts of perishable materials, principally wood busts of adult males and females, that were deposited as special offerings in the spring (figs. 1, 2). The objects recovered from El Manatí were deposited there over a period of six hundred years (1600–1000 B.C.). The long and continued ritual use of the spring and its immediate surroundings indicates that El Manatí was a sacred place.

Cerro Manatí rises amidst the swamps and lagoons of the Coatzacoalcos basin and stands out against the coastal plain. Currently the information shows the existence of at least three important phases of use, each with distinctive characteristics in their uses of space and types of offering (Ortiz and Rodríguez 1989a, 1989b, 1989c, 1994; Ortiz et al. 1990). In this essay we describe briefly the three major periods of ritual use of El Manatí and the principal classes of offerings left there. For each class of offerings, we consider their meaning and significance. Offerings placed in the spring included clusters of jade axes, many pieces of carved wood sculpture, rubber balls, animals, and human infants.

The Chronological Sequence at El Manatí and Sacred Time

Cultural deposits from the oldest phase (Manatí A) date to 1600–1500 B.C. and are associated with an ancient streambed formed by water that coursed down the west side of the Cerro Manatí. The bottom of the spring was stabilized by a layer of sandstone rocks that vary in size from 10–30 centimeters to 1.5 meters (fig. 3). The larger rocks were arranged along a north-south axis, and many show traces of human alteration from use in polishing axes. These traces consist of V-shaped cuts and rounded depressions of varying diameters (figs. 4, 5), similar to markings seen on some basalt monuments at San Lorenzo, La Venta, and Chalcatzingo.

We have encountered fragments of broken ceramic vessels dispersed throughout this lowest stratum, with sherd concentrations among the rocks as though ceramic vessels had been thrown into the spring, perhaps as offerings holding special foodstuffs. Also significant is the presence of stone bowls—shallow mortars—decorated with notching (figs. 6, 7), as well as a considerable quantity of fire-cracked rocks used in cooking. Fragments of obsidian are rare; we have recovered only twenty flakes and blade fragments in this deposit. The same low frequency characterizes the figurines: only one small figurine head came from this context, and it may have formed part of a necklace with jade beads. In short, the frequencies of certain

1. View of the 1992 excavations at El Manatí
Photograph: Proyecto Manatí

2. Closer view of excavations showing details of stratigraphy
Photograph: Proyecto Manatí

3. Bed of worked boulders in the lowest levels of the excavation
Photograph: Ignacio Montes

4. View of a worked boulder showing the axe-sharpening marks
Photograph: Ignacio Montes

5. View of a worked boulder showing axe-sharpening marks and a sinuous groove
Photograph: Proyecto Manatí

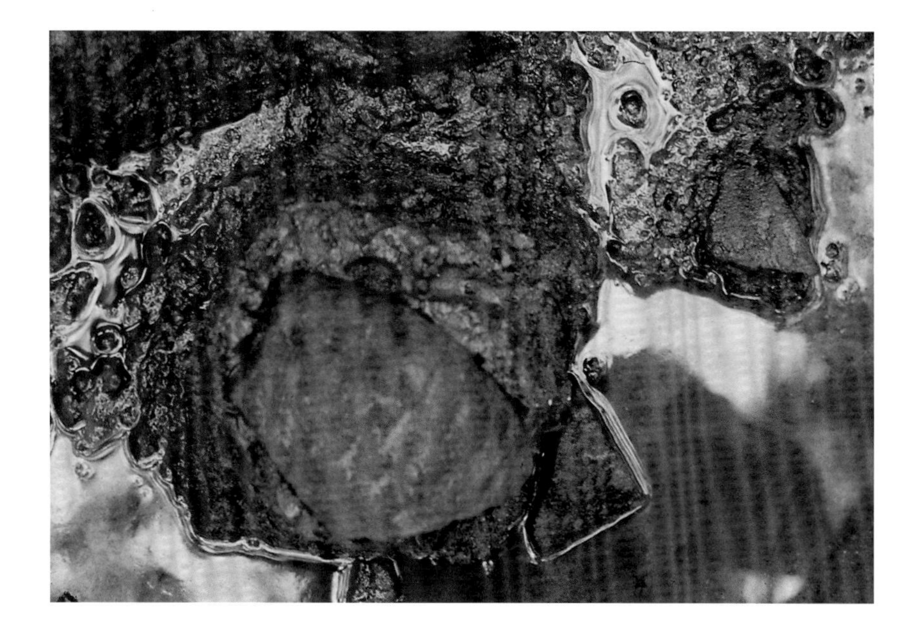

6. Fragment of a stone mortar in situ; note the elaborate design that mimics fingernail punctation in ceramic vessels
Photograph: Proyecto Manatí

7. Fragments of stone mortars from El Manatí, Early Formative period
Photograph: Curtis Craven

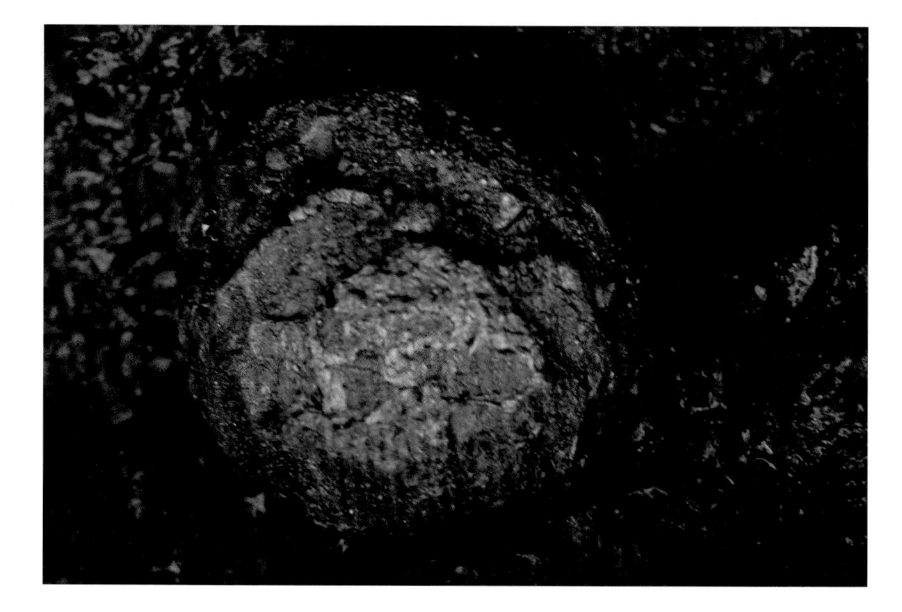

8. Jadeite and greenstone axes from the Manatí A phase
Photograph: Ignacio Montes

9. Rubber ball associated with the axes shown in figure 8
Photograph: Proyecto Manatí

artifacts in the spring suggest that we are not dealing with normal domestic refuse.

Axes and beads, many of high-quality jade, were found dispersed throughout this stratum of rocks and gravel (fig. 8). Until the 1992 field season, we had encountered three rubber balls, all approximately 15 centimeters in diameter, within the same context (fig. 9). During the 1996 field season, a group of six balls of various sizes was found. One ball measures almost 40 centimeters in diameter and was found associated with forty fine stone axes and some seeds (figs. 10–13). These rubber balls are impressive evidence of the existence of the ball game in this early period (c. 1600 B.C.), but they also indicate to us that rubber had other ritual uses as well (see below).

The radiocarbon dates from this deposit corroborate the ceramic evidence. The ceramics include diagnostic tecomate forms, neckless jars with narrow openings and encircling grooves below their rims (fig. 14), as well as plates with vertical exterior and interior grooves below the everted rim. The vessels were covered with red specular hematite slip, and brown and black slip, similar to the pottery styles of the Barra and Locona complexes described for the Pacific Coast region of Chiapas (Clark 1994; Lowe 1975, 1978; Ceja 1985; Clark and Pye, this volume).

During the Manatí B phase (c. 1500–1200 B.C.), the bottom of the spring was covered by a layer of organic material about 5–20 centimeters thick. This layer of peat sealed the earlier offerings described above. Nevertheless, the use of the spring for ritual offerings and sacred space continued. After the accumulation of the peat, the narrow channel began clogging up with fine layers of organic silt and clay. We still do not know how much time passed between the accumulation of the peat layer and the channel clogging up. On top of these strata, the Olmecs continued depositing their most precious objects—jade axes and other fine stone objects that were polished to a mirror-like finish (fig. 15).

Then a change in ritual practices occurred, with the placement of offerings becoming more complex. Axes were still offered, but they were no longer randomly cast into the spring. Instead, they were buried or placed in the mud in formal patterns: arranged lines following the north-south axis either singly or in groups, always maintaining symmetry. Highlighting these groups were special arrangements of axes, placed in tight circles with their bits pointing upward, like petals of a flower (fig. 16). Others were bundles of three to twelve axes grouped together.

We have not found any associated ceramics in this deposit, but we did recover rubber balls, all about 20 centimeters in diameter. The change in offering patterns through time suggests a change in the conceptualization of sacred events. In the Manatí B phase, planned layouts characterized the axe offerings (fig. 17). They continued as communal, collective offerings, but still conformed to preconceived patterns. These

10. Unidentified seeds from El Manatí
Photograph: Proyecto Manatí

11. Fruit pits from *jobo* (hog plum) from the Manatí A phase
Photograph: Proyecto Manatí

12. Fragments of otate (species of bamboo) from the Manatí A phase
Photograph: Proyecto Manatí

13. Piece of *copal,* a tree resin used for incense in native ceremonies
Photograph: Proyecto Manatí

14. Grooved ceramics from the Manatí A phase
Photograph: Proyecto Manatí

15. Finely polished axes of jadeite and greenstone
Photograph: Andrés Curtis Craven

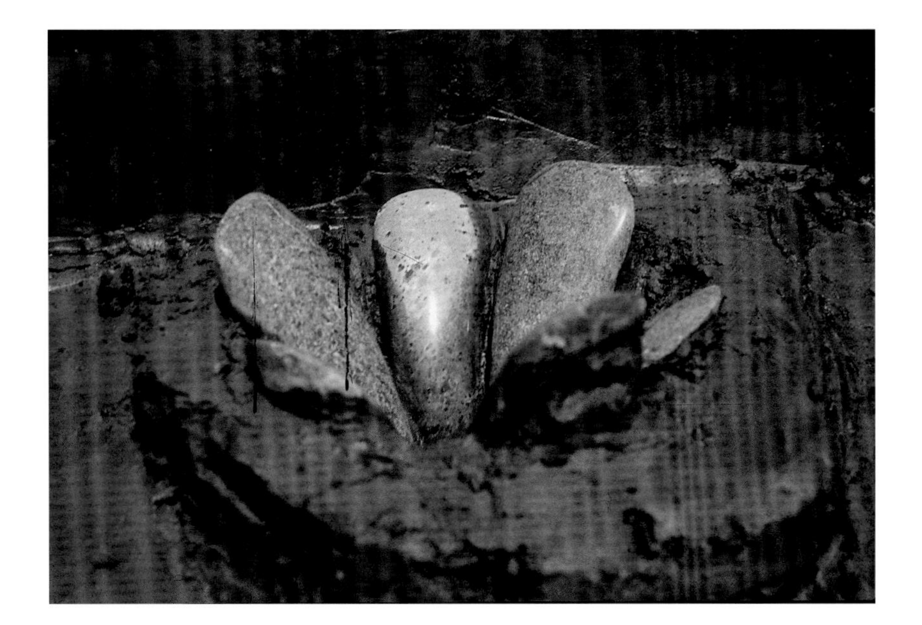

16. Greenstone axes in a "flower" arrangement from the Manatí B phase
Photograph: Proyecto Manatí

17. Axe offering from the Manatí B phase
Photograph: Proyecto Manatí

18. Rocks covering an offering of wood sculpture
Photograph: Proyecto Manatí

19. Group of wood sculptures 18, 19, and 20 (also known as Macario, Guicho, and Dani) from El Manatí
Photograph: Proyecto Manatí

ritual axe offerings, first evident at El Manatí, were precursors to later offerings known for La Venta (Tabasco), San Isidro (Chiapas), and La Merced in the municipality of Hidalgotitlán, Veracruz, a site recently discovered and excavated by members of the Manatí Project (see Rodríguez and Ortiz, this volume). After these axe group offerings, the bottom of the spring was subsequently covered by very fine silty clay. It was rose colored in the lower half and dark gray in the upper half, reaching a thickness of 2–4 meters.

During the subsequent Macayal A phase (1200–1000 B.C.), a great ritual event occurred at the spring: a massive burial of anthropomorphic wood busts (figs. 18, 19) accompanied by a great quantity of important paraphernalia (for example, branches of plants, axes, hematite balls, wood scepters, pectorals and earrings, and dismembered bones of children; see figs. 20–24). There is no clear pattern evident in the arrangement of the burials, but three groups of sculpture follow an east-west axis toward the hill. Bundles of leaves, plants, and reeds played an important role within the ceremony of the sculpture interments, and each appears to have been accorded treatment similar to that given to people. The plants were wrapped like mortuary bundles and offered in a careful and sophisticated ritual (fig. 19). While the data indicate that the wood sculpture and the plant bundles occurred as a single offering event, the possibility cannot be ruled out that many of the items were separate offerings. It is also possible that the spring was used for later offerings.

The evidence demonstrates that this singular space was used for sacred purposes through various generations over a span of six centuries. There can be little doubt that the memory and use of the sacred spring were maintained through these years. How and why did this happen? Although its full significance continues to elude us, the ritual deposits at El Manatí indicate a significant time depth in Olmec religious practices, as well as a semiotic complexity related to the elements recovered.

El Manatí as a Sacred Place

El Manatí was a spectacular setting for rituals. Three thousand six hundred years ago, Cerro Manatí was covered by dense tropical vegetation and inhabited by forest animals: jaguars, ocelots, iguanas, wild boars, monkeys, and a variety of colorful birds. Perhaps a cleared area was maintained where preparations for the ritual offerings occurred. There may have been houses for the priests or shamans who watched over the place and were in charge of rituals. Perhaps they received pilgrims who came bearing valuable, exotic gifts for their gods. The manufacture and acquisition of these gifts surely had a high cost and, therefore, would have brought elevated prestige to the donor within the small, local community. Obviously, the expensive offerings were by elites, but commoners may also have participated.

According to Mircea Eliade (1991, 1994), sacred space is an area delimited by the profane space that surrounds it, making communication possible with the sacred; the hierophanies that occur there serve to maintain its sacredness. As noted, the earliest known use of the spring was ritual in nature. The artifacts in the bottom level of the spring do not constitute a full domestic artifact assemblage. There is little variation in vessel forms, lithic instruments are primarily pristine jade axes, and there is a virtual absence of obsidian and figurines—objects typically associated with domestic habitats. El Manatí was not occupied by a permanent hamlet, and there is no evidence of ceremonial constructions or nearby habitations, as was the case at the excavated site of El Macayal, where domestic units were recovered. This separation from domestic (profane) space strengthens the identification of El Manatí as a sacred space.

We have suggested elsewhere (Ortiz and Rodríguez 1994) that El Manatí as a sacred place combined three important elements of Mesoamerican ideology: a hill, natural springs, and ferrous pigments, such as hematite. The cult of hills was intimately related to the cult of water, springs, and caves. In Mesoamerica, springs were considered sacred places, and ceremonies were performed at them that were related to fertility. We are probably recovering evidence of ancient rituals at El Manatí performed in honor of the "Lord of the Mountain," controller of the rains, lightning, and thunder, who held within himself a space filled with primordial waters from which flowed the springs that provided access to the mansion of the rain god.

In her study of the Mesoamerican rain god, María del Carmen Anzures y Bolaños (1990: 122) writes that "the water that falls from the sky as rain originates in springs and underground currents, from whence it ascends by evaporation, and then returns to earth as life-giving drops to resurrect all of nature, which dies each year and returns to be reborn. For this reason it is said that water circulates

20. The head portion of a red-painted staff with a shark tooth inset
Photograph: Ignacio Montes

21. Detail of a wood bust; note the polished axes beneath the sculpture and the wood staff or "sword" above the base of the sculpture
Photograph: Proyecto Manatí

22. Detail of the axe offering associated with the wood sculpture shown in figures 20 and 21
Photograph: Proyecto Manatí

23. Wood bust with a wood pectoral in situ
Photograph: Proyecto Manatí

24. Another view of the wood bust shown ready for removal
Photograph: Proyecto Manatí

through the veins of the earth as blood through the human body." As for Tlaloc, the Aztec rain god, Johanna Broda (1991: 466) comments that this being "was not only the patron of rain and storms, but also of the hills; in this sense he was an ancient god of the earth. It was said that the rain came from the mountains from whose peaks the clouds were born. For the Aztecs, mountains were sacred and conceived of as rain gods. They were identified as tlaloques, small beings who created storms and rain and constituted a group of servants to the god Tlaloc. These beliefs are amply documented in seventeenth-century sources."

The course of the Avenue of the Dead at Teotihuacán connects the sacred mountain north of the city to the zone of springs in the south, while another axis crosses from east to west, "where the constellation Pleiades arose to mark the annual renewal of time" (Townsend 1993: 43). The significance of the location at the foot of an important hill also coincides and fits with what is observed at Chalcatzingo (Grove 1987), Las Bocas (Coe 1965), and Teopantecuanitlán (Martínez 1986), where the communities were placed on the west side of important hills in their respective regions.

Mountains and hills had a fundamental importance within the *cosmovisión* of different Mesoamerican cultures, as well as other world cultures. Mountains and hills functioned as nexus points between earth and sky and were considered the center of the world, or its *axis mundi* (see Eliade [1991] for full discussion of *axis mundi*). In Mesoamerica, hills were also considered the houses of rain gods and sources of life-giving rains and springs; they were the abodes of nature's custodians who controlled water, lightning, and thunder. These rainmakers fed the earth, permitting the growth of all living things, and therefore insuring the perpetuity of humankind.

Anzures y Bolaños (1990: 121) affirms that "in Mesoamerican history and mythology, and even beyond its borders to the northeast, there existed and still persists today the belief in a supernatural being, the lord of nature, of mountains and valleys, of vegetation, of the rivers and springs that give life, and of all the animal kingdom. Dwarfs and hunchbacks serve this lord as his messengers, collaborators and confidants, and guardians of the underworld. This lord watches over and cares for the fountains of life that supply human sustenance and through man supply the food of the gods." Examples of the cult of the sacred mountains abound, but one site, Chalcatzingo, pertains to the Olmec era (see Grove, this volume). Jorge Angulo (1987a, 1987b) analyzed the iconography at this site and concluded that Chalcatzingo was considered not only a sacred mountain but also an oracle. Certain mythicoreligious concepts were developed there and possibly explain why the rites and ceremonies depicted in the iconography were performed. Similar rituals to rain gods and earth lords likely occurred at El Manatí.

At the site of Cerro Estrella in the Valley of Mexico, "they had a singular strategic and religious position," according to Broda (1991: 466), "when every 52 years the New Fire ceremony was celebrated there, held in the month of November when the Pleiades passed the meridian at midnight, the astronomical date that in this latitude corresponded to the nadir of the sun." Similar beliefs are known for other sites. At Teotihuacán, Cerro Gordo was considered the principal sacred mountain and was vital in the urban planning of the site (Pasztory 1993). The annals of Chalco Amecameca mention that ceremonies to water were performed on the summits of these mountains and that here "lived the commoners named xochtecas, olmecas, quiyahuiztecos, cocolcas . . . they were rain sorcerers who could provoke rain" (Anzures y Bolaños 1990: 136). The cult of the hills is amply documented throughout Mesoamerica. According to Eduardo Matos (1982) and Leonardo López Luján (1993), the Templo Mayor in Tenochtitlán (present-day Mexico City) was modeled after the Cerro Coatepec, birthplace of Huitzilopochtli, and its architectural layout validated these myths.

Axes

The axe offerings at El Manatí demonstrate the ceremonial use of the hill spring by the Olmecs during the Manatí A phase. It is obvious that axes were symbols reproducing objects used in daily life. Axes as tools were vital in day-to-day domestic activities such as forest clearance and cultivation, cutting wood and thatch for making houses, and constructing canoes and other wooden goods. Axes may also have been used in warfare. One might think that axe symbolism was related to concepts pertaining to the original function of the instrument, perhaps related to agricultural rites. But the context in which the axes have been found at El Manatí, their quantity, and, above all, the extant differences between domestic and ceremonial axes, suggest to us that the relationship between the objects as symbols (ceremonial axes) and as tools (domestic axes) was more arbitrary and polyvalent. The symbolism transcended the relationship and significance associated directly with each axe's original function.

In contrast to the domestic ones, ceremonial axes show great variation in the combination of formal attributes. The greater variation could be partly due to limitations of original raw material and artisanal skill in manufacturing. Alternatively, the great quantity of ceremonial axe forms, compared with the domestic ones, could also be explained as ritual characteristics, since the ceremonial forms were not determined by specific functions. Freedom from functional requirements would have permitted a greater creativity and imaginative use of the material.

During Manatí A and B phases, with the exception of limestone pseudo-celts, axes in general were carefully carved and polished into a variety of petaloid forms. To minimize raw material defects, the maximum thickness of each axe could be located either in the middle or at either end, but the maximum width had to be located between the middle and the axe's cutting edge. One notes almost an obsession for the surface finish, the material, and the color of the axes. The axes had soft lines, with smooth and brilliant surfaces with no irregularities (figs. 15–17). Very few of the axes show pits, and, when present, they are limited to those caused by postmanufacture knocks or blows but not from wear due to use. In contrast, the poll ends of the axes were rarely polished, and many polls are irregular, as if this part had been detached from the mother rock. All of this implies that the ceremonial object was important in and of itself and that, to be effective, the offering sought to highlight the material, the form, the color, and the surface finish.

In the later Macayal phase, however, the overall form of axes was neglected, and the surface finish was emphasized. Formal defects were reduced, but with little attention to symmetry of form. More fragile raw materials were also employed. What appears to have been important is that the offerings were still generically axes. That axes were fabricated from fine materials and used frequently in magicoreligious contexts indicates that they represented an idea or generalized concept within Olmec society. To mark clearly their ritual character and to differentiate them from common axes, artisans used sacred and exotic materials, such as jade, serpentine, andesite, or schist—all foreign materials that had to be imported, thereby incurring high costs and requiring a wide network of commercial exchange. As with all symbols, the axes had polyvalent meanings, and their significance varied according to the ritual contexts in which they were used.

The sandstone boulders at the bottom of the spring are another important element of the rituals. These rocks are of regular size and have grooves from grinding axes (figs. 3–5). Also relevant is the fact that the largest rocks are found aligned on a north-south axis in an intentional arrangement. As mentioned above, we postulate that these boulders could have served as grinding stones for sharpening domestic axes; however, the evidence suggests that they may have been used in a religious practice to obtain the manna or the magic power from the sacred spring. The markings on the rocks are also seen on various monuments at San Lorenzo (some colossal heads) and also appear on monuments from La Venta (Drucker et al. 1959) and Chalcatzingo (Grove 1987). Michael Coe believes that these marks relate to symbolic destruction of the monuments after a palace revolution, and for this reason some colossal heads were buried in the plazas of San Lorenzo (Coe and Diehl 1980). David Joralemon (1971) associates these markings with ritual practices occurring in later eras as a way to obtain the ritual power the sculptures were believed to have possessed. David Grove (1981) believes that the monuments were destroyed symbolically to "ritually" kill the ruler portrayed by them.

Returning to the El Manatí data, we propose other ideas and speculations. The domestic artifacts found in the Manatí A phase are highly standardized, perhaps indicating that the individuals who discarded or threw these objects into the spring had followed a special diet. If the site had been watched over by priests or ritual specialists, it is possible that these individuals followed dietary regimens somewhat different from those of the rest of the population. Their diet may have emphasized vegetables, tubers, or plants in their effort to maintain a greater tie with nature, and, therefore, they would not have required domestic artifacts such as cutting instruments.

It is also possible that the evidence for limited domestic activities corresponds to occasional offerings—discarded by-products of ritual use of the spring by pilgrims who came to the site for calendrical rituals, perhaps ceremonies performed at the appearance of the Pleiades and the arrival of the rainy season. Speculation aside, we did not find at El Manatí any evidence of domestic objects for the Macayal phase; their absence indicates a change in the use of space. Although it continued to be maintained as a sacred site, apparently at this later time there were no resident ritual specialists guarding the spring.

The Wood Olmecs

As to the function of the numerous wood busts found at El Manatí and their significance, it seems obvious that they were related to the cult of water and hills, given their placement in the spring. In other words, one perceives a strong relationship to the cult of fertility, and perhaps ancestors, as represented by the wood images. Olmec religion has been considered totemic, and, as such, the social organization would have been based on clans. Román Piña Chan (1985: 16) considers that the greenstone, mosaic offering floors at La Venta represented stylized jaguar faces and could have been sacred burials of the totem god. If this type of offering occurred for the apical ancestor of the clan, it could also have occurred for lineage ancestors. The clan could have included one or more lineages. The common ancestor of clan members was mythic and totemic, being represented in this case by a jaguar or a serpent. In contrast, lineage members descended from a common human ancestor, represented naturalistically.

It is likely that the wood busts of adult males and females represented common ancestors of lineage members. The divine force possessed by each bust was preserved by fashioning sacred bundles similar to the Aztec *tlaquimilolli.* These were referred to by chroniclers such as Fray Jerónimo de Mendieta (1945: 85–86, citing Fray Andrés de Olmos): "and these devoted servants of the dead gods wrapped these cloths around certain staffs, and making a notch or hole in the staff they put for a heart some small green stones, and the skin of a snake and a jaguar, and this bundle they called *tlaquimilolli,* and each one they gave the name of that demon that had given them the cloth and this [demon] was the principal idol that they held in much reverence, and they did not have as much [reverence] for this [demon] as for the beasts or stone figures or the staff that they had made." This same Fray Andrés de Olmos mentions that "in Tlalmanalco was found one of these idols wrapped in many cloths, although [the cloths were] already half rotted from the idol having been hidden."

From their fine finish, we infer that the wood busts from El Manatí had a specific function prior to, and perhaps unrelated to, their burial in the spring. Their unambiguous individuality would suggest that they were representations of real, historic persons, perhaps of chiefs, leaders, or persons of high prestige who were memorialized in wood (figs. 19, 22). The wood knives and scepters (figs. 20, 21) and the stone axes (fig. 22) buried with the busts may have been insignia of the power that in life they once represented. Hierarchical differences could have been indicated by the location of the interment of each sculpture and by their accompanying objects.

From an aesthetic point of view, the busts display diverse qualities that suggest they are works by different artists, although they could well have been made by a single artisan. In some of the works, one notes great artistic mastery; in this regard, the great force of Olmec aesthetic values comes into play. We have not detected a definite pattern in the placement of these offerings. What was constant was the axis of orientation of both the groups and the isolated sculpture in forming groups of three east-west axes toward the hill.

The Lords of Water and Child Sacrifice

One could think analogically that the wood sculpture represented the helpers of Tlaloc, the tlaloques, chaneques, or dwarfs—bringers of rain, denizens of the hills and springs, and the lords of water who with their staffs or scepters struck the clouds to release this vital element, as are represented in the scenes on Stelae 2 and 3 at La Venta (Drucker et al. 1959). Personages carrying scepters are also common on other, later stelae and have been interpreted as symbols of rulership, but they could be images of leaders or players of the ball game.

The piles of rock that we call "funerary biers" had to have had an important significance (fig. 18), perhaps in a symbolic manner referring to the same hill where the gods of water, or tlaloques, are found. Piles of stone were venerated even at the time of the Conquest, and were and are seen at cardinal points and roads. Fray Diego de Landa (1978) reports them in the Maya area.

Another aspect of the Manatí offerings that merits emphasis is the presence of two primary burials and dispersed bones of others, which include long bones, cranial fragments, vertebrae, ribs, and phalanges associated with some of the wood sculpture. These bones were originally thought to have been of monkeys and other mammals, and we interpreted them as animals accompanying the sculpture, that is, we thought they were some kind of animal alter egos or animal spirit companions. Nevertheless, the recent identification by Norma Valentín (1989) indicates that these are human bones of newborns, perhaps neonates. The majority of these bones did not appear in the anatomical position of primary burials; they were dismembered and then buried, unlike the burial associated with sculptures 12 and 13, which was a primary burial in the fetal position. These recent identifications completely change our original interpretation and elevate the ancient ritual practices at El Manatí to a greater level of complexity. We now have before us evidence of possible child sacrifices as offerings to Olmec gods—and perhaps even ritual cannibalism, as the dismemberment could indicate.

We know from the depictions on the smaller Olmec statuary, stelae, and altars that infants played a fundamental role in Olmec religious beliefs and were associated in later eras with the cult of the rain god. It remains to be seen whether more information can be obtained by physical anthropologists from these human remains from El Manatí, particularly looking for evidence of cannibalism and whether the bones were of normal children or of children with pathologies.

From the chroniclers (Sahagún 1981; Durán 1967) we learn that in later times child sacrifice was a common practice and was especially associated with the cults of water and fertility. Recent discoveries of child sacrifices to the rain god in the Templo Mayor at Tenochtitlán are an eloquent example of such practices (Román 1990). Child sacrifice in ceremonies related to water and fertility continued until the Conquest. Infants with their weeping and their tears propitiated the rains, and we know that they occupied a preponderant role in Olmec representations. For this reason, some investigators have suggested the notion that these "child-gods," born of mountains, hills, or caves, reenact the Olmec origin myth. Perhaps, as Joralemon (1971: 91) speculates, it was one of the ceremonies used to bring the return of the rain god to the world of men; such ceremonies, he says, "may have marked the beginning of the Mexican rainy season and were almost certainly accompanied by the sacrifice of infants and small children."

The sacrifice or burial of the children provides a basis for arguing that these offerings at El Manatí may have had a conceptual and ritual link to Olmec beliefs of the creation of the world and the equilibrium or harmony that must exist in nature for the well-being and continuity of human beings. Their world had to reproduce itself through a rite that showed its regeneration and abundant sustenance: the earth's fertility was closely related to water, and water was vital.

All sacrifices, says Yolotl González Torres (1985: 74), "were performed at special places that share a basic requirement: sacredness, a characteristic they acquired because communication with the deity occurred there. The sacred nature of these sites was permanent because they had some special characteristic, such as natural springs, mountaintops, eddies of water, intersections of roads, or had been places of some consecration."

Rubber Balls

The finding of fourteen rubber balls in archaeological context, many of them corresponding to the earliest phases, demonstrates the importance that offerings of rubber had through time as cult objects at El Manatí (see fig. 9). It is the first time in the history of Olmec archaeology that convincing evidence has been uncovered for the use of this material and its importance in Olmec rituals.

The use of rubber is also documented by the chroniclers, not only in the ball game, but also in a great number of ceremonies related to the cult of the water gods. Fray Bernardino de Sahagún (1981: 49, 149, 151) reports that at the fiesta

25. Blocks of white clay with an axe embedded in the center
Photograph: Proyecto Manatí

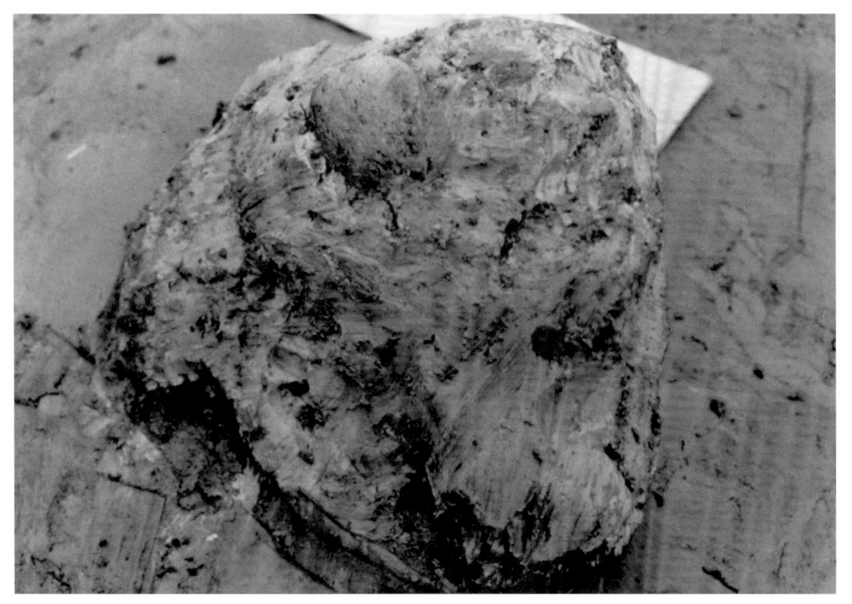

26. Block of white clay with an axe offering
Photograph: Proyecto Manatí

of Etzalcualiztli, dedicated to the god Tlaloc, images were made of the gods using rubber which were called Ulteteotl, "rubber gods." The water deities were adorned with papers sprinkled with melted rubber, and these same papers also served as an offering (see Heyden 1978). There could have existed an equivalence between latex that springs from the tree as sap and blood from a human body and from all living beings.

Other Offerings

Another important element in the offerings during the Macayal phase was a series of white clay blocks, the majority with a small greenstone axe embedded in their center, with the axe edge protruding from the block and pointing upward (figs. 25, 26). We do not understand the significance of these offerings, but we do have some ideas. The color of the blocks could have represented clouds, and the axes, fixed to the symbolic center, could have represented the cleavage of these same clouds that would cause the rain to fall. We accept the idea that axes are, like other objects with cutting edges, associated with thunder and lightning that cut the sky and release rain (see Taube, this volume). Obsidian, on the other hand, is associated with lightning strikes. In southern Veracruz and other areas, greenstone is still called "lightning stone," and where these greenstones are found, it is believed that a bolt of lightning had fallen.

Conclusion

In southern Veracruz and the inland archipelago in the swampy region where El Manatí is located, and at other Olmec zones such as the island of La Venta in Tabasco, the problem was not water shortage (see Rodríguez and Ortiz, this volume). Instead, it was the need for sweet and fresh water of natural springs versus the insalubrious, stagnant water of the permanent swamps. This need, no doubt, led to the idea of freshwater springs as sacred spaces. In the Olmec region, water caused problems in several ways. The inhabitants fought against the swamps, and the long rainy seasons frequently inundated hamlets and devastated planted fields—all of which surely provoked serious crises and shortfalls of basic resources. Paradoxically, this is similar to what happened in the highlands with unexpected droughts that obliged people to implore their gods for aid and perform propitiatory rites. With what objective, then, would the Olmecs have performed their ceremonies laden with elements of the cult of fertility, water, and hills? Were they propitiating the gods of rain or begging for clemency against constant inundations?

Of course, there are many aspects that we must evaluate before we can understand ancient Olmec ritual practices at El Manatí. For the time being, we need to keep in mind that, for the Manatí region, the most critical thing may have been too much water, with its attendant dangers, and that the ceremonies undertaken at the El Manatí spring may have been major events of supplicating rain gods to be more benevolent.

In summary, we believe that the offerings at El Manatí reveal an elaborate ritual in which various communities may have participated. It is difficult to know the motives that drove these people to perform the great ritual, which consisted of the burial of dozens of wood sculptures, jadeite and serpentine axes, as well as humans, animals, and other sacred objects. The offerings surely exceeded the mere zeal of propitiatory rites. It must have been an exceptional event.

The ritual implied the participation of many people and a great quantity of sacred or magic objects. It was carefully planned and executed. The result was extremely interesting, not only due to the classes of materials recovered and their artistic qualities, but because careful analyses of the site and the contexts of the offerings will permit deeper understanding of the magicoreligious thinking of the Olmecs, their beliefs, their myths, and even their gods.

BIBLIOGRAPHY

Angulo, Jorge

1987a The Chalcatzingo Reliefs: An Iconographic Analysis. In *Ancient Chalcatzingo,* ed. David Grove, 132–158. Austin.

1987b Los relieves del Grupo IA en la montaña sagrada de Chalcatzingo. In *Homenaje a Román Piña Chan,* organized by Barbro Dahlgren, Carlos Navarrete, Lorenzo Ochoa, Mari Carmen Serra, and Yoko Sugiura, 191–228. Mexico City.

Anzures y Bolaños, María del Carmen

1990 Tlaloc, señor del monte y dueño de los animales: Testimonios de un mito de regulación ecológica. In *Historia de la religión en Mesoamérica y áreas afines, coloquio 2,* ed. Barbro Dahlgren. Mexico City.

Broda, Johanna

1991 Cosmovisión y observación de la naturaleza: El ejemplo del culto de los cerros en Mesoamérica. In *Arqueoastronomía y etnoastronomía,* ed. Johanna Broda, Stanislaw Iwaniszewski, and Lucrecia Maupome, 461–500. Mexico City.

Ceja Tenorio, Jorge Fausto

1985 *Paso de la Amada: An Early Preclassic Site in the Soconusco, Chiapas.* Papers of the New World Archaeological Foundation 49. Provo, Utah.

Clark, John E.

1994 Antecedentes de la cultura olmeca. In *Los olmecas en Mesoamérica,* ed. John Clark, 31–41. Mexico City and Madrid.

Coe, Michael D.

1965 The Olmec Style and Its Distribution. In *Archaeology of Southern Mesoamerica, Part 2,* ed. Gordon Willey, 739–775. Handbook of Middle American Indians, vol. 3. Austin.

Coe, Michael D., and Richard Diehl

1980 *In the Land of the Olmec,* 2 vols. Austin.

Drucker, Philip, Robert F. Heizer, and Robert J. Squier

1959 *Excavations at La Venta, Tabasco, 1955.* Bureau of American Ethnology Bulletin 170. Washington.

Durán, Fray Diego

1967 *Historia de las Indias de Nueva España y Islas de Tierra Firme.* 11th ed. Mexico City.

Eliade, Mircea

1991 *Tratado de historia de la religión.* Mexico City.

1994 *Lo sagrado y lo profano.* Bogotá.

González Torres, Yolotl

1985 *El sacrificio humano entre los Mexicas.* Mexico City.

Grove, David C.

1981 Olmec Monuments: Mutilation as a Clue to Meaning. In *The Olmec and Their Neighbors,* ed. Elizabeth Benson, 49–68. Washington.

1987 (Editor) *Ancient Chalcatzingo.* Austin.

Heyden, Doris

1978 Deidad del agua encontrada en el metro. *Boletín del Instituto Nacional de Antropología e Historia* 40.

Joralemon, Peter David

1971 *A Study of Olmec Iconography.* Washington.

Landa, Fray Diego de

1978 *Relación de las cosas de Yucatán.* Mexico City.

López Luján, Leonardo

1993 *Las ofrendas del Templo Mayor de Tenochtitlán.* Mexico City.

Lowe, Gareth W.

1975 *The Early Preclassic Barra Phase of Altamira, Chiapas.* Papers of the New World Archaeological Foundation 38. Provo, Utah.

1978 Eastern Mesoamerica. In *Chronologies in New World Archaeology,* ed. Robert Taylor and Clement Meighan, 391–393. New York.

Martínez Donjuán, Guadalupe

1986 Teopantecuanitlán. In *Primer coloquio de arqueología y etnohistoria del Estado de Guerrero,* 55–82. Mexico City and Chilpancingo.

Matos Moctezuma, Eduardo

1982 *El Templo Mayor de Tenochtitlán.* Boletín de Antropología Americana 1. Mexico City.

Mendieta, Fray Jerónimo de

1945 *Historia eclesiástica indiana, Tomo 1.* Mexico City.

Ortiz, Ponciano, and María del Carmen Rodríguez

1989a Proyecto Manatí 1989. *Arqueología,* 2d series, 1: 23–52. Mexico City.

1989b Proyecto Manatí: Propuesto Segunda Temporada. Report in the Archivo Técnico del Centro Regional Veracruz, Instituto Nacional de Antropología e Historia, Mexico City.

1989c Proyecto Manatí, 1989. *Revista Arqueología,* Instituto Nacional de Antropología e Historia 1: 23–53.

1994 Los espacios sagrados olmecas: El Manatí, un caso especial. In *Los olmecas en*

Mesoamérica, ed. John Clark, 69–92. Mexico City and Madrid.

Ortiz, Ponciano, María del Carmen Rodríguez, Paul Schmidt, Alfredo Delgado, Lourdes Hernández, Luis Heredia, Ricardo Herrera, Eric Juárez, Jorge Bautista, César Corre, Julio Chan, Steve Nelson, and Ignacio Montes
1990 Proyecto Manatí. Informe final, temporada 1989. Report in the Archivo Técnico del Centro Regional Veracruz, Instituto Nacional de Antropología e Historia, Veracruz, Mexico.

Pasztory, Esther
1993 El mundo natural como metáfora cívica en Teotihuacán. In *La antigua América: El arte de los parajes sagrados,* ed. Richard Townsend, 135–146. Chicago.

Piña Chan, Román
1985 *Quetzalcoatl, serpiente emplumada.* Mexico City.

Román Berrelleza, Juan Alberto
1990 *Sacrificio de niños en el Templo Mayor, México.* Mexico City.

Sahagún, Fray Bernardino de
1981 *Historia general de las cosas de la Nueva España.* Mexico City.

Tibón, Gutierre
1983 *El jade en México.* Mexico City.

Townsend, Richard F.
1993 Introducción: Paisaje y símbolo. In *La antigua América: El arte de los parajes sagrados,* ed. Richard Townsend, 29–48. Chicago.

Valentín Maldonado, Norma
1989 Análisis del material óseo procedente del Sitio Manatí. Report submitted to the Archivo de la Subdirección de Servicios Académicos, Instituto Nacional de Antropología e Historia, Mexico City.

SUSAN D. GILLESPIE
University of Illinois at Urbana-Champaign

The Monuments of Laguna de los Cerros and Its Hinterland

Stone sculpture has played a prominent role in the interpretations of Olmec culture and society. The quantity, size, technology, and style of stone carvings have been used to reconstruct the Olmecs' social and political complexity, the origins and legacies of Olmec culture, and the extent of Olmec influence beyond the Gulf Coast heartland. The Olmecs have been judged Mesoamerica's first "civilization," in large part because they were the first to sculpt monumental images in stone on a grand scale (Coe 1968). The presence of so many huge stones moved over long distances is taken to indicate that the Olmec people were divided into social ranks or classes, with a small elite group able to control the labor of hundreds, if not thousands, of individuals (for example, Coe 1968: 109–111; Coe and Diehl 1980, 2: 147; Drucker 1981: 30–31, 45; Velson and Clark 1975: 22). The emphasis on the human form and the presence of portraiture among the monuments—which Beatriz de la Fuente (1981: 86; this volume) characterized as "homocentric art"—have led scholars to suggest exactly how the elite members of society (thought to be portrayed in stone) gained and exercised their political power (see Gillespie 1999).

The monuments have been especially critical in determining sociopolitical relationships among the various Gulf Coast Olmec polities. A concentration of monuments, together with mound architecture, was the original basis for identifying the primary Olmec centers: San Lorenzo, La Venta, Laguna de los Cerros, and Tres Zapotes (Drucker 1981: 38–39), although this last site actually has very few Olmec-style stone carvings (Grove 1984: 16; 1994: 227; Pool, this volume). The carvings' stylistic characteristics have been used, with little reliability, to date the occupations of the centers and secondary sites within the Olmec and post-Olmec periods (for example, Clewlow 1974; Medellín 1971; Milbrath 1979). Differences in the sculpture from the three centers have been characterized as denoting distinctive "styles" or "schools" of art (Clewlow 1974; de la Fuente 1977, this volume); these differences have also been taken as evidence of these centers' political independence (Drucker 1981: 43). At the same time, the majority of the carvings from all these sites share the recognizable canons of Early and Middle Formative Olmec sculpture. In some cases, very similar monuments have been found at distant sites, indicating a high degree of cultural contact and some chronological overlap. Finally, the presence of smaller sites with one or a few carvings has been used to define a "hinterland" around each center and to speculate on possible relationships whereby the hinterland or secondary sites were integrated into a larger political organization with the primary centers (Grove 1994).

The sculpture from La Venta and San Lorenzo, the two centers that have had a long history of excavation, is fairly well known to scholars and becoming more familiar to the general public because of exhibitions in museums in Mexico and other countries. But for the

View of Laguna de los Cerros
Photograph: Courtesy of New World Archaeological Foundation

third center with numerous Olmec-style monuments, Laguna de los Cerros, very little is known, especially the degree to which it compares to San Lorenzo and La Venta in terms of overall size, construction of mound architecture, sociopolitical complexity, and hegemony over a surrounding area during the Early and Middle Formative periods. Limited test excavations were carried out at Laguna de los Cerros by Alfonso Medellín Zenil in 1960, and the brief publications that resulted from them concentrated on descriptions of only some of the monuments (Medellín 1960, 1971), so we still lack complete information on the monument corpus and the archaeological (and hence social and chronological) contexts for the monuments.

My objective in this essay is to summarize briefly what is known about the Laguna de los Cerros monuments (commenting on general sculptural themes with less emphasis on technical details), providing information on more recent discoveries and unpublished carvings. This summary takes a regional perspective, incorporating monuments from within the Laguna de los Cerros hinterland. Newer information on stone carvings from the hinterland comes from the 1991 Proyecto Arqueológico La Isla-Llano del Jícaro (Gillespie 1994; Grove 1994). This project involved excavations at La Isla, a secondary center with several known monuments, and at Llano del Jícaro, a monument quarry-workshop previously investigated by Medellín in 1960 (1960, 1971). As part of this project, we investigated a few carvings that had been discovered by inhabitants in the area (Grove et al. 1993). The monuments from the hinterland not only add to the total Laguna de los Cerros corpus for comparative purposes but also shed light on how the distribution and placement of monuments outside the main center may have integrated the hinterland with its center. In addition, recent excavations at San Lorenzo (see Cyphers 1993, 1995, 1996, 1999) have yielded more monuments and augmented our knowledge of Olmec stone-carving traditions in general, which may change our assessment of how similar or different the Laguna de los Cerros corpus is from its counterparts elsewhere. Finally, previous comparative analyses have failed to deal explicitly with the *absence* of major monument types at Laguna de los Cerros, but this is an important point to consider when attempting to demonstrate the degree of cultural contacts and contemporaneity among the three Olmec centers. I discuss this factor in the final section of the essay.

Laguna de los Cerros and Its Monuments

One reason why more information is greatly needed from Laguna de los Cerros in terms of determining how the different primary centers may have interacted with one another is that this site provides important data on the environmental variability within Olmec culture. It is an "upland" Olmec site (Grove 1994), a term referring to a major distinction in Olmec ecology and settlement patterns between the uplands and the lowlands, the latter region being the location of both San Lorenzo and La Venta (Arnold, this volume). Laguna de los Cerros commands a large area of rolling hills, upland plains, and plateaus broken by valleys that extend outward from the southwestern flank of the Tuxtla Mountains, whose foothills begin about 20 kilometers to the north (Bove 1978: 6). The Tuxtlas are the source of Cerro Cintepec basalt, a stone type used to make many of the San Lorenzo and La Venta carvings that were transported to the lowlands, as well as those from nearby Laguna de los Cerros (Williams and Heizer 1965).[1] Within Laguna de los Cerros' hinterland is the only known Olmec monument quarry-workshop, Llano del Jícaro, where surface boulders of Cerro Cintepec basalt were readily available to stone carvers. Because of its easy accessibility to the raw material, it is quite possible that Laguna de los Cerros provided preformed monuments or simple boulders from this and other outcrops to San Lorenzo and La Venta, adding an important economic aspect to the interrelationships between or among these centers (Gillespie 1994; see also Drucker 1981: 29).

Problems concerning Our Knowledge of Laguna de los Cerros

Laguna de los Cerros is about 5 kilometers south of Corral Nuevo, a town located between Juan Díaz Covarrubias and Acayucan on Highway 180 (fig. 1); its location is worth noting because Laguna de los Cerros and nearby Llano del Jícaro are often mislocated on maps of the Olmec region. Medellín (1960: 86) conducted test excavations (pits and trenches) at Laguna de los Cerros during the short period from 13 March to 8 May 1960. He described the site as

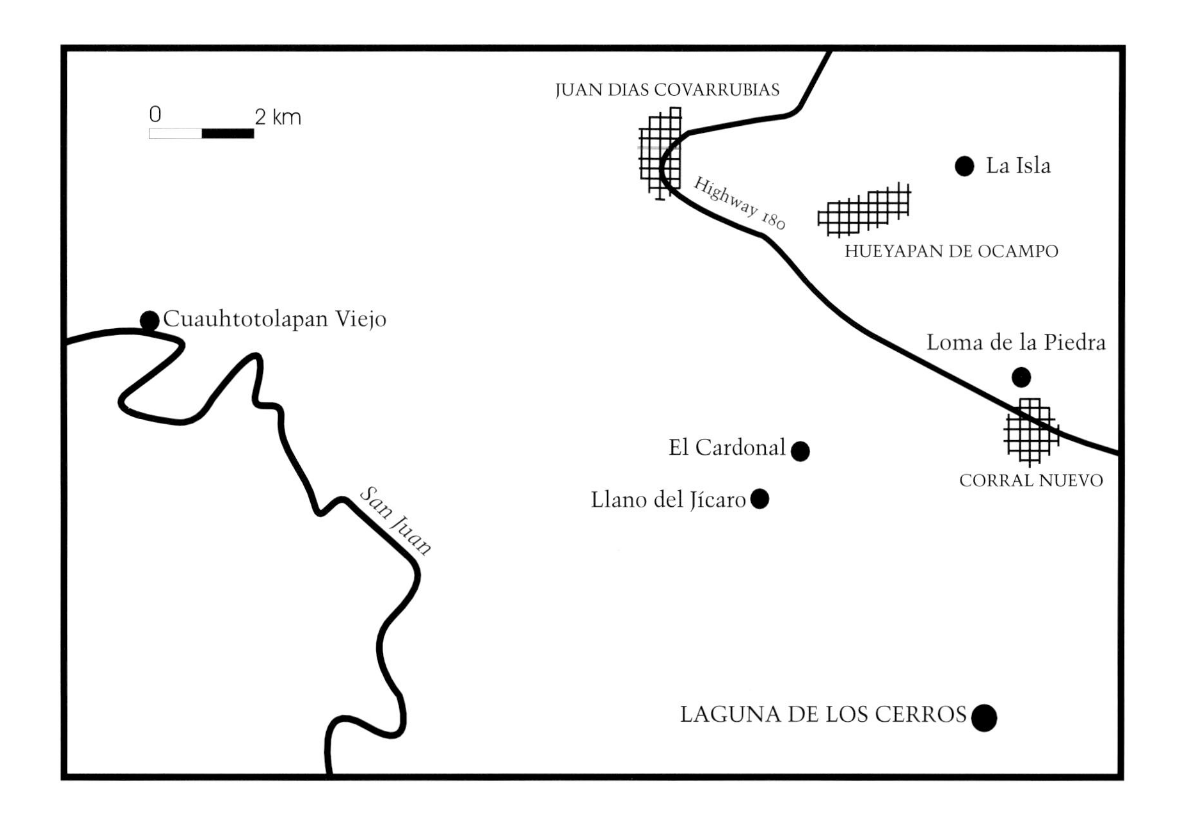

1. Map showing sites in the Laguna de los Cerros hinterland; cross-hatched areas are modern towns on Highway 180

a major ceremonial center surrounded by five smaller mound groupings. The site map that was produced at that time shows ninety-five mounds, ranging in height from 1 to 30 meters, extending over an area of some 40 hectares (Bove 1978). It is uncertain whether that map includes the five smaller mound sites together with the main ceremonial center, as described by Medellín (Bove 1978: 9). Frederick Bove cited a personal communication from Medellín (in 1975) indicating that these secondary mound groups extended from 1 to 1.5 kilometers from the site center in various directions, so it seems unlikely that they are part of the map.

The dating of occupation at Laguna de los Cerros has been a contentious issue. Medellín (1971: 17) was convinced that the site's monuments dated to the Classic period and that Olmec culture flourished during that period, an opinion not shared by other archaeologists working in the region. His reasons for making this chronological assessment were (1) his interpretations of the style of Olmec monuments, for which he found Classic and Postclassic analogues (see also Medellín 1963), and (2) the finding of Classic period pottery and other artifacts at Laguna de los Cerros in association with many sculptures.[2] Tatiana Proskouriakoff (1968: 126) made note of this latter fact when she suggested a comparison between two sculptures from Laguna de los Cerros (Mons. 3 and 19) and two remarkably similar carvings from Toniná of the Classic Maya culture a thousand years later. However, Terence Grieder, in 1966, and Bove, in 1975, reanalyzed the ceramics excavated by Medellín's 1960 project (Bove 1978: 10; Proskouriakoff 1968: 133). Both concluded that the site experienced a long occupational history, extending from the Early Formative to the Early Postclassic. According to their analyses, early ceramic sherds and figurine heads found in the deepest excavations are comparable to the San Lorenzo phase artifacts (1150–900 B.C.) at San Lorenzo. The Early Postclassic fine orange pottery (equivalent to Villa Alta phase at San Lorenzo, A.D. 900–1100, and Tres Zapotes Superior) occurs in the upper layers of mound fill. This later pottery is found over much of the site, especially in the northern mound groups, which Bove suggested were probably constructed at that time (Bove 1978: 10, 23, 32–33).[3]

Bove (1978: 9) concluded that "whatever the original placement of these sculptures, many of them had been reset by a Late Classic-Postclassic reoccupation of the site, accounting for the preponderance of Late Period pottery types found in association with the sculptures and almost always from the upper levels of the site." This was the opinion expressed earlier by Michael Coe (in Proskouriakoff 1968: 134) and Ignacio Bernal (1969: 69)—that at least some of the monuments were of definite Olmec style and must have been reused by later peoples (see also de la Fuente 1977: 259). Beyond that generalization, however, opinions differed as to the dating of the individual monuments. For instance, Bernal (1969: 65) and Tillie Smith (1963: 133) argued that the atypical standing figure, Monument 19, postdated the Olmec occupation, while Coe (in Proskouriakoff 1968: 132), commenting specifically on this carving, declared that in its smallest details it demonstrated that the Laguna de los Cerros monuments "belong to the full corpus of 'classic' Olmec sculpture" (of the Formative period). De la Fuente (1977: 259) concluded that the majority of known artworks are Olmec in style, including Monument 19, but doubted the Olmec attribution of three others—Monuments 4, 17, and 26 (de la Fuente 1973: 271–272).

In addition to attempts to date individual pieces, there were also variable results from studies that strove to place the Laguna de los Cerros monument corpus in its entirety in a chronological context by comparing it to those from the other centers. Thus Susan Milbrath's (1979: 48) stylistic seriation placed the Laguna de los Cerros statues in the Early Formative, contemporary with some of the sculpture from San Lorenzo (and La Venta), while C. William Clewlow's (1974: 147) study dated many of them even earlier than their counterparts at the other two centers (pre–San Lorenzo phase). These conclusions matched an expectation suggested earlier by several scholars that the origins of monument carving should be found in the Tuxtla Mountains, the source of the basalt stone (in Milbrath 1979: 44; also Clewlow 1974: 147–148). Laguna de los Cerros is the closest of all three centers to the mountains.

A major reason why the chronological placement of the Laguna de los Cerros monuments has been difficult to resolve is that so little information is available concerning them. The sculpture has never been completely published; in fact, a list of the entire monument sequence is not available in print, so a fundamental problem is determining precisely which objects belong to the corpus of artworks. What few data were collected concerning their archaeological contexts and proveniences have been only minimally reported. Some monuments numbered in the Laguna de los Cerros sequence actually originated from surrounding sites. The monuments themselves are in generally poor condition, having suffered a high degree of mutilation, perhaps because so many of the ones that Medellín encountered were reused by later peoples.

The Laguna de los Cerros Monuments

Medellín reported twenty-seven carvings from Laguna de los Cerros in his 1960 publication, and a Monument 28 appears in his 1971 work. However, he published information and photographs for only fourteen of them, those that were the least mutilated and had the most distinct forms. Unfortunately, most of these fourteen are very incomplete (which suggests that the unpublished monuments are even more fragmentary or shapeless). The anthropomorphic statues are headless and often lack arms and legs. Brief descriptions or labels are provided for a few more of the Laguna de los Cerros numbered monuments by de la Fuente (1973, 1977), but about one-half of the numbered sequence lacks full descriptions or illustrations.[4]

Table 1 provides information I obtained on the Laguna de los Cerros monuments and those from nearby sites thought to lie within its hinterland to the north and west.[5] The published carvings, which will not be considered in detail here, include two large heads of "supernaturals"—non-naturalistic anthropomorphic faces—with shallow cavities ground into their top surfaces (Mons. 1, 2); four seated anthropomorphic statues (Mons. 3, 6, 8, 11); one standing anthropomorph (Mon. 19); two or three small altars (Mons. 5, 28; Mon. 4 shows two eroded seated figures in shallow niches and has also been called an altar fragment [Winfield Capitaine 1987: 13], but its original form is impossible to determine [de la Fuente 1977: 277]); a figure seated on a block of stone (Mon. 9); a bird or man-bird sculpture (Mon. 13); a kneeling figure atop a supine figure (Mon. 20); a disk with a bas-relief of a face (Mon. 27); and the bas-relief of a standing figure later reworked into a stair cover (Mon. 26).

Only some of the monuments excavated by

Table 1. Laguna de los Cerros Area Monuments

Site	Description	Height (cm)	Weight (tons)	Location	Sources
Laguna de los Cerros					
Monument 1	supernatural head with cavity	75	0.81	Xalapa 00422	Medellín 1960: 86–88, pls. 14–15; 1971: 33, pl. 32; de la Fuente 1973: 135–137, fig. 98; 1977: 261–263, color pl. 18, pl. 70
2	supernatural head with cavity	80	0.79	Xalapa 00324	Medellín 1971: 33, pl. 33; de la Fuente 1973: 137–138, fig. 99; 1977: 263–265, pl. 71
3	seated statue	59	0.04	Xalapa 04025	Medellín 1960: 89–90, pls. 16–17; 1971: 35, pl. 34; de la Fuente 1973: 138–139, fig. 100; 1977: 268–269, pl. 74
4	sculpture with 2 seated humans	50	0.4	Xalapa 10956	de la Fuente 1973: 271; 1977: 276–277
5	altar	61	0.2	Xalapa 00334	Medellín 1960: 90–91, pl. 19; 1971: 35, pl. 35; de la Fuente 1973: 140–141, fig. 101; 1977: 270–271
9	seated human on block of stone	38	0.3	Xalapa 10935	Medellín 1971: 39, pl. 44; de la Fuente 1973: 145–146; 1977: 276
10	disk with bas-relief			?	de la Fuente 1973: 146
11	high-relief seated statue	72	0.55	Xalapa 00332	Medellín 1960: 94, pl. 23; 1971: 37, pl. 37; de la Fuente 1973: 146–147, fig. 106; 1977: 269–270, pl. 75
13	"bird" or man-bird statue	36	0.15	Xalapa 00323	Medellín 1971: 39, pl. 43; de la Fuente 1973: 148; 1977: 275–276
16	flat block with central depression			?	de la Fuente 1973: 149
17	oval stone with relief design			?	de la Fuente 1973: 271–272
18	U-shaped stone with convex sides			?[1]	de la Fuente 1973: 149
19	standing statue	160	2.2	Xalapa 00333	Medellín 1960: 94, pls. 24–25; 1971: 37, pl. 38; de la Fuente 1973: 149–151, fig. 110; 1977: 273–274, pl. 78
20	kneeling human on prostrate human	80*a*		?	Medellín 1960: 95, pls. 27–28; de la Fuente 1973: 151; 1977: 274–275
23	stone with projections on flat surface			?	de la Fuente 1973: 152
24	rectangular slab with depressions			?	de la Fuente 1973: 152
26	relief reworked into stair step			Xalapa?	Medellín 1960: 95–96, pl. 29; 1971: 37, pl. 39; de la Fuente 1973: 272; 1977: 276
27	disk with relief of face	15*a*		Xalapa?	Medellín 1960: 96, pl. 30; 1971: 37, pl. 40; de la Fuente 1973: 152; 1977: 260–261
28	altar	82	0.3	Xalapa 10909	Medellín 1971: 39, pl. 41; de la Fuente 1973: 153–155; 1977: 271–272
(A)	high-relief seated statue	43	0.2	Xalapa 10947	Winfield Capitaine 1987: 12
(B)	box with jade symbols	42	0.62	Xalapa 10925	Winfield Capitaine 1987: 19
(C)	statue?	30*b*		on site[2]	
(D)	altar	>115*b*		on site	
(E)	"throne" raised on four lcgs			on site	
(F)	lidless box			on site[3]	

Table 1, continued

Site	Description	Height (cm)	Weight (tons)	Location	Sources
Near Laguna de los Cerros center					
Monument 6	seated statue	65	0.25	Xalapa 00329	Medellín 1971: 39, pl. 42; de la Fuente 1973: 141–142, fig. 102; 1977: 270, pls. 76–77
Llano del Jícaro					
	worked stones of defined shape				
Monument 8	seated statue	195	4	Xalapa 00341	Medellín 1960: 92–93, pl. 22; 1971: 35, pl. 36; de la Fuente 1973: 143–144, fig. 103; 1977: 265–267, pls. 72–73
Monument 12	"jaws of jaguar"?			?	Ortiz 1986; Medellín's (1960: 93) "Mon. 21"?
WS 1	tabletop altar	128*b*		on site	Gillespie 1994: 233–234, figs. 3–4
WS 3	rectangular block	120*b*		on site	Gillespie 1994: 235, fig. 6
La Isla					
Monument 1a	seated statue with knuckle-dusters	72	0.47	Xalapa GOB094	Grove et al. 1993: 93
1b	supernatural head of Monument 1a	56*b*		Hueyapan[4]	Grove et al. 1993: 94
2	supernatural statue head	67	0.48	Xalapa GOB093	Grove et al. 1993: 93
3	skeletal face with cavity	69	0.4	Xalapa GOB098	Winfield Capitaine 1987: 14
Rancho El Cardonal					
	seated statue on pedestal	95*b*		on site	Grove et al. 1993: 93
Loma de la Piedra					
	seated statue	95*b*		on site	Grove et al. 1993: 92
Cuauhtotolapan Viejo					
	seated statue	151	3	Xalapa 10960	Medellín 1971: 23, pl. 6; de la Fuente 1973: 129–130; 1977: 311–312, color pl. 21, pl. 90

Notes: Measurements from the *Guía de monumentos* (Winfield Capitaine 1987) except where noted: *a* = Medellín (1960, 1971), *b* = Gillespie. The registration number is provided for monuments on display in the Xalapa Museum of Anthropology (from Winfield Capitaine 1987).

1. Description may indicate a trough or drainage stone.
2. Resembles description of Monument 17.
3. Resembles description of Monument 16.
4. Last seen in private hands in the town of Hueyapan de Ocampo.

2. Monument "C," headless torso of an anthropomorphic figure wearing a banded cape, Formative period, basalt
Photographed in the main plaza at Laguna de los Cerros, 1989: David Grove

3. Monument "D," fragment of an altar, Formative period, basalt
Photographed in the main plaza at Laguna de los Cerros, 1989: David Grove

the 1960 project at Laguna de los Cerros were removed from the site and taken to the museum (now the Museum of Anthropology in Xalapa). Michael Coe (in Proskouriakoff 1968: 132) reported "a lot of sculpture" still at the site in the mid-1960s. Some of the carved objects found and not formally reported were trough-shaped stones similar to those from San Lorenzo and La Venta and presumed to have been used as drain stones (Medellín, 1975 personal communication to Bove [1978: 9]); these are said to have been "dumped and buried in a plaza" at the site (Michael Coe in Proskouriakoff 1968: 134). On trips to the site in 1989 and 1991, Ponciano Ortiz, David Grove, and I observed at least four large fragments of carved objects among the vegetation in the main plaza. (Some or all of them, we presume, were exposed by Medellín's 1960 project.)

At least two of these sculptures appear stylistically to be Olmec, including an oval fragment (Mon. "C") that I interpret as the headless torso of a figure wearing a banded cape that extends along the curvature of the back (fig. 2). The estimated height of this fragment is 30 centimeters. This carving might be Medellín's Monument 17; it resembles de la Fuente's (1977: 277) description of Monument 17 as a "gran piedra de forma oval con diseño de ondulaciones en relieve" ("a large oval-shaped stone with a design of undulations in relief"), and she indicated (1973: 329) that its location in the 1970s was at Laguna de los Cerros.[6] The other probable Olmec monument is Monument "D," a section of an apparent tabletop altar partially buried with only the upper front corner exposed (fig. 3). Carved in bas-relief on the tabletop ledge is the "upside-down-U-bracket" or "caiman jaw" design, similar to the motif that decorates the ledge of La Venta Altar 4 (de la Fuente 1973: 25). The estimated height of the visible portion of the altar is 115 centimeters.

Two other monuments we saw on the plaza seem to be post-Olmec in date, based on stylistic comparisons with other sculptures. Monument "E" lies on the surface, upside down. It is a "throne" or seat raised on four square legs, one at each corner, of which only three are intact (fig. 4). The legs have incised designs (we did not move the stone to determine whether the seat area has designs). It is similar in overall form to the Late Formative Throne 1 at Izapa on the Pacific coast of Chiapas (Norman 1973: pl. 63) and to the Incensio Throne from Late Formative Kaminaljuyu, Guatemala (Kaplan 1995: figs. 1, 2). Monument "F" is a fragment of what appears to be a rectangular box (fig. 5) that somewhat resembles a plain stone box from Tres Zapotes (Mon. B; Stirling 1943: pl. 7a). The Laguna de los Cerros box is shorter and has thicker walls and a more shallow concavity than its Tres Zapotes counterpart. This carving may match the description of Monument 16 in the Laguna de los Cerros sequence, a flat block with a central depression (de la Fuente 1973: 149).

In addition to these and possibly other excavated monument fragments that were left at Laguna de los Cerros, there are at least two sculptures attributed to Laguna de los Cerros in the Xalapa Museum of Anthropology that have no monument numbers attached to them. One (Mon. "B") is described as a box with jade symbols (Winfield Capitaine 1987: 19). The other, Monument "A," is more definitely Olmec in style. This decapitated statue depicts an individual sculpted in high relief against a flat, plain background that connects the space between the torso and the arms (that is, the entire back of the sculpture is flat). The person is seated cross-legged on a low platform. The entire figure, with background, tilts slightly forward. The person wears a belt and a cape tied at the neck with a looped cord. His right arm is raised, bent at the elbow with the hand at the shoulder. The left arm is broken, but the left hand rests on the right knee. The right leg is gone, but the toes of the right foot show beneath the left knee. This combination of high relief against a flat background and the use of a low (6 cm high) platform also characterizes Monument 11, another decapitated seated figure (Clewlow 1974: 52). Monument 19, the unique standing statue, has also been described as a high-relief sculpture in which the full-length cape functions as both a backdrop and a technical device to prevent the statue from toppling (Clewlow 1974: 74); compare this sculpture to the caped seated figure from La Venta, Monument 77 (Benson and de la Fuente 1996: 172–173).

As noted above, the Laguna de los Cerros monument sequence includes sculpture that was found at secondary sites. One of these is Monument 6, a torso fragment said to come from "a site near the ceremonial center" (Medellín 1971: 39); this was presumably one of the five secondary sites that lie a short distance from Laguna de los Cerros. In addition, at least four monuments were located at another site approximately 5 kilometers to the northwest, Llano del Jícaro (Ortiz 1986; Gillespie 1994), which was also investigated by Medellín's 1960 project (Medellín 1960: 92–93). Of these four monuments, only one was taken to the Xalapa museum and subsequently published—the

4. Monument "E," four-legged "throne," Formative period, basalt
Photographed in the main plaza at Laguna de los Cerros, 1989: David Grove

5. Monument "F," fragment of a plain stone box, Formative period, basalt
Photographed in the main plaza at Laguna de los Cerros, 1989: David Grove

seated statue labeled Monument 8 in the Laguna de los Cerros sequence. Monument 12 also came from this site (Ortiz 1986); this may or may not be the same one briefly referred to as "Mon. 21" by Medellín (1960: 93). The Llano del Jícaro carvings are described below as part of the hinterland group.

One reason for the lack of agreement on how to date the monuments stylistically, to the point that several have been considered non-Olmec, is the unusual degree of formal variation within the Laguna de los Cerros monument corpus (de la Fuente 1977: 259). According to de la Fuente's (1977: 259–281) analysis, the majority of the monuments *are* assignable to the Olmec period by their stylistic and technical qualities, but local variation, developed to the highest degree at Laguna de los Cerros, makes it difficult to create a single chronological seriation applicable to all the monuments found within the Olmec heartland (such as attempted by Clewlow [1974] and Milbrath [1979]). She suggested (de la Fuente 1977: 280–281) that the monuments known for the site likely represent a long temporal sequence, but there is as yet no objective (nonstylistic) evidence to place individual sculptures within that sequence as being earlier or later.

In addition to showing internal formal variation, the entire corpus has been said to represent a sculptural "school" distinct from that of La Venta and San Lorenzo. In particular, the Laguna de los Cerros monuments have been noted for their "dynamic quality" (de la Fuente 1977: 259, 273, 280; see also Clewlow 1974; Medellín 1960, 1971); dynamism was earlier considered not to characterize the general Olmec style (Smith 1963: 143). The posture exhibited by the anthropomorphic figures from Laguna de los Cerros is most often asymmetrical, with arms and legs positioned at different angles, as if frozen in movement. The seated figures are also exceptionally well modeled, with delicate and realistically proportioned necks and other body parts and with great attention to representing musculature (Clewlow 1974: 53). These qualities were also considered not to be well represented in the sculpture from other Olmec sites.

However, a new monument from San Lorenzo does compare favorably in these respects with the Laguna de los Cerros corpus. A mutilated torso from the Xochiltepec *ejido* (Potrero Nuevo, near San Lorenzo) portrays a well-costumed seated figure lacking head, arms, and legs. Enough remains to show that the arms and legs were asymmetrically positioned, the right leg hanging down vertically while the left leg was bent under the body. The left arm extends forward, and the right arm appears to have been raised. In addition to its dynamic quality, this sculpture is well modeled with realistic body proportions (Cyphers 1993: 48–49).

Several earlier comparative studies linked individual Laguna de los Cerros monuments with those from elsewhere in the Olmec realm (for example, Clewlow 1974; de la Fuente 1977; Drucker 1981; Milbrath 1979). They include the following items, and I have added additional comparisons with some of the newer sculpture from San Lorenzo.

(1) Monument 27, a disk with the relief of a supernatural Olmec face, may be compared with a disk of unknown provenience in the Santiago Tuxtla museum (de la Fuente 1977: 260). Clewlow (1974: 91) reported that the unprovenienced disk was said to come from the vicinity of Tres Zapotes.

(2) The human figure on the Monument 5 altar has a close counterpart in the figure on the front of the larger altar from San Lorenzo, Monument 14 (Coe and Diehl 1980, 1: 321), who wears the same collar and pectoral (de la Fuente 1977: 271).

(3) The wing motif on Monument 13 has a correspondence with the paw-wing motif on the back of La Venta Altar 1 (de la Fuente 1977: 276; Milbrath 1979: 16). In both cases the paw-wing is accompanied by a spiral motif. Monument 13, though sometimes characterized as a bird (de la Fuente 1973: 148), even a duck, and hence compared to the duck-shaped drain stone at San Lorenzo, Monument 9 (Clewlow 1974: 108), has also been described as a crouching human figure with added paw-wings on each side (Milbrath 1979: 16), perhaps as a kind of disguise. The paw-wing motif is not uncommon on Early Formative ceramics (for example, Joralemon 1971: 40–41; Milbrath 1979: 16), so its presence on monuments from La Venta and Laguna de los Cerros need not indicate a direct tie between those two centers.

(4) Laguna de los Cerros Monument 20 and Tenochtitlan (near San Lorenzo) Monument 1 (Coe and Diehl 1980, 1: 371) both depict a human figure with the right leg bent up and the left leg tucked under in a kneeling position atop a supine second figure (Clewlow 1974:

83; de la Fuente 1977: 275; Drucker 1981: 41; Milbrath 1979: 12). The upper figures on the monuments from the two sites differ most notably in their clothing.

(5) Monument 9 and San Lorenzo Monument 15 (Coe and Diehl 1980, 1: 322) have a remarkable similarity. They both depict human figures (mostly destroyed) seated atop a rectangular block on which has been carved knotted cords, as if each block were a stone tied up to be moved (de la Fuente 1977: 276).[7] The cords are tied in a similar fashion on both blocks, but the design is repeated on the Laguna de los Cerros monument. The remains of the two legs are barely visible on the more destroyed San Lorenzo monument.

(6) On the large supernatural heads, Laguna de los Cerros Monuments 1 and 2, the mouths are covered with dissimilar, fanged buccal masks, and the eye areas are covered with rectangular plaques with carved designs. The buccal mask of Monument 1 is similar to that found on La Venta Monument 11. The left eye of Monument 1, which has a clear "X" or St. Andrew's cross in bas-relief, is like that of San Lorenzo Monument 30 (Coe and Diehl 1980, 1: 339), a profile serpentine figure carved in very low relief whose right eye also has an "X" within a squarish plaque (de la Fuente 1977: 263). David Joralemon (1971: fig. 125) suggested that the right eye of Monument 1 has a U-shape with a dot in the center, a motif that frequently is paired with the "X" in the eyes (for example, on a mask of unknown provenience [Joralemon 1971: fig. 153]) or above the eyes (for example, on a large supernatural severed head from La Venta pictured in Benson and de la Fuente [1996: 176]).

Another unusual feature of the two heads is their curly or "kinky" hair, created by drilling depressions at irregular intervals into the top, sides, and back of the head. Clewlow (1974: 27) suggested that this was an experimental technique indicative of the precocious beginnings of stone carving at Laguna de los Cerros. However, the technique for making the hair compares to that used on a carving discovered in 1995 by the San Lorenzo project. Referred to as a "mutilated head" (Cyphers 1996: 58), it is a composite sculpture consisting of the right half of a human head juxtaposed with an amorphous mass created by drill holes and perforations like the hair on the Laguna de los Cerros heads. In addition, the projecting quadrangular eye plaques and a well-defined mouth area with protruding outcurving fangs occur on a rather delicately carved feline sculpture also found at San Lorenzo in 1995 (Cyphers 1996: 57); the feline's outstretched front legs touch a column on which a descending, helmeted human figure is sculpted in bas-relief. There are no bas-relief designs on the feline's eye plaques, however.

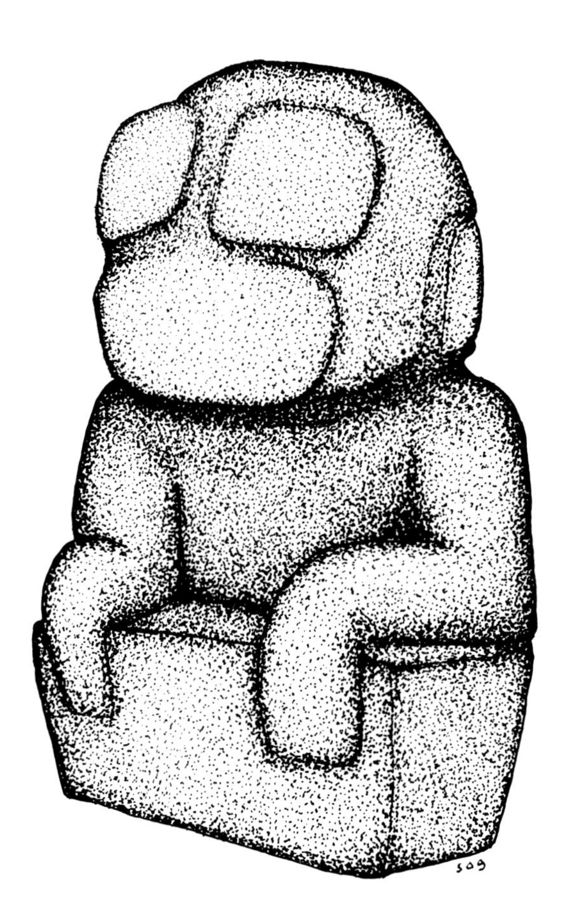

6. Drawing of Monument 8, Llano del Jícaro, unfinished statue of a seated anthropomorph probably intended to have supernatural features

In sum, despite the stylistic differences noted for the Laguna de los Cerros monument corpus, there are quite a few similarities of sculptural themes and individual motifs between some Laguna de los Cerros monuments and those of other sites, especially San Lorenzo.

Hinterland Monuments

Another unique member of the Laguna de los Cerros numbered series is Monument 8, a massive intact statue of a seated personage almost 2 meters tall (fig. 6). What makes it so very different from other Olmec sculpture is that the entire body is represented by three great geometric forms: the oversized rounded head, the upper torso, and a rectangular lower portion representing the area of presumably crossed legs and arms atop them. Details such as hands, legs, and facial features are merely hinted at. Scholars have disagreed as to whether this work represents some achievement of abstract art among the Olmecs (for example, de la Fuente 1977: 265, pls. 72, 73; Medellín 1971: 35; Smith 1963: 133) or is an unfinished piece, probably planned as a composite creature with a face like that of Monuments 1 and 2, in a seated cross-legged pose with the hands near the knees (for example, Clewlow 1974: 52; Medellín 1960: 93; Gillespie 1994: 232). The head of Monument 8 is approximately the same size as the Monuments 1 and 2 heads, and like them has eyes marked by two projecting rectangular plaques, with a similar projection covering the mouth area, as if in anticipation of sculpting a buccal mask.

One reason this sculpture appears to be a finished work is that the entire outer surface is well smoothed by fine pecking; that is, it does not bear the scars of stone flake removal that one might expect for a sculpture that was halted in progress. However, an argument for its unfinished state is its original location. As mentioned, this is one of the four monuments in the Laguna de los Cerros sequence that were found at Llano del Jícaro, the monument workshop located northwest of Laguna de los Cerros in the *municipio* of Hueyapan de Ocampo (Medellín 1960: 92; 1971: 35; Gillespie 1994).

7. Worked Stone 1, an unfinished tabletop altar at Llano del Jícaro, Formative period, basalt
Photographed after excavation, 1991

Other carvings still at this site reveal the same smoothed surfaces on their unfinished portions. Survey and excavations at this site in 1991 revealed nine unfinished carved or worked stones still in situ (Gillespie 1994).[8] Two of them were previously noted by Medellín, according to Ponciano Ortiz (1986), who had access to Medellín's unpublished field notes, but we were unable to locate the third one that should still have been there, Monument 12. This carving was interpreted by Medellín as an attempt to sculpt the open jaws of a jaguar. Ortiz could not find it when he visited the site in 1979 (Ortiz 1986), nor did our 1991 project reveal the presence of a stone that fit this rather specific description.

The other two carvings reported by Medellín are probably among the worked stones located by the 1991 project, although I am unaware of what monument numbers they were given in 1960. One was described by Medellín as a large rectangular stone with trimmed sides; this is probably the unfinished carving we labeled Worked Stone (WS) 3 (Gillespie 1994: 235). It is a very large rectangular slab with a flattish upper surface, 3.3 meters long and 2.6 meters wide. It had been dragged up onto other boulders to raise it so that the carvers could work on the sides. Our investigations revealed great quantities of debitage in the form of large and small flakes, as well as a hammerstone and fragments of other stone tools immediately adjacent to the worked stone. The carvers had nicely shaped one short side but were still in the process of removing stone from the other sides and smoothing the top surface when work was abandoned. In its unfinished state, WS 3 compares with San Lorenzo Monument 51, which Coe and Diehl (1980, 1: 360) called a "flat altar."

The other unfinished carving reported by Medellín is one he called the "split stone," our WS 1 (Gillespie 1994: 233–234). It is a recognizable tabletop altar or "throne" whose top half had broken off the base sometime in the past (fig. 7). It was apparently tipped up and lying on its back, the two halves split apart, when found in 1960. Medellín's workers righted the altar onto its base, placed the top portion onto the base half, moved the monument slightly in so doing, and then excavated for ceramic artifacts in the place where it had stood. The carvers had removed large portions of stone from all four sides and the top, by per-

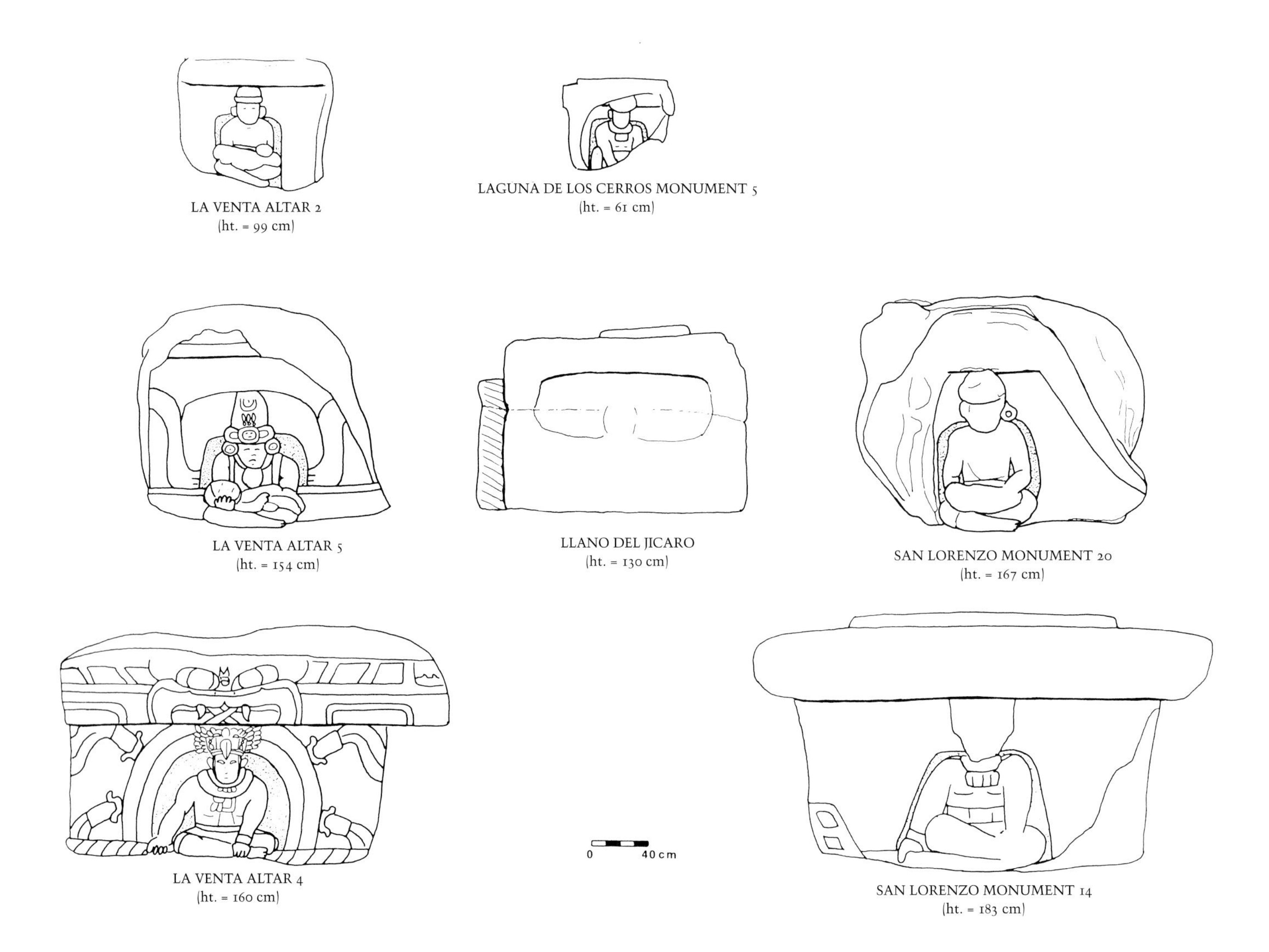

8. Comparison of sizes of altars from San Lorenzo, La Venta, and the Laguna de los Cerros area

cussion, and were in the process of straightening and smoothing those surfaces by pecking and grinding in small delimited areas. This work left raised rectangular projections that were destined to be removed, but the process gave even those projections a smooth surface that might appear to us to be "finished." On what we recognize as the front, they had begun to remove stone to form the area below the tabletop ledge. A curious feature is a rectangular tab projecting from one back corner of the altar the entire height of the stone. It is very smoothed and well shaped, but we suspect it was intended to be completely removed at a later time, possibly after the altar reached its final destination, because no other altar has such a tab.

Scholars (for example, Clewlow 1974: 123; de la Fuente 1977: 272) have commented on the "atypically" small size of the two reported altars (Mons. 5 and 28) from Laguna de los Cerros. Monument 5 is just under 50 centimeters high in its fragmentary state, while Monument 28 is only slightly taller at 66 centimeters. However, adding WS 1 from Llano del Jícaro, which is 128 centimeters tall, to the total corpus of the Laguna de los Cerros area sculpture yields a better comparison in terms of altar size with the other two Olmec centers, whose altars also exhibit quite a range of sizes (fig. 8). As noted above, there is also the large portion of another altar still in situ in the main plaza at Laguna de los Cerros. Interestingly, the Monument 28 altar lacks a niche for the figure to sit within, unlike Monument 5, which has this more typical trait; thus Monument 28 compares to a late altar at La Venta, Altar 6, which also lacks a niche. It is unknown whether WS 1 was intended to have a niche, or whether one appears on the altar still in the plaza.

Another important hinterland site that has

yielded several Olmec carvings is La Isla, which may have been a secondary center (it has several earthen mounds) under the hegemony of Laguna de los Cerros. Sculpture fragments were recovered from the site by people living in the area, and several of these are now in the Museum of Anthropology in Xalapa, Veracruz, with their proveniences labeled "Hueyapan de Ocampo" (Winfield Capitaine 1987), the town adjacent to La Isla. In addition, we were shown a carved head from the site which is in private hands. Informants told us that all these carvings were recovered from the river, which has cut into La Isla Mound D. The brief excavations carried out at La Isla yielded no new sculpture but did provide evidence to suggest that the Olmec monuments had likely been redeposited in Classic period constructions (Grove 1994: 226), of which Mound D is one, a situation similar to that which Medellín encountered in Laguna de los Cerros.

9. La Isla Monument 1b, head of a supernatural being, Formative period, basalt
Photographed in Hueyapan de Ocampo, 1991: David Grove

We renumbered all the sculpture from La Isla to properly indicate its provenience. The ones we designated La Isla Monuments 1 and 2 (Grove et al. 1993) are two supernatural statue heads severed from their bodies.[9] Monument 1 (in private hands) is eroded and lacks visible eyes, and its rectangular ear pieces are broken (fig. 9). The mouth area is the most distinct feature: a prominent downturned upper lip meets a bulbous and broken nose area. What looks like a projecting "tongue" reaches down to the chin and defines the lower corners of the mouth which were created by drilling circular holes. The blocky shape's cleft head, broad headdress band just above the eyes, and general snarling mouth resemble the features on the heads of Estero Rabón Monument 5 near San Lorenzo (Medellín 1960: 75–76, pl. 1), several monuments from La Venta—Monuments 9, 64 (de la Fuente 1973: 65–66, 111), and the large unnumbered head that has the X- and U-shaped motifs above the eyes (Benson and de la Fuente 1996: 176)—and also the head of San Lorenzo Monument 10 (see Symonds, this volume, fig. 10). Monument 10 (Coe and Diehl 1980, 1: 317) is a more intact sculpture in which the head is shown to belong to a stocky seated figure with arms bent and held in front of the body, each hand holding a "knuckle-duster."

The resemblance to Monument 10 is even more significant when another La Isla monument from Mound D is considered—a torso fragment of a seated individual holding two knuckle-dusters (now in the Xalapa museum), virtually identical to Monument 10 (fig. 10). The legs are missing. Like Monument 10, this figure wears a very wide band worn above the waist to mid-chest, and it also has what appears to be a narrow loincloth showing between the buttocks. My analysis of the size and shape of fracture areas and the pattern of irregularities in the stone for both La Isla pieces indicates that the Monument 1 head belongs to this torso (fig. 11). We accordingly numbered the head Monument 1b and the torso as Monument 1a (Grove et al. 1993: 93–94). This carving is yet another instance of sharing of a very specific sculpture type between Laguna de los Cerros and San Lorenzo.

The other Olmec-style head from La Isla, Monument 2, has a flattish rounded top with no visible headdress, heavy projecting brow

10. La Isla Monument 1a, torso of an anthropomorph holding two knuckle-dusters, Formative period, basalt
Photographed in Hueyapan de Ocampo, 1984: David Grove

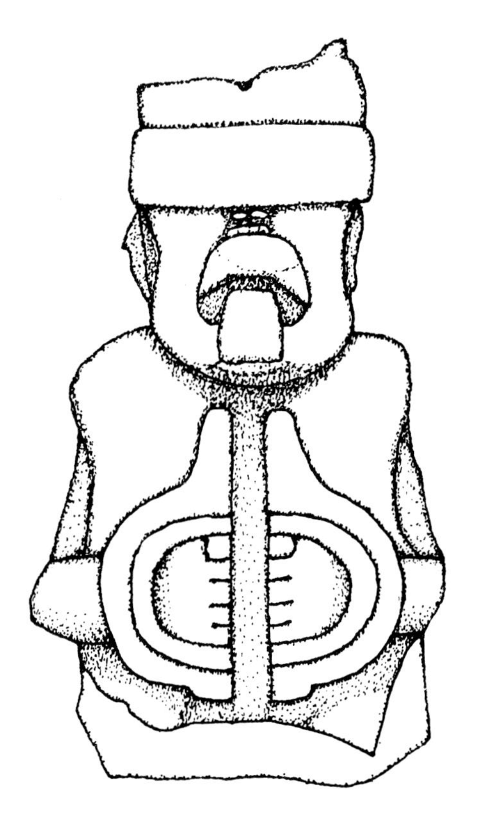

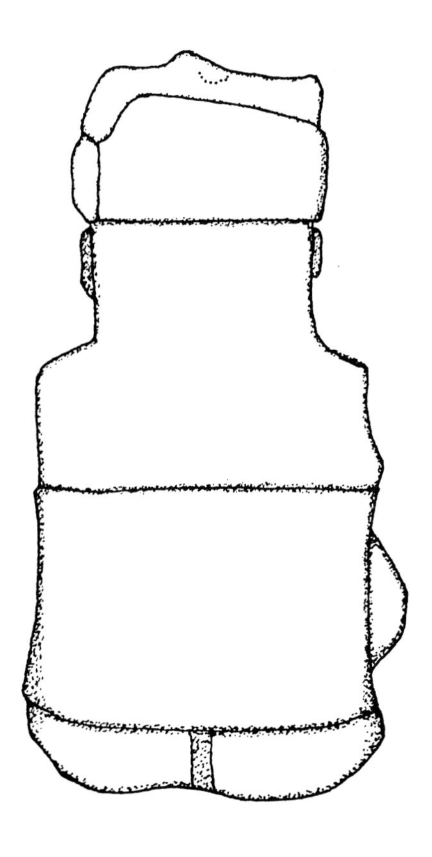

11. Tentative reconstruction drawing uniting the two known fragments of La Isla Monument 1

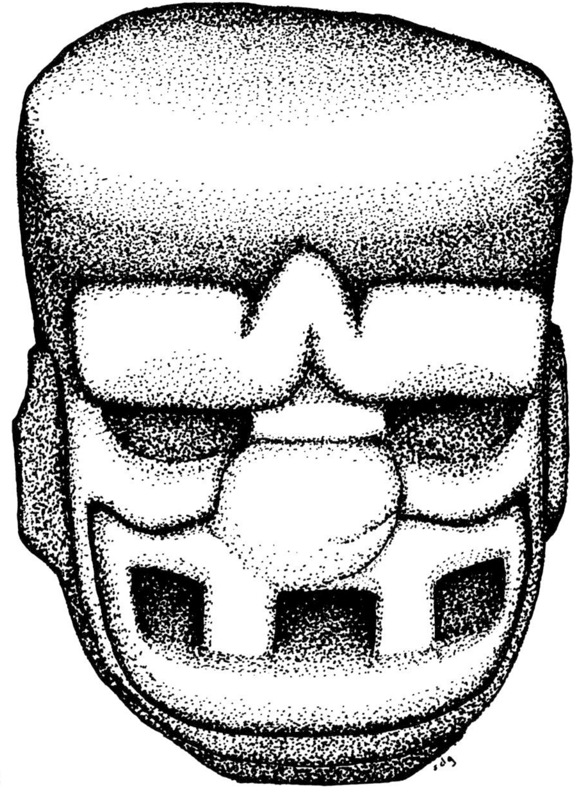

12. La Isla Monument 2, head of a supernatural being
Drawing based on photographs taken in Hueyapan de Ocampo, 1984

ridges, a bulbous eroded nose area, and a buccal mask with two widely spaced rectangular teeth projecting down from the upper mandible (fig. 12). The rectangular ear pieces are broken (Grove et al. 1993: 93). The brow treatment compares to La Venta Monument 8 (de la Fuente 1973: 64), but the face is otherwise dissimilar.

In addition to finding these figures from secondary sites in the Laguna de los Cerros hinterlands, we were also shown two other carvings, both highly mutilated seated statues (Grove et al. 1993). The first, designated the Loma de la Piedra carving, was found on a low hill north of the town of Corral Nuevo, while the other, from the Rancho El Cardonal, was recently discovered by the landowner at a location not far from Llano del Jícaro. Both monuments were mutilated in the past, like all the other finished carvings from the Laguna de los Cerros area.

The Loma de la Piedra sculpture depicts a seated person wearing a narrow belt (fig. 13). The head and most of the arms and legs have been broken off. The legs were asymmetrically positioned, the right leg apparently horizontal, the knee bent, while the left leg may have been raised or with the knee up (compare to Laguna de los Cerros Monument 11). Unlike the Laguna de los Cerros seated figures, the torso is larger than life-size and very blocky, rather than delicate and rounded, and the personage leans strongly forward (perhaps to distribute the weight of the stone [see Drucker 1981: 39]). The height of the sculpture fragment, including a shallow platform on which the person is seated, is 95 centimeters (Grove et al. 1993: 92). The general posture, size, and massive quality compare to another, previously published Laguna de los Cerros hinterland monument also located in the *municipio* of Hueyapan de Ocampo: the seated statue from Cuauhtotolapan Viejo (Medellín 1971: 23, pl. 6), retrieved from the river bottom in two pieces. With its head restored to the body, this sculpture has a total height of 163 centimeters. The Loma de la Piedra and Cuauhtotolapan Viejo monuments are similar in overall appearance to other large, forward-leaning seated figures with crossed legs and arms in front of their knees, such as the Cruz del Milagro, Sayula, Monument 1 sculpture (Medellín 1971: 41, pl. 48) and La Venta Monument 10 (de la Fuente 1973: 68). The Loma de la Piedra monument differs from these others in the asymmetrical placement of the limbs.

In contrast to these two hinterland monuments, the Rancho El Cardonal carving is smaller than life-size and more delicately modeled, which is typical of the finished anthropomorphic statues from Laguna de los Cerros (fig. 14). The legs are only loosely crossed, and the toes of the right foot are well defined. The upper torso and head were removed, as were the arms, which rested on the legs. The only vestige of costume is what appears to be a single narrow ribbon cascading down the center of the back, as if from a headdress (compare to the wider and more elaborate headdress ribbons on the back of Laguna de los Cerros Mon. 6). This carving is unusual because it is seated upon a very tall pedestal that is oval in cross section. The base of the pedestal has been mutilated, and it has a slightly projecting flange around the perimeter near the bottom edge. The broken height of the figure is only 29 centimeters, while the height of the entire fragment is 95 centimeters (Grove et al. 1993: 93).

The El Cardonal monument is similar in position and size to decapitated carvings of seated personages on rounded pedestals from the site of Sin Cabezas, Escuintla, Guatemala,

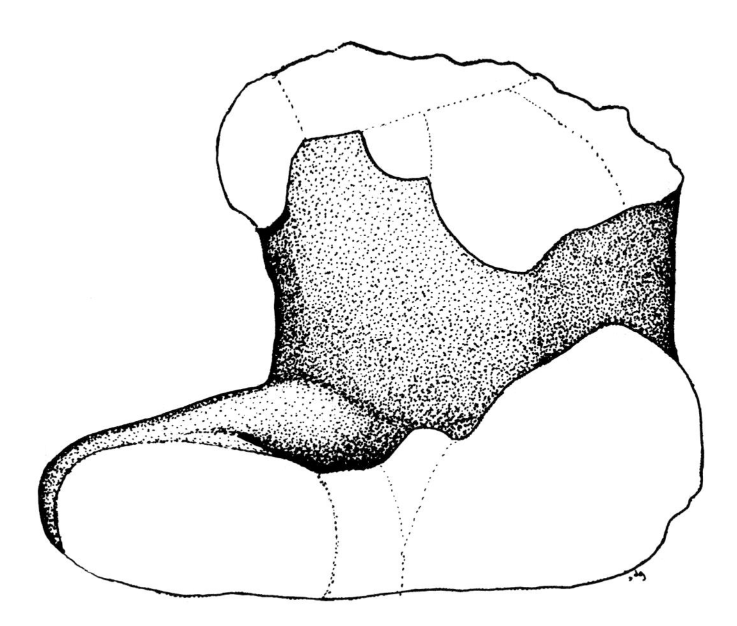

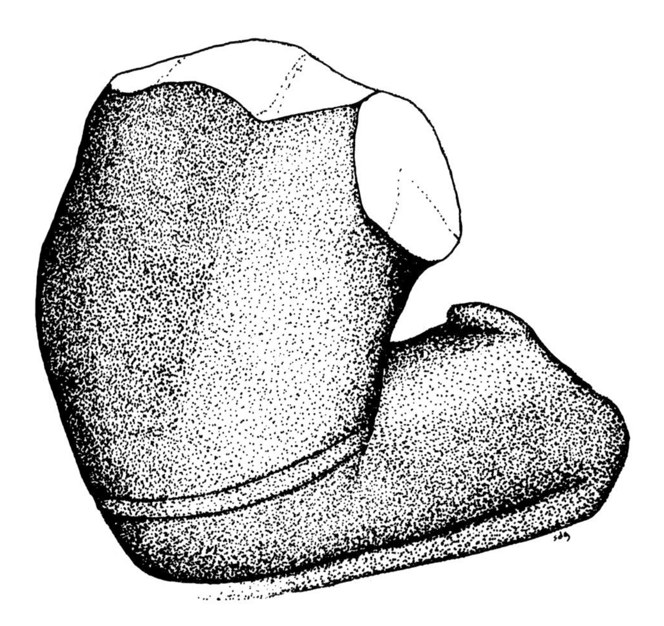

13. Two views (a and b) of the Loma de la Piedra monument of a seated anthropomorph
Based on field observations and photographs, 1990

most especially to Monument 1 (total height of Mon. 1 is 105 cm; height of the seated figure is 35 cm [Parsons 1986: fig. 15]). Lee Parsons dated this site's monuments on stylistic grounds to the late Middle Formative, 700–500 B.C. (the time when La Venta and Chalcatzingo both flourished), which he considered a transitional period between "Olmec" and later monument carving traditions (1986: 14). Nevertheless, he considered the naturalistic, full-round pedestaled figures of Monuments 1 and 2 to "reflect prior Olmec canons," and Sin Cabezas Monument 1 is further characterized as "the most Olmec-looking" (1986: 20).

A significant fact concerning these two hinterland carvings is that they were placed in locations where surface indications failed to show any evidence of prehistoric occupation. We have suggested (Grove et al. 1993: 94) that, assuming these monuments were placed there during the periods when Laguna de los Cerros was a regional power, they may have served as a form of boundary marker, delimiting sacred or political space. The Loma de la Piedra statue sits on a low hill several kilometers north of Laguna de los Cerros, while the El Cardonal carving is a few kilometers to the northwest. This sculpture sits at the edge of the same plateau where the monument workshop is located, and from El Cardonal one can look down into the valley toward Laguna de los Cerros.

Grove (1999) has shown for San Lorenzo and La Venta that the spatial positioning of monuments within a center conforms to recognizable patterns. The carvings were part of a symbolic system activated in ritual practices that integrated the center as a unity and defined its relationship to its hinterland or periphery. So, too, the monuments assigned to the hinterland should not be considered in isolation from their possible relationship to the patterning at the larger center. They should be seen as part of the greater spatial unity defined, in part, by monuments that extended far beyond the center itself. Therefore, just as much more work needs to be done at Laguna de los Cerros to understand better how it functioned as a primary Olmec center—an assessment thus far based entirely on the number of battered Olmec monuments it has yielded—so, too, a fuller understanding of its role as a center in a complex settlement hierarchy depends on investigations of its hinterland sites and monuments.

Implications of Comparative Studies

The recent findings of monuments in the Laguna de los Cerros hinterland and elsewhere in the Olmec area, especially at San Lorenzo, have increased the number of similarities that can be described between the upland and lowland sites since the earlier comparative studies of the 1970s, revealing further and often striking correspondences. The closest similari-

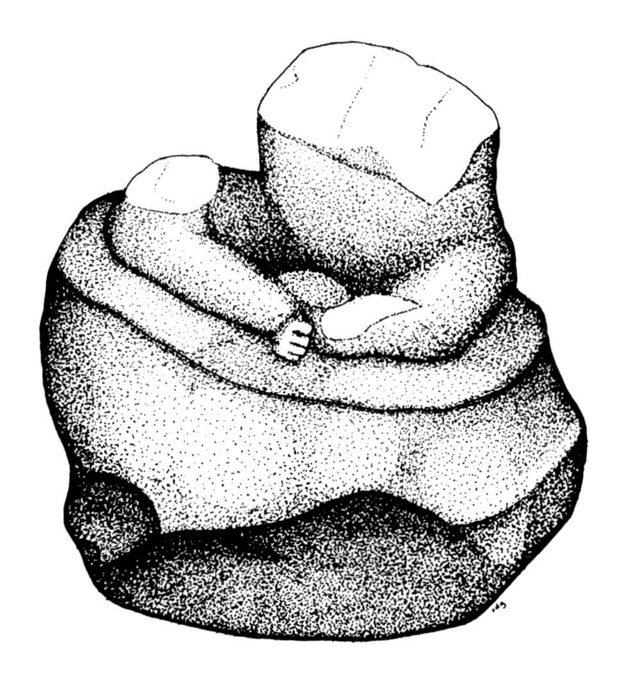

14. Rancho El Cardonal monument of an anthropomorph seated on a pedestal
Drawing (a) based on field observations and photographs (b) taken in 1991

ties between centers are noted for Laguna de los Cerros and San Lorenzo, which lies approximately 65 kilometers to the southeast. This fact has implications for both the dating of Laguna de los Cerros' Olmec occupation and the degree of cultural contact between the two sites, including the possibility, as yet unproven, that Laguna de los Cerros provided basalt boulders or unfinished monuments to San Lorenzo during the San Lorenzo phase (1150–900 B.C.). The monuments also demonstrate, through stylistic links, occupation in the Middle Formative (some similarities to La Venta and the El Cardonal pedestaled statue like those of Sin Cabezas) and into the early Late Formative, with resemblances to Tres Zapotes carvings (Mon. 27, and the four-legged throne and plain stone box still in situ at Laguna de los Cerros). This continuity of settlement generally matches the preliminary evidence from the ceramic artifacts as analyzed by Bove (1978: 23), although the emphasis in the ceramic reanalyses has been on the affinities to the San Lorenzo phase and not to these later periods.

Despite these similarities, the Laguna de los Cerros carvings, as a corpus, are distinctive for various reasons, in terms of both style and of how representative the corpus is of the entirety of Olmec monumental art (see also de la Fuente, this volume). While earlier claims that the Laguna de los Cerros carvings were different in being more dynamic, delicate, and realistically proportioned now may not have as much validity, thanks to some of the newer finds at San Lorenzo that also have these qualities, Laguna de los Cerros still has some unique pieces, including Monument 19, the statue of a standing human figure. Furthermore, in order to evaluate the relationships Laguna de los Cerros may have had with other primary and secondary centers on the basis of its known monuments, another issue must be addressed, namely, what typical Olmec monument types are missing? Monument 19 is so far the largest Olmec sculpture known for the site of Laguna de los Cerros itself, at 160 centimeters tall and weighing 2.2 tons. What this implies is that, despite its location close to the source of basalt boulders, Laguna de los Cerros thus far *lacks* the massive stone carvings found at San Lorenzo, La Venta, and also Tres Zapotes.

Especially significant is the absence at Laguna de los Cerros of colossal heads, one of the most distinctive Olmec sculpture types.

Ten heads are known from San Lorenzo, four from La Venta, and three from the Tres Zapotes area. Many scholars believe that the colossal heads are giant portraits of rulers or their ancestors, who were portrayed wearing headdresses that further signaled their identity (for example, Clewlow 1974: 150; Coe 1972: 5; Cyphers 1995: 45; de la Fuente 1992: 14; Grove 1981: 61; Stirling 1965: 733). I suspect that the lack of colossal heads, along with any other unmutilated naturalistic or "portrait" heads (except on the two small altars), is one reason why the Laguna de los Cerros monuments seem less familiar to us. We are drawn to the massive and compelling faces that we believe depict individual Olmec personages, but at Laguna de los Cerros the paramounts of Olmec society remain faceless and anonymous (see Pasztory, this volume).

Heads are important beyond the emotional responses they may evoke. David Grove (1981) has suggested that colossal heads and other representations of faces and headdresses can provide evidence of the interaction of important individuals between the various centers. He noted the similar facial features and headdress of La Venta Colossal Head Monument 4 (de la Fuente 1973: 55–57) and the person depicted in bas-relief on the side of the great San Lorenzo altar, Monument 14 (Coe and Diehl 1980, 1: 321); both have slightly projecting upper teeth and a headdress with a big "feline paw" on top. If both carvings are meant to represent the same person, then this constitutes evidence of personalized interrelationships between these two centers.[10]

It is possible that future excavations will finally add colossal heads to the Laguna de los Cerros corpus, with the potential to provide valuable comparative data with other sites. This was the opinion optimistically expressed by Michael Coe in 1967 (in Proskouriakoff 1968: 134): "There must be big heads there. Most of the monuments must still be underground just as most of the monuments of San Lorenzo must still be underground" (as his and later excavations have shown true). Furthermore, it was from the deepest excavation units at Laguna de los Cerros that the late Early Formative ceramic artifacts were recovered (especially Trench 14, excavated to a depth of 6.3 meters [Bove 1978: 16]).

It is nevertheless interesting to note that in addition to the absence of colossal heads, Laguna de los Cerros has no other large monuments, no stelae (like those of La Venta), and no large altars like San Lorenzo Monument 14 and La Venta Altar 4 (see fig. 8). In fact, the few large carvings in the Laguna de los Cerros area all come from the hinterland sites—the large unfinished statue (Mon. 8), the altar (WS 1), and the great rectangular slab (WS 3) from Llano del Jícaro, and the Cuauhtotolapan Viejo and Loma de la Piedra seated statues. If this absence of large monuments is real and not a product of limited excavations at Laguna de los Cerros, then it suggests that the paramounts of the site may have purposely limited themselves to smaller monuments. Their counterparts at San Lorenzo and La Venta imported the largest stones over the longest distances to their home sites, where such stone is completely absent and its inherent value was correspondingly very high. In contrast, in the Laguna de los Cerros area, where massive boulders are close by and abundant, perhaps the huge size of the stone itself was less important for conveying the meanings or fulfilling the functions of the monuments there.

NOTES

The 1991 archaeological investigations at Llano del Jícaro and La Isla were undertaken with the permission of Mexico's Instituto Nacional de Antropología e Historia. The Llano del Jícaro project was funded by the Wenner-Gren Foundation for Anthropological Research and the work at La Isla by the National Science Foundation. Ponciano Ortiz lent invaluable assistance in the field, and David Grove helped me enormously, both in the field and with the writing of this paper. John Clark and David Webster provided valuable insights on comparisons of some of the monuments. I gratefully acknowledge the help and cooperation of these persons and institutions.

1. "Cerro Cintepec" as a type of stone refers to a coarsely porphyritic, olivine-augine basalt of Plio-Pleistocene age resulting from volcanic flows in the southern and eastern area of the Tuxtla Mountains. It appears on the surface in various places, eroded into large boulders (Williams and Heizer 1965: 3, 5).

2. Medellín (1971) frequently reported as associated ceramics the artifacts from test excavations placed where he *suspected* that the carvings were originally positioned, namely, on top of mounds, even though he actually recovered the monuments from other locations, such as the plazas below.

3. As for the earthen mound architecture that is present at Laguna de los Cerros, it is difficult to say how much of it dates to the Olmec period. Bove (1978: 32) noted that the main mound group was oriented to 8 degrees west of north, like the Formative ceremonial centers of La Venta and also San José Mogote, Oaxaca.

4. Furthermore, there was some early confusion concerning the numbering system, so reports such as those of Clewlow (1974) and Bove (1978) refer to Mon. 1a (= Mon. 2), Mon. 3a (= Mon. 6), and use no numbers when describing Monuments 9 and 28, although de la Fuente's 1973 catalogue lists the correct numbers for all these sculptures.

5. Table 1 does not include the "small, crouched jaguar on boulder from Laguna de los Cerros" reported by Clewlow (1974: 101). According to de la Fuente (1977: 277), the provenience of this eroded sculpture, which was in the Museum of Anthropology in Xalapa, is unknown.

6. Ann Cyphers (personal communication, 1996) informed me that this monument fragment has since disappeared from the site.

7. David Webster (personal communication, 1996) brought to my attention a fascinating similarity between these two monuments, each showing a person atop a block of stone seemingly tied with cords (carved on its surface), and a photograph taken before 1939 from South Nias, Indonesia, showing a large stone tied up with real cords, in order to be dragged a great distance, upon which two men were standing (in Bellwood 1979: 225). Such stone-dragging events are not unusual in Indonesia (Bellwood 1979: 226) and have been described ethnographically, for example, in Kodi, West Sumba, where certain "big men" engaged the labor of thousands to haul huge stones to mark their graves (Hoskins 1986). More attention should be paid to these ethnographic analogues to help explain how, as well as why, the Olmecs may have transported huge boulders and carvings, and whether an advanced chiefdom or archaic state organization is necessarily indicated by the presence of large imported monoliths, as is usually assumed for the Olmecs.

8. Five of the worked stones from Llano del Jícaro were rectilinear blocks in which a lengthwise channel or groove was being cut in the upper surface. While in their general form they appeared to resemble the making of trough or drainage stones, such as are known for La Venta and San Lorenzo, and which Medellín indicated were present at Laguna de los Cerros (see above), their dimensions do not match any of the published drain stones (Gillespie 1994: 235).

9. A third head from La Isla, Monument 3, is post-Olmec in style: a crude "skull" face on a tall, almost cylindrical form, with a shallow cavity ground into the upper surface. Its overall form and the carving of the eyes—circular depressions surrounded by shallow channels that extend to the sides of the face—strongly resemble the stone "mask" from Medias Aguas, Sayula, Veracruz (Mon. 1; Medellín 1960: pls. 4, 5; 1971: pl. 10). The latter object is larger and has a feline mouth with projecting fangs instead of exposed human teeth that give the La Isla face a skeletal appearance. Medellín (1971: 25) dated the Medias Aguas monument to the Late Classic period on the basis of associated ceramics.

10. The bas-relief on the San Lorenzo altar shows better than the colossal head what the headdress worn by this individual actually looked like—a tall, broad-brimmed hat with the big "jaguar paw" on top. On La Venta Head 4, this headdress is reduced and depicted in very low relief, like the ear ornaments, while the facial features are shown in higher relief to give a more realistic three-dimensional representation. Scholars have long commented on the round, close-fitting helmetlike headdress worn by virtually all colossal heads (for example, Covarrubias 1957: 65; Cyphers 1995: 45), somewhat resembling old-fashioned American football helmets (Covarrubias 1957: 65; repeated by Diehl 1996: 32). In fact, the headdress as "helmet" is not naturalistically represented; instead, it is a product of the technique used to carve the colossal heads, made from rounded boulders that were only minimally modified (Drucker 1981: 40). To try to duplicate realistically on such a massive scale the elaborate headdress actually worn by the head would have required the removal of a great quantity of stone, starting with a much larger boulder, and would have been technically very difficult to achieve (Stirling 1965: 733–734). We must therefore rely on the bas-reliefs and some smaller three-dimensional representations of headdresses to realize the nature of Olmec headgear as worn by the persons depicted on the colossal heads.

BIBLIOGRAPHY

Bellwood, Peter
1979 *Man's Conquest of the Pacific: The Prehistory of Southeast Asia and Oceania.* New York.

Benson, Elizabeth P., and Beatriz de la Fuente
1996 (Editors) *Olmec Art of Ancient Mexico* [exh. cat., National Gallery of Art]. Washington.

Bernal, Ignacio
1969 *The Olmec World,* trans. Doris Heyden and Fernando Horcasitas. Berkeley.

Bove, Frederick J.
1978 Laguna de los Cerros: An Olmec Central Place. *Journal of New World Archaeology* 2(3).

Clewlow, C. William, Jr.
1974 *A Stylistic and Chronological Study of Olmec Monumental Sculpture.* Berkeley.

Coe, Michael D.
1968 *America's First Civilization: Discovering the Olmec.* New York.

1972 Olmec Jaguars and Olmec Kings. In *The Cult of the Feline,* ed. Elizabeth Benson, 1–18. Washington.

Coe, Michael D., and Richard Diehl
1980 *In the Land of the Olmec,* 2 vols. Austin.

Covarrubias, Miguel
1957 *Indian Art of Mexico and Central America.* New York.

Cyphers, Ann
1993 Escenas escultóricas olmecas. *Antropológicas,* new series, 6: 47–52.

1995 Las cabezas colosales. *Arqueología Mexicana* 12: 43–47.

1996 Recent Discoveries at San Lorenzo, Veracruz. In *Olmecs.* Special edition of *Arqueología Mexicana,* 56–59. Mexico City.

1999 From Stone to Symbols: Olmec Art in Social Context at San Lorenzo Tenochtitlán. In *Social Patterns in Pre-Classic Mesoamerica,* ed. David Grove and Rosemary Joyce, 155–181. Washington.

de la Fuente, Beatriz
1973 *Escultura monumental olmeca: Catálogo.* Mexico City.

1977 *Los hombres de piedra: Escultura olmeca.* Mexico City.

1981 Toward a Conception of Monumental Olmec Art. In *The Olmec and Their Neighbors,* ed. Elizabeth Benson, 83–94. Washington.

1992 *Cabezas colosales olmecas.* Mexico City.

Diehl, Richard A.
1996 The Olmec World. In *Olmec Art of Ancient Mexico,* ed. Elizabeth Benson and Beatriz de la Fuente, 29–33 [exh. cat., National Gallery of Art]. Washington.

Drucker, Philip
1981 On the Nature of Olmec Polity. In *The Olmec and Their Neighbors,* ed. Elizabeth Benson, 29–47. Washington.

Gillespie, Susan D.
1994 Llano del Jícaro: An Olmec Monument Workshop. *Ancient Mesoamerica* 5: 231–242.

1999 Olmec Thrones as Ancestral Altars: The Two Sides of Power. In *Material Symbols: Culture and Economy in Prehistory,* ed. John Robb, 224–253. Carbondale, Ill.

Grove, David C.
1981 Olmec Monuments: Mutilation as a Clue to Meaning. In *The Olmec and Their Neighbors,* ed. Elizabeth Benson, 49–68. Washington.

1984 *Chalcatzingo: Excavations on the Olmec Frontier.* London.

1994 La Isla, Veracruz, 1991: A Preliminary Report, with Comments on the Olmec Uplands. *Ancient Mesoamerica* 5: 223–230.

1999 Public Monuments and Sacred Mountains: Observations on Three Formative Period Sacred Landscapes. In *Social Patterns in Pre-Classic Mesoamerica,* ed. David Grove and Rosemary Joyce, 255–299. Washington.

Grove, David C., Susan D. Gillespie, Ponciano Ortiz C., and Michael Hayton
1993 Five Olmec Monuments from the Laguna de los Cerros Hinterland. *Mexicon* 15: 91–95.

Hoskins, Janet A.
1986 So My Name Shall Live: Stone-Dragging and Grave-Building in Kodi, West Sumba. *Bijdragen Tot de Taal-, Land- en Volkenkunde* 142: 31–51.

Joralemon, Peter David
1971 *A Study of Olmec Iconography.* Washington.

Kaplan, Jonathan
1995 The Incienso Throne and Other Thrones from Kaminaljuyu, Guatemala: Late Preclassic Examples of a Mesoamerican Throne Tradition. *Ancient Mesoamerica* 6: 185–196.

Medellín Zenil, Alfonso
1960 Monolitos inéditos olmecas. *La Palabra y el Hombre* 16: 75–97.

1963 The Olmec Culture. In *The Olmec Tradition* [exh. cat., Museum of Fine Arts]. Houston.

1971 *Monolitos olmecas y otros en el Museo de la Universidad de Veracruz.* Mexico City.

Milbrath, Susan
1979 *A Study of Olmec Sculptural Chronology.* Washington.

Norman, V. Garth
1973 *Izapa Sculpture. Part 1: Album.* Papers of the New World Archaeological Foundation 30. Provo, Utah.

Ortiz Ceballos, Ponciano
1986 Proyecto Arqueológico Laguna de los Cerros y su Area de Interacción Cultural. Manuscript on file, Instituto Nacional de Antropología e Historia, Veracruz.

Parsons, Lee A.
1986 *The Origins of Maya Art: Monumental Stone Sculpture of Kaminaljuyu, Guatemala, and the Southern Pacific Coast.* Washington.

Proskouriakoff, Tatiana
1968 Olmec and Maya Art: Problems of Their Stylistic Relation. In *Dumbarton Oaks Conference on the Olmec,* ed. Elizabeth Benson, 119–134. Washington.

Smith, Tillie
1963 The Main Themes of the "Olmec" Art Tradition. *The Kroeber Anthropological Society Papers* 28: 121–213. Berkeley.

Stirling, Matthew W.
1943 *Stone Monuments of Southern Mexico.* Bureau of American Ethnology Bulletin 138. Washington.

1965 Monumental Sculpture of Southern Veracruz and Tabasco. In *Archaeology of Southern Mesoamerica, Part 2,* ed. Gordon Willey, 716–738. Handbook of Middle American Indians, vol. 3. Austin.

Velson, Joseph S., and Thomas C. Clark
1975 Transport of Stone Monuments to the La Venta and San Lorenzo Sites. *Contributions of the University of California Archaeological Research Facility* 24: 1–39. Berkeley.

Williams, Howel, and Robert F. Heizer
1965 Sources of Rocks Used in Olmec Monuments. *Contributions of the University of California Archaeological Research Facility* 1: 1–39. Berkeley.

Winfield Capitaine, Fernando
1987 *Guía de monumentos del Museo de Antropología de Xalapa.* Xalapa.

PHILIP J. ARNOLD III
Loyola University Chicago

Sociopolitical Complexity and the Gulf Olmecs: A View from the Tuxtla Mountains, Veracruz, Mexico

During the Early and Middle Formative periods (1500–400 B.C.), the southern Gulf Coast of Mexico witnessed the advent of social complexity at a degree not previously recognized in Mesoamerica. This complexity was expressed in megalithic sculpture, monumental architecture, and an intricate iconography. Perhaps less impressive, but no less important, these developments were intimately linked to the seasonal rhythms of a lowland coastal habitat.

Many of the papers in this volume speak to the aesthetic characteristics and artistic achievements of the Gulf Olmecs. Rather than add another small voice to this ever-expanding chorus, the following discussion takes a different direction. Here I explore the issue of Gulf Olmec complexity and the internal variation that may have characterized Early Formative occupation along the Gulf Coast. Despite several decades of fieldwork, researchers still lack a well-balanced understanding of basic aspects of Gulf Olmec existence, including settlement organization and domestic behavior. This gap is especially apparent when one moves beyond the immediate hinterland of the better-known Gulf Olmec centers such as San Lorenzo and La Venta.

In this study I discuss archaeological research recently conducted within the Tuxtla Mountains of southern Veracruz, Mexico. Although firmly ensconced within the traditional "Olmec Heartland," the Tuxtla region has received only cursory attention with regard to Early and Middle Formative occupation. This lack of attention is somewhat surprising given the agreement among scholars that the natural resources of the Tuxtlas were intensively exploited by occupants of Gulf Olmec centers (see R. Diehl 1996). In fact, *olmequistas* once proposed that the Gulf Olmecs may have originated within the Tuxtlas region (Coe 1968: 89; Heizer 1968: 22).

The present discussion, however, is not about finding the first Olmec. Rather, by concentrating on the Tuxtlas, I hope to emphasize the environmental diversity that characterizes the Gulf Coast lowlands and highlight the variation in adaptations that may have resulted from these differences. Referring specifically to the Tuxtlas, David Grove (1994) has recently called attention to the difference between what he terms the "upland" versus the "lowland" Gulf Olmecs. Recent settlement survey and excavation within the Tuxtlas support Grove's distinction and suggest an occupation and settlement organization unlike that known for areas around San Lorenzo and La Venta. These findings argue for an amplified approach to Gulf Olmec settlement and subsistence patterns and an appreciation of the internal diversity that characterized Gulf Olmec lifeways (Arnold 1995; Santley et al. 1997).

I organize the following discussion around several themes. First, in order to contextualize our research in the Tuxtlas, I review what is actually known about Gulf Olmec subsistence and settlement activities. I note that previous characterizations of the Gulf Olmecs tend to

Panorama of the Tuxtla Mountains, looking west from Lake Catemaco overemphasize the relationship between corn agriculture and sociopolitical complexity, often at the expense of detailed residential data from Early Formative Gulf Coast sites. Next, I provide information on the Tuxtla Mountains and discuss the archaeology that relates to Formative period occupation. Third, I discuss the site of La Joya and contrast the Late Formative and the Early Formative occupations there. Although the Late Formative at La Joya was clearly a maize-based agrarian occupation, the Early Formative settlement suggests a seasonal, residentially mobile system based on intensive collecting and hunting. I conclude with some thoughts about the implications of these findings for a broader understanding of Gulf Olmec occupation.

Corn and Complexity in Gulf Olmec Research

Overviews of the Gulf Olmecs are legion, so I will refrain from yet another accounting here. Instead, this section is designed to bring two issues to the foreground. The first issue involves subsistence; simply put, characterizations of the Gulf Olmecs as a corn-based agrarian society have outdistanced the direct evidence that would support these assertions. I do not disavow the *presence* of domesticated corn at Gulf Olmec sites. Rather, I question the degree to which the available evidence indicates that corn farming was the dominant component of Early Formative Gulf lowland subsistence.

The second issue concerns scales of complexity used to interpret Gulf Olmec lifeways. This discussion usually assumes the form of a debate, whereby those who champion a "chiefdom" level organization square off against those who prefer a "state" level model. Often lost in such exchanges is the fact that a reliance on these two societal types invokes a false dichotomy that artificially collapses the considerable variation found within either possibility. Given the range of variation within each sociopolitical type, and the potential overlap between them, attributions of one over another to the Gulf Olmecs ring hollow.

Corn Agriculture and the Gulf Olmecs

By all accounts, the Early and Middle Formative periods marked an important watershed in the formation of hierarchical society along the south Mexican Gulf Coast of present-day Veracruz and Tabasco (fig. 1). Initial excavations at two of the largest Gulf Olmec sites, San Lorenzo (Coe and Diehl 1980a; Cyphers 1996) and La Venta (Drucker 1952; Heizer et al. 1968), produced evidence suggesting that the Gulf Olmecs constituted the earliest complex society in Mesoamerica. Following the general acceptance of this antiquity, research attention turned toward reconstructions of Gulf Olmec subsistence activities, social organization, and models for their cultural origins (Benson 1968, 1981; Bernal 1969; Coe 1968).

Ironically, much of this discussion proceeded in the absence of continued fieldwork along the southern Gulf Coast (see Diehl 1989: 30; Sharer 1989). Nonetheless, research into Early and Middle Formative occupations in other regions of Mesoamerica did move forward, often with important implications for Gulf Olmec studies (see Fowler 1991; Sharer 1989). For example, some early discussions suggested that the Gulf Olmecs constituted the "earliest civilization" or the *cultura madre* (mother culture) of Mesoamerica (Bernal 1969; Coe 1968). This characterization is now suspect, particularly in light of research along the Pacific Coast of Mesoamerica that documents a complex, sociopolitical organization apparently antedating the "precocious" Gulf Olmecs (Clark 1991, 1994; Clark and Blake 1994; Clark and Pye, this volume; Love 1991).

Research outside the Gulf Coast also raised questions about the very definition of "Olmec," leading some scholars to suggest that the stylistic traits often used to identify Gulf Olmec "influence" derive as much from highland Mexican contexts as they do from Gulf lowland sites (Flannery and Marcus 1994; Grove 1993). In fact, many archaeologists view the Gulf Olmecs as simply one of several Mesoamerican complex societies that arose over the course of the Early-to-Middle Formative era, thereby deemphasizing the role of diffusion and implicating a process of development that was not confined to a single set of circumstances (Demarest 1989; Flannery and Marcus 1994; Grove 1993; Hammond 1989; Love 1991; Sharer 1989). In sum, research outside the Gulf lowlands has prompted significant reconsideration of the Formative period sociopolitical landscape in Mesoamerica.

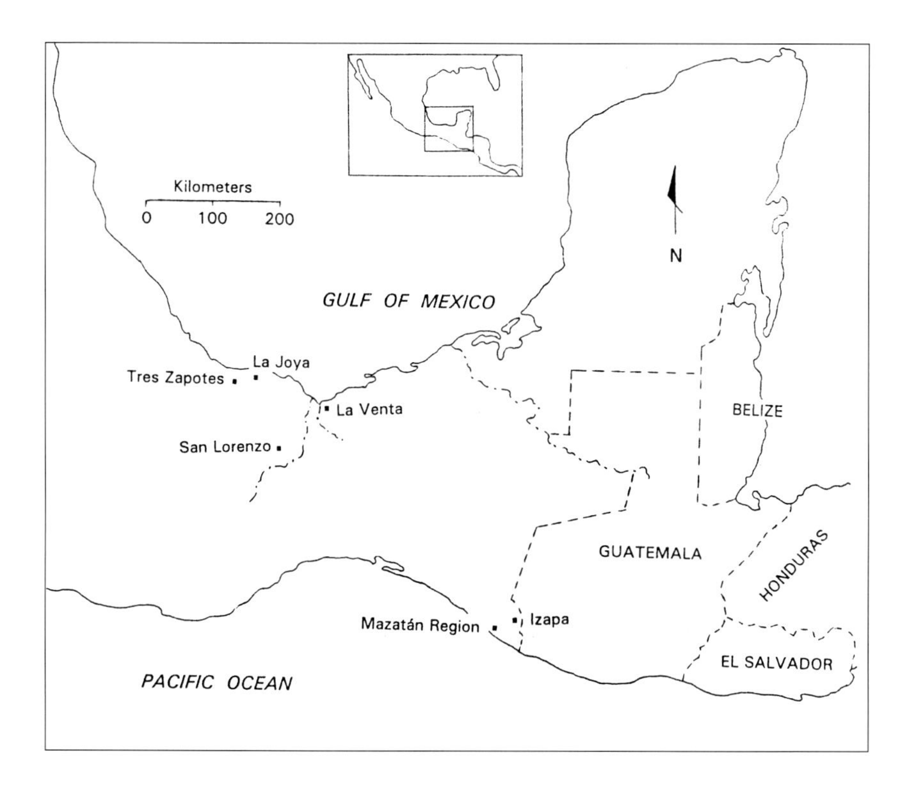

1. Mesoamerica, indicating Gulf Coast and Pacific Coast Formative period occupations discussed in the text

Although outside views of the Gulf Olmecs in relation to greater Mesoamerica may be changing, archaeologists working within the Gulf lowlands have lagged in reconsidering Gulf Olmec occupation. For example, despite the relative dearth of botanical data, most reconstructions of Gulf Olmec society continue to posit, either implicitly or explicitly, a subsistence economy based primarily on maize agriculture (Cyphers 1996; R. Diehl 1996). Apart from some recent evidence for the presence of maize around La Venta (Rust and Leyden 1994), there is practically no published botanical evidence for Gulf Olmec subsistence agriculture. In fact, direct evidence for agricultural activities continues to be one of the weakest links in models of Gulf Olmec lifeways (Diehl 1989: 23–26; Flannery 1982).

Corn agriculture has certainly received the lion's share of attention in discussions of Formative period subsistence in the Gulf lowlands (Coe 1981; Heizer 1960; Rust and Leyden 1994; Santley 1992). Much of this emphasis derives from attempts to construct and validate sociopolitical models for the formation of Gulf Olmec complexity (Diehl 1989: 23–26). As noted, these attempts were advanced with almost no direct evidence for maize cultivation. Instead, reconstructions of corn agriculture have generally relied on indirect evidence such as ground stone artifacts (Coe and Diehl 1980b: 144) or the presence of supposed "corn" iconography on Gulf Olmec sculpture. Ironically, direct evidence for subsistence activities, including faunal and estuarine exploitation, has traditionally generated only perfunctory mention (see Wing 1981).

Available data now suggest that there are reasons to question the assumed connections between Gulf Olmec sociopolitical complexity, sedentism, and corn agriculture. First, the presence of milling stones is actually a poor reflection of an agrarian lifestyle; numerous nonagricultural groups make and use such tools. In fact, a better index of agriculture is the type and size of ground stone, especially manos, that occur on a site (M. Diehl 1996; Mauldin 1993). Unfortunately, the data presented by Michael Coe and Richard Diehl (1980a: 223–231) for San Lorenzo cannot be used systematically to explore variation in mano dimensions through time. These data do indicate, however, that the meager mano assemblage does not change appreciably from the Chicharras phase (1250–1150 B.C.) through the San Lorenzo A phase (1150–1050 B.C.), when complexity was experiencing its greatest spurt (Coe and Diehl 1980a: table 5-1). A significant increase in the type and frequency of manos occurs during San Lorenzo B (1050–900 B.C.), the period that marks the end of the major Gulf Olmec occupation at San Lorenzo (Coe and Diehl 1980a: 258). This pattern is not what one would expect if corn agriculture was important in the initial formation and development of Gulf Olmec complexity.

Research conducted around La Venta also suggests that significant intensification in maize cultivation did not occur prior to the appearance of social stratification (Rust and Leyden 1994). Ratio calculations of milling stones to area excavated and *Zea mays* fragments to area excavated are basically constant from the Late Bari (1400–1150 B.C.) through the Early La Venta (1150–800 B.C.) periods (Rust and Leyden 1994: table 12.3). Significantly higher ratios do not occur until Late La Venta (800–500 B.C.), well after the site was founded and social hierarchies were in place (Rust and Leyden 1994: 199). Also noteworthy is the authors' assertion that access to basalt imported for manos and metates was apparently not restricted or otherwise manipulated throughout the Early Formative and Middle Formative sequence (Rust and Leyden 1994: 195). Again, it seems somewhat inconsistent that, while access to corn and agricultural land supposedly underwrote increasing sociopolitical stratification at La Venta (Rust and Leyden 1994: 199; Rust and Sharer 1988), access to imported milling stones, the means by which corn was transformed into a consumable, was not differentially impacted.

Assertions that maize was important based on its iconographic occurrence (R. Diehl 1996: 31) may also require rethinking. Karl Taube (this volume) argues that corn imagery is primarily a Middle Formative rather than an Early Formative phenomenon (fig. 2). Again, this temporal association is counterintuitive if corn farming and control of agricultural land were essential to the Early Formative origins of Gulf Olmec complexity. Furthermore, the degree to which the depiction of corn is a reference to agricultural production has been questioned. Brian Stross (1989: 152–153) argues, for example, that the appearance of what is thought to be maize on some Olmec monuments and artifacts may be a rebus device indicating "excellence" or "beauty" and thus was not intended to highlight corn as a subsistence linchpin.

Finally, data derived from Early Formative contexts outside the Gulf Coast cast doubt on the strong relationship between corn agriculture and sociopolitical complexity. Research along the Pacific Coast of Mesoamerica indicates that early sedentary societies developed and flourished without a reliance on maize. Although these data include botanical evidence for corn, stable carbon isotope analyses of human bone from this time period do not support the presence of a corn-based diet (Blake, Chisholm, et al. 1992). Nor do artifactual indices, such as frequencies of milling stones per phase, suggest that corn was intensively processed. In fact, John Clark (1994: 236) characterizes the Barra phase (1550–1400 B.C.) ground stone industry in Mazatán as "unspecialized, inefficient, and light weight." In sum, data from the Pacific Coast indicate that "the transition in subsistence practices from Late Archaic to Early Formative was gradual rather than abrupt" and that "changes in the subsistence system were probably not the cause" of increased Early Formative sociopolitical complexity in that part of Mesoamerica (Clark 1994: 247). In conjunction with the ambiguous evidence for early maize agriculture along the Gulf lowlands, these findings call into question the assumption that corn farming and control of agricultural land were pivotal factors in the development of Gulf Olmec complex society.

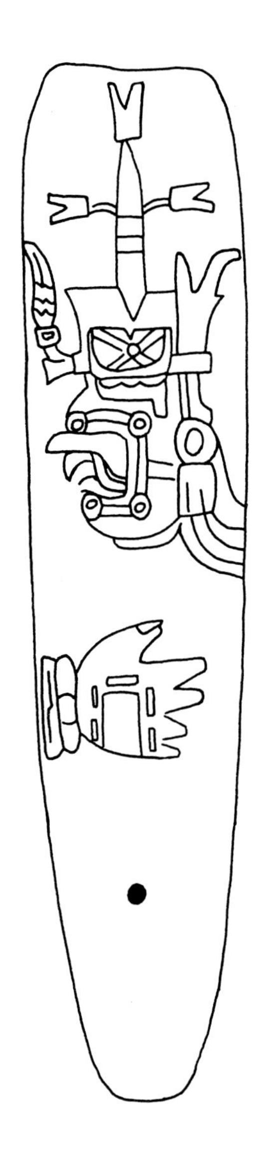

2. Middle Formative period corn imagery on portable jade celts. Figure on left from Río Pesquero, Veracruz, and on right from Tabasco (Redrawn after Benson and de la Fuente 1996: cats. 117 and 116 respectively)

Cultural Complexity and the Gulf Olmecs

Gulf Olmec research also suffers in the way in which discussions of sociopolitical complexity have been framed. Conventional approaches to the development of Gulf Olmec sociopolitical complexity generally downplay possible variation within Gulf Olmec society throughout the coastal lowlands. Two factors contribute significantly to this situation. First, the overwhelming majority of current knowledge regarding Early and Middle Formative occupation along the southern Gulf lowlands derives from only two sites: San Lorenzo and La Venta. It is worth stressing that the same monumental sculpture, elaborate offerings, and large-scale architecture that prompted the intense initial interest in these sites also distinguishes them from other Early and Middle Formative Gulf lowland settlements. Thus these two sites probably reflect a relatively restricted, specialized suite of activities that may not have occurred elsewhere along the southern Gulf lowlands (see Grove 1994; Santley and Arnold 1996; Santley et al. 1997).

Perhaps more important, discussions of sociopolitical organization that inform much of the research at these sites is often phrased in terms that oversimplify complex issues. For example, there is a long-standing debate over whether Gulf Olmec society was organized along the lines of a "state" or a "chiefdom" (Diehl 1989). The literature is filled with claims and counterclaims involving agricultural productivity, ancient demography, labor requirements, and other potential indices of system scale. That these arguments were advanced without firm archaeological information is only part of the difficulty. Equally problematic is the inadvertent reliance on typological thinking and the implications of this thinking for understanding ancient cultural process.

Couching the Gulf Olmec argument with reference to "chiefdoms" or "states" emphasizes differences between idealized, static types. Left unexplored in most discussions of Gulf Olmec development and complexity is the range of variation that is masked and subsumed within these sociopolitical categories. In fact, scholars have questioned the degree to which such typologies are appropriate for investigating issues related to cultural organization and transformation (see Feinman and Neitzel 1984; Upham 1990). These concerns are legitimate because the dynamic interworkings of a system are often glossed over when discussion centers on more abstract categories or types (Crumley 1987; Earle 1989).

Rather than framing the question in terms of "how complex were the Gulf Olmecs," a more fruitful approach would be to explore "how were the Gulf Olmecs complex" (compare Nelson 1995). Complexity in this sense is not simply a function of system scale but also an index of the internal variation within Gulf Olmec society. In other words, to what degree were all members of Early Formative Gulf lowland society participating in the same kinds of activities that are traditionally suggested for San Lorenzo or La Venta? To what degree were all Gulf Olmec people agrarian and/or residents of permanent farming communities? To what degree did environmental differences within the Gulf lowlands foster differences in the adaptation of Early Formative peoples? These questions require an orientation that looks beyond the important, but numerically few, Gulf Olmec centers and considers occupation outside the immediate hinterland of San Lorenzo and La Venta.

Gulf Olmec Archaeology in the Tuxtla Mountains

Mesoamerican scholars have long suggested that the Tuxtla Mountains of southern Veracruz, Mexico, played a significant role in the economy, ideology, and even possible origins of the Gulf Olmec culture (Coe and Diehl 1980a; Heizer 1968: 22; Williams and Heizer 1965). The Tuxtlas include a low, volcanic range that covers approximately 4,500 square kilometers along the coast of southern Veracruz (fig. 3). The Tuxtla region actually comprises two distinct uplifts or massifs, separated by the spring-fed waters of Lake Catemaco, the largest self-contained body of fresh water along the southern Gulf Coast.

Although the highest volcanic cones of the Tuxtlas reach an elevation above 1,600 meters, the overwhelming majority of the region lies below 1,000 meters. Average temperatures in the Tuxtlas remain above 20 degrees C, and annual precipitation is well over 1,000 millimeters (Arnold 1991). As a result of the low elevation, high temperatures, and heavy seasonal precipitation, the Tuxtlas fall within the category of humid, *tierra caliente* (hot country) that includes all of the southern Gulf lowlands (Stark and Arnold 1997). Nonetheless, the volcanic uplands provide an environment and suite of resources distinct from those of the surrounding coastal plain (West 1965: 377). Soils in the Tuxtlas are fertile, well drained, and highly productive, especially in contrast to the comparatively poor cropland surrounding Gulf Olmec ceremonial centers (see Sanders 1953: 66, cited in Bernal 1969: 18).

Research into the paleoecology of the west-

3. Panorama of the Tuxtla Mountains, looking west from Lake Catemaco

ern Tuxtlas (Byrne and Horn 1989; Goman 1992) provides evidence for early, albeit limited, maize cultivation. Data from a sediment core indicate that maize was present in the Tuxtlas at least by 4250 B.P. (Goman 1992: 33), several hundred years earlier than the maize pollen reported from the Early Bari phase deposits near La Venta (Rust and Leyden 1994). Despite the evidence for maize, the remaining pollen profile from the same core indicates minor forest clearing and limited soil erosion during the Early Formative period. Thus, while these findings indicate the *presence* of maize, they also suggest minimal investment in agricultural activities at the beginning of the Formative period (Goman 1992: 38–39). Furthermore, given the restricted range for maize pollen dispersal, it remains unclear to what degree even this limited maize use extended throughout the Tuxtla region.

In addition to the region's rich flora and fauna, the Tuxtlas contain mineral resources important to Gulf Olmec adaptations. The mountains were the source of the basalt used for monumental sculpture, stone for elite tombs, and utilitarian ground stone artifacts at Gulf Olmec centers (Coe and Diehl 1980a; Gillespie, this volume; Williams and Heizer 1965). Kaolin clay and salt deposits may also have attracted Gulf Olmec interests in the region (R. Diehl 1996; Lowe 1989: 36). In fact, the Tuxtla region was an important focus of natural resources during the entire Pre-Columbian era (Arnold et al. 1993; Coe 1965; Stark 1978).

Over the last decade, archaeological research in the Tuxtla Mountains has produced evidence for a Gulf Olmec occupation coeval with that at San Lorenzo and La Venta (fig. 4). Excavations at the Classic period center of Matacapan encountered small quantities of Early and Middle Formative period material (Santley and Ortiz 1985; Santley et al. 1984). A considerably more extensive Formative period occupation was documented during a 400 square kilometer regional settlement survey within the western Tuxtlas massif (Santley and Arnold 1996; Santley et al. 1997). Most recently, excavations at the site of La Joya encountered several Early Formative and later Formative deposits (Arnold et al. 1996, 1997). Taken together, these findings provide important data for developing a more comprehensive picture of the potential variation that characterized the entire Gulf

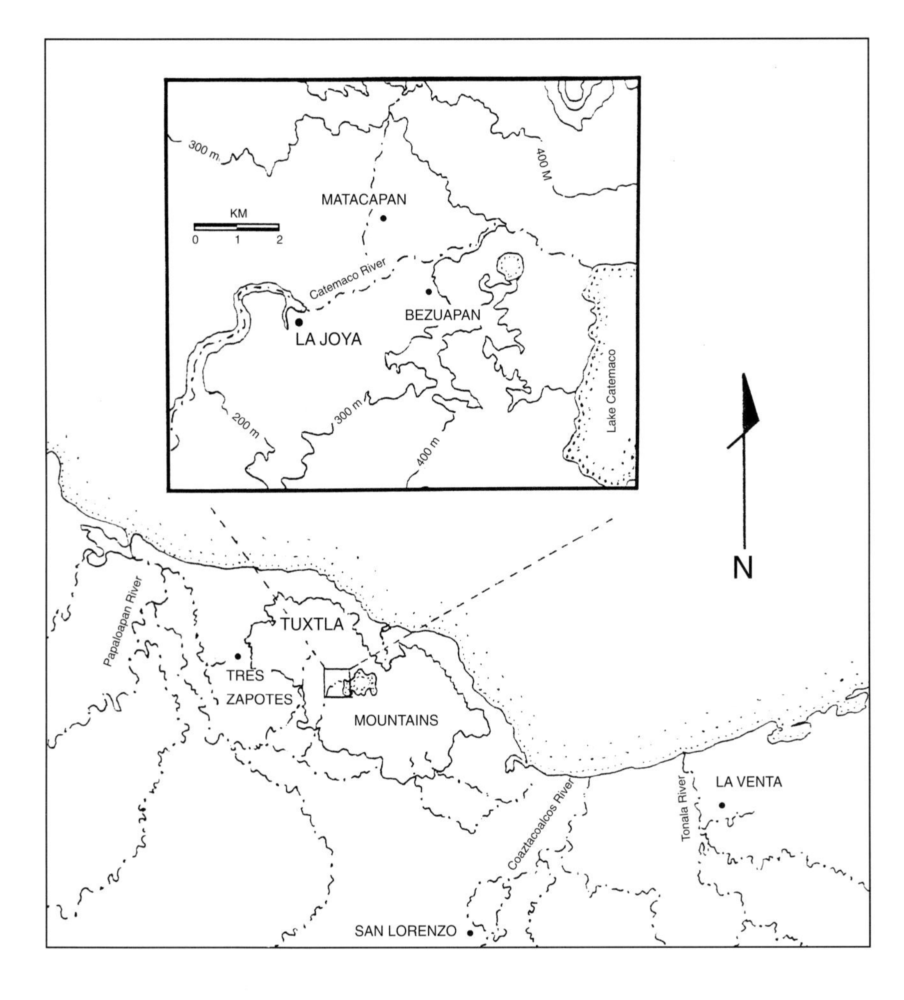

4. Formative period Tuxtlas archaeological sites discussed in the text and their relationship to Gulf Olmec centers

Olmec lowland occupation (Arnold 1995; Grove 1994).

Archaeological Evidence from Matacapan

Excavations at Matacapan encountered the remnants of a ridged field, possibly dating to the Early or Middle Formative period (Diehl 1989: 26; Santley 1992; Santley et al. 1984: 32). This feature consists of several parallel crests and swales overlain by a deposit of volcanic ash (Santley et al. 1984: fig. 9). Unfortunately, no botanical remains were recovered from these deposits, probably because of field clearing prior to the volcanic eruption. Consequently, any suggestion as to the types of plants grown in the plot must remain speculative. According to Payson Sheets (1982: 113), soil ridging provides a means to improve drainage and to control erosion. This interpretation is reasonable for the Tuxtlas given the heavy seasonal rains that fall across the region. In fact, this type of field maintenance seems to have occurred in the Tuxtlas throughout the pre-Hispanic era (Arnold et al. 1997; Pool et al. 1993; Santley et al. 1984).

Based on a combination of excavated and surface evidence, Robert Santley (1992) has proposed a model for Early Formative residential land use and site structure within the Tuxtlas. His study combines the archaeological data from Matacapan (Santley and Ortiz 1985; Santley et al. 1984) with Thomas Killion's (1987, 1990) ethnoarchaeological research on peasant agriculture in the Tuxtlas. Based on these data, Santley (1992) infers an agricultural strategy that included infield and kitchen garden cultivation. The Matacapan survey and excavation data suggest that plots closer to the residence were cultivated by cooperative groups, while fields farther away were farmed by individual families (Santley 1992: 166). Finally, the presence of infields implies an emphasis on maize agriculture coupled with a "moderately high population density" (Santley 1992: 161). Despite the suggestive data, Santley (1992: 179–181) underscores the preliminary nature of his interpretations and cautions that independent subsistence evidence and evaluation of alternative possibilities are required.

One such alternative would be that the ridged field encountered in the Matacapan excavations was cultivated primarily to provide dietary supplements rather than as a component in a more intensive agricultural regime. While the ridged field implies intensive cultivation, the plot itself was rather small. The field was noted in only one 3 by 3 meter unit, and excavations in the immediate vicinity failed to expose additional portions of the feature (Santley and Ortiz 1985; Santley et al. 1984: 30–32). An excavation immediately to the north, however, revealed an associated line of rocks, suggesting a residence in close proximity (Santley et al. 1984: 35). Although the ridged field almost certainly reflects some form of cultivation, it need not indicate an agrarian adaptation. Rather, it may represent a subsistence strategy in which cropping assumed a role comparable to that of hunting, collecting, fishing, and fruit tree management (Blake, Clark, et al. 1992).

Finally, Santley's (1992) analysis turned on the limited Formative period evidence available from the Matacapan excavations. More recent fieldwork provides new information relevant to the issue of Early and Middle Formative period occupation and land use in the Tuxtlas. These additional data suggest a possible alternative to the infield-outfield model, one that places less emphasis on agriculture and implicates a more extensive and generalized subsistence strategy.

Settlement Data from the Tuxtlas

In 1991 and 1992 we undertook a regional settlement survey within the western massif of the Tuxtlas (Santley and Arnold 1996). This survey included a full-coverage pedestrian survey of an area that measured just under 400 square kilometers. The primary goal of this research was to investigate Classic period economic interaction within the Tuxtlas at a regional scale. A bonus of this survey was the considerable data on Formative period occupation that were also collected (Santley et al. 1997) (fig. 5).

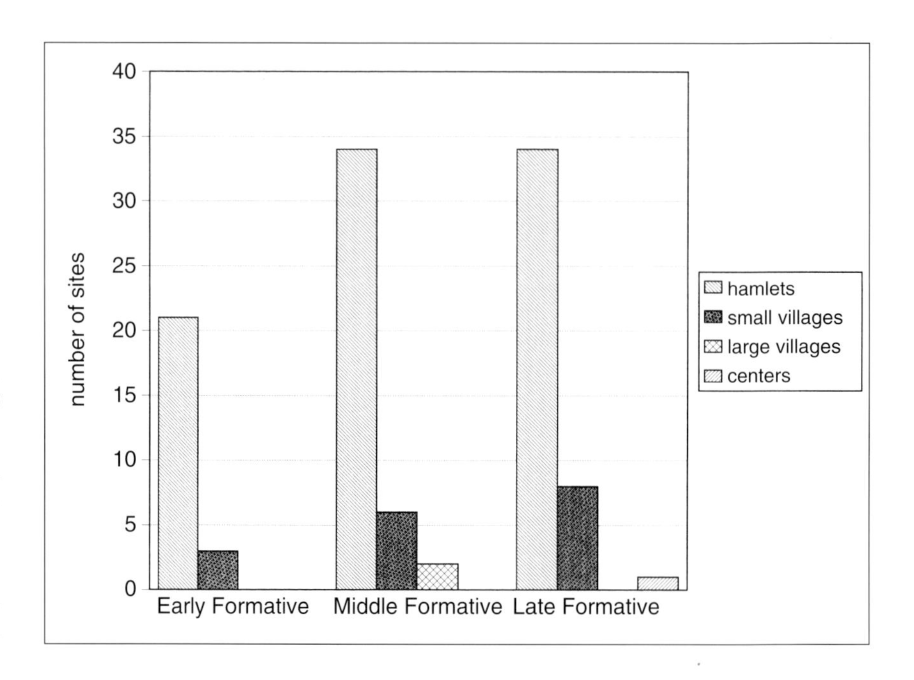

5. Formative period settlement frequencies from the Tuxtlas survey

Survey crews located twenty-four Early Formative sites. The overwhelming majority of these sites (n = 21) were classified as small hamlets, defined by light surface evidence of occupation and the absence of mounded architecture. Three sites were classified as small villages, as evidenced by more extensive areal distribution of artifacts and possibly representing a larger resident population. Rank-size plots of estimated regional site populations indicate that the Early Formative period pattern is relatively convex in appearance. Such a pattern results from the existence of several communities of similar size, as opposed to a single site that dominates the settlement system. The convex pattern suggests overall political segregation (Santley et al. 1997).

Population within the survey region grew during the Middle Formative. The number of sites almost doubled (n = 42), with thirty-four settlements characterized as hamlets, six settlements typed as small villages, and two settlements thought to be large villages. Despite the apparent three-tiered settlement hierarchy for the Middle Formative, additional analyses do not support an interpretation of increased sociopolitical complexity and settlement integration. Although mounds are present at some villages, these mounds date to later, Classic period occupations. Nor is there a significant relationship between the presence of mounds and estimated Middle Formative site populations. Finally, rank-size distributions continue to implicate a political landscape free of a dominant regional center. In sum, settlement survey data indicate that the Middle Formative political system was not functionally differentiated (Santley and Arnold 1996; Santley et al. 1997).

Regional settlement growth was minimal during the Late Formative. The number of sites increased (n = 43), with hamlets continuing to dominate the settlement system (n = 34). Eight sites are classified as small villages, with one site characterized as a small center. This site includes several mounds and covers approximately 45 hectares, an area almost twice the size of the next largest settlement. Furthermore, there is a notable clustering of sites around this small center. This patterning suggests that the center and the surrounding hamlets may have formed a single polity.

In sum, the regional survey information indicates that a multitiered settlement hierarchy did not appear in the Tuxtlas until the Late Formative period, well after the development of sociopolitical complexity at San Lorenzo and La Venta. Furthermore, the artifactual data demonstrate that Early and Middle Formative period sociopolitical complexity in the survey region never approached the pronounced differentiation reflected in the monumental art and architecture of the Gulf Olmec lowland centers. Thus settlement organization in the

Tuxtlas was notably different from Gulf Olmec occupation in the remaining Gulf lowlands (see Arnold 1995; Santley et al. 1997).

Contrary to Santley's (1992) initial model, data from the regional survey indicate that agriculture may have played a less prominent role in Early Formative adaptations in the Tuxtlas. Population densities during this period were comparatively low, estimated at about four persons per square kilometer (Santley and Arnold 1996: 228). These figures contradict the earlier proposition that Early Formative infield cultivation resulted from "moderately high population densities" (Santley 1992: 161). In fact, the population densities reflected in the regional settlement data could easily have been supported by exploitation of the rich natural resources of the Tuxtlas (Andrle 1964; Gómez-Pompa 1973) without recourse to an agrarian lifestyle. The weakly developed Early Formative settlement organization and limited evidence for craft production also imply a relatively egalitarian sociopolitical organization (Santley et al. 1997). Finally, the frequency of milling stones from the surveyed Early Formative sites in the Tuxtlas suggests that grinding activities were not intensive, especially relative to later, corn-dependent Classic occupations (Scott Wails, personal communication, 1995). In sum, these data indicate that minimal sociopolitical complexity and subsistence based on hunting/collecting, silviculture, and horticulture may have been the Early Formative norm in the Tuxtlas.

Archaeological Evidence from La Joya

Excavations at La Joya were designed specifically to investigate the relationships between Formative period land use, subsistence activities, and residential occupation in the Tuxtlas. La Joya is located along the southern bank of the Catemaco River, approximately 4 kilometers southwest of Matacapan. This area lies along a geologic boundary separating volcanic and sedimentary soils, thereby providing easy access to the diverse flora, fauna, and mineral resources that characterize these distinct zones (Andrle 1964; Killion 1987; Pool 1990). The Catemaco River not only affords ready access to riverine resources, but also represents an important communication and transportation corridor that linked La Joya with Lake Catemaco upriver and with the lowland coastal estuaries to the south and west (Arnold et al. 1993; Santley et al. 1989).

La Joya was initially identified during the regional survey of the Tuxtla Mountains (Santley and Arnold 1996). Surface ceramics indicated an occupation that spanned the Formative period and also included a Classic period presence. Unfortunately, the limited information on the Formative period ceramic sequence in the Tuxtlas occasionally made chronological placement difficult. Moreover, our reliance on the pottery chronologies from archaeological contexts outside the Tuxtla uplands meant that cross-dating would necessarily emphasize ceramic similarities and downplay the differences between material culture in the Tuxtlas and other Gulf lowland sites (Arnold 1995). Consequently, research at La Joya was also designed to gather ceramic data and chronological information directly relevant to Formative period occupation within the Tuxtla Mountains.

Based on initial survey information, La Joya was described as one of several small, spatially discrete sites along the Catemaco River (Santley 1991). A second season of intensive surface survey allowed us to group these separate occupations into a larger, single settlement (Santley and Arnold 1996). However, our recent excavations suggest that occupation at the site during certain periods was not as intensive as the spatial distribution of surface material might otherwise indicate. There is a general lack of architecture on the site; the single visible mound is approximately 1 meter high and residential in function. Subsurface exploration suggests that this mound dates to the Late Formative period, rather than earlier (Arnold et al. 1997; see below). High-density surface concentrations of Early and Middle Formative period artifacts are not mirrored in subsurface deposits in many parts of the site (Arnold et al. 1996). Rather than directly reflecting ancient cultural patterns, these high-density surface concentrations appear to result from erosion, slope wash, and other natural transformations.

The data from La Joya are in the process of analysis, so the following comments are preliminary and subject to revision. Nonetheless, archaeological material at the site exhibits sufficient patterning to propose a model of Formative occupation. In the following discussion I argue that Late Formative occupation at La Joya was sedentary and supported by maize-based subsistence. This settlement/subsistence pattern is contrasted with a semipermanent, nonagrarian adaptation that characterized Early Formative settlement at the site. Support for this distinction comes from several independent lines of evidence, including residential architecture, subsurface storage and refuse features, ground stone artifacts, and patterning within the ceramic assemblage.

Late Formative La Joya

Similar to occupation elsewhere along the Gulf lowlands, the Late Formative settlement at La Joya was apparently the product of a sedentary, agrarian adaptation (see Pool, this volume). Surface survey indicates that Late Formative material is continuously distributed across the site and covers an area of approximately 20 hectares. Almost all areas that exhibited Late Formative artifacts on the surface contained subsurface deposits dating to the same period. In fact, the Late Formative probably represents the most intensive occupation of La Joya throughout the pre-Hispanic era.

As noted above, mounded architecture at the site is minimal. The single visible mound was constructed during the Late Formative; the earthen fill of this residential platform included debris from earlier time periods mixed with several burials that dated to the Late Formative. Stratigraphic evidence indicates that these burials were not later intrusions into the mound but rather were incorporated into the mound during its construction. The maintained, active surface of the mound was overlain by a lens of volcanic ash. This ashfall was the same as that noted in other Late Formative contexts across the site. Furthermore, the physical characteristics of the ash are comparable with the volcanic ashfall identified in Late Formative deposits at Bezuapan, a site approximately 8 kilometers east of La Joya (Pool et al. 1993; Pool 1997).

Subsurface pits also reflect the intensity of occupation and agricultural activities that characterized Late Formative settlement at La Joya. These bell-shaped features are large, with volumes ranging between 2 and 2.5 cubic meters. The original function of these pits was most likely storage, but they were later given over to refuse disposal. In fact, the majority of Late Formative period ground stone artifacts recovered in subsurface contexts came from such features. Macrobotanical remains from these same pits include corn kernels and possibly squash seeds. Finally, an adult human burial was encountered at the bottom of one of these large features. In summary, these pits were used intensively and repeatedly through time, again mirroring the pattern seen at Late Formative period Bezuapan (Pool 1997).

Ground stone artifacts recovered from Late Formative period contexts suggest an increased investment in plant processing by grinding. Two-handed manos appear for the first time during the Late Formative period, and footed slab metates were present. The average surface area of manos is greater than the milling stones from earlier deposits, suggesting that grinding activities had intensified (M. Diehl 1996; Mauldin 1993).

Finally, the remains of ridged fields were encountered in several excavation units. Our current data suggest that these features represent a single large plot rather than several discrete, smaller gardens. If accurate, these findings indicate that intensive cultivation was taking place at La Joya during the Late Formative.

The Late Formative period occupation at La Joya conforms nicely to expectations involving sedentary, agricultural activities. There is evidence for investment in residential, mounded architecture, coupled with large storage features used repeatedly over a period of time. Evidence from the ground stone industry indicates intensive plant processing, and remnants of a Late Formative agricultural field were encountered. Finally, macrobotanical remains from domestic refuse indicate that corn and other domesticates were a regular component of the diet.

Early Formative La Joya

In contrast to the Late Formative, the Early Formative complex at La Joya indicates a very different settlement organization. Early Formative occupation was less extensive. Furthermore, these few Early Formative "hot spots" revealed no evidence for substantial investment in architecture. Rather, the evidence of the earliest occupation of the site consists primarily of packed earthen surfaces associated with lower-density sheet scatters of refuse.

Excavations did encounter the remains of one possible structure dating to the Early For-

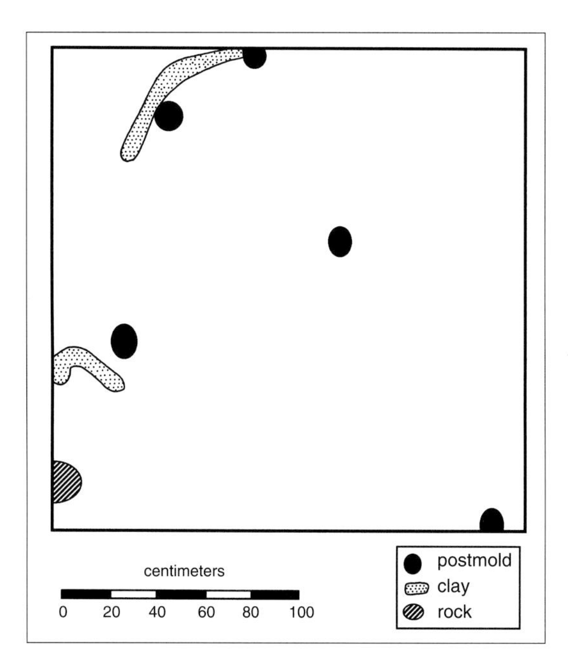

6. Early Formative period postmold pattern from La Joya (north is to the top of the figure)

mative. Construction evidence includes a series of four postholes with a larger, interior post also indicated (fig. 6). These supports were apparently arranged in an oval or apsidal shape. Associated areas of fired clay indicate that the walls may have consisted of a daub covering. We found no evidence, however, of stone foundations, prepared walls, or other indications of more intensive labor investment in construction. Outside the possible structure was a hard-packed surface and an associated pit feature. No burials were encountered in or around the structure nor were any recovered from any Early Formative contexts at La Joya.

In general, Early Formative pits differed from those of later occupations at La Joya. Early Formative pits are generally shallow, oval-shaped features, approximately 70 by 40 by 30 cubic centimeters, or about 60,000 cubic centimeters—approximately one-thirtieth the size of the Late Formative pit features. Furthermore, unlike the Late Formative pits, the earlier features are usually devoid of domestic refuse. Early Formative pits occasionally contain fire-cracked rock, and many exhibit a "band" of fired clay that lines the upper two-thirds of the pits' interiors. Evidence of feature construction, such as lip/collar preparation and clay bottoms, are absent. By all accounts these early pits are significantly different from the large storage facilities that characterized later Formative habitation at La Joya.

Of particular interest is the pattern of distribution that is found among the Early Formative features. These features rarely occur in isolation and instead are found in clusters of two to five. Moreover, there is a tendency for these features to cut into one another in palimpsest fashion. In other words, it appears that individuals opted to excavate a pit whenever needed, rather than cleaning and reusing a preexisting pit. At the same time, there was an apparent preference for certain areas within the site for the activities related to using these pits. Thus Early Formative activities associated with these pits were designed to reuse areas rather than reusing facilities. In organizational terms, these Early Formative features reflect a more "expedient" strategy of activity organization, in contrast with the more "curated" strategy represented by the Late Formative storage pits at La Joya.

Finally, the Early Formative artifact assemblage is different from the Late Formative assemblage. Early Formative stone grinding tools were smaller, suggesting less intensive grinding activities. Two-handed manos are not present, but basalt mortars do occur. Ground stone pestles, with evidence of grinding on both ends, were also recovered from Early Formative deposits.

The overwhelming majority of chipped stone artifacts are flakes and reduction debris. The current evidence indicates that bipolar reduction was the most common technique for making flake tools. Flake sizes and the frequency of tools with cortex suggest that raw material was originally small, golf ball–size pieces of obsidian, probably from surface deposits associated with the Guadalupe Victoria source (see Cobean et al. 1991; McCormack 1996; Stark et al. 1992). Both the nature of the raw material and the more expedient nature of production are congruent with an adaptation based on seasonal mobility.

Finally, locally manufactured tecomates (neckless jars) dominate the Early Formative ceramic assemblage (fig. 7). Elsewhere I argue that tecomates constitute multifunctional vessels that would perform well within the context of Early Formative residential mobility (Arnold 1999). The formal properties of the tecomate are consistent with performance demands that require a compromise among transportability, durability, and cooking effectiveness. Tecomate decoration at La Joya is also multifunctional; decorations include slipping, burnishing, and surface treatments such as punctation and rocker stamping. These types of decoration are relatively simple to execute and are usually not labor intensive. I suggest that these types of decoration are often associated with "overelaborated" assemblages; that is, multipurpose vessels whose prospective functions include both domestic food preparation as well as food presentation in socially important contexts. Thus both the formal and stylistic properties of the Early Formative ceramic assemblage at La Joya are consistent with an emphasis on multipurpose activity performance (Arnold 1999).

In sum, there is nothing in the Early Formative assemblage at La Joya that would necessarily demonstrate a livelihood based on maize cultivation and/or sedentism. In fact, ignoring the presence of pottery for the moment, it would be easy to assimilate the Early Formative La Joya occupation within the patterns of many nonsedentary hunting/fishing/collecting societies. Pottery alone is insufficient to alter this interpretation. Although some Mesoamerican scholars view pottery as "that index fossil of fully sedentary life" (Coe 1994: 38), recent research across the globe demonstrates that pottery developed and flourished in nonsedentary contexts (see Hoopes and Barnett 1995). The current evidence from La Joya indicates that Early Formative occupation at the site was impermanent and possibly seasonal in character. There is no direct evidence for a sedentary, agrarian adaptation, and the artifacts suggest a broad, flexible subsistence strategy that likely included exploitation of fish, fowl, and wild plants.

The available data from the Tuxtlas, therefore, suggest an Early Formative adaptation that differed from the settlement/subsistence pattern proposed for other Gulf Olmec sites. Rather than the sedentary, corn-based society that has been argued for San Lorenzo, Early Formative occupation in the Tuxtlas may have been seasonal and not tied to agricultural activities. Again, this is not to say that maize was not present in the Tuxtlas by the Early Formative. Rather, the current evidence indicates that maize farming was not a primary subsistence activity during this period. Sometime during the Middle Formative, however, corn agriculture became increasingly important until by the Late Formative a sedentary, maize-based farming system was present at La Joya and elsewhere in the Gulf Olmec uplands.

7. Early Formative period tecomate from La Joya with rocker stamping and red-painted rim

Discussion

This diachronic model of residential mobility during the Early Formative, supplanted by an agricultural adaptation by the Late Formative, departs from other reconstructions of Formative period Gulf lowland adaptations (Coe 1981; Diehl 1989: 23–26; Rust and Leyden 1994: 199). These latter reconstructions consistently downplay nonagrarian subsistence and instead emphasize the importance of corn agriculture and the control of circumscribed, agriculturally productive land. Furthermore, these studies imply considerably higher population densities (although specific population estimates are rarely provided). Finally, conventional models for Early Formative Gulf lowland occupation emphasize distinct sociopolitical inequality, as opposed to the nonhierarchical society implied by the Tuxtlas settlement pattern data and the Early Formative occupation at La Joya.

The Tuxtlas scenario is not very different from the model of Early Formative adaptations recently proposed for areas along the Mesoamerican Pacific Coast (Clark 1991, 1994; Clark and Blake 1994). In fact, information from the Mazatán region of coastal Chiapas indicates that maize cultivation, although present, made a minor contribution to the subsistence diet (Blake, Chisholm, et al. 1992; Blake, Clark, et al. 1992; Clark and Blake 1994: 24). Instead, Early Formative occupation along the Pacific Coast relied on a "true, mixed subsistence economy" (Clark 1991: 16). It is noteworthy that estimated population densities for this occupation range from twelve to eighteen persons per square kilometer (Clark 1991: 18), almost four times the density proposed for the Early Formative Tuxtlas.

These findings raise interesting questions for understanding the development of sociopolitical complexity along the ancient Gulf lowlands. The data from the Pacific Coast demonstrate that agriculture was not a necessary prerequisite for complex society in Early Formative coastal Mesoamerica. If true, why would corn agriculture have been necessary for the development of sociopolitical inequality along the Gulf Coast? And if corn agriculture was so important, why did the Gulf Olmecs not take advantage of the highly productive agricultural land in the Tuxtlas?

I suggest that corn agriculture was not the single most important factor in the development of sociopolitical inequality along the Gulf lowlands. Rather, it is possible that restricted access to other resources may have played as large a role. For example, the seasonal flooding that characterizes the southern Gulf lowlands generates a number of backwater lakes that form as floodwaters begin to recede. These oxbow lakes trap fish and other aquatic resources, thereby providing a reliable concentration of food as the seasonal lakes dry up. In the area around contemporary San Lorenzo, for example, work parties of ten to twelve individuals are organized to take advantage of these resources, using nets up to 30 meters long and occasionally building bamboo fences that trap fish and turtles as the waters recede (Coe and Diehl 1980b: 107–120).

The formation of these natural "holding tanks" provides an excellent context for the development of sociopolitical complexity. These conditions include a relatively abundant resource that must be acquired and processed over a relatively short period of time. Furthermore, the timing and formation of these lakes is relatively predictable since they are a consequence of the seasonal rains. Acquiring and controlling these resources would require labor mobilization and would involve decisions regarding rights to resource access. The need for labor mobilization, decisions involving access rights, and a predictable, but temporally restricted, resource are among the most common ingredients in models for the development of sociopolitical inequality (Earle 1989; Hayden and Gargett 1990).

Corn may have been important in this scenario as an additional means of exploiting the backwater lakes. For example, modern-day maize cultivation around San Lorenzo may include a dry season (locally called *tapachol*) crop, which is planted during November and harvested by June (Coe and Diehl 1980b: 69). Similarly, the Gulf Olmecs may have planted corn along the banks of oxbow lakes as the rainy season ended and the floodwaters drained. This type of "backslope" agriculture has been discussed for other portions of lowland Mesoamerica (Siemens 1983) and may have characterized Gulf Olmec cultivation as well. In this way, corn cultivation would have been "grafted onto" a preexisting pattern of land use and resource acquisition. In fact, cultivating corn in and around these oxbow lakes may have helped a group "mark" or otherwise solidify their access rights to the seasonal resource areas even during the drier season. Thus, while the corn produce could have augmented the power of individuals controlling the oxbow lakes, the control of corn itself would not have been the principal mechanism by which sociopolitical complexity was institutionalized among the Early Formative Gulf Olmecs.

This model would also account for the general absence of sociopolitical complexity and corn cultivation in the Tuxtlas during the Early Formative. The upland Tuxtlas are not subject to the same flooding conditions that characterize other portions of the lowlands. Thus there would have been no short-term concentrations of important resources such as fish and no need to organize labor to access and possibly control the resources. Instead, foodstuffs from Lake Catemaco and the Catemaco River could have been available year round and could be acquired on a more individual basis. Furthermore, despite the more fertile soils of the volcanic uplands, it is unlikely that maize farming in the Tuxtlas would have been adopted as readily since there may not have been a prior condition that provided an easy entrée for planting as a way of life. At least in the Tuxtlas, it appears that agriculture and sedentism were adopted as a package. The precise timing and the relationship of these events are subjects for future investigations.

Conclusion

The available archaeological data from the Tuxtlas indicate a pattern of Early Formative lifeways that differed significantly from reconstructions of contemporaneous Gulf Olmec occupations. Rather than sedentary, maize-based societies, the Tuxtlas were likely occupied by residentially mobile groups who practiced hunting, collecting, and fishing as their primary mode of subsistence. This pattern may have changed during the Middle Formative, but it was not until the Late Formative that direct evidence for a sedentary, agrarian adaptation appeared within the Tuxtlas survey region.

There are two ways to approach the current Tuxtlas data vis-à-vis the Gulf Olmecs. One position would be that the Early Formative Tuxtlas represent an aberration of sorts, a kind of "country cousin" to the Gulf Olmecs. The Tuxtla occupants were relatively late in adopting corn agriculture and never achieved the degree of sociopolitical complexity represented at San Lorenzo or La Venta. Thus it was not until the Classic period that long-term, complex society was established in the region (for example, Arnold et al. 1993; Santley et al. 1987).

A second, perhaps more extreme position would be that Early Formative occupation within the Tuxtlas was basically no different from that characteristic of other Gulf lowland regions. Direct evidence for Early Formative corn agriculture is modest throughout the Gulf lowlands; while corn was *present* in all regions, it may not have become a dietary staple until the Middle Formative. Furthermore, occupation at some sites may not have been as intensive as previously suggested. For example, Ann Cyphers (1997) has shown that the San Lorenzo plateau was not the product of a single construction event (that is, an effigy mound) but rather resulted from the combination of geomorphological uplift, terracing along the side of the plateau, and the accumulation of occupation through time. Moreover, Cyphers' (1997) study indicates that the residential mounds originally attributed to Early Formative occupation are much later in date, and the "artificial ponds" that dot the San Lorenzo plateau are probably post-Conquest period features.

It is reasonable to assume that the reality of Gulf Olmec sociopolitical complexity falls somewhere between these two positions. As noted at the beginning of this essay, the question of Gulf Olmec complexity should center on internal variation as much as variation in scale. Thus the Gulf Olmecs may well have been complex, but not because they were either a "chiefdom" or a "state." Rather, the Early Formative Gulf Olmec adaptations may have included a wide range of residential and subsistence behaviors. Understanding how these differences were interwoven across the coastal lowlands should prove more informative than attempts to validate one or another category of complexity for the Gulf Olmecs.

Considerable additional research is needed to address these questions. A regional approach to Gulf Olmec studies is only now under way, and as Richard Diehl (1989: 25) laments, "as is often the case in Olmec studies, we have a set of plausible ideas but no information with which they can be tested." This paper, and contributions by others (see Pool, this volume; Symonds, this volume), are designed to provide a first step toward addressing such issues. But more important, these studies should serve as points of departure that will inspire others to put shovel to ground and expand our understanding of Gulf Olmec complexity.

ACKNOWLEDGMENTS

I would like to thank Mary Pye and Joanne Pillsbury for organizing the National Galley Olmec symposium and John Clark and Mary Pye for editing this volume. Many of the more interesting ideas that appear in this paper, especially the notion of maize as a "marker" of access, developed from conversations with Shannon Fie. Fieldwork in the Tuxtlas has been supported by the National Science Foundation, the H. J. Heinz, III Charitable Trust, and Loyola University Chicago.

BIBLIOGRAPHY

Andrle, Robert F.

1964 A Biogeographical Investigation of the Sierra de los Tuxtlas in Veracruz, Mexico. Ph.D. dissertation, Louisiana State University, Baton Rouge.

Arnold, Philip J., III

1991 *Domestic Ceramic Production and Spatial Organization: A Mexican Case Study in Ethnoarchaeology.* Cambridge.

1995 Ethnicity, Pottery, and the Gulf Olmec of Ancient Veracruz, Mexico. *Biblical Archaeologist* 58: 191–199.

1999 *Tecomates,* Residential Mobility, and Early Formative Occupation in Coastal Lowland Mesoamerica. In *Pottery and People: A Dynamic Interaction,* ed. James Skibo and Gary Feinman, 159–170. Salt Lake City.

Arnold, Philip J., III, Christopher A. Pool, Ronald R. Kneebone, and Robert S. Santley

1993 Intensive Ceramic Production and Classic-Period Political Economy in the Sierra de los Tuxtlas, Veracruz, Mexico. *Ancient Mesoamerica* 4: 175–191.

Arnold, Philip J., III, Valerie J. McCormack, Eric Omar Juárez V., Scott A. Wails, Ricardo Herrera B., Guillermo de Jesús Fernandez S., and Charles A. Skidmore

1996 El Proyecto Arqueológico La Joya: Informe final de campo—Temporada 1995. Report submitted to the Instituto Nacional de Antropología e Historia, Mexico City.

Arnold, Philip J., III, Valerie J. McCormack, Scott A. Wails, Lourdes Ligia Mercado, Leonora Pohlman, Eric Omar Juárez V., Ricardo Herrera B., Guillermo de Jesús Fernandez S., Antione Lona, and Elizabeth E. Jindrich

1997 El Proyecto Arqueológico La Joya: Informe final de campo—Temporada 1996. Report submitted to the Instituto Nacional de Antropología e Historia, Mexico City.

Benson, Elizabeth P.
1968 (Editor) *Dumbarton Oaks Conference on the Olmec.* Washington.

1981 (Editor) *The Olmec and Their Neighbors.* Washington.

Benson, Elizabeth P., and Beatriz de la Fuente
1996 (Editors) *Olmec Art of Ancient Mexico* [exh. cat., National Gallery of Art]. Washington.

Bernal, Ignacio
1969 *The Olmec World.* Berkeley.

Blake, Michael, Brian S. Chisholm, John E. Clark, Barbara Voorhies, and Michael W. Love
1992 Prehistoric Subsistence in the Soconusco Region. *Current Anthropology* 33: 83–94.

Blake, Michael, John E. Clark, Brian S. Chisholm, and Karen Mudar
1992 Non-Agricultural Staples and Agricultural Supplements: Early Formative Subsistence in the Soconusco Region, Mexico. In *Transitions to Agriculture in Prehistory,* ed. Anne Gebauer and T. Douglas Price, 133–151. Madison, Wisc.

Byrne, Roger, and Sally P. Horn
1989 Prehistoric Agriculture and Forest Clearance in the Sierra de los Tuxtlas, Veracruz, Mexico. *Palynology* 13: 181–193.

Clark, John E.
1991 The Beginning of Mesoamerica: Apologia for the Soconusco. In *The Formation of Complex Society in Southeastern Mesoamerica,* ed. William Fowler Jr., 13–26. Boca Raton, Fla.

1994 The Development of Early Formative Rank Societies in the Soconusco, Chiapas, Mexico. Ph.D. dissertation, University of Michigan, Ann Arbor.

Clark, John E., and Michael Blake
1994 The Power of Prestige: Competitive Generosity and the Emergence of Rank Societies in Lowland Mesoamerica. In *Factional Competition and Political Development in the New World,* ed. Elizabeth Brumfiel and John Fox, 17–30. Cambridge.

Cobean, Robert H., James R. Vogt, Michael D. Glascock, and Terrence R. Stocker
1991 High-Precision Trace-Element Characterization of Major Mesoamerican Obsidian Sources and Further Analysis of Artifacts from San Lorenzo Tenochtitlán, Mexico. *Latin American Antiquity* 2: 69–91.

Coe, Michael D.
1965 Archaeological Synthesis of Southern Veracruz and Tabasco. In *Archaeology of Southern Mesoamerica, Part 2,* ed. Gordon Willey, 679–715. Handbook of Middle American Indians, vol. 3. Austin.

1968 *America's First Civilization: Discovering the Olmec.* New York.

1981 Gift of the River: Ecology of the San Lorenzo Olmec. In *The Olmec and Their Neighbors,* ed. Elizabeth Benson, 15–39. Washington.

1994 *Mexico: From the Olmecs to the Aztecs,* 4th ed. New York and London.

Coe, Michael D., and Richard A. Diehl
1980a *In the Land of the Olmec, Vol. 1: The Archaeology of San Lorenzo Tenochtitlán.* Austin.

1980b *In the Land of the Olmec, Vol. 2: The People of the River.* Austin.

Crumley, Carol L.
1987 A Dialectical Critique of Hierarchy. In *Power Relations and State Formation,* ed. Thomas Patterson and Christine Gailey, 155–169. Washington.

Cyphers, Ann
1996 Reconstructing Olmec Life at San Lorenzo. In *Olmec Art of Ancient Mexico,* ed. Elizabeth Benson and Beatriz de la Fuente, 61–71 [exh. cat., National Gallery of Art]. Washington.

1997 Olmec Architecture at San Lorenzo. In *Olmec to Aztec: Settlement Patterns in the Ancient Gulf Lowlands,* ed. Barbara Stark and Philip Arnold, III, 98–114. Tucson, Ariz.

Demarest, Arthur A.
1989 The Olmec and the Rise of Civilization in Eastern Mesoamerica. In *Regional Perspectives on the Olmec,* ed. Robert Sharer and David Grove, 303–344. Cambridge.

Diehl, Michael W.
1996 The Intensity of Maize Processing and Production in Upland Mogollan Pithouse Villages, A.D. 200–1000. *American Antiquity* 61: 102–115.

Diehl, Richard A.
1989 Olmec Archaeology: What We Know and What We Wish We Knew. In *Regional Perspectives on the Olmec,* ed. Robert Sharer and David Grove, 17–32. Cambridge.

1996 The Olmec World. In *Olmec Art of Ancient Mexico,* ed. Elizabeth Benson and Beatriz de la Fuente, 29–34 [exh. cat., National Gallery of Art]. Washington.

Drucker, Philip
1952 *La Venta, Tabasco: A Study of Olmec Ceramics and Art.* Bureau of American Ethnology Bulletin 153. Washington.

Earle, Timothy K.
1989 The Evolution of Chiefdoms. In *Chief-*

doms: Power, Economy, and Ideology, ed. Timothy Earle, 1–5. Cambridge.

Feinman, Gary M., and Jill Neitzel
1984 Too Many Types: An Overview of Sedentary Prestate Societies in the Americas. In *Advances in Archaeological Method and Theory,* vol. 7, ed. Michael Schiffer, 39–102. San Diego, Calif.

Flannery, Kent V.
1982 Review of *In the Land of the Olmec. American Anthropologist* 84: 442–447.

Flannery, Kent V., and Joyce Marcus
1994 *Early Formative Pottery in the Valley of Oaxaca.* Memoirs of the Museum of Anthropology 27. University of Michigan, Ann Arbor.

Fowler, William R., Jr.
1991 Approaches to the Study of the Formation of Complex Society in Southeastern Mesoamerica. In *The Formation of Complex Society in Southeastern Mesoamerica,* ed. William Fowler Jr., 1–11. Boca Raton, Fla.

Goman, Michelle
1992 Paleoecological Evidence for Prehistoric Agriculture and Tropical Forest Clearance in the Sierra de los Tuxtlas, Veracruz, Mexico. Master's thesis, University of California, Berkeley.

Gómez-Pompa, Arturo
1973 Ecology of the Vegetation of Veracruz. In *Vegetation and Vegetational History of Northern Latin America,* ed. Alan Graham, 73–148. Amsterdam.

Grove, David C.
1993 "Olmec" Horizons in Formative Period Mesoamerica: Diffusion or Social Evolution? In *Latin American Horizons,* ed. Don S. Rice, 83–111. Washington.

1994 La Isla, Veracruz, 1991: A Preliminary Report, with Comments on the Olmec Uplands. *Ancient Mesoamerica* 5: 223–230.

Hammond, Norman
1989 Cultura Hermana: Reappraising the Olmec. *Quarterly Review of Archaeology* 9: 1–4.

Hayden, Brian, and Rob Gargett
1990 Big Man, Big Heart? A Mesoamerican View of the Emergence of Complex Society. *Ancient Mesoamerica* 1: 3–20.

Heizer, Robert F.
1960 Agriculture and the Theocratic State in Lowland Southeastern Mexico. *American Antiquity* 26: 215–222.

1968 New Observations on La Venta. In *Dumbarton Oaks Conference on the Olmec,* ed. Elizabeth Benson, 9–36. Washington.

Heizer, Robert F., Philip Drucker, and John Graham
1968 Investigations at La Venta, 1967. *Contributions of the University of California Archaeological Research Facility* 5: 1–39. Berkeley.

Hoopes, John W., and William K. Barnett
1995 The Shape of Early Pottery Studies. In *The Emergence of Pottery: Technology and Innovation in Ancient Societies,* ed. William Barnett and John Hoopes, 1–7. Washington.

Killion, Thomas W.
1987 Agriculture and Residential Site Structure among Campesinos in Southern Veracruz, Mexico: Building a Foundation for Archaeological Inference. Ph.D. dissertation, University of New Mexico, Albuquerque.

1990 Cultivation Intensity and Residential Site Structure: An Ethnoarchaeological Examination of Peasant Agriculture in the Sierra de los Tuxtlas, Veracruz, Mexico. *Latin American Antiquity* 1: 191–215.

Love, Michael W.
1991 Style and Social Complexity in Formative Mesoamerica. In *The Formation of Complex Society in Southeastern Mesoamerica,* ed. William Fowler Jr., 47–76. Boca Raton, Fla.

Lowe, Gareth W.
1989 The Heartland Olmec: Evolution of Material Culture. In *Regional Perspectives on the Olmec,* ed. Robert Sharer and David Grove, 36–67. Cambridge.

Mauldin, Raymond P.
1993 The Relationship between Ground Stone and Agricultural Intensification in Western New Mexico. *Kiva* 58: 317–330.

McCormack, Valerie J.
1996 Formative Community Organization at La Joya, Veracruz, Mexico. Paper presented at the 61st Meeting of the Society for American Archaeology, New Orleans.

Nelson, Ben A.
1995 Complexity, Hierarchy, and Scale: A Controlled Comparison between Chaco Canyon, New Mexico, and La Quemada, Zacatecas. *American Antiquity* 60: 597–618.

Pool, Christopher A.
1990 Ceramic Production, Resource Procurement, and Exchange in Southern Veracruz: A View from Matacapan. Ph.D. dissertation, Department of Anthropology, Tulane University, New Orleans.

1997 The Spatial Structure of Formative Houselots at Bezuapan. In *Olmec to Aztec: Settlement Patterns in the Ancient Gulf Lowlands,* ed. Barbara Stark and Philip Arnold, III, 40–67. Tucson, Ariz.

Pool, Christopher, Patty Wright, and Georgia Mudd Britt
1993 Formative Houselot Structure in Bezuapan, Veracruz, Mexico. Report submitted to the H. J. Heinz, III Charitable Trust, Pittsburgh.

Rust, William F., III, and Barbara W. Leyden
1994 Evidence of Maize Use at Early and Middle Preclassic La Venta Olmec Sites. In *Corn and Culture in the Prehistoric New World,* ed. Sissel Johannessen and Christine Hastorf, 181–201. Boulder, Colo.

Rust, William F., III, and Robert J. Sharer
1988 Olmec Settlement Data from La Venta, Tabasco. *Science* 242: 102–104.

Sanders, William T.
1953 The Anthropogeography of Central Veracruz. *Revista Mexicana de Estudios Antropológicas* 12: 27–78.

Santley, Robert S.
1991 Final Field Report: Tuxtlas Region Archaeological Survey, 1991 Field Season. Report to the National Science Foundation, Washington.

1992 A Consideration of the Olmec Phenomenon in the Tuxtlas: Early Formative Subsistence Pattern, Land Use, and Refuse Disposal at Matacapan, Veracruz, Mexico. In *Gardens in Prehistory: The Archaeology of Settlement Agriculture in Greater Mesoamerica,* ed. Thomas Killion, 150–183. Tuscaloosa, Ala.

Santley, Robert S., and Philip J. Arnold, III
1996 Prehispanic Settlement Patterns in the Tuxtla Mountains, Southern Veracruz, Mexico. *Journal of Field Archaeology* 23: 225–259.

Santley, Robert S., and Ponciano Ortiz
1985 Reporte final de campo, Proyecto Matacapan: Temporada 1983. *Cuadernos del Museo de Universidad Veracruzana* 4: 3–98.

Santley, Robert S., Ponciano Ortiz, Thomas W. Killion, Philip J. Arnold, III, and Janet M. Kerley
1984 *Final Report of the Matacapan Archaeological Project: The 1982 Season.* Latin American Institute Research Paper 15. Albuquerque, N.M.

Santley, Robert S., Ponciano Ortiz, and Christopher A. Pool
1987 Archaeological Research at Matacapan, Veracruz: A Summary of Results of the 1982–1986 Field Season. *Mexicon* 9: 41–48.

Santley, Robert S., Philip J. Arnold, III, and Christopher A. Pool
1989 The Ceramic Production System at Matacapan, Veracruz, Mexico. *Journal of Field Archaeology* 16: 107–132.

Santley, Robert S., Philip J. Arnold, III, and Thomas P. Barrett
1997 Formative Period Settlement Patterns in the Tuxtla Mountains. In *Olmec to Aztec: Settlement Patterns in the Ancient Gulf Lowlands,* ed. Barbara Stark and Philip Arnold, III, 174–205. Tucson, Ariz.

Sharer, Robert J.
1989 Olmec Studies: A Status Report. In *Regional Perspectives on the Olmec,* ed. Robert Sharer and David Grove, 3–7. Cambridge.

Sheets, Payson
1982 Prehistoric Agricultural Systems in El Salvador. In *Maya Subsistence,* ed. Kent Flannery, 99–118. Cambridge.

Siemens, Alfred H.
1983 Wetland Agriculture in Pre-Hispanic Mesoamerica. *Geographical Review* 73: 166–181.

Stark, Barbara L.
1978 An Ethnohistoric Model for Native Economy and Settlement Patterns in Southern Veracruz, Mexico. In *Prehistoric Coastal Adaptations: The Economy and Ecology of Maritime Middle America,* ed. Barbara Stark, 211–238. New York.

Stark, Barbara L., and Philip J. Arnold, III
1997 Introduction to the Archaeology of the Gulf Lowlands. In *Olmec to Aztec: Settlement Patterns in the Ancient Gulf Lowlands,* ed. Barbara Stark and Philip Arnold, III, 3–32. Tucson, Ariz.

Stark, Barbara L., Lynette Heller, Michael D. Glascock, J. Michael Elam, and Hector Neff
1992 Obsidian-Artifact Source Analysis for the Mixtequilla Region, South-Central Veracruz, Mexico. *Latin American Antiquity* 3: 221–239.

Stross, Brian
1989 Olmec Vessel with a Crayfish Icon: An Early Rebus. In *Word and Image in Maya Culture,* ed. William Hanks and Don Rice, 143–164. Salt Lake City.

Upham, Stedman
1990 Decoupling the Process of Political Evolution. In *The Evolution of Political Systems,* ed. Stedman Upham, 1–17. Cambridge.

West, Robert C.
1965 The Natural Regions of Middle America. In *Natural Environment and Early Cultures,* ed. Robert West, 363–383. Handbook of Middle American Indians, vol. 1. Austin.

Williams, Robert, and Robert F. Heizer
1965 Sources of Rocks Used in Olmec Monuments. *Contributions of the University*

of California Archaeological Research Facility 1: 1–39. Berkeley.

Wing, Elizabeth S.
1981 A Comparison of Olmec and Maya Foodways. In *The Olmec and Their Neighbors,* ed. Elizabeth Benson, 21–28. Washington.

AYAX MORENO 99

AYAX MORENO 99

CHRISTOPHER A. POOL
University of Kentucky

From Olmec to Epi-Olmec at Tres Zapotes, Veracruz, Mexico

How, why, and when did Olmec culture collapse and what do we mean by the concept of a collapse in this context?

Richard A. Diehl, 1989

. . . nothing is known about the Olmec-post-Olmec transition beyond the bare fact that San Lorenzo and La Venta were abandoned at approximately this time. The limited information we have on Tres Zapotes suggests that research there will provide important insights into this transition.

Richard A. Diehl, 1989

The end of Olmec culture is often described as a decline or a collapse, and the subsequent Epi-Olmec culture as epigonal or decadent (Bernal 1969: 112; Diehl 1989: 32, 1996: 32; Diehl and Coe 1995: 13; Miller 1986: 37). In recent years, however, the discovery of La Mojarra Stela 1 has reminded us that the Gulf Coast successors to the Olmecs made impressive strides in the development of writing, calendrical systems, and political institutions (Justeson and Kaufman 1993). As Richard Diehl observes in the epigraph, we understand very little about the transition from Olmec to Epi-Olmec society. Our ignorance has both chronological and geographical components; research has slighted both the Late Formative period and the ancestral Olmec culture in the western heartland where Epi-Olmec society flourished.

Tres Zapotes, Veracruz, is a logical place in which to investigate the fate of the Olmecs. Located on the western margin of the Olmec heartland, the site contains a long archaeological sequence that includes Olmec and Epi-Olmec components in addition to later Classic and Postclassic occupations. Although Tres Zapotes has been studied longer than any other major Formative site in the Olmec heartland, previous studies failed to ascertain the overall extent of the site or to produce an accurate site map, much less provide detailed information on the organization and history of settlement of the site. In 1995 I initiated a new phase of research at Tres Zapotes to address questions concerning the evolution of political and economic organization in the western heartland. For two seasons the Recorrido Arqueológico de Tres Zapotes (RATZ) mapped and conducted an intensive surface collection program to obtain chronologically sensitive household-scale data on the distribution of residential occupation and craft production. In this essay I consider the surface distributions of Formative period ceramics collected in the 1995 season, their relationship to mounded construction and sculpture, and their implications for political changes accompanying the Olmec to Epi-Olmec transition.

I begin by summarizing previous research at Tres Zapotes and discussing the significance of the site's regional ecological setting, then describe the physical organization of architecture and artifact distributions as revealed by our recent investigations. Next, I provide

Reconstructed front and back views (from two fragments) of Stela C, Tres Zapotes, Veracruz, showing one of Mesoamerica's earliest Long Count calendar dates (32 B.C.)
Drawing by Ayax Moreno. Courtesy of New World Archaeological Foundation

an updated interpretation of site chronology and apply it to a reconstruction of the occupational history of Tres Zapotes. This reconstruction provides the basis for the subsequent discussion of continuity from Olmec to Epi-Olmec culture and the evolution of political organization at Tres Zapotes. I conclude with a model of political evolution that takes into account the ecological setting of Tres Zapotes, the history of regional political and economic systems, and the development of new forms of political expression.

1. Tres Zapotes Monument A, the Cabeza Colosal de Hueyapan, Formative period, basalt

2. Stela C, upper portion showing Initial Series glyph and baktun coefficient of Long Count date, Formative period, stone

History of Research

Tres Zapotes first attracted scholarly attention in 1869 when José Melgar reported the discovery of a colossal head by a *campesino* on the Hacienda Hueyapan (fig. 1). Seventy years later, in 1939, Matthew Stirling initiated the first modern exploration of an Olmec site at Tres Zapotes. His discovery of Stela C, and Marion Stirling's reconstruction of a Cycle 7 baktun coefficient for its inscribed Long Count date, provided early support for a Formative placement of Olmec culture (fig. 2) (Stirling 1940). Working with Stirling, Philip Drucker (1943) conducted the first stratigraphic excavations in an Olmec center and worked out a general ceramic chronology, later revised by Michael Coe in 1965 and refined by Ponciano Ortiz in 1975. The stone monuments of Tres Zapotes, which now number more than forty, have been the subject of several studies (Porter 1989), including Howell Williams' and Robert Heizer's (1965) landmark petrographic analysis, and the obsidian assemblage of the site was one of the first in Mesoamerica to be characterized by physicochemical means (Hester et al. 1971).

Although Tres Zapotes figured prominently in the early history of Olmec studies, it was soon eclipsed by the spectacular finds at La Venta (Stirling 1943, 1947; Drucker 1952; Drucker et al. 1959) and San Lorenzo (Stirling 1947; Coe 1968; Coe and Diehl 1980). As these eastern sites became the paragons of Olmec culture, ecological explanations of Olmec evolution came to focus on the peculiarities of their lowland riverine settings, and Olmec social complexity became the "Gift of the River" (Coe 1981). As a result, scholars have underappreciated the significance of variation in the regional settings of heartland Olmec sites.

Regional Setting

The westernmost of the major Formative period centers in the Olmec heartland, Tres Zapotes occupies an area of rolling sedimentary uplands between the volcanic massif of the Sierra de los Tuxtlas on the east and the alluvial plain of the Río Papaloapan and its tributaries on the west (fig. 3). This ecologically diverse setting provided the people of Tres Zapotes with most of the resources they required for their basic livelihood. The lakes and swamps of the Papaloapan basin teemed with aquatic resources, and the alluvial plain provided vast expanses of fertile agricultural land. If, as Drucker (1943: 8) believed, the sedimentary uplands were less intensively cultivated, they would have provided diverse forest resources in addition to underlying deposits of high-quality pottery clays. Most significantly, the inhabitants exploited the nearby slopes of Cerro El Vigía and the ravines descending from them for the distinctive porphyritic basalt from which they fashioned stone monuments and grinding implements. The only commonly used material that was not available nearby was obsidian; it does not occur naturally in the Sierra de los Tuxtlas. Chemical analyses indicate that the people of Tres Zapotes looked westward for sources of obsidian, the bulk of which they obtained from the Pico de Orizaba, Guadalupe Victoria, Zaragoza, and Oyameles sources in central Veracruz and Puebla (Hester et al. 1971).

As David Grove (1994: 227–228) has emphasized, the upland environment of Tres Zapotes differs significantly from the riverine and estuarine settings of the more intensively studied eastern heartland sites of San Lorenzo and La Venta. Taking note of the environmental diversity of the Olmec heartland, Grove has recently argued that the distribution of major Olmec centers and their association with specific sets of natural resources reflect a system of cooperative exchange based on zonal complementarity, which would have been under the control of chiefs who may have reinforced the ties between centers through marriage alliances (Grove 1994: 228; see also Arnold, this volume). I argue here that the location of Tres Zapotes vis-à-vis other Gulf Coast centers and natural resource zones is important for understanding the history of its growth and sociopolitical organization. First, however, I update the picture of the site's geography as it has been revealed through recent archaeological fieldwork.

Site Layout

The archaeological site of Tres Zapotes covers about 450 hectares on either side of a large bend in the Arroyo Hueyapan (fig. 4). Alluvial terraces bound the floodplain of the arroyo to the east and west. Cerro Rabon and Cerro Nestepe, two hills formed by resistant volcanic ash deposits, or *laja,* rise above the plain on the east bank of the arroyo. A broad ravine delimits the northern edge of the site.

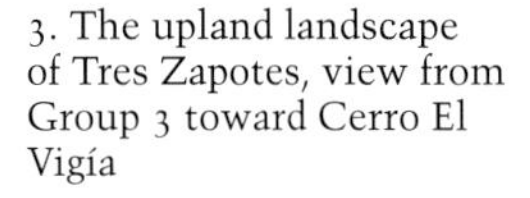

3. The upland landscape of Tres Zapotes, view from Group 3 toward Cerro El Vigía

Most of the mounds at Tres Zapotes, including the three major formal mound groups, are located on the floodplain and terraces to the west of the Arroyo Hueyapan. The three major mound groups are separated from one another by distances of .5 to 1 kilometer. Stirling (1943) and Drucker (1943) identified these as Group 1, Group 2, and Group 3. Clarence Weiant (1943) identified Group 1 as the Cabeza Group for the colossal head (Mon. A) that was found there, and the other two as the Arroyo Group and the North Group for their locations. Group 1 and Group 2 have several features in common: rectangular plazas oriented a few degrees north of east (84° and 80°, respectively), long mounds on the northern edges of plazas, prominent conical mounds located at either end of plazas, low mounds on center lines within plazas, and prominent flanking mounds on the eastern ends of groups. The pattern of a long mound and a conical mound framing the north and western edges of a plaza is repeated at a smaller scale to the east of the Arroyo Hueyapan in the Nestepe Group.

Group 3 diverges from this characteristic plan in that its plaza is oriented about an axis running approximately 9 degrees east of true north, its principal conical mound is located on the north edge of the plaza, and it lacks a comparable long mound. The four tallest mounds delimit a small plaza, which measures about 100 meters on a side, seven smaller mounds cluster around the southern and eastern edges of the group, and two broad platforms with heavy concentrations of material are located on the southern edge of the terrace. The more crowded distribution of mounds in Group 3 may reflect its location on a narrow spur of the upper terrace, which drops off sharply to the north, east, and south.

Group 3 contains several additional features of interest. The lower portion of Stela C was discovered by Stirling directly south of Mound A. It was set on its side next to a circular altar. The upper half of the stela was found nearby thirty years later. Two broken basalt columns rest on the summit of Mound E, a small mound on the northern edge of the terrace. Two irregular rows of boulders extend from the columns down the southern face of the mound. Three other basalt columns are set in a small projection of the terrace jutting out to the east of Mound D.

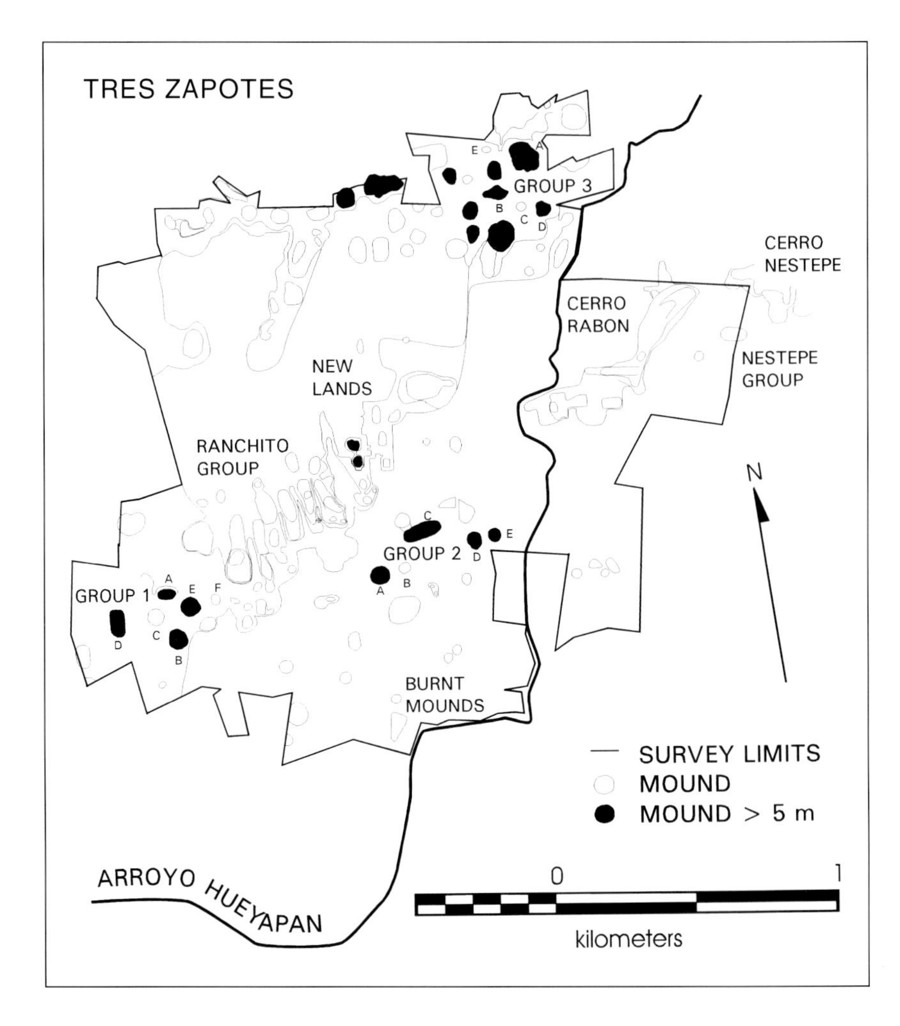

4. Tres Zapotes, within the 1995 survey boundaries
Map by Michael Ohnersorgen and Christopher A. Pool

The scale of mound construction at Tres Zapotes is not particularly impressive, although the placement of many mounds on natural terraces and hills enhances their elevations. The tallest mounds, Mound A of Group 2 (known locally as Loma Camila for a previous owner) and Mound A of Group 3, both rise about 12 meters above the current ground surface. The remaining mounds in the three principal mound groups are all less than 8 meters tall. Other mounds between 5 and 8 meters tall are located on the east-west ridge to the west of Group 3 and on the upper terrace in the New Lands locality. Smaller formal mound groups occur to the east of the Arroyo Hueyapan on Cerro Rabon and on the valley floor.

In addition to formal mound groups, the 1995 RATZ survey detected eighty-five residential mounds, less than 2 meters in height, which were distributed in two broad zones. The southern zone encompasses the Ranchito, New Lands, and Burnt Mounds groups reported by

Drucker (1943: 5–9) but is more extensive. The northern zone comprises a series of residential terraces and platforms scattered along the ridge that extends westward from Group 3.

The distribution of visible architecture, however, gives only a partial picture of ancient settlement at Tres Zapotes. In 1995 we obtained 3,103 surface collections from 3 meter-square units over an area of 320 hectares, using a combination of full coverage survey and systematic transect interval sampling techniques. A heavy concentration of ceramic artifacts stretches along the alluvial terrace from the Ranchito Group through an area devoid of residential mounds to Group 3 (fig. 5). Another heavy concentration of ceramics occurs on Cerro Rabon. Moreover, moderate ceramic densities of between 10 and 100 sherds per collection extend over a broad area of the upper terrace between the northern and southern zones of residential construction, suggesting that nonmounded architecture occupied large portions of the site or that plowing has destroyed residential platforms in this area. Pieces of daub used in house construction were recovered from these areas of elevated ceramic densities, corroborating their identification as residential zones. On the alluvial plain, high ceramic densities tend to occur on housemounds or in discrete circular concentrations, which probably represent mounds flattened by decades of plowing in sugarcane fields. Low artifact densities on the alluvial plain should not be taken as conclusive evidence of less intensive occupation, however; both Drucker (1943: 29–34) and Ortiz (1975) found deep sherd-bearing deposits below sterile alluvium in and around the Burnt Mounds Group.

In summary, the 1995 survey revealed numerous mounds and extensive areas of residential occupation extending over more than 300 hectares. The current site pattern, however, is the result of two millennia of occupation. Reconstructing the growth of Tres Zapotes requires an understanding of the site chronology.

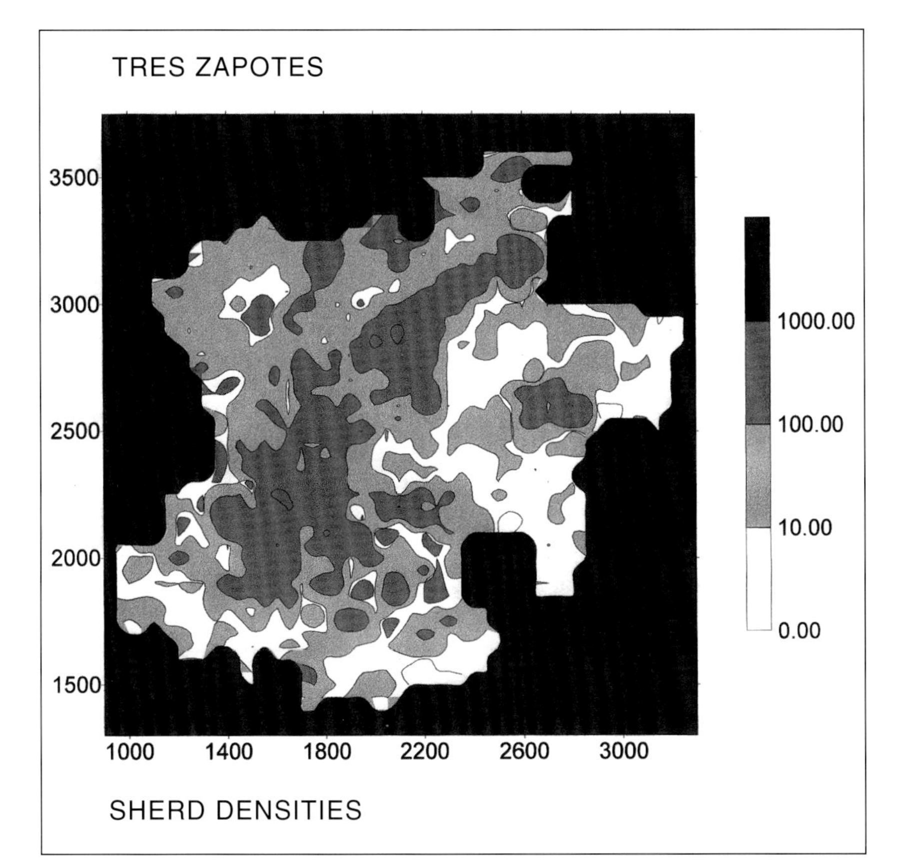

5. Isopleth map of total sherd frequencies from 1995 transect collections at Tres Zapotes

Chronology

The long sequence of essentially continuous occupation at Tres Zapotes stretches from the Formative period through the Classic period with a minor intrusive occupation in the Early Postclassic (table 1). The inception of the Formative period occupation has been the subject of considerable debate and revision. Drucker (1943: 118–120) considered deposits sealed below a bed of volcanic ash on the valley plain to be Late Formative in date, and Coe (1965a: 694–696) concurred. Ignacio Bernal (1969), however, placed the inception of occupation in pre-Olmec times, and James Chase (1981) suggested that the volcanic ash fell at the end of the Middle Formative period, causing a depopulation of Tres Zapotes. These investigators relied on the ceramic analyses conducted by Drucker and Weiant in the 1940s and on stylistic seriations of the monuments. My own interpretation of the occupational sequence at Tres Zapotes is based on more recent excavations by Ortiz (1975) into the subash levels at Tres Zapotes and comparisons with excavated ceramic sequences at Matacapan (Ortiz and Santley 1989) and Bezuapan (Pool et al. 1993) in the central Sierra de los Tuxtlas, and at San Lorenzo in the Río Coatzacoalcos drainage (Coe and Diehl 1980), as well as Gareth Lowe's (1989) synthesis of Olmec chronology.

Ortiz (1975: 132) recovered a handful of Early Formative ceramics in the lowest subash levels

Table 1. Archaeological Phases at Tres Zapotes

	Mesoamerican periods	Olmec periods (Lowe 1989)	Tres Zapotes phases Coe (1965a)	Tres Zapotes phases Ortiz (1975)
1500				
	Late Postclassic			
1200				
	Early Postclassic		TZ V	
1000				
	Late Classic		TZ IV	
600				
	Early Classic		TZ III	
300				
	Protoclassic		TZ II	
100				
A.D.	Late Formative	Epi-Olmec		Nextepetl
B.C.			TZ I	
300				
		Terminal Olmec		Hueyapan
600	Middle Formative			
		Intermediate Olmec		Tres Zapotes phase
900				
		Initial Olmec		
1200	Early Formative			
		Pre-Olmec		"Ocós"
1500				

of his stratigraphic excavations. He was probably correct in his belief that these sherds were redeposited by the arroyo, but hollow babyfaced figurines and multiperforate ilmenite cubes recovered in Stirling's excavations and our own survey confirm an Early Formative occupation (Lowe 1989: 53; Weiant 1943: pls. 18, 19, and 76). The two colossal heads from Tres Zapotes, Monuments A and Q, may also date to the Early Formative (Clewlow 1974: 26, 28, table 5; Drucker 1981: 39–40; Lowe 1989: 43, 51), although some scholars regard one or both as later in the Olmec sequence (de la Fuente 1977; Porter 1989: 21).

Ortiz (1975: 79–80, table 21) assigned more substantial assemblages containing tecomates, white-rimmed black wares and white wares (Baño Blanco and Crema Natural) to a Middle Formative Tres Zapotes phase (900–300 B.C.), which probably extends back into the Early Formative. The characteristic types of the Tres Zapotes phase continue to be present in reduced proportions through the succeeding Hueyapan phase, while a polished orange type, Naranjo Pulido, which is present throughout the Formative levels, achieves its maximum representation at 17 percent. Ortiz (1975: 80, table 21) dated the Hueyapan phase to the Late Formative period (300–100 B.C.), but a Terminal Olmec date (600–300 B.C.) is more likely, given the widespread association of polished red-orange wares with the late Middle Formative period in eastern Mesoamerica (Lowe 1989: 59).

According to Ortiz (1975: 223–225), the defining ceramic types of the subsequent Nextepetl phase include fine paste differentially fired wares and fine paste Polished Black (Negro Pulido de pasta fina). Coarse brown jars with brushed shoulders (Rastreado) increase to more than 50 percent of the assemblage, and Fine Orange and Fine Gray types appear toward the end of the phase. In addition, differentially fired black wares with tan rims (Black and Tan), which are widely distributed in surface collections at Tres Zapotes, are a common component of Nextepetl phase assemblages at Bezuapan in the central Sierra de los Tuxtlas (Pool et al. 1993; Pool 1997). Ortiz (1975: 81, table 21) regarded the Nextepetl phase as Protoclassic (100 B.C.–A.D. 300). Recently analyzed radiocarbon dates from the Nextepetl phase deposits at Bezuapan support the extension of the phase to the third century A.D. On the other hand, incised motifs on Polished Black pottery and flat-bottomed, white-rimmed black bowls correlate the Nextepetl phase with the Remplas phase of San Lorenzo, which Coe and Diehl (1980: 208–211) assign a Late Formative age of 300–100 B.C. (see also Lowe 1989: table 4.1). The Nextepetl phase therefore represents the Epi-Olmec occupation at Tres Zapotes between 300 B.C. and A.D. 300.

A volcanic ash caps the Nextepetl phase deposits in Ortiz' excavation. The volcanic eruption does not appear to have caused a major disruption of occupation at Tres Zapotes, however, for Early and Late Classic period occupation covers much of the site. A close examination of sherd counts reported by Ortiz (1975: table 1) indicates considerable stratigraphic overlap among several of his diagnostic types, lending support to Drucker's (1943: 120) view that there is substantial cultural continuity from the Middle to Late Formative in the western Olmec heartland. Although some of this overlap may be attributed to the alluvial setting of the subash deposits, the sherds

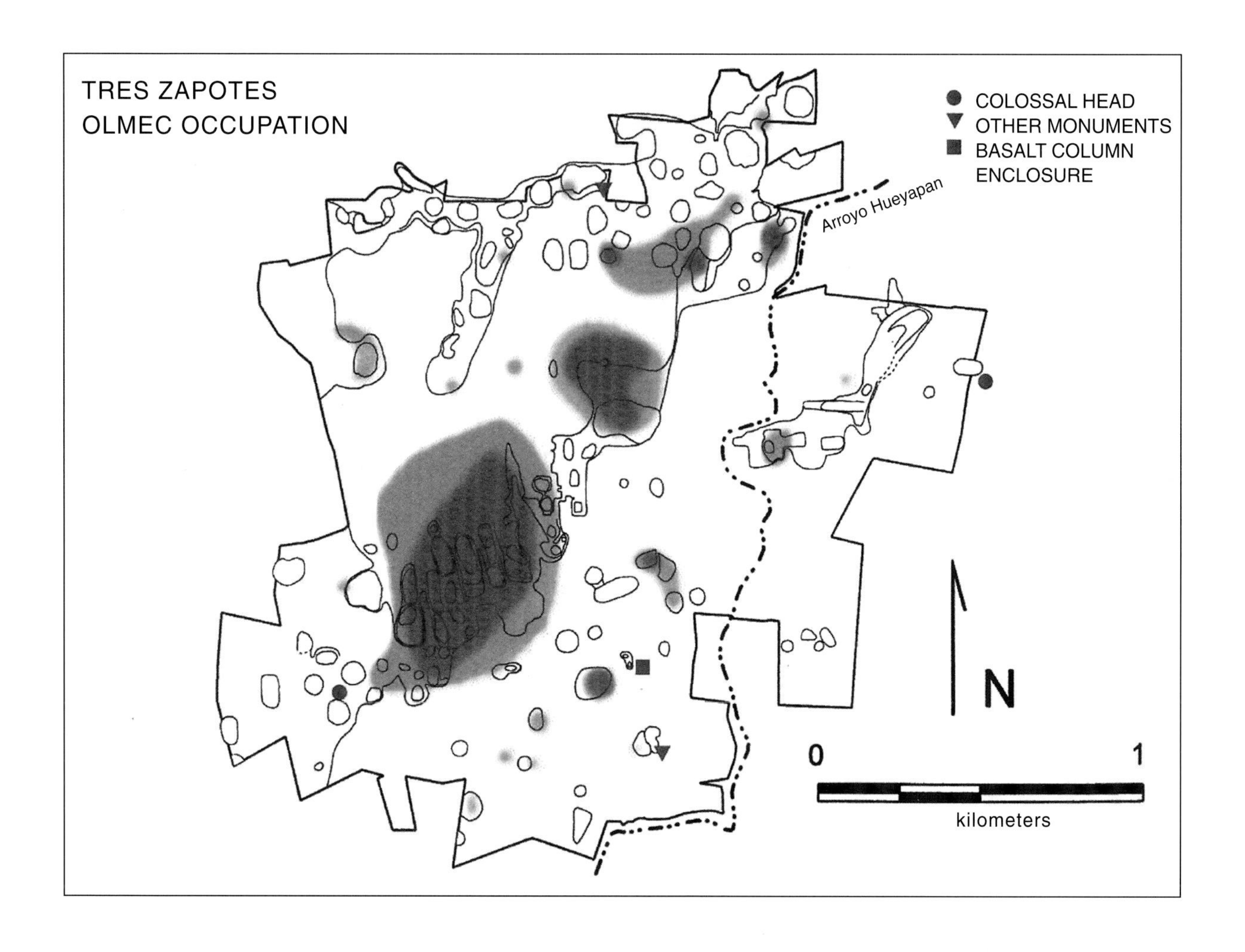

6. Distribution of Olmec occupation and monuments at Tres Zapotes

in Ortiz' type collection are large and well preserved, suggesting minimal fluvial transport. Furthermore, auger tests conducted in 1996 encountered the daub-rich remains of a housemound below the volcanic ash on the east side of the arroyo, confirming Formative period residential occupation on the alluvial plain.

Occupational History

The distribution of diagnostic rim sherds in our systematic transect surface collections reveals significant differences in the organization of Olmec and Epi-Olmec occupation at Tres Zapotes.

Early to Middle Formative diagnostics at Tres Zapotes include white-rimmed black wares and white wares. Although tecomate rims are also diagnostic of Early to Middle Formative occupation, I have not included them in this analysis because their functional equivalents in the Late Formative period are nondiagnostic striated coarse ware ollas, which continue in large frequencies in the Classic period. I have also not separated Early from Middle Formative phases. The most diagnostic Middle Formative wares are white wares, which are quite rare and occur in association with Black and White ceramics and tecomates in Ortiz' collections; separating them creates a probably erroneous impression of population decline in the Middle Formative. Furthermore, discriminating between Late Formative and Protoclassic occupation is difficult due to the erosion of the diagnostic Polished Orange sherds of the Hueyapan phase in surface collections. For these reasons the following analysis only distinguishes between Olmec (Early to Middle Formative) and Epi-Olmec (Late Formative to Protoclassic) occupations.

Surface materials of the Olmec occupation are concentrated on the elevated terrace to the west of the arroyo and on Cerro Rabon to the east of the arroyo (fig. 6). The 1996 survey also encountered Olmec ceramics on the lower slopes of terrace remnants farther to the east. Concentrations of Olmec ceramics on the valley plain are associated with mounds and undoubtedly represent old deposits incorporated in later mound fill. We do not at present know the extent of Olmec occupation beneath the alluvium of the valley plain. Nevertheless, the distribution of Olmec sherds derived from the shallower deposits of the alluvial terrace re-

7. Tres Zapotes Monument Q, Formative period, stone

8. Tres Zapotes Monument H, Formative period, stone

veals a pattern of small, discrete communities covering 1 to 40 hectares separated by zones with little or no occupation.

Mound construction does not appear to have been typical of the Olmec occupation. Of the fourteen mounds sectioned by Stirling's project, none produced assemblages assignable exclusively to the Olmec occupation (Drucker 1943; Weiant 1943). The only possible exception is represented by Mound E in Group 1 (fig. 4). The initial construction stage consisted of a red clay mound about 1 to 1.5 meters tall with sandstone steps (Weiant 1943: 6–7). Unfortunately, Stirling only excavated a corner of this basal mound, and it was apparently sterile. A single incised Black ware sherd found just above the surface of the red mound probably dates to the Late Formative period. Rather than constructing mounds, the Tres Zapotes Olmecs appear to have taken advantage of natural eminences, perhaps filling and leveling them, as may be the case on Cerro Rabon and on the projecting ridges of the Ranchito Group. This method of construction parallels that recently reported from San Lorenzo by Ann Cyphers (1996: 69–70).

Though scholars disagree about the temporal placement of several monuments at Tres Zapotes, most accept as Olmec the two colossal heads (Mons. A and Q) (figs. 1, 7), two seated figures (Mons. I and J), and the head of a were-jaguar statue (Mon. H) (fig. 8) and assign most of the remaining monuments to the Late Formative period (Lowe 1989: 43; Milbrath 1979; Porter 1989: 97–100). A basalt column chamber, excavated in 1978 in Group 2, is similar to Tomb A at La Venta (Lowe 1989: 60). The chamber contained a rectangular stone slab pierced by a circular hole in which was placed an upright serpentine "plug" (Mons. 33 and 34), a damaged piece of dressed stone (Mon. 32), and a basalt column with a crude petroglyph face (Mon. 31).[1] On the basis of their context, these may also be counted among the later Olmec monuments of Tres Zapotes. The spatial distribution of the known Olmec sculpture reinforces the impression of small, discrete communities but does not correspond closely to the ceramic distributions (fig. 6). The colossal heads, for example, were found in plazas that do not exhibit high frequencies of diagnostic Olmec sherds. The most likely expla-

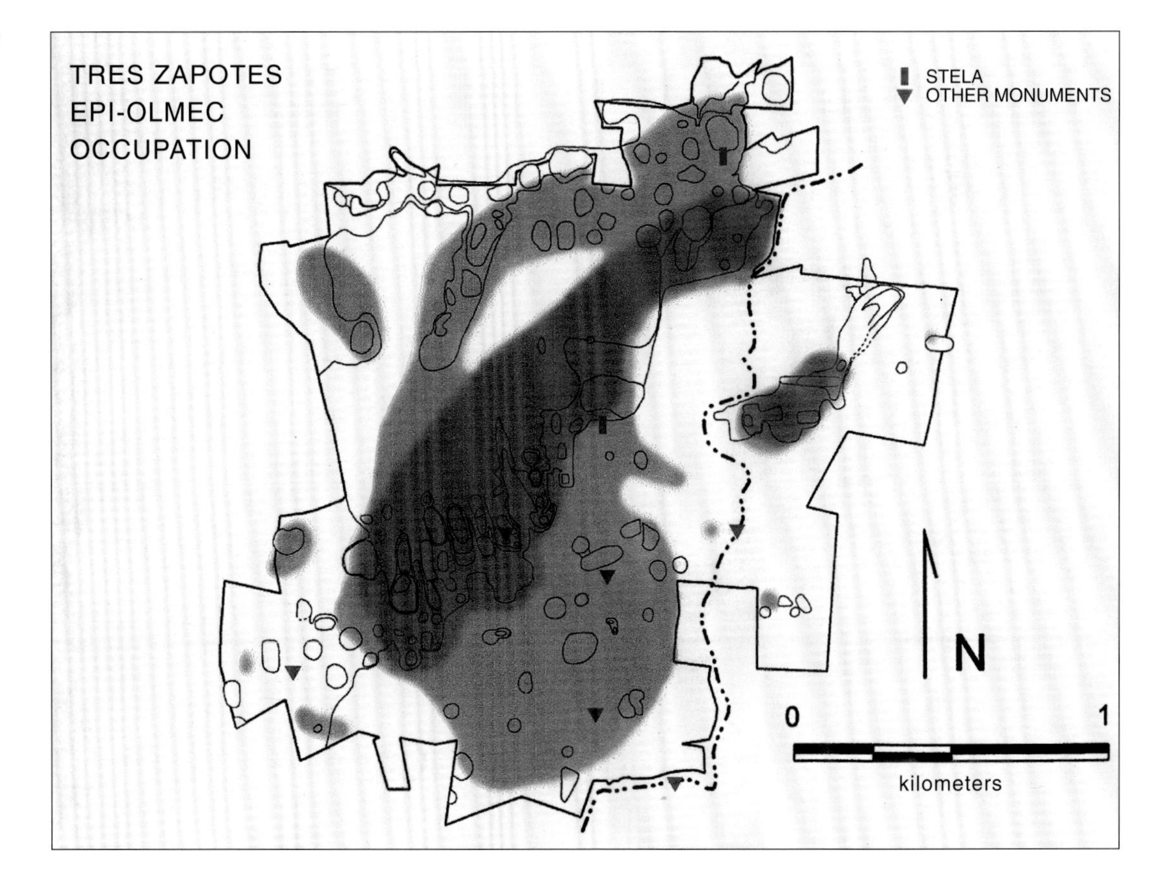

9. Distribution of Epi-Olmec (Late Formative) occupation and monuments at Tres Zapotes

10. Tres Zapotes Monument 19, Late Formative period, stone

11. Tres Zapotes Stela A, Late Formative period, stone

12. Tres Zapotes Monument C, Late Formative period, stone
After Stirling 1943: pl. 6c

nations for this pattern are that the Olmec occupation in these areas is too deeply buried to be detected on the surface or that the Olmec monuments were reset in subsequent occupations. Unfortunately, the stratigraphic data necessary to resolve the question do not exist, and any diagnostic artifacts that may have been associated with the monuments were not recorded.

Late Formative diagnostic sherds (Black and Tan ware and Polished Black ware) are much more widely distributed than Olmec ceramics (fig. 9). Once again, Late Formative sherds cluster along the edge of the alluvial terrace and on Cerro Rabon, but they are also common in collections from the alluvial plain and to the west of the terrace bluff. Late Formative sherds are also widely distributed on hills and terraces to the north and east of the 1995 survey limits. In all, the Late Formative occupation probably encompassed an area in excess of 300 hectares.

In general, mound construction appears to have been initiated during the Late Formative period, although the first construction stage in Mound E of Group 1 may be earlier, as noted above. Strong evidence for Late Formative construction is reported by Weiant (1943: 13) for the initial stage of construction in the Long Mound (Mound C of Group 2) and by Drucker (1943: 25–27, 144–145) for an early construction stage of Mound A in Group 3 (fig. 4). Both of these construction stages contained abundant diagnostic pottery and figurines of the Late Formative period and lacked Classic period diagnostics. Mound B of Group 2, and a U-shaped mound on the eastern Ranchito ridge (Weiant's Mound D?), are also likely Late Formative constructions (fig. 4) (Weiant 1943: 14, map 3; Drucker 1943: 17). Weiant's (1943: 11–12) description of a trench placed between Mounds J and K outside the Ranchito Group appears to indicate deposits with Late Formative materials above Classic period deposits. This reversed stratigraphy may have resulted from the erosion of exclusively Late Formative fill from these two mounds.

Sculpture of probable Late Formative manufacture has been recovered from Group 1 (Mon. 19) (fig. 10), Group 2 (Stela A and Mon. C) (figs. 11, 12), Group 3 (Stela C) (fig. 2), the Ranchito Group (Mon. G) (fig. 13), the Burnt Mounds Group (Mon. F) (fig. 14), and along the course of the Arroyo Hueyapan (several monuments, including a bar-and-dot date, Mon. E). Stela D, a magnificent example of Late Formative sculpture, was found in Group 4, which is best considered an outlying settlement to the northwest of Tres Zapotes (fig. 15). Although many of these monuments may have been reset in the Classic period, they correspond more closely to the distribution of Late Formative ceramics and certainly reflect an expansion of occupation in the Late Formative (fig. 9).

Cultural Continuity and Evolution of Political Organization

Incomplete as it is, the evidence from sculpture, architecture, and artifact distributions provides clues to the nature of Olmec and Epi-Olmec political organization at Tres Zapotes. Leaders of one or more of the small Olmec communities that existed within the Tres Zapotes zone evidently possessed sufficient prestige and authority to commission colossal portraits and have them transported to their seats of power. As compared to their fellow leaders at San Lorenzo and La Venta, however, their portraits were smaller and transported shorter distances, their subject communities were less extensive and provided a smaller labor force, and their construction programs, whether consisting of mound construction or modifications to natural features of the landscape, were less impressive.

As Tres Zapotes expanded in the Late Formative, its rulers embarked on a program of mound construction. Even so, their architectural efforts were not particularly impressive, nor were mounds concentrated in a single ceremonial complex. Groups 1, 2, and 3 all appear to have been active at some point during the Late Formative period, and no one group appears to have been markedly larger than the others. Whether the three mound groups were occupied sequentially or simultaneously, it appears that political hierarchy was not strongly developed at Late Formative Tres Zapotes.

Grove's hypothesis of zonal complementarity provides a possible explanation for the developmental sequence observed at Tres Zapotes. Of the four sites frequently identified as major Olmec centers, Tres Zapotes and Laguna de los Cerros are the most similar in terms of their ecological settings and their access to geological resources (see Gillespie, this volume). If Grove is correct, we may expect that the proximity of Laguna de los Cer-

13. Tres Zapotes Monument G, Late Formative period, stone

14. Tres Zapotes Monument F, Late Formative period, stone

15. Tres Zapotes Stela D, Late Formative period, stone
Photograph: Charles Knight

ros to San Lorenzo and La Venta should have afforded it a preferred position to Tres Zapotes in an intraregional exchange system based upon zonal complementarity during the Early and Middle Formative periods (see Pye and Clark, this volume, fig. 1). During Olmec times the only clear advantage that Tres Zapotes would have had over Laguna de los Cerros was its position closer to central Mexican sources of obsidian, including the Pico de Orizaba sources. However, alternative sources in Guatemala were also used by the inhabitants of San Lorenzo and La Venta (Cobean et al. 1971), precluding the possibility of a Tres Zapotes monopoly on obsidian trade into the Olmec heartland. In sum, if Olmec chiefly power and prestige were supported by participation in such an exchange system, we may expect sociopolitical hierarchy at Tres Zapotes to have been less fully developed during the Early and Middle Formative periods (compare Stark, this volume).

In contrast, the Late Formative expansion of Tres Zapotes coincides with the rise of centers such as Cerro de las Mesas to the west in La Mixtequilla, the abandonment of the eastern Olmec centers, and the increasing use of central Mexican obsidian sources in the Sierra de los Tuxtlas. Recent evidence from the Sierra de los Tuxtlas and the Mixtequilla as well as Tres Zapotes indicates a widespread shift in obsidian tool manufacture from a flake core technology to a prismatic blade core technology concurrent with the change in preferred sources (Barrett 1996; Hester et al. 1971; Pool 1997; Stark et al. 1992). Applying Grove's arguments to the Late Formative, if exchange between ecologically complementary zones continued to provide a base for political power and social prestige, the shifting political and economic landscape of the Late Formative would have placed the elites of Tres Zapotes in a more favorable position relative to population centers requiring highland products.

The transition from the Olmec to Epi-Olmec culture at Tres Zapotes was more gradual than the catastrophic collapse that is often depicted. In the ceramic assemblages, the persistence of differential firing and black wares in the Late Formative reflects technological continuity. Moreover, Ortiz (1975) found no depositional hiatus or stylistic disjunction in his excavations of subash levels below the alluvial plain.

Olmec to Epi-Olmec cultural continuity is also evident in the sculptural corpus of Tres Zapotes. Claims of pervasive Izapan and Mayan influence at Tres Zapotes are unconvincing, except in the case of Monument C, an elaborately carved stone box covered with weapon-bearing human figures struggling amidst watery scrolls (fig. 12). Although James Porter (1989: 84) identifies the cluttered style of this box as typically Mayan, Coe (1965b: 773) considered the box to be transitional between Olmec and Izapan styles. I see very little that is Olmec in the design on the box. Instead I would attribute the style of carving (which emphasizes incision to indicate detail on surfaces that are defined by removing the background), the scroll-like representation of water, and the composition of the scene to contemporaneous Izapan influence (see also Smith 1984: 44–45, 47). Nevertheless, Izapan influence does not extend to other Late Formative monuments at Tres Zapotes.

Thematic and stylistic continuity from Olmec times is most strongly represented in the stelae of Tres Zapotes. Stelae A and D each depict compositions of three figures within a niche. In Stela D the niche is formed by the gaping mouth of a feline whose face forms the upper register of the carving as in La Venta Stela 1 (fig. 15). Two standing figures face a kneeling figure, while a fourth, rather indistinct figure floats above them, peering downward.

Stela A is even more Olmec in its composition and execution. The central figure is carved in the round, bears a tall headdress, and faces forward (fig. 11). Two standing figures in bas-relief face the central figure on either side, and dragon masks frame the niche both above and below. The upper mask finds its closest parallel in the face of the Olmec Dragon carved on La Venta Monument 6, a sandstone sarcophagus, while the half-round execution, forward stance, and tall headdress of the central figure and low-relief treatment of secondary figures call to mind La Venta Stela 2 (fig. 16). The right side of the stela presents low-relief carvings of a feline and a serpent. On the left side are two damaged human figures carved in low relief. The upper one is upside down, and the lower one, which is right side up, holds a staff or baton in his hands. These two small, plump figures likewise invoke the floating dwarfs on La Venta Stelae 2 and 3 (fig. 17).

The front of Stela C, whose obverse bears the famous 32 B.C. Long Count inscription,

16. La Venta Stela 2, Middle Formative period, basalt
Redrawn after Bernal 1969: pl. 4

17. La Venta Stela 3, Middle Formative period, basalt
After Drucker, Heizer, and Squier 1959: pl. 55

depicts a leftward-facing head amid curved, upward-radiating lines above the cleft brow of an abstract were-jaguar mask (fig. 18) (see also Porter 1989: pl. 5a and my fig. 2). The Olmec affinity of the mask has been defended by Coe (1965b: 756) and Porter (1989: 49–50). The upper portion of the design, however, was found later and has been discussed less frequently. The leftward-facing head in this part of the carving calls to mind figures on celts from Río Pesquero, and elsewhere, which Reilly (1995: 38–39) identifies as representations of the ruler as the *axis mundi* or world tree, thus reinforcing the Olmec conception of this celtiform stela.

In contrast to the Early Formative colossal heads, the Late Formative stelae of Tres Zapotes and its environs present a pronounced change in sculptural themes related to rulership, from static representations of rulers to depictions of legitimizing acts. This shift does not represent an abandonment of Olmec themes, however, but a shift in emphasis already presaged in La Venta Stelae 2, 3, and 5, for example. The recording and display of such events suggest a greater concern with historicity, a development that is expressed most explicitly in the Long Count date of Stela C and that reaches its greatest elaboration on the Gulf Coast in the inscription on La Mojarra Stela 1 (fig. 19).

Joyce Marcus (1992) has recently argued that early writing and calendrical systems in Mesoamerica developed in response to competition among chiefly elites who legitimized their status through propaganda directed at peers and subordinates. In this context, the historical accuracy of an inscription would have been less important than the relation of elite activities to the mythical past and the prophetic future. The Terminal Olmec stelae of La Venta and the Epi-Olmec stelae of Tres Zapotes and La Mojarra appear to document the evolution of this practice from its nonliterate roots to its literate climax as rulers sought new modes of legitimation in an increasingly competitive political landscape. Indeed, at Tres Zapotes, competitors for rulership may have been as near as the next mound group.

Conclusion

Our continuing archaeological survey has helped clarify the nature of the Olmec occupation at Tres Zapotes and has documented the Epi-Olmec growth of the site. As has long

18. Tres Zapotes Stela C, upper fragment, front
Author photograph

19. La Mojarra Stela 1

been suspected, Tres Zapotes no longer can be considered a major Olmec center on a scale equivalent to La Venta or San Lorenzo. Rather, Olmec occupation at Tres Zapotes was distributed among several small communities. Nevertheless, at least two chiefs in the Tres Zapotes zone were able to commission colossal head portraits in stone, emulating the rulers of the eastern centers. These chiefs probably extended their control over nearby villages, and they may have exerted broader influence on their contemporaries in the western periphery of the Olmec heartland.

Although further analyses and investigation will be required to isolate the Middle Formative component at Tres Zapotes, at present the evidence from ceramic complexes and stratigraphy provide little support for a significant disjunction in occupation at the end of the Middle Formative. Olmec villages appear to have expanded and coalesced to form a site extending over more than 300 hectares in the Late Formative period. The Epi-Olmec growth of Tres Zapotes coincided with the abandonment of La Venta, the growth of centers beyond the western margin of the Olmec heartland, and a pronounced change in obsidian technology and resource utilization both at Tres Zapotes and in the nearby Sierra de los Tuxtlas. I have suggested in this essay that the underdevelopment of political hierarchy in the Olmec period and the expansion of the site in the Epi-Olmec period are consistent with a hypothesis of zonal complementarity in regional exchange systems of the Formative period.

Reinterpretation of earlier mound excavations at Tres Zapotes suggests that the construction of formal mound groups began in the Late Formative period and continued into the Classic period. The principal mound groups are widely dispersed and of similar scale, suggesting a weakly developed political hierarchy. If true, this raises the possibility that rulership may have been negotiated among elites with competing claims to authority. Under the model proposed above, that authority would have extended to control over resource zones, exchange networks, and productive labor.

A prominent feature of mound groups at Tres Zapotes is their association with Late Formative stelae that appear to record events, either visually, as in Stelae A and D, or textually, as in Stela C. Following Marcus' (1992) arguments, these monuments are interpretable as propagandistic declarations to subordinates and competing elites, which drew their legitimacy from references to myth, legend, and prophecy. Moreover, they form part of a developmental sequence of increasingly explicit mythicohistorical references beginning in the Terminal Olmec phase of La Venta and culminating in the Protoclassic La Mojarra stela.

In conclusion, the rumors of an Olmec collapse have been greatly exaggerated. Instead, the Olmec to Epi-Olmec transition marks a time when the inhabitants of the western Olmec heartland successfully adapted their Olmec traditions to the political and economic landscape of the Late Formative Mesoamerican world.

NOTES

1. The first seventeen monuments found at Tres Zapotes (Mons. A through Q) are identified by the letters originally assigned to them by Matthew Stirling and others (see de la Fuente 1973). James Porter (1989) assigned numbers to the thirty-four monuments from Tres Zapotes known to him when he wrote his dissertation, and his designations are used for Monuments 18 through 34. The Recorrido Arqueológico de Tres Zapotes has identified nine other monuments and has continued the numerical sequence of designations established by Porter.

BIBLIOGRAPHY

Barrett, Thomas P.
1996 Formative Obsidian on the Gulf Coast of Mexico: Industry Development in the Tuxtlas Region. Paper presented at the 61st Annual Meeting of the Society for American Archaeology, New Orleans.

Bernal, Ignacio
1969 *The Olmec World.* Berkeley.

Chase, James E.
1981 The Sky Is Falling: The San Martín Tuxtla Volcanic Eruption and Its Effects on the Olmec at Tres Zapotes, Veracruz. *Vínculos* 7: 53–69.

Clewlow, C. William, Jr.
1974 *A Stylistic and Chronological Study of Olmec Monumental Sculpture.* Berkeley.

Cobean, Robert H., Michael D. Coe, Edward A. Perry Jr., Karl K. Turekian, and Dinkar P. Kharkar
1971 Obsidian Trade at San Lorenzo Tenochtitlán, Mexico. *Science* 174: 666–671.

Coe, Michael D.
1965a Archaeological Synthesis of Southern Veracruz and Tabasco. In *Archaeology of Southern Mesoamerica, Part 2,* ed. Gordon Willey, 679–715. Handbook of Middle American Indians, vol. 3. Austin.

1965b The Olmec Style and Its Distribution. In *Archaeology of Southern Mesoamerica, Part 2,* ed. Gordon Willey, 739–775. Handbook of Middle American Indians, vol. 3. Austin.

1968 *America's First Civilization: Discovering the Olmec.* New York.

1981 San Lorenzo Tenochtitlán. In *Archaeology,* ed. Jeremy Sabloff, 117–146. Supplement to the Handbook of Middle American Indians, vol. 1. Austin.

Coe, Michael D., and Richard A. Diehl
1980 *In the Land of the Olmec,* 2 vols. Austin.

Cyphers, Ann
1996 Reconstructing Olmec Life at San Lorenzo. In *Olmec Art of Ancient Mexico,* ed. Elizabeth Benson and Beatriz de la Fuente, 61–71 [exh. cat., National Gallery of Art]. Washington.

de la Fuente, Beatriz
1973 *Escultura monumental olmeca: Catálogo.* Mexico City.

1977 *Los hombres de piedra: Escultura olmeca.* Mexico City.

Diehl, Richard A.
1989 Olmec Archaeology: What We Know and What We Wish We Knew. In *Regional Perspectives on the Olmec,* ed. Robert Sharer and David Grove, 17–32. Cambridge.

1996 The Olmec World. In *Olmec Art of Ancient Mexico,* ed. Elizabeth Benson and Beatriz de la Fuente, 17–32 [exh. cat., National Gallery of Art]. Washington.

Diehl, Richard A., and Michael D. Coe
1995 Olmec Archaeology. In *The Olmec World: Ritual and Rulership,* 11–26 [exh. cat., The Art Museum, Princeton University]. Princeton.

Drucker, Philip
1943 *Ceramic Sequences at Tres Zapotes, Veracruz, Mexico.* Bureau of American Ethnology Bulletin 140. Washington.

1952 *La Venta, Tabasco: A Study of Olmec Ceramics and Art.* Bureau of American Ethnology Bulletin 153. Washington.

1981 On the Nature of Olmec Polity. In *The Olmec and Their Neighbors,* ed. Elizabeth Benson, 29–48. Washington.

Drucker, Philip, Robert F. Heizer, and Robert J. Squier
1959 *Excavations at La Venta, Tabasco, 1955.* Bureau of American Ethnology Bulletin 170. Washington.

Grove, David C.
1994 La Isla, Veracruz, 1991: A Preliminary Report with Comments on the Olmec Uplands. *Ancient Mesoamerica* 5: 227–228.

Hester, Thomas R., Robert N. Jack, and Robert F. Heizer
1971 The Obsidian of Tres Zapotes, Veracruz, Mexico. In *Papers on Olmec and Maya Archaeology,* ed. John Graham, 65–131. Berkeley.

Justeson, John S., and Terrence Kaufman
1993 A Decipherment of Epi-Olmec Hieroglyphic Writing. *Science* 259: 1703–1711.

Lowe, Gareth W.
1989 The Heartland Olmec: Evolution of Material Culture. In *Regional Perspectives on the Olmec,* ed. Robert Sharer and David Grove, 33–67. Cambridge.

Marcus, Joyce
1992 *Mesoamerican Writing Systems: Propaganda, Myth, and History in Four Ancient Civilizations.* Princeton.

Melgar, José M.
1869 Antigüedades mexicanos. *Boletín de la Sociedad Mexicana de Geografía y Estadística,* 2d series, 1: 292–297.

Milbrath, Susan
1979 *A Study of Olmec Sculptural Chronology.* Washington.

Miller, Mary E.
1986 *The Art of Mesoamerica from Olmec to Aztec.* New York.

Ortiz Ceballos, Ponciano
1975 La cerámica de los Tuxtlas. Licenciatura thesis, Universidad Veracruzana, Xalapa.

Ortiz Ceballos, Ponciano, and Robert Santley
1989 La cerámica de los Tuxtlas. Manuscript on file, Department of Anthropology, University of New Mexico, Albuquerque.

Pool, Christopher
1997 The Spatial Structure of Formative Houselots at Bezuapan. In *Olmec to Aztec: Settlement Patterns in the Ancient Gulf Lowlands,* ed. Barbara Stark and Philip Arnold, III, 40–67. Tucson, Ariz.

Pool, Christopher, Patty Wright, and Georgia Mudd Britt
1993 Formative Houselot Structure in Bezuapan, Veracruz, Mexico. Report submitted to the H. J. Heinz, III Charitable Trust, Pittsburgh.

Porter, James B.
1989 The Monuments and Hieroglyphs of Tres Zapotes, Veracruz, Mexico. Ph.D. dissertation, University of California, Berkeley.

Reilly, F. Kent, III
1995 Art, Ritual, and Rulership in the Olmec World. In *The Olmec World: Ritual and Rulership,* 27–46 [exh. cat., The Art Museum, Princeton University]. Princeton.

Smith, Virginia G.
1984 *Izapa Relief Carving: Form, Content, Rules for Design and Role in Mesoamerican Art History and Archaeology.* Washington.

Stark, Barbara L., Lynette Heller, Michael D. Glascock, J. Michael Elam, and Hector Neff
1992 Obsidian-Artifact Source Analysis for the Mixtequilla Region, South-Central Veracruz, Mexico. *Latin American Antiquity* 3: 221–239.

Stirling, Matthew W.
1940 *An Initial Series from Tres Zapotes, Veracruz, Mexico.* Washington.

1943 *Stone Monuments of Southern Mexico.* Bureau of American Ethnology Bulletin 138. Washington.

1947 On the Trail of La Venta Man. *National Geographic* 91(2): 137–172.

Weiant, Clarence W.
1943 *An Introduction to the Ceramics of Tres Zapotes, Veracruz, Mexico.* Bureau of American Ethnology Bulletin 139. Washington.

Williams, Howell, and Robert F. Heizer
1965 *Sources of Rocks Used in Olmec Monuments.* Berkeley.

MARÍA DEL CARMEN RODRÍGUEZ
Instituto Nacional de Antropología e Historia

PONCIANO ORTIZ
Instituto de Antropología, Universidad Veracruzana

A Massive Offering of Axes at La Merced, Hidalgotitlán, Veracruz, Mexico

Water and aquatic resources were critical concerns for the Olmecs inhabiting the swampy, tropical Gulf Coast lowlands of Tabasco and Veracruz, Mexico. The swamps, lakes, and jungles of this lowland zone provided Olmec communities important resources for subsistence as well as surpluses for exchange. Studies of Olmec imagery clearly demonstrate that their religious concepts were tied to this environment. Jaguars, terrestrial and water serpents, crocodiles, and certain fish and birds are the most common representations, and they are thought to have been associated with the cult of water, the earth, and fertility (Joralemon 1971, 1976; Pohorilenko 1977, 1986; Coe 1972; Diehl 1989; Grove 1968, 1972, 1987).

The problem of excess water—swamps, lakes, and the frequent inundations—led lowland Olmecs to construct great drainage systems, such as those found at San Lorenzo (Coe and Diehl 1980), La Venta (Heizer et al. 1968), and Laguna de los Cerros (Ortiz 1986). Hydraulic engineering also had a pragmatic as well as sacred purpose, for despite the wet environment, potable water was in great demand. Hence, natural springs were valued, and sophisticated systems were designed to transport potable water to settlements. Ethnohistoric data and recent offerings found in sacred areas at El Manatí (see Ortiz and Rodríguez, this volume), and possibly at La Merced, demonstrate the locations of many important early cult centers, and some of these regions continue to have ritual significance today for indigenous communities (Ortiz et al. 1988, 1989, 1990, 1996; Ortiz and Rodríguez 1989, 1995, 1997; Rodríguez and Ortiz 1994; compare Eliade 1991, 1994).

From the beginning, we considered it a priority to continue investigations at Cerro Manatí, and at other sites like El Macayal and La Merced, to understand the broader sociocultural context for Olmec ritual offerings at both the local and regional levels. More information is needed from these sites and others in the region to provide insight into the motivations for Olmec society to create large-scale offerings. Did they include nearby communities, and perhaps some even farther away like San Lorenzo, Portrero Nuevo, and other settlements still undiscovered?

We undertook the survey at La Merced during the 1994 season, creating a map with data on topography, activity areas, and the location of stratigraphic units excavated in the site center and in domestic spaces on the outskirts (fig. 1). The site zone was divided into sectors according to the spatial arrangement of structures. The site center was named the Ceiba Group, while the area with low and dispersed mounds located toward the south was designated the Cocuite and Tiznada Groups.

The Archaeological Zone

The archaeological zone of La Merced is located scarcely 2 kilometers in a straight line northeast of the site of El Macayal, which was likely only a few minutes by water when the area

Anthropomorphic axe "El Bebé" (detail) from La Merced, Early Formative period, stone
Photograph: Proyecto Manatí

was inundated. La Merced forms part of a group of islets that we have called the archipelago of El Manatí, where modern and ancient populations have lived (fig. 2). At present there is a small cooperative community *(ejido)* that has recently sprung up, although most of the site center is on private property utilized for cattle raising. The site takes its name from the modern community of La Merced to the north.

La Merced is located on the highest part of an island and was possibly filled over in some areas during ancient times. Site planning was not well defined, as seen by the irregular distribution of structures. Nevertheless, the layout follows a common pre-Hispanic community pattern: platforms and pyramidal structures distributed around open spaces that form plazas and public and residential areas.

Taking advantage of the higher natural topography to the north is a residential area, consisting of a complex with small rooms, some bordered by *patios*. To the west of this area, a residential group occupies a low rise and consists of a small plaza surrounded by elongated parallel platforms with mounds closing off the plaza at its north and south ends. This residential group is located on the highest elevation at the site, and the slopes were possibly modified to function as containment walls in the event of flooding. In addition, it is likely that canals were dug out, thereby providing quick access to the interior public and habitational zones of the site.

The site center, the Ceiba Group, is located to the south and is defined by a plaza, which is formed by two platforms and a mound closing off the east end and a small platform on its west end. A great mound rises to the east, but at a considerably lower elevation, and could therefore be associated with this elevated plaza. However, it would seem that the mound's principal facade faces east—the direction of the lake rather than the plaza. It is possible that this mound was constructed before the great plaza and was incorporated functionally into the plaza at a later date.

In the northeast section of the central plaza, the constructions consist of large platforms arranged in an L shape. To the southeast, next to one of the main platforms of the plaza, the terrain was modified to form terraces that lead down to what was likely a pier or quay on an artificial canal leading to La Merced Lake. This canal provided access to the religious center, arriving directly at the principal mound and then branching off in other directions. Ceramics from excavations here indicate that the most recent occupation at the site dates to the Late Classic period, but Early Formative materials were found occasionally in the deepest levels (Ortiz and Rodríguez 1997).

Various stratigraphic excavations over two seasons in 1994 and 1995 were also carried out in the Cocuite and Tiznada Groups to locate and define the earliest Olmec occupations. Small mounds, both isolated and in groups,

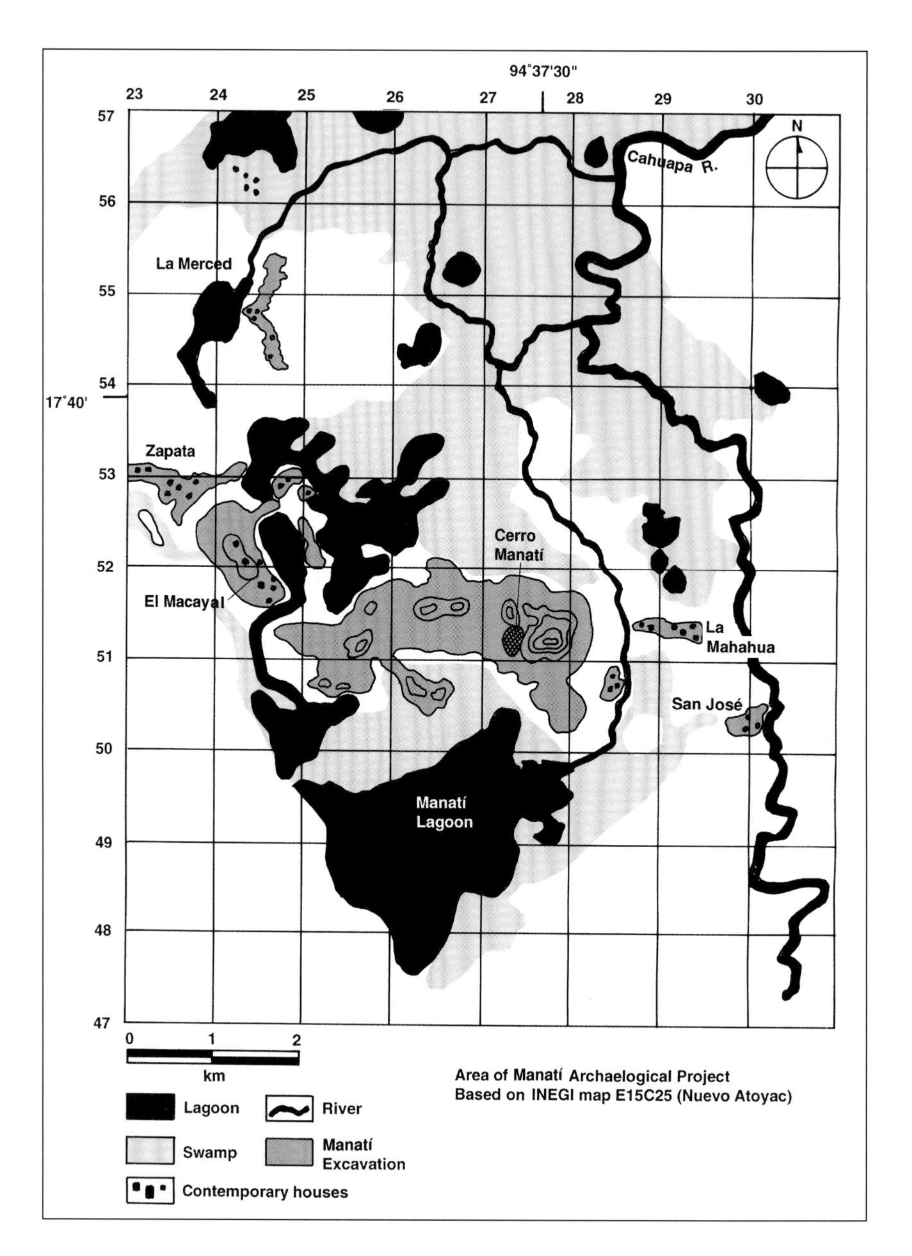

1. Map showing the location of La Merced
Photograph: Proyecto Manatí

2. View of the site during the dry season
Photograph: Proyecto Manatí

3. View of the La Merced excavations
Photograph: Proyecto Manatí

4. View of the lowest levels of the excavation showing the domestic refuse and ceramics
Photograph: Proyecto Manatí

forming plazas with platforms extend out from the central area and correspond to distinct phases. Excavations uncovered an Early Formative settlement (fig. 3).

Located southeast of the monumental zone, Unit 3 of the Ceiba Group revealed the most interesting information of all the excavation units. Initially it was outlined as a stratigraphic pit measuring 1.5 by 1.5 meters, oriented north-south; however, various concentrations of axes were discovered, and it was necessary to extend the unit. In the end, a total area of 30 by 30 meters was excavated, encompassing a massive offering of more than six hundred axes, the majority of which were carved from limestone and kaolin. These axes were found with ceramics and other artifacts that date to the end of the Early Formative period and were perhaps contemporaneous with the offerings of serpentine mosaics found at La Venta.

We present here only a preliminary interpretation of the data, based on our observations during excavations at the site; a detailed analysis of the materials is still pending. From the stratigraphy, we infer that the space where the offerings were placed witnessed three separate events later than the domestic midden found in the deepest levels (fig. 4).

The first and oldest offering contains axes of the smallest dimensions and the most well defined forms. These axes were arranged in open semicircles, either in groups of four or five axes or with individual axes standing apart. The small axe with the incised human-feline personage was found in this offering. The natural stratum where the offering was located had sedimented in a way that preserved the original placement of these objects. This layer (IV) was located low on a slope with regular deposition.

The second axe offerings, located in layer IIId, expand to the east. With these events, the most important and abundant offerings were put in place. Some changes are noteworthy, particularly the technique of making the axes, the different axe forms and dimensions, and

the lesser quality of axe material, now primarily limestone and kaolin stone. A new type of axe arrangement is also apparent: the axes were placed with their cutting edges pointing upward and poll ends down (fig. 5). The surface finish of the axes tends to be better, with clear definition of axe forms and their polls, which tend to be more rectangular. However, the overall forms lack the symmetry seen for the axes from the earlier event.

While the area of this second offering was extensive, the greatest concentration was found toward the southeast where the anthropomorphic sculpture "El Bebé" (The Baby), was found surrounded by many axes, stone axe preforms and nodules, tecomates, and fragments of pyrite mirrors (figs. 6–8). Also found in this southeast zone is a probable sculpture located during this 1996 season (S3E4), which also had associated axes, fragments of hematite mirrors, and a tecomate (figs. 9–11).

The third offering is observed in layer IIIb where, in general, stone preforms, nodules, and unworked stone predominate (fig. 12). From this layer came the stela or worked stone with a human-feline face, but the number of axes diminished considerably, and tecomates and hematite mirror fragments are absent. This last offering is concentrated in the southern part of the unit.

At this time, the site still retained a sacred character but could have been losing importance, or alternatively, the new characteristics of the offerings could well have signified changing ritual patterns.

Stratigraphy

The stratigraphy at La Merced is similar to that described for the 1994 season (Ortiz and Rodríguez 1995), except for some modifications in nomenclature by Antonio Flores, an investi-

5. Offering of axes at La Merced, Early Formative period (c. 900–800 B.C.); note that the axes were positioned vertically, with the poll ends in the ground and the sharp and wide end upward
Photograph: Proyecto Manatí

6. Concentrations of axes found in association with the anthropomorphic axe
Photograph: Proyecto Manatí

7. View of the excavation of the axe offerings at La Merced
Photograph: Proyecto Manatí

8. Anthropomorphic axe in situ
Photograph: Proyecto Manatí

9. Ceramic vessel (tecomate) with an axe offering
Photograph: Proyecto Manatí

10. Petaloid axe found in association with small hematite mirrors
Photograph: Proyecto Manatí

11. Details of axe offerings showing the vertical position of some of the axes
Photograph: Proyecto Manatí

12. View of the various stages of excavation at La Merced showing the stone deposits of the latest phase of excavation
Photograph: Proyecto Manatí

gator from Servicios Académicos of the Instituto Nacional de Antropología e Historia, who demonstrated that the strata, in general, showed similar characteristics and pertained to the same overall matrix. There were some distinctive soil lenses caused by the fluctuation of the water table that helped us to better define the stratigraphy and the sequences of the offerings. The significant strata are described in table 1. These strata numbers correspond to those mentioned above for the various massive offerings.

The Stone Mask

This flat stone, Monument 1, has a rectangular shape, 72 centimeters in total length, although its carved length is 63 centimeters. It has a maximum width of 40 centimeters and a thickness of 9 centimeters. Only one surface is carved (fig. 13). Each of the four corners shows four small rectangles. A V-shaped cut occurs in the upper part of the stone, while the right lower flank has what appear to be crudely outlined, open eyes. Toward the center of the stone was another carved V-shaped cut, with a conical oval cap appearing to emerge behind the cut.

Below the upper rectangles, a face was carved. The elongated eyes had slightly curved irises, giving the image the appearance of squinting. The nose is wide, and the nostrils seem to bring forth a liquid draining over its upper lip. The tip of the nose is formed by a small square that seems to pass behind and below the lip and delineates teeth. The mouth is the most complicated element and somewhat atypical (fig. 14). The upper lip is very thick and elevated from the surface and has drooping corners. Toward the center of the mouth emerges a shell-shaped flower similar to the teeth of a feline or shark. Below this element is another feature that could represent the gum, while

Table 1. Description of Strata from Excavations at La Merced

Level	Munsell color	Description of level
I	10YR 3/2, dark gray	Medium texture and consistency due to high humus content, contains some quartziferous gravel of medium size (2–5 mm). Average thickness of layer is 8 cm. Seen throughout the excavation area.
II	10YR 4/3, light brown to yellow brown	Medium texture and loose consistency; contains some sand and quartziferous gravel. Average thickness of layer is 50 cm. Root and animal holes were common with a high density of archaeological materials.
IIIa	5YR 5/6 dry, 5YR 4/5 wet, reddish orange	Sandy clay, semicompacted with medium texture.
IIIb	10YR 5/8 dry, 10YR 4/6 wet, yellowish brown	Clay with some sand, semicompacted with medium texture. Thickness of layer varied from 50–60 cm. Very dense concentration of archaeological materials.
IIIc	5YR 5/2, grayish cream, 2.5YR 6/2 and 10YR 6/2, reddish brown	Grayish cream clay lens with veins of reddish brown clay. Occurs in quadrants N3W3 and N3W4.
IIId	7.5YR 5/6–5/8, brown, 2.5YR 6/2 and 10YR 6/2, light gray-brown to pale brown	Brown clay with light gray-brown to pale brown veins of fine sand. Quartziferous gravel is abundant and allows for significant compaction with a medium to thick texture. Found throughout excavation area; contains the highest concentration of archaeological materials, deposited during the second offering.
IV	5YR 3/4 to 7.5YR 4/4–4/6, dark reddish brown to dark brown, 10YR 6/2, gray	Sandy clay with gray veins. The sand and clay varied according to contact with and fluctuation of water table, with sand generally occurring in lower half and clay predominant in the upper. The sandy area contained lenses of pure clay. More lenses were observed in the southeast area of excavation with more consistent sandy clay in the northeast.
IVa	yellow	Sand lens with medium texture and semicompacted, located in the northern area.
IVb	yellow	Sand lens at the water table; sterile fine gray sand located beneath it.

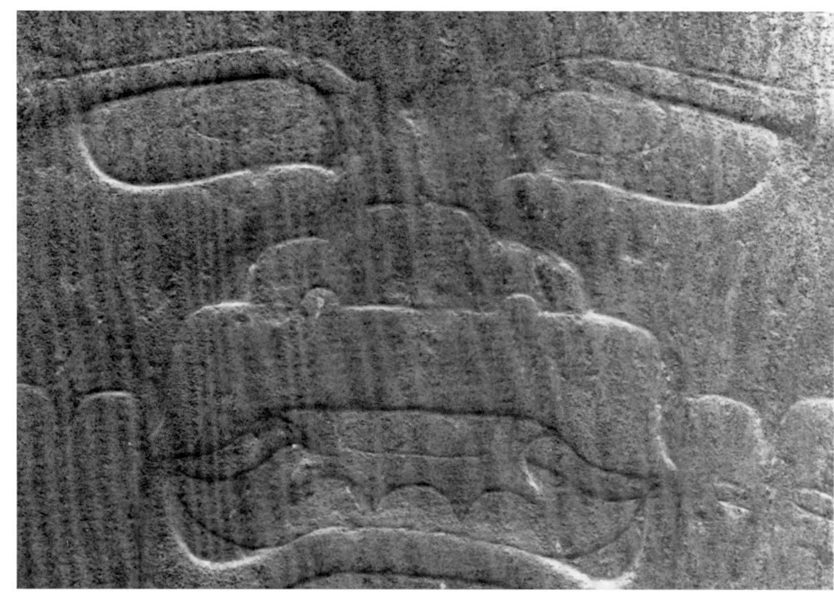

13. La Merced Monument 1, Early Formative period, stone
Photograph: Hernando Gómez Rueda

14. Detail of the mouth of the image carved on La Merced Monument 1
Photograph: Proyecto Manatí

15. Anthropomorphic axe "El Bebé" (detail) from La Merced, Early Formative period, stone
Photograph: Proyecto Manatí

further down in the plane of the lower relief is a tongue. The carving of the thin lip is at the same height as that of the gum, while just below the lip is another small square.

The lower part of the monument has a carved tang or stem that is broken on the right side, perhaps caused by a defect in the primary material.

Anthropomorphic Sculpture "El Bebé"

This piece was equally interesting. It measures 40 centimeters in length, with a maximum width of 23 centimeters and a thickness of 8 centimeters. The first impression upon viewing it is that of an infant crying with the eyes closed and swollen (fig. 15).

The personage is standing. The forehead has a V-shaped cleft, and the closed eyes were carved with a horizontal line that continues almost unbroken toward its extremities, interrupted only by the nose. The eyelids seem inflamed and frame the eyes. The nose is flat but short; the mouth is open and occupies almost half of the face. The lips are shaped like brackets; the upper lip is thick with the corners pointed upward. The neck is marked by a single line that separates the trunk or chest. The arms are crossed over the chest, and each hand holds a downward-pointing axe. The legs are plump, as are the feet and fingers. The ears are worked in the shape of rectangles. As with the stela, there is a V-shaped cleft on the forehead, but not the conical cap. Arms are defined in its upper half. The buttocks are heightened; the legs are short and chubby.

Olmec literature reports at least fourteen objects with similar characteristics. Each is a standing anthropomorphic axe that represents head, neck, body, and extremities. Each has a wide, flattened nose; the upper lip of the mouth is prominent, with a downturned mouth, toothless visible gums, and the arms crossed over the chest.

While the objects are not identical, the shared formal elements are numerous. Each of them, as in the example from La Merced, represents the head with the cleft, similar eyes, a mouth with canine teeth, and the lower extremities; and some carry an axe with the edge pointing downward. The best-known example is the Kuntz axe in the American Museum of Natural History, New York, of unknown provenience.

16. Stone preform
Photograph: Proyecto Manatí

Incised Axe with Human-Feline Personage

This axe is really an irregular oval-shaped nodule, with one of its polished faces crudely carved with an anthropomorphic depiction of a human-feline personage. The eyes have the feline appearance with the irises outlined, and they appear to be squinting. The eyebrows are incised, incurved lines. The nose is wide, and the lower lip is thin, while toward the center of the upper lip one notes a "tooth." The lower edge of the face is indicated by a horizontal line. In the forehead is a V-shaped cut. The arms cross over the chest, with hands tucked under the arms, and are barely incised. The piece resembles a seated feline with its upper paws crossed over the chest. David Joralemon mentions a single axe from Cuauhtla that has a similar hand position (Joralemon 1971: 76, fig. 220).

Small Axe with Relief

The object in question is very small (10 centimeters) in relation to the two previous examples. It depicts a standing individual with the legs spread and the arms extended downward. The right leg is slightly raised as in the poise of a dancer or walker.

The face is framed by a rectangular hair arrangement that hangs toward the sides and covers the ears. There is a V-shaped cut in the forehead, and from this cleft rises a cone. The

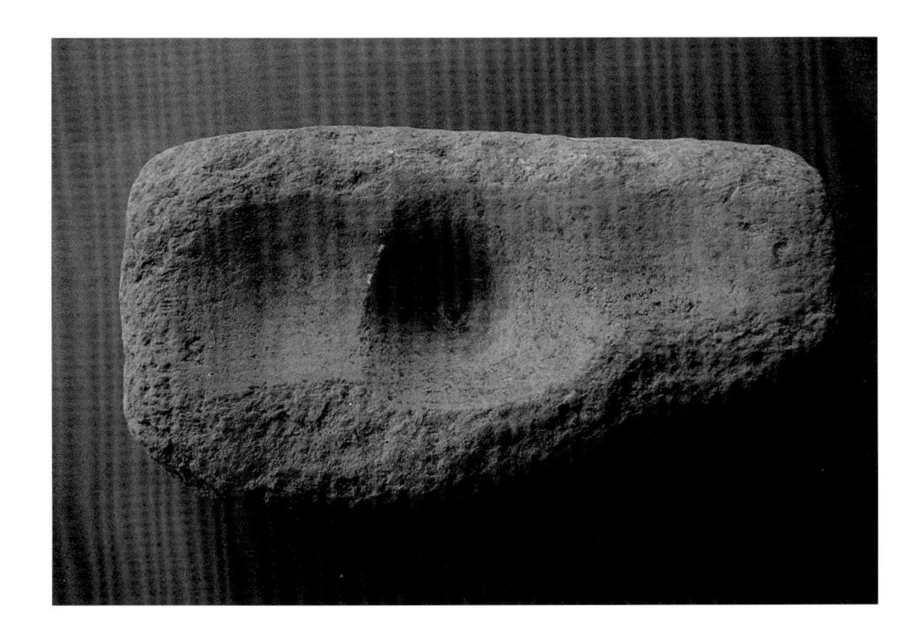

17. Worked stone from La Merced
Photograph: Proyecto Manatí

18. Unworked stone, or raw material, found in association with the worked stone
Photograph: Proyecto Manatí

eyes are indicated by incised lines. The mouth is open and thick, although not very visible due to erosion. The nose is very wide. The figure wears a loincloth that covers the groin and has what appears to be a sash around the waist holding up the loincloth.

Preliminary Discussion

From the data obtained, it is clear that the La Merced offerings were deposited at various times. The oldest offering is associated with domestic activity, to judge by the presence of the midden located at the edge of the offering and what could have been a riverbed with permanent but slow-moving water. A deposit of clays with lenses of sand and gravel was located in the lowest zone under the water table that formed the riverbed. The forms and decorative characteristics of the ceramics in these layers probably date to the end of the Early Formative period.

Subsequently, while layer IIId was forming, an axe offering was interred, with some of the axes intruding into the earlier midden. Most of the greenstone and limestone axes were positioned horizontally rather than on end.

After layer IIId was deposited, judging by the abundance of axes and lithic preforms and nodules of primary material, the most important offering was ritually interred. Also placed with these axes were sculpture and anthropomorphic axes, tecomates, vases, polished black plates, and fragments of hematite that probably were parts of mosaics and mirrors (fig. 10).

The last offering included the mask, some worked stones without decoration, stone nodules, and other amorphous objects of primary material (figs. 16–18). The decreased number of axes was noteworthy. The data suggest that those involved in the rituals of which the axe offerings are our only remaining testimony must have had special motives for selecting La Merced to deposit their most valuable objects, whether of jade, other fine stone, or local materials.

The offerings of La Merced were probably associated with a spring, old riverbed, or other source of water for the lake. The offering events may have been associated with agricultural cults, perhaps propitiatory rituals to maintain the equilibrium of rainfall—to save harvests or perhaps to improve them. If true, these were likely to have been performed at critical moments, for reasons due to a lack of or an excess of water. Or perhaps "they corresponded to a celestial event that was repeated each year and had a great effect on the spectators, for example, the first appearance of the Pleiades on the day the sun crossed its zenith" (Pasztory 1993: 139), or also to the disappearance of the Pleiades during the month of May when the rains became more intense.

This offering involved the appropriation of primary local and foreign resources and the work of a good number of people and artisans. Nevertheless, the quality and finish of the objects were apparently not the most important feature. The importance of the items derived from their symbolic or ritual significance, a fact that exceeded their sumptuary and luxury character. It also suggests that common people in some cases could acquire the primary material. When the techniques of manufacture were unknown, or could not be acquired, they perhaps created the objects themselves, albeit more crudely, giving them the proper form as ritual objects which were then offered.

This is a different phenomenon from that seen at El Manatí, where the quality of the material, as well as the execution, was always very careful and important, especially during the earliest periods (see Ortiz and Rodríguez, this volume). Through time this tendency also changed, beginning with the offering of the wood busts (Ortiz and Rodríguez 1997), when the axes show a preference for the material, rather than the quality of the completed object. In this case, the pattern had become more similar to La Merced and could be indicative of its contemporaneity. While we observe an evolution in the significance of the axes at El Manatí, axes at La Merced already have a formal but distinctive imagery: an axe with carved human features and associated with other symbolic elements, such as figures holding axes, the V-shaped cut on the foreheads, and thick lips.

Nevertheless, the quality of stone at El Manatí is superior to that at La Merced. To date, no limestone or other material of local origin has been recovered at El Manatí, with the exception of a sandstone example. At El Manatí, one notes a close relationship between the primary material, form, and significance or symbolism. The use of fine or precious stone at El Manatí required a great labor investment, including the acquisition of the primary material, its movement over great distances, and its fabrication into axes by specialized artisans, who were likely in the service of those who sponsored the offering, most likely a high-ranking social group.

The Symbolism of the Axe

The axe as representation of an idea was also probably a metaphor for a myth (see Leach 1978: 52). In reality, however, we do not have specific evidence that indicates what precisely were the ideas symbolized by the axes (see Taube, this volume). They may have represented water and, as such, be an indicator of a water cult, particularly for having been carved primarily in jade or greenstone. In later Mesoamerican cultures there was an equivalence between jade, water, and the color green (Tibón 1983). The axes' petaloid forms are also reminiscent of raindrops and ears of corn, items associated with the fertility of mother earth. At La Merced, as at other sites where Olmecs offered axes, the axes' domestic significance likely transformed into a sacred and primordial element in ceremonies related to the cult of the deities of water (Anzures y Bolaños 1990).

Although distant in time, and always used with care, analogies to the data provided by the chroniclers, indigenous sources, and contemporaneous ethnography contribute numerous ideas for interpretations of some possible Olmec religious practices. Many present-day indigenous groups preserve their myths and beliefs. Among the "Cakchiqueles de Comalapa wedge-shaped green stones (ancient objects [axes] that are found in fields) were called 'lightning axes'" (Broda 1991: 468).

In a transcription by Fray Gregorio García on the Mixteca, one reads: "And on the highest [part] of the house [palace] and habitation of these [creator] gods, there was a copper axe, with the cutting edge pointing upward, upon which was the sky" (Dahlgren 1990: 236). A significant percentage of axes found at La Merced were placed intentionally with their edges pointing skyward.

The Chols believe that lightning, known as the Lord of Storms, possesses an axe with which he splits trees that, upon falling, sometimes reveal an axe at the foot of the tree where lightning once fell. The association of axe-lightning-rain explains the myth. Also, obsidian is commonly called "lightning stone" because it is thought that where one finds it, a lightning bolt had fallen. This is a widespread concept in southern Veracruz.

This idea apparently has a universal character, given that among various African groups this axe-lightning-rain association has also been documented (Luzuy 1978). In this sense it is interesting that Philippe Luzuy (1978: 255) affirms that, in reference to a communal African ceremony, "it is known that throughout all the eras, in all of the countries of the world, all carved axes have been considered 'lightning stones'; among the attributes of Jupiter, one finds these lightning stones. The first prehistoric discoveries were by men looking for 'lightning stones' to possess them as protective talismans, such as those presently used in Brittany, where they place them in the framework of houses."

Along the Gulf Coast, many stories abound of children who, in the distant past, were lost in the forest and rescued by old people who lived in a magic hill. From this hill, they fabricated swords or axes and produced winds on which they flew, wearing capes. In some versions, it is a flying axe that carries the child to the old owners of lightning; in others it is a deer. In all, the youth disobeys the prohibition against touching the magic instruments of lightning, provoking a catastrophe in which he submits himself to being tied to the bottom of the sea, converting himself into the "Old King." The Mixes have this belief, as well as the Totonacs, Tepehuas, Nahuas, and the Popolucas (Williams 1980; Técnicos Bilingües 1985).

Shamans making rain (called "lightning men" in southern Veracruz and "men of hail" in the states of Mexico and Morelos) and the spirits to whom they dedicate their rites and offerings (that is, Spirit of the Volcanoes, dwarfs, old lightning) seem to have a common origin and in many cases are related to the origin myths of the Maize God. It is unsettling to note the parallel of the paraphernalia of these shamans with the effigy axes and Olmec sculptures that carry "padlocks," "gauntlets," "torches," and wear "capes."

The axe was a tool of the gods of water and was, by extension, a symbol of this same element. As with all symbols, it had a polyvalent character, and its significance transformed or varied according to the ritual in which it was used.

In other cases the axes symbolized power and status, as was suggested by the Olmec anthropomorphic figurines that typically hold fine stone axes in their hands or those that have perforations at their heels to be suspended as pendants. The two personages on Altar 18 from San Lorenzo hold an axe between their hands with arms crossed over their chests; one carries an axe in the left hand with the edge pointing downward, while the other figure carries the axe in his right hand with the edge pointing upward. Also, on Monument 8 from San Lorenzo, known as the "billiard table," are six impressions that seem to be axes and are located on one of its flat surfaces, as if they had been embedded in the monument (Coe and Diehl 1980, 1: 313). Similar impressions appear on a basalt plaque from Laguna de los Cerros (Ortiz 1986).

But the real function of the axes in agriculture, that is, cutting and burning, also had to have been related to some deity of the woods. In this sense, the representation of the tool used in deforestation would be the logical offering to the spirits of the forest so that they would not harm those responsible for the cutting; the instruments used would likely have had to have been buried in the same place where the act had occurred.

Among the indigenous groups of southern Veracruz, the dwarf is the owner of the forest and animals. He is in charge of punishing those who excessively cut down the forests and those hunters who indiscriminately kill the animals. These small dwarfs lived near springs, rivers, lakes, and any body of water; to avoid them, one had to smoke a cigar or wear his clothing inside out.

By their association with water, axes also relate to the helpers of Tlaloc, or tlaloques; the Aztecs believed that water was guarded within the mountains in large caves by the tlaloques, who eventually emptied or broke their clay vessels over the fields and at the four cardinal points, thereby causing rain. The tlaloques also regularly smoke cigars, for the smoke forms clouds, which then provoke rainfall. As we know, Tlaloc lived in paradise or Tlalocan, also called the "house of turquoises" or jades. The description of these dwarfs coincides perfectly with the personages carved on Olmec altars, like that at Corral Nuevo; and while they seem to represent magical entities, we do not know whether they were considered owners of the forests as the dwarfs are today or as tlaloques of the Aztecs.

Conclusion

Given that the central problem of the Olmecs was not, as in many other centers of civilization, the shortage of water but its excess, the ritual activity had to be directed toward its containment and control rather than entreaties for its abundance. In fact, the axes and other objects in the offerings such as ceramic vessels, figurines, and fine stone masks may have been hurled into the springs, rivers, arroyos, wells, and estuaries to call the rains, to conjure storms, or to exercise an effective control over the waxings of the moon, as the data of El Manatí, La Merced, or Arroyo Pesquero may suggest.

The discovery and archaeological investigation of offerings like those at El Manatí or La Merced will help explain somewhat better the religious concepts of the Olmecs, in particular the meaning behind the ceremonial axes, masks, portable figurines, and other objects that have been admired in the world's museums for their artistic quality and style. Museum pieces, as products of looting, lack provenience and context and therefore provide minimal help in interpreting the events in which they played an important, signaling role. Almost all anthropomorphic axes or carved reliefs of personages carrying axes are found in private or museum collections. The only ones that come from controlled excavations are, to date, those from La Merced and El Manatí. To the degree that scholars and aficionados can unite to prevent looting of precious Olmec artifacts and to recover the important contextual information for them, to that degree we will enrich our knowledge of their history, beliefs, and ritual practices.

BIBLIOGRAPHY

Anzures y Bolaños, María del Carmen
1990 Tlaloc, señor del monte y dueño de los animales: Testimonios de un mito de regulación ecológica. In *Historia de la religión en Mesoamérica y áreas afines, coloquio 2*, ed. Barbro Dahlgren. Mexico City.

Broda, Johanna
1991 Cosmovisión y observación de la naturaleza: El ejemplo del culto de los cerros en Mesoamérica. In *Arqueoastronomía y etnoastronomía*, ed. Johanna Broda, Stanislaw Iwaniszewski, and Lucrecia Maupome, 461–500. Mexico City.

Coe, Michael D.
1972 Olmec Jaguars and Olmec Kings. In *The Cult of the Feline*, ed. Elizabeth Benson, 1–18. Washington.

Coe, Michael D., and Richard A. Diehl
1980 *In the Land of the Olmec*, 2 vols. Austin.

Dahlgren, Barbro
1990 *La mixteca: Su cultura e historia prehispánica*, 4th ed. Mexico City.

Diehl, Richard A.
1989 Olmec Religion. In *Encyclopedia of Religion*, vol. 11. New York.

Eliade, Mircea
1991 *Tratado de historia de la religión*. Mexico City.

1994 *Lo sagrado y lo profano*. Bogotá.

Grove, David C.
1968 The Pre-Classic Olmec in Central Mexico: Site Distribution and Inferences. In *Dumbarton Oaks Conference on the Olmec*, ed. Elizabeth Benson, 179–185. Washington.

1972 Olmec Felines in Highland Central Mexico. In *The Cult of the Feline*, ed. Elizabeth Benson, 153–164. Washington.

1987 (Editor) *Ancient Chalcatzingo*. Austin.

Heizer, Robert, John Graham, and Lewis Napton
1968 The 1968 Investigations at La Venta. *Contributions of the University of California Archaeological Research Facility* 5: 127–205. Berkeley.

Joralemon, Peter David
1971 *A Study of Olmec Iconography*. Washington.

1976 The Olmec Dragon: A Study in Pre-Columbian Iconography. In *Origins of Religious Art and Iconography in Preclassic Mesoamerica*, ed. Henry Nicholson, 27–71. Los Angeles.

Leach, Edmund
1978 *Cultura y comunidad. La lógica de la conexión de los símbolos: Una introduc-*

ción al uso del análisis estructuralista de la antropología social. Mexico City.

Luzuy, Philippe
1978 Los llamadores de la lluvia: Ritos mágicos para vivir. *Revista Geografía Universal,* año 3, 6(2). Mexico City.

Ortiz, Ponciano
1986 Laguna de los Cerros y su área de interacción cultural: Propuesta de investigación. Submitted to the Archivo Técnico del Instituto de Antropología, Universidad Veracruzana, Xalapa, Mexico.

Ortiz, Ponciano, and María del Carmen Rodríguez
1989 Proyecto Manatí 1989. *Arqueología,* 2d series, 1: 23–52. Mexico City.

1995 Informe técnico de la temporada de campo 1994 del Proyecto Manatí. Report in the Archivo Técnica del Centro Veracruz del Instituto Nacional de Antropología e Historia, Veracruz, Mexico.

1997 Informe Técnico de la temporada de campo 1996 del Proyecto Manatí. Report in the Archivo Técnica del Centro Veracruz del Instituto Nacional de Antropología e Historia, Veracruz, Mexico.

Ortiz, Ponciano, María del Carmen Rodríguez, and Alfredo Delgado
1996 *Las investigaciones arqueológicas en el Cerro Sagrado Manatí.* Universidad Veracruzana, Xalapa, Mexico.

Ortiz, Ponciano, María del Carmen Rodríguez, and Paul Schmidt
1988 El Proyecto Manatí: Informe preliminar. *Arqueología* 3: 141–154. Mexico City.

Ortiz, Ponciano, María del Carmen Rodríguez, Paul Schmidt, Alfredo Delgado, Luis Heredia, Lourdes Hernández, Ines Gheno, Eric Juárez, Jorge Bautista, Martha Osorio, Judith Zunita, César Corre, Julio Chan, Ignacio Montes, Daniel Nahmad, and Feruccio Hasta
1989 Proyecto El Manatí 1988: Informe final de temporada. Report in the Archivo Técnico del Centro Regional Veracruz, Instituto Nacional de Antropología e Historia, Veracruz, Mexico.

Ortiz, Ponciano, María del Carmen Rodríguez, Paul Schmidt, Alfredo Delgado, Lourdes Hernández, Luis Heredia, Ricardo Herrera, Eric Juárez, Jorge Bautista, César Corre, Julio Chan, Steve Nelson, and Ignacio Montes
1990 Proyecto Manatí. Informe final, temporada 1989. Report in the Archivo Técnico del Centro Regional Veracruz, Instituto Nacional de Antropología e Historia, Veracruz, Mexico.

Pasztory, Esther
1993 El mundo natural como metáfora cívica en Teotihuacán. In *La antigua América: El arte de los parajes sagrados,* ed. Richard Townsend, 135–146. Chicago.

Pohorilenko, Anatole
1977 On the Question of Olmec Deities. *Journal of New World Archaeology* 2(1): 1–16.

1986 The Structure and Development of the Olmec Representational System. Manuscript on file, Department of Anthropology, Tulane University, New Orleans.

Rodríguez, María del Carmen, and Ponciano Ortiz
1994 *El Manatí: Un espacio sagrado olmeca.* Universidad Veracruzana, Xalapa, Mexico.

Técnicos Bilingües de Acayucan
1985 *Agua, mundo, montaña. Narrativa Nahua, Mixe y Popoluca del sur de Veracruz.* Mexico City.

Tibón, Gutierre
1983 *El jade en México.* Mexico City.

Williams, Robert
1980 Tradición oral de Tajín. Report submitted to the Dirección General de Culturas Populares, Instituto de Antropología, Universidad Veracruzana, Xalapa, Mexico.

CHRISTINE NIEDERBERGER
Instituto Nacional de Antropología e Historia

Ranked Societies, Iconographic Complexity, and Economic Wealth in the Basin of Mexico toward 1200 B.C.

At the end of the second millennium B.C., large regional centers, constituting the expression of a new type of territorial organization, appeared in various zones of Middle America, from Guerrero to the Gulf Coast. Emerging from a rather homogeneous social landscape of independent farming villages, these new regional centers were greater in size, and with higher population densities and more varied functions, than earlier villages and were able politically and economically to control their surrounding territories. Behind this observable archaeological phenomenon, characteristic of the emergence of Mesoamerican civilization, lay a plurality of interrelated factors and accumulated changes that had occurred since early Holocene times.

As suggested by general archaeological evidence, and by the study of Helladic Greece in particular, the term "civilization" is not necessarily synonymous with "urbanism." In Mesoamerica, "civilization" can be related to the rise of cities, centers of regional integration, that I have defined elsewhere (Niederberger 1987) in the Latin sense of *caput* rather than *urbs.* Certain criteria considered necessary to identify the emergence of cities in Old World archaeology, such as writing or metalworking, do not apply in Mesoamerica. If we postulate that a community attains the status of a city when one can observe the coexistence of (1) some forms of elaborated political and religious power, (2) clear social ranking, (3) planned public architecture, (4) a group of highly specialized craftspersons, (5) control and active participation in interregional trade networks, and (6) complex intellectual achievements such as a sophisticated, codified iconography for the permanent recording of certain concepts or events, then we must accept that cities were already emerging in Mesoamerica at the end of the second millennium B.C. The data described here indicate that this was certainly the case for some sites in the Basin of Mexico. At the same time period we also observe, in numerous zones, the development of a distinctive style and iconography based on the crystallization of a set of beliefs that would eventually constitute the roots of the Mesoamerican mental universe.

Since the 1930s, this particular stylistic expression has been designated *Olmec,* a name even then considered misleading by pioneer researchers such as Wigberto Jiménez Moreno (1959: 1022). Over time, the semantic ambiguity of *Olmec* has greatly increased, especially for scholars working outside the Gulf Coast (Niederberger 1976: 265–266; Grove 1989), as it also implies the belief in a one-way, direct or indirect impact from Gulf Coast inhabitants on other Mesoamerican communities.

In opposition to this postulate, I have proposed a nondiffusionist model that explains the relative homogeneity of iconography and related beliefs in Early Formative societies by a long-established *dual system* of interregional exchanges of commodities and information between culturally dynamic groups in differ-

Rupestrian paintings at Tlapacoya, probably from the Ayotla–Manantial phases ent regions of ancient Mesoamerica (Niederberger 1974b; 1976: 265–266).

Within this conceptual framework, my corollary contention is that each regional entity participating in the gradual buildup of this specific cultural configuration or early facet of Mesoamerican civilization pertained to a similar level of sociocultural complexity (Niederberger 1976: 265–266; 1987: 732–752). Consequently, I do not use the now unavoidable term *Olmec* to allude to unicentric theories of *Olmec* colonizers or to refer to a particular people. Instead, I limit its use to two concepts: "style," in a Saussurian linguistic sense, and, more broadly, "civilization," defined in this context as pan-Mesoamerican and multiethnic in nature.

In this brief synopsis of the Basin of Mexico's pre-800 B.C. archaeological levels, I limit my discussion to a few general comments concerning the variety and productivity of ancient landscapes, the evidence related to a sociopolitical organization based on clearly ranked societies, from the end of the second millennium onward, and the concomitant development of regional centers, earthen architecture, complex codified graphic symbols, craft specialization, and the dynamic implications of interregional trade and exchange systems. It is worth stressing that since the pioneer work of Miguel Covarrubias, the chronological framework and sequence of the pre-Teotihuacán societies of the Basin of Mexico have drastically changed (Tolstoy and Paradis 1970; Tolstoy 1978; Niederberger 1970, 1976, 1987), and a long-lasting in situ development, from archaic times onward, has been uncovered (Niederberger 1979). It also seems that the systematic twentieth-century destruction of crucial zones of Early Formative sites has led many scholars to a certain blindness concerning the dynamic and precocious Basin of Mexico communities within the nascent Mesoamerican interaction sphere, despite the data published in this field.

Paleoenvironments of the Basin of Mexico

Today the Basin of Mexico environment offers but a withered image of the singular ecological bounty of past landscapes, a fact too often overlooked by Mesoamericanists unfamiliar with this region. In my study of Basin of Mexico paleolandscapes and ancient economy (Niederberger 1987: 46–168), I have analyzed the components and high productivity of this remarkable zone for the pre-1900 period, the time before drainage of the lakes, deforestation, erosion, and chemical and organic pollution transformed this ancient Eden into an ecological disaster. To deal with the emergence of complex societies in temperate lacustrine basins, such as the Basin of Mexico, it is useful to move beyond the traditional view that divides Middle America into two broad ecological zones: the "semi-arid" highlands and the "fertile" lowlands. This dichotomy has sparked

1. Basin of Mexico, Chalco area: (a) restoration of ancient freshwater lacustrine expanses in the eastern zone of the Chalco subbasin, dominated by snowy Iztaccihuatl volcano; today, coots, shovelers, spoonbills, herons, and other aquatic birds find their traditional ecological niche; (b) representation of freshwater white fish *(Chirostoma humboldtianum)*, characteristic of ancient Lake Chalco fauna, incised on a white-slipped vessel from the Manantial phase (1000–800 B.C.) of Tlapacoya-Zohapilco
Author photographs

irrelevant and unfruitful debates, the principal one being the controversy between those who view the origins of complex societies in the lowlands and those who concede priority to the highlands.

The issue is more complex as such a dichotomy can be observed within the Basin of Mexico itself. The northern part of the basin, as well as the eastern regions of Texcoco located in a rain shadow of the Sierra Nevada, shows a relative dryness, with intermittent rivers. In these regions, the first significant human occupation dates to between 1000 and 800 B.C. and parallels the development of irrigation systems (Nichols 1982); I have termed this period the Manantial phase (Niederberger 1974a). In contrast, and this point deserves emphasis, the western and southern regions of the basin were among the most favorable habitats in Middle America in pre-Hispanic times for the establishment of a sedentary way of life and development of early complex societies (see table 2 and Niederberger 1979). The western area received all the rain discharge from the clouds coming over the Sierra Nevada, and, with this high rainfall, good humic and volcanic soils, as well as numerous perennial rivers (now piped and drained northward), made this zone favorable for early agriculture. Archaeological evidence demonstrates that the zone was exploited by large agrarian communities since at least the middle of the second millennium B.C. at sites such as Tlatilco.

As for the landscape of the southern part of the basin (fig. 1), it was deeply marked by the presence of a large freshwater lake, nurtured by important perennial rivers and numerous springs. The lacustrine area was surrounded by fertile forest soils (today below the Pedregal lava flow) and rich alluvial deposits in the southeast. These included the Chalco plains, famous in protohistoric times for their high productivity and prized varieties of maize. Both archaeological and ethnohistoric data indicate the profusion and variety of ancient faunal resources in this region, particularly of fish and resident and migratory waterfowl. This zone was occupied by sedentary settlements by the end of the sixth millennium B.C., as shown by archaeological work carried out at the Tlapacoya-Zohapilco site, and eventually became the setting of complex intensive agrosystems (Armillas 1971) and one of the most heavily occupied regions of Pre-Columbian America.

The Basin of Mexico Formative Sequence: Past and Present

Within the interpretive schemes of Early Formative Mesoamerica, of all the areas concerned, "it is perhaps the Basin of Mexico that has been most unfairly treated" (Flannery and Marcus 1994: 390). Kent Flannery and Joyce Marcus comment further on the Basin of Mexico environment: "It is now clear that it could not have been the high, cold, marginal area it was once portrayed to be" and that its inhabitants "produced some of the best and most sophisticated ceramics of the early horizon" (Flannery and Marcus 1994: 390). If so, the natural question that arises is why the basin developments have been misconstrued and misunderstood for so long.

The fact that the Basin of Mexico played a significant role in the emergence of pan-Mesoamerican technoeconomic strategies and cultural patterns at the end of the second millenium B.C. has long been obscured by a series of unfortunate occurrences. First, a critical misinterpretation, the inversion of the relative and absolute chronology of the pre-Teotihuacan occupations (an error repeated in all the archaeological literature from the 1940s to the late 1960s), led to the false conviction that the late El Arbolillo-Zacatenco sites, excavated by George Vaillant in the 1930s (Vaillant 1930, 1935), represented not only the "first villages" of the basin (wrongly dated to about 2000–1500 B.C.) but also characterized the cultural stasis and primitiveness of the region during the Formative period. It is worth noting here, however, that at the time of his investigations Vaillant did not ascribe such an antiquity to his sites. He qualified them as "Middle or Intermediate Cultures." Nevertheless, in the 1940s, when Olmec-style ceramic vessels and figurines were discovered in the basin, first at Tlatilco, they were considered to be coeval with Zacatenco cultures and to reflect unmistakable evidence of culturally more advanced intruders, among primitive peasant (Zacatenco) societies (Covarrubias 1950).

Today a coherent set of radiocarbon dates and excavations carried out in the Basin of Mexico from the end of the 1960s onward has swept away the view of early Zacatenco primitive villages, and supposed external influence upon them, and has exposed the erroneous assumption of exogenous-elite/local-peasantry

Table 1. Basin of Mexico, Archaeological Sequence

From Early Sedentarism to the Rise of Proto-urban Regional Centers

Sidereal time (B.C.)	Radiocarbon time (b.c.)	Characteristic pottery styles and decorations	Dominant clay figurine types	Cultural phases	Major sites	Socioeconomic characteristics
(see R. M. Clark 1975)	100					
	200	Ticoman	H		CUICUILCO	
			G L M N	Ticomán		
	300		E, I			• Rise of proto-urban regional centers
450	400					
	500	"Zacatenco" Ceramic assemblage described by G. Vaillant with carinated bowls	A, B, F,		SUB PEDREGAL SITE ?	
	600		C3 C1, C2	Zacatenco		
880	700	Earlier styles deculturation	C7	Tetelpan		
950	800	Tlatilco style and incised fluid rendering of pan-Mesoamerican symbols	Pahuacan Tenayo K, O D1, D2, D3	Manantial		• First evidence of canal irrigation in the northern area
	900				TLATILCO	• Intensification of interregional exchanges
1250	1000				COAPEXCO	
	1100	Excised rendering of pan-Mesoamerican symbols	Isla Pilli (ex C9)	Ayotla	TLAPACOYA	• Emergence of regional capitals *(caput,* not *urbs)*
	1200					• Development of ranked societies
1600	1300	Fine red-slipped and red on buff wares	Tlalpan ?	Nevada		• Well-established agricultural economy. Large metates and two-handed milling stones
	1400					
1835	1500			?		
	2000					
2920	2300	Protoceramic no utilitarian ceramic found	Zohapilco clay figurine	Zohapilco		• Village life. Among cultivated plants: *Amaranthus leucocarpus, Cucurbita, Physalis, Sechium, Capsicum annuum.* Larger average size of *Zea* pollen grains than in previous phases and frequency trebled. Standardized grinding tools with short manos.
	2500			?		
4500	3500			Playa II		
	4500	Preceramic				(Meridional zone) • Proto-agrarian early sedentarism. Exploitation of varied biotopes and resources well distributed throughout the annual cycle. Nonstandardized grinding tools.
6000	5500			Playa I		

Table 1. Excavations carried out at Tlapacoya-Zohapilco led to the detection and definition of the following cultural phases: Playa I and II, Zohapilco, Nevada, Manantial, and Tetelpan (Niederberger 1976, 1979, 1987). The Ayotla phase was first named and dated by Paul Tolstoy at Tlapacoya-Ayotla (Tolstoy and Paradis 1970) and then amply documented through the study of the Tlapacoya-Zohapilco site archaeological finds. At this site, the analysis of the Manantial level components indicates that Robert Heizer's *Tertium Quid* (1958), as well as the Tlatilco style assemblage first described by Román Piña Chan (1958) and by Muriel Porter (1953)—and for decades enigmatic as to their cultural affinities and chronological positions—can now be ascribed to this important post-Ayotla and pre-Zacatenco cultural phase. The upper limit of the Tetelpan phase can be estimated at c. 700 or 600 B.C. Names and definitions of the Zacatenco and Ticomán phases derive from George Vaillant's pioneer investigations at Zacatenco (1930), El Arbolillo (1935), and Ticomán (1931). Vaillant considered that the artifacts were already highly elaborated, and, in the absence of absolute dating, he qualified Zacatenco-Ticomán levels as "Middle Cultures," that is, intermediate between still unknown earlier cultural levels and proto-Teotihuacán deposits, today well defined in numerous studies (Manzanilla 1988). However, in pioneer times from 1942 on, the great artist and researcher Miguel Covarrubias (1950, 1957), and his immediate followers, held the postulate that the El Arbolillo-Zacatenco levels corresponded to the most ancient agrarian and egalitarian villages in the basin, dated c. 1500–2000 B.C., villages later colonized by a sophisticated elite from the Gulf Coast. Now the sequence has been reversed. The Ayotla phase precedes the Zacatenco levels by 500 to 600 years, and today's data show that the Ayotla ranked societies developed in situ, in the context of a pan-Mesoamerican and multidirectional interregional exchange system of goods and ideas.

relationships at Tlatilco. We now know that Zacatenco occupations date some six hundred years after the first Olmec-style stratigraphic levels in the basin and were contemporaneous with proto-urban centers such as Cuicuilco (table 1).

Notwithstanding the recent data on the Early Formative, the belief that Formative sites of the basin, such as Tlatilco, were simple villages inhabited by relatively egalitarian villagers still persists in many recent publications. In other words, it is not fully understood that the impact of this new perspective goes well beyond the field of chronological reappraisals; it affects the very basis of our knowledge of the sociopolitical and cultural nature and dynamics of the ancient Formative communities of the Basin of Mexico. The continuing repetition and reification of this factual error is probably due, in part, to the fact that few early structural remains have survived the destructive effects of three successive and powerful urban centers of pre-Hispanic and modern times: Teotihuacán, Tenochtitlán, and Mexico City. This could be seen as the fate of many archaeological sites, but in this specific case, it must be noted that the "coup de grâce" has been struck in quite recent times and could have been avoided.

Two Formative Regional Centers

One of the tragedies of Pre-Columbian archaeology has been the relatively recent, systematic destruction in the Basin of Mexico of Olmec-style horizon, regional centers such as Tlatilco and Tlapacoya. The astonishing disinterest in the Formative period altogether remains evident today at the still poorly understood Cuicuilco site, arguably the earliest urban center in the basin, where a commercial multistoried building has just been built right in the middle of the archaeological site. (It seems as surrealistic and incongruous as if one were to discover, one morning, a modern skyscraper at Teotihuacán nestled between the pyramids of the Sun and Moon.)

Tlatilco

Tlatilco, a site massively looted since the 1930s for masterpieces of Formative ceramic art, was very well situated in the western Hondo River fertile plains and adjacent foothills. Long erroneously considered as a burial site and the most important necropolis of Formative times, Tlatilco was, in fact, a city with public structures. These structures included clay-surfaced earthen platforms, as apparent in the observation of mounds, terraces, and steps in the profiles of fresh cuts at the site exposed during excavations dedicated to the explorations of burials (Porter 1953 and personal communication). Cross-correlations of ceramic artifacts with the master sequence recently established for Tlapacoya-Zohapilco indicate that Tlatilco had a significant population between 1200 and 700 B.C. But the site, a clay source for brickmaking, has been destroyed, and most of its material evidence—including domestic and nondomestic earthen structures and foundations, refuse middens, bell-shaped pits, and hundreds of burials associated with these features—has been removed during sixty years of continuous looting. What is left of Tlatilco now lies beneath highways and factories.

Fortunately, the study of more than four hundred burials, rescued during several field seasons of excavations carried out from 1942 to 1969 (Covarrubias 1950, 1957; Piña Chan 1958, 1971; Romano 1967; Porter 1953, n.d.; Lorenzo 1965; Faulhaber 1965; García Moll et al. 1991), offers irreplaceable and extremely valuable evidence concerning the clearly ranked societies of that time, their material and cultural wealth, the arts and knowledge of their craftspersons, and their involvement in long-distance exchange (Niederberger 1987: 677–692). Analysis of the contents of 213 burials by Muriel Porter (n.d.) reveals the hierarchical nature of Tlatilco society (Niederberger 1987: 704–709). This sample of Ayotla and Manantial phase burials includes those lacking nonperishable offerings (nos. 11, 24, 25, 27, 57, and 73), those with just a few sherds (nos. 19 and 29), graves with three or fewer pottery vessels (nos. 23, 26, and 83), individuals with specialized tool kits of bone needles and awls (nos. 28, 30, 40, and 168), graves with rich and varied offerings but no exotic goods (nos. 42, 29, 79, and 90), and other burials with opulent offerings containing imported items such as seashells, jadeite and serpentine celts and ornaments, and iron-ore mirrors (nos. 10, 37, 60, 137, and 172). Finally, the existence of rich infant burials with exotic goods, such as Burial 161, is testimony of a system of inherited status. Burials with exotic items, such as the famous Burial 154 reported by Arturo Romano (1967), document the systematic importation to the Basin of Mexico of prized commodities through regular, interregional exchange systems.

Burial 154, a male individual with cranial deformation and intentional dental mutilation, attested on only 3 percent of the exhumed individuals (Faulhaber 1965: 89), is but one example of the systematic acquisition by residents of Tlatilco of foreign goods. Offerings included faceted quartz "polishers" or amulets, ground to a near optical polish, similar to those reported from Guerrero (Griffin 1981: 218–219), jade earplugs, graphite, bitumen, and an effigy vessel of an acrobat (Romano 1967). It is worth recalling, also, a particular burial with splendid funerary offerings, reported in Tlatilco in the 1940s, consisting of 806 blue-green jade beads, some carved in squash forms, and 20 light green jade beads associated with a bowl of red ocher, pieces of iron ore, and twelve Manantial phase, fine pottery vessels. The great archaeologist Pedro Armillas made a study of the drill holes of the beads and concluded that it was the largest jade necklace ever discovered at that time in the Americas.

Within Tlatilco elite funerary offerings, the presence of seashell is particularly noteworthy, as evident by the important report of 214 burials of Tlatilco field season IV (1962–1969) described by Roberto García Moll and his colleagues (1991). Three radiocarbon dates are associated with field season IV excavations. These dates of 1230 ± 120 b.c., 1140 ± 100 b.c., and 970 ± 80 b.c. (see García Moll et al. 1991: 13) fit well within the time span of the Ayotla and Manantial phases defined at Tlapacoya. Marine shell burial offerings include conchs and pendants, bracelets, beads, and zoomorphic plaques made of the nacreous pearl oyster *(Pinctada mazatlanica)* of the Pacific Coast, whose importance within Formative exchange networks has already been described by Jane Wheeler Pires-Ferreira (1976, 1978b). Entire valves were also valued and stored at Tlatilco, as demonstrated by the presence of complete shells within offerings of Manantial phase Burial 27, together with a pearl oyster triangular pendant and 54 beads of serpentine (García Moll et al. 1991: 27–28). Marine turtle shells (*Pseudemys* sp.) as well as remains of regional fauna such as mountain lions *(Felis concolor)*, owls *(Bubo virginianus)*, turkeys, ducks, and pelicans are also reported in mortuary offerings or in excavations (Alvarez 1976). It is fascinating to observe that, along with ducks, grebes, spoonbills, and herons, pelicans are today making a notable return in the ecological reserve near Texcoco (fig. 2).

2. Basin of Mexico, Texcoco area, rehabilitation of part of the saline Texcoco Lake and return of migratory waterfowl, such as these pelicans *(Pelecanus erythrorhynchus)*
Author photograph

In sum, Tlatilco mortuary data indicate that the social group was segmented into categories having unequal access to certain resources, particularly to long-distance trade items. All the characteristics discussed by Joseph Tainter (1978) for distinguishing hierarchical societies were present, in particular, considerable individual variation of offerings, with no coincidence with age or sex, and evidence of inherited social status as evident in child burials with prized exotic goods.

Tlapacoya

The Formative site of Tlapacoya, located on an ancient island (fig. 3a) in Lake Chalco, has also been the target of irremediable destruction. In pre-Hispanic times, and until 1900 when the lacustrine expanses were artificially drained, Tlapacoya was surrounded by the freshwater Chalco-Xochimilco Lake and was exceptionally rich in edible resources, such as fish including *Atherinidae, Goodeidae* and *Cyprinidae* families, amphibians, as well as a considerable number of species of resident and

3. (a) The ancient volcanic island of Tlapacoya, with several water sources and formerly surrounded by Lake Chalco freshwater expanses, with an array of biotic resources and well situated on primary communication routes, was densely populated during the Formative period and has always been a favorable location for human occupation; (b) rupestrian paintings at Tlapacoya, probably from the Ayotla–Manantial phases
Author photographs

migratory aquatic birds, well represented in Formative subsistence remains and on Ayotla-Manantial ceramic iconography.

In pre-Hispanic times the volcanic island of pink andesite of Tlapacoya reflecting in the lake would have constituted an impressive sight and may have been conceived, with its grottoes and springs, as a sacred place, as were other isolated dome-shaped mountain sites (see Ortiz and Rodríguez, this volume; Grove, this volume).

For the last fifty years, Tlapacoya has been exploited as an andesite quarry, the rock being blasted free with dynamite. It came as a surprise in 1992, therefore, to discover some paintings left on untouched zones of the nearby cliff. Some of them seem to pertain to the Olmec-style horizon period, such as the representation of a chubby chin, baby-face profile and oval cartouche with cross-hatching (fig. 3b). These designs are similar to some on pottery found in archaeological deposits.

Tragic for our understanding of highland early regional capitals has been the eradication of the Tlapacoya ancient Formative zone, in large part bulldozed away in 1958 to provide building material for the Mexico-Puebla highway. In the process, a large-scale earthen platform, which projected eastward from the hill toward the ancient lake (of which some external limits can still be observed), was destroyed. People aware of the site's significance bought, at that time, complete pieces and also sacks of earth from which to sort out any artifacts. Now Olmec-style horizon ceramic vessels, figurines, greenstone celts (fig. 5a), jade and serpentine ornaments, seashell bracelets and pendants, iron-ore mirrors (fig. 5b), and other elaborate burial offerings that were associated with this structure are in the Roch Collection, donated to the Universidad Nacional Autónoma de México (UNAM), in local private haciendas, and in Mexican and American museums, such as the Museum of the American Indian in New York (Porter 1967).

At the edge of this devastated zone has remained, by luck, the Ayotla zone excavated by Paul Tolstoy and the Zohapilco ancient shores, where I have excavated a long series of human occupations that span six millennia. In 1967, Tolstoy was the first scholar to observe in the deep deposits of Tlapacoya of his Ayotla excavation that the Olmec-horizon artifacts were situated well below the El Arbolillo-Zacatenco levels containing C type figurines (Tolstoy and Paradis 1970). This crucial discovery of the true Formative sequence was confirmed by radiocarbon dating. But the fact that the Ayotla excavation was of reduced size, yielding only twenty-eight figurines (Reyna Robles 1971), and was excavated by artificial levels, resulting in some mixing between distinct deposits, constituted an obstacle for building a convincing post-Ayotla sequence and placing the cultural deposits within a broader economic and ecological context. Moreover, the excavation was stopped just below the

Ayotla levels, giving the impression that this cultural level, with its sophisticated potteries, was a result of external influence.

Definition of a Long Sequence of Regional Development at Tlapacoya-Zohapilco

The excavations sponsored by the Instituto Nacional de Antropología e Historia that I carried out some years later in the Tlapacoya-Zohapilco ancient lacustrine shores followed the natural and cultural stratigraphy and interpreted these strata within a multidisciplinary approach. Excavations yielded 709 figurines, 130,000 sherds, and nearly 6,000 lithic artifacts (Niederberger 1976, 1987, 1996a). The evidence first permitted me to define a pre-Ayotla ceramic cultural level that I named Nevada. Nevada phase artifacts show many similarities with those of the Tierras Largas phase of Oaxaca (Flannery 1976; Flannery and Marcus 1994; Winter 1984). The excavation also allowed me to define two post-Ayotla occupations: the well-documented and important phase that I named Manantial and the Tetelpan phase (a period of Olmec-style deculturation), both preceding the El Arbolillo-Zacatenco-Ticomán levels originally defined by Vaillant. The recovered artifacts also permitted the amplification of the original definition of the Ayotla phase (see table 1). But most interesting was the discovery at Zohapilco of a series of archaic and prepottery levels (Playa I, Playa II, and Zohapilco phases) dating from the sixth millennium B.C. onward. These levels allow assessment of the regional development of sedentary life, the agrarian economy, and the direct antecedents to pre-urban settlements.

I have reported in *Science* (Niederberger 1979) the technoeconomic and cultural characteristics of these early occupations. In brief, paleoenvironmental data and faunal and pollen analyses show that Chalco lakeshore communities of Playa I and Playa II times had direct or ready access to spatially close and diversified biotopes (rich lacustrine environment, humic alluvial soils, and pine-oak-alder forests) and that all were actually exploited (see table 2). The year-round regular distribution of natural food resources during the bioclimatic optimum of the Playa phases, together with the attested early manipulation of certain plants, such as teosinte, amaranths, *Cucurbita*, and *Physalis*, led Playa peoples to a sedentary occupation of their territory. The artifact assemblage of Playa times consists of andesite macroblades and grinding stones, notched basalt tools, blunt-backed knives and scrapers, obsidian cores, utilized flakes, and projectile points, as well as wooden tools, such as small, burnished pointed sticks—probably part of combs—and long sticks with burned and ground distal ends.

The following Zohapilco phase, apart from showing an irreversible trend toward an expanding agrarian economy, with cultivated plants such as *Amaranthus leucocarpus*, chayote (a plant of the genus *Sechium*), and *Capsicum annuum*, is characterized by the presence of stone bowls and the development of standardized grinding stones, with basalt one-hand manos of excellent craftsmanship. *Zea* maize

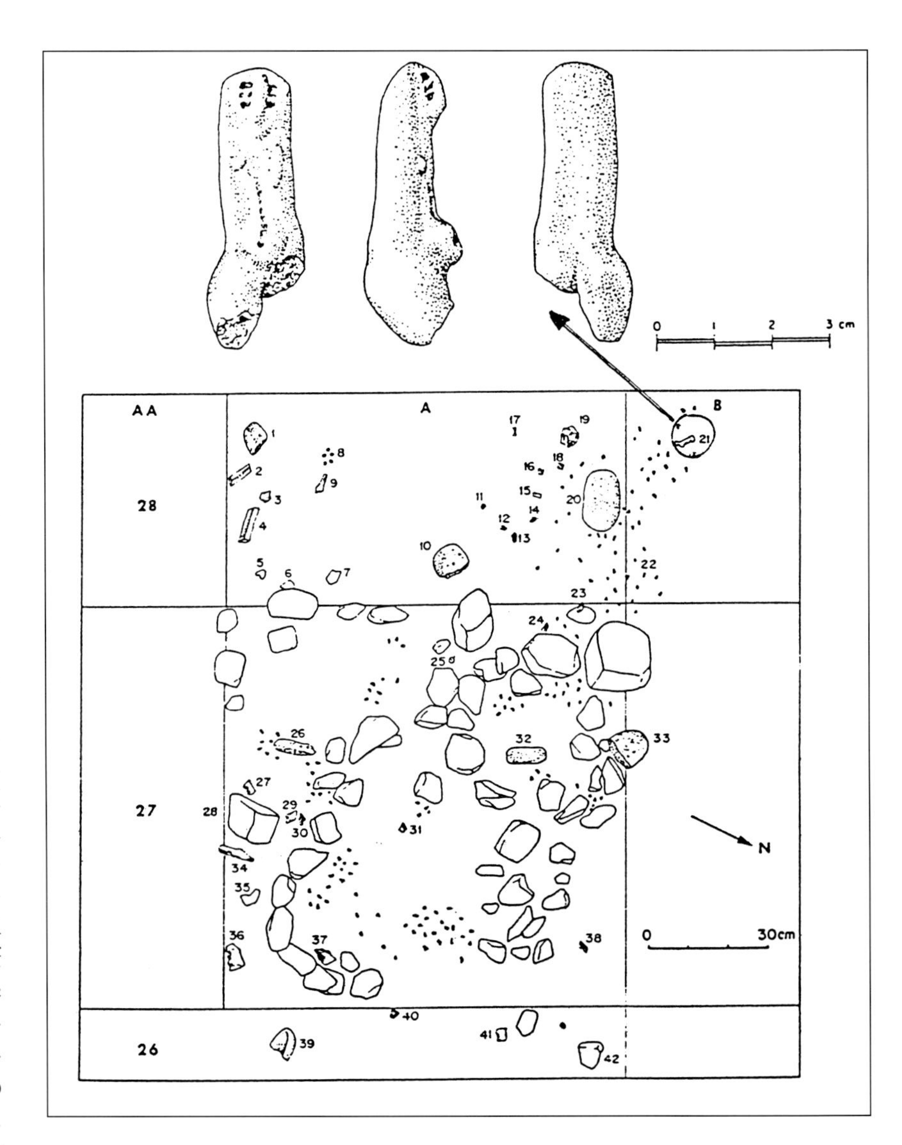

4. Tlapacoya-Zohapilco site (Basin of Mexico), hearth cluster, Zohapilco phase, prepottery levels with evidence of growing agrarian activities and milling stones of excellent craftsmanship; the earliest baked clay figurine known to date in an archaeological context in Middle America was found in situ near this feature and associated with a radiocarbon date of 2300 ± 110 b.c. (2920 B.C. sidereal time)

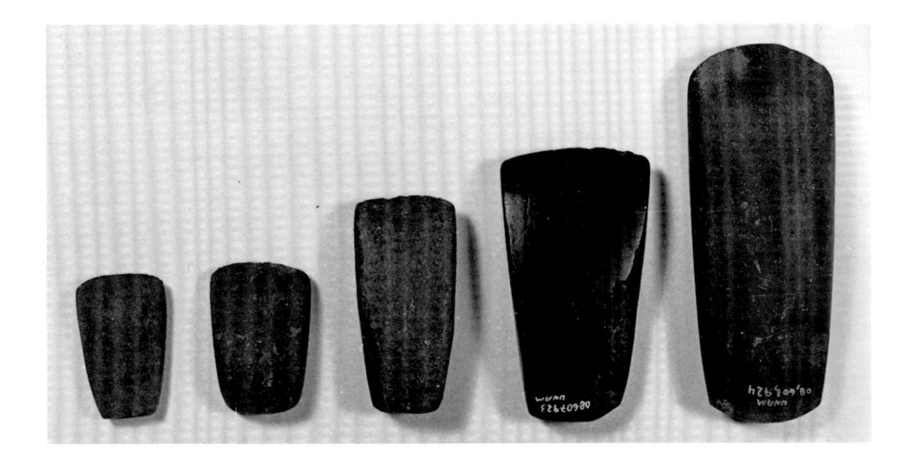

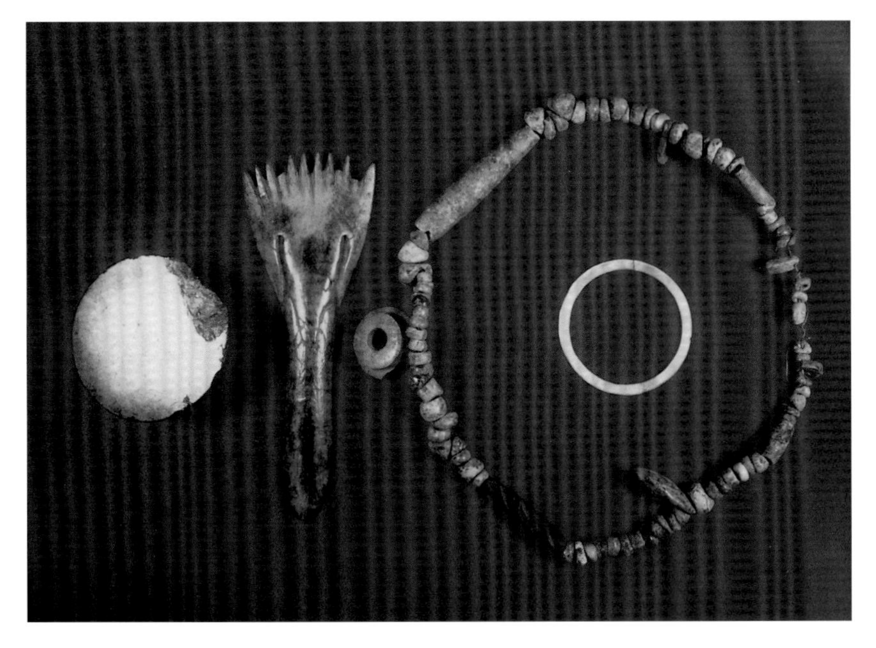

5. (a) Greenstone polished celts from Tlapacoya; (b) polished iron-ore mirror, bone comb, greenstone necklace, and seashell ring from Tlapacoya
Photographs: Victor Lagarde, courtesy of Universidad Nacional Autónoma de México

pollen grains from these levels are, on average, of greater dimensions than those of the previous phase, and their frequency tripled. This level also yielded the earliest known Middle America clay figurine found in situ—in a prepottery context. Global structural analyses have interestingly shown the independent recurrence of the "mute" (without mouth) and "multi-eyed" figurines, with armless columnar body, in homotaxial—but not necessarily contemporaneous—prepottery levels, in particular in Eurasian early Neolithic cultures (see fig. 4).

The most ancient pottery levels known at present in the Basin of Mexico correspond to the Nevada phase of the Tlapacoya-Zohapilco sequence. These occupations date to 1360 ± 110 b.c. (radiocarbon time), or 1675 B.C. ± 140 (sidereal time). The ceramic assemblage has a significant proportion of fine vessels with thin walls, tecomates with fine vertical grooves, flat-based dishes, and bottles. Plastic decoration of vessels included rocker stamping and fine incisions of clustered, parallel lines on the interior bases of flat-bottomed dishes. The most common painted decoration is represented by red-slipped geometrical motifs, often with specular hematite, on light brown ware.

In summary, this multimillennial trajectory offers the first possibility to perceive, through the study of fossil pollens, macroplant remains, and their dated cultural contexts, some aspects of the regional development of an agrarian economy, as well as the natural and manmade evolution of paleolandscapes, through a long diachronic perspective. It also permits us to follow the gradual in situ development toward the specific technoeconomic and cultural complexity observed in the Basin of Mexico at the end of the second millennium B.C.

The Rise of Regional Centers, Complex Belief Systems, and Iconography

Site Distribution and Function

With the rise and development of regional centers in the Basin of Mexico during the Ayotla and Manantial phases, quantitative and qualitative changes took place (Niederberger 1987: 704–717). Current data, including those from archaeological excavations, surveys (Parsons 1971; Parsons et al. 1982), and salvage operations, have led to a better understanding of the distribution and, in certain cases, the relative size of contemporaneous Early Formative sites. Information on site composition and distribution suggests the existence of a growing hierarchy among sites, beginning about 1250 B.C. (Niederberger 1987: 728–729 and figs. 600–601). Tlapacoya, Tlatilco, and perhaps one sub-Pedregal site, apparently were higher-order sites in the Basin of Mexico; they were greater in size, sustained greater and denser populations, and supported more varied activities and functions than contemporaneous villages and hamlets. Leaders of these larger communities were able to control, politically and economically, a constellation of smaller satellite villages in their surrounding territories (Niederberger 1987: 692–704). This pattern of settlement hierarchy

Table 2. Tlapacoya-Zohapilco Site, Basin of Mexico, Playa I Phase

REGULAR ANNUAL FOOD RESOURCES EXPLOITED BY SEDENTARY COMMUNITIES TOWARD 5500 B.C.

Early food resources recovered at the site of Zohapilco (c. 5500 B.C.)	Month of availability											
	Dry season					Rainy season						
	Nov.	Dec.	Jan.	Feb.	March	April	May	June	July	Aug.	Sept.	Oct.
Ducks												
Aythya spp.	●	●	●	●	●							
Spatula clypeata	●	●	●	●	●							
Anas acuta	●	●	●	●	●							
Anas platyrhynchos	●	●	●	●	●							
Querquedula sp.	●	●	●	●	●							
Anas diazi	●	●	●	●	●	●	●	●	●	●	●	●
Grebes												
Podiceps caspicus	●	●	●	●	●							
Podilymbus podiceps	●	●	●	●	●	○	○	○	○	○	○	○
Aechmophorus sp.	●	●	●	●	●	○	○	○	○	○	○	○
Geese												
Branta spp.	●	●	●	●	●							
Coots												
Fulica americana	●	●	●	●	●	○	○	○	○	○	○	○
Amphibians												
Ambystoma						●	●	●	●	●	●	●
Turtles and snakes												
Kinosternon						●	●	●	●	●	●	●
Thamnophis						●	●	●	●	●	●	●
Fish												
Chirostoma spp.	●	●	●	●	●	●	●	●	●	●	●	●
Girardinichthys sp.	●	●	●	●	●	●	●	●	●	●	●	●
Cyprinids	●	●	●	●	●	●	●	●	●	●	●	●
Mammals												
Odocoileus virginianus	●	●	●	●	●	○	○	○	○	○	○	○
Sylvilagus cunicularius	●	●	●	●	●	●	●	●	●	●	●	●
Canids	●	●	●	●	●	●	●	●	●	●	●	●
Rodents						●	●	●	●	●	●	●
Plants from alluvial soils												
Zea	●									○	●	●
Amaranthus	●										●	●
Cucurbita	●							●	●	○	○	●
Physalis											●	●
Leafy vegetables	○	○					●	●	●	●	●	●

Seasonal and perennial food resources available in the ancient Chalco-Xochimilco lacustrine basin. Closed circles indicate maximum availability; open circles represent minimum availability.

6. Tlapacoya (Basin of Mexico), Ayotla phase (1250–1000 B.C.), clay figurine (ht. = 20.5 cm) wearing sophisticated ball-game paraphernalia, including wrist and ankle bands, waist yoke with a circular ornament (perhaps a concave iron-ore mirror), hip pads, and elaborate tier headdress
Photograph: Victor Lagarde, courtesy of Universidad Nacional Autónoma de México

fits a general trend observable throughout ancient Mesoamerica toward the end of the second millennium B.C. and reflects the development of new types of settlement units and territorial organization (Bray 1978: 94).

As to the size of ancient Formative capitals *(caput,* not *urbs)* in the Basin of Mexico, more information is badly needed. The installation of water mains around Mount Tlapacoya allowed me and my students, on several occasions, to map and estimate the spatial distribution of Ayotla, Manantial, and Tetelpan phase artifacts (Niederberger 1987: 697–704; Gámez Eternod 1993). Salvage operations carried out at Tlapacoya in 1992 by the Instituto Nacional de Antropología e Historia, and directed by Olivia Torres, discovered Manantial phase stone and earthen structures associated with "Pahuacan"-style figurines. Based on these observations, it now seems that my 1987 estimate of 35 hectares for Manantial phase Tlapacoya was too conservative and should probably be doubled to 70 hectares. As to the important site of Coapexco, during the Ayotla phase it is estimated to have been 50 hectares in extent (Tolstoy and Fish 1973). All these data on site size and complexity indicate the existence of a growing hierarchization among communities and villages from 1250 B.C. onward (Niederberger 1987: 728–729, figs. 600–601).

Archaeological Information from Figurines

Although ancient Formative public architecture remains have been destroyed, a coherent set of evidence indicates such features were present at Tlapacoya and Tlatilco. Specific groups of figurines and iconographic elements show that these major sites were the settings of elaborate public ceremonies. These ceremonies may have included the Mesoamerican ritual ball game, as suggested particularly by the Tlapacoya evidence. At that site I found, in Ayotla and early Manantial strata, a large number of unusually dressed figurines, already known to occur in great numbers there (Coe 1965; Bradley and Joralemon 1993). Many of them wear sophisticated ball-game paraphernalia, including wrist and ankle bands, heavy protective belts or waist yokes, often adorned with what appears to be a concave iron-ore mirror, hip pads, and impressive multitier headdresses (fig. 6). Other, more enigmatic figures also portray extremely elaborate attire—with no apparent relationship to the ball game—that may have signaled specific political/religious events (Niederberger 1987: 439, fig. 288).

Ayotla levels are characterized by Pilli- and Isla-type figurines described at length in earlier works (Niederberger 1987: 417–444). They correspond to the ancient C9 group (Covarrubias 1957, fig. 8) figurine category long utilized by archaeologists when it was believed that Vaillant's Zacatenco C1-C2 type figurines were anterior to them. The sequence must now be

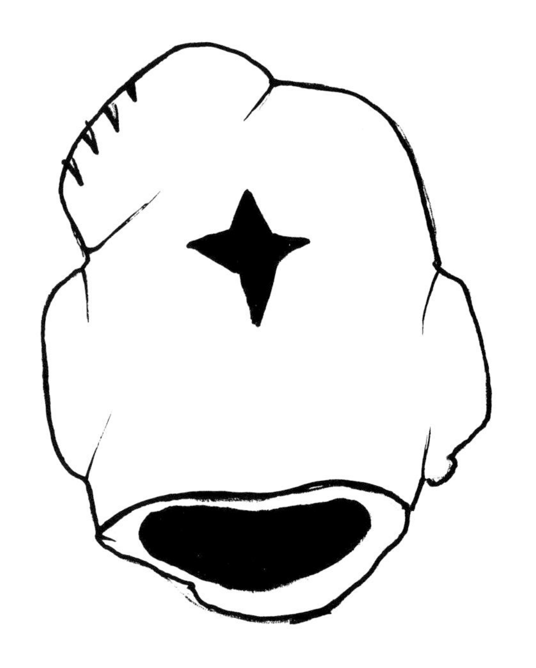

a

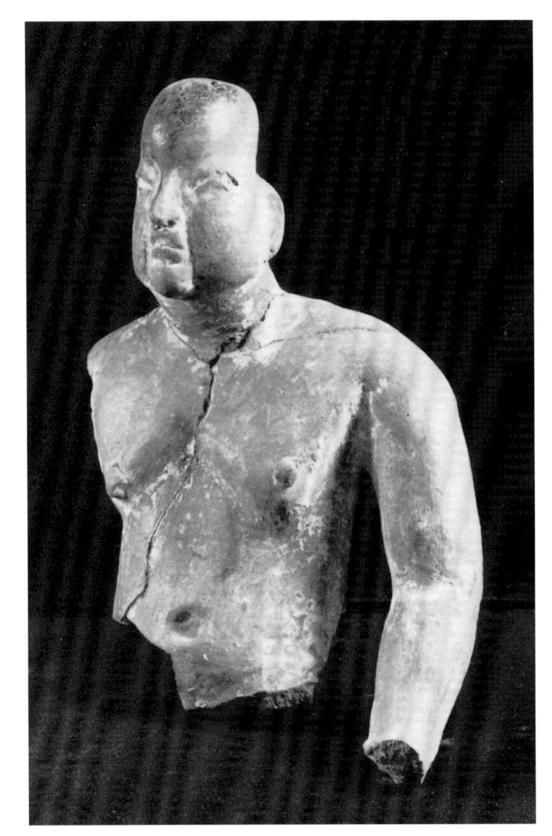

b

c

7. Tlapacoya-Zohapilco site (Basin of Mexico), Ayotla phase (1250–1000 B.C.), Pilli-type figurines: (a) hollow, 8 cm high, the back displaying an opening in the shape of a "star" symbol; (b) solid, 18 cm high, depicting intentional cranial deformation; (c) hollow, 7.5 cm high

reversed as Pilli and Isla figurines—having nothing in common with Vaillant's late C type figurine tradition—are much earlier in date (see table 1). The interesting point for our theme is that some large-sized, hollow or solid figurines of the Pilli group, although rendered following the stylistic canons of the type, offered nevertheless singular and individualistic features and could correspond to actual portraits of eminent persons. These representations are sometimes associated with a sophisticated sign, inscribed on the back side of their head, such as the four-elongated-sides lozenge, known as a "star" symbol (fig. 7a). As shown by complete or semicomplete specimens, the figurines are generally male and range in height from 20 to 40 centimeters. The head is totally or partially shaved and displays a high grade of intentional cranial deformation (fig. 7b). We still lack information—through study of osteological remains—to determine whether intentional cranial deformation was a relatively general practice or was the exclusive prerogative of high-status members of the community. Shaved, deformed heads can also be observed on more standardized Pilli figurines, but these smaller figurines more commonly show a large variety of headdresses, including "helmets" and "turbans."

Masked Tlapacoya and Tlatilco figurines can be classified into several categories. Most common are the representations of musicians, dancers, and actors with particular disguises, which strongly evoke the existence of *cofradía*-type associations (civic-religious groups that channel wealth communitywide through ceremonies and fiestas, while also conferring status and prestige) with specific ritual responsibilities, engaged in public performances at given dates, such as observed with historical Amerindian groups (see Flannery 1976: 336; Niederberger 1987: 710–711). More sporadic are sophisticatedly dressed and masked personages that evoke specialized religious agents who temporarily embody a supernatural category of the mythological system. Noteworthy figurines of this category, whose faces are characterized by large quadrangular or round eyes as well as a central pointed tooth with lateral curving fangs, associated in Tlatilco with a U-bracket symbol, seem to be related to a pristine expression of a rain icon (see Reyna Robles n.d.: 304; Niederberger 1987: 435, 712; Taube 1995: 98).

The Iconography and Information of Pottery Vessels and Stamps

The regional centers of Tlapacoya and Tlatilco may also have become focal points for information storage, including the production, reception, and redistribution of elaborate graphic symbols and messages. The evidence suggests that Tlapacoya and Tlatilco, as well as Las Bocas in the highlands, manipulated one of the most complex sets of iconographic symbols of ancient Mesoamerica (see Lesure, this volume).

Geologic and pedological studies of the composition of Tlapacoya clays and deposits from surrounding zones (Reyes Cortés 1986; Limbrey 1986), together with petrographic and mineralogical analyses of randomly selected pan-Mesoamerican, Olmec-style sherds in Tlapacoya (see analysis reported in Niederberger 1976: 112–142), indicate that ceramic vessels with masterfully executed mythological hybrid creatures, diamond-shaped or star symbols, hand-paw-wing motifs, four-petaled flowers, crossed bands, cleft heads, fangs, four-dots-and-bar motifs, and X, L, or U symbols were made from local or regional clays and manufactured by local craftspersons, experts not only in the ceramic arts but also in a complex, hermeneutic knowledge (fig. 8a). On the other hand, clear evidence of imported clays or vessels from extraregional or distant sources, such as Oaxaca, the Panuco region, and perhaps Morelos, come from recent analyses of Tlapacoya's Atoyac Fine Grey, Xochilepec White, and Tlapizahua White ceramic groups.

Atoyac Fine Grey (Niederberger 1976: 129–130) is characterized by the presence of metamorphic elements absent in the Basin of Mexico geology. Comparative petrographic and mineralogical analysis, carried out by Wayne Lambert (see appendix A in Niederberger 1976), of Atoyac Fine Grey sherds from Tlapacoya and sherds of Delfina Fine Grey from the San José phase of Oaxaca, kindly provided by Kent Flannery, have brought out the ample similarities between the two groups and permitted the verification of the Oaxacan origin of Tlapacoya's Atoyac Fine Grey vessels or components, already suspected by Muriel Porter (1967: 29) (see also Flannery and Marcus 1994: 259–268). As to Xochiltepec White (Niederberger 1976: 128–129), made of a white amorphous fine paste with dominant kaolinite, the raw clay of these vessels could have been acquired

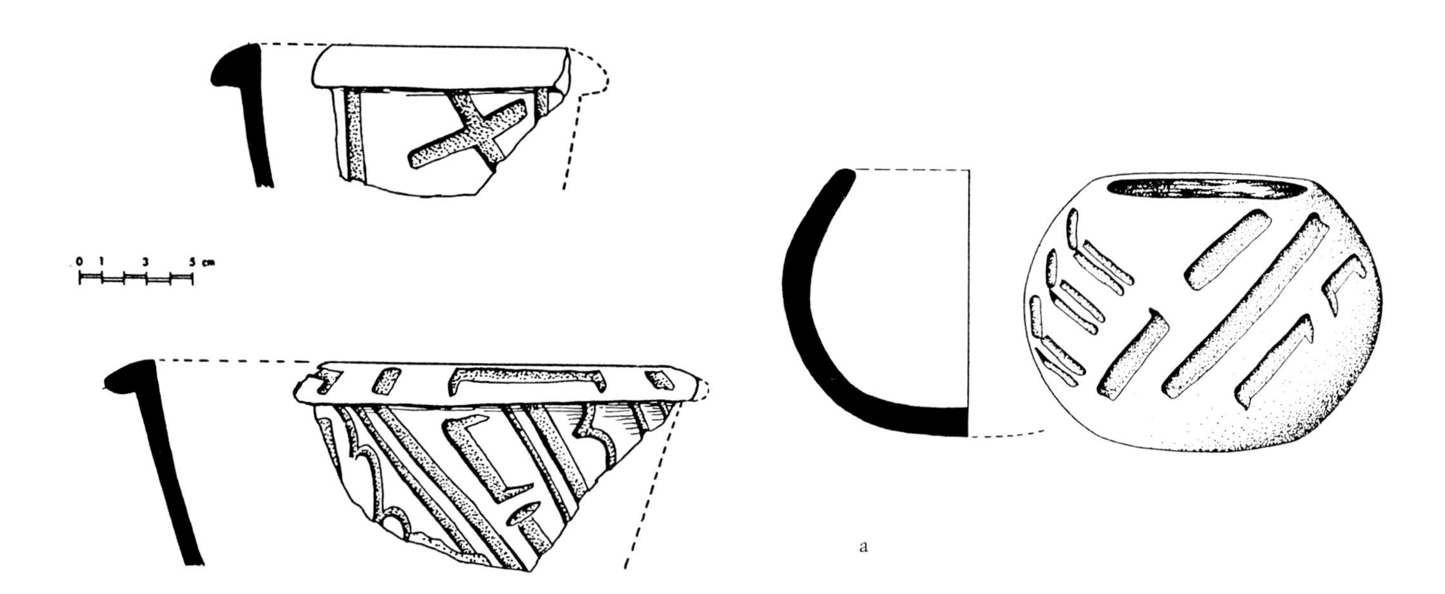

8. Clay vessels with iconography at Tlapacoya, Basin of Mexico, Ayotla phase (1250–1000 B.C.): (a) Tlapacoya-Zohapilco, black-slipped burnished ceramics with carved motifs (Niederberger 1976); (b) Tlapacoya
Courtesy of Museo Nacional de Antropología, Mexico City

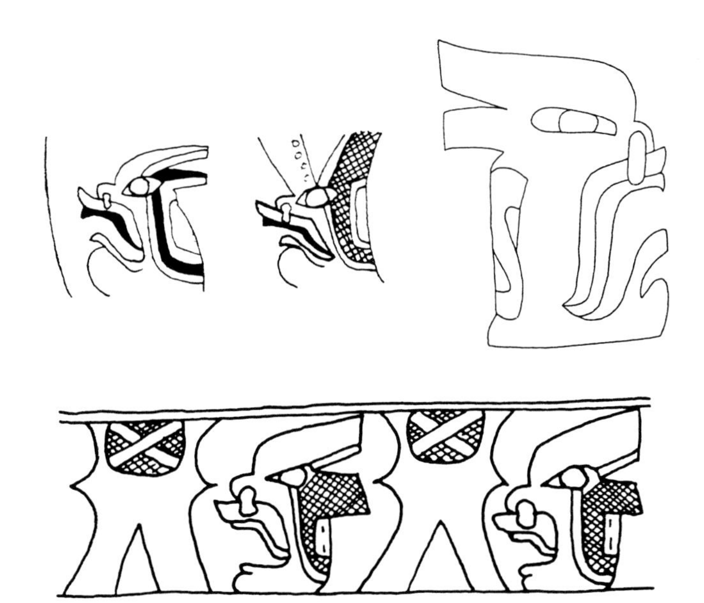

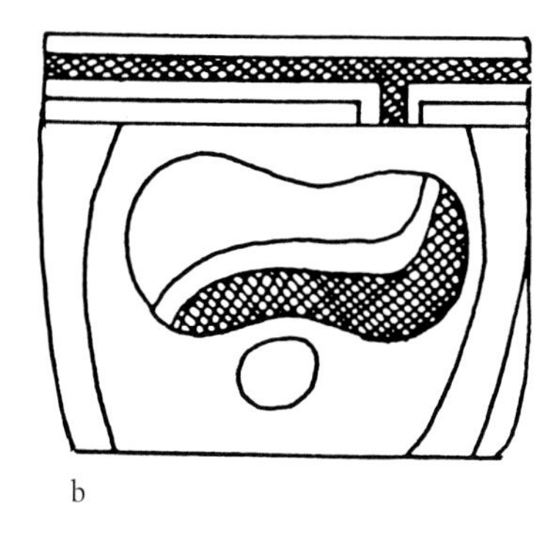

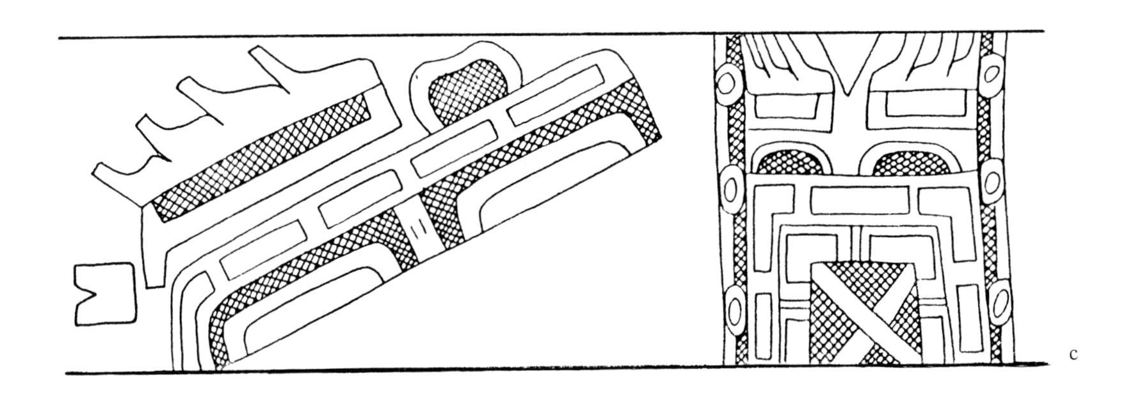

9. Clay vessels with complex iconography at Tlapacoya, Basin of Mexico (see Joralemon [1971] and Niederberger [1987])

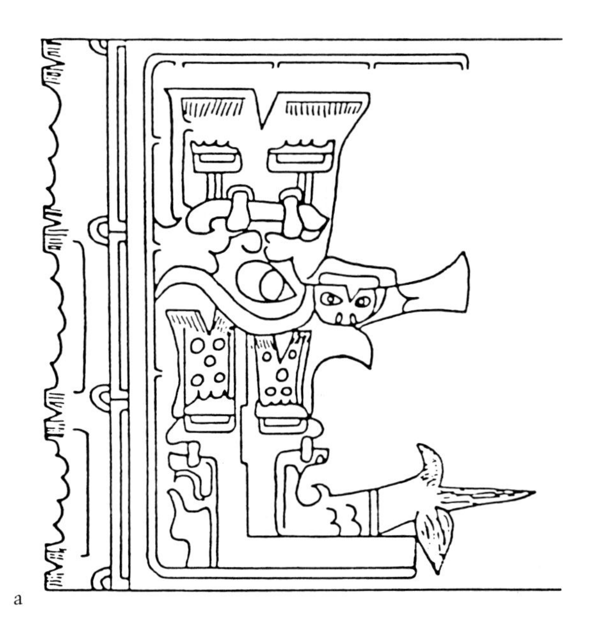

a

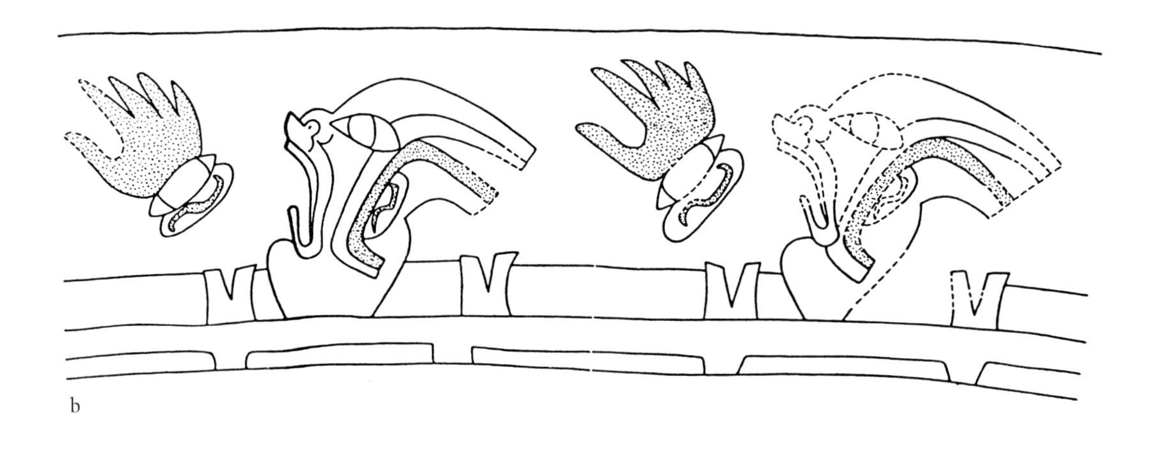

b

10. Clay vessels with complex iconography at Tlapacoya, Basin of Mexico: (a) see Joralemon 1971 and Niederberger 1987; (b) see Parsons 1980

from the area of Chalcatzingo (Morelos) where kaolinite sources have been reported by David Grove (1987: 383–385). Finally, Tlapizahua White (Niederberger 1976: 141–142), with fine rosy paste and very fine (0.1 to 0.3 millimeter) inclusions of a metamorphic rock derived from gneiss, represents a small Tlapacoya sample (225 sherds) identical to the important Aguilar Red ceramic group of the Panuco region (MacNeish 1954) that I had the opportunity to study at the New York Museum of Natural History, thanks to the graciousness of Gordon Ekholm. To the same group pertains Golfo Grey (18 sherds in the Tlapacoya-Zohapilco collection) but, in this case, Golfo Grey vessels were fired in a reducing atmosphere, thereby causing the gray color of the paste and vessel surface. In short, based on analyses of ceramic pastes, it is difficult to detect any direct or indirect influence from San Lorenzo within the Tlapacoya assemblage, as a long-lasting tradition postulates.

As to ceramic designs and iconography, I can only briefly consider a few examples of the complex repertory of symbols found at Tlapacoya. These symbols may have constituted a sort of metalanguage related to cosmological and religious beliefs and, in some cases, probably associated with political power. Tlapacoya offers an impressive number of a particular pan-Mesoamerican Olmec-horizon theme: the head seen in profile, and sometimes in frontal view, with an open mouth (a metaphor for cave and infraworld entrance) of a hybrid being with anthropomorphic features (figs. 8b, 9a,c). Even more striking is the different set of symbolic attributes sometimes associated with these representations. A developed design of a Tlapacoya vessel (see Parsons 1980) with this cleft-headed image seems to constitute an extraordinary evocation of a sacred political force. It represents, in my view, a clear abridged statement of power and leadership, with the profile of this mighty hybrid creature associated with three significant symbols: the constantly informed ears and eyes and the commanding hand (fig. 10b).

Another striking case of the permanent recording on fired clay of a hermeneutic knowledge possessed by specialized groups within the regional capital is the highly sophisticated codified information registered on a Tlapacoya vessel in the fluid rendering typical of Manantial phase vessels (Joralemon 1971: 50, fig. 146; Niederberger 1987: 552). It also shows several faces, in frontal and profile positions, intricately superposed and associated with vegetation, cleft, and glyphlike five-dots motifs (fig. 10a). Men holding a torch are represented on Tortuga Polished type vessels. One of the most ancient representations of the Mesoamerican death symbol with a fantastic hybrid creature, a man-fish-amphibian-feline with a closed eyelid crossed with a vertical band, can be observed on the flat interior base of an Ayotla phase plate (fig. 9d) (Joralemon 1976: 34; Niederberger 1987: 513). This early theme (Nicholson 1976: 164–165) also occurs on one of the head profiles of the Las Limas statuette (Joralemon 1976: 32–33) and on a remarkable clay vessel from the Chalcatzingo area (Grove 1987; Grove, this volume), demonstrating again one of the main functions of the regional capital to produce, record, and transmit complex sacred messages.

At Tlatilco, glyphlike symbols, isolated in

a

c

b

11. Tlatilco (Basin of Mexico): (a) clay stamp (Kelley 1966); (b) metallic gray-slipped bottle (ht. = 22.5 cm) with raptorial bird clawprint motif; (c) black-slipped vessel (ht. = 11.5 cm) with crossed-band motifs in a cartouche
(b) and (c) Courtesy of Museo Nacional de Antropología, Mexico City

a sort of cartouche, such as a hybrid being profile, the four-petaled flower, and a cleft head with dots, have also been observed on a clay stamp. They have been interpreted by David Kelley (1966) as ideograms and a pristine form of glyphic writing (fig. 11a). I have analyzed elsewhere why they could perhaps be defined as "mythograms," that is, graphic symbols having an accurate meaning deprived of a systematic phonetic counterpart (Niederberger 1987: 715–717; 1996a: 90) but also considered as antecedents to writing systems (Leroi-Gourhan 1964). But the question remains open. It must be noted that several graphic symbols on Tlapacoya clay vessels are associated with one, five, seven, or nine dots. A particular Pilli White-type vessel (fig. 9b), probably from early Manantial phase archaeological deposits (Joralemon 1971: 26, fig. 46; Niederberger 1987: 551), is engraved with a "motion" symbol motif and a "number one" dot. The possibility exists that it could represent a true ideogram, with phonetic correspondence, and have been part of a ritual calendar. Within a general perspective, one of the fundamental roles of a regional capital is to organize time. This would not be an isolated case: in other archaeological sites of the early first millennium B.C., independent motifs, such as the glyphs of Oaxaca's Monument 3 of the Rosario phase (700–500 B.C.), which could correspond to a calendar glyph "1 Earthquake" (Flannery and Marcus 1983: 53–54), or the reptilian-avian head associated with six dots of the Oxtotitlan grotto, in Guerrero (Grove 1970: 18–20), have been interpreted as number glyphs.

Finally, it is essential to observe that among the concomitant phenomena observed with the rise of cities, one of the most striking is the almost explosive development of interregional long-distance exchanges. I shall briefly deal with this subject in my final comments.

The Basin of Mexico and Interregional Exchange Systems

General data from Tlapacoya, as well as the study of Tlatilco burials, now placed within an accurate chronological framework, document the existence in the Basin of Mexico of wealthy and clearly ranked societies that manipulated a coherent and complex system of codified graphic symbols some six hundred years before the advent of Zacatenco cultures. The data also show that Tlatilco and Tlapacoya, as regional centers, held a regular and strong control over economic activities and were important, active links within complex regional and interregional exchange networks of goods and ideas. Although the threefold typology proposed by Karl Polanyi (1957) to classify economic exchanges (reciprocal, redistributive, or market-oriented) has been widely adopted by archaeologists, and the redistributive type of exchanges characteristic of chiefdom-level polities is also thought to have been an important component of Ayotla-Manantial exchange systems, Frederic Pryor (1977) and Kenneth Hirth (1984a: 288–290) have stressed that societies can seldom be classified satisfactorily by a single form of economic transaction. Different types of exchanges can take place at the same time and side by side within local and regional exchange systems.

In the Basin of Mexico, the disparity between northeastern and southwestern pluvial distribution, the zonal repartition of some important stone resources, the diversity of faunal and plant resources between freshwater or salty lacustrine expanses, as well as the natural specificity of different altitude levels, would have early fostered regional exchanges among communities, with some exchanges of goods and services probably being carried out through barter. In any case, at the Tlapacoya-Zohapilco site, artifacts made of *Pinus* sp. from higher altitudes, as well as Otumba obsidian, are found in cultural remains in lacustrine settings as early as Playa times. The archaeological inventory of nonperishable material, exchanged between 1250 and 700 B.C., also includes nodular and naturally laminated basalt, volcanic tuff used in the manufacture of grinding tools, chalcedony, obsidian, clay, and chunks of *tepetate* or hardpan, used as building components (Niederberger 1987: 678–685).

As to the interregional circulation of utilitarian goods and high-valued luxury items during Formative times, a remarkable increase is apparent throughout Mesoamerica from the end of the second millennium onward (Pires-Ferreira 1976; Flannery et al. 1976; Lee and Navarrete 1978; Hirth 1984b). The Basin of Mexico was significantly active within these organized long-distance networks. Obsidian from the Basin of Mexico had been circulating in Middle America for millennia. Three major sources of obsidian—Pachuca (Cerro de las

Navajas), Paredón, and Otumba (Barranca de los Estetes)—are located in the northeastern zone of the basin (García Bárcena 1972; Charlton et al. 1978; Charlton 1984). Tlapacoya, strategically located on the obsidian route from the northeastern quarries of the basin toward Morelos and *tierra caliente* (warm regions) as well as Coapexco, dominating the Amecameca pass (Tolstoy and Fish 1975; Tolstoy et al. 1977), may have developed some organizational features to control part of the exchange system.

Through neutron activation analysis of Formative obsidian samples, the presence of Basin of Mexico obsidian has been detected in the archaeological deposits of numerous regions (compare Pires-Ferreira 1978a), such as Puebla (Las Bocas, Acatepec, Moyotzingo), Morelos (San Pablo, Cerro Chacaltepec), Oaxaca (Tierras Largas, San José Mogote), as well as Veracruz (San Lorenzo) (Cobean et al. 1971) and Chiapas (La Libertad) (Clark and Lee 1984: 260). As far as the Basin of Mexico's obsidian is concerned, gray, dark-banded Otumba obsidian is nearly the only source represented at those sites between 1200 and 700 B.C. Green obsidian from Pachuca appears in small amounts at the end of this period (Pires-Ferreira 1978a).

In exchange for obsidian, centripetal movements of exotic goods toward the basin included a wide range of commodities from neighboring or distant regions. They included iron-ore mirrors and a type of gray pottery with metallic shine from Oaxaca; kaolin; pottery from the Panuco region; flint and travertine onyx from Puebla or Guerrero; pigments; rock crystal; mica; bitumen from the Gulf Coast; schist, blue-green jadeite, serpentine, and other greenstones, probably from Guerrero (see Mastache 1988; Niederberger n.d.); cotton (*Gossypium* sp.) from *tierra caliente,* found in Formative burials during salvage operations at Coyoacan (L. González Quintero, personal communication), as well as sea turtle and numerous marine shells, such as the pearl oyster *(Pinctada mazatlanica)* from the Pacific Coast, which was probably circulating through Oaxaca or Guerrero's Teopantecuanitlan gateway site, where a pearl oyster workshop has been excavated in the domestic residential group of Lomeríos (Niederberger 1996b: 102). The presence at Tlatilco of toucan and parrot effigy vessels may relate to a custom of importing exotic birds as domestic animals or to exploit their plumage. Thus Basin of Mexico data document dynamic relationships with multiple economic partners throughout ancient Mesoamerican territory.

Conclusions

Within Mesoamerican Formative exchange networks, it is of interest to note that the Ayotla and Manantial phase communities did not develop privileged links with the Gulf Coast, and even less a passive linear route of reception from this region, as postulated by some still vivacious unicentrist and diffusionist currents of interpretation. In fact, the Basin of Mexico's early interregional exchange system included multidirectional contacts. Data show a particularly well defined and regular relationship with Oaxaca and the Pacific Coast.

The position I have held (Niederberger 1974b; 1976: 265–266; 1987: 678–692, 750–751) concerning ancient Formative interregional exchanges—and implying the existence of multiregional contacts and the active participation of multiple partners—is no longer an isolated stand. Similar views have been formulated more recently. One of the most elegantly and clearly expressed analyses comes from a study by Arthur Demarest (1989: 337) that proposes a "lattice-like model of interregional interaction" for ancient Mesoamerica. Since the early 1970s, I have also postulated that these multiple partners, with ranked societies and efficient agrarian economies, were situated at the same level of technoeconomic and sociopolitical complexity, a conviction that is gaining ground in today's Formative research with the growing use in Mesoamerican Formative studies of the conceptual tool of "peer polities," refined by Colin Renfrew (1986), pioneer architect of nondiffusionist approaches in Old World archaeology.

Related to this issue, it must be noted that, since the first clearly formulated refutation (Flannery 1968) of the old belief concerning the imperialism of Gulf Coast polities and their domination of highlands and other communities, whether by invasions, colonization, or proselytizing expeditions, most archaeologists have rallied to the idea that interregional interactions were still based on the indirect impact, through more subtle processes, of culturally complex Gulf Coast communities upon less advanced ethnic groups. This dichotomous view between more complex/less advanced groups or, in other words, between Promethean versus culturally static, contemporaneous societies, still persists in the Formative literature. But new trends are now clearly emerging. In this context, Gulf Coast communities, even though their achievements are perfectly acknowledged, are no longer considered as the center and exclusive force of Formative dynamism and changes (Hammond 1991; Flannery and Marcus 1994).

Expressed in one way or another, the "peer polities" postulate is indeed a central notion in the study of already complex agrarian societies for building an alternative scheme to diffusionist models and ungrounded interpretations, which always tend to explain cultural changes or similarities by dominance or direct or indirect influences from a single zone (Renfrew and Bahn 1996: 364). As to the cultural similarities observed in ancient Formative communities, I have analyzed at length in previous works how, as already stressed long ago by Marcel Mauss (1924) in his "Essai sur le Don," all structured systems of trade and exchange have a noneconomic dimension and are combined with a parallel system of regular exchange of messages and information. This parallel network explains, in my view, the simultaneous development of a common set of specific visual symbols, mythological systems, and semantic fields gradually built up and shared by early Mesoamerican ranked societies.

BIBLIOGRAPHY

Alvarez, Ticul
1976 Restos óseos de las excavaciones de Tlatilco, Estado de México. *Apuntes para la arqueología. Cuadernos de Trabajo* 15. Mexico City.

Armillas, Pedro
1971 Gardens on Swamps. *Science* 174: 653–661.

Bradley, Douglas E., and Peter D. Joralemon
1993 *The Iconography of Power and Fertility in Preclassic Mesoamerica.* Notre Dame, Ind.

Bray, Warwick
1979 From Village to City in Mesoamerica. In *The Origins of Civilization,* ed. Peter Moorey, 78–108. London.

Charlton, Thomas H.
1984 Production and Exchange: Variables in the Evolution of a Civilization. In *Trade and Exchange in Early Mesoamerica*, ed. Kenneth Hirth, 17–42. Albuquerque, N.M.

Charlton, Thomas H., David C. Grove, and Philip K. Hopke
1976 The Paredón, Mexico, Obsidian Source and Early Formative Exchange. *Science* 201: 807–809.

Clark, John E., and Thomas A. Lee
1984 Formative Obsidian Exchange and the Emergence of Public Economies in Chiapas, Mexico. In *Trade and Exchange in Early Mesoamerica,* ed. Kenneth Hirth, 235–274. Albuquerque, N.M.

Cobean, Robert H., Michael D. Coe, Edward A. Perry, Jr., Karl K. Turekian, and Dinkar P. Kharkar
1971 Obsidian Trade at San Lorenzo Tenochtitlán. *Science* 174: 666–671.

Coe, Michael D.
1965 *The Jaguar's Children: Pre-Classic Central Mexico.* New York.

Covarrubias, Miguel
1950 Tlatilco: El arte y la cultura preclásica del Valle de México. *Cuadernos Americanos* 11: 149–162.

1957 *Indian Art of Mexico and Central America.* New York.

Demarest, Arthur A.
1989 The Olmec and the Rise of Civilization in Eastern Mesoamerica. In *Regional Perspectives on the Olmec,* ed. Robert Sharer and David Grove, 304–344. Cambridge.

Faulhaber, Johanna
1965 La población de Tlatilco caracterizada por sus entierros. In *Homenaje a Juan Comas,* 2: 83–121. Mexico City.

Flannery, Kent V.
1968 The Olmec and the Valley of Oaxaca: A Model for Inter-Regional Interaction in Formative Times. In *Dumbarton Oaks Conference on the Olmec,* ed. Elizabeth Benson, 79–110. Washington.

1976 (Editor) *The Early Mesoamerican Village.* New York.

Flannery, Kent V., and Joyce Marcus
1983 (Editors) *The Cloud People.* New York.

1994 *Early Formative Pottery in the Valley of Oaxaca.* Memoirs of the Museum of Anthropology 27. University of Michigan, Ann Arbor.

Gámez Eternod, Lorena
1993 Crecimiento del sitio de Tlapacoya, Estado de México, durante el horizonte formativo. In *A propósito del formativo,* ed. María Teresa Castillo Mangas, 11–32. Mexico City.

García Bárcena, Joaquim
1972 Obsidian Hydration Dating in Central Mexico: Preliminary Results. *Atti del XL Congresso Internazionale degli Americanisti.* Rome.

García Moll, Roberto, Daniel Juárez Cossío, Carmen Pijoan Aguade, María Elena Salas Cuesta, and Marciela Salas Cuesta
1991 *San Luis Tlatilco, México. Catálogo de entierros de San Luis Tlatilco, México: Temporada IV.* Mexico City.

Griffin, Gillett G.
1979 Olmec Forms and Materials Found in Central Guerrero. In *The Olmec and Their Neighbors,* ed. Elizabeth Benson, 209–222. Washington.

Grove, David C.
1970 *The Olmec Paintings of Oxtotitlan, Guerrero, Mexico.* Washington.

1987 "Torches," "Knuckle Dusters," and the Legitimization of Formative Period Rulerships. *Mexicon* 9: 60–65.

1989 Olmec: What's in a Name? In *Regional Perspectives on the Olmec,* ed. Robert Sharer and David Grove, 8–14. Cambridge.

Hammond, Norman
1991 Cultura Hermana: Reappraising the Olmec. *Quarterly Review of Archaeology* 9: 1–4.

Heizer, Robert
1958 Review: *Indian Art of Mexico and Central America* by Miguel Covarrubias. *American Antiquity* 24(2): 201–203.

Hirth, Kenneth
1984a The Analysis of Prehistoric Economic Systems: A Look to the Future. In *Trade and Exchange in Early Mesoamerica,* ed.

Kenneth Hirth, 281–302. Albuquerque, N.M.

1984b (Editor) *Trade and Exchange in Early Mesoamerica.* Albuquerque, N.M.

Jiménez Moreno, Wigberto
1959 Síntesis de la historia pre-tolteca de Mesoamérica. In *Esplendor del México antiguo,* 1019–1096. Mexico City.

Joralemon, Peter D.
1971 *A Study of Olmec Iconography.* Washington.

1976 The Olmec Dragon: A Study in Pre-Columbian Iconography. In *Origins of Religious Art and Iconography in Preclassic Mesoamerica,* ed. Henry Nicholson, 27–71. Los Angeles.

Kelley, David H.
1966 A Cylinder Seal from Tlatilco. *American Antiquity* 31: 744–746.

Lee, Thomas A., and Carlos Navarrete
1976 (Editors) *Mesoamerican Communication Routes and Cultural Contacts.* Papers of the New World Archaeological Foundation 40. Provo, Utah.

Leroi-Gourhan, André
1964 *Le geste et la parole.* Paris.

Limbrey, Susan
1984 Analysis de suelos y sedimentos. In *Tlapacoya: 35000 años de historia del lago de Chalco,* ed. José Luis Lorenzo and Lorena Mirambell, 67–75. Mexico City.

Lorenzo, José Luis
1965 *Tlatilco: Los artefactos,* vol. 3. Mexico City.

MacNeish, Robert S.
1954 An Early Archaeological Site near Panuco, Veracruz. *Transactions of the American Philosophical Society* 4(5).

Manzanilla, Linda
1988 La arqueología sobre los períodos preclásico superior y clásico en la Cuenca de México. In *La antropología en México,* ed. Carmen García Mora, 14: 81–104. Mexico City.

Mastache, Alba Guadalupe
1988 El trabajo de lapidaria en el estado de Guerrero: Una artesanía actual inspirada en formas prehispánicas. *Arqueología* 2: 197–216. Mexico City.

Mauss, Marcel
1924 Essai sur le Don. Forme et raison de l'échange dans les sociétés archaïques. *L'Année Sociologique*, 2d series, 1. Paris.

Nichols, Deborah
1982 A Middle Formative Irrigation System near Santa Clara Coatitlán in the Basin of Mexico. *American Antiquity* 47: 133–144.

Nicholson, Henry B.
1976 Preclassic Mesoamerican Iconography from the Perspective of the Postclassic Problems in Interpretational Analysis. In *Origins of Religious Art and Iconography in Preclassic Mesoamerica,* ed. Henry B. Nicholson, 159–175. Los Angeles.

Niederberger, Christine
1970 Excavations at Tlapacoya, Mexico. Cultural Remains II. Paper presented at the 35th Annual Meeting of the Society for American Archaeology.

1974a Inicios de la vida sedentaria en América Media. In *Historia de México* 1: 39–120. Barcelona.

1974b Zohapilco. Manuscript, Escuela Nacional de Antropología e Historia, Mexico City.

1976 *Zohapilco: Cinco milenios de ocupación humana en un sitio lacustre de la Cuenca de México.* Mexico City.

1979 Early Sedentary Economy in the Basin of Mexico. *Science* 203: 131–142.

1987 *Paléopaysages et archéologie pré-urbaine du Bassin de Mexico,* 2 vols. Mexico City.

1996a The Basin of Mexico: A Multimillennial Development toward Cultural Complexity. In *Olmec Art of Ancient Mexico,* ed. Elizabeth Benson and Beatriz de la Fuente, 83–93 [exh. cat., National Gallery of Art]. Washington.

1996b Olmec Horizon Guerrero. In *Olmec Art of Ancient Mexico,* ed. Elizabeth Benson and Beatriz de la Fuente, 95–103 [exh. cat., National Gallery of Art]. Washington.

n.d. Nacar, "jade" y cinabrio: Guerrero y las redes de intercambio en la Mesoamérica antigua (1000–600 A.C.). In *Colección Guerrero. Volumen arqueología,* ed. Christine Niederberger. Guerrero.

Parsons, Jeffrey R.
1971 *Pre-Hispanic Settlement in the Texcoco Region, Mexico.* Memoirs of the Museum of Anthropology 43. University of Michigan, Ann Arbor.

Parsons, Jeffrey R., Elizabeth Brumfiel, Mary Hrones Parsons, and David J. Wilson
1982 *Prehispanic Settlement Patterns in the Southern Valley of Mexico: The Chalco-Xochimilco Region.* Memoirs of the Museum of Anthropology 14. University of Michigan, Ann Arbor.

Parsons, Lee A.
1980 *Pre-Columbian Art. The Saint Louis Museum.* New York.

Piña Chan, Román
1958 *Tlatilco.* Mexico City.

1971 Preclassic or Formative Pottery and Minor Art of the Valley of Mexico. In *Archaeol-*

ogy of Northern Mesoamerica, ed. Gordon Ekholm and Ignacio Bernal, 157–178. Handbook of Middle American Indians, vol. 10. Austin.

Pires-Ferreira, Jane
1976 Shell and Iron-Ore Mirror Exchange in Formative Mesoamerica, with Comments on Other Commodities. In *The Early Mesoamerican Village,* ed. Kent Flannery, 311–328. New York.

1978a Obsidian Exchange Networks: Inferences and Speculations on the Development of Social Organization in Formative Mesoamerica. In *Cultural Continuity in Mesoamerica,* ed. David Browman, 49–78. The Hague.

1978b Shell Exchange Networks in Formative Mesoamerica. In *Cultural Continuity in Mesoamerica,* ed. David Browman, 79–100. The Hague.

Polanyi, Karl
1957 The Economy as Instituted Process. In *Trade and Market in the Early Empires,* ed. Karl Polanyi, Conrad Arensberg, Harry Pearson, 243–269. Glencoe, Ill.

Porter, Muriel
1953 *Tlatilco and the Preclassic Cultures of the New World.* New York.

1967 *Tlapacoya Pottery in the Museum Collection.* Heye Foundation, Museum of the American Indian, New York.

n.d. Unpublished field notes from Tlatilco, manuscript.

Pryor, Frederic
1977 *The Origins of the Economy.* New York.

Renfrew, Colin
1986 Introduction: Peer Polity Interaction and Socio-political Change. In *Peer Polity Interaction and Socio-political Change,* ed. Colin Renfrew and John Cherry, 1–18. Cambridge.

Renfrew, Colin, and Paul Bahn
1996 *Archaeology: Theories, Methods, and Practice.* 2d ed. London.

Reyes Cortés, Manuel
1984 Geología. In *Tlapacoya: 35000 años de historia del lago de Chalco,* ed. José Luis Lorenzo and Lorena Mirambell, 57–65. Mexico City.

Reyna Robles, Rosa María
1970 Las figurillas preclásicas. Master's thesis, Instituto Nacional de Antropología e Historia, Mexico City.

Romano, Arturo
1967 Tlatilco. *Boletín del Instituto Nacional de Antropología e Historia* 30: 38–42. Mexico City.

Tainter, Joseph A.
1978 Mortuary Practices and the Study of Prehistoric Social Systems. In *Advances in Archaeological Method and Theory,* ed. Michael Schiffer, 105–141. New York.

Taube, Karl
1996 The Rainmakers: The Olmec and Their Contributions to Mesoamerican Belief and Ritual. In *The Olmec World,* 83–104 [exh. cat., The Art Museum]. Princeton.

Tolstoy, Paul
1977 Western Mesoamerica before A.D. 900. In *Chronologies in New World Archaeology,* ed. Robert Taylor and Clement Meighan, 214–329. New York.

Tolstoy, Paul, and Susan Fish
1975 Surface Evidence for Community Size at Coapexco, Mexico. *Journal of Field Archaeology* 2: 98–104.

Tolstoy, Paul, and Louise Paradis
1970 Early and Middle Preclassic Culture in the Basin of Mexico. *Science* 167: 344–351.

Tolstoy, Paul, Susan Fish, Martin Boksenbaum, Kathryn Vaughn, and C. Earle Smith
1977 Early Sedentary Communities of the Basin of Mexico. *Journal of Field Archaeology* 4: 91–106.

Vaillant, George C.
1930 *Excavations at Zacatenco.* Anthropological Papers of the American Museum of Natural History 32(1). New York.

1931 *Excavations at Ticomán.* Anthropological Papers of the American Museum of Natural History 32(2). New York.

1935 *Excavations at El Arbolillo.* Anthropological Papers of the American Museum of Natural History 35(2). New York.

Winter, Marcus
1984 Exchange in Formative Highland Oaxaca. In *Trade and Exchange in Early Mesoamerica,* ed. Kenneth Hirth, 179–214. Albuquerque, N.M.

RICHARD G. LESURE
University of California, Los Angeles

Animal Imagery, Cultural Unities, and Ideologies of Inequality in Early Formative Mesoamerica

What is the source of the ancient cultural unity of Mesoamerica? While most cultural continuities across this region can be traced to a rich history of innovation and interaction in the Formative, Classic, and Postclassic epochs, there have been persistent suggestions that it is possible to find manifestations of a more ancient substratum of belief that was common to Mesoamerican groups of the preceramic era (Furst 1995; Lathrap 1974; Marcus et al. 1983). There is little material evidence from the Archaic period, or even the initial Early Formative, that can be used to evaluate these ideas. Most attempts to reconstruct an ancient cultural legacy focus on Olmec art of the latter part of the Early Formative, especially the stylized motifs that appear on pottery across much of Mesoamerica. A persuasive body of interpretation identifies these motifs as abstract representations of mythological creatures combining traits of different animals from the natural world (Joralemon 1976; Marcus 1989; Pohorilenko 1977). In many areas these motifs are the earliest known examples of iconographic representations in which designs illustrate subjects. The striking thing about these late Early Formative motifs is that similar or even identical motifs appear in many different regions.

Researchers have explained these similarities in a variety of ways. According to one longstanding interpretive trend, the Olmec iconographic system arose on the Gulf Coast, and its use spread to other areas during the Early Formative period (for example, Clark 1990; Diehl and Coe 1995; Tolstoy 1989). An alternative interpretation holds that many regions contributed to late Early Formative iconographies, and the Gulf Coast was not the primary locus of innovation (Grove 1989; Flannery and Marcus 1994; Niederberger 1987). In this view, similarities in motifs derive either from a sharing of innovations among different regions during the Early Formative period or from the development of new ways of expressing elements of a much older substratum of belief (common to all Mesoamerican peoples) that was already in place by the Early Formative period. In this alternative view, it is not appropriate to term the shared iconography "Olmec" because it did not derive from the Gulf Coast.

The debate over the source of the shared motifs is of far more than antiquarian interest. At issue are basic understandings of the social processes that led to the emergence of complex societies in Mesoamerica. In addition, tracing the sources of Olmec iconography is an important step toward sorting out a complicated set of transformations in belief systems that took place in the Early Formative period. For instance, what cosmological changes accompanied the shift from hunter-gatherer to sedentary lifestyle? How did ideologies of social inequality arise? What was the history of beliefs that came to justify and naturalize social hierarchies of the late Early Formative and Middle Formative periods?

I do not pretend to be able to resolve all these long-standing debates in this short essay.

Fish Effigy Vessel,
Early Formative period,
blackware ceramic
Museo Nacional de Antropología,
Mexico City

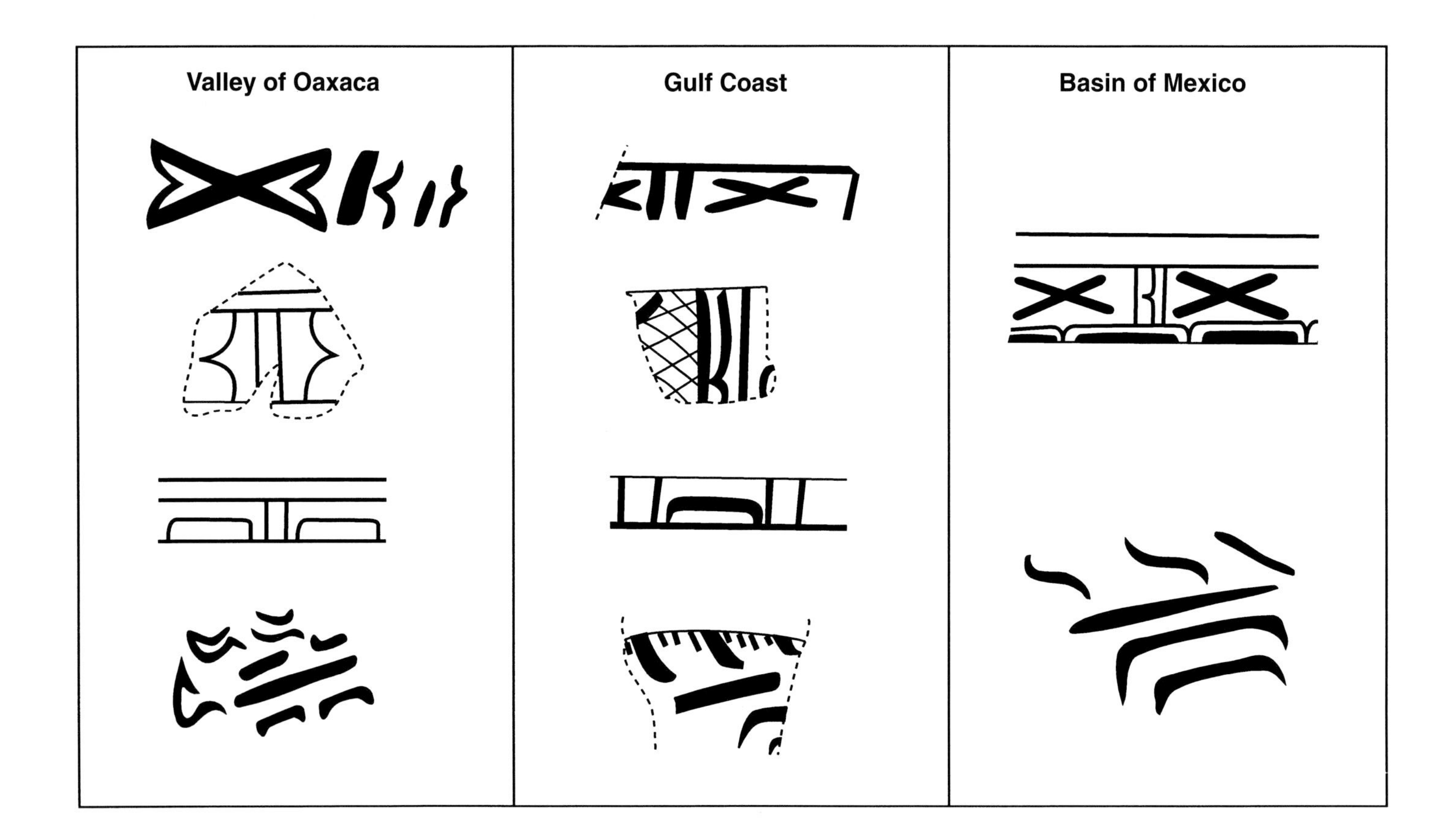

1. Comparison of motifs on pottery vessels from three different areas of Mesoamerica indicates strong similarities of elements and motifs. Redrawn (modified, not to scale) after: for Oaxaca, Flannery and Marcus (1994: figs. 12.4, 12.75) and Whalen (1981: fig. 36); for Gulf Coast, Coe and Diehl (1980: figs. 139, 141, 142); for Basin of Mexico, Niederberger (1987: figs. 398, 471)

Instead, my goal is to present new data from the Soconusco region of Chiapas, Mexico, suggesting that Olmec motifs were *not* part of an ancient heritage common to all Mesoamerican peoples. The intriguing aspect of the Soconusco case is that the appearance of stylized motifs corresponds with the disappearance of a completely different system of zoomorphic imagery that involved naturalistic representations of animals from the local environment. I argue that the stylized motifs replaced the local system of naturalistic representations and were therefore not part of an Archaic legacy already present in the area from preceramic times. What can this change in representational systems tell us about the content of a shared substratum of belief in Mesoamerica and its transformation or transmutation into an ideational basis for social hierarchy?

The Issues

I will use the expressions "Early Olmec motifs" (or just "Olmec motifs") and "late Early Formative motifs" interchangeably to describe the stylized designs that appeared across Mesoamerica from 1150 to 850 b.c. (dates in uncalibrated radiocarbon years). The logic of my analysis does not require any a priori assumptions about the geographical source of these motifs or the number of cultures that may have contributed to their creation.

The idea that elements of this Early Olmec iconography were part of an ancient cultural heritage shared among many regions is based on the appearance of similar iconographic elements across great geographical distances (fig. 1), the variability in the use of these elements in different areas (Grove 1989, 1993), and the complexity of this system at the time of its first emergence. For this last point, it is not just that the designs themselves are complex but that the mythological subject matter depicted is richly developed. The fact that this iconographic system appears fully formed on late Early Formative ceramics could mean that it developed in a perishable medium and was only later transferred to ceramics. If this were the case, what we observe in the late Early Formative would be not the origin of the system itself but, rather, the origin of the practice of inscribing its elements on durable media such as ceramics and stone. A preceramic origin for the system and the widespread sharing of both the motifs and their mythological subject matter would seem reasonable in this light.

Recent findings in the Soconusco challenge the notion that the later motifs were already part of a cultural heritage this area shared with the rest of Mesoamerica. There a different system of zoomorphic representations preceded the appearance of the late Early Formative iconography on ceramics. If the inhabitants of the Soconusco developed one system of zoomorphic representations and then abandoned it for another, it would seem more probable that the new system was either a recent innovation or an import rather than something that had always been around even during the development of the first system.

There are two potential problems with this line of argument. The first derives from the observation that two or more representational systems can be present in any one society (see Morphy 1977). Since we are missing the perishable material assemblage from Early Formative Soconusco, it is conceivable that the system of abstract motifs was in use at the same time as the naturalistic effigies, but that it was restricted to wood or other perishable media. At present this seems an unlikely possibility. Naturalistic animal effigies in the early period appear on implements used for a number of different purposes in different social contexts (ceramic vessels of various sorts, figurines, whistles, jade pendants, incense burners, and, in one case, a stone bowl). The evidence suggests a pervasive use of naturalistic imagery in a wide variety of social contexts and the absence of the mythological imagery known from later times in any of these contexts. Of course, as long as we lack perishable items, this issue cannot be definitively resolved one way or the other.

The second problem is more the subject of this essay: even if there was a change from one representational system to another, does a change in representations necessarily imply a change in meaning? We may identify what a representation depicts (its "subject matter" or simply "subject") but still understand little of its meaning, since the subjects of representations often connote more abstract ideas. As Robert Layton (1991: 126) puts it, "the ideas signified by visual motifs themselves stand for other ideas." It is conceivable that a change of representational system and subject matter might occur without any fundamental change in the more abstract messages being conveyed. The Early Formative inhabitants of the Soconusco might have switched representational vehicles without changing the more general meanings they sought to express. According to this scenario, despite the changes in animal imagery in the Soconusco during the Early Formative, key ideas conveyed by the later representational system could still have been part of a much more ancient cultural heritage the Soconusco shared with other areas. I will present a qualified argument against this view, concluding that the observed change in representations does indeed reflect significant discontinuities in both subject matter and more abstract symbolism.

Analyzing Representations

Although design systems can be purely decorative, without any underlying symbolism (Layton 1991: 125–126), such systems do not appear to be typical. Representations usually convey ideas. If we are to make headway in the analysis of these systems, it is important to think in terms of a dimensionality or structure to the ideas once conveyed by artifacts and designs on artifacts. At least three conceptual levels can be distinguished. First, there is the representational system itself, which includes the designs as mental constructs. Second is the subject matter of the representations, what the representations "look like" or illustrate, again to be thought of as a set of concepts rather than entities in the physical world. Third, there is what I will refer to as the symbolism of the images, those abstract ideas to which the subjects refer but which are not explicitly depicted in the designs.

It is important also to bear in mind that artifacts with motifs are more than simply vehicles for investigating ideas. They are also evidence of the entrance of ideas into social life. Objects bearing effigies or motifs were deployed and manipulated by social actors. The subject matter and symbolism of the representations would thus have been a potential resource for people negotiating social relationships.

From this theoretical perspective, shared cultural legacies in Mesoamerica may themselves have been dimensional. For instance, certain basic symbols shared by Early Formative societies might have derived from a shared ancient legacy. At the same time, understandings that selected metaphors for those beliefs, and practices that introduced the metaphors into social interactions, might both have been innovations of the Early Formative period. The contribution of a shared cultural substratum to representations, subjects, symbolism, and modes of social interaction in Early Formative Mesoamerica is thus an empirical question that must be investigated with archaeological data from particular areas.

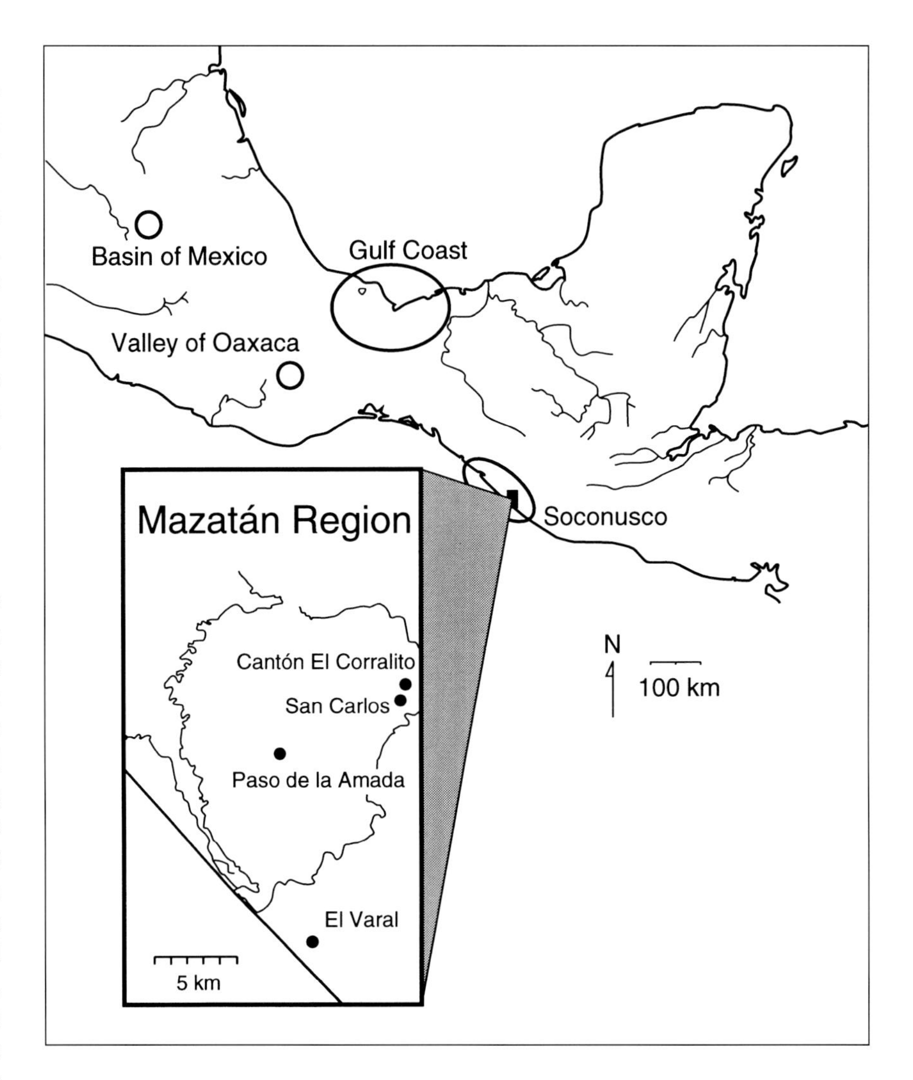

2. Map of Mesoamerica showing regions discussed in the text; inset shows locations of sites in Mazatán area

The Soconusco and the Mazatán Area

The materials analyzed for this study come from recent excavations in the Mazatán area of the Soconusco, a coastal region that runs along the southern coast of Mesoamerica from Mapastepec, Chiapas, southeast to just across the Guatemalan border (fig. 2). The coastal plain between the ocean and the steeply rising Sierra Madre is just 20 kilometers wide but is characterized by a number of different biotic zones that parallel the line of the coast in thin strips. These include estuaries, mangrove swamps, lagoons, and savanna lands (Coe and Flannery 1967: 9–15). A large variety of fish, reptiles, mammals, and birds inhabited this region. This diversity of wildlife seems to have provided the inspiration for the wide variety of zoomorphic depictions, described below, that appeared during the first part of the Early Formative period.

The importance of initial Early Formative (c. 1550–1100 b.c.) developments in the Soconusco has been known since Michael Coe's (1961) work on Ocós phase materials from La Victoria and Gareth Lowe's (1975) discovery of earlier, Barra phase assemblages in the Mazatán area. Coe (1961) and Jorge Ceja (1985), for La Victoria and Paso de la Amada, respectively, were the first to identify the tradition of naturalistic ceramic effigies analyzed here. Recent work by John Clark and Michael Blake (1989, 1994; Blake et al. 1995), again in the Mazatán area, has further refined the Early Formative ceramic sequence and generated a detailed model of sociopolitical changes during this time period. These authors suggest that small-scale chiefly polities arose in the region after 1400 b.c. and persisted until around 1000 b.c., when most of the study region was organized into a single complex chiefdom (see also Clark and Pye, this volume). Clark (1990, 1994a) argues that sociopolitical developments and material culture changes in late Early Formative Soconusco (including the appearance of Olmec-style motifs on ceramics) were profoundly affected by developments on the Gulf Coast.

I turn now to a description of the two sequential systems of zoomorphic imagery in Early Formative Soconusco. The early pattern of naturalistic representations characterizes the initial Early Formative of the region but continues into the late Early Formative, perhaps to around 1000 b.c.[1] The onset of the late Early Formative in the Mazatán study area is indicated by significant changes in the material culture assemblage beginning around 1100 b.c. Those changes included shifts in the shapes

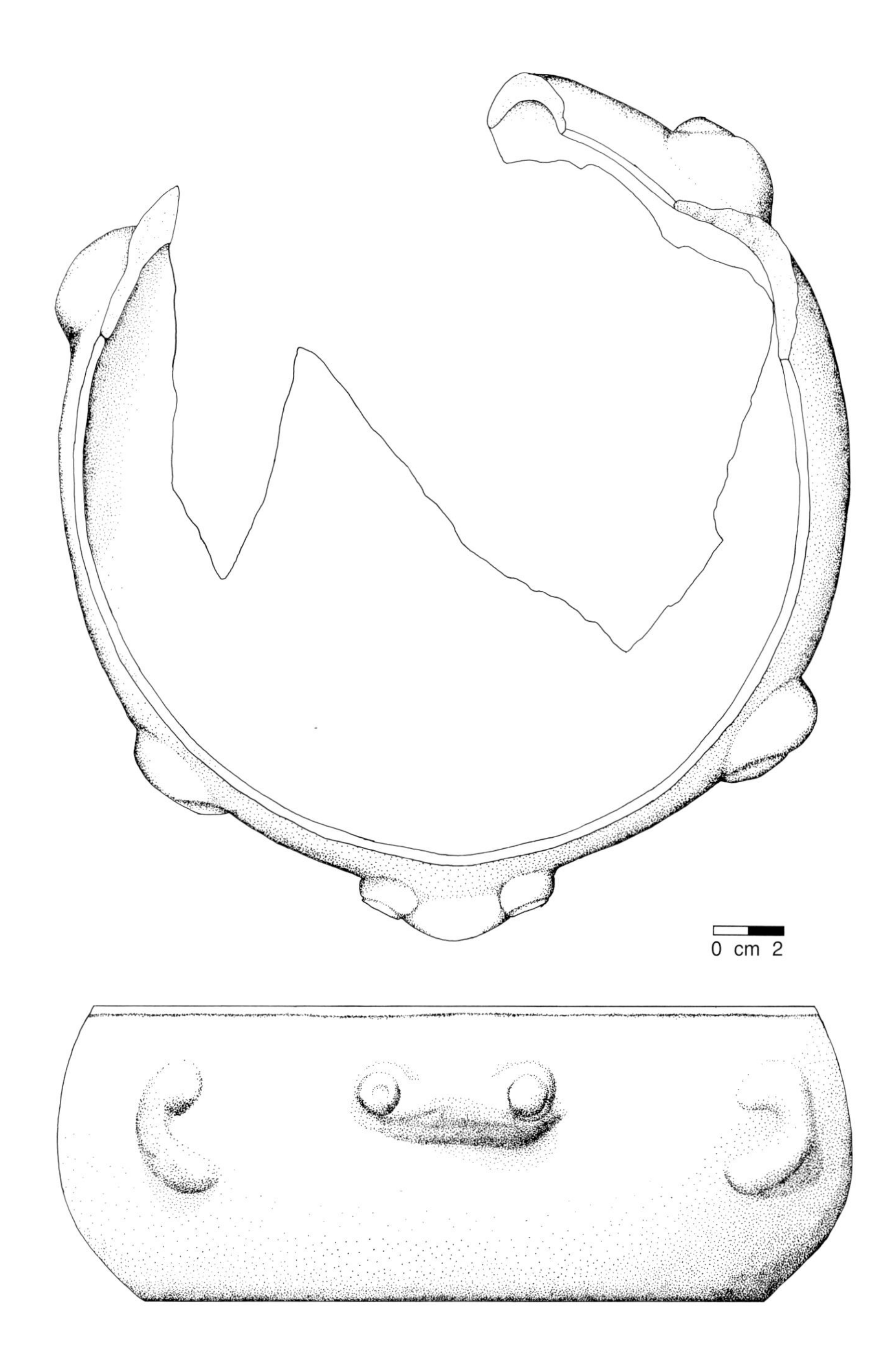

3. Ceramic bowl with toad effigy, Paso de la Amada, 1250–1100 b.c.; scale, 2 cm throughout

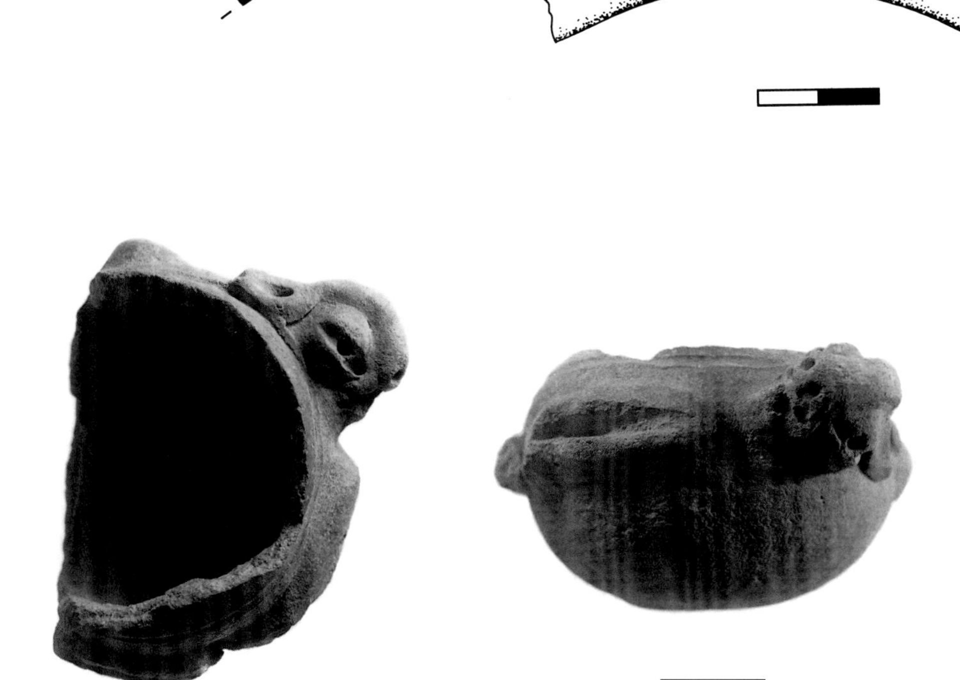

4. Ceramic bowl with fish effigy, Paso de la Amada, 1400–1000 b.c.

5. Top and side views of miniature ceramic vessel with rabbit effigy, Paso de la Amada, 1400–1000 b.c.

and colors of pottery vessels as well as the appearance of iron-ore mirrors, cylinder seals, white slipping on figurines, and new (Olmec) head styles and body positions for figurines. These changes demonstrate the participation of the inhabitants of Mazatán in the pan-Mesoamerican stylistic horizon of the late Early Formative and probably reflect intensive contact with complex societies on the Gulf Coast and other areas of Mesoamerica as well.

Artifacts and Representations, 1400–1000 b.c.

Zoomorphic imagery of the period 1400–1000 b.c. is characterized by naturalistic figures hand modeled in clay. The study collection consists of 159 identifiable animal heads or head fragments and 126 identifiable body or limb fragments from recent excavations at Paso de la Amada. Many more unidentifiable fragments (generally body or limb pieces) were not analyzed for this study. Most figures appear as effigies on vessels. Some of these vessels are unique creations, but most effigies are modeled heads and other features affixed to otherwise typical vessel forms. The ceramic representations depict a wide range of animals from the local environment. All kinds of representations appear in refuse throughout the site of Paso de la Amada. Most or all households seem to have used these items in daily activities.

Artifacts

Most prevalent among effigy vessels were appliqué animal heads and limbs on what were otherwise quite typical pots. Most appliqué effigies appear on neckless jars (tecomates) with unslipped bodies or on red-slipped, rounded-wall bowls (typically with flat bases). Effigies were occasionally affixed to other bowl forms as well. For rounded-wall bowls used in food service, rim diameters of vessels with effigies are significantly smaller than those of similar vessels without effigies.[2] Interestingly, the rim diameter distribution of these serving bowls is bimodal, and all except one of the thirty effigies in the sample appear on vessels in the smaller size mode. It is possible that these different size modes represent individual-portion serving bowls, approximately 13–21 centimeters in diameter, and family-portion serving bowls, most commonly 26–35 centimeters in diameter (see Henrickson and McDonald 1983). I suggest below that the occurrence of effigies almost exclusively on individual-portion vessels indicates that the deployment of effigies mediated small-scale social interactions or personal identities.

Effigy heads affixed to all kinds of vessels were oriented in one of two ways. Usually the head faced straight out from the side of the pot so that an observer looking down on the vessel would look down on the animal as well (fig. 3). For heads oriented in this latter fashion, the pot itself seems to have represented the body of the animal, and limbs and tails were often added in appropriate positions around the perimeter of the vessel. In other cases, the head faced along the exterior circumference of the vessel, so that an observer looking straight down on the pot from above would see the animal in profile (figs. 4–5).

In the case of the most elaborate effigy vessels, the whole vessel was specially molded to form the body and appendages of the animal depicted (fig. 6). Because each of these vessels appears to have been unique and the collection is very fragmentary, it is not possible to reconstruct any of these very elaborate vessels from the tantalizing pieces available.

The least elaborate effigy vessels were a rare set of miniature bowls that are distinct from typical serving vessels in their size and relative crudity of surface finish. Although they may have a slip or wash, they are usually unburnished or only lightly burnished. The surfaces of some are very roughly finished. The actual effigies appearing on these pots can, however, be quite sophisticated (fig. 5). Rim diameters range from 3 to 8 centimeters, and maximum pot diameters vary from 4 to 9 centimeters. The three bases of these small vessels are all slightly blackened on the exterior, but there is no evidence of heavy burning. The uses of these vessels are unknown. The fact that they are so small, with surface treatments so different from typical serving vessels, may indicate that they were used for some purpose besides serving food.

Two effigy incense burners were recovered by Michael Blake from Mound 6 at Paso de la Amada. One represents a fish; the other probably depicted a dog. Both consist of a flat clay slab that had three or four small, solid supports. The upper surfaces of these and other (non-effigy) incense burners are heavily burned and blackened.

Animal imagery appears on other ceramic artifacts besides vessels. Rare animal figurines are small or miniature in comparison to human figurines of the same period and are occasionally pierced for suspension. Bird-effigy whistles are small, hollow figures with a blow hole formed with a flat reed or twig and a few other small round holes in the hollow body. Some anthropomorphic figurines appear to be depicted wearing masks that include animal features. I have analyzed these with the human

6. Fragment of ceramic effigy vessel molded in the form of a duck, Paso de la Amada, 1100–1000 b.c.

figurines and will not consider them here (Lesure 1997).

Representations

A wide range of animals, including mammals, fish, reptiles or amphibians, and birds, is represented among the effigies, figurines, and whistles (figs. 7–9). The distribution of representations among various classes of animals is shown in tables 1 and 2, along with the frequency of these same animals in a large sample of faunal remains from a nearby site of the same period.[3] Reptiles and amphibians are the most numerous class of animals among the representations. This is because toad effigies make up a full 27 percent of all identifiable head fragments. Among the mammals, dogs, rabbits, peccaries, and armadillos are well represented. There are a variety of different birds that are difficult to identify precisely. Judging from the beak forms, these include waterfowl, birds of prey, and songbirds. Fish are much rarer than their importance in the diet might lead one to expect, and they appear rather stylized. I have not attempted to divide them into different species.

The different animal representations are not distributed evenly among the different vessel and figurine forms noted above. Mammals (primarily dogs) predominate on the elaborate molded vessels (69 percent). Toads are by far the most common appliqué effigies on regular serving bowls (62 percent) and are the most common appliqué on tecomates as well (30.3 percent). Only one probable toad appeared among the miniature bowls. Instead, the most common representations on these pots were dogs (60 percent) and rabbits (27 percent). Solid figurines were primarily armadillos (58 percent) and birds (25 percent). The twenty-four identified whistles were all birds, though many of these had two heads and were not in that sense naturalistic. There may have been shifts over time in the animals represented, but I am unable to show this convincingly with my sample.

Interestingly, despite the pervasive naturalism in the imagery, some of the effigies depict subtle mixtures of human and animal characteristics. One human feature is the inclusion of ear ornaments and occasionally humanlike ears. At least two depictions of what I interpret to be crocodiles (for example, fig. 8, upper right) appear to wear some sort of headdress. I distinguish between essentially animal figures with a few humanlike features (which appear as effigies on vessels) and the basically human figures with animal masks mentioned above (which appear as small, solid figurines). There are not enough specimens to know whether these two categories might actually grade into each other.

7. Mammal effigies and figurines, Paso de la Amada, 1400–1000 b.c., ceramic. Top from left: dog, peccary snout. Middle: dog, monkey figurine, armadillo figurine (seen from top). Bottom: coati, rabbit, deer

Frequencies

In the overall assemblage at Paso de la Amada, animal effigies, figurines, and whistles were rare. In a large sample of rim sherds of the period 1400–1000 b.c., less than 1 percent of all rims, or slightly more than 1 percent of all bowl rims, showed evidence of having been part of an effigy vessel. However, these pat-

8. Reptile and fish effigies, Paso de la Amada, 1400–1000 b.c., ceramic. Top from left: tortoise (note beaked mouth and placement of nostril), crocodile with headdress (note protrusion of teeth outside jaws). Middle: toad, unidentified reptile. Bottom: toad, fish

9. Bird effigies and figurines, Paso de la Amada, 1400–1000 b.c., ceramic. Top from left: hooked (raptorial) and straight beaks. Middle: crested bird with short beak, waterfowl with long beak, bird figurine. Bottom: vulture, possible owl

terns varied through time, reaching a peak in the period 1250–1100 b.c., when 1.6 percent of bowl rims show evidence of having been part of an effigy vessel. It should be noted that half or more of the rim sherds from an effigy vessel would show no evidence of the effigy. Depending on the placement of the effigy and the degree of breakage, it is possible that none of the rim sherds from an effigy vessel would show evidence of the effigy. A reasonable estimate might be that from 2 to 4 percent of serving bowls and a somewhat smaller proportion of tecomates were effigy vessels.

Contexts

Animal effigies and figurines were encountered in occupation surfaces, middens, and fill. No effigy pots have yet been recovered with burials, but the sample of burials is still quite small. Contexts of recovery suggest that effigy vessels, figurines, whistles, and censers were used in household contexts and discarded with other household refuse. There appear to have been various social contexts for the use of animal imagery within households. Animal effigies were sometimes affixed to vessels used to serve food, but plain tecomates that seem more appropriate for transport or storage of water or other liquids also occasionally had effigies. Household ritual activities may have involved the miniature bowls, but more certainly the small, slablike incense burners.

Artifacts and Representations, 1000–850 b.c.

Zoomorphic imagery of the period 1000–850 b.c. is characterized by very abstract representations of supernatural creatures; indeed, it is primarily by comparison to other regions, where very similar designs appear at this time, that motifs from the Mazatán region are convincingly identifiable as zoomorphic (fig. 10).

Table 1. Classes of Animals among Effigies Compared to Classes of Animals in Faunal Assemblage from Nearby Early Formative Site

Class of animal	Animal effigies and figurines from Paso de la Amada (%)	Faunal remains from Feature 6, Aquiles Serdán (%MNI)[a]
reptile or amphibian	37.1	7.4
mammal	34.0	6.5
bird	19.5	4.6
fish	6.9	81.5
fantastic creature	2.5	n/a
sample size	159 identifiable head fragments	

[a]Data from Clark (1994b: fig. 69); see also Blake et al. (1992: tables 1 and 2). MNI = minimum number of individuals.

Table 2. Different Kinds of Reptiles/Amphibians and Mammals Represented by Effigies Compared to Frequencies of the Same Animals in Faunal Assemblage

Category of animal	Animal effigies and figurines from Paso de la Amada (%)	Faunal remains from Feature 6, Aquiles Serdán (%MNI)[a]
Reptiles or amphibians		
toads	72.9	0
crocodile/cayman	13.6	17.5
turtle/tortoise	5.1	30.5
other reptiles or amphibians	8.5	52.0
Mammals		
dog	33.3	15.4
rabbit	14.8	7.7
peccary	13.0	3.8
armadillo	9.2	3.8
deer	3.7	19.2
tepezcuitle	3.7	0
coatimundi	1.8	0
other mammals	20.4	50.0

[a]Data from Clark (1994b: fig. 69) and Blake et al. (1992: tables 1 and 2). MNI = minimum number of individuals.

Study of the late Early Formative in the region is less advanced than study of the initial Early Formative; a comprehensive treatment of late Early Formative representational systems is not attempted here. Recent excavations by Tomás Pérez at Cantón el Corralito (Mz-257) recovered a large and well-preserved sample of decorated vessels from this era, and future studies by Pérez will expand considerably the brief sketch provided here.

For this study, a detailed analysis of 2,065 rim sherds from twenty-six provenience units in the sites of Cantón el Corralito, San Carlos, and El Varal was undertaken. (During this time period, the site of Paso de la Amada, the source of the initial Early Formative assemblage described above, had only ephemeral occupation.) Of the rim sherds analyzed, 95 sherds from bowls and thin-walled tecomates bore evidence of incised or excised motifs. Motifs incised around the rims of unslipped tecomates do not fit so obviously into the pan-Mesoamerican stylistic horizon of the late Early Formative and were not considered for this study. To develop a better qualitative understanding of the designs and motifs, incised sherds in type collections from the Mazatán area, housed at the New World Archaeological Foundation in San Cristóbal de Las Casas, Chiapas, were also examined.

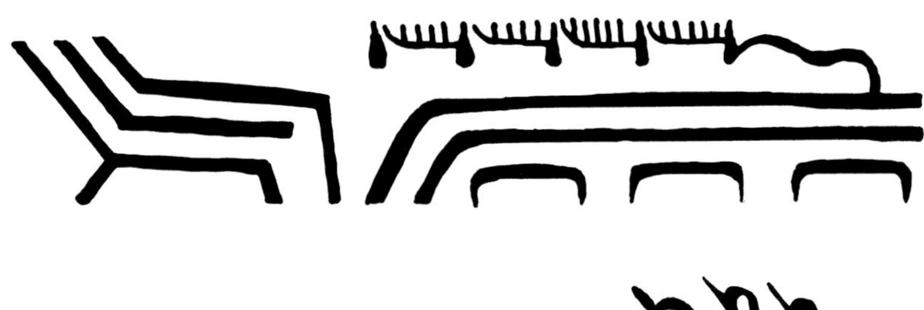

10. Comparison of recognizably zoomorphic (at top, dragon profile facing right) and very abstract motifs from Tlatilco showing similarities of elements that allow interpretation of the latter as zoomorphic representations. Note that "fire-serpent" motifs (bottom row) are zoomorphic
Redrawn after Covarrubias 1957: fig. 9

Artifacts

A striking contrast between assemblages of this period and those of the immediately preceding era is the extreme rarity of molded effigies. Many of the effigies that do appear are much cruder than their counterparts from before 1000 b.c., appearing as generalized faces that could be either animal or human (fig. 11). Although the sample of these is quite small, favored locations for effigies are the necks of large jars, a new vessel form. A number of very crude effigies formed by cane impressions also appear on large tecomates. Pérez' recent excavations at Cantón el Corralito recovered a few fragments of more naturalistic animal effigies from this time period, but in general his findings support the idea that such representations were extremely rare after 1000 b.c. The tradition of detailed representations of a wide variety of species essentially disappears.

11. Effigies from after 1000 b.c., such as these from El Varal (1000–850 b.c., ceramic), are no longer naturalistic representations of animals

Instead of effigies or other forms of plastic decoration such as modeling of the rim, serving vessels by 1000 b.c. were decorated with abstract, incised, or excised motifs. Vessels decorated in this manner are generally black, gray, or differentially fired black and white. The primary forms bearing decoration are open bowls with outslanting sides, cylindrical bowls, and bolstered-rim bowls. Rare forms that are sometimes decorated are small jars with low vertical or outsloping necks; small, thin-walled tecomates; and jars with tall, vertical necks in a variety of sizes. In contrast to the effigy vessels of the preceding period, which tended to be smaller than their noneffigy counterparts, there was no statistically significant difference in rim size between bowls bearing motifs and undecorated bowls. This pattern holds for each of the three main forms (outsloping walled, cylindrical, and bolstered-rim bowls).[4]

The only other ceramic artifacts that may bear a similar iconography are rare cylinder seals or roller stamps. Interestingly, these show up in small numbers in Mazatán assemblages beginning around 1100 b.c., about a century earlier than the iconography appears on the ceramics. The fragmentation and rarity of these artifacts preclude any meaningful discussion of representations or frequencies; they were apparently used and discarded in household contexts.

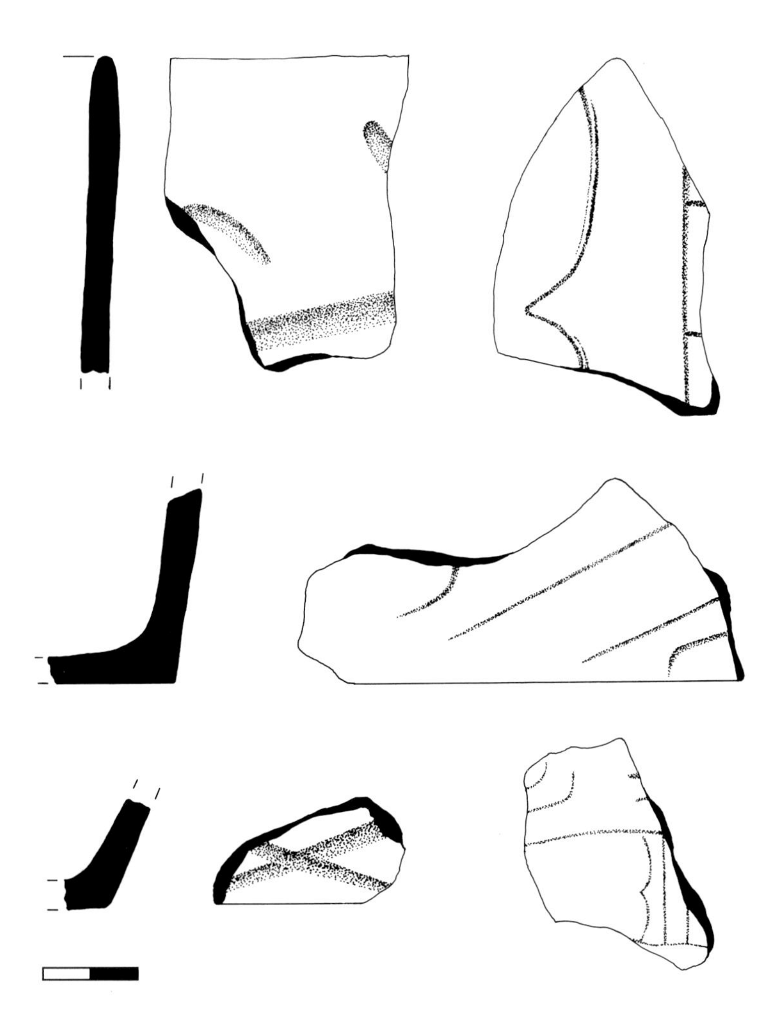

12. Abstract motifs from El Varal and San Carlos, 1000–850 b.c., ceramic

Representations

Although the collection of motifs on vessels is fragmentary and complete designs are difficult to reconstruct, it is clear that the Mazatán assemblage includes many motifs familiar from late Early Formative collections of other regions. Elements present in Soconusco assemblages include crossed bands, music brackets, and flame-eyebrows (figs. 12–14). Complex designs include fire-serpent and paw-wing motifs. Along with these pan-Mesoamerican or Olmec designs there appear to be motifs with more localized distributions, especially after 900 b.c. An expanded sample and more detailed analysis are needed to piece together the full representational system. For the present study, the crucial observation concerning the late Early Formative representational system is that pan-Mesoamerican (Olmec) motifs are prominent in the Mazatán assemblage. The subjects of these representations were mythological creatures with zoomorphic attributes.

Frequencies

Among all bowl rims in the sample for the period 1000–850 b.c., 7.7 percent bear evidence of motifs. Half the incised sherds, however, came from a single remarkable deposit excavated by John Clark at Cantón el Corralito. This may have been an elite midden. If this sample is removed, the overall percentage of bowl rims bearing motifs falls to 4.4 percent. Since inspection of the most complete incised vessel fragments suggests that more than half the rim sherds from an incised bowl would bear evidence of the motifs, a reasonable estimate of the frequency of bowls bearing motifs in typical assemblages would be 6 to 7 percent. Like the earlier effigies, the abstract motifs are consistently present in assemblages of their epoch but are not common. I present an overall estimate of motif frequency mainly to support the idea that the earlier effigies and the later motifs are broadly comparable as representational systems. This estimate should be taken with a large grain of salt until data are available to conduct a detailed study of variations within sites, between sites, and over time in the frequencies of vessels bearing abstract motifs. The sample from Cantón el Corralito, in which 23.8 percent of bowl rims in a possible high-status midden bore evidence of incised motifs, emphasizes the potential for complex patterns of distribution. Pérez' recent excavations at the same site confirm this basic pattern in a greatly enlarged sample. Patterned distribution of vessels with abstract motifs would constitute a significant difference between those and the earlier effigies, where within-site and between-site patterns have not been identified.

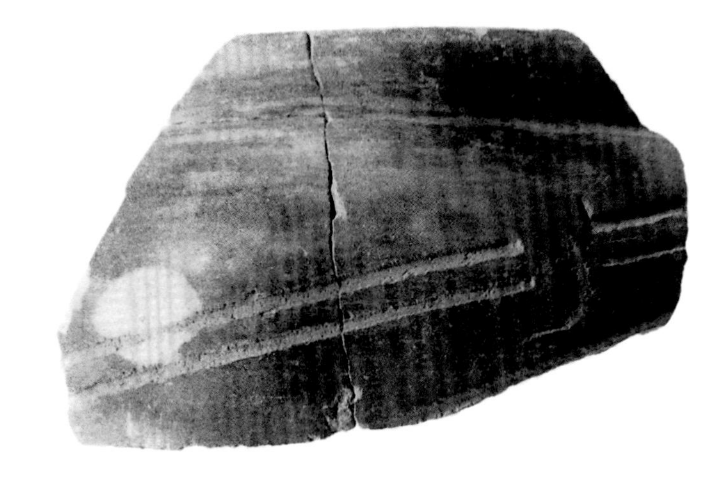

13. Abstract "fire-serpent" motif from El Varal, 1000–850 b.c., ceramic

Contexts

Vessels bearing abstract motifs were encountered primarily in middens and fill. No vessels bearing motifs have been recovered in burials, but the sample of burials is quite small. Contexts of recovery suggest use in residences for the serving of food. The appearance of similar imagery on cylinder seals shows that the motifs were deployed in other social contexts besides food consumption.

A Basis for Comparison

Interpretations presented below of the change from naturalistic animal effigies to stylized representations of supernatural creatures explore a series of contrasts between the two representational systems. Before such contrasts can become meaningful, however, it is important to establish some sort of frame in which the two systems can be seen as analogous. I consider the two systems similar in the sense that both appear to reflect the symbolic manipulation of ideas about the natural and supernatural worlds and the deployment of those ideas in the negotiation of social relationships, especially those relationships activated in the presentation and consumption of food (the "social relations of consumption"). Such a complicated proposition will necessarily remain an assumption of my analysis, but a number of lines of evidence can be marshaled in its support.

One consideration is whether these representational systems were really symbolic rather than purely decorative. The symbolic claim seems easier to support for the stylized motifs. David Joralemon (1976) and Anatole Pohorilenko (1977) convincingly demonstrate the coexistence of ideas about the natural and supernatural worlds in early Olmec iconography and identify key images as representations of mythological or supernatural creatures bearing traits drawn from a variety of natural creatures. The fact that the iconography of the ceramics also appears on large stone monuments at sites like San Lorenzo underscores its symbolic importance. It seems likely that the stylized motifs on late Early Formative pots in the Soconusco were important and meaningful images.

The question of whether the earlier effigies were also symbols reflecting abstract beliefs about the natural and supernatural worlds is less clear-cut, though Pohorilenko (1996: 130) does interpret them as evidence of animistic religions. If the effigies were actually nothing more than decorative elements, perhaps reflecting what was eaten in the pots, then any exploration of fine-grained contrasts between the two representational systems (one symbolically charged and one purely decorative) would be meaningless. Some evidence against the "mere decoration" argument can be adduced from the materials themselves. It is clear from tables 1 and 2 that the system of animal representations was much more than a simple reflection of subsistence concerns, since the

14. "Fire-serpent" motifs from El Varal, 1000–850 b.c., ceramic

frequency with which different animals appear as effigies does not reflect their importance in the diet. In addition, the occasional subtle mixtures of human and animal characteristics described above (such as the appearance of a human ear and ear ornament on an otherwise naturalistic animal) may reflect symbolic elaboration of the idea that humans can transform themselves into animals. This is a recurring theme in the ethnography of the Americas, and the Mazatán effigies may well reflect such beliefs. The best reason, however, for rejecting the idea that the naturalistic effigies were merely decorative is simply the general and pervasive cosmological importance of animals throughout Native America. On comparative grounds, it seems likely that animal metaphors were important in Early Formative villagers' cosmologies and that their carefully modeled effigies were symbolically rich images.

Once one accepts both effigies and motifs as symbolic objects, the next issue for consideration is the claimed importance of these objects for social relationships. Did people really use these representations as sources of metaphors for interpreting or negotiating social interactions in terms of cultural symbols? And, if so, were the two systems of representations used in comparable sets of interactions or activities? The answer to the second question seems clear: since both the effigies and motifs appear predominantly on pottery vessels, especially on vessels appropriate for the presentation and consumption of food and drink, it is likely that they were used in similar kinds of activities. The first question is more difficult to answer and must remain a hypothesis. Certainly many vessels used in food service did not bear zoomorphic imagery. A small but relatively consistent percentage of vessels (2–4 percent for effigies, 6–7 percent for the later motifs) did bear such imagery, however, and would have been familiar items at meals. It would perhaps be surprising if people did not incorporate these symbolic resources in strategies they devised for navigating the social relations of consumption.

Interpretations

The representations of initial and late Early Formative Soconusco are thus comparable to the extent that they were deployed in social interactions involving the presentation and consumption of food, where they invoked symbolism of the natural and supernatural worlds. The appearance of the motifs at the time of the disappearance of effigies raises the possibility that the motifs replaced the effigies. By referring to the observed changes as "replacement," I suggest that there was a causal relation between the disappearance of the one and the appearance of the other—that one form of representational expression was deliberately abandoned and another adopted as a result of as yet unknown social and historical conditions. To investigate the implications of this possible replacement, I explore differences in representations, subject matter, and symbolism between the earlier effigies and the later motifs.

Representations

Setting aside for a moment the difference in subject matter of the representations, the most obvious distinction between the earlier and later images is one of representational style. In the early period, representations were naturalistic. Effigies were modeled to resemble the three-dimensional form of their subjects. In the later period, representations continued to illustrate subjects, but in a more stylized way. The motifs are two-dimensional abstractions composed of straight, curved, and hooked lines. Only a careful comparison among different images has enabled analysts to demonstrate that this is zoomorphic imagery (fig. 10).

The shift from naturalism to stylization may signal an increase in the potential for ambiguity in the messages conveyed. In the Yolngu art of Australia analyzed by Howard Morphy (1980), both geometric and figurative elements appear. Morphy (1980: 33) points out that "precisely because Yolngu figurative representations are intended to look like another object and be interpreted as such, they are less ambiguous, less productive and have less potential for multivalency than the geometric art." Indeed, several Yolngu informants told Morphy that "part of the function of geometric art is to obscure meanings" (1980: 32). I do not take Morphy's analysis to suggest that geometric art is always more ambiguous than figurative art. Nevertheless, the possibilities Morphy raises would seem worth investigating when a naturalistic and a stylized system are juxtaposed in some way, either because both appear in a single cultural context or because one was abandoned in favor of the other.

The latter would apply to Early Formative Soconusco. Of course, the later imagery there is not pure abstraction; there does appear to have been a resemblance, however stylized, between illustration and subject. But as we attempt to explain the shift from naturalism to stylization, it seems worth considering the possibility, raised by the Yolngu case, that this shift was linked to an increase in symbolic ambiguity. Interpretation of the stylized imagery required knowledge of a code, while the naturalistic imagery invited interpretation even from those unfamiliar with its meanings. The code associated with the stylized images might have been open and well known, but there was a new potential for restricting access to meaning. More ambiguous imagery could have provided greater scope for the development of esoteric interpretations that could be guarded as secret by a special segment of the community.

Subject Matter

In the earlier period, subjects were drawn from the animals with which villagers came into contact in their daily lives. After 1000 b.c., subjects were supernatural entities imagined as fantastic creatures bearing traits drawn from various animals. The subjects of zoomorphic representations changed from the creatures of everyday existence to those of special, numinous experiences; there was a shift in focus from the ordinary to the extraordinary. It is important not to go overboard with this observation. The ancient inhabitants of the Soconusco are unlikely to have made the sharp distinctions western peoples make today between the pragmatic and the spiritual. Indeed, I argued above that animals were likely to have had important cosmological and supernatural implications.

The crucial point here is a symbolism of access. The creatures depicted in the effigies had real-life counterparts accessible to everyone. Adults killed them, skinned them, and ate them. Children poked at them with sticks. The supernaturals represented in the abstract motifs were removed from this concrete existence. Although it is quite possible that many people interacted with these creatures in such contexts as dreams or visions, the removal of the concrete dimension of interaction created a new potential for restrictions in access. Although people continued to use zoomorphic symbolism in negotiating the social relations of consumption, the new subject matter was removed from everyday life and was thus no longer impervious to manipulation by a single social segment.

Abstract Symbols

An important issue raised at the outset of this essay was whether representational systems and subject matter could have changed while, at a more abstract level, the messages conveyed remained constant. The extent of the changes in subjects observed above suggests some general but important changes in the realm of abstract symbolism, especially if we imagine symbols to have been continually at play in the processes of social reproduction (rather than existing remote from and remaining unaffected by people's lived experiences). After 1000 b.c., villagers in the Soconusco chose a whole new set of ideas for negotiating social relations of consumption. The change from local animals to supernaturals suggests a shift of focus from the creatures of everyday life to those of extraordinary experience. Such a shift could signal a significant increase in the level of generality of symbolism applied to certain important domains of social activity (such as the presentation and consumption of food).

This claim for increased symbolic generality is based on the assumption that Early Formative cosmologies would have been hierarchically organized into levels of increasing generality, with distinctions among animals occupying a lower level than composite supernaturals. I say "distinctions among animals" rather than simply "animals" for good reason. Particular animals could easily have been key cultural symbols with a high degree of generality, and if the Soconusco effigies represented just two or three different animals, the assumption I am proposing would be much more tenuous. As it is, the prevalence of toads among the effigies suggests that this creature had a special kind of symbolic importance. The overall pattern among the effigies, however, is the representation of many different kinds of animals. It is this aspect of the system that suggests a fairly low level of cosmological generality. This characterization would fit the modern cosmology of the Mixe of Oaxaca (see Lipp 1991: 24–50), whose language is probably closely related to that spoken by the Early Formative inhabitants of the Soconusco (Lowe 1977). This would also appear to be compatible with Marcus' (1989) model of Early Formative cosmologies in Oaxaca in which the mythological subject matter of late Early Formative motifs symbolized high-order supernatural forces identified with earth and sky.

If I am right to interpret the switch from animal effigies to abstract motifs as indicative of a shift in symbolism to higher-order cosmological concepts, it does not necessarily follow that the observed material changes actually signal the first appearance of a new level of generality in cosmologies of the Soconusco. Higher levels of generality could have been present in initial Early Formative times without ideas from those levels being applied to the social interactions in which they later became significant. What the representational change does signal is a reorganization of the relations between different parts of the cosmological system and different domains of experience such that social acts took on new dimensions of symbolism. In particular, activities involved in the presentation and consumption of food took on more general cosmological implications.

Symbols and Social Interactions

A change to a representational system with more general cosmological implications suggests that social interactions were being interpreted in new ways. What were the specific aspects of social interaction that were becoming more important? One possibility that would accord nicely with the proposed symbolic changes is that people found it increasingly important to signal memberships in large-scale groups or social categories. Patterns relating to the appearance of effigies and motifs on ceramic vessels may provide support for that idea. As described above, effigies of the earlier period appeared on individual-portion bowls to the near exclusion of family-portion bowls. This may be because the symbolism of naturalistic effigies mediated small-scale social relations, such as individual interactions and personal identities. In contrast, the higher-order supernaturals represented in the later period were placed on both small and large pots without preference. If personal identities became less important than allegiances to lineages, status groupings, or even a generalized human community, then it would not be surprising to find just such a pattern of distribution of motifs. The distinctions and achievements of individuals within families were no longer emphasized; what was significant was a common identity and solidarity. Thus images that linked social groups or categories to basic cosmological principles appeared on pots of all sizes. This proposal for the Soconusco fits comfortably with mortuary data from highland Mexico, where late Early Formative motifs appear to have conveyed messages about social groupings such as clans or lineages (Marcus 1989: 169–170; Pyne 1976; Tolstoy 1989: 290).

Social Inequality

In the last few sections I have set up something of a contradiction, first suggesting that the later representational system was appropriate for control by an elite because it was more ambiguous and more remote from everyday life than its predecessor, and then claiming that it evoked more general cosmological principles that were of interest to people as they emphasized the solidarity of large-scale social groupings or categories. Were these images divisive or uniting? An analysis of the representations from the perspective of social inequality suggests that they were both.

The appearance of abstract imagery in the Soconusco coincides with settlement pattern and other changes that Clark and Blake (1989) interpret as the formulation of a regional paramount chiefdom. In other words, the observed changes in zoomorphic imagery are coeval with sociopolitical transformations toward greater centralization and political inequality. Were vessels with abstract motifs elite goods that symbolized social status?

Elite households do seem to have used more of these vessels than commoner households. At the late Early Formative site of Cantón el Corralito, 23.8 percent of serving bowls in one midden sample bore incised motifs. Pérez' recent tests in the same midden found, in addition to much more decorated pottery, jade ornaments and magnetite mirrors. Evidence suggests that this is an elite midden. The percentages of bowls with motifs in two samples of the same phase from the adjacent site of San Carlos were 3.7 and 9.4 percent. Despite an apparent tendency for elites to have more decorated pottery, use of the stylized zoomorphic imagery was by no means restricted to the elite. Excavations at a variety of sites in the Mazatán area clearly show that everyone had access to decorated vessels. The change from naturalistic effigies to abstract motifs occurred at both large inland villages and small estuary hamlets. These were not exclusively "elite goods."

The new representational system could nevertheless have suited elite interests in at least two respects. First, claims of special (elite-controlled) knowledge would have been more plausible for ambiguous symbols removed from everyday experience than for naturalized images whose living referents were accessible to everyone. The meanings of the abstract images could have been organized hierarchically, with ordinary people having access to only a limited range of the associations understood by elite exegetes. For instance, everyone might have known that propitiation of these forces was crucial to community well-being, while only the elite knew how to perform rites of propitiation. This scenario would be especially likely if the symbolism itself bore an element of foreignness (see below). Second, an emphasis on allegiances to large-scale social groupings or categories, along with a concomitant increase in the level of generality of animal symbolism, would also have been advantageous to the elite of an increasingly divided society by providing social cohesion at a higher level. One message of the motifs might have been, "We are the same because we are all under the protection of this supernatural." The seeming contradiction between my two interpretations (that the new representational system fostered solidarity while providing a vehicle for divisive claims to esoteric knowledge) is deliberate. Such a contradiction, ideologically cloaked and properly mystified, could have been an important element in the constitution of chiefly power in the Soconusco. The chief would have benefited from the mystification of unequal social relations provided by supernaturals as symbols of solidarity, while at the same time claiming, through superior knowledge, to be the source of that solidarity.

Effigies and Motifs in Other Areas

The previous discussion makes such a nice logical package—the appearance of marked sociopolitical inequality being accompanied by the appearance of a more ambiguous and less accessible representational system more amenable than its predecessor to manipulation and control by an elite—that it might be tempting to think of this as a general model for ideological change in Early Formative Mesoamerica. That would be a mistake. The dramatic shift in zoomorphic imagery in villages of the Soconusco region, from naturalistic to fantastic and abstract, does not occur in other areas. Perhaps the best examples are the Central Mexican sites of Las Bocas, Tlapacoya, and Tlatilco (see

Niederberger, this volume). Although representational systems of the initial Early Formative are poorly understood at those sites, some of their best-known pieces from the late Early Formative are beautifully molded ceramic effigy vessels, some of which even bear Olmec motifs (see frontispiece, also Benson and de la Fuente 1996: cats. 27–28; Niederberger 1987: figs. 414–415, 497). At these sites, naturalistic depictions of birds, fish, and other animals appear together with abstract representations of mythological creatures. Although the initial Early Formative system is unknown, it is clear that the appearance of stylized motifs did not coincide with any disappearance of naturalistic imagery.

This observation may at first seem to pose problems for the analysis presented here, but it actually makes sense given the nature of ideological change and helps clarify what kinds of transformations were going on in the Soconusco. Concerning ideological change, Chantal Mouffe (1979: 193–194), commenting on Gramsci, points out that "ideological struggle . . . consists of a process of *disarticulation-rearticulation* of given ideological elements in a struggle between two hegemonic principles to appropriate these elements; it does not consist of the confrontation between two already elaborated, closed world-views. Ideological ensembles existing at a given moment are, therefore, the result of the relations of forces between the rival hegemonic principles and they undergo a perpetual process of transformation" (original emphasis). Ideologies thus weave together bits or elements from an existing symbolic field. The subject of social struggle is the structural relations among symbolic elements, since different sets of structural relations among elements can yield radically different patterns of empowerment and disempowerment.

If we imagine Early Formative Mesoamerica as a landscape of local ideological struggles (the widespread shift from egalitarian to hierarchical social systems during the course of this period certainly supports that perspective), then what we may be seeing in the Soconusco and Central Mexico are different solutions to the articulation of symbolic elements into an ideology of social inequality. It is probable that, in both areas, certain kinds of social interactions in which personal identities and achievements had been negotiated took on new implications as new distributions of power and knowledge emerged. In the Soconusco, these processes led to the abandonment of a local tradition of elaborating ceramic serving vessels with naturalistic depictions of animals from everyone's daily experience and its replacement by a system of abstract representations of mythological subject matter more remote from everyday life and with more general social/cosmological referents. Social relations of consumption were a site of ideological struggle, and the resulting articulation of symbolic elements counterpoised naturalistic and fantastic/abstract representational modes. The results of what must have been an analogous struggle in villages of Central Mexico produced a very different set of relations among elements in which multiple representational modes flourished alongside one another.

Conclusion

What was the source of ideological elements that supported the formation and reproduction of social hierarchies in late Early Formative Mesoamerica? Were most of these elements derived from a shared ancient substratum of belief? These questions have been difficult to address because in many areas the first iconographic representations to appear in the archaeological record date to the late Early Formative itself; we can only speculate on the character of earlier belief systems. Data from the Soconusco provide an important new perspective on this problem since a well-developed system of zoomorphic imagery appears here during the initial Early Formative period. The abandonment of this system around 1000 b.c., and its replacement by an equally well-developed but very different representational system, suggest that the later system was an Early Formative import to the Soconusco rather than an element of shared cultural heritage the Soconusco held in common with the rest of Mesoamerica. I noted two potential problems with that line of argument. The first is the possibility that the later representational system had actually been present in the Soconusco from earlier times, but only in perishable media that are lost to us. This cannot be resolved definitively in the absence of any actual perishable remains, but the fact that the earlier naturalistic representations appear on objects of different kinds in a variety of media while the later abstract imagery does not appear at all provides a basis for suspecting that the latter was simply absent in earlier times.

The second potential problem is the possibility that representational systems could have changed while the "ideas" associated with them remained constant. Investigation of this issue required some sort of model of the dimensionality of ideas once associated with ancient representational systems. I identified three sets of ideas that could have been associated with the modelings and incisions we observe on Early Formative pottery. These are representational systems, subject matter of the representations, and abstract symbols signified by these subjects. In addition to viewing ideas as dimensional, it is important to view symbols as embedded in people's lived experiences; social acts reproduce and redefine symbols at the same time as those acts are interpreted in symbolic terms.

Analyzing the representational change in Early Formative Soconusco from this perspective suggests significant change in "ideas" and their links to social life; it also suggests some potential areas of continuity. The most important change seems to have been that, after 1000 b.c., social acts involved in the presentation and consumption of food took on new symbolic implications that put these human interactions into a higher-order cosmological framework than they had been seen in before. People organized ideas within this framework by imagining one or more fantastic creatures whose attributes stood for important cultural symbols. A system of abstract imagery provided material representations of these creatures.

What the Soconusco data suggest was critically absent from a widely shared substratum of belief was a structure that interpreted social relations of consumption at this level of symbolic and cosmological generality. Also missing was a representational system for expressing such symbols in material media and a set of social practices involving the deployment of these representations and ideas in the presentation and consumption of food. This nexus of representations, beliefs, and practices does not appear to have developed in the Soconusco. It was invented elsewhere in Mesoamerica and was adopted by the inhabitants of the Soconusco during the late Early Formative in the course of an intricate local trajectory of sociopolitical development.

I will leave the modeling of this process of adoption to others, but it is important to note hints that inhabitants of the Soconusco interpreted their adopted representational system in local ways. In the Soconusco, restructuring of beliefs and practices during the late Early Formative resulted in the abandonment of a rich tradition of naturalistic imagery that had previously provided a medium for interpreting social relations of consumption. After 1000 b.c., naturalistic effigies are virtually absent. In other regions, such as Central Mexico, abstract Olmec imagery appears together with naturalistic effigies during the late Early Formative. The sequence of change in the Soconusco is not precisely reflected in other regions because the inhabitants of the Soconusco were adopting a particular set of beliefs and practices rather than a whole way of living. New beliefs and practices had to be articulated to local structures; it would appear to be this local process of articulation that resulted in the abandonment of the naturalistic tradition in the Soconusco.

It is important to add that some general aspects of late Early Formative belief systems of the Soconusco could derive from a much more ancient cultural heritage this area shared with the rest of Mesoamerica. There could well have been a sharing of certain cosmological principles of the order referenced by the later motifs. Supporting this view would be the facility with which new representations and subjects were embraced by villagers of the Soconusco. The observed representational changes may reflect new ways of expressing long-shared symbols or cosmological principles and new ways of linking these to social life. Elements of long-standing traditions were reorganized, reformulated, and applied in novel ways. It is unclear whether to include in this category the subject matter of the later representations (the mythological or supernatural creatures) or simply the more abstract ideas they represented. Villagers of the Soconusco might have adopted the creatures along with their representations as a means of reorganizing and reconceptualizing certain long-held beliefs, or the creatures could have had a much longer history in the region. Either way, cosmological ideas of this order had previously been remote from everyday social interactions, and something important happened during the late Early Formative to draw them to the foreground.

In conclusion, it seems unlikely that the ideologies of social inequality that developed in Formative period Soconusco emerged directly either from an Archaic belief substratum or as an imported total system. Borrowed elements, local innovations, and elements derived from ancient traditions assumed a complexly structured form in Early Formative belief systems. Ideas from different structural positions or levels were drawn on to interpret the changing dimensions of social life. A reorganization of social relations such as the development of permanent hierarchies required a reorganization of belief systems perhaps best imagined in Mouffe's (1979) sense of "ideological struggle." As the result of such struggles, "old" beliefs were articulated with social activities and relationships in new ways, generating the need for new vehicles of symbolic expression and commentary. It is possible that the naturalistic imagery of the initial Early Formative was increasingly ill-suited to the expression of emergent social differences. The system that replaced it helped to draw new ideas into the interpretation of transformed social relationships, ideas more relevant to the fields of contention in late Early Formative ideological systems.

NOTES

My 1992 work at Paso de la Amada was supported by a Fulbright (IIE) Fellowship and dissertation grants from the Wenner-Gren Foundation for Anthropological Research, the Social Science Research Council, the New World Archaeological Foundation (Brigham Young University), and the University of Michigan. Michael Blake generously supported my 1993 work under a grant from the Social Sciences and Humanities Research Council of Canada. I would like to thank especially Lorena Mirambell and the Consejo de Arqueología of the Instituto Nacional de Antropología e Historia, Mexico, for permission to carry out the fieldwork. John Clark and Michael Blake generously provided access to effigies and incised sherds from Paso de la Amada, Cantón el Corralito, and San Carlos. Their guidance and encouragement were especially important during both the fieldwork and the long period of analysis that followed. Barbara Arroyo, Michael Blake, Deborah Cembellin, John Clark, Vicki Feddema, Dennis Gosser, Warren Hill, Tomás Pérez, Mary Pye, and Michael Ryan were wonderful as field companions and always generous with their ideas and suggestions. The penetrating questions of participants in the National Gallery's Olmec conference and John Clark's insightful comments contributed greatly to my thinking as I prepared the revised version of this paper.

1. For Soconusco dates I rely on Blake et al. (1995). What I refer to as the initial Early Formative includes the Barra (1550–1400 b.c.), Locona (1400–1250 b.c.), and Ocós (1250–1100 b.c.) phases. The late Early Formative includes the Cherla (1100–1000 b.c.), Cuadros (1000–900 b.c.), and Jocotal (900–850 b.c.) phases. I follow Blake et al. (1995) in using uncalibrated radiocarbon years instead of calendar years.

2. For rounded-wall bowls, all vessels less than 9 cm in diameter were eliminated from the analysis since these were primarily miniature vessels that may not have been used in food service. Elimination of miniature rounded-wall bowls left 30 with effigies and 192 without. Rim diameter ranges in the two samples were 10–26 and 9–43 centimeters, respectively, with median rim diameters of 14 centimeters for effigy bowls and 18 centimeters for bowls without effigies. A Mann-Whitney U test from the program Statview was chosen instead of a t-test because the distributions were not normal. The test found the distributions significantly different with a p-value of .0005 (U = 1735, U′ = 4025, z-value = -3.500, no. ties = 25, tied z-value = -3.505, tied p-value = .0005). A similar pattern is found among unslipped tecomates, where effigies are most common on vessels with diameters less than 13 centimeters.

3. Analysis of faunal remains from Paso de la Amada is currently being conducted by Thomas Wake at the University of California, Los Angeles, Institute of Archaeology. Preliminary results indicate that the general patterns suggested by the Aquiles Serdán sample in tables 1–2 are present at Paso de la Amada as well.

4. Among open-walled bowls from the period 1000–900 b.c., 23 bore motifs and 86 did not; median rim diameters were 26 and 29 centimeters, respectively. The Mann-Whitney U test found no significant difference between these, with a p-value of .1375. Among bolstered-rim bowls, 19 bore motifs and 18 did not; median rim diameters were 22 and 22.5 centimeters, respectively. The Mann-Whitney U test found no significant difference between these, with a p-value of .9274. Among cylindrical bowls, 6 bore motifs and 6 did not; median rim diameters were 12.5 and 15 centimeters, respectively. The Mann-Whitney U test found no significant difference between these, with a p-value of .4233.

BIBLIOGRAPHY

Benson, Elizabeth P., and Beatriz de la Fuente
1996 (Editors) *Olmec Art of Ancient Mexico* [exh. cat., National Gallery of Art]. Washington.

Blake, Michael, John E. Clark, Brian S. Chisholm, and Karen Mudar
1992 Non-Agricultural Staples and Agricultural Supplements: Early Formative Subsistence in the Soconusco Region, Mexico. In *Transitions to Agriculture in Prehistory,* ed. Anne Gebauer and T. Douglas Price, 133–151. Madison, Wisc.

Blake, Michael, John E. Clark, Barbara Voorhies, George Michaels, Michael W. Love, Mary E. Pye, Arthur Demarest, and Barbara Arroyo
1995 Radiocarbon Chronology for the Late Archaic and Formative Periods on the Pacific Coast of Southeastern Mesoamerica. *Ancient Mesoamerica* 6(2): 161–184.

Ceja Tenorio, Jorge Fausto
1985 *Paso de la Amada: An Early Preclassic Site in the Soconusco, Chiapas.* Papers of the New World Archaeological Foundation 49. Provo, Utah.

Clark, John E.
1990 Olmecas, olmequísmo, y olmecquización en Mesoamérica. *Arqueología,* 2d series, 3: 49–55. Mexico City.

1994a El sistema económico de los primeros olmecas. In *Los olmecas en Mesoamérica,* ed. John Clark, 189–202. Mexico City and Madrid.

1994b The Development of Early Formative Rank Societies in the Soconusco, Chiapas, Mexico. Ph.D. dissertation, Department of Anthropology, University of Michigan, Ann Arbor.

Clark, John E., and Michael Blake
1989 El origen de la civilización en Mesoamérica: Los olmecas y mokaya del Soconusco de Chiapas, México. In *El preclásico o formativo: Avances y perspectivas,* ed. Martha Carmona, 385–403. Mexico City.

1994 The Power of Prestige: Competitive Generosity and the Emergence of Rank Societies in Lowland Mesoamerica. In *Factional Competition and Political Development in the New World,* ed. Elizabeth Brumfiel and John Fox, 17–30. Cambridge.

Coe, Michael D.
1961 *La Victoria, an Early Site on the Pacific Coast of Guatemala.* Papers of the Peabody Museum of Archaeology and Ethnology 53. Cambridge, Mass.

Coe, Michael D., and Richard A. Diehl
1980 *In the Land of the Olmec. Volume 1: The Archaeology of San Lorenzo Tenochtitlán.* Austin.

Coe, Michael D., and Kent V. Flannery
1967 *Early Cultures and Human Ecology in South Coastal Guatemala.* Smithsonian Contributions to Anthropology 3. Washington.

Covarrubias, Miguel
1957 *Indian Art of Mexico and Central America.* New York.

Diehl, Richard A., and Michael D. Coe
1995 Olmec Archaeology. In *The Olmec World: Ritual and Rulership,* 11–25 [exh. cat., The Art Museum, Princeton University]. Princeton.

Flannery, Kent V., and Joyce Marcus
1994 *Early Formative Pottery of the Valley of Oaxaca.* Memoirs of the Museum of Anthropology 27. University of Michigan, Ann Arbor.

Furst, Peter T.
1995 Shamanism, Transformation, and Olmec Art. In *The Olmec World: Ritual and Rulership,* 69–81 [exh. cat., The Art Museum, Princeton University]. Princeton.

Grove, David C.
1989 Olmec: What's in a Name? In *Regional Perspectives on the Olmec,* ed. Robert Sharer and David Grove, 8–14. Cambridge.

1993 "Olmec" Horizons in Formative Period Mesoamerica: Diffusion or Social Evolution? In *Latin American Horizons,* ed. Don Rice, 83–111. Washington.

Henrickson, Elizabeth, and Mary M. A. McDonald
1983 Ceramic Form and Function: An Ethnographic Search and an Archaeological Application. *American Anthropologist* 85: 630–643.

Joralemon, Peter David
1976 The Olmec Dragon: A Study in Pre-Columbian Iconography. In *Origins of Religious Art and Iconography in*

Preclassic Mesoamerica, ed. Henry Nicholson, 29–71. Los Angeles.

Lathrap, Donald W.
1974 The Moist Tropics, the Arid Lands, and the Appearance of Great Art Styles in the New World. In *Art and Environment in Native America,* ed. Mary King and Idris Traylor Jr., 115–158. Texas Tech University, Lubbock.

Layton, Robert
1991 *The Anthropology of Art.* Cambridge.

Lesure, Richard G.
1997 Figurines and Social Identities in Early Sedentary Societies of Coastal Chiapas, Mexico, 1550–800 b.c. In *Women in Prehistory: North America and Mesoamerica,* ed. Cheryl Claassen and Rosemary Joyce, 225–248. Philadelphia.

Lipp, Frank J.
1991 *The Mixe of Oaxaca: Religion, Ritual, and Healing.* Austin.

Lowe, Gareth W.
1975 *The Early Preclassic Barra Phase of Altamira, Chiapas.* Papers of the New World Archaeological Foundation 38. Provo, Utah.

1977 The Mixe-Zoque as Competing Neighbors of the Lowland Maya. In *The Origins of Maya Civilization,* ed. Richard Adams, 197–248. Albuquerque, N.M.

Marcus, Joyce
1989 Zapotec Chiefdoms and the Nature of Formative Religions. In *Regional Perspectives on the Olmec,* ed. Robert Sharer and David Grove, 148–197. Cambridge.

Marcus, Joyce, Kent V. Flannery, and Ronald Spores
1983 The Cultural Legacy of the Oaxacan Preceramic. In *The Cloud People: Divergent Evolution of the Zapotec and Mixtec Civilizations,* ed. Kent Flannery and Joyce Marcus, 36–39. New York.

Morphy, Frances
1977 The Social Significance of Schematisation in Northwest Coast American Indian Art. In *Form in Indigenous Art: Schematisation in the Art of Aboriginal Australia and Prehistoric Europe,* ed. Peter Ucko, 73–76. Australian Institute of Aboriginal Studies, Canberra.

Morphy, Howard
1980 What Circles Look Like. *Canberra Anthropology* 3(1): 17–36.

Mouffe, Chantal
1979 Hegemony and Ideology in Gramsci. In *Gramsci and Marxist Theory,* ed. Chantal Mouffe, 168–204. London.

Niederberger, Christine
1987 *Paléopaysages et archéologie pré-urbaine du Bassin de Mexico,* vol. 2. Mexico City.

Pohorilenko, Anatole
1977 On the Question of Olmec Deities. *Journal of New World Archaeology* 2: 1–16.

1996 Portable Carvings in the Olmec Style. In *Olmec Art of Ancient Mexico,* ed. Elizabeth Benson and Beatriz de la Fuente, 119–131 [exh. cat., National Gallery of Art]. Washington.

Pyne, Nanette M.
1976 The Fire-Serpent and Were-Jaguar in Formative Oaxaca: A Contingency Table Analysis. In *The Early Mesoamerican Village,* ed. Kent Flannery, 272–282. Orlando, Fla.

Tolstoy, Paul
1989 Western Mesoamerica and the Olmec. In *Regional Perspectives on the Olmec,* ed. Robert Sharer and David Grove, 275–302. Cambridge.

Whalen, Michael E.
1981 *Excavations at Santo Domingo Tomaltepec: Evolution of a Formative Community in the Valley of Oaxaca, Mexico.* Memoirs of the Museum of Anthropology 12. University of Michigan, Ann Arbor.

JOHN E. CLARK
Brigham Young University

MARY E. PYE

The Pacific Coast and the Olmec Question

In this chapter we report and evaluate the evidence of Olmec-style artifacts from the Pacific Coast region of Chiapas, Mexico, and adjacent Guatemala. These artifacts include stone sculpture, incised jades, ceramic figurines, and carved pots. The Olmec question alluded to in our title concerns the possibility that the Olmecs had a significant influence on peoples living along the Pacific coastal plain. The evidence currently available is extremely uneven but does signal periods of strong influence followed by periods of lesser impact.

Any assessment of Olmec influence presupposes that Olmec and Olmec-style artifacts can be distinguished from non-Olmec ones. Moreover, a consideration of the temporal-spatial placement of Olmec artifacts clearly must precede any narrative dependent on such data. In this essay, therefore, we first consider briefly questions of who or what is "Olmec" and then questions of the chronological placement of Olmec artifacts found in the Pacific Coast region. We then present an overview of coastal prehistory, from the earliest Formative societies to the rise of the ceremonial center of Izapa toward the close of the Middle Formative period.

Olmec monument at Chalchuapa, El Salvador, showing a royal personage with an elaborate cape and staff
Photograph: Courtesy of New World Archaeological Foundation

Who or What Is Olmec?

Olmecs Were People

As with other primordial queries, the essentialist question of "what is Olmec" is more frequently raised than answered, and its answer is probably less critical than many suppose. Current usage is a mere archaeological convention to designate an ancient culture known only archaeologically. Currently the term refers to a "culture" or, better stated, a closely interacting group of societies that shared the same cultural practices, including a unique style of representation evident in carved monuments, excised ceramic vessels, terracotta figurines, incised and polished jades, and other artifacts.

It is ironic that the "Olmec" label has generated so much controversy because archaeologists have been lax in their skepticism of most labels. If scholars had to make a rigorous archaeological case for the legitimate use of labels such as "Zapotec" and "Maya," few would pass muster. There remains a significant difference, however. The terms *Zapotec, Mixtec, Aztec, Maya,* and so forth refer to groups of living peoples, their languages, and their current practices, while the term *Olmec* does not and cannot. The archaeological usage of linguistic or ethnic terms implies a clear connection between the peoples whose material remains are found archaeologically and supposed living descendants. But the connections are mostly assumed rather than demonstrated, and current confidence in these generalizations is incommensurate with the evidence.

This brings us back to the label *Olmec.* First and foremost the term designates a group of people, or peoples, who shared a suite of cultural practices. We can be confident that they spoke an intelligible language, perhaps a form of proto-Mixe-Zoque. This is not to say, however, that all speakers of this language, whatever it was (Mixe-Zoque or Maya), shared the same cultural practices. Nor does it mean that all those people who shared the same practices were native speakers of the same language. They may have been, but such an assumption is unwarranted and unnecessary. What is important here is the patterned way of life, or cultural practices, that the participants followed, regardless of their biological, linguistic, or cultural backgrounds.

A simple example will highlight the problem. If we suppose that the peoples whom we consider Olmecs had ancestors and descendants who spoke the same language and shared many of the same practices and beliefs, then it makes little sense to claim that Olmec culture "began" about 1300 B.C. and "ended" a thousand years later. Presumably, many of their biological descendants still plant and harvest corn today and engage in other activities. In what sense, then, did Olmec culture die out if there has been biological, linguistic, ethnic, and spiritual continuity? The only sense that does *make sense* is a cessation of specific cultural practices and/or their material representations. In short, the term *Olmec* refers to a historic phenomenon evident in a particular suite of practices and representations—a particular episode in a longer and broader history of a people. Rather than viewing *Olmec* as a parallel term to *Maya,* it would be more accurate to class it with such terms as *Victorian, Carolingian, Roman,* or *Byzantine,* designations that convey a sense of cultural and/or political commitment to certain beliefs, practices, and material representations and that had a definite temporal and spatial distribution but do not encompass the entire history of a people, considered either biologically or linguistically.

Identification of such entities is based upon the homogeneity of material culture that resulted from a consistency of practices. For the most extensively distributed Olmec artifacts (carved pots and ceramic figurines), it is clear that several ethnic-language groups must have been involved. In the case of the Gulf Coast lowlands, due to its more limited extent, a unity of culture, language, dialect, and ethnic group is generally assumed. It is worth reiterating, however, that such unity has not been demonstrated. The archaeological Olmecs may have included several ethnic groups and language families; at least the possibility ought to be left open. We think it best to consider Olmec a politicoreligious entity (or several) of societies and peoples with deeply shared cultural practices. The borders of the Olmec entity, and its constituent units, fluctuated through time and varied across space.

To anticipate subsequent discussion, we think that the Olmecs of the Gulf Coast at 1300 B.C. were speakers of Mixe-Zoque (MZ), as argued by Lyle Campbell and Terrence Kaufman (1976), and that most inhabitants of the greater isthmian and Pacific Coast regions spoke this same language (Clark and Blake 1989; Lowe 1977). But the MZ speakers living outside the Gulf Coast region were not Olmecs; they followed different cultural practices and had different representational systems (see Lesure, this volume). We use the term *Mokaya* (an invented MZ term meaning "corn people") to refer to the early inhabitants of the Pacific Coast region (Clark and Blake 1989). Much of the following narrative concerns the ancient interactions between the Mokaya and their Olmec neighbors.

Olmec Artifacts Were Not People

In archaeology, all difficult questions eventually are reduced to debates about artifacts and their contexts. The Olmec question is no different. We identify the presence of Olmec peoples by finding Olmec artifacts—and we know they are Olmec artifacts because they were made by Olmec peoples. Phrased so indelicately, the vicious circularity of the Olmec problem is patent. The two obvious solutions to this illogical circle have given rise to the two main contending models of the Olmecs' impact, or lack of impact, on greater Mesoamerica. The "mother culture" model sees pervasive and significant Olmec presence almost everywhere in early Mesoamerica, and its inverse image, the "sister culture" model, denies that such influence or impact took place (compare Lesure, this volume).

The Olmec style is now well known and amply illustrated in the contributions to this book. Artifacts considered stylistically Olmec appear all across Mesoamerica in contexts dating to about 1100–700 B.C. Clearly, the various societies who made and/or used such objects were in frequent contact with one another, but given the wide spatial distribution of Olmec artifacts, surely many different language and culture groups were represented. Dispersal of Olmec artifacts, or Olmec-style artifacts, may have involved three different forms of interaction among peoples of different regions: the movement of (1) peoples, (2) objects, or (3) knowledge. For the Pacific Coast region, there is good evidence that shows all three modes of interaction at different times during the Formative period.

The alternative solution for breaking out of the vicious circle is to decide the matter of Olmecness by fiat. Some scholars have decreed that the term *Olmec* is suitable only for the peoples of the Gulf Coast lowlands, the region with the most obvious, most concentrated, and most spectacular remains in the Olmec style, and in the greatest range of media. Richard Diehl (this volume) argues for the use of *Olman* (meaning the place or land of the Olmecs) for this region.[1] Dictating the shape of prehistory by fiat, we hope, will prove an ephemeral fad. But granting the benefit of the doubt to these proposals, we can at least take the material record of Olman as the best single indicator of "Olmecness" and of Olmec cultural practices. We do so here.

The most striking elements of the Olmec pattern are colossal basalt sculpture located at regional and subregional centers (see Symonds, this volume), pottery carved with representations of supernaturals (see Niederberger, this volume), and ceramic figurines (see Lesure, this volume). These special artifacts, colloquially known as "Olmec art," are found in Olman in the same archaeological deposits as plain ceramic and stone artifacts, the latter presumably used in everyday activities. These utilitarian artifacts are also stylistically distinct. To be consistent in the identification of "Olmec," the same criteria for identifying Olmec culture in Olman should suffice for identifying it elsewhere—even if outside Olman. We argue below that the Mazatán zone of the Pacific Coast region shows precisely such a pattern about 1100 B.C. and that some Olmecs may actually have moved into this zone and reorganized the resident Mokaya populations there (Clark and Blake 1989; Clark 1997).

This claim has already generated discomfort in some circles, with the easy objections being critiques of the degree of fit in the artifact patterns. How close is the artifactual pattern in Mazatán to that in Olman? Are the so-called Olmec artifacts in Mazatán really Olmec? Or are they merely local productions in the Olmec style? Both imported objects and local objects are represented at different times. Questions of manufacturing origins, however, deflect attention from the real issues: questions of style and timing. Where did the Olmec style originate? Why and how did the Olmec style subsequently spread to other regions? More specifically, which types of Olmec artifacts and icons spread to which regions, when, and why? In the Pacific Coast region, Olmec artifacts included sculpture, jades, and ceramic vessels and figurines. Our story of Pacific Coast prehistory considers this whole range of artifacts. In the following section we describe recent finds of special Olmec artifacts and the problems of dating them correctly.

Expanding the Olmec Corpus

The best treatment of Olmec artifacts found in the Pacific Coast region of Chiapas and Guatemala remains Carlos Navarrete's (1974) summary of sculpture and jades. In the course of our recent research in the Mazatán region of Chiapas, Mexico, several more Olmec objects have come to light. We have also examined most of the sculpture reported by Navarrete and have made additional observations. We update here the information on some of the known sculpture and describe some of the new finds, beginning with the sculpture and then considering jade and related greenstone artifacts. The major sites and locations of the artifacts discussed are shown in figure 1.

Olmec Sculpture

Several dozen sculptures in the distinct Olmec style are known for the Pacific Coast, an area stretching from the Isthmus of Tehuantepec in Mexico to El Salvador (see Parsons [1986] for a recent summary of the sculpture from the region). These include bas-relief carvings on boulders as well as a few sculptures in the round. The best-known sculptures are the bas-relief panels from Pijijiapan, Chiapas (figs. 2, 3), and the more varied corpus of early sculpture from Abaj Takalik, Guatemala (see illustrations in Graham 1981; Graham et al. 1978; Orrego 1990). We have not examined the sculp-

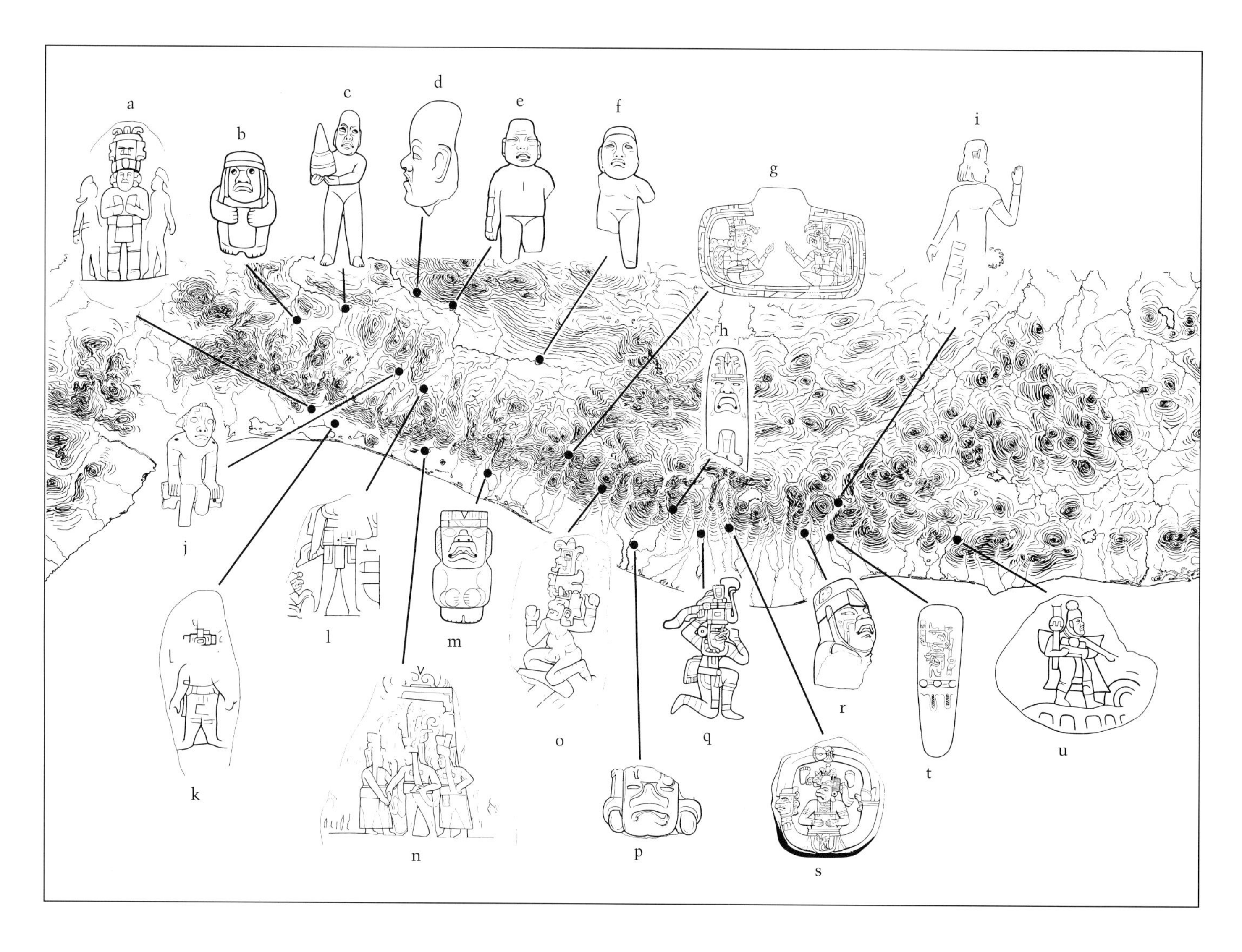

ture in Guatemala or El Salvador (see Anderson 1978; Boggs 1950; Sharer 1989) and thus confine our observations here to sculpture from the Chiapas Coast.

Pijijiapan Monument 1 (fig. 2) is of particular interest. Over the years, this stone has suffered from local vandalism. About fifteen years ago the low-relief figures were outlined in crimson paint by a teacher to highlight the human figures for the benefit of his grade school class, and just two years ago a highway-crew worker attempted to push the stone over with a bulldozer. He was unsuccessful in uprooting the stone but did manage to break away about a third of the low relief. Most recently, restoration efforts by personnel from the Tuxtla Gutiérrez, Chiapas, Regional Center of the National Institute of Anthropology and History have reversed some of the recent damage by removing most of the oil-based paint from the granite monolith and cementing the spalled-off portions of the carving back in place.

Recent damage to the stone is senseless and tragic, but the original scene can once again be appreciated today. We have had the monument carefully redrawn under raking light at night to capture additional details not evident in Navarrete's original photographs (fig. 2) or drawings made from them (fig. 3a). It is now clear that the central male figure is flanked by two women, both in elaborate attire and with one or two attendants (shown in the diminutive) standing behind each, only traces of which are now currently evident (fig. 3b). Also, the upper frame of the panel is not an Izapa-like sky panel as previously supposed and argued. Overall, the addition of details, and corrections of others, make this scene more complex than previously supposed, and it appears to be a Middle Formative style more akin to the art

1. Map of the Pacific Coast region and immediate interior showing the locations of Olmec artifacts: (a) Tiltepec, (b) Miramar, (c) Ocozocuautla, (d) Chiapa de Corzo, (e) Acala, (f) Laguna Francesa, (g) Motozintla, (h) San Marcos, (i) Amatitlan, (j) Villa Flores, (k) Tzutzuculi, (l) Padre Piedra, (m) Mapastepec, (n) Pijijiapan, (o) La Union, (p) La Blanca, (q) Abaj Takalik, (r) El Baul, (s) Suchitepéquez, (t) Escuintla, (u) Chalchuapa

2. Photograph by Carlos Navarrete of Monument 1 at Pijijiapan, Chiapas, Mexico, Middle Formative period, stone

a

b

3. Drawings of Monument 1 at Pijijiapan: (a) drawing published by Carlos Navarrete (1974: 5, fig. 3); (b) recent drawing of the monument by Ayax Moreno

of La Venta than that at San Lorenzo. The carving has recently been interpreted as a possible marriage scene (Clark and Pérez 1994: 269).

Other monuments described by Navarrete (1974) from Ojo de Agua and Buena Vista are shown in figures 4 and 5 and were also redrawn by Ayax Moreno to obtain the best possible rendering of the details. These sculptures are each made on local andesite boulders readily available in the piedmont zone of the southern Chiapas Coast. It is important to note here that all details of the technical drawings were rechecked under varying conditions; only those details that were sufficiently clear were rendered on the drawings.

The sculptures from Buena Vista and Ojo de Agua are both from the Mazatán region and are of special interest because they are small sculptures in the round, a rarity for Olmec stone sculpture outside Olman. The Ojo de Agua sculpture depicts a figure in elaborate garb and headdress, and with an elaborate chest plate upon which is shown a male seated cross-legged on a throne, portrayed in a cave. According to the eyebrow clues discussed by David Grove (this volume and personal communication, 1997), the monster framing the "cave" and the underworld serpent face on the throne denote an underworld or otherworld setting for this throne.

Arguably, the most important Olmec sculpture from the Mazatán region has never been adequately described or illustrated, although it has long been known. Thomas Lee (1989: 218, fig. 9.6d) presents a crude sketch of the Alvaro Obregon sculpture in his summary of the Olmec presence in Chiapas. As evident in figure 6, the monument is now decapitated and legless. It is a three-dimensional torso fragment of a standing male depicted in elaborate dress, which includes a short cape and tied waistband from which hang a pair of crocodile paws (or the paw-wing motif). The only other large standing Olmec sculptures of which we are aware are Monument 19 from Laguna de los Cerros, Veracruz (see Gillespie, this volume), also depicted in an elaborate cape, Monument 42 from Abaj Takalik (Orrego 1990: 83), and Monuments 1 and 4 from Los Naranjos in Honduras (Baudez and Becquelin 1973: 82, fig. 65). These last three monuments probably date to the early Middle Formative period. The Alvaro Obregon figure may be attired in ball-playing gear; he is shown holding a ball and a club or

4. Reconstruction of light andesite sculpture from Ojo de Agua, Chiapas, now in the Regional Museum of Anthropology, Tapachula, Chiapas, Mexico
Drawing by Ayax Moreno

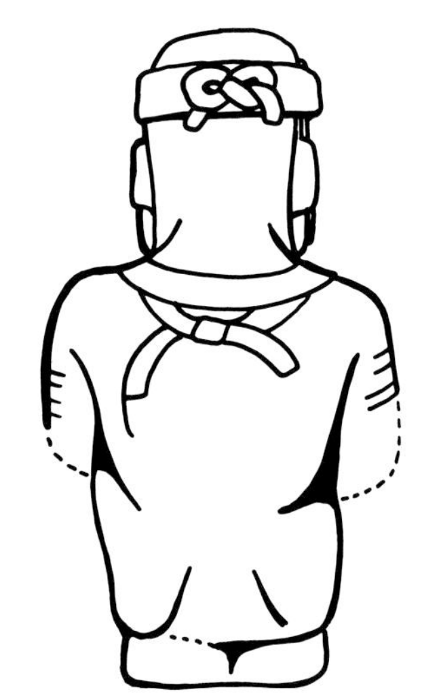

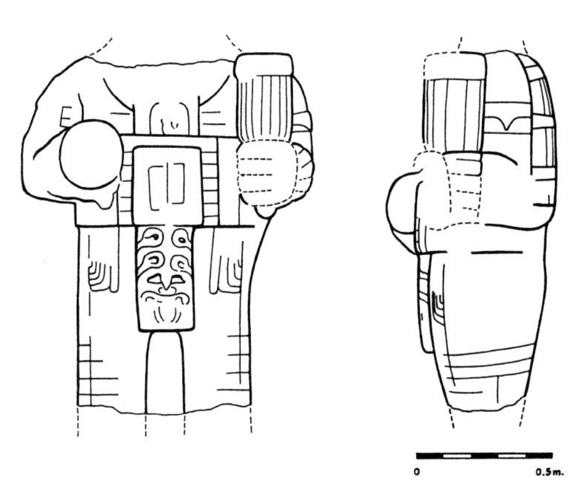

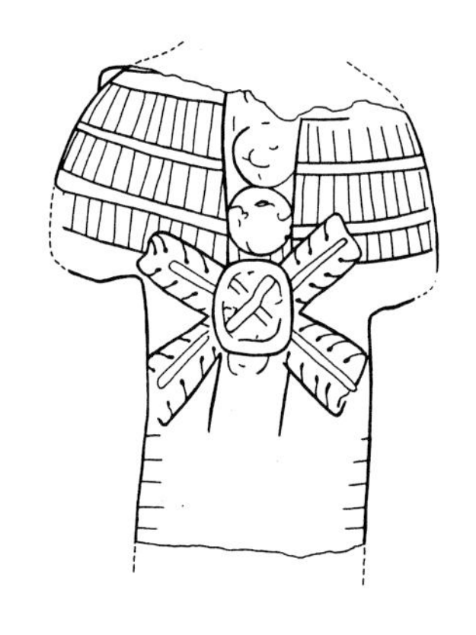

short bat. The arms are tight to the body and poorly rendered. The sculpture is of hard, dark andesite and is larger than lifesize. The completed sculpture would have weighed several tons.

The sculpture is on permanent display in the main plaza at Alvaro Obregon and is cemented into a concrete block. Details of the part embedded in the cement were reconstructed from an early photograph taken by Carlos Navarrete and on file with the New World Archaeological Foundation. The sculpture was supposedly found at the large Protoclassic site on the south side of town and must have been moved there from elsewhere in ancient times. The Ojo de Agua and Buena Vista sculptures are from the same general area around Obregon. Although we know where most of these smaller sculptures were found, they all lack specific archaeological contexts. One of us (Clark) recently was able to examine a private collection of figurine heads and a jade axe found in loose association with the Buena Vista sculpture, and they date to the Cuadros phase (c. 1100–950 B.C.). Such a date is consistent with the style of the monument. As described below, given the history of the Mazatán region, it is likely that all the Olmec sculpture in this region predates 850 B.C.

Figure 7 depicts a high-relief carving from La Union, a site located just north of Izapa in the piedmont and in a major pass to the highlands of Guatemala. The portrayed figure is of a partially kneeling male, with upraised arms, wearing a tall, elaborate headdress. The stone is eroded or defaced, and details of the head and face are difficult to discern. It is most similar to Monument 1 at Abaj Takalik (see fig. 15k), a near neighbor to La Union and located in a similar environmental setting. The stone was investigated by Carlos Navarrete and is currently on display in the Anthropology Museum in Tapachula. Garth Norman (1976: 300, fig. 6.12) illustrated this monument and described its similarities to Izapan stelae. We find the stylistic similarities to late Olmec sculpture the more compelling comparison.

5. Dark andesite sculpture from Buena Vista, Chiapas, now in a private collection in Tapachula, Chiapas, Mexico

6. Sculpture fragment from Alvaro Obregon, Chiapas, from a sculpture of a standing male in elaborate dress, possibly of a ballplayer

7. High-relief sculpture from La Union, Chiapas, currently on display in the Regional Museum of Anthropology, Tapachula, Chiapas, Mexico

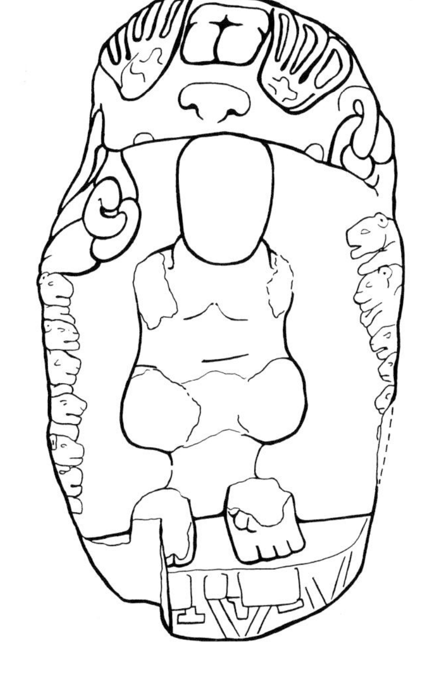

8. Drawing of "El León," Monument 2 from Izapa, Chiapas, showing a crouching personage in a cave of the earth monster, represented by the jaguar face at the top of the cave

9. The Tuxtla Chico dancing jaguar, Middle Formative period, stone
Museo Regional de Antropología e Historia, Tuxtla Gutiérrez, Chiapas

The sculpture known as "El León" from Izapa has long been thought to be the oldest sculpture at the site, as it is reminiscent of the Olmec style (Lowe et al. 1982: 100, fig. 6.10). It is carved in the round and shows a figure in a niche or cave. A recent redrawing of this monument (fig. 8) shows that the upper panel is a jaguar snout and paws. Jaguars carved in low relief, and stacked one atop the other, frame the sides, and the basal panel is a high relief in a style akin to the "earth" panels on other stelae at the site (see Norman 1976).

The eroded (or defaced) head, shoulders, and feet of the individual in the niche are still evident. The legs and arms have been broken off, leaving just the stubs of the arms and feet. Initially we thought that El León portrayed a figure seated in a cave/niche, but careful examination of the stone and its breakage patterns revealed that the full figure was in a crouched position, with the knees flexed, and with the hands and forearms in front of the body, a position similar to that known for the Tuxtla Chico statue (fig. 9). The crouching figurine in the niche could very well be the same person in costume, or the same creature, shown in the freestanding Tuxtla Chico sculpture. If true, the headdress of this being could account for what otherwise appears to be a very oversized head on the El León niche figure. Perhaps the figure represented a ruler in jaguar costume, or one in transformation to a jaguar, as argued for other Olmec figurines (see Furst 1995; Reilly 1989). On stylistic grounds, we place the El León sculpture toward the middle of the Middle Formative period, about 600–500 B.C., contemporaneous with all the pieces of small Olmec lapidary found in the region.

A head and torso of two other sculptural fragments from Izapa match the Tuxtla Chico statue in size, theme, and technical execution; the two sculpture fragments are of different stones, however, suggesting that there were at least three monuments of the same size representing the dancing or crouched jaguar. Susanna Ekholm (1993) recovered the reworked head of one jaguar sculpture in mound fill that dates to 600–300 B.C., suggesting that the three jaguar sculptures may date to as early as 600 B.C. and are contemporaneous with or earlier than El León.

10. Drawing of a greenstone axe from the Mapastepec area of Chiapas currently in a private collection in Tapachula, Chiapas, Mexico

Jade and Greenstone Artifacts

Six pieces of jade or greenstone Olmec lapidary from the general vicinity of the Chiapas Coast have recently come to light; we have been able to examine five and verify the discovery and description of a sixth. Three appear to have come from the general area of Mapastepec, located south of Pijijiapan and near Pampa el Pajón (see fig. 1), the latter famous for a burial of a young male with tabular-erect cranial deformation in the style portrayed on long-headed, Olmec jade figurines (see Lowe 1994: 117, fig. 7.4; Paillés 1980: 97–103, figs. 54–60). All the artifacts reported here are independent finds in different collections. We currently know of no large, inland Middle Formative site in the Mapastepec zone, but, given the recent finds, the zone deserves to be surveyed systematically to search for such sites.

The first artifact is a votive axe made from local, igneous stone, probably gabbro or related stone with a high concentration of dark green minerals. This piece of stone is unusual because it is from a vein of dense, dark mineral in granitic rock. The face of the axe is dark green, and the back is white. The color contrast of the stone was deliberately selected and worked into the piece to have the piebald effect of a dark face and light back. Unfortunately, some of the softer plagioclase minerals have eroded, and so it is now extremely difficult to appreciate the original quality and design of this artifact. As evident in figure 10, the axe was carved in high relief, with additional details of the design rendered by fine incisions. Originally the axe had a mirror finish, which is still evident in patches on some of the harder crystals, but it has since eroded and now has the appearance of rough sandstone. The incised design is difficult to see without raking light. The axe supposedly came from a ranch south of Mapastepec, near the estuary. It is now in the private collection of Javier León in Tapachula.

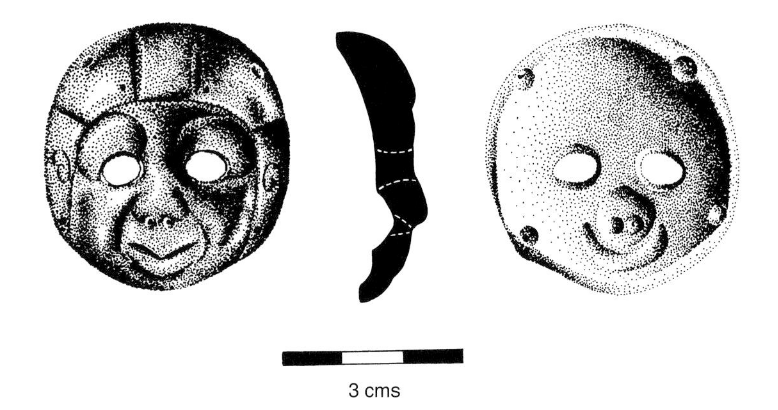

11. Small maskette of high-quality, blue-green jade said to be from the Mapastepec region of Chiapas, now in a private collection in Tapachula, Chiapas, Mexico

Another piece in a different collection in Tapachula is of fine, blue-green jade. It is a small maskette with suspension holes, per-

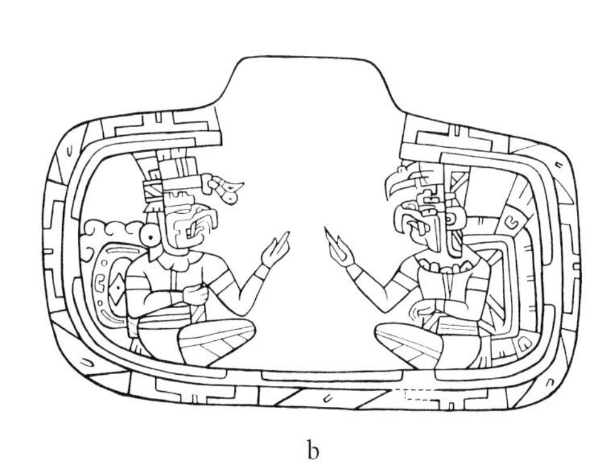

12. Greenstone plaque and figurine fragment from the Chiapas Coast: (a) small figurine of greenstone showing an individual wearing a large chest plaque, perhaps such as from Motozintla; (b) large plaque said to have been found in the Motozintla area of Chiapas, the major pass from the Pacific Coast to the interior valleys, currently in the Regional Museum of Anthropology, Tuxtla Gutiérrez, Mexico

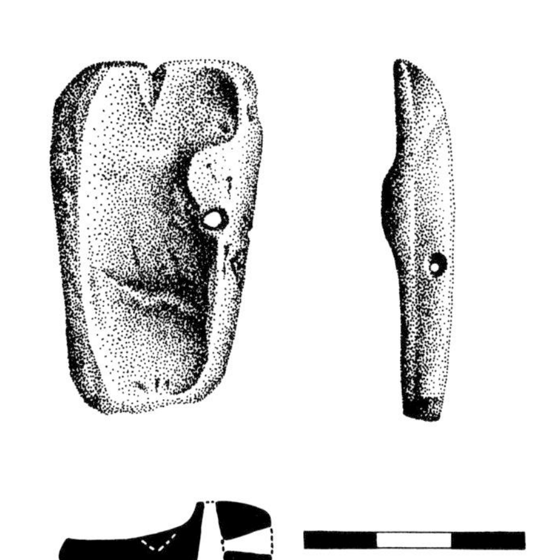

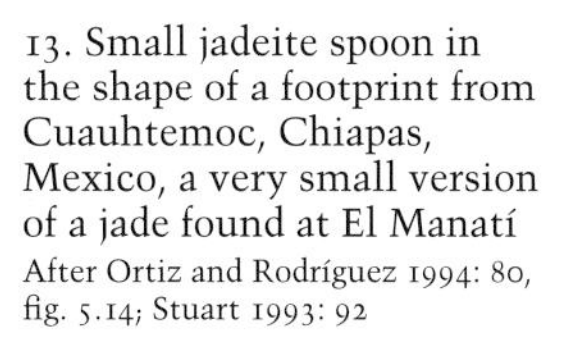

13. Small jadeite spoon in the shape of a footprint from Cuauhtemoc, Chiapas, Mexico, a very small version of a jade found at El Manatí
After Ortiz and Rodríguez 1994: 80, fig. 5.14; Stuart 1993: 92

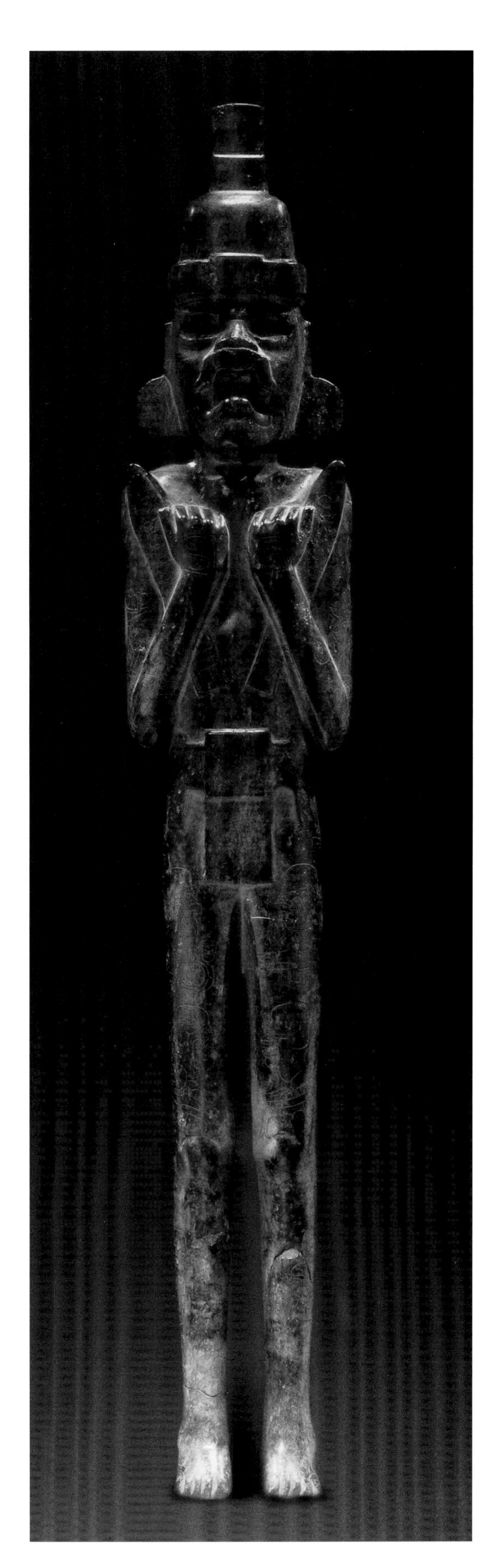

14. Serpentine statuette known as the "Young Lord," Middle Formative period, said to be from either La Blanca, Guatemala, or Atiquizaya, El Salvador
Private collection

haps for wearing around the neck (fig. 11). The representation is not obviously in the Olmec style, but we have identified it as such on the basis of its raw material and workmanship. The piece is very delicately carved and polished to a mirror finish.

A third greenstone artifact from the general Mapastepec area, and donated to the Regional Museum of Anthropology in Tapachula, is illustrated by Gareth Lowe (1994: 118, fig. 7.5) in his summary article on the Olmec presence in Chiapas. It is of a softer greenstone, perhaps serpentine, not native to the zone. The stone figurine fragment is clearly in the Olmec style and is of special interest because of the large chest plaque that the figure is shown wearing (fig. 12a). This ornament may be similar to that shown in figure 12b, a large pectoral recently discovered by Mario Tejada in the storeroom of the regional Museum of Anthropology in Comitán (Tejada 1993). The piece, now on display in the Regional Museum of Anthropology in Tuxtla Gutiérrez, is said to have come from the Motozintla area. Motozintla is located just on the inland side of the major pass from the southern Chiapas Coast into the interior river valleys on the northern side of the Sierra Madre (fig. 1). As evident, the inscribed design of two personages attired in avian costumes on this polished, serpentine plaque is complex and reminiscent of the La Venta narrative style, probably dating toward the end of the Middle Formative period.

The last "new" artifact that we illustrate here comes from the site of Cuauhtemoc, located at the extreme tip of the south coast of Chiapas, about 15 kilometers from the Guatemalan border and across from the well-known site of La Victoria (see Coe 1961). It is a small "spoon" in the shape of a footprint (fig. 13), such as recently reported from El Manatí (see Ortiz and Rodríguez 1994: 80, fig. 5.14; Stuart 1993: 92). Another small jadeite spoon was found at Cuauhtemoc, and one is reported in the literature from Altamira, Chiapas, a site in the Mazatán region (Lowe 1967: 129, fig. 97d). What is particularly interesting about Cuauhtemoc, however, are the ones that got away. In 1966, John Clark and Ayax Moreno spent a week pursuing rumors of an Olmec axe that had supposedly been found there in recent ditch-digging operations of the banana plantation. They could not verify the rumor of the axe, but they did obtain secure testimony of the discovery of a jade figurine in an urn burial. The tractor driver who had had the piece in his possession for several years described the highly polished figurine of dark green jade as slightly bent at the knees, with the face of a "gorilla," and as holding a ball near his chest. The urn burial would have dated to the late Conchas phase, or about 750 B.C. We suspect that the site of Cuauhtemoc may have been part of the La Blanca polity, located about half a day's walk to the east in Guatemala.

La Blanca was probably the most important regional center in the Pacific Coast region at the beginning of the Middle Formative period (see Love 1989, 1991; Jackson and Love 1991). The jade figurine known as "Slim," or the "Young Lord," is said to have been found at La Blanca (see fig. 14) or Atiquizaya, El Salvador.[2] The complexity of its iconography suggests a Middle Formative date. Two fragments of Olmec sculpture in the round are also known for this site (Love 1991). All of the greenstone and jade artifacts reported here probably date to the Middle Formative, some probably to the very end of the period.

Toward a Chronology of the Olmec Artifacts

As noted, most of the artifacts just described lack specific temporal or spatial context, but such context is critical to understanding the Olmec question as it applies to the Pacific Coast. In some cases, we have a specific or general idea of the location at which an artifact or sculpture was found. Placing them in time, however, remains a critical problem. Here we describe our recent speculations on the matter.

As a general rule of thumb, we believe that the archaeology of Olmec sites in Olman shows a basic chronological progression from sculpture in the round (common at San Lorenzo) to high-relief and then low-relief sculpture (more common at La Venta). These same data indicate that incised jade axes and jade figurines are also Middle Formative phenomena. The iconography and composition of incised images on the jades also correspond well with the scenes shown on Olmec stelae (compare Taube, this volume).

Three of the sculptures described here come from the Mazatán region, and all are carved in the round. They vary substantially, however, in theme, technical execution, and style. On stylistic grounds, we are confident that the sculpture from Alvaro Obregon (fig. 6) and Buena Vista (fig. 5) date to the Cuadros phase (1100–950 B.C.) of the Early Formative and that the sculpture from Ojo de Agua (fig. 4) dates to the Jocotal phase (950–850 B.C.). The Alvaro Obregon sculpture has the paw-wing motif, a characteristic of Cuadros phase pottery, shown suspended from the belt, thus suggesting a date to this phase. The Mazatán region was virtually abandoned by the end of the Jocotal phase, and so this provides a convenient termination date for the Olmec sculpture in this region. A nondescript fragment of Olmec sculpture, made of the same soft andesite as the Ojo de Agua sculpture, was recovered in a Jocotal context at the site of San Carlos, so we know that sculpture dates at least to this period. The major center of the time was in the Ojo de Agua zone. Numerous low mounds are dispersed around two very long mounds, the taller of which is about 15 meters high and 110 meters long. The Ojo de Agua ranch was part of this Jocotal site which we now call El Silencio, in honor of the ranch on which the principal mounds are located.

The Olmec boulder sculpture reported here probably postdate the Jocotal phase. Navarrete (1974: 7) originally suggested that the Pijijiapan sculpture dated to the Cuadros/Jocotal phase, but the few sherd diagnostics he reports could be earlier than the carvings. Sherds recently taken from the adjacent brickyard are also too early (Ocos or Cherla phases, 1350–1100 B.C.). But these artifacts do indicate that the site was known and occupied in pre-Olmec times, long before the bas-reliefs were carved. It is worth stressing that the Pijijiapan sculptures are part of a much broader chronological problem, as they are thematically and technically similar to boulder sculpture elsewhere in Mesoamerica, including those from El Salvador, Chalcatzingo, Guerrero, Veracruz, and the inland jungle of Chiapas. Many of these sculptures are shown in figure 15.

Three monuments of this style in Chiapas have been assigned dates based upon relative archaeological association. The Olmec sculpture up the coast at Tzutzuculi (see figs. 1k and 15f) dates to the Middle Formative, or between 650 and 450 B.C. (McDonald 1983: 37). The sculpture at Padre Piedra (figs. 1l and 15g) (Green and Lowe 1967: 33, fig. 42), just across the Sierra Madre, dates to the Dili or Chiapa II phase, or about 850–700 B.C. (Green and Lowe 1967: 36). And the sculpture at Xoc (fig. 15i) is associated with later Chiapa III pottery, but probably is earlier (Ekholm-Miller 1973: 23). It is worth pointing out that the dating in all of these cases is ambiguous and is also an estimate of the latest date for each monument. We used to think that the Pijijiapan monument was iconographically earlier than these others, but this impression was a consequence of the simplicity of the original drawings. The recent drawing of Monument 1 at Pijijiapan (fig. 3b) shows that it is stylistically similar to the other bas-relief monuments.

Our working assumption for these monuments is that they were part of a short-lived, widespread phenomenon, as indicated by similarities in representations, media, and carving techniques. The phenomenon was pan-Mesoamerican and not just limited to Chiapas. We think the data available allow us to bracket these low-relief monuments temporally between the end of the Jocotal phase and the beginning of the Chiapa III phase, or about 850–700 B.C. One of the characteristics of these monuments in Chiapas is that they appear to be isolated pieces unassociated with major archaeological sites. This may be true, or it may merely be our perception based upon the absence of large pyramids at the sites in which they were found. We take as our working hypothesis that the monuments were placed close to important sites, but sites lacking pyramids. The significant observations concerning these monuments, we think, can be accounted for if they date to the time before erection of earthen pyramids became popular, or before 700 B.C. (see Lee 1989; Lowe 1989a, 1989b).

We consider it likely, therefore, that the low-relief Olmec sculpture dates to the early Conchas phase (850–750 B.C.) and is related to the "double-line-break" horizon (Dili or Chiapa II phase in the Chiapas interior), which was also a pan-Mesoamerican phenomenon. Of course, some of the sites at which the Olmec sculpture is found do have pyramidal structures (for example, Tzutzuculi, La Blanca, and Chalcatzingo), but these pyramids may have been constructed subsequent to the carving of the monuments. On the Pacific Coast, the monument that most impresses us at Tzutzuculi, Monument 3 (fig. 15f), could have been relocated there from elsewhere (McDonald 1983: 39). For the cases of immovable boulder sculp-

15. Summary of early low-relief sculpture in Mesoamerica: (a) San Miguel Amuco, Guerrero, (b) Chalcatzingo, Morelos, (c) El Viejón, Veracruz, (d) La Venta, Tabasco, (e) Tiltepec, Chiapas, (f) Tzutzuculi, Chiapas, (g) Padre Piedra, Chiapas, (h) Pijijiapan, Chiapas, (i) Xoc, Chiapas, (j) La Union, Chiapas, (k) Abaj Takalik, Guatemala, (l) Chalchuapa, El Salvador

16. Summary of the chronology of Olmec artifacts from the Pacific Coast and the Olmec heartland

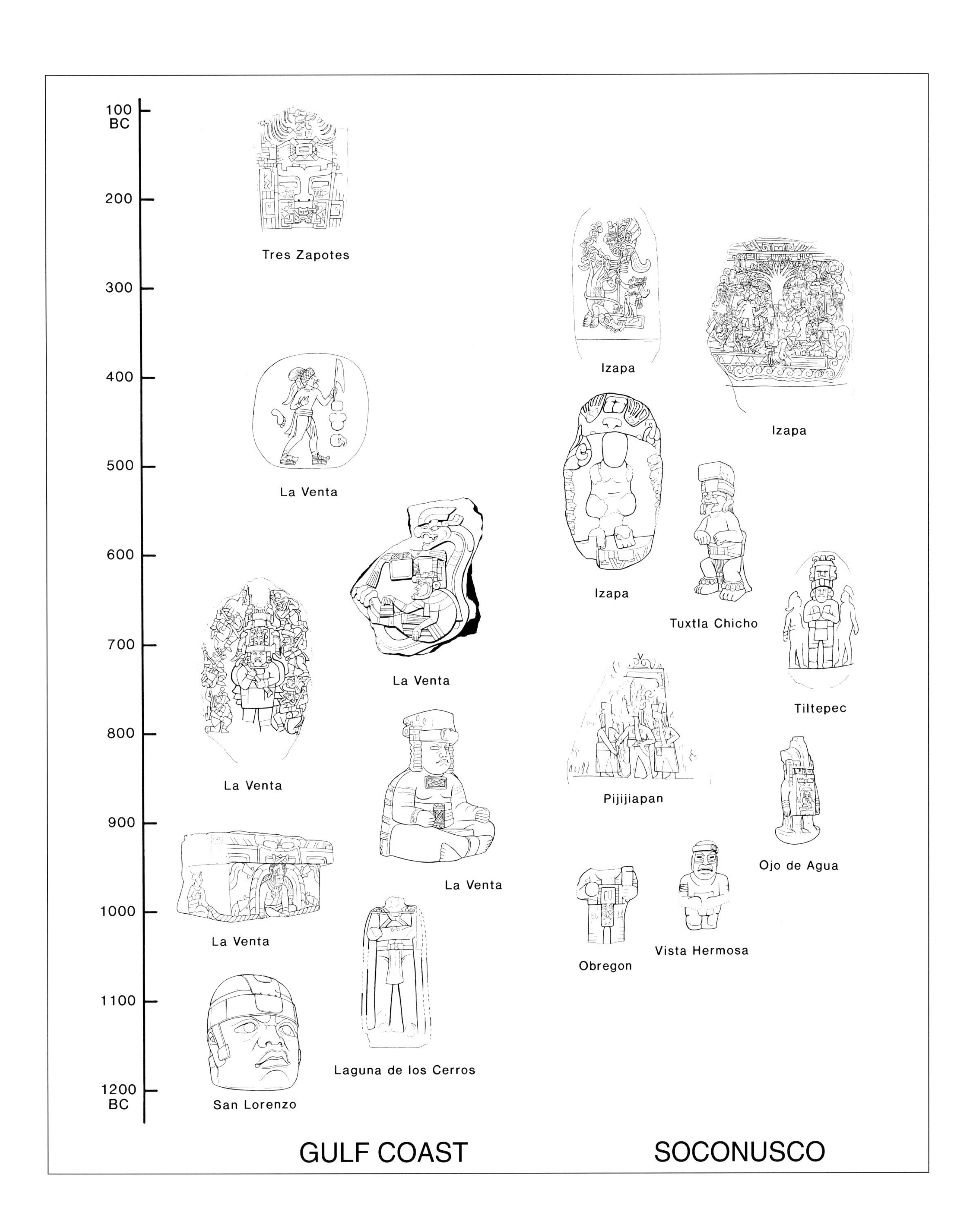
100
BC
200
300
400
500
600
700
800
900
1000
1100
1200
BC
Tres Zapotes
La Venta
La Venta
La Venta
La Venta
La Venta
San Lorenzo
Laguna de los Cerros
Izapa
Izapa
Izapa
Tuxtla Chicho
Tiltepec
Pijijiapan
Ojo de Agua
Vista Hermosa
Obregon
GULF COAST
SOCONUSCO

ture, such as at Pijijiapan, the largest Middle Formative sites may have postdated the monuments and have been located elsewhere as different considerations of optimal settlement came into play.

Each of these speculations is subject to numerous objections, and we will continue to question them in the future. But for now, our best guess at a sculptural chronology is that the Mazatán Olmec sculpture dates to the end of the Early Formative and that the low-relief carvings shown in figure 15 date to the early Conchas phase on the coast or to the Dili phase (Chiapa II) of the interior. The El León sculpture at Izapa is probably directly related to the Tiltepec style (see Parsons 1986) that probably dates to the Chiapa III phase, or about 700–500 B.C., and is related to the Tres Zapotes style (see figs. 15e, 16).

We can say less about the lapidary items because we cannot yet pinpoint them to specific sites. Except for the small "spoon" (fig. 13) from Cuauhtemoc, which dates to the Conchas phase, all of them probably date to the Chiapa III phase (Escalón phase in the Izapa sequence). We find polished axes in Cuadros contexts, but none of them are incised, so we think that incised axes, and perhaps masks, date to the beginning of the Middle Formative (early Conchas) and later. For the Pacific Coast, the Olmec lapidary objects may postdate the era of low-relief carvings. If true, it would suggest a change in the importing or local copying of Olmec art objects, as noted by Lee (1989: 216–217). We think that the uneven data currently available indicate that this was the case. The best data for making this assessment come from recent research in the Mazatán zone of the Soconusco region, a favorable spot occupied by the Mokaya, predecessors and subsequent neighbors of the Olmecs of Olman.

17. Reconstruction of Barra phase (1700–1500 B.C.) ceramic vessels from the Mazatán region
Drawing by Ayax Moreno

18. Reconstruction of Locona phase (1500–1350 B.C.) ceramic vessels from the Mazatán region
Drawing by Ayax Moreno

A Millennium of Contact

The Early Mokaya Tradition

The Soconusco region of the greater Pacific Coast region is one of the few places in Middle America with attested Late Archaic and Early Formative societies (Clark 1994a). The transition to sedentary village life occurred about 2000–1800 B.C., with the first Mokaya villages in the Mazatán region being evident during the Barra phase (c. 1700–1500 B.C.). Evidence of these early village societies was first discovered by Michael Coe at the site of La Victoria on the Guatemalan coast. He named this early complex "Ocos" after the nearby port town (Coe 1961). Gareth Lowe (1967, 1975) subsequently discovered an even earlier ceramic complex that he dubbed the "Barra" complex, thought to date from about 1800–1500 B.C. Both of these complexes are well known in the literature. We have since identified and named two more early complexes (see Blake et al. 1995), and we refer to all four as the Mokaya tradition.

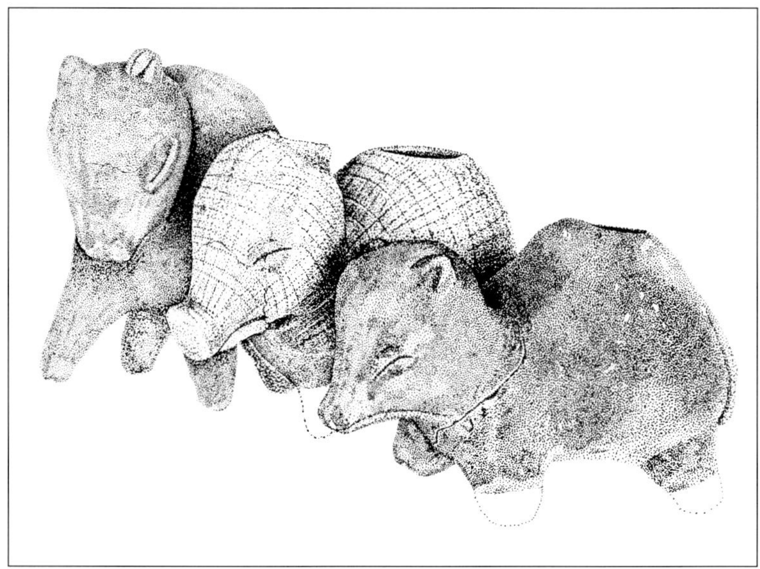

19. Locona figurines from the Mazatán region of coastal Chiapas, Mexico

20. Locona effigy vessels from the Mazatán region
Drawing by Jared Clark

Our best data for the Mokaya tradition come from the Mazatán region of the Chiapas coast (see fig. 1). The earliest known villages date to the Barra phase, the time of the first use of ceramics (fig. 17). These early ceramic vessels were elaborate and well made, and they appear to have been used exclusively for processing and serving special beverages, perhaps corn beer or chocolate (Clark and Blake 1994). Although elaborate ceramics appear rather suddenly in the archaeological record and lack local precedents, John Clark and Dennis Gosser (1995) argue that the vessels were made by local peoples who adopted foreign technologies from peoples living in Central America. These earliest Mokaya were horticulturalists and are thought to have been organized in small, egalitarian villages organized by aggrandizers or bigmen (Clark 1994a, 1994b). Many of the early changes and innovations seen in the archaeological record potentially could have been effected through attempts at self-aggrandizement by these leaders. The basic subsistence economy of the time was mixed, with hunting and fishing being of prime importance. Corn was cultivated but does not appear to have become a major staple until a few centuries later (Blake et al. 1992; compare Arnold, this volume).

About 1500 B.C. the local populations appear to have become organized into an interlocked network of rank societies or simple chiefdoms—large villages directed by chiefs. In terms of the local chronology, this occurred during the Locona phase (1500–1350 B.C.). The ceramic assemblage had changed significantly by this time (fig. 18) to include a variety of fancy serving dishes and plates and the first cooking and storage pots. Clay figurines also show up in greater frequencies, and they include large, hollow, slipped, elaborate figurines, predominantly of males, and small, crude, unslipped female figurines (fig. 19). A variety of animal effigy pots were also produced (fig. 20).

Of particular interest is the presence of large, central villages, each with a singular, elite domestic residence placed on an elevated platform (see figs. 21, 22) and surrounding small villages and hamlets. We think that these large residences were chiefs' houses. As such, they would have housed the chief, his wives, children, and other dependents and also have served public functions from time to time. Warren Hill and Michael Blake recently recovered clear evidence of an 80 meter-long ballcourt at the

21. Structure 4, Mound 6 at Paso de la Amada, Chiapas, Mexico, a large domestic structure, possibly a chiefly residence

22. Reconstruction of Structure 4 at Paso de la Amada
Drawing by Ayax Moreno

site of Paso de la Amada that dates to the beginning of the Locona phase (Hill 1996; Hill et al. 1998). Its proximity to the chiefly residence at that same site suggests the possibility that the ballcourt was maintained and controlled by the chief and his close followers.

In the following Ocos phase, we detect no major changes in regional organization. Each large village center continued to be occupied. Population tended to aggregate, however, a bit more in large villages, and the space between the large villages was less inhabited than before. The inventory of ceramic vessels changed to simpler, less-complex forms, colors, and more subtle surface textures (fig. 23); the hand-modeled figurine tradition continued, only now most of the figurines were unslipped, solid figurines (fig. 24). Of particular interest are figurines of seated, fat males depicted wearing animal masks and/or costumes (fig. 25). We suggest that these may have been portrayals of village shaman-chiefs (Clark 1991).

The final phase of the Mokaya tradition, the Cherla phase (1200–1100 B.C.), is of particular interest here because it was a time of rapid and pervasive change. The pottery changed from a red-ware tradition (Barra, Locona, Ocos) to a black-and-white-ware tradition (fig. 26). Items

23. Reconstruction of Ocos phase (1350–1200 B.C.) ceramic vessels from the Mazatán region
Drawing by Ayax Moreno

24. Reconstruction drawing of an Ocos female figurine from Aquiles Serdán in the Mazatán region
Drawing by Ayax Moreno

25. Reconstruction drawings of Ocos male figurines from the Mazatán region, possibly portraying shaman chiefs
Drawings by Ayax Moreno

of personal adornment (clay earspools, greenstone beads, and small iron-ore mirrors) reached an all-time high frequency in the region. Long-distance trade also appears to have achieved its greatest extent. Some of Mazatán's imports appear to have been fine-paste ceramic vessels and clay figurines from Olman (fig. 27). These were precursors of things to come.

The Olmecization of the Mokaya

The Mokaya appear to have gradually come under Olmec influence during Cherla times and to have adopted Olmec ways. We use the term *olmecization* to describe the processes whereby independent groups tried to become Olmecs, or to become like the Olmecs (Clark 1990). Our data from Mazatán suggest that this occurred in at least three sequential stages. During the Cherla phase, we see clear evidence of significant trade contacts with the Olmecs. Obsidian and jade from highland Guatemala passed through the Mazatán region on their way to Olman. The principal local export from Mazatán was probably chocolate (cacao beans). As noted, a few imported ceramic vessels and figurines from Olman appear at this time. These imports were rare, but they gave rise to local imitations. Local copies were made of the imported ceramic vessel forms and the seated, slipped figurines. One reason that the Cherla ceramic vessels appear so different is that the Mokaya tried to copy the ceramic vessels characteristic of Olman, but they did so with their own techniques and did not get the appropriate technical knowledge for differential firing of white-rimmed black vessels until later.

The final stage of olmecization was the actual presence of Olmecs in the region and a nearly full conversion of local artifacts to Olmec norms. This occurred at the beginning of the Cuadros phase (1100–950 B.C.), the local equivalent of the San Lorenzo phase defined at San Lorenzo. By this time, all of the serving wares had been transformed from red ware to black or white wares. Olmec dragon designs were carved or painted on the pots, and the storage and cooking vessels had gone from thin tecomates to thick, brushed tecomates (fig. 28). Also at this time, all of the local female figurines dropped out of the sequence, and the figurine assemblage became almost exclusively of seated Olmec solid and hollow male figurines (fig. 29).

26. Reconstruction drawing of Cherla phase (1200–1100 B.C.) ceramic vessels from the Mazatán region
Drawing by Ayax Moreno

27. Reconstruction of Cherla figurines from the Mazatán region
Drawings by Ayax Moreno

As noted, Olmec sculpture appeared in the Mazatán region at this time. The earliest sculpture (Alvaro Obregon and Buena Vista) portrays males in elaborate dress or special headdresses. We still know too little of this critical phase, but current data suggest that a significant decrease in local population occurred and that all the local chiefdom societies were reorga-

28. Reconstruction drawing of Cuadros phase (1100–950 B.C.) ceramic vessels from the Mazatán region
Drawing by Ayax Moreno

29. Reconstruction of Cuadros figurine from Aquiles Serdán in the Mazatán region
Drawings by Ayax Moreno

nized into one larger chiefdom administered from a regional center located in the middle of the region at the site of Cantón Corralito (Clark 1997). The few Olmecs who came into the region may have resided in this local capital center. The frequency of jade artifacts, carved pottery with Olmec designs, imported fine-paste vessels, Olmec figurines, obsidian prismatic blades, and mirrors is much greater at this center than for any other site (see Lesure, this volume). We still do not know how the Olmecs were able to gain such a strong foothold in Mazatán nor why they would have wanted to do so. Clark (1997) speculates that better control of trade may have been one primary motivation. He further suggests that local chiefs, or those striving to become chiefs, may initially have solicited help from their Olmec trade partners in gaining local ascendancy. Any Olmec help offered to the particular local factions may eventually have played to the long-term advantage of the Olmecs.

In the future, DNA studies of skeletal populations may provide a firm indication that some Olmecs indeed infiltrated the Mazatán zone and had a major impact there. But even should this prove not to have been the case, we would still consider the inhabitants of the Mazatán zone during the Cuadros phase to have been Olmecs because they adopted and internalized Olmec practices and the material representations of them. In all respects, they signaled their commitment to the Olmec system. And as Richard Lesure (this volume) demonstrates, there was no local precedent for the Olmec system in Mazatán. To the contrary, the Mokaya had a vibrant representational system based upon naturalistic portrayals of people and animals that was replaced by an abstract system of supernaturals or mythological creatures. The success of the Olmec system in Mazatán appears to have paralleled, step for step, its success at San Lorenzo. With the fall of San Lorenzo about 900 B.C. (see Coe and Diehl 1980), things in Mazatán began to fall apart.

Getting Back to Basics

The Jocotal phase along the Pacific Coast is still poorly understood. In many ways it appears as a clear continuation of the Cuadros phase. As evident in figure 30, much of the pottery continued as before. But there are still clear differences. In the Mazatán region, the dominant regional center appears to have shifted from Cantón Corralito to the other side of the Coatan River to the site of El Silencio. We find thin traces of Jocotal occupation nearly everywhere in the Mazatán zone but rarely in significant densities. On the face of it, the Jocotal phase appears to have been a time of rapid population increase (Clark 1994a). Much of this expansion, however, may be more apparent than real, being the result of a shift in the permanence of settlement, perhaps from settled villages to greater reliance on shifting farmsteads. Until we have excavated more sites, we cannot evaluate the significance of the regional distribution of the Jocotal phase materials.

30. Reconstruction drawing of Jocotal phase (950–850 B.C.) ceramic vessels from the Mazatán region
Drawing by Ayax Moreno

We do know, however, that this phase witnessed a significant use of the estuaries along the Pacific Coast, including the sites of Altamira (Lowe 1967), Los Alvarez (Ceja 1974), the Navarijo mound (Shook and Hatch 1979), and Salinas La Blanca (Coe and Flannery 1967). Three additional sites present evidence for specialized production of foodstuffs, perhaps salt or fish products: El Mesak in Guatemala (Demarest et al. 1988; Pye and Demarest 1991; Pye 1995) and Pampa el Pajón (Paillés 1980) and El Varal in Chiapas (Lesure 1993). These sites are located within 2.5 kilometers of the coast, either on a mangrove-estuary or a tributary leading to an estuary. All three are multicomponent sites and consist of a single, large Jocotal period mound at least 4 meters in height and 60 meters in diameter, or larger. All show a rapid buildup of dense midden deposits rich in artifacts, especially broken and burned tecomates or hemispherical jars. Other vessels are present and suggest a full domestic assemblage, albeit one with little obsidian (Paillés 1980; Lesure 1993; Pye 1995: 88). The size of these mounds and the midden deposits are particularly notable, since the Jocotal period lasted only some fifty years (Blake et al. 1995) to at most one hundred years (Pye 1995).

Other pertinent features at these estuary sites include large, deep hearths, both circular and oval in shape (Paillés 1980; Pye 1995; Lesure 1993: 213). These features are similar to deep hearths uncovered at the Late Formative site of Guzman (Nance 1992), while at nearby Salinas La Blanca, Michael Coe and Kent Flannery reported the Cerro del Tiestal complex at sites around salt flats and believed that these had been engaged in salt production (1967: 90–92). Other parallels include Güegüensi, a Late Postclassic mangrove site in the Bay of Fonseca, also argued by Claude Baudez (1973) to have been a salt production site. The Soconusco area was known for salt production according to Colonial period accounts (Estrada and de Niebla 1977; Andrews 1983: 16). Alternatively, some kind of fish product may have been produced, such as a fish sauce or paste; such items were widely produced and distributed in coastal areas of the Mediterranean during the Roman Empire (Peacock 1986: 35–36).

It remains unclear why intensive food or salt production began in this period, although it would seem that the quantities produced were beyond the requirements of the inhabitants at these sites. The Pacific Coast communities had been participants in trade networks along the Pacific Coast, both local and long distance, as far back as the Archaic; Barbara Voorhies recovered El Chayal obsidian from highland Guatemala at Chantuto (c. 3000–2000 B.C.) sites in coastal Chiapas (Nelson and Voorhies 1980). Not far from El Chayal is the Motagua Valley jade source—a raw material that was likely moved along the same network. For the Jocotal phase, two jade or greenstone axes were recovered from El Mesak, one of which came from an excavated level (Pye and Demarest 1991). This find substantiates the proposed dating for the Olmec lapidary items recovered from Chiapas. Additionally, it was at the estuary site of Pampa el Pajón that the burial of a twelve-year-old child with a cranium exhibiting "tabular erect, fronto-occipital type [deformation]" was recovered (Paillés 1980: 89)—a physical trait typical of Olmec jade figurines. These small hamlets in Pacific Coast mangrove swamps were participating in the broader Mesoamerican interaction of goods and symbols.

Another category of artifact consistently found at all Jocotal period sites along the Pacific Coast are ceramics with Olmec motifs. As previously described, Early Formative period ceramics with Olmec iconographic motifs date from 1200 to 950 B.C. and are found at many sites in Mesoamerica. Forms include shallow to deep bowls with straight or outflared walls, tecomates, and jars slipped a dark color or composed of dark-colored pastes. The distinguishing decorative characteristic is a carved surface, which was cut away with a sharp, regular-edged tool prior to firing while the vessel surface was still in the leather-hard stage. Decorative motifs are variable, with flame-eyebrows, clefts, slanted clefts and lines, and crossed bands, among others (see Lesure, this volume).

In the subsequent Middle Formative period, dating from roughly 950 to 500 B.C., Olmec motif ceramics generally occur on thin-walled cylinders and outflared-wall bowls typically slipped white, although they can also occur in gray, red, or black. The decorative technique shifted from carving to a combination of incision and scraping of the surface slip. In contrast to the previous period, often no specific tool appears to have been used, and the quality of design execution varied widely. The motifs include Olmec faces in profile and more abstract designs like clovers, variations on the double-line-break,[3] and geometric patterns. These Olmec motif ceramics have been largely defined by materials from outside the Gulf Coast area, particularly Central Mexico and the valleys of Oaxaca, Morelos, and Puebla; La Venta ceramics are still poorly understood and await further analysis from ongoing excavations (González 1988, 1996). As described below, the Pacific Coast motif set consists of Olmec profile faces, circles, clovers, and geometrics.

Design Elements: Olmec Profile Faces and Circles. Typically appearing on whiteware cylinders, Olmec profile faces depict a distinctive cleft atop the head or curving back to the right (see Taube, this volume, for a discussion of this iconography). Unprovenienced cylinders with this motif are believed to have originated from sites in the valleys of Mexico, Puebla, and Morelos (fig. 31) (Coe 1965: 27–28; Feuchtwanger 1989: 199–201; Joralemon 1971; Benson and de la Fuente 1996: 202–203). Christine Niederberger has since related these unprovenienced examples to a specific Ayotla phase (1250–1000 B.C.) ceramic type, Paloma Negativo, recovered from the Tlapacoya site in the Valley of Mexico. Black or negative resist was used to help create the design, together with incised lines and cross-hatching, while some examples have red paint or slip overlying areas of white slip (Niederberger 1976: 126–127, 179). Also carrying the incised designs with Olmec motifs are Pili Blanco and Pili Rojo—plainer white-ware versions of Paloma Negativo (Niederberger 1976: 123–137, 175). Niederberger has identified sherds of Paloma Negativo from materials found at San José Mogote households in the Valley of Oaxaca (Flannery and Marcus 1994: 286).

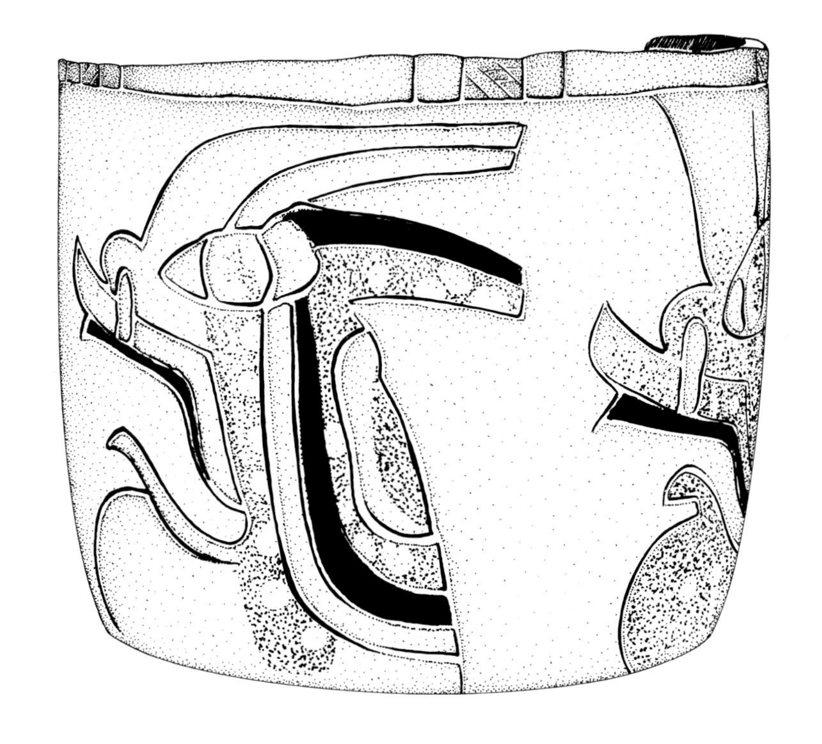

Ceramics from the Pacific Coast region feature a similar Olmec profile face and use black resist, red slip, and incision for design, although the Pacific Coast examples are less elaborate than Paloma Negativo from Central Mexico (fig. 32). The motif ceramics exhibit a variety of paste types, which range from compacted, fine paste with mica to a coarser paste without mica. The gradient of paste quality, presence of mica, and the quality of executed design all vary independently, making it difficult to distinguish likely imported examples from local copies, the only potential exception being kaolin paste sherds.

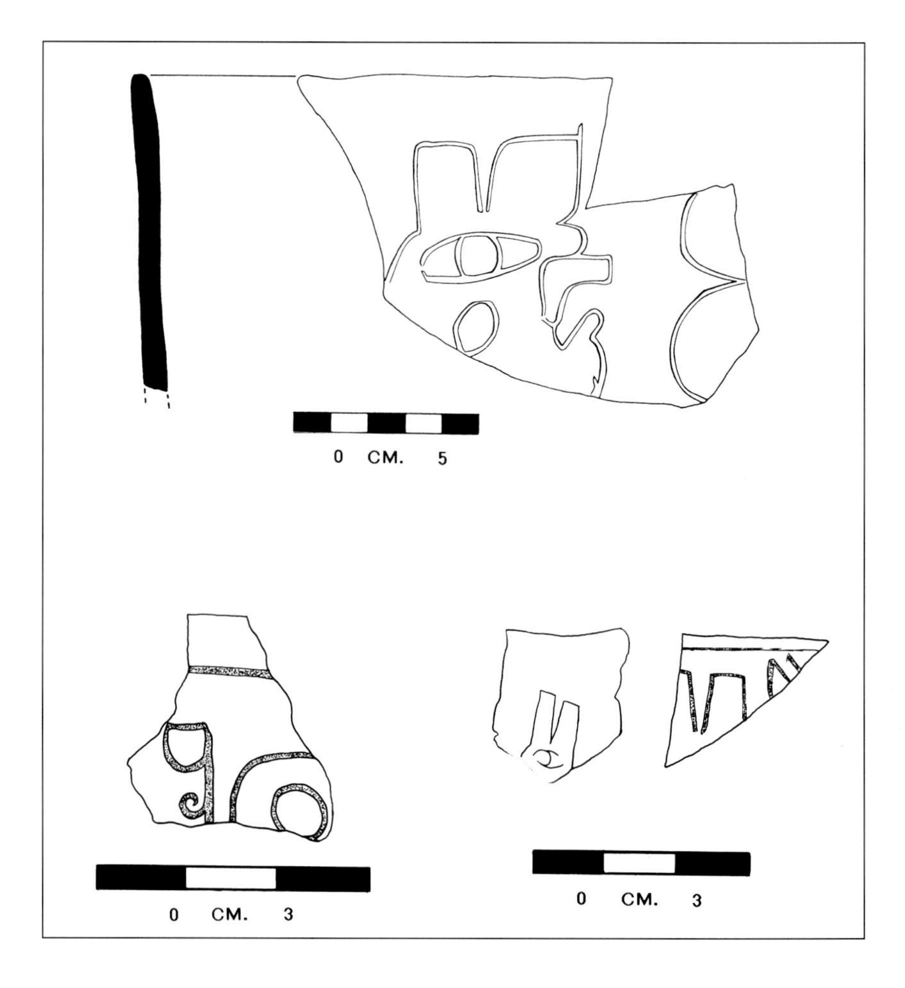

An element related to the Olmec profile face is the circle, which is formed by either an incised line, scraped surface removal of slip, or resist (fig. 33). Circle elements occur on some Olmec profile face cylinders from Central Mexico and the Pacific Coast region, or as individual elements (see Niederberger, this volume, for a discussion of iconography). The El Mesak example has a "teardrop" circle (fig. 32); one occurs above an Olmec face on a La Blanca vessel (Love 1991: fig. 15), and there is a somewhat crude example from Altamira (fig. 32). However, the most numerous occurrence of these circles is found at Chalcatzingo, Morelos, where they are seen on Amatzinac White vessels that

31. Unprovenienced vessel with Olmec profile face defined as the Paloma Negativo type
Redrawn by Fernando Luín and John Clark after Soustelle 1984: color plate insert

32. Examples of Pacific Coast ceramics with Olmec profile face motifs. Top: El Mesak (after Pye and Demarest 1991: 94); bottom, left: La Victoria (redrawn after Coe 1961: fig. 25); bottom, middle and right: Altamira (redrawn after Lowe 1967: 119, 117)

33. Circular elements. Top: Amatzinac White motifs, Chalcatzingo (redrawn after Cyphers 1987: 218 aa, kk); bottom: El Varal (redrawn after Richard Lesure field notes 1992)

34. Brackets and geometric. Top, left: Pyne's Motif 8, Leandro Grey cylinder from San José Mogote (redrawn after Flannery and Marcus 1994: 143c); top, right and bottom: El Mesak (after Pye and Demarest 1991: 93)

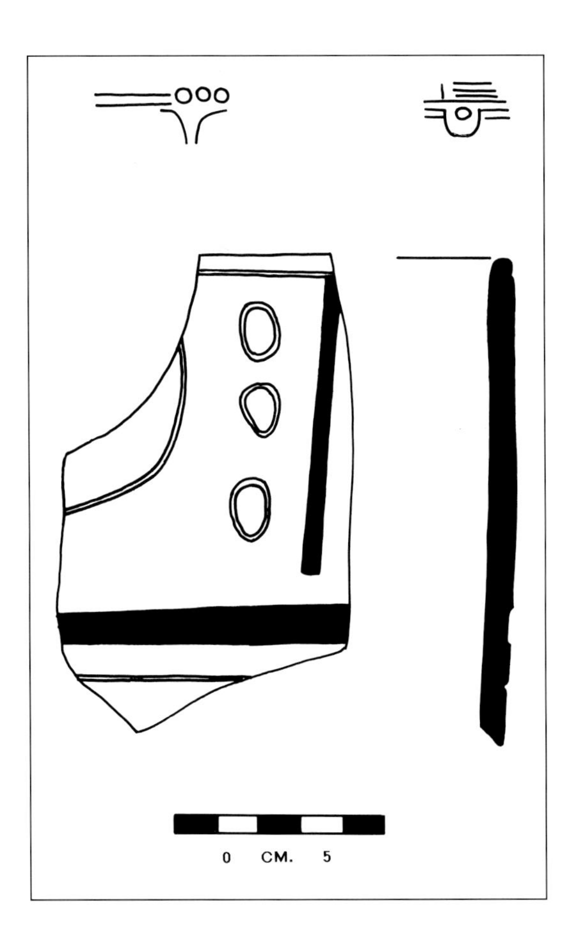

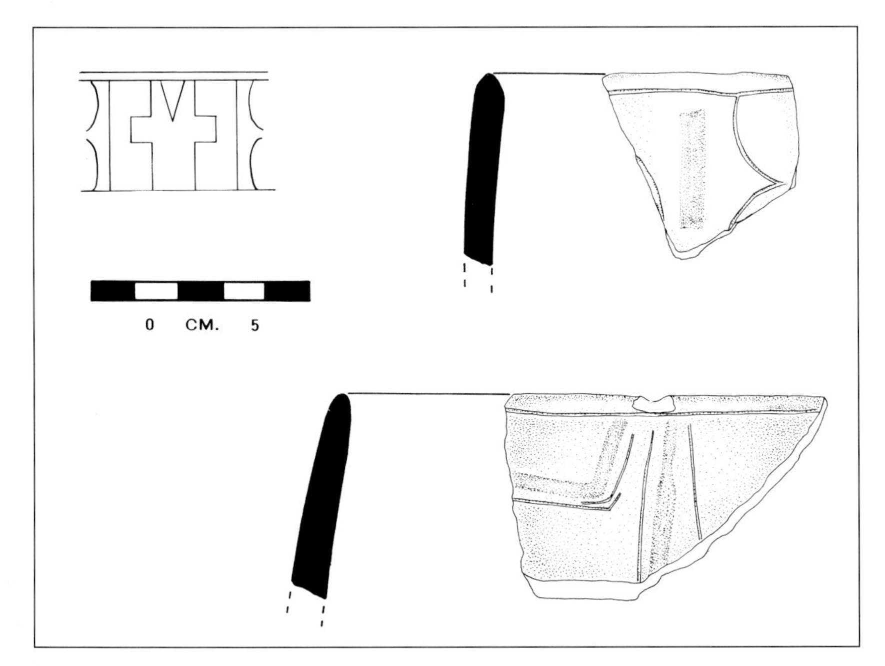

carry the double- and triple-line-break, using incised and scraped techniques, typically around the rim of these whiteware bowls (fig. 33) (Cyphers 1987: 218, fig. 13.23; 220–222, fig. 13.26–13.27). On the Pacific Coast materials, these circles likewise occur with the incised and rasped lines (Pye and Demarest 1990: fig. 25). Also seen are groups of circles, such as the example from El Varal, Chiapas (fig. 33).

Design Elements: Clovers and Geometrics. Used as framing devices are clover, "bracket" (Flannery and Marcus 1994), or "star" (Love 1991) elements, all common in the Pacific Coast motif set. These vertical clefts seem to function as a frame for a group of elements, or to broadly enclose a design. The origin of this particular motif may be outside the Pacific Coast; they appear at San Lorenzo (Coe and Diehl 1980: fig. 141) and commonly in Oaxacan materials. Nanette Pyne (1976: 272–274) identified the clover or "bracket" as Motifs 8 and 11 in her iconographic motif study (fig. 34). These elements occur in both straight and curved forms (Flannery and Marcus 1994: 143, fig. 12.9–12.10; 201, fig. 12.75c; 214, fig. 12.89).

Pyne's Motif 8 (fig. 34) depicts a distinct frontal view of an abstract cleft-head image, with a clover or bracket framing either side. The design layout is echoed in the El Mesak Olmec profile face cylinder, only the frontal view abstract were-jaguar motif in Oaxaca has been replaced by the profile Olmec face. This would suggest that these images—frontal abstract and profile face—are interchangeable within the clover elements. Other Pacific Coast elements alternate with the Olmec profile face, particularly contiguous geometric elements, including squares, rectangles, and trapezoids (fig. 34). In one partial cylinder from El Mesak, a large clover appears on one side, while the other has three stacked trapezoids and a black resist pattern of half circles overlying the surface (see Lesure, this volume, fig. 12, top left; Pye and Demarest 1990: fig. 23). The use of these geometric elements has not been described elsewhere in Mesoamerica and appears to be unique to the Pacific Coast.

Chronology of Olmec Motif Ceramics. The change in Olmec motif ceramics from Early Formative to Middle Formative in Mesoamerica is not as discrete as is implied by the labels "Early" and "Middle." The modes of Early Formative Olmec motif ceramics (shallow and deep bowls, excision, flame-eyebrow motif, and dark-colored slips and pastes) and those of the Middle Formative (cylinders and outflared-wall bowls, white wares, incision and scraping with interior decoration, and double-line-break motifs) overlapped at Formative sites. During the Ayotla phase (1250–1000 B.C.) at Tlapacoya, ceramic types such as Atoyac Gris and Valle Borde Negativo, exhibit many "Early Formative" modes, while Paloma Negativo exhibits the "Middle Formative" modes (Niederberger 1976, 1987). Temporal priority is demonstrated for the Early Formative modes. For example, there are more deep bowls and excised decoration occurring in the Ayotla phase than in the subsequent Middle Formative Manantial (1000–800 B.C.); Niederberger explicitly notes the temporal primacy of excision for the Central Mexican materials (1987, 1: 278).

Atoyac Gris, believed to be an import to the Valley of Mexico, occurs in Oaxaca during the coeval San José Mogote phase (1150–850 B.C.). Kent Flannery and Joyce Marcus concur and place Atoyac Gris as being Delfina Fine Grey and Leandro Grey (1994: 165). Interestingly, the imports that occur in Oaxaca are Paloma Negativo and Cesto Blanco (1994: 377). Cesto Blanco, which includes outflared-wall bowls with rim and interior decoration (grater bowls), is primarily a Middle Formative Central Mexican type. During the Manantial phase (1000–800 B.C.), Cesto Blanco ceramics experience an "explosive development" of double-line-break and multiple parallel lines (Niederberger 1976: 268). Flannery and Marcus note that these imports occur in late San José phase contexts (1994: 377).

In Oaxaca, the horizon marker type of the San José phase, Leandro Grey, is dark-colored, reduced-fired ware with flat-bottom bowls evincing a variety of wall angles; it was also "a major medium for excised pan-Mesoamerican motifs" (Flannery and Marcus 1994: 149). Atoyac Yellow-White, however, also occurs in this phase and carries incision, with double-line-break beginning in the mid-San José phase. By late San José, there was an increase in cylindrical bowls and a diversification in motifs. Atoyac Yellow-White became the dominant type during the subsequent Guadalupe phase (900/850–700 B.C.) in Oaxaca.

Overlap of Early and Middle Formative modes is likewise noted at Chalcatzingo. Late Amate phase (1250–1100 B.C.) has a Veredas Gris that Ann Cyphers likens to Calzadas Carved from San Lorenzo (Cyphers 1992: 25), a gray ware with excised motifs (Coe and Diehl 1980, 1: 162–169) and equivalent to Leandro Grey of Oaxaca. The first Amatzinac White forms also appear at this time, although few in number; this type does not proliferate until the subsequent Barranca phase (1100–700 B.C.), when the changing and diversifying motifs "formed the base for distinguishing the subphases of the Barranca phase" (Cyphers 1992: 27).

The earliest dating of the profile Olmec faces, double-line-break, clovers, and other motifs along the Pacific Coast is during the Jocotal period (950–850 B.C.) at El Mesak (Pye and Demarest 1991: 91, 93–94; Blake et al. 1995: 163) and Salinas La Blanca (Coe and Flannery 1967: 42–45) in Guatemala, and at El Varal (Lesure 1993: 212, 221), Altamira (Green and Lowe 1967: 20; Lowe 1967: 116–120), and Pampa el Pajón (Paillés 1980: 70, 73) in Chiapas. Greater quantities occur in the subsequent Middle Formative, particularly at La Blanca in Guatemala, including a whiteware cylinder with an elaborate profile Olmec face and inverted cleft (Love 1991: 65–71).

The Pacific Coast whitewares are most interesting for what appears to be the selection of various elements from a Mesoamerican symbol set that referenced widespread concepts and regional variations to create a distinctive Pacific Coast style. While there was a broad symbol set, which would include the double-line-break, clovers, and Olmec faces, unique regional and site preferences were also in place, whether in Oaxaca, Central Mexico, or at the site of Chalcatzingo. Although the demarcation of periods obscures the development of the whitewares and motifs of this second Olmec motif wave, by at least 1000 B.C. the first Olmec motif ceramics were on the wane and the second were becoming popular. This suggests communication and interaction in central and southeastern Mesoamerica, but with clear autonomous development of regional styles.

The Jocotal period remains an elusive era of the coastal sequence; nevertheless, it was a moment of transition that may hold the key to some of the critical questions concerning Olmecs. Unlike the preceding Cuadros phase, the derivative Jocotal phase was largely a local phenomenon. There is nothing quite like it in Olman or anywhere else in Mesoamerica. This Jocotal complex may have represented an attempt at continuity in the face of the demise of the San Lorenzo polity. During this transition to the more hierarchical Middle Formative period, rapid social change may have led to nativistic or revitalization movements represented by the development of new regional styles along with the search for new status markers.

The designs on Jocotal ceramics have always been identified as Olmec and doubtlessly will continue to be so in the future. But it is important to stress that they are not Olmec in the same sense as their predecessors discussed above. Considering the total picture of early Middle Formative Mesoamerica, we think that the few clues available indicate a shift in the balance of power or influence from Olman to outside regions (all of which had previous, significant ties to Olman) about 950 B.C. and then back again about 800 B.C. In short, in the brief interval from 1100 to 800 B.C., we think that at least three significant types of "Olmec" can be discerned in the archaeological record.

The standard story, best told by Paul Tolstoy (1989), sees two Olmec traditions: the San Lorenzo Complex of the Early Formative and the La Venta Complex of the Middle Formative. Continuity and succession from one to the other is assumed. But this has not been demonstrated, and it is becoming less credible in light of recent evidence from the Mexican highlands and the Pacific Coast. We see no convincing evidence of a Manantial-Jocotal/Conchas development in Olman. We suppose that the demise of the San Lorenzo polity may have created a local power vacuum for nearly a century. And this was a time of florescence in the highlands and along the Pacific Coast. If a label is needed to think clearly about this episode, we can think of none better than the Manantial or Tlapacoya horizon.

We cannot address the local developments of other regions, but in the Mazatán region, the Jocotal complex was a clear derivative of the preceding complex of strong Olmec presence and influence. The Jocotal complex was probably also an independent development along the Pacific Coast, almost a regionalization of the Olmec patterns adopted earlier from Olman during the Cuadros phase.

Before considering the rest of the Middle Formative, it is worth drawing out some of the implications of the preceding observations and speculations. First, during Manantial times the phenomenon called "Olmec" became significantly different from its predecessor, at least at the level of representations and possibly also at the level of practices. And this Olmec may not have originated in Olman. Second, the social groups that appear to have had the most significant influence in the pan-Mesoamerican pattern of representations were probably in the Mexican highlands (the valleys of Mexico, Morelos, and Oaxaca, and Guerrero). Third, all of these exciting developments are irrelevant to the original Olmec question. The spread of Olmec artifacts and practices during the Middle Formative does not inform us of their original spread or significance at an earlier time. Just as there are several types of Olmec, or Olmec horizons, so too are there a corresponding number of Olmec questions (San Lorenzo, Tlapacoya, La Venta, and Tres Zapotes, to mention the obvious horizons). Consequently, the elaboration of Olmec designs or iconography at highland sites in Manantial times, such as San José Mogote in Oaxaca and Tlapacoya in the Basin of Mexico, in no way informs us about the Early Formative origins of these designs (*contra* Flannery and Marcus 1994; Grove 1989; Niederberger 1987). Clearly, it is inappropriate, on the basis of extant evidence, to attribute these complicated motifs to any source in Olman, but their antecedents are there. Consequently, it is inappropriate to retrodict this observation of design complexity to argue against a mother culture phenomenon some two centuries earlier (see Clark 1997).

A Time of Shifting Alliances

Data from Michael Love's (1989, 1991) excavations at La Blanca, Guatemala, suggest that the early Conchas phase peoples participated in the Manantial Olmec horizon. Complex designs incised through white slips were dominant decorations. In most other ways, the Conchas complex was a clear technological continuation of the Jocotal complex. Locally, however, there were significant changes.

La Blanca appears almost from nowhere to become the dominant capital center of the Pacific Coast at the beginning of the Middle Formative (Love 1991, 1999). The Mazatán region to the west (Clark 1994a, 1994b) and the El Mesak region to the east were both virtually abandoned by this time (Pye 1993, 1995). It appears that the Jocotal inhabitants of these adjacent regions were enticed into the La Blanca polity and region, and their immigration there explains La Blanca's demographic boom. La Blanca was the first center on the coast known to have erected an earthen pyramid. Dating to about 850 B.C., this pyramid was about 25 meters high and 100 meters square at the base (Love 1999).

We reconstruct the rest of the story of the late Middle Formative from the regional pattern of Olmec sculpture along the coast (fig. 1). As argued above, we think the bas-relief sculpture dates to Conchas times and that Olmec lapidary items may date to slightly later times (fig. 16). By 800 B.C., we think that the kings of La Venta had also become major players on the Mesoamerican scene, thus filling the power void left vacant by the rulers of San Lorenzo.

As evident in figure 15, the iconography and representations of the La Venta horizon were very consistent over the broad expanse of Mesoamerica. Middle Formative peoples were clearly involved in significant interaction. The distribution of Olmec monuments and lapidary along the Pacific Coast shows a pattern of regularly spaced loci (fig. 1). Also significant is the pairing of coastal artifacts with inland monuments or artifacts, usually at major passes from the coast to the interior. This looks to us like marked way stations or rest stops along a trade route—a coastal and a parallel inland route—with connecting spurs between the two at major passes. Kenneth Hirth (1978) argued that these Olmec low-relief carvings were strategically placed in dendritic systems with a focus on controlling trade. We think the additional evidence from the Pacific Coast, and amplification of the pattern, support his trade thesis but not the notion of gateway communities. Along the Pacific Coast, the pattern is extensive but not obviously tied to major centers. The earliest centers that we do know of are La Blanca, Abaj Takalik, and Izapa. The really obvious growth in regional centers occurred in the next phase.

The Olmecs, of course, did not run around Mesoamerica setting up monuments for the convenience of future archaeologists. Why, then, were the monuments carved, and what meanings did their images convey? Karl Taube (this volume) argues that most of the images on the Middle Formative bas-relief monuments show individuals with corn fetishes and that we may be seeing, in these monuments, the spread of an Olmec corn cult across Mesoamerica. We agree that maize, because of felicitous genetic transformations, crossed a threshold of productivity (larger cob sizes) to become a basic staple all across Mesoamerica during the Middle Formative. Reliance on new and improved maize allowed some regions to come into ascendancy, such as La Blanca, and other regions to be populated with settled village agriculturalists for the first time, such as the Maya Lowlands. The corn symbolism noted on Middle Formative sculpture and votive axes suggests that corn was the rage and that its cultivation was tied in with elites and perhaps the gods.

The Pijijiapan monuments, however, appear to be of another sort. If Monument 1 depicts a marriage scene (fig. 3b), we may be seeing the commemoration of an elite marriage alliance between a local lord and an Olmec woman, or an Olmec lord and a local woman. Ann Cyphers (1984) has argued that Monument 21 at Chalcatzingo, which shows a woman, may have been an Olmec lady who married into a local dynasty (see Grove, this volume). The forging of alliances between the La Venta Olmecs and outlanders would fit the overall pattern of wide-open communication and trade characteristic of the Middle Formative. The spread of a corn cult directed by elites would also have been beneficial for redirecting local subsistence economies and fostering the generation of surplus (see Taube, this volume).

Kings Everywhere but No Olmecs

It is a characteristic of many systems that they are undercut by their own successes. This may have happened to the Olmecs. They appear to have spread a particular suite of cultural practices all across Mesoamerica, and when these practices actually took hold, Mesoamerica witnessed a proliferation of complex chiefdoms or petty kingdoms organized after the Olmec pattern. The initial success of these kingdoms was basic for the overall trading and alliance strategy of the Olmecs at La Venta. Closely related trade partners kept the goods and services funneling into Olman. Prolonged success of the kingdoms outside Olman, however, eventually led to the isolation of Olman from the major arteries of trade and communication. As political power wielded by Olmecs of Olman waned toward the end of the Middle Formative, they were progressively cut out of most of the action. The Olmecs of Olman set the processes in motion that resulted in their own marginalization in the Mesoamerican world system. This explanation supposes that issues of political economy were paramount at this time.

Our argument for trade, based in part on the regular spacing of Olmec artifacts along the Pacific Coast, only works if one ignores the chronological distinctions between sculpture and lapidary items that we argued for above. Of course, our distinction could be in error, with the pieces dating to the same part of the Middle Formative. But the distribution of Olmec lapidary objects in the Chiapas interior (see Lee 1989; Lowe 1994) in the absence of any sculpture suggests that this was not the case. We think a more likely explanation is that there was continuity of populations in the general vicinities of the initial spots that were marked with Olmec sculpture.

Data from the Pacific Coast for the remainder of the Middle Formative is rather coarse grained, and we base our speculations for this period on the general developments in Chiapas and Guatemala. The last part of the Middle Formative (locally the Chiapa III and IV phases, c. 600–300 B.C.) witnessed a proliferation of pyramid centers, importation of jade jewelry, and the wide distribution of splotchy-resist orange pottery and round-headed figurines. We do not see any iconography that is clearly Olmec of any stripe. We suspect that the Olmec lapidary objects date to the Chiapa III phase and were special objects manipulated by paramount chiefs. Many of these artifacts may already have been heirlooms by this time.

We suspect that these paramounts considered themselves "kings" according to the ancient Olmec pattern, although in anthropological jargon we would consider them "chiefs." Many of these kings may have been literal descendants of Olmec kings from Olman through strategic marriage alliances from an earlier era that disseminated the royal line to subsidiary centers (Clark and Pérez 1994). Olmec paraphernalia, such as incised axes or scepters, would have been material proof of a king's connections to royal blood. The Olmec artifacts manipulated by regional kings, therefore, would have functioned differently from Olmec artifacts from earlier times, more as markers of blood relations with Olmec kings in Olman rather than trade relations.

In a literal sense, the proliferation of kingdoms across Mesoamerica in Middle Formative times represented a clear continuation of Olmec practices of social stratification, kingship, a pantheon of gods, and conspicuous consumption of jade, feathers, textiles, and so on. But the style of representation changed, and so scholars say that Olmec culture "ceased." It would be closer to the truth to say that the basic practices and beliefs did not change significantly—they merely underwent a face-lift as the same old practices were rewrapped in new garb. The first radical shift in style is represented by the Izapa monuments, which probably date to about 400–300 B.C. (Lowe et al. 1982). But the Izapan narrative style is clearly derivative of the late Olmec narrative style present at La Venta. We do not know what gave rise to the Izapa style and its local repackaging of traditional Olmec concepts. Nor do we know why the people at Izapa chose to erect so many monuments. But with the rise of Izapa on the Pacific Coast, we can no longer see anything in the Olmec style, and the same is true of the societies in Olman, such as Tres Zapotes (see Pool, this volume).

Toward a History of Olmec Contact

As we currently understand the data from the Pacific Coast, the Olmec presence there toward the end of the Early Formative period was a brief historical interlude in a much longer history of interaction between the Mokaya and peoples of Olman, mostly Olmecs. The civilizational impact of the Olmecs on the Mokaya was profound and long lived. At the beginning of the Early Formative, the Mokaya of the Soconusco were clearly independent of other peoples of Mesoamerica. Early forms of rank society, or simple chiefdoms, evolved in the Pacific Coast region, and these institutions were quickly adopted by neighboring peoples, including those living in Olman (see Clark 1994a; Clark and Blake 1994). There is clear archaeological evidence of early contact between the peoples of the Pacific Coast and those of Olman in pre-Olmec times, most apparent in similarities in ceramic assemblages and the types of obsidian imported into each region. The Mokaya's impact on the first villagers of Olman remains to be determined, but we think it was significant (see Clark 1990; Clark and Blake 1989).

Some contact was maintained between the two groups throughout the Formative period, but after the initial close contact at the beginning of the Early Formative the peoples in the Soconusco and Olman developed along separate paths. The peoples in Olman created the cultural patterns and representational systems that we now call "Olmec," and the Mokaya of the Soconusco continued much as before. About 1200 B.C. the Olmecs of Olman and the Mokaya of the Mazatán region once again began to interact with greater frequency. As noted, we think that considerations of trade were involved for both partners in the enterprise. Trade, however, does not adequately explain the impact of the Olmecs on the Mokaya. Many of the people living in the Mazatán region at the time gave up traditional practices in order to imitate Olmec canons of pot decoration, figurines, and so on. Why did they do so?

One of the more plausible explanations of the social dynamic of the time is that postulated by Flannery (1968) for the relationship between the inhabitants of the Valley of Oaxaca and the early Olmecs. Flannery argued that it was in the best interests of nascent elites in the Valley of Oaxaca to adopt the symbol system of their more sophisticated Olmec trading partners in order to gain political leverage and influence on the local scene.[4] This model has the double merit of specifying the types of players involved in the interaction and their likely self-interested motives for engaging in it. A variant of this phenomenon may have been in effect for the Mokaya. Clark (1996) argues that during the time of their greatest interaction, the Olmecs of Olman (at least at San Lorenzo) had already developed a system of social stratification based upon divine kingship. Consequently, the interaction between the Mokaya and the Olmecs was between peoples of significantly different social systems and levels of complexity and was probably asymmetrical (Clark 1997). The highest-ranking individuals and chiefs of the Mazatán zone may have seen the Olmec system as superior to their own along a number of dimensions and have tried to copy it locally for their own selfish reasons of expanding and consolidating their power bases.

Adoption of the Olmec system of social stratification resolved the major problem with the Mokaya rank system: the problem of long-term legitimacy. In the Mokaya system, rank and prestige were gained and maintained through public displays of largesse, such as feasting and ritual drinking (see Clark and Blake 1994). A leader's status was in large part based upon what he had done for his followers most recently. In contrast, the Olmecs developed a more complex form of political legitimization based upon social stratification in which one's right to rule was based upon circumstances of birth rather than upon periodic dispersal of perks. To rule, one's genealogy was more critical than one's generosity. The most serious questions of political legitimacy were deflected into the realm of the past and the supernatural rather than the here and now. We do not know how the Olmecs pulled off this masterful coup of divine kingship, but this is a question for researchers working in Olman and is not critical in our analysis because the Olmecs came onto the Middle American scene as major players about 1200 B.C. after they had developed social stratification and kingship. Compared to the political institutions in place among their neighbors, Olmec institutions were particularly attractive to the big-men and petty chiefs who held sway over these other societies.

To tap into the Olmec system, local leaders would have required material signs of their connections to the superior system, and they would have to have been committed to its basic precepts. Viable connections could have been demonstrated by the actual possession of special goods from Olman, such as pots carved with representations of supernatural creatures or small ceramic statuettes of Olmec kings. But possession of props would soon have become old news, and stronger ties would have been required to keep up appearances. In this conception of the interregional dynamic, local leaders would have been the cultural brokers between two different systems and the principal movers and shakers for getting local peoples to modify their ways and to conform to Olmec practices. Realistically, in a system of small, competitive chiefdoms, leaders of some polities, and some aspirants to leadership in others, would have found it in their best interests to pursue traditional ways and to represent a clear alternative position to the leaders pushing for increased foreign entanglements.

The evidence of an Olmec presence in Mazatán suggests that some of the local leaders actually pulled off the adoption of Olmec ways and convinced their principal followers to do the same. They eventually invited Olmecs from Olman to come and participate in local governance (Clark 1997). Part of this presence may have been establishment of marriage alliances between the Mokaya of Mazatán and nobles from Olman. At this point in their history, the local polities of Mazatán were all consolidated into a larger polity, with radically different results for the antecedent, village chiefdoms. Most of the former seats of political power, such as at Paso de la Amada (fig. 22), were abandoned, and new, smaller centers were set up nearby. One of the local polities (San Carlos/Cantón Corralito) became the new seat of power in the zone. It looks as if the petty chiefs in Mazatán had differential access to Olmec connections, and some won and others lost when Olmecs from Olman actually came into the zone.

Eventually the political fortunes of those who were tied directly to Olman may have failed them as a result of the failure of the mother system in Olman. During the Jocotal period, the capital center in Mazatán shifted across the river, and the local basis of its power may have also. Our reconstruction of subsequent developments during the Middle Formative is incomplete, but we do see a period of stone carving and one of dispersal of lapidary objects. In the simplest terms, the erection of stone monuments, or carving of boulders, was a clear demarcation of space, perhaps the creation of sacred or secular geography of particular interest to the Olmecs at La Venta. The images on these stones indicate the spread of Olmec ideas of kingship, perhaps including the notion of divine "corn" kings, and perhaps the related notion of elite marriages between local elites and royal houses of Olman. If true, the first part of the Middle Formative saw a concerted effort of Olmec royal lines to marry out and to establish cadet lines in the frontiers, especially along the most critical trade routes—or seen from the opposite perspective, of local elites to tie into the royal Olmec houses.

The distribution of Olmec jades, of all sorts, can be seen as the logical extension of this emphasis on royal blood and connections. The complex iconography on these special goods would have been material evidence of one's royal claims. John Clark and Tomás Pérez (1994) speculate that this development was the beginning of the end for the Olmecs. In a sense it ensured the immortality of the Olmec system but also the rapid demise of the last Olmec polities. The fundamental Olmec system of social stratification, as well as all of its foundational rituals and material paraphernalia, was widely disseminated across Mesoamerica. After this occurred, the Olmecs had nothing left to offer outlanders other than claims of being the original hearth of civilization. But such claims would diminish in time with the prolonged success of local kingdoms and cadet dynasties. Origins would be buried in the mythic past along with the notion of stranger kings, the idea that the original kings came from elsewhere.

Developments of the Middle and Late Formative can be seen as a regionalization of complex chiefdoms all across Mesoamerica. With regionalization came stylistic divergence and diversity and the dissipation of anything that looked stylistically Olmec. The Olmecs did not die, they merely receded into the background as more dynamic peoples or polities took center stage. With the emergence of the Izapa art style, the Olmec style was clearly superseded, although most of the fundamental practices they developed and fostered persisted.

Conclusion

Recent archaeological data from the Pacific Coast demonstrate some of the complexity inherent in the Olmec problem. Rather than one Olmec "question," there is actually a family of related questions. To address them adequately, one must place each in its appropriate temporal, spatial, and cultural frame. We have tried to be careful here in our use of labels for distinguishing the peoples involved, the times and places of their interactions, the nature of their interactions, and the effects of their interactions on each other. We have also engaged rather freely in speculation. Currently, our major problem in understanding the Pacific Coast is the lack of clear understanding of the developments in Olman. It would help to understand the processes by which social stratification arose in that region and the local and regional political dynamics of its nascent kingdoms.

Much of the current debate about the Olmecs concerns the traditional mother culture view. For us this is still a primary issue. Our data from the Pacific Coast show that the mother culture idea is still viable in terms of cultural practices. The early Olmecs created the first civilization in Mesoamerica; they had no peers, only contemporaries. Creation of this first stratified society involved the forging and crystallization of social, political, and religious institutions that became the hallmarks of Mesoamerica itself. As with all historical entities and cultural configurations, this was not creation *ex nihilo* but from preexistent matter. The Olmecs clearly were influenced by their predecessors and neighbors, such as the Mokaya, in significant ways, but they also created essentially new institutions on their own, and for this reason they hold the founding position in Mesoamerican history.

Once the Olmecs had devised hierarchical forms of social and political life, their continuing interactions with their more rustic neighbors served to impart these beliefs and practices to others who, for reasons of personal advantages, adopted them. In short, the earliest Olmecs created Mesoamerica by disseminating a particular way of life and view of the cosmos. Mesoamerica as both a cultural and geographic reality was historically constituted by the spatial distribution of the societies that shared in basic Olmec institutions and representational systems. Along the Pacific Coast, this first occurred about 1100 B.C., but this first system did not last. The Middle Formative transmission of Olmec institutions did take hold, however, and eventually evolved into the Izapa system. These developments at the end of the Middle Formative are still poorly understood but are clearly tied to the cessation of Olmec culture. Future investigations ought to tackle the difficult problem of how one system transformed itself into another.

NOTES

We gratefully acknowledge the thoughtful comments of Michael Blake, Gareth W. Lowe, and David T. Cheetham on earlier drafts of this essay. We particularly thank the New World Archaeological Foundation and the College of Family, Home and Social Sciences, both of Brigham Young University, Dumbarton Oaks Research Library and Collection, and the National Gallery of Art for providing the funding to carry out this research. Much of the artwork was provided by Ayax Moreno of the New World Archaeological Foundation; we greatly appreciate his contribution.

1. As Jiménez Moreno (1942: 119) noted years ago, "*Olmeca* es un gentilico derivado de *Olman,* '(donde) está el hule' *(Olli mani),* o 'donde se coge hule.'" [Olmec is a name of a people derived from Olman, '(where) the rubber is' *(Olli mani),* (the Nahuatl term) or 'where the rubber is collected.'"] The use of *Olman* for this region has historic precedent. The term refers only to the region, "the place of rubber," rather than a people, and thus is equivalent to the use of the term *Soconusco* (a Nahuatl term meaning "place of the prickly pear") for the southeastern half of the Chiapas Coast and the very northwestern portion of the coast of Guatemala. The radicalness of Diehl's proposal is to shift the emphasis from place to people. In Diehl's usage, the region takes its name from the people who inhabit it. In Jiménez Moreno's usage, the people take their name from the region and one of its principal identifying attributes, the ability to produce rubber. To avoid future complications, we recommend that such a term be used only with reference to geography, thereby leaving open the ability to speak of non-Olmecs in Olman and of Olmecs outside Olman.

2. The "Young Lord" statuette illustrates some of the difficulties and hazards of trying to study looted pieces sold on the international art market. "Slim" was definitely sold in Guatemala, but the statuette has conflicting, and equally credible, possible histories that derive it either from La Blanca, Guatemala, or Atiquizaya, El Salvador—a small mound site several kilometers west of Chalchuapa. The owner of the Antiquizaya mound supposedly has a picture of the large figurine found on his property, so it should be possible eventually to verify or reject an El Salvador provenence for this piece. In either event, "Slim" appears to have come from the Pacific Coast region.

3. Using data from Oaxaca, the double-line-break has been argued by Flannery and Marcus (1994: 140–141, 377–381) to have evolved from cleft imagery. The issue of double-line-break is beyond the scope of this analysis.

4. Flannery and Marcus (1994) have repudiated Flannery's (1968) earlier argument for the Olmec influence in Oaxaca, but we still find the earlier argument to be the more persuasive.

BIBLIOGRAPHY

Anderson, Dana
1978 Monuments. In *The Prehistory of Chalchuapa, El Salvador,* vol. 1, ed. Robert Sharer. Philadelphia.

Andrews, Anthony
1983 *Maya Salt Production and Trade.* Tucson, Ariz.

Baudez, Claude F.
1973 Les camps de saliniers de la côte méridionale de Honduras: Données archéologiques et documents historiques. In *L'homme, hier et aujourd'hui. Recueil d'études en hommage à André Leroi-Gourhan,* 507–520. Paris.

Baudez, Claude F., and Pierre Becquelin
1973 *Archéologie de Los Naranjos, Honduras.* Mexico City.

Benson, Elizabeth P., and Beatriz de la Fuente
1996 (Editors) *Olmec Art of Ancient Mexico* [exh. cat., National Gallery of Art]. Washington.

Blake, Michael
1991 An Emerging Early Formative Chiefdom at Paso de la Amada, Chiapas, Mexico. In *The Formation of Complex Society in Southeastern Mesoamerica,* ed. William Fowler, Jr., 27–46. Boca Raton, Fla.

Blake, Michael, Brian Chisholm, John Clark, Barbara Voorhies, and Michael Love
1992 Prehistoric Subsistence in the Soconusco Region. *Current Anthropology* 33: 83–94.

Blake, Michael, John Clark, Barbara Voorhies, George Michaels, Michael Love, Mary Pye, Arthur Demarest, and Barbara Arroyo
1995 Radiocarbon Chronology for the Late Archaic and Formative Periods on the Pacific Coast of Southeastern Mesoamerica. *Ancient Mesoamerica* 6: 161–183.

Boggs, Stanley
1950 *"Olmec" Pictographs in the Las Victorias Group, Chalchuapa Archaeological Zone.* Notes on Middle American Archaeology and Ethnology 99. Washington.

Campbell, Lyle, and Terrence Kaufman
1976 A Linguistic Look at the Olmec. *American Antiquity* 41: 80–88.

Ceja Tenorio, Jorge
1974 Coatán, una provincia preclásica temprana en el Soconusco de Chiapas. Paper presented at the 41st Congreso Internacional de Americanistas, Mexico City.

Clark, John E.
1990 Olmecas, olmequismo y olmequización en Mesoamérica. *Arqueología* 3: 49–56.

1991 The Beginnings of Mesoamerica: Apologia for the Soconusco Early Formative. In *The Formation of Complex Society in Southeastern Mesoamerica,* ed. William Fowler, Jr., 13–26. Boca Raton, Fla.

1994a The Development of Early Formative Rank Societies in the Soconusco, Chiapas, Mexico. Ph.D. dissertation, Department of Anthropology, University of Michigan, Ann Arbor.

1994b Antecedentes de la cultura olmeca. In *Los olmecas en Mesoamérica,* ed. John Clark, 30–41. Mexico City and Madrid.

1996 Craft Specialization and Olmec Civilization. In *Craft Specialization and Social Evolution: In Memory of V. Gordon Childe,* ed. Bernard Wailes, 187–199. University Museum Monograph 93. University of Pennsylvania, Philadelphia.

1997 The Arts of Government in Early Mesoamerica. *Annual Review of Anthropology* 26: 211–234.

Clark, John E., and Michael Blake

1989 El origen de la civilización en Mesoamérica: Los olmecas y mokaya del Soconusco de Chiapas, México. In *El preclásico o formativo: Avances y perspectivas,* ed. Martha Carmona, 385–403. Mexico City.

1994 The Power of Prestige: Competitive Generosity and the Emergence of Rank Societies in Lowland Mesoamerica. In *Factional Competition and Political Development in the New World,* ed. Elizabeth Brumfiel and John Fox, 17–30. Cambridge.

Clark, John E., and Dennis Gosser

1995 Reinventing Mesoamerica's First Pottery. In *The Emergence of Pottery: Technology and Innovation in Ancient Society,* ed. William Barnett and John Hoopes, 209–221. Washington.

Clark, John E., and Tomás Pérez Suárez

1994 Los olmecas y el primer milenio de Mesoamérica. In *Los olmecas en Mesoamérica,* ed. John Clark, 261–276. Mexico City and Madrid.

Coe, Michael D.

1961 *La Victoria, an Early Site on the Pacific Coast of Guatemala.* Papers of the Peabody Museum of Archaeology and Ethnohistory 53. Harvard University, Cambridge, Mass.

1965 *The Jaguar's Children: Preclassic Central Mexico.* New York.

Coe, Michael D., and Richard Diehl

1980 *In the Land of the Olmec,* 2 vols. Austin.

Coe, Michael D., and Kent V. Flannery

1967 *Early Cultures and Human Ecology in South Coastal Guatemala.* Washington.

Cyphers, Ann

1984 The Possible Role of Women in Formative Exchange. In *Trade and Exchange in Early Mesoamerica,* ed. Kenneth Hirth, 115–123. Albuquerque, N.M.

1987 Ceramics. In *Ancient Chalcatzingo,* ed. David Grove, 200–251. Austin.

1992 *Chalcatzingo, Morelos: Estudio de cerámica y sociedad.* Mexico City.

Demarest, Arthur, Mary Pye, James Myers, and Rosalinda Mendez

1988 El Proyecto Mar Azul/El Mesak. Report submitted to the Instituto Nacional de Antropología e Historia, Guatemala City.

Drucker, Philip

1952 *La Venta, Tabasco: A Study of Olmec Ceramics and Art.* Bureau of American Ethnology Bulletin 179. Washington.

Drucker, Philip, Robert F. Heizer, and Robert J. Squier

1959 *Excavations at La Venta, Tabasco, 1955.* Bureau of American Ethnology Bulletin 170. Washington.

Ekholm, Susanna

1993 La escultura más temprana excavada en Izapa, Chiapas. In *Antropología, historia e imaginativa: En homenaje a Eduardo Martínez Espinosa,* ed. Carlos Navarrete and Carlos Alvarez, 67–76. Ocozocoautla de Espinosa, Chiapas, Mexico.

Ekholm-Miller, Susanna

1973 *The Olmec Rock Carving at Xoc, Chiapas, Mexico.* Papers of the New World Archaeological Foundation 32. Provo, Utah.

Estrada, Juan, and Fernando de Niebla

1977 Descripción de la provincia de Zapotitlan y Suchitepequez. Año 1579. *Anales de la Sociedad de Geografía e Historia* 28: 68–83.

Feuchtwanger, Franz

1989 *Cerámica olmeca.* Mexico City.

Flannery, Kent V.

1968 The Olmec and the Valley of Oaxaca: A Model for Interregional Interaction in Formative Times. In *Dumbarton Oaks Conference on the Olmec,* ed. Elizabeth Benson, 79–117. Washington.

Flannery, Kent V., and Joyce Marcus

1994 *Early Formative Pottery in the Valley of Oaxaca.* Memoirs of the Museum of Anthropology 27. University of Michigan, Ann Arbor.

Furst, Peter

1995 Shamanism, Transformation, and Olmec

Art. In *The Olmec World: Ritual and Rulership,* 69–81 [exh. cat., The Art Museum, Princeton University]. Princeton.

González Lauck, Rebecca
1988 Proyecto Arqueológico La Venta. *Arqueología* 4: 121–165.

1996 La Venta: An Olmec Capital. In *Olmec Art of Ancient Mexico,* ed. Elizabeth Benson and Beatriz de la Fuente, 73–82 [exh. cat., National Gallery of Art]. Washington.

Graham, John A.
1981 Abaj Takalik: The Olmec Style and Its Antecedents in Pacific Guatemala. In *Ancient Mesoamerica: Selected Readings,* ed. John Graham, 163–176. Palo Alto, Calif.

Graham, John A., Robert F. Heizer, and Edwin M. Shook
1978 Abaj Takalik 1976: Exploratory Investigations. *Contributions of the University of California Archaeological Research Facility* 36: 85–109. Berkeley.

Green, Dee, and Gareth W. Lowe
1967 *Altamira and Padre Piedra, Early Preclassic Sites in Chiapas, Mexico.* Papers of the New World Archaeological Foundation 20. Provo, Utah.

Grove, David C.
1989 Olmec: What's in a Name? In *Regional Perspectives on the Olmec,* ed. Robert Sharer and David Grove, 8–14. Cambridge.

Hill, Warren D.
1996 Mesoamerica's Earliest Ballcourt and the Origins of Inequality. Paper presented at the 61st Annual Meeting of the Society of American Archaeology, New Orleans.

Hill, Warren D., Michael Blake, and John E. Clark
1998 Ball Court Design Dates Back 3,400 Years. *Nature* 392 (6679): 878–879.

Hirth, Kenneth G.
1978 Interregional Trade and the Formation of Prehistoric Gateway Cities. *American Antiquity* 3: 35–45.

Jackson, Thomas, and Michael W. Love
1991 Middle Preclassic Obsidian Exchange and the Introduction of Prismatic Blades at La Blanca, Guatemala. *Ancient Mesoamerica* 2: 47–59.

Jiménez Moreno, Wigoberto
1942 El enigma de los olmecas. *Cuadernos Americanos* 5(5): 113–145.

Joralemon, Peter David
1971 *A Study of Olmec Iconography.* Washington.

Lee, Thomas A., Jr.
1989 Chiapas and the Olmec. In *Regional Perspectives on the Olmec,* ed. Robert Sharer and David Grove, 198–226. Cambridge.

Lesure, Richard G.
1993 Salvamento arqueológico en El Varal: Una perspectiva sobre la organización sociopolítica olmeca de la costa Chiapas. In *Segundo y Tercer Foro de Arqueología de Chiapas,* ed. M. Pedrero Corzo, 211–227. Tuxtla, Chiapas, Mexico.

1995 Paso de la Amada: Sociopolitical Dynamics in an Early Formative Community. Ph.D. dissertation, Department of Anthropology, University of Michigan, Ann Arbor.

Love, Michael W.
1989 Early Settlements and Chronology of the Rio Naranjo. Ph.D. dissertation, University of California, Berkeley.

1991 Style and Social Complexity in Formative Mesoamerica. In *The Formation of Complex Society in Southeastern Mesoamerica,* ed. William Fowler, Jr., 47–76. Boca Raton, Fla.

1999 Economic Patterns in the Development of Complex Society in Pacific Guatemala. In *Pacific Latin America in Prehistory: The Evolution of Archaic and Formative Cultures,* ed. Michael Blake, 89–100. Pullman, Wash.

Lowe, Gareth W.
1967 Appendix: Results of the 1965 Investigations at Altamira. In *Altamira and Padre Piedra, Early Preclassic Sites in Chiapas, Mexico,* 81–133. Papers of the New World Archaeological Foundation 15. Provo, Utah.

1975 *The Early Preclassic Barra Phase of Altamira, Chiapas.* Papers of the New World Archaeological Foundation 38. Provo, Utah.

1977 The Mixe-Zoque as Competing Neighbors of the Maya. In *The Origins of Maya Civilization,* ed. Richard Adams, 197–248. Albuquerque, N.M.

1989a Algunas aclaraciones sobre la presencia olmeca y maya en el preclásico de Chiapas. In *El preclásico o formativo: Avances y perspectivas,* ed. Martha Carmona, 363–384. Mexico City.

1989b The Heartland Olmec: Evolution of Material Culture. In *Regional Perspectives on the Olmec,* ed. Robert Sharer and David Grove, 33–67. Cambridge.

1994 Comunidades de Chiapas relacionadas con los olmecas. In *Los olmecas en Mesoamérica,* ed. John Clark, 113–118. Mexico City and Madrid.

Lowe, Gareth W., Thomas A. Lee, Jr., and Eduardo Martínez Espinosa
1982 *Izapa: An Introduction to the Ruins and Monuments.* Papers of the New World Archaeological Foundation 31. Provo, Utah.

McDonald, Andrew J.
1983 *Tzutzuculi: A Middle Preclassic Site on the Pacific Coast of Chiapas, Mexico.* Papers of the New World Archaeological Foundation 47. Provo, Utah.

Nance, Roger
1992 Guzman Mound: A Late Preclassic Salt Works on the South Coast of Guatemala. *Ancient Mesoamerica* 3: 27–46.

Navarrete, Carlos
1974 *The Olmec Rock Carvings at Pijijiapan, Chiapas, Mexico and Other Olmec Pieces from Chiapas and Guatemala.* Papers of the New World Archaeological Foundation 44. Provo, Utah.

Nelson, Fred W., and Barbara Voorhies
1980 Trace Element Analysis of Obsidian Artifacts from Three Shell Midden Sites in the Littoral Zone, Chiapas, Mexico. *American Antiquity* 45: 540–550.

Niederberger, Christine
1976 *Zohapilco: Cinco milenios de ocupación humana en un sitio lacustre de la Cuenca de México.* Mexico City.

1987 *Paléopaysages et archéologie pré-urbaine du Bassin de Mexico,* 2 vols. Mexico City.

Norman, V. Garth
1976 *Izapa Sculpture, Part 2.* Papers of the New World Archaeological Foundation 30. Provo, Utah.

Orrego, Miguel
1990 *Investigaciones arqueológicas en Abaj Takalik, El Asintal, Retalhuleu, Año 1988.* Reporte 1. Instituto Nacional de Antropología e Historia and Ministerio de Cultura y Deportes, Guatemala.

Ortiz, Ponciano, and María del Carmen Rodríguez
1994 Los espacios sagrados olmecas: El Manatí, un caso especial. In *Los olmecas en Mesoamérica,* ed. John Clark, 69–92. Mexico City and Madrid.

Paillés, Mari Cruz
1980 *Pampa el Pajón: An Early Middle Preclassic Site on the Coast of Chiapas, Mexico.* New World Archaeological Foundation 44. Provo, Utah.

Parsons, Lee A.
1986 *The Origins of Maya Art: Monumental Stone Sculpture of Kaminaljuyu, Guatemala, and Its Southern Pacific Coast.* Washington.

Peacock, David
1986 *Amphorae and the Roman Economy.* London.

Pye, Mary E.
1993 Patrones de asentamiento en la region del Río Jesús, departamento de Retalhuleu. In *IV Simposio de Investigaciones Arqueológicas en Guatemala, 1992,* ed. Juan Pedro Laporte, Hector Escobedo, and Sandra Villagran, 337–352. Guatemala City.

1995 Settlement, Specialization, and Adaptation in the Rio Jesus Drainage, Retalhuleu, Guatemala. Ph.D. dissertation, Department of Anthropology, Vanderbilt University, Nashville.

Pye, Mary E., and Arthur A. Demarest
1990 Análisis cerámico preliminar. In Informe preliminar de los resultados del análisis de laboratorio del Proyecto El Mesak, ed. Mary Pye, 6–21, figs. 1–36. Report submitted to the Instituto de Antropología e Historia, Guatemala City.

1991 The Evolution of Complex Societies in Southeastern Mesoamerica: New Evidence from El Mesak, Guatemala. In *The Formation of Complex Society in Southeastern Mesoamerica,* ed. William Fowler, Jr., 77–100. Boca Raton, Fla.

Pyne, Nanette
1976 The Fire-Serpent and Were-Jaguar in Formative Oaxaca: A Contingency Table Analysis. In *The Early Mesoamerican Village,* ed. Kent Flannery, 272–282. Orlando, Fla.

Reilly, F. Kent, III
1989 The Shaman in Transformation Pose: A Study of the Theme of Rulership in Olmec Art. *Record of the Art Museum, Princeton University* 48: 4–21.

Sharer, Robert J.
1989 The Olmec and the Southeast Periphery of Mesoamerica. In *Regional Perspectives on the Olmec,* ed. Robert Sharer and David Grove, 247–271. Cambridge.

Shook, Edwin, and Marion Hatch
1979 The Early Preclassic Sequence in the Ocos-Salinas La Blanca Area, South Coast of Guatemala. *Contributions of the University of California Research Facilities* 41: 149–195. Berkeley.

Shook, Edwin, and Robert Heizer
1976 An Olmec Sculpture from the South (Pacific) Coast of Guatemala. *Journal of New World Archaeology* 1: 1–18.

Soustelle, Jacques
1984 *The Olmecs: The Oldest Civilization in Mexico.* Garden City, New York.

Stuart, George E.
1993 New Light on the Olmec. *National Geographic* 184(5): 88–115.

Tejada B., Mario
1993 Nota preliminar sobre un nuevo pectoral olmeca proveniente de los alrededores de Comitán, Chiapas. *Instituto Chiapaneco de Cultura, Anuario 1993*: 299–302. Chiapas, Mexico.

Tolstoy, Paul
1989 Coapexco and Tlatilco: Sites with Olmec Materials in the Basin of Mexico. In *Regional Perspectives on the Olmec,* ed. Robert Sharer and David Grove, 85–121. Cambridge.

Zeitlin, Robert
1979 Prehistoric Long-Distance Exchange on the Southern Isthmus of Tehuantepec, Mexico. Ph.D. dissertation, Department of Anthropology, Yale University, New Haven.

BEATRIZ DE LA FUENTE
Universidad Nacional Autónoma de México

Olmec Sculpture: The First Mesoamerican Art

San Lorenzo Monument 11, c. 1200–1000 B.C., basalt
Museo de Antropología de Xalapa, Universidad Veracruzana

Mesoamerica's first true art was created by the archaeological culture now known as the Olmecs. Although there were numerous artistic figurines and other objects that clearly preceded the development of Olmec art, some of them with patterns similar to decorations applied to Olmec clay vessels, I agree with those who consider true art to be the conjunction of forms and meanings, as first evident in the great number of Olmec objects spread throughout early Mesoamerica. The qualities of Olmec art have been observed since the 1920s and have been enriched by almost every scholar attracted by the Olmecs. What is important here is the recognition that these Olmec traits can be found in objects in distant regions, especially dating to the Middle Formative period. My purpose in this essay is to discuss Olmec art, its themes, and its stylistic variations or artistic schools.

The Olmec Art Style

Olmec Art would seem to be a self-evident category, but both parts of the term have been the center of controversy. What is meant by *Olmec,* and what is meant by *art*? As noted, I take art to be the conjunction of form and meaning. As to *Olmec,* many hypotheses have been proposed as to the precise meaning of this term and its acceptable usage. Some see the Olmec phenomenon as indicative of a unity based on religion, ethnicity, language, or art style. I remain faithful to the last idea because it corresponds to the original sense given by Marshall Saville (1929) and later reinforced by Matthew Stirling (1943), Miguel Covarrubias (1944), and Michael Coe (1965), and more recently by several other scholars (The Art Museum 1996). In the apprehension of similar traits and qualities in a wide range of objects, these scholars discovered a new style of forms and iconographic representations, which they attributed to the Olmecs. By the time the name was established, the greatest concentration of monuments known with these qualities came from southern Veracruz and eastern Tabasco, Mexico, an area considered the "climax" zone by American archaeologists (Coe 1965) and the "metropolitan" area by Mexican archaeologists (Bernal 1968). Nowadays Olmec traits are known to occur in a much wider region than the Gulf Coast and Mexican highlands; Olmec-style objects occur in the Mexican states of Guerrero and Chiapas, Guatemala, and portions of lower Central America.

There has been much discussion about the unity of the Olmec style, and I must emphasize that such unity may be relative since different communities in diverse geographical areas interpreted fundamental qualities in accordance with their own traditions. By "unity" I mean the consistency of traits in form and iconography. Some traits dominated at certain times, but they appeared as a uniform complex when the style expressed moments of greater cultural integration. Thus one can speak of the Olmec style as a global concept or, alternatively, can also refer to its regional stylistic variations in time and space.

As part of a formal pattern, I have long stressed (de la Fuente 1977) the use of the convention of the golden mean established in the classical moment of Olmec art and extended and defined in the metropolitan area. The use of this sculptural convention began to diminish in late Olmec times as other conventions for formal presentation became more important (de la Fuente 1977). Changes in late Olmec art are also evident in the iconography and general themes of the sculpture and objects.

Olmec Iconography

The main themes of Olmec art and iconography have been discussed by several scholars (Saville 1929; Stirling 1943; Covarrubias 1944; Coe 1965; de la Fuente 1977; Joralemon 1971; Reilly 1996). All of these proposals, however, remain hypothetical as none has yet been demonstrated fully. Since written testimony for Olmec times is lacking, scholars must rely for their interpretations of the meaning and functions of Olmec art on universal religious experience as revealed in nonliterate cultures and comparative assessments of these experiences.

Art is the fundamental expression of underlying concepts: religious, political, social, technological, or economic. However, it is difficult to establish universal patterns for human conduct because, in the course of history, differences in human activities have been hard to isolate. Based on a common human experience, I think we can appreciate some matters that deal with cosmogony. They are present in the themes and meanings of monumental Olmec sculpture. Generally, it is the human figure that is rendered as primordial in Olmec art.

The first group of Olmec iconographic cosmogony is supported by the depiction of mythical themes. They all deal with myths of creation, possession of the Earth by fertilizing it, such as Monument 1 from Tenochtitlán (fig. 1), or by humans emerging from the cave of Earth in a clear origin myth of Olmec peoples, as seen in Monument 5 of Laguna de los Cerros (fig. 2). It is the ancestral, terrestrial matrix that gives birth to whole-figured men. Some variations of this theme are evident on La Venta Monument 5, in which sacrifice as a

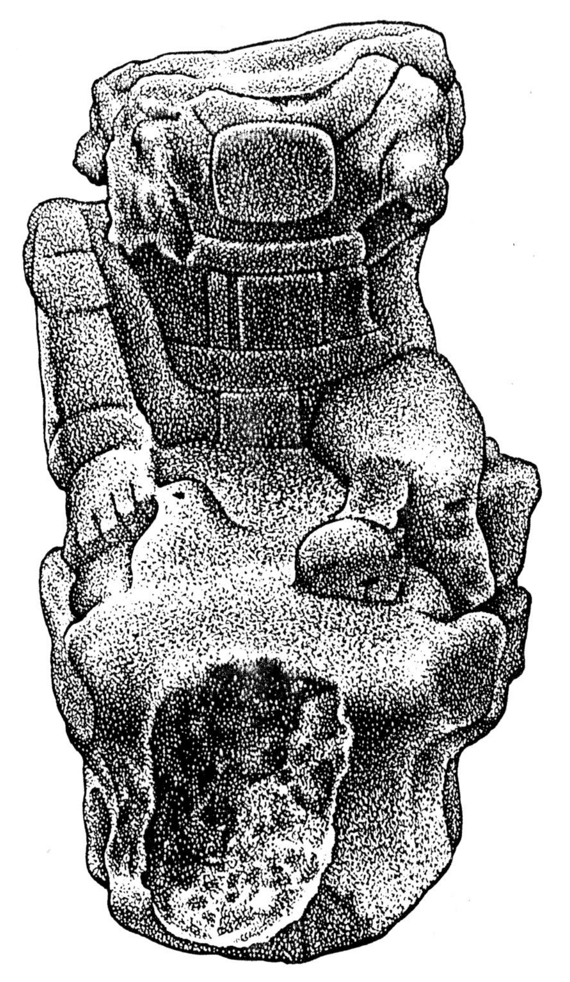

1. Tenochtitlán Monument 1, c. 1200–1000 B.C., basalt
Museo Nacional de Antropología, Mexico City

2. Laguna de los Cerros Monument 5, c. 1200–800 B.C., basalt
Museo de Antropología de Xalapa, Universidad Veracruzana

3. Las Limas Monument 1, c. 1200–800 B.C., basalt
Museo de Antropología de Xalapa, Universidad Veracruzana

4. "El Principe" from Cruz del Milagro, c. 1200–800 B.C., basalt
Museo de Antropología de Xalapa, Universidad Veracruzana

5. San Lorenzo colossal head 8, c. 1200–1000 B.C., basalt
Museo de Antropología de Xalapa, Universidad Veracruzana

need for purification and sacredness is the essential theme depicted. Variations also exist in sculpture such as the Las Limas figure, where natural rocky shelters might have served as a substitute for otherwise depicted caves (fig. 3).

Another cluster of thematically related monuments is constituted by figures that incorporate features of animals into their essential human aspect and others that are merely combinations of fantastic and visual characters. Elsewhere I have considered them as "supernatural" beings (de la Fuente 1977). They refer, of course, to what has been the pivotal explanation of the meaning of the totality of Olmec art: the jaguar, the were-jaguar, the humanized jaguar, and the baby jaguar. Certainly these images were related to mythical beings; they themselves were part or symbols of the myth.

The group of monuments of principal importance is constituted by images whose characteristics are exclusively human. In this group I include those with personal physical attributes, such as the "Prince" of Cruz del Milagro (fig. 4), and those that show unique personality. I refer to the portraits of kings in the seventeen colossal heads: ten from San Lorenzo (fig. 5), four from La Venta, and three from Tres Zapotes and its environs.

6. San Lorenzo Monument 11, c. 1200–1000 B.C., basalt
Museo de Antropología de la Universidad Veracruzana, Jalapa

7. El Azuzul, feline sculpture, c. 1200–800 B.C., stone, in situ

8. San Lorenzo, feline and man, c. 1200–800 B.C., basalt
Museo Comunitario de San Lorenzo

Schools of Olmec Art

As evident above, one recognizes a major style and a plurality of regional, local, and perhaps personal styles entailed within it. Style obtains its climax of cultural unity, but as a process it is always mutable and modifies itself by internal laws of change or by inevitable external expressions. Style, either general or particular, has its proper and peculiar trace; it is always dynamic, develops cycles, and reaches moments where cultural homogeneity is expressed in greater similarities of works of art. Here I consider the local Olmec sculptural styles of the major centers in the metropolitan area. The main reason why it is now possible to distinguish styles at these sites is because we have large samples of monuments from each, and it is possible to make a general and analytical survey of the sculpture.

The sculptural school of *San Lorenzo* was perhaps a long-lasting workshop where novices were taught by the masters of stone carving and then transmitted their learning to subsequent generations. I include with San Lorenzo the smaller sites surrounding it, namely, Potrero Nuevo, Tenochtitlán, El Azuzul, and Los

9. La Venta Throne (altar) 4, c. 1000–600 B.C., basalt
Parque Museo La Venta

10. La Venta Stela 2, c. 1000–600 B.C., basalt
Parque Museo La Venta

Idolos. The prominent characteristic of this school is the ideal approach to visual reality (see Pasztory, this volume); the images that dominate in volume or in bas-relief are mostly human (fig. 6). Most of the sculpture conveys the feeling of absolute concordance between form and meaning. The regional style of San Lorenzo has its own "grammar," internal order, and expressiveness.

The highlights of the San Lorenzo school include all those characteristics mentioned for the Olmec style in general (volume, monumentality, heaviness, and internal rhythm), as well as a preference for rounded forms that cover acute geometrism and maintain equilibrium based on perfect harmony, as is true of the animal figures such as the felines (fig. 7). The arrest of momentum evident in the San Lorenzo sculpture changes through time. In later times, the restful serenity we have seen before is substituted with soft dynamism, scenic resources, exaggeration in traits, and, in general, a more eclectic expression (fig. 8).

The *La Venta* school seems to have been more versatile than that at San Lorenzo because of the diversity of themes portrayed on its monuments. Noteworthy is the near equivalence in the number of human and composite figure representations (the "supernaturals" mentioned above that integrate human and animal characteristics in fantastic combinations). This may mean that a greater diversity of myths was present in La Venta culture. At its beginning, the style was characterized by solid figures of geometric forms. The volume sometimes seems to have been obscured by bas-reliefs on the sides of monuments, such as seen in the combinations between volume (one main figure) and scenes carved on the sides in relief, as on Thrones 4 and 5 (fig. 9).

Over time, the La Venta style displayed an increase of geometrism and synthetic forms, plastic movement produced by the release of volume into space, and a wider discourse of scenic narrative. It seems to me that the final expressions of the La Venta style, the narrative historical scenes depicted on enormous stone slabs such as Stelae 2 and 3 (fig. 10), were a sort of bridge between mythical and historical narratives such as seen in Maya times.

The site of *Laguna de los Cerros*, the locus of the third artistic school, has some of the most impressive sculptural masterpieces of any Olmec site (see Gillespie, this volume).

The art from Laguna de los Cerros does not conform to the compact naturalistic style of San Lorenzo nor to the impersonal geometrism of La Venta climax art. Until a larger corpus of sculpture is available from this region, however, I dare say only that the Laguna style represented an eclectic school that fully mastered stone carving but showed different forms and levels in its iconography. At the same time, one appreciates the powerful quality of the priest or king depicted in Monument 19 (fig. 11), the classical, sensual forms of the seminude torsos (Monument 6; fig. 12), the baroque, noncolossal heads (Monuments 1 and 2; fig. 13), and a surprising combination of synthetic corporal forms with an enormous head and abstract facial traits (Monument 8; fig. 14).

There are many other sites with few works of monumental sculpture; stylistically, they can either be forced into one of the substyles just described or left apart until more evidence is available. It is difficult at the moment to propose evidence for a sculptural chronology. I leave this matter to archaeologists and specialists in the field. My main purpose here is to draw attention to the outstanding forms and meanings of Mesoamerica's first art style, as it is evident in sculpture from sites in the Gulf Coast lowlands of Mexico.

11. Laguna de los Cerros Monument 19, c. 1000–600 B.C., basalt
Museo de Antropología de Xalapa, Universidad Veracruzana

The Question of Twins

In the course of writing this paper, several unusual monuments piqued my interest. These monuments portray mythical images and supernatural beings and are part of the primordial cosmogony of Mesoamerica dealing with twins. These are evident in the duality present in monumental Olmec sculpture and in ceramic figurines of the Middle Formative period. I want to emphasize this cosmogonic myth here because it seems, thus far, that Olmec deities and myths are supposed by scholars to have been essentially based on jaguar themes, some thought to have been induced by psychoactive drugs introduced into the body or by auto-sacrifice.

I like to think that Pre-Columbian man had similar experiences as people from other parts of the world and shared conceptions of nature, the universe, earth, and the human being. Of course, this experience would have included the stage of animal power (in the Olmec case, that of the jaguar, the monkey, the toad, the eagle, the crocodile, and so on) and the con-

12. Laguna de los Cerros Monument 6, c. 1000–600 B.C., basalt
Museo de Antropología de Xalapa, Universidad Veracruzana

13. Laguna de los Cerros Monument 1, c. 1000–600 B.C., basalt
Museo de Antropología de Xalapa, Universidad Veracruzana

14. Laguna de los Cerros Monument 8, c. 1000–600 B.C., basalt
Museo de Antropología de Xalapa, Universidad Veracruzana

solidation of the seeded earth. Experiences in this early process of human development related to the adaptation to and dominion of nature. Consequently, man created myths to explain and defend against it.

There was a myth precisely depicted in Olmec times, and until now not wholly recognized, at its origin a radical Mesoamerican myth that is also a common theme in global mythology. I refer to the twins depicted in the sculptures from El Azuzul (fig. 15), the ones in Monument 2 of Potrero Nuevo (fig. 16), and most probably in San Martín Pajapan and Monument 44 of La Venta. Let us first remember the universality of myths of hero twins and later refer to some of the sculpture depicting this myth in its Mesoamerican setting. The myth of founding twins represents a continuity of belief from Olmec to Mexica times.

All cultures and all mythologies reveal particular interest in twins. Even though the birth of twins is a common natural phenomenon, it always arouses surprise and admiration. In mythology, twins can be portrayed as equals or opposites. One of them may be luminous, while the other is obscure; one may represent heaven and the other the earth; they may represent other paired dualities of day and night, black and white, hot and cold, or red and blue. They express duality, the basic principle of Mesoamerican ideology. Dualism, in both spiritual and material senses, approaches the profound meaning of life and the cosmos.

Some twins are absolutely alike, doubles, or copies of each other, as is the case of the Azuzul twins, the Maya hero twins of the *Popol Vuh,* or the Mexica eagle warriors of the Templo Mayor, Tenochtitlán. They express the unity of a balanced duality, like a mirror image. Moreover, these twins symbolized the ambivalence of the mythical universe. In all world traditions, twins (as gods or heroes) dispute, struggle, or even charm, giving them an ambivalent character.

André Virel (1965) argues that twin images are the internal tension of a permanent situation, the reduction of a multiple to a unity. Twin images symbolize contrary interior and exterior forces; they are at the same time opposite and complementary, relative or absolute principles to be resolved in an eternal creative tension.

A general survey of early world mythologies shows evidence of the twins' symbolic myth,

15. El Azuzul, twins, c. 1200–800 B.C., stone, in situ

16. Potrero Nuevo Monument 2, c. 1000–800 B.C., basalt
Museo de Antropología de Xalapa, Universidad Veracruzana

17. Tlatilco, bicephalous figure, c. 800–600 B.C., clay
Museo Nacional de Antropología, Mexico City

18. El Azuzul, twins, c. 1200–800 B.C., stone, in situ

19. Mexica *Ehecatl* standard bearers, c. 1350–1500 B.C., stone
Museo Nacional de Antropología, Mexico City

for example, the Vedic Ashwins, Mitra-Varuna, Romulus-Remus, Isis-Osiris, Apollo-Artemis, and Castor-Pollux. In some myths there is a third brother, as with Castor and Helena or Osiris and Set. Could these be something equivalent to the third image, the standing jaguar, at El Azuzul? In all cases, either twins or triad, they are mythical beings with a natural appearance, or mixed with animals descended from an immortal father and a mortal mother. They are hierogamic because of the integration of soul (immateriality) and flesh (corporeality).

Conclusion

In this essay I have considered the general qualities, form, and meaning of Olmec art, as expressed by its sculpture, as well as the defining attributes of the San Lorenzo, La Venta, and Laguna de los Cerros regional substyles. I also stressed the importance of a cosmogonic myth, that of the hero twins depicted in several colossal human figures. It is important to note that this myth of hero twins goes together with dualism in ancient Mexico.

The earliest depiction of twins I have found

in America comes not from Mexico but from Ecuador and dates to c. 2000 B.C. (Early Valdivia phase). It shows two anthropocentric female branches that emerge from the same pedestal. Later, from 1200 to 600 B.C., we see the concept in Mesoamerica in ceramic figurines and stone sculpture. Figurines are frequent at Tlatilco, in the Basin of Mexico, and depict bicephalism or two faces integrated in one head (fig. 17); the concept of life and death is clearly exhibited in a well-known mask from the same site. The magnificent twins from El Azuzul are the earliest known depiction of these twins in monumental sculpture (fig. 18).

Another important example is that of the double twin heroes of the *Popol Vuh,* the primary document of Maya spirituality. Some of the scenes on Classic Maya vessels and bone objects have been interpreted as depictions of the *Popol Vuh* myth. Here scholars recognize the resurrection of the maize god Hun Hunahpu and his two sons, Hunahpu and Xbalanque. The monkey scribe appears with them in a late Maya vase. Also important is the Postclassic twin myth of Quetzalcoatl, as Venus or Xolotl, as described in the sixteenth-century sources. This is also the period of the twin double pyramids in ancient Tenochtitlán. Other examples from late figurative art include the Mexica standard bearers (fig. 19) and the twin eagle warriors found in the chamber of that name at the Templo Mayor in Mexico City.

Olmec art was the earliest in Mesoamerica, and it established an artistic unity, both formal and conceptual, at the foundation of Mesoamerica. Civilization was whole and continuous, but styles changed at different times and in different places. As with all true art, the most outstanding expressions of Mesoamerican art, such as Olmec Art, have taken their place among the world's masterpieces.

BIBLIOGRAPHY

The Art Museum
1996 *The Olmec World: Ritual and Rulership* [exh. cat., The Art Museum, Princeton University]. Princeton.

Bernal, Ignacio
1968 *El mundo olmeca.* Mexico City.

Coe, Michael D.
1965 The Olmec Style and Its Distribution. In *Archaeology of Southern Mesoamerica, Part 2,* ed. Gordon Willey, 739–775. Handbook of Middle American Indians, vol. 3. Austin.

Covarrubias, Miguel
1944 El arte "olmeca" o de La Venta. *Cuadernos Americanos* 28(4): 153–179.

Cyphers, Ann
1997 (Editor) *Población, Subsistencia y Medio Ambiente en San Lorenzo Tenochtitlán.* Mexico City.

de la Fuente, Beatriz
1977 *Los hombres de piedra: Escultura olmeca.* Mexico City.

Joralemon, Peter David
1971 *A Study of Olmec Iconography.* Washington.

Reilly, Kent F., III
1996 Art, Ritual, and Rulership in the Olmec World. In *The Olmec World: Ritual and Rulership,* 27–46 [exh. cat., The Art Museum, Princeton University]. Princeton.

Saville, Marshall
1929 Votive Axes from Ancient Mexico. *Indian Notes* 6(3): 266–299. Museum of the American Indian, Heye Foundation, New York.

Stirling, Matthew W.
1943 *Stone Monuments of Southern Mexico.* Bureau of American Ethnology Bulletin 138. Washington.

Virel, André
1965 *Histoire de notre image.* Geneva.

ESTHER PASZTORY
Columbia University

The Portrait and the Mask: Invention and Translation

How, then should we interpret the great divide, which runs through the history of art and sets off the few islands of illusionist styles, of Greece, of China, and of the Renaissance, from the vast ocean of "conceptual" art?

Ernst Gombrich 1963

The Olmec portrait heads astonish westerners—who come upon them usually in a dimly lit museum hall—by their scale and realism. There are now seventeen heads found at three sites, the last as recently as 1994. These massive basalt heads were pecked and carved with simple flint and basalt hammerstones and required enormous effort to sculpt. San Lorenzo Monument 1, for example, is 2.75 meters high and weighs 16 tons (fig. 1). Westerners used to colossal modern engineering and buildings respond positively to the size of the heads on this account alone. But the westerner is also used to realism in art. According to the model developed by Johann Winckelmann (1968) in the eighteenth century, and still so presented in survey books, art began in rigid stylization as in Egypt and only in time became realistic in the hands of the Greeks.

Various types of realism have been the favorite styles of the West. Only two epochs, the Middle Ages and the twentieth century, favored nonrealistic styles. Whether the modern viewer prefers realism or abstraction, western thought has long associated realism with higher cultures. The Olmec heads are amazing not only because they were transported over a long distance (70 kilometers from the quarry) but also because such realistic effects were created with crude stone tools at the very beginning of an artistic tradition (c. 1200–700 B.C.). The westerner has seen many realistic images but is *still* impressed by the wrinkled brow, parted lips as if speaking, pupils in the eyes, and fleshy jowls of the Olmec colossal heads. These are the Pre-Columbian waxworks of rulers long gone by. We do not know whether they were in fact rulers, but most informed opinion thinks so.

The Pre-Columbian viewer probably saw the heads in bright sunshine or rain, set up in rows outdoors. As far as we can surmise, nothing in earlier art prepared him or her for the scale of the heads. Earlier and contemporary arts were in ceramic or wood and probably smaller in scale. Nothing prepared the viewer for that realistic gaze either. It was as if the rulers of the past had come back to life in a colossal, permanent stone form. They were so near and lifelike that they may have seemed real and so big as to be frightening. To the Olmec viewer, I imagine that the stone heads did not so much signify a high degree of cultural development as an enormous presence of power.

San Martín Pajapan, kneeling figure with mask headdress, 1000–800 B.C., stone
Museo de Antropología de Xalapa, Universidad Veracruzana; photograph: Studio Beatrice Trueblood

Naturalism and Portraiture

In the western paradigm of art history, the naturalism of Greek art is intimately related to democracy and the concept of individual freedom. In contrast, the stiff and rigid conventionalization of Egyptian art, from which it supposedly derived, was related to the absolute power of Pharaonic rule. Already in Winckelmann's (1968) history it is clear that certain forms of art were associated with certain forms of political rule. In the works of many subsequent art historians, including Ernst Gombrich (1960), nonwestern arts take the place of Egypt as the primitive "others" against which to play the miracles of Classical civilization. Egypt, with its animal-headed deities and idol worship, is reminiscent of Hindu or Pre-Columbian civilizations. Had the Olmec heads looked conventionalized like the ones from Easter Island, they would have occasioned little surprise as works of nonwestern art. The colossal heads' evocative likenesses to real persons—even to a racial type—have been a source of fascination. Although earlier scholars supposed that the more naturalistic heads were made last, and thus a conventionalization-to-naturalism development could be suggested for the heads themselves (see Graham 1989), the best archaeological evidence suggests that the most realistic ones are the earliest, and the development proceeds in the other direction (Milbrath 1979).

Olmec art is surprising not only due to the possible portraiture in the heads but also in the freedom of design in the lifesize carvings of bodies. Although hands and feet are often rudimentary, on several sculptures bodies are asymmetrical and twist about their axes in a manner that occurs in Greek art only relatively late. One sculpture had arms inset into sockets, presumably for an even greater illusion of movement (fig. 2).

Because Pre-Columbian art emerged outside the Old World, it is a testing ground for theories based on Old World art. Olmec art allows one to examine the issue of naturalism and the development of art in a comparative context. Does naturalism have to occur gradually, or can it develop suddenly? If it does not develop according to the Egyptian-to-Greek paradigm, how does one account for its appearance?

Not all Olmec art is equally naturalistic. Many other figures, particularly human were-jaguar combinations, are much more stylized (fig. 3). Instead of the well-developed pectorals and calves, these figures have much more schematic bodies and grotesque heads with angular elements. Art history based on European models has sought to create lawlike patterns in the development of style that were based on the consistency of form. Pairings such as "Classical" and "Baroque" (Wolfflin 1922) created various classifications of line and form that were mutually exclusive. On this basis Gombrich (1960) divided art into the "perceptual" and the "conceptual." In the perceptual mode, the artist seeks to match the image to reality and to create the illusion that it is indeed real. It is a physical, psychological, and philosophical vision that Gombrich associated with relatively secular and "free" societies. In the conceptual mode, the artist creates what he already knows or imagines in his mind without an outside referent. To Gombrich, this represented the

1. San Lorenzo Monument 1, colossal head, c. 1200 B.C., basalt
Museo de Antropología de Xalapa, Universidad Veracruzana; photograph: Studio Beatrice Trueblood

2. San Lorenzo Monument 34, kneeling figure, c. 1200 B.C., stone
Museo de Antropología de Xalapa, Universidad Veracruzana; photograph: *Arqueología Mexicana*, Marco Antonio Pacheco/Raíces

3. San Lorenzo Monument 52, were-jaguar canal stone, c. 1200 B.C.
Photograph: *Arqueología Mexicana*, Marco Antonio Pacheco/Raíces

epitome of a religious worldview and, developmentally speaking, was anterior to perceptual art. Realism was related to the humanism of the Classical and Renaissance worlds.

In the case of the Olmecs, however, the perceptual and the conceptual coexist. The "conceptual" San Lorenzo Monument 52 is coeval with the "perceptual" colossal heads and with Monument 34. We therefore have to look for an explanation that allows for the existence of naturalism in the beginning of a tradition, intermixed with conventionalization, outside of a Classical context.

The Olmec situation is rare in art but not unique. A similar phenomenon occurs in two other places in the world, at Ife/Benin in Africa and Moche in the Andes (Griffin 1976; Peterson 1981). It is the presence of naturalistic heads that have made both of these traditions favorites of westerners with a Classical viewpoint. The terracotta and brass heads of Ife (fig. 4) and the ceramic effigy vessels of the Moche (fig. 5) are both believed to represent rulers in an idealized youthful-mature age. The heads are similar in the representation of racial types, idealized good looks, and some personal specificity (fat or thin faces, an occasional smile). The period of realistic representation does not last a very long time in either area. Moreover, as in the case of the Olmecs, bodies and other figures are not necessarily treated equally realistically. Bodies may be proportionately short or schematized. In all three art styles, there is an easy continuum between the realistic and the conventionalized. And in all three some aspects of the figures are detailed and realistic, as in a close-up, while other aspects are simpler (for example, the ears of the colossal heads are quite stylized).

It is not certain that any of these remarkably idealistic heads are portraits. Nevertheless, scholars studying each art style have felt that the heads were meant to represent rulers, despite a wide variety of contexts. According to one theory, the Ife heads were dressed with the regalia of the *oni* and presented as an effigy on a funerary occasion (Willett 1967). Or, possibly, they held crowns and regalia (Drewal 1989). The Moche vessels are found in burials, but in the burials of men other than the ruler himself, since they exist in moldmade multiples (Donnan 1976; Strong and Evans 1962).

4. Brass head from Ife, thirteenth century
British Museum, London

5. Stirrup spout Moche vessel, 300–500 B.C., ceramic
The Art Institute of Chicago

The Olmec heads were on permanent display (Ann Cyphers, personal communication, 1996).

One can try to find an answer to the question of the development of naturalism in the sociopolitical integration of these three cultures. It is my impression that in all cases the societies were highly stratified and were either complex chiefdoms or states. Each area had an agricultural base and trade in exotic materials, such as fine stones or metals. In chiefdoms, as defined by Elman Service (1962, 1975), societies focus on chiefs and the hierarchies surrounding them, but rulers may rule by consensus only and not have absolute power. Such rulers often play important ceremonial roles. Large and complex chiefdoms have built some impressive architectural structures, such as the Polynesian *marae,* and have set up large monuments, such as the Easter Island heads.

States are generally defined as polities with greater executive power in the hands of the ruler and classlike divisions in the populations. Usually, states build impressive monuments, roads, and irrigation canals and engage in other engineering projects that require a large, well-organized labor force. The difference between the rulers and the ruled is much more sharply defined in states than in chiefdoms in which lineages may have titled members. Nevertheless, the difference between a powerful chiefdom and a small state may not be easy to see in the archaeological record. Olmec, Ife, and Moche fit into this borderland category of social integration types. It is striking that such portraiture and realism should be associated with this type of social integration in which a great deal of attention is lavished on powerful rulers. Evidently, realism may be a feature of the art of such societies, but it is by no means a standard or necessary feature. The Easter Island heads, erected in the context of a chiefdom, for example, are quite schematic. The

6. Greenstone mask,
800–600 B.C.
Dumbarton Oaks Research Library and Collection, Washington

7. Iroquois False Face Society wooden mask, twentieth century
American Museum of Natural History, New York

notion of realistic portraiture, therefore, needs to have a more specific context beyond that of the chiefdom or state.

Masks and Masking

While the West sees portraits and naturalism as unexpected wonders in other cultures, masks are seen as nonwestern par excellence. The grotesque Olmec mask in the Dumbarton Oaks collection is a perfect embodiment of the "primitive" as seen in the West (fig. 6). Indeed, masks are among the most important works of art in village societies. I see the relationship of art and society in the contexts, as defined by anthropologists, to be quite different from chiefdoms. Village societies are not usually stratified into ranks or titles. Rather, authority is usually in the hands of elders and, more specifically, delegated to the spirit world. Ancestor cults are usually important, and ancestors and nature spirits often visit the village and oversee initiations and curing rituals and reinforce social norms. These spirits are usually impersonated by villagers wearing masks. While the portrait is presumably a likeness of the self devoid of cover, the mask is a constructed identity covering a real self. Such a central role for masquerades is usually found in societies with relatively egalitarian social structures, where humans may literally hide behind the spirits in enforcing social norms. No one person is meant to be important enough to be represented by portraiture. Ancestral images may be "portraits" in terms of scarification designs or by being named but not in terms of outward appearance. In this sense, the portrait with physiognomic likeness is the opposite of the mask.

Enormous variety characterizes the masks of village societies, usually made of a perishable material such as wood (fig. 7). Many of the spirits are powerful and dangerous, and sharply conventionalized, dramatic, "cubistic" shapes are felt to be appropriate to them. Beautiful and serene faces also occur, but they too are often simplified into abstract forms rather than portraiture. Sometimes they are coupled, as in the "beauty and beast" masks of Nigeria. Village cultures, masking, and conventionalized art styles appear to go together.

In chiefdoms and states, masks do not have a central role for the obvious reason that authority is in the person and court of the ruler and not in a masking society of elders. Masking societies sometimes disappear once a village becomes a chiefdom, or often the society is attached to the court and becomes an arm of the ruling power. The form and meaning of the masks do not disappear entirely in states and chiefdoms. They are often turned into chiefly regalia: headdresses, pectorals, and loincloth adornments. The Benin Oba wore beautiful ivory mask pendants at his waist. Moreover, these mask images may be transferred from the perishable material of wood into rare and costly treasures such as ivory or greenstone. Much of the art of chiefdoms consists of the insignia of the ruler in costly and exotic materials. While the art of villages is dramatic but rough, the art of chiefdoms is lustrous and smooth.

It is only possible to sketch the artistic situation prior to Olmec times in the Basin of Mexico. Given the quantity of masks in later Mesoamerican art, and of the importance of masking in colonial and even in modern times, it seems reasonable to suppose that early Mesoamerica might have had strong traditions of masking. The existence of a single Olmec wooden mask (from Guerrero) in the American Museum of Natural History indicates that masking existed in Olmec times. There are finds of masks and masked figurines from sites such as Tlatilco in the Basin of Mexico that date around 900 B.C. (Coe 1965).

The evidence of representations also indicates that the Olmec rulers also employed the usual strategies with masking: they appropriated it to the uses of power and prestige in the form of insignia, thereby indicating that access to the supernatural was not through independent societies but through the ruler and aristocracy. Many Olmec pectorals survive with masked faces of the jaguar/human supernatural with his cleft head and angular mouth. Some human figures with portraitlike faces wear stylized were-jaguar masks as headdresses (fig. 8). The forms of these masks are dramatic and reminiscent of village art. Their very purpose, in my view, was to conserve continuity with a past and to present its long traditions in a new form. Indeed, if their meaning is traditional, and in order to maintain the traditional in meaning, their form would have had to have been kept as well.

It is no accident that the supernaturals in Olmec art all derive from or are related to these grotesque mask forms. Their bodies are not grotesque, although they are often child-size. The head, however, is a mask (fig. 3). Even the confusing multiplicities of Olmec deities that have been so difficult to tease apart may go back to various masking personae. The mask form was such a powerful icon among the Olmecs that it was even used in symbolic designs incised on celts or on figures, such as the one from Las Limas. As such, it becomes a frame for a variety of facial features and markings that in their complexity resemble glyphs. While none of the Olmec designs are considered writing, they bear both a superficial and structural resemblance to Maya glyphs. Many Maya glyphs, especially such basic ones as the head variants of numbers, have masklike

8. San Martín Pajapan, kneeling figure with mask headdress, 1000–800 B.C., stone

Museo de Antropología de Xalapa, Universidad Veracruzana; photograph: Studio Beatrice Trueblood

flames that function in a similar manner and may be descendants of Olmec mask designs.

The mask form in Mesoamerica underwent a complex series of translations, with each descendant possibly coexisting with the parent form: actual masks in wood, ritual masks in greenstone, ruler insignia, deity face, sign system, and glyph. One of the ways in which art forms develop is through the creative translation of one image into the other, from one medium to another, from three dimensions to low relief, and so on. I am calling these transformations "translations" to indicate both the continuity and the magnitude of the changes. The term *translation* puts the emphasis on the translators who were charged with finding idioms in the language of the current time and practices for the language of the past. Translation may try to minimize change, but change is unavoidable due to new circumstances. Translation is an outwardly conservative process that nevertheless results in creative change. The history of art is an endless series of translations.

9. San Lorenzo colossal head found in 1994, c. 1200 B.C., basalt
Photograph: Ann Cyphers

Why Olmec Naturalism?

Unlike the Olmec masks and supernaturals for which I have suggested earlier sources, the colossal heads and figures have no known prototypes. They appear in the archaeological record as sudden and surprising inventions. Ife and Moche portraiture are similarly sudden within their own contexts. Instead of long developmental periods, we have to assume that certain ruler/patrons and their artists conceived of such a new way of representation for their purposes. The power of a ruler to change the canons of art and begin something completely new and radical is illustrated by the historic account of Akhenaton, whose political and religious agenda included a veristic artistic one. It does not take more than one ruler of vision to sponsor a new style. The invention happens once as the subsequent rulers usually continue the new tradition, or in Akhenaton's case, discontinue it. Thus all Olmec colossal heads, Ife bronzes, and Moche portrait vessels bear family likenesses as a result of continuity after initial invention (fig. 9).

It is significant for the how-to aspect of these portraits that both Ife and Moche art is, or is based on, easily modeled clay forms and not carvings. Because of the rich evidence of clay modeling of various types of figures in the Olmec area, I am postulating that the Olmec made clay models of their sitters—or of that first sitter—and subsequently carved the stones from them.

Why the choice for naturalistic representation? Reception theory may suggest some answers. Conventionalized styles keep their viewers at an emotional distance. The Olmec jaguar supernaturals, for example, have a mystery about their non-natural forms that distance them from this world. Masks in general suggest that another reality lies underneath their rigid and nonmoving forms. Naturalistic art, by contrast, implies that one is not in the presence of an artifact but of the "real" and draws one in seductively. (This is not to say that a stylized work cannot be felt to have power within it, but that it is more through the mystery of the strange than through the insinuation of the familiar.) We respond to portraits as if they were real beings before we have decided that they are real or not.

Many twentieth-century writers and artists dislike realism's power for attracting viewers and undermining their intellectual faculties. Jean Baudrillard (1987) has written extensively about the effect of modern realistic images in film and advertising that blur the borders between the real and the manmade in an instantaneous emotional reaction. According to him, naturalism encourages passive viewing and passivity in general (for example, *The Evil Demon of Images*). Some hyperrealist, modern artists have explored the various facets of this illusion of the real. All over the United States people bump into and take their pictures with hyperrealistic modern bronze sculptures (by J. Seward Johnson) set up outside shops and in parks. George Segal's white plaster figures are also in public places like passengers in a bus station (Hunter 1989). Most colorful of all are the works of Duane Hanson, whose ladies in curlers and museum guards are meant to fool the eye of the sophisticated museum goer in the museum itself (Bush 1976). The aim of such verism is to scramble the perceptions of the viewer. The impact of all of these figures has to do with the question of their reality. We are used to naturalistic images, and our artists have to develop many tour-de-force tricks to create this illusion of the real for us. The viewing audience of the Olmec colossal heads was probably less jaded to the effects of naturalism, and therefore the impact of the colossal stone head(s) must have been correspondingly greater.

10. Laguna de los Cerros Monument 19, standing figure in cape, c. 1000 B.C., stone
Museo de Antropología de Xalapa, Universidad Veracruzana; photograph: Studio Beatrice Trueblood

The secret of naturalistic representation is not so much the acquisition of a particular "vision," as Gombrich (1960) thought, but the desire to create the illusion of the "real" for a particular purpose. The illusion is created by relatively well known means. Conceptual art focuses on the denotative features of the face—the eyes, nose, and mouth—but however detailed they are, they remain abstract if the intervening areas are not developed. The illusion of reality is created by modulating and developing the "insignificant" intermediate areas of the cheeks and eye sockets and situating the features within. In Norman Bryson's (1983) terms, such images are overarticulated and informationally expensive. Olmec artists also understood that strict symmetry and regularity read as pattern and not as "life." The eyes and lips of San Lorenzo Monument 1 (fig. 1) are all slightly asymmetrical; the figure emerging from the niche on La Venta Monument 4 has asymmetrically arranged arms, and so on. The illusion of Olmec realism is but a bag of artistic tricks, and their purpose might have been to astonish and overwhelm. Naturalistic rendering, as such, is a form of mysterious and miraculous knowledge and therefore also a form of power. Such power belonged to the ruler and his circle and was not available to others.

Presentation of the Body

Besides the choice of naturalism, the Olmecs also chose to represent themselves and their power through the body (fig. 10). There is little emphasis on costume or headdresses, and when they exist, they are secondary in importance to the body. This emphasis on the body coincides with the three-dimensionality that is the preferred form. The Olmec rulers claimed power in themselves as physical entities. They are shown as a physically powerful group with heavy muscles and heavy jowls. Their hands, often clenched, hold ropes or staffs. Their faces scowl, and their gazes are fierce. By contrast, in the art of later Mesoamerica, most rulers claim legitimacy through costume and insignia that relate to their ancestors or to the spirit world, not through their bodies and faces (the Herrera stela dated A.D. 36 is an example). In later art, writing and glyphs bolster up the claims of rulers. Information is given visually in a two-dimensional form, and the physical presence of the figure is lost in the process.

Naturalism is most impressive and awesome when the subject is the human face and body. The choice of portraiture in the experimentation with naturalism is not accidental. My argument is that naturalism is always potentially available for the artist—that is, it does not take generations to master it—but only at certain times has it been chosen as a preferred visual language. Art develops through two major processes: translation and invention. Realism is often an invention in the midst of conventionalized styles. Why then is it as rare as Gombrich has pointed out?

Conclusion

Not all cultures share the joy of realism. Robert Thompson (1971: 376–377) describes the Yoruba whose aesthetic ideal is "'mimesis at midpoint'—i.e., the siting of art at a point somewhere between absolute abstraction and absolute likeness. . . . Portraiture in the Western manner is considered virtually sinister by traditional Yoruba. It is interesting that Hans Himmelheber was told by a Guro artist on the Ivory Coast: 'I am afraid to carve the face of a particular man or girl, for if that person should die soon after, people might attribute death to this portrait.'"

Reading such ethnographic detail makes it seem that "primitives" are frightened of realism, while the more "civilized" are not. David Freedberg's (1989) *Power of Images* tries to undo these tropes by arguing that even the most "civilized" person has a response to images that operates before aesthetic appreciation or any other kind of analysis takes place, and that this response could be innate. It is normal and common to confuse the image with what it is supposed to be. Although he suggests that we have a response to all images, hyperrealistic ones evoke a particularly strong reaction. He analyzes the extremely lifelike European wax images, emphasizing the fear they cause in the viewer: "We are arrested by these images at least partly out of fear that they might just come alive, just open their mouths, just begin to move. We fear the lifelike because the dead substance of which the object is made may yet come alive" (Freedberg 1989: 231). "Of course we marvel at the skill of the maker, at mechanical contrivance, and the artistry that makes objects seem real: but at the same time, fear of the lifelike haunts the warring perceptions of the image as reflection and the image as reality" (Freedberg 1989: 221). For Freedberg, the waxwork figures are merely the end points in verisimilitude, but objects all along the continuum of abstraction to naturalism have some uncanny power to move the beholder.

The choice of realistic human representation and portraiture is an investment in a new kind of power and emotional manipulation of the viewer. The rarity of such representation indicates avoidance. Its presence suggests the purposeful transgression of something of a representational taboo. Rather than being the benign signs of cultures at a "higher level of civilization," they suggest profoundly complex deployments of power.

The aim of all realistic art, whether it is the nineteenth-century novel, the twentieth-century film, or Olmec portraits, is the eradication of distance between the viewer and the object viewed. A realistic image suggests that we are in the actual presence of the person depicted, despite the fact that we know that it is only celluloid, paint, or stone. Realistic depiction works on the emotional level to create intimacy. The more realistic Olmec heads, for instance, are experienced as "closer" and friendlier than the stylized ones. The western preference for realistic styles has suppressed their uncanny features except in extreme examples.

The rarity of naturalistic arts elsewhere indicates that naturalism signifies not only intimacy but a certain kind of undesirable power. I see the creation of Olmec portrait heads as a strategy invented by the rulers in creating images of immediacy and thus making their rule appear accessible, personal, and perhaps inescapable. At the same time, they represent that power of the ruler that can come to life at any time in a colossal incarnation. Friendly as they appear to us, in their own time they must have been more awesome and frightening than the jaguar-human supernaturals.

BIBLIOGRAPHY

Baudrillard, Jean
1987 *The Evil Demon of Images.* Sydney, Australia.

Bryson, Norman
1983 *Vision and Painting.* New Haven, Conn.

Bush, Martin H.
1976 *Duane Hanson.* Witchita, Kans.

Coe, Michael D.
1965 *The Jaguar's Children.* New York.

Donnan, Christopher
1976 *Moche Art and Iconography.* Los Angeles.

Drewal, Henry John
1989 Ife: Origins of Art and Civilization. In *Yoruba: Nine Centuries of African Art and Thought,* ed. Alan Wardwell, 45–76. New York.

Freedberg, David
1989 *The Power of Images.* Chicago.

Gombrich, Ernst
1960 *Art and Illusion.* Princeton.

1963 *Meditations on a Hobby Horse.* Chicago.

Graham, John
1989 Olmec Diffusion: A Sculptural View from Pacific Guatemala. In *Regional Perspectives on the Olmec,* ed. Robert Sharer and David Grove, 227–246. Cambridge.

Griffin, Gillett
1976 Portraiture in Palenque. In *The Art, Iconography, and Dynastic History of Palenque, Part III,* ed. Merle Greene Robertson, 137–147. Pebble Beach, Calif.

Hunter, Sam
1989 *George Segal.* New York.

Milbrath, Susan
1979 *A Study in Olmec Sculptural Chronology.* Washington.

Peterson, Jeanette
1981 On Portraiture: African and Precolumbian. Paper presented at the College Art Association Annual Meeting, San Francisco.

Service, Elman
1962 *Primitive Social Organization.* New York.

1975 *Origins of the State and Civilization.* New York.

Strong, William D., and Clifford Evans
1962 *Cultural Stratigraphy in the Viru Valley in Northern Peru.* New York.

Thompson, Robert D.
1971 Aesthetics in Traditional Africa. In *Art and Aesthetics in Primitive Societies,* ed. Carol Jopling, 374–381. New York.

Willet, Frank
1967 *Ife in the History of West African Sculpture.* New York.

Winckelmann, Johann J.
1968 *History of Ancient Art.* New York.

Wofflin, Heinrich
1922 *Principles of Art History.* New York.

DAVID C. GROVE
University of Illinois at Urbana-Champaign

Faces of the Earth at Chalcatzingo, Mexico: Serpents, Caves, and Mountains in Middle Formative Period Iconography

The Olmecs were the first Mesoamerican society to create monumental art, and those stone monuments are one of their indisputable distinguishing traits. The presence of such monuments within a limited geographical area of Mexico's southern Gulf Coast has enabled archaeologists to define and delimit the basic Olmec realm and to identify the three sites with the preponderance of monuments—La Venta, San Lorenzo, and Laguna de los Cerros—as major Olmec centers. While stone monumental art seems to have been exclusive to the Olmecs' Gulf Coast realm prior to c. 800 B.C., a limited number of sites in Central Mexico and along the Pacific Coast of southern Mesoamerica also erected somewhat similar carved stone monuments during a two- or three-hundred-year period after 800 B.C. Because there are no known antecedents to monumental art in Mesoamerica other than those of the Gulf Coast, the carvings created at the Pacific Coast and Central Mexican sites were most probably produced using a technology ultimately derived from Olmec roots (see Clark and Pye, this volume). The additional fact that the non–Gulf Coast monuments also adhere to many of the basic stylistic canons of Olmec monumental art reinforces that observation.

The site of Chalcatzingo, in the highlands of Central Mexico, has more than thirty Formative period carvings, the largest quantity known outside the Olmec domain. Archaeological research conducted at Chalcatzingo over the last few decades has shown that those monuments were displayed in and around a major village site (fig. 1) (Grove 1984, 1987a). That ancient village is situated on the terraced hillslopes at the base of two massive stone hills—the Cerro Chalcatzingo and the Cerro Delgado—that dominate the flat landscape of the surrounding Amatzinac valley. A settlement had existed at Chalcatzingo as early as 1500 B.C., but all archaeological and stylistic data indicate that the site's monuments were created c. 700–500 B.C., the period during which the settlement also reached its maximum size and importance. The 700–500 B.C. temporal range for Chalcatzingo's carvings makes them contemporaneous with many of the monuments at the Olmec center of La Venta, Tabasco. Indeed, although Chalcatzingo is situated more than 250 mountainous miles west of that Olmec center, there are specific iconographic motifs that occur on monuments only at Chalcatzingo and La Venta (Grove 1989), suggesting that significant interaction took place between the two centers, yet the form of that interaction remains to be determined. However, Chalcatzingo also shares equally distinctive but different iconographic symbols with the Formative period centers of Teopantecuanitlán and Oxtotitlán, Guerrero, to the southwest, indicating interaction with that region as well.

At Chalcatzingo there is a direct correlation between the themes communicated by individual monuments and the area of the site at which they were erected (that is, displayed), thus facilitating an understanding of Chalcatzingo's

Monument 1 at Chalcatzingo, Morelos, depicting a personage seated within a mountain cave
Artistic interpretation by Ayax Moreno; drawing courtesy of New World Archaeological Foundation

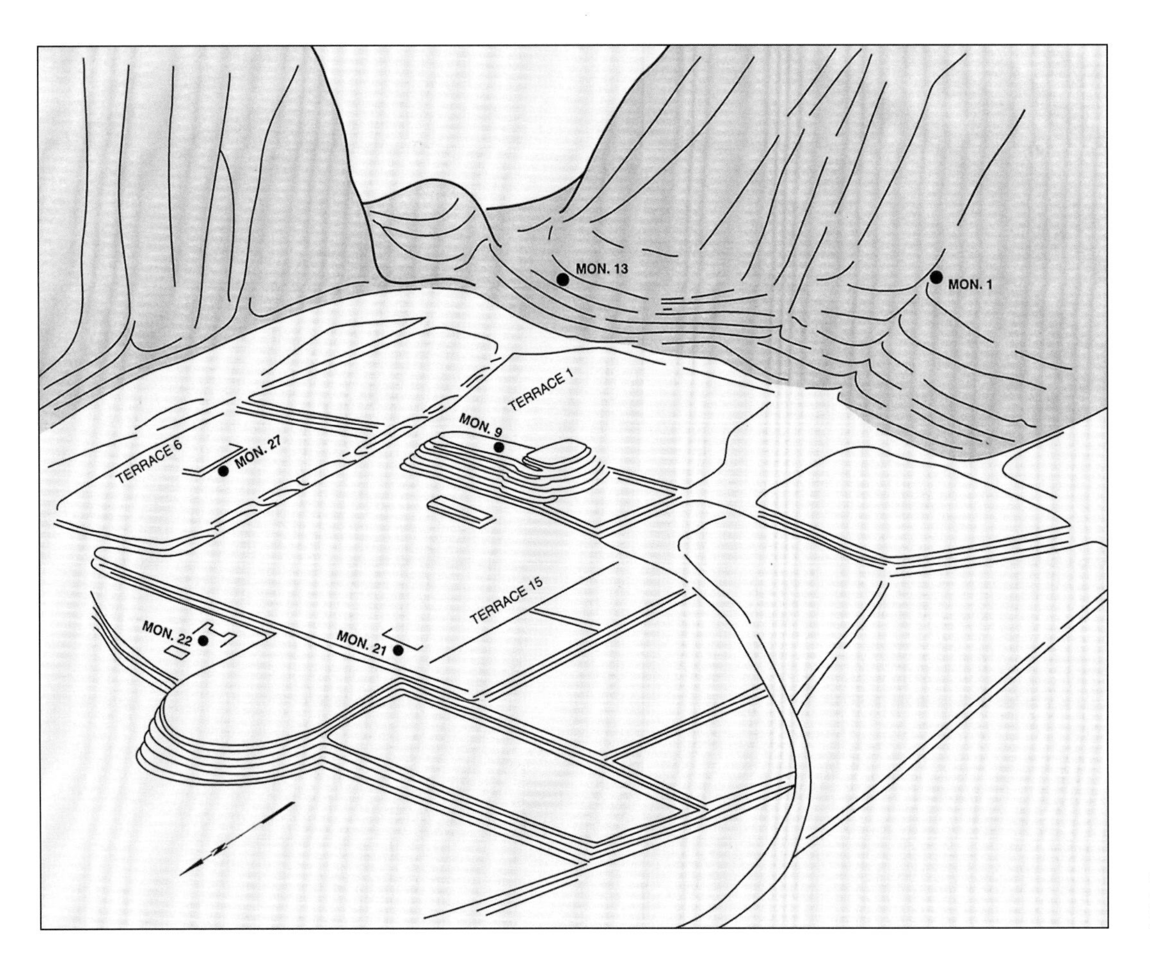

1. Chalcatzingo, a schematic map of the site showing monuments and site locations discussed

spatial organization or "sacred landscape" (Grove 1999). There is a thematic dichotomy to that organization. In the southern site sector, carvings occur on the cliffs and talus slopes of the Cerro Chalcatzingo, a mountain that was clearly sacred to the ancient villagers who lived at its base and at settlements in the surrounding region (see Angulo 1987: 140; Cook 1967: 63–64; Grove 1987b: 430–432). The carvings on that sacred mountain convey mythico-religious themes, and many depict supernatural animals. In contrast, the monuments erected in the northern site sector, within the actual village area, portray particular personages and contain iconography that is related to rulership (Grove 1984: 449–468, 109–122; 1987b: 431–432; 1999).

This essay uses a set of iconographic images at Chalcatzingo, the "earth monster faces" of Monuments 1, 9, 13, 21, and 22, to address two significant topics. The first is the nature of the site's monumental art: just how Olmec are those images? The long-held notion that the Gulf Coast Olmecs substantially influenced contemporaneous societies across Mesoamerica has understandably led scholars to focus on what is "Olmec" about monuments at non–Gulf Coast sites. In doing so, we have perhaps neglected to inquire whether there is also anything non-Olmec about them. The second topic pertains to the iconographic aspects of the monumental art. Early scholars described many of the images in Olmec art as "feline" or "jaguar" (see Covarrubias 1942, 1944, 1946; Saville 1929; Stirling 1940, 1943), and those generic "feline" identifications still heavily influence perceptions and interpretations of Formative period art today. Nevertheless, various studies over the past few decades have demonstrated that a variety of supernaturals, in zoomorphic and anthropomorphic form, are represented in the images that are labeled as "jaguar" (Joralemon 1971, 1976; Stocker et al. 1980; Joyce et al. 1991; also Bonifaz Nuño 1988, 1989; Luckert 1976).

In the following pages, Chalcatzingo's five "earth monster face" carvings are individually analyzed and their important iconographic motifs are discussed in detail. The analyses often utilize iconographic data from sites other than Chalcatzingo when such data are useful to an understanding of Formative period iconography, and thus the discussions of individual Chalcatzingo monuments will sometimes make momentary digressions into those other data. The results of that overall examination not only highlight the eclectic nature of Chalcatzingo's monumental art, but also provide evidence that the site's "earth monster faces" are not jaguars, but instead carry the iconography of serpent supernaturals, one of which is even further distinguished as a *sky* serpent. On a more general level, the analyses also offer some new and different insights into certain widely spread Formative period motifs. In this regard, some of the interpretations presented here are significantly different from the iconographic identifications made by friends and colleagues (including some contributors to this book) whose work has helped illuminate our understanding of Formative period iconography.

The analysis begins with the first major monument discovered at Chalcatzingo, Monument 1, located at the southern periphery of the site, and concludes with Monument 22, one of the northernmost carvings.

2. Chalcatzingo Monument 1, Middle Formative period, granodiorite

Chalcatzingo Monument 1

The largest and most famous of Chalcatzingo's carvings is Monument 1, a large bas-relief executed on a vertical rock face high on the Cerro Chalcatzingo. Monument 1 is an appropriate starting point for discussing the site's five "earth monster faces"; it is the best known of those images, and its iconographic details also aid in understanding aspects of the other faces. The overall scene of Monument 1 depicts an elaborately decorated personage seated within a U-shaped niche (fig. 2). Large scrolls issue outward from the niche, plants grow from its exterior surface, and trilobed rain clouds with falling raindrops float above it. An oval eye motif with crossed-band, on the upper side of the niche, distinguishes the U-shaped niche as an "earth monster face" shown in side (profile) view. Ever since the discovery of this magnificent carving (Guzmán 1934), it has been recognized that the U-shaped "earth monster face" symbol represents a cave. Most discussions of Monument 1, while describing the cave/niche, have nevertheless focused primarily on the personage seated within the cave (for example, Angulo 1987: 135–141; Guzmán 1934: 238–243; Oliveros 1996). However, by studying several motifs "decorating" the "earth monster face" niche, additional details about the image's symbolism can be ascertained.

Serpent Attributes

The identification and understanding of Formative period supernatural imagery was greatly facilitated by the discovery in 1965 of a large greenstone statuette at the site of Las Limas, Veracruz, on the southern periphery of the Olmec domain (Beltrán 1965; Medellín 1965). That carving, "El Señor de Las Limas," is a personage holding a supernatural baby. The personage is decorated with engraved iconography that includes a different supernatural face on each shoulder and each knee (see Medellín 1965: fig. 10). The four faces shown are those of supernaturals commonly depicted in other Formative period art, and thus Michael Coe (1968: 114; 1972; 1989: 71–76) and other investigators have found the Las Limas representations to be extremely useful in their interpretations of various aspects of Formative period art and iconography. Over the last two decades the supernatural faces have been identified. They include a saurian (or "dragon"; left shoulder; fig. 3b), a serpent (right knee; fig. 3c), and a fish (or "shark"; left knee; fig. 3d) (Grove 1987c; Joralemon 1971: nos. 126, 232, 249, 253; Joyce et al. 1991; see Joralemon 1996: 53–54 and Reilly 1991: 154 for alternative interpretations of the upper images). The fourth face (fig. 3a) is more anomalous, but a face with similar iconographic attributes is depicted on a jade plaque in the collection of the Museo Nacional de Antropología in Mexico (fig. 4) (Benson and de la Fuente 1996: 138, 247; Joralemon 1971: no. 233), where it occurs in a Maya-like "Jester God" position. The fourth Las Limas face may therefore have carried a similar rulership-related value in Middle Formative period art.

The positioning of the supernatural faces on the statuette is important, for if the body of the Las Limas personage is seen as a simple cosmological model ("upperworld": shoulders/earth's surface: waist/"underworld": knees), then the location of the saurian, serpent, and fish supernaturals within the basic "upperworld/underworld" dichotomy of the Formative period cosmos is clarified. It is also informative that the supernaturals of the underworld (serpent and fish) are legless, and the upperworld (saurian [and/or bird]) are legged (see below).

Two decades ago I characterized Monument 1's cave/niche image as an "earth monster mouth" (Grove 1968: 486) and as a "jaguar-monster mouth" (1972: 159–161). A reexamination of the carving in the light of the Las Limas faces indicates that the cave/niche is neither a generic "earth monster" nor is it a "jaguar monster" image but is instead the face of the serpent supernatural. Serpent iconography, as elucidated by the face on the right knee of the "Señor de Las Limas,"[1] has three distinguishing attributes (figs. 3c, 5): (1) the distinctive upcurve in the corner of the mouth (fig. 5d); (2) the unusual shape of the elongated eye, narrowed by the upcurved mouth (fig. 5c); and (3) the oval eyeball containing a crossed-band motif (fig. 5b). Although those three attributes appear together on the Las Limas engraving, they do not always co-occur in every iconographic representation of the serpent supernatural. For example, the serpent painted deep within Juxtlahuaca cave, Guerrero (fig. 6) (Gay 1967: 30; Grove 1970: fig. 35; Joralemon 1971: no. 248), exhibits only the curved eye and the eyeball with crossed-band motif. In other in-

3. The heads of the Las Limas figure, Middle Formative period, etched greenstone: (a) face with "band and dot" motif symbol; (b) saurian/dragon; (c) serpent; (d) fish/shark

4. A Middle Formative jade plaque showing "Jester God"-like image (shaded)
Drawing after plaque in the Museo Nacional de Antropología, Mexico City

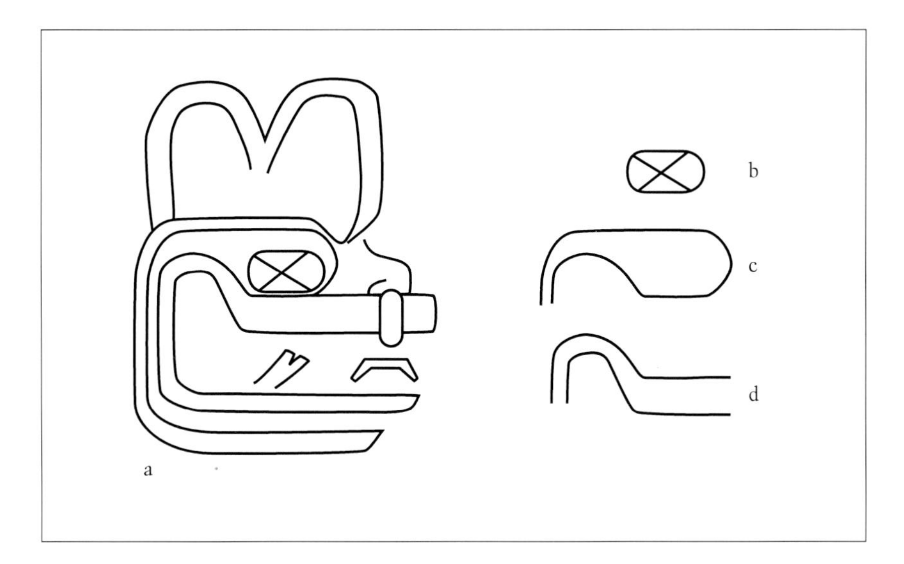

5. Serpent face from Las Limas figure and its distinguishing attributes, Middle Formative period: (a) complete face; (b) oval eyeball containing a crossed-band motif; (c) the elongated eye, narrowed by the upcurved mouth; (d) the mouth with its distinctive upcurved corner

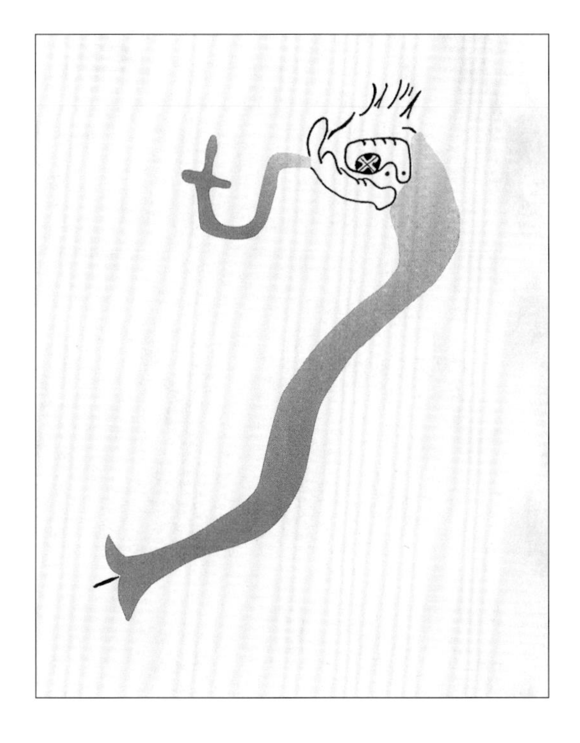

6. Painting 2, Juxtlahuaca cave, Guerrero, Middle Formative period

stances, a single attribute can function to identify the complete image *(pars pro toto)*, and that is true in the case of Chalcatzingo's Monument 1. Although an upcurved serpent mouth and elongated eye are absent from the U-shaped niche face, the presence of the eyeball with crossed-band motif nevertheless identifies the image as a serpent face. That the cave/niche is symbolized as a serpent face should not be surprising since the metaphorical relationship between serpent and cave is ancient in Mesoamerican iconography (for example, Gillespie 1993).

Fang Motifs

A second detail of the Monument 1 face is elucidated by analogous representations on the large polychrome mural (Mural 1) painted above the south grotto of Oxtotitlán cave, Guerrero (figs. 7, 8) (Grove 1970: frontispiece). That mural depicts a personage seated upon a large frontal supernatural face, and the latter clearly exhibits the distinctive mouth, eye, and eyeball attributes of the serpent supernatural (Grove 1970: fig. 4f, g). The location of that mural above an actual cave mouth reiterates the correlation of serpent mouth and cave in Middle Formative art. The Oxtotitlán serpent face also displays two large fangs that protrude down and outward from the upper jaw row. It has been my observation over the years that in frontal views of supernatural images, such fangs can often be a significant cosmological referent: outcurved fangs indicate that the image is that of a "sky" supernatural or within the sky register, while incurved fangs denote the earth register and its associated supernaturals.[2] Those fang referents are particularly evident in Late Formative monumental art at Izapa (fig. 9) but appear to have carried the same symbolic significance in Early and Middle Formative art and in the art of later periods as well.

The outcurved fang motifs of the Oxtotitlán serpent face therefore identify it as a *sky* serpent supernatural. Viewing Chalcatzingo Monument 1 with that insight, it can be noted that fangs—albeit curled fangs—occur at both the upper and lower inner extremes of the U-shaped mouth (fig. 2). Significantly, they curl outward, again presenting a *sky* referent for this large supernatural serpent face. Sky affiliations for both the Chalcatzingo and Oxtoti-

7. Mural 1, Oxtotitlán cave, Guerrero, Middle Formative period

8. Mural 1, Oxtotitlán cave, Guerrero, Middle Formative period

9. Izapa Stela 4, showing sky and earth fang referents, Late Formative period, stone
After Norman 1973: pl. 7

tlán faces are understandable when those images are placed within their proper geographical context. Both occur high on the sides of mountains, above the terrestrial plane. They are caves within the sky realm.

The Quatrefoil Motif

Kent Reilly and I (working together and also independently) have reached several similar conclusions about the significance of the "U-shaped" form of the Monument 1 face. The first is also the most apparent—that the U-shape is a half-section or "profile view" of a quatrefoil face, such as the image shown in full frontal view on Chalcatzingo Monument 9 (fig. 11a) (Reilly 1994: fig. 15.18). Second, the frontal quatrefoil face, when sectioned horizontally (as if buried in the ground to its midpoint) (fig. 11b) (Reilly 1994: figs. 15.20, 15.21), has a close iconographic counterpart in the mountain-glyph/place-glyph utilized at Monte Albán (and some other sites in the Oaxaca area) during periods Monte Albán II and III (fig. 12) (see also Gillespie 1993: 88–89; Marcus 1980: 59; 1992: 395–396, figs. 11.36–11.44; Marcus and Flannery 1996: 196–198, figs. 233–236, 256, 258–260). In line with my comments above regarding fang motifs, it is worth noting that the Monte Albán II period mountain-glyph/place-glyphs on Building J at that site are also often marked by outcurving fangs, indicating that they too symbolize "sky mountains" (fig. 12) (Marcus 1992: 395–396, figs. 11.36–11.38). A major iconographic meaning of the quatrefoil motif at Chalcatzingo is clearly that of *mountain.* The quatrefoil face displayed on Monument 1 is therefore not only a *sky serpent* cave, but also specifically a *mountain* cave.

Susan Gillespie (1993: 74–75) has discussed the quatrefoil motif as a cosmogram and the quatrefoil's interior as symbolic of the "cosmic center" (see also Angulo 1987: 140, for Monument 1 as "heart of the mountain"). It is significant that the creators of Monument 1 made the quatrefoil shape the dominant image—to the point that two major iconographic attributes of the serpent supernatural, the upturned mouth and elongated eye, could not be accommodated to the rigid quatrefoil form. The utilization of the quatrefoil face as the primary image is particularly significant in view of the fact that it is not an icon used by the Gulf Coast Olmec in their monumental art. In fact, the serpent eye and sky fangs that reiterate the overall meaning of the "mountain cave" image are, themselves, relatively rare in Olmec monuments.

Chalcatzingo Monument 13

A fragment of another "earth monster face" carving, Monument 13, was found on the lower slopes of the Cerro Chalcatzingo in 1972 (fig. 13) (Grove and Angulo 1987: 122, fig. 9.13; Angulo 1987: 141, fig. 10.12; Grove 1984: fig. 32). The bas-relief image is executed on a rock slab, and, although incomplete, it is in many respects a smaller version of Monument 1. It depicts an anthropomorphic figure seated within a quatrefoil mouth, and plant motifs "grow" from the exterior of the quatrefoil. There are reasons to believe that the quatrefoil face was

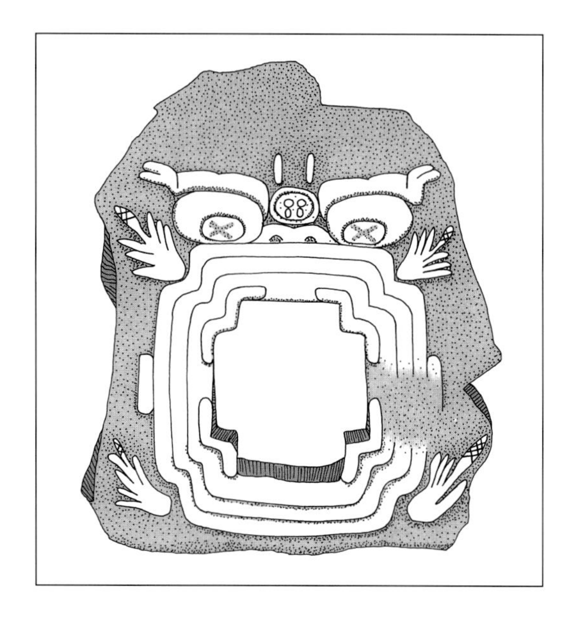

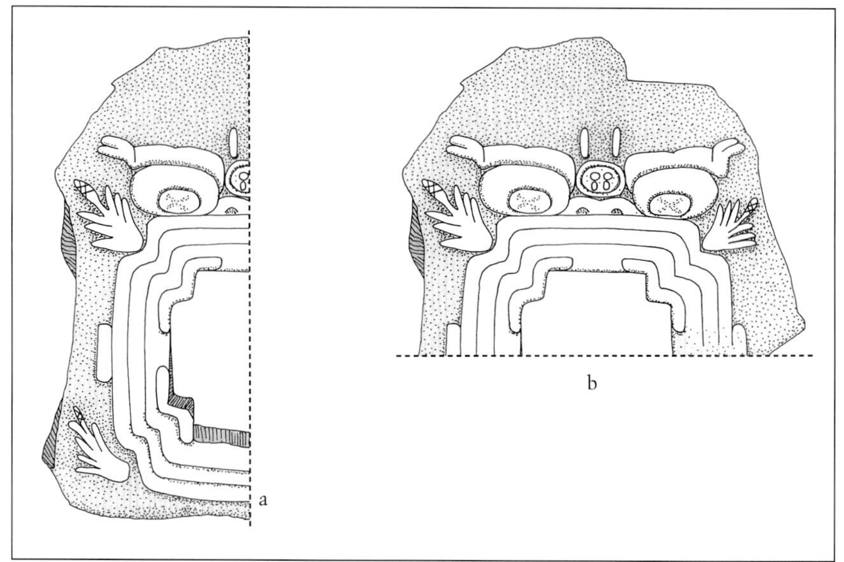

10. Chalcatzingo Monument 9, Middle Formative period, granodiorite

11. Chalcatzingo Monument 9, cross-sectioned (a) vertically, (b) horizontally

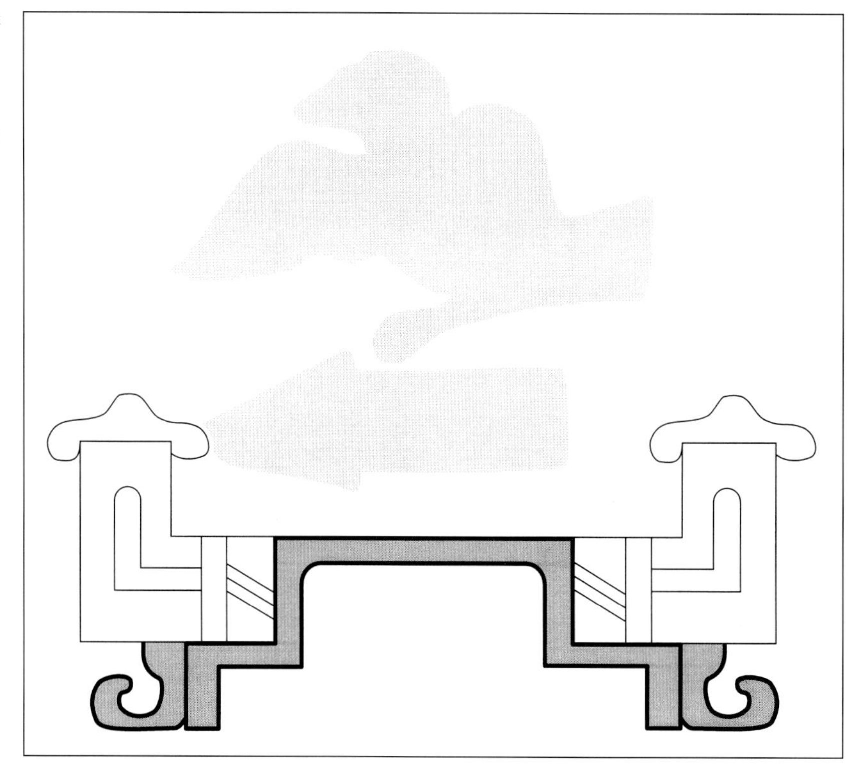

12. Monte Albán II period mountain-glyph/place-glyph, stone, Building J, Monte Albán

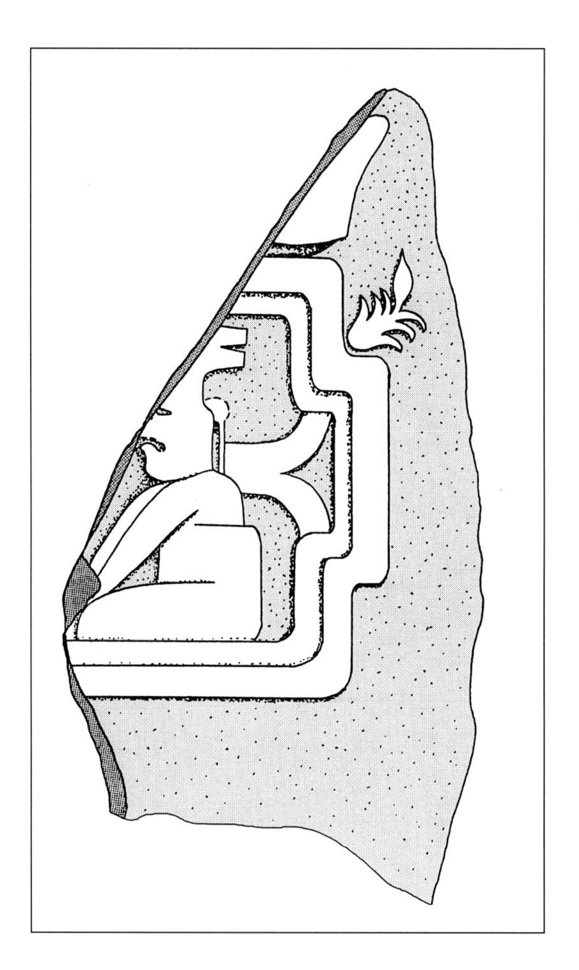

13. Chalcatzingo Monument 13, Middle Formative period, granodiorite

shown in profile, but with the opening to the left rather than to the right (as in Monument 1). Only a small section of the upper area of the quatrefoil exists, but two features barely visible on that section suggest that the iconography of this face differed from the Monument 1 face: a narrow "slit" eye and a large "flame-eyebrow." Unfortunately, little more can be said about this carving beyond the fact that it is a second example of a quatrefoil face.

Chalcatzingo Monument 9

The broken fragments of this carving, a bas-relief on a thick stone slab, were unearthed in the 1960s by a farmer preparing the upper surface of Chalcatzingo's massive Middle Formative period earthen platform mound (PC-4) for planting (Grove and Angulo 1987: 124). The carving was illegally removed from the site and now resides, reconstructed (fig. 10) (Benson and de la Fuente 1996: 178–179; Grove and Angulo 1987: fig. 9.17), at an art institute in the United States. The monument's image is a full frontal quatrefoil surmounted by two large oval eyes, unusual eyebrow motifs, and a circular motif between the eyes and nostrils. The carving is unique among all known Middle Formative monuments because the center of the quatrefoil—the mouth—is hollow and passes entirely through the stone. If the carving had been erected in a vertical position at the northern upper edge of the PC-4 platform mound (its location when discovered), its great quatrefoil image would have been easily visible to the peoples living in the ancient village surrounding the mound, and any ritual activities associated with the monument would likewise have had community visibility. Such ritual activities may have included the passage of objects or people through the supernatural's open "cave" mouth (for example, Grove 1972: 161; 1984: 50), and, as Gillespie (1993: 75) has commented, "to go through this doorway was to enter the supernatural world at its cosmic center and to have access to the power . . . there."

In the first published description of this monument, I characterized the image as a "jaguar's face" (Grove 1968: 489–490) and soon thereafter as a "jaguar-monster mouth" (Grove 1972: 159–161). I now believe that this carving is also more likely the face of a serpent supernatural. The quatrefoil is again the dominant icon. David Joralemon (1971: no. 141) illustrates crossed-band motifs within the oval eyes, yet if crossed bands were once present, they have since eroded to the extent that they are not readily apparent today. Nevertheless, even in their absence, a second feature of the face also suggests that it is a serpent image—undulating eyebrows that end in outturned cleft motifs.

Eyebrow Motifs

For at least fifty years scholars have recognized the prominence of flame-eyebrows in the depiction of Formative period supernatural images. Any inspection of images with such flame-eyebrows reveals variation in eyebrow treatment, yet little attention has been paid to those differences, and the term *flame-eyebrow* continues to be used generically. Recently, however, the correlation of different eyebrow treatments with particular supernaturals has been made possible through another "mini–Rosetta Stone," an anthropomorphic stone figurine referred to in the literature as the

"Young Lord" (Benson and de la Fuente 1996: 213–215; Joralemon 1996: 53–56; also known as "Slim," Reilly 1991: 152–166). Like the Las Limas statuette, the "Young Lord" is decorated with engraved designs that include a representation of a legged zoomorph (a caimanlike creature) on the figure's left leg (fig. 14b) and a legless zoomorph (serpent and/or fish) on the right leg (fig. 14a).

As noted above, the dichotomy of legged versus legless supernaturals seen on the "Young Lord" is also a structural principle exhibited in the supernatural faces on "Señor de Las Limas." Associated with each zoomorph depicted on the "Young Lord" are six unique anthropomorphic faces in profile, each with distinctive eyebrow treatments. Many of those profiled faces have counterparts in Formative period portable art, and thus their association here with either the legged ("upperworld") or legless ("underworld") zoomorphic supernaturals is instructive. Of interest to this essay is the fact that eyebrows ending with *outturned* cleft motifs occur only on the faces associated with the legless/serpent zoomorph (fig. 14a). The eyebrows of the serpent zoomorph itself are undulating and also terminate in an outturned cleft; thus they are similar to the eyebrow treatment on Chalcatzingo Monument 9. Therefore, although the dominance of Monument 9's quatrefoil motif lends the appearance of a jaguarlike cave-mouth face, the image may instead be a serpent face.[3]

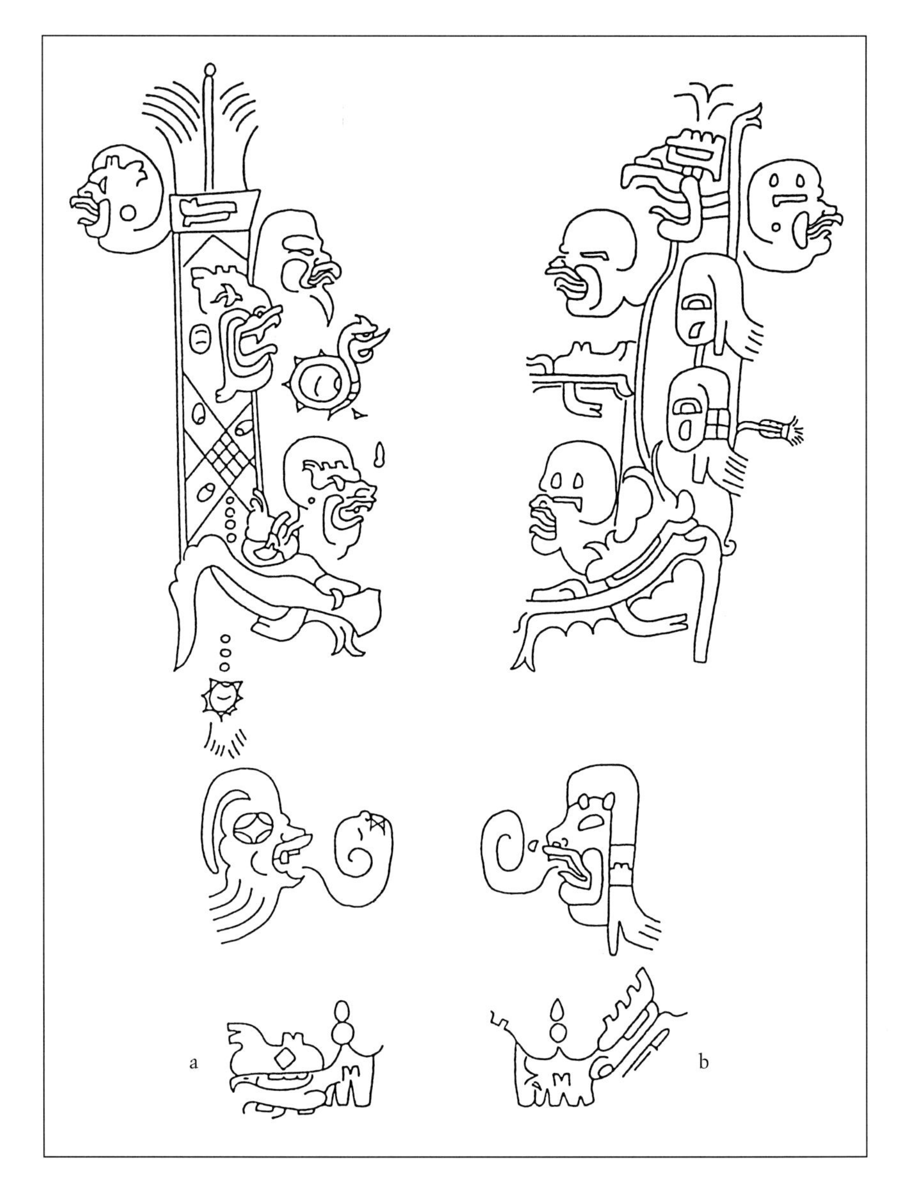

14. Zoomorphic motifs engraved on the legs of the "Young Lord" figure, Middle Formative period, greenstone: (a) legless serpent and/or fish zoomorph, right leg; (b) legged saurian, left leg
After Benson and de la Fuente 1996: 213

Chalcatzingo Monument 21

The face images and archaeological contexts of Monuments 21 and 22, displayed in the northern sector of the site, differ markedly from those described above. Monument 21 is a carved stela and had once been erected beside a small, low, rectangular stone-faced platform construction on Terrace 15. Similar low stone-faced platforms, with stelae, also occur on adjacent terraces, and all are Middle Formative period in date (Grove 1984: 57–65; Prindiville and Grove 1987: 65). The "earth monster face" found on Monument 21 is of secondary importance in the bas-relief scene. The primary image is that of a woman whose outstretched arms touch a tall vertical object (fig. 15). She is one of the few known females depicted in Mesoamerican monumental art of this early time period (see Clark and Pye, this volume), and Ann Cyphers (1984) has suggested that her portrayal on this monument may have commemorated a marriage alliance between elite families at Chalcatzingo and those at another center. In this regard, it is worth observing that the tall vertical object she touches contains a motif known at only one other site, Teopantecuanitlán, Guerrero (Grove 1987b: 429; 1989: 142–145, fig. 7.14).

The "earth monster face" forms the lower register of the scene and acts as an earth referent. The woman stands upon the face, and thus she stands upon the surface of the earth. The "earth monster" face is not a quatrefoil. Instead, it is primarily created by extremely large incurved fangs and unusual trilobed "eyes" or "eyebrows." It lacks any obvious attributes of a serpent supernatural, probably because in this context the face is not communicating the idea of an entrance into the earth but rather serves to denote that the woman stands on the earth's surface.

Chalcatzingo Monument 22

The "earth-monster" face located on Terrace 25 differs from the others at the site in that it is not carved on a stela or rock face, nor was it apparently intended to have the wide visibility of those other monuments. Instead, the face decorates an "architectural" construction, Monument 22, the only Olmec-style tabletop altar (throne) ever found outside the Gulf Coast (fig. 16) (Fash 1987; Grove 1984: 65–68). The relative "invisibility" of this monument is due to its positioning: it is situated within a large sunken rectangular stone-walled patio, and its upper surface (metaphorically the "earth's surface") is level with the top of the patio wall and the modern ground surface (fig. 17). Monument 22 was built into the sunken patio's south wall and therefore is also part of the wall's architecture.

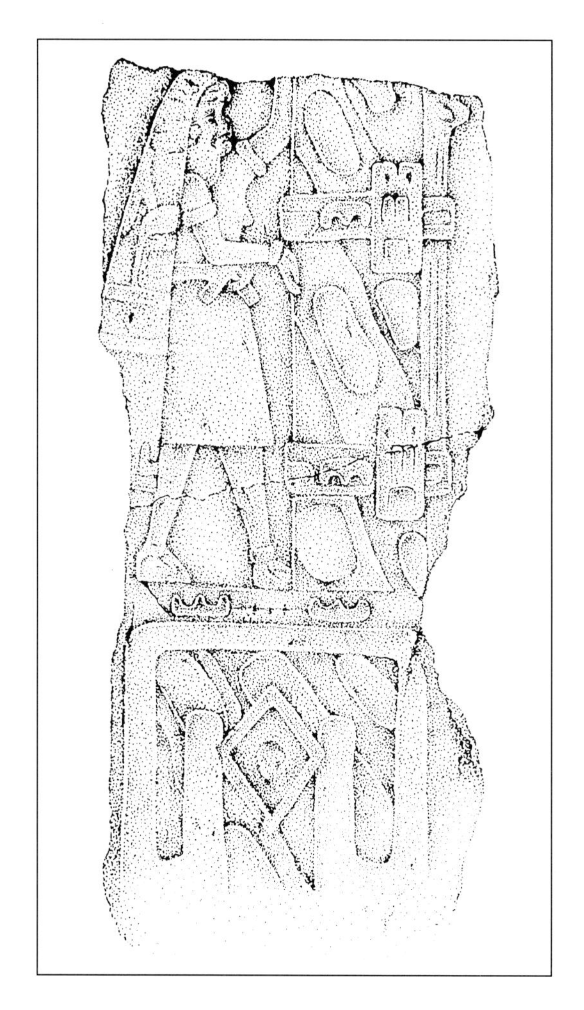

15. Chalcatzingo Monument 21, a woman standing on an earth image, Middle Formative period, granodiorite
Drawing by Barbara Fash

Beyond the fact of its uniqueness outside the Gulf Coast, Chalcatzingo's tabletop altar presents several inconsistencies when compared to its Olmec counterparts. Gulf Coast tabletop altars are monolithic carvings that were created from multiton blocks of stone brought to Olmec centers from distant stone sources at a great expenditure of human labor. Monument 22 is a more modest construction created by stacked stone slabs—even though suitable altar-sized boulders occur only a few hundred meters away. The front sides of Gulf Coast tabletop altars are characterized by a central niche (symbolic cave entrance) with seated personage (see fig. 18). Monument 22 lacks such a niche (and personage), and its front surface is decorated only with a pair of distinctively shaped elongated eyes carved in bas-relief: the eyes of the serpent supernatural (figs. 16, 17). However, even those serpent eyes are unusual, for the oval eyeballs within the eyes do not contain the crossed-band elements that occur on the Las Limas serpent face, Oxtotitlán Mural 1, Juxtlahuaca Painting 2, or Chalcatzingo Monument 1.

The most economical explanation for the absence of a central niche on Monument 22 and its replacement with a partial serpent face is one of symbolism vis-à-vis context. The faces of Chalcatzingo Monuments 1, 9, and 13 are iconographically identified as *entrances into the earth and underworld,* specifically via mountain caves. The frontal niches of Gulf Coast tabletop altars similarly symbolize *entrances into the earth and underworld* (see Gillespie 1993: 76; Grove 1973, 1981). Chalcatzingo Monument 22 lacks entrance symbolism in its iconography, yet it is placed within a sunken patio, and that subsurface enclosure is itself a symbolic *entrance to the underworld.*[4] Thus, just as the south grotto of Oxtotitlán cave substitutes for the mouth of the great serpent face painted above the grotto, the sunken patio serves as Monument 22's mouth/niche, making an actual niche in the tabletop altar both redundant and unnecessary.

The absence of crossed-band motifs in Monument 22's serpent eyes is perhaps also explicable as due to the monument's subterranean context. Crossed-band motifs occur in the eyes

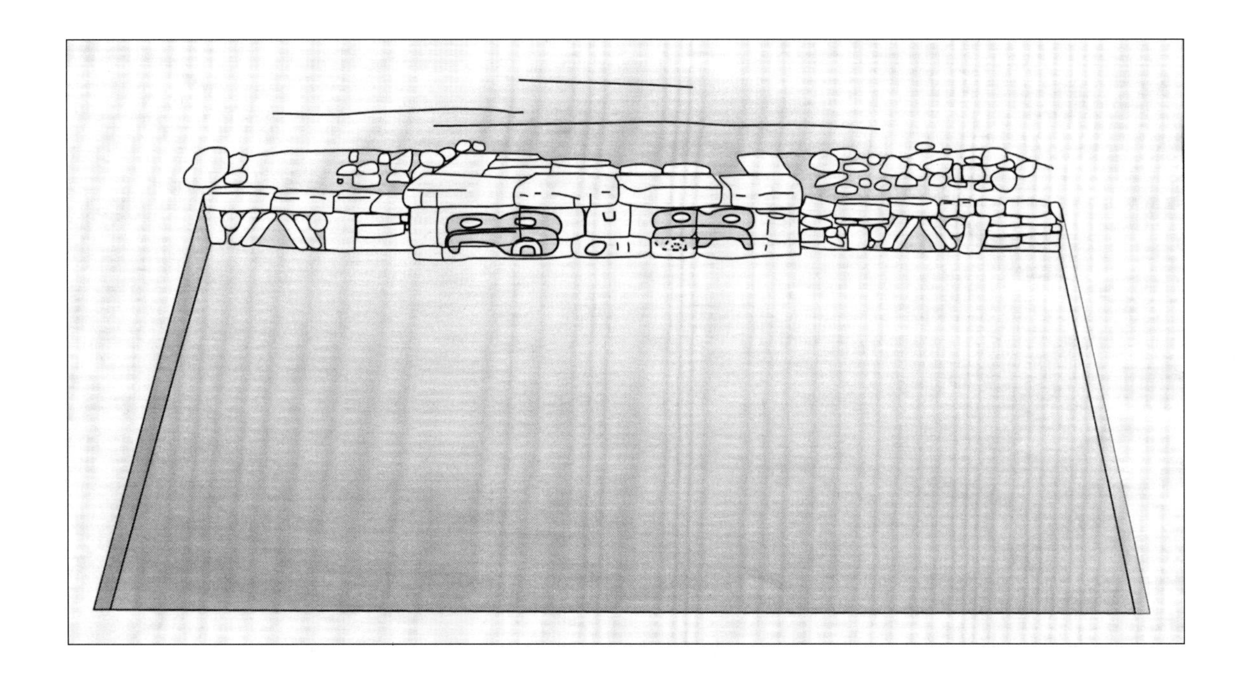

16. Chalcatzingo Monument 22, a tabletop altar/throne positioned within a stone-walled sunken patio, Middle Formative period, granodiorite. Note "faces" with inverted V-shaped mouths built into the walls (and compare those to inverted V-shaped mouths in fig. 20b)

17. Drawing of Chalcatzingo Monument 22

18. La Venta Altar 4, Middle Formative period, basalt

of Monument 1 and Oxtotitlán's Mural 1, images that are located on mountains and that also carry additional motifs linking them with the *sky* realm. From these two examples it could perhaps be inferred that their crossed bands carried a *sky* symbolism (as the motif does much later in Maya iconography). From such a perspective, the absence of crossed bands in association with Monument 22 could be considered appropriate because the monument is not in a *sky* context.

Such an explanation is not entirely satisfactory, however, for a far more common use for crossed-band motifs in Formative period art is as the symbol for *entrances into the earth and otherworld* (Joyce 1980). An excellent example of that iconographic use is found with the image of the supernatural "jaguar"[5] face that decorates the tabletop ledge of La Venta Altar 4 (fig. 18). That image, with a crossed-band motif in its mouth, occurs directly above the altar's central niche, and the crossed band apparently marks the niche as an *entrance.* The same iconographic meaning occurs earlier in images on Early Formative period pottery (c. 1100–900 B.C.). Perhaps the most explicit example is found on a cylindrical pottery bowl from the site of Tlapacoya in the Basin of Mexico (fig. 19) (Benson and de la Fuente 1996: 201; Joralemon 1971: no. 120). This vessel carries two images: a saurian head in profile (fig. 19a; often labeled as a "fire serpent") and a frontal face with a crossed-band motif in its gaping mouth (fig. 19b; often termed a "were-jaguar" face). The images actually represent two views of the same saurian earth supernatural. Significantly, the profiled head of the supernatural is raised upward at an angle, showing that its mouth is open—and in its frontal image the open mouth is marked by the crossed-band motif to show that it is an opening, an *entrance into the earth* (see also fig. 20a). Thus, as Rosemary Joyce (1980) has noted, the crossed bands in the eyes of Chalcatzingo Monument 1 may have symbolized *entrance* rather than *sky.* However, such openings are not always explicitly marked (for example, fig. 20b), and, as discussed above, the absence of crossed-band motifs on Monument 22 may simply reflect its association with the large sunken patio.

This discussion not only shows that the symbolism of motifs can vary over both space and time, but, in the case of temporal change, highlights an important transformation. Serpent images are extremely rare in the art of the Early Formative period (c. 1100–900 B.C.), and the iconographic data indicate that "earth entrance" iconography was associated with the saurian supernatural during that period (for example, figs. 19, 20). In contrast, overall serpent imagery and the serpent association with "earth entrances" is more common in the Middle Formative period (c. 900–500 B.C.) and supplants the saurian imagery, particularly in elite monumental and portable art. That transformation, one of many aspects of the social evolution that took place over those six centuries of the Early and Middle Formative periods, is significant. However, it is also beyond the scope of this essay (but see Grove 1993).

Mountain Faces, Mountain Symbols

Various facial images in Early and Middle Formative period monumental and portable art have been identified as "feline," yet, as the iconography of those periods becomes better understood, most of those identifications become questionable. In particular, there seems little evidence beyond superficial appearances to support the notion of jaguar imagery in "earth entrance" iconography during those periods. Chalcatzingo's three complete major "earth monster faces," Monuments 1, 9, and 22, carry attributes of the serpent supernatural as expressed on the Las Limas figure. In Mesoamerican cosmology, serpents have a symbolic association with caves and entrances into the earth (or sky), particularly as *conduits* between realms (Gillespie 1993). *Entrance into the earth and underworld* relationship is clear for the images discussed above, in spite of the iconographic differences in their images. Many of those differences seem directly correlated with the location of the images within the site's natural sacred geography and constructed sacred landscape.

The quatrefoil *mountain-cave* motif is the dominant icon of the two images displayed on the Cerro Chalcatzingo (Monuments 1, 13), while monuments on the flat terraced hillside away from the cerro (Monuments 21, 22) lack the quatrefoil mountain form. However, the one exception to the latter is Monument 9 (fig. 10), the quatrefoil image erected on the PC-4 platform mound, near the midpoint of the ancient village (fig. 1). Monument 9's positioning on the site and its *mountain-cave* iconog-

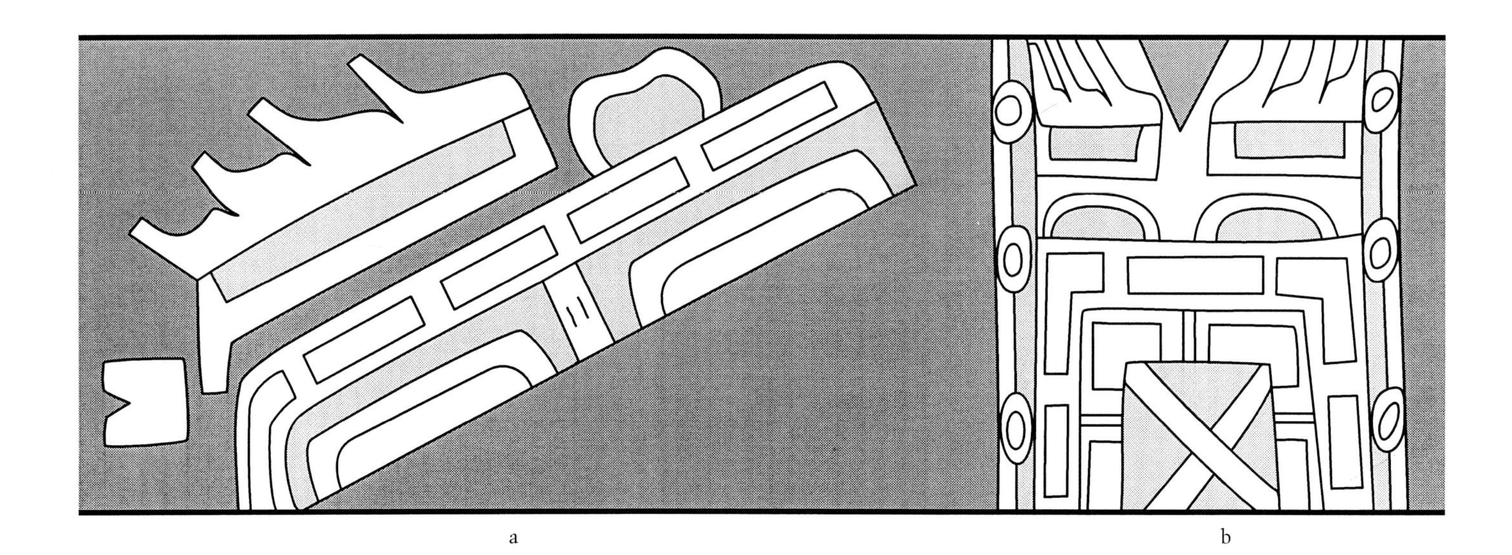

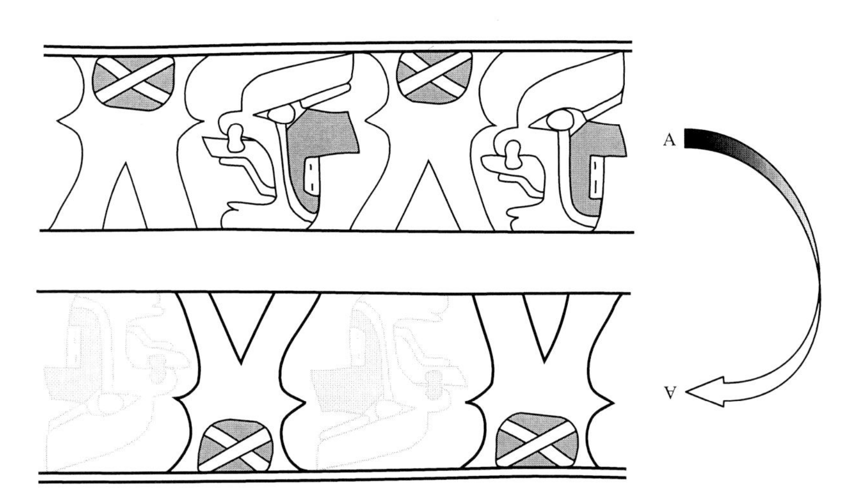

19. Decoration from Early Formative vessel showing (a) profile and (b) frontal view of the saurian supernatural, with mouth open as "entrance"
After Joralemon 1971: no. 120(b)

20. Early Formative vessels with anthropomorphic heads separated by inverted frontal saurian faces: (a) saurian faces with open mouths marked with crossed-band motifs, (b) saurian faces lacking crossed-band motif
After Joralemon 1971: nos. 237, 235

raphy strongly suggest that its quatrefoil facial image marked or distinguished that tall central mound as a "sacred mountain"—a constructed "sacred mountain" within the site's constructed "sacred landscape" (Grove 1999). If correct, the act of using monumental art to identify major mounds as "sacred mountains" has interesting implications beyond Chalcatzingo.

The 1955 research at La Venta disclosed two large stelae, Monuments 25/26 and 27, at the southern base of the site's 100 foot-tall earthen pyramid (Mound C-1; Drucker et al. 1959: 204–209). The major image on both stelae is a large frontal supernatural face with outcurved (sky) fangs (fig. 21) (Drucker et al. 1959: figs. 59, 60 [shown upside down], pls. 53, 54; Porter 1992: figs. 7, 8). The faces also have eyebrow elements with outturned cleft elements (see discussion of Chalcatzingo Monument 9, above). Recent excavations by Rebecca González in the area immediately adjacent to those 1955 discoveries have uncovered two additional—and nearly identical—stelae, Monuments 88 and 89 (González 1996: 76). Therefore, four large stelae with identical face images had been displayed in a line along the southern base of the pyramid, facing out toward Plaza B, the site's major "public plaza." If Chalcatzingo's Monument 9 symbolically identified that site's platform mound as a "sacred mountain," then it is equally probable that La Venta's four stelae depict "mountain faces" that likewise served to designate Mound C-1 as a "sacred mountain" (Grove 1999). The La Venta "mountain faces" are remarkably different from those at Chalcatzingo, yet both can be considered regional Middle Formative equivalents to the *witz* (mountain) faces that decorate some Maya pyramids and distinguish those structures as sacred mountains as well.

The display of four "mountain face" stelae has additional implications. In Mesoamerican cosmological concepts, sacred mountains (or similar geographic features) are positioned at the four cardinal directions. If the La Venta stelae are mountain symbols, then the set of four may likewise symbolize the sacred mountains of the four cardinal directions, even though displayed in an alignment at the front of the site's pyramid. Reilly has arrived at a similar conclusion regarding the set of four Middle Formative face images at the site of Teopantecuanitlán, Guerrero (see Reilly 1994: 252–255; Martínez Donjuán 1982, 1985, 1986, 1995).

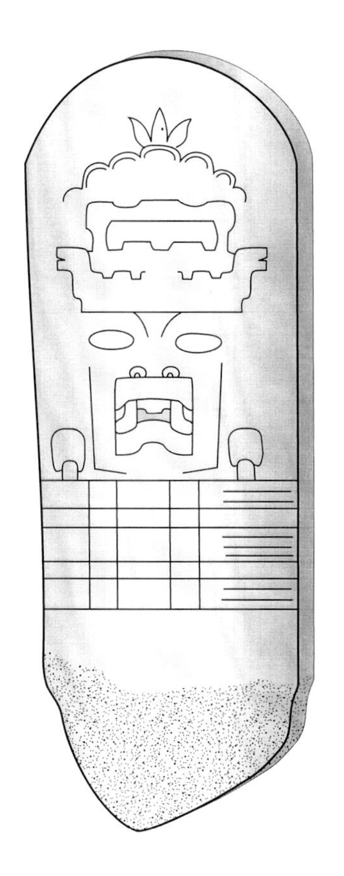

21. La Venta Stela 27, Middle Formative period, basalt, simplified drawing to highlight details of the large frontal supernatural face
After Drucker et al. 1959: fig. 60; Porter 1992: fig. 7

22. Teopantecuanitlán, Guerrero, supernatural face, one of four identical images, Middle Formative period, stone
After Martínez Donjuán 1985: figs. 7–10

These carvings, four large inverted T-shaped monoliths, each with virtually identical bas-relief faces (fig. 22), were set within the north and south walls of Teopantecuanitlán's large stone-walled sunken patio,[6] and, as Reilly (1994: 255) has observed, "the monuments . . . could have represented the four directional mountains to the priests conducting rituals in the sunken patio."

Few scholars would have doubted the presence of such common Mesoamerican cosmological principles of directionality among Formative period societies. However, the various mountain images discussed here seem to document their presence and also indicate that by the Middle Formative period the concept of sacred mountains in the four cardinal directions was beginning to be incorporated into the programs of monumental art and architecture of diverse Mesoamerican societies.

Conclusion

Because of the attention that the Olmecs have received over the last half century, scholars have generally focused on what seems "Olmec" about the images on portable and monumental art found at the sites outside the Gulf Coast. Yet it is equally important to understand what is also non-Olmec about them, for without a balanced perspective we can never expect to understand the cultural interactions and motivations that led to their creation.

In the case of Chalcatzingo's carvings, there are numerous obvious similarities with Gulf Coast Olmec monumental art, but there are also some remarkable differences, such as the use of the quatrefoil motif. Archaeological research at Chalcatzingo suggests that the site's inhabitants were part of the indigenous highland population (Grove 1987b), and linguistic research (Hopkins 1984: 30–52; Manrique Castañeda 1975: maps 5, 7) indicates that they probably spoke a language related to the Zapotec and Mixtec languages of Oaxaca. As a major Formative period highland center, Chalcatzingo interacted not only with Gulf Coast centers but also with chiefdoms in Guerrero, the Valley of Mexico, Puebla, Oaxaca, and along the southern Pacific Coast of Mesoamerica (Grove 1987d: 434–437). That "internationalism" seems to be reflected in the eclectic mix of iconography that characterizes Chalcatzingo's monumental art.

NOTES

1. This Las Limas face was first recognized as a serpent by David Joralemon (1971: 82–84).

2. See also Miller (1996: 256 note 17).

3. A colleague has remarked that Monument 9's face could not be a serpent because it has prominent nostrils. However, nostrils are depicted on the serpent of Middle Formative period La Venta Monument 19 and on numerous serpent images in later Mesoamerican art, including Postclassic serpent balustrades, and the serpent heads adorning Teotihuacán's Temple of the Feathered Serpent.

4. The sunken patio's stone wall also incorporates two quite simple niche faces (see figs. 16, 17, and similar motifs in fig. 20b).

5. Although the face on the tabletop ledge of La Venta Altar 4 looks jaguarlike, its mouth symbol has an upward curve similar to that of the serpent's mouth.

6. Teopantecuanitlán's sunken patio is larger in size than Chalcatzingo's.

BIBLIOGRAPHY

Angulo, Jorge
1987 The Chalcatzingo Reliefs: An Iconographic Analysis. In *Ancient Chalcatzingo,* ed. David Grove, 132–158. Austin.

Beltrán, Alberto
1965 Reportaje gráfico del hallazgo de Las Limas. *Boletín del Instituto Nacional de Antropología e Historia* 21: 9–26.

Benson, Elizabeth P., and Beatriz de la Fuente
1996 (Editors) *Olmec Art of Ancient Mexico* [exh. cat., National Gallery of Art]. Washington.

Bonifaz Nuño, Rubén
1988 Los olmecas no son jaguares. *Chicomóztoc* 1: 51–58. Mexico City.

1989 *Hombres y serpientes: Iconografía olmeca.* Mexico City.

Coe, Michael D.
1968 *America's First Civilization: Discovering the Olmec.* New York.

1972 Olmec Jaguars and Olmec Kings. In *Cult of the Feline,* ed. Elizabeth Benson, 1–18. Washington.

1989 The Olmec Heartland: Evolution of Ideology. In *Regional Perspectives on the Olmec,* ed. Robert Sharer and David Grove, 68–82. Cambridge.

Cook de Leonard, Carmen
1967 Sculptures and Rock Carvings at Chalcatzingo, Morelos. *Contributions of the University of California Archaeological Research Facility* 3: 57–84. Berkeley.

Covarrubias, Miguel
1942 Origen y desarollo del estilo artístico "olmeca." In *Mayas y Olmecas, segunda reunión de Mesa Redonda sobre problemas antropológicas de México y Centro América, Tuxtla Gutiérrez, Chiapas,* 46–69. Mexico City.

1944 La Venta: Colossal Heads and Jaguar Gods. *Dyn* 6: 24–44. Mexico City.

1946 El arte "olmeca" o de La Venta. *Cuadernos Americanos* 28: 153–179.

Cyphers, Ann
1984 The Possible Role of a Woman in Formative Exchange. In *Trade and Exchange in Early Mesoamerica,* ed. Kenneth Hirth, 115–123. Albuquerque, N.M.

Drucker, Philip, Robert F. Heizer, and Robert J. Squier
1959 *Excavations at La Venta, Tabasco, 1955.* Bureau of American Ethnology Bulletin 170. Washington.

Fash, William, Jr.
1987 The Altar and Associated Features. In

Ancient Chalcatzingo, ed. David Grove, 82–94. Austin.

Gay, Carlo
1967 Oldest Paintings of the New World. *Natural History* 76: 28–35.

Gillespie, Susan
1993 Power, Pathways, and Appropriations in Mesoamerican Art. In *Image and Creativity: Ethnoaesthetics and Art Worlds in the Americas,* ed. Dorothea Whitten and Norman Whitten, Jr., 67–107. Tucson, Ariz.

González Lauck, Rebecca
1996 La Venta: An Olmec Capital. In *Olmec Art of Ancient Mexico,* ed. Elizabeth Benson and Beatriz de la Fuente, 73–82 [exh. cat., National Gallery of Art]. Washington.

Grove, David C.
1968 Chalcatzingo, Morelos, Mexico: A Reappraisal of the Olmec Rock Carvings. *American Antiquity* 33: 468–491.

1970 *The Olmec Paintings of Oxtotitlán Cave, Guerrero, Mexico.* Washington.

1972 Olmec Felines in Highland Central Mexico. In *The Cult of the Feline,* ed. Elizabeth Benson, 151–164. Washington.

1973 Olmec Altars and Myths. *Archaeology* 26: 128–135.

1981 Olmec Monuments: Mutilation as a Clue to Meaning. In *The Olmec and Their Neighbors,* ed. Elizabeth Benson, 49–68. Washington.

1984 *Chalcatzingo: Excavations on the Olmec Frontier.* London.

1987a (Editor) *Ancient Chalcatzingo.* Austin.

1987b Comments on the Site and Its Organization. In *Ancient Chalcatzingo,* ed. David Grove, 420–433. Austin.

1987c "Torches," "Knuckle Dusters," and the Legitimization of Formative Period Rulerships. *Mexicon* 9(3): 60–65.

1987d Chalcatzingo in Broader Perspective. In *Ancient Chalcatzingo,* ed. David Grove, 434–442. Austin.

1989 Chalcatzingo and Its Olmec Connection. In *Regional Perspectives on the Olmec,* ed. Robert Sharer and David Grove, 122–147. Cambridge.

1993 "Olmec" Horizons in Formative Period Mesoamerica: Diffusion of Social Evolution? In *Latin American Horizons,* ed. Don S. Rice, 83–111. Washington.

1999 Public Monuments and Sacred Mountains: Observations on Three Formative Period Sacred Landscapes. In *Social Patterns in Pre-Classic Mesoamerica,* ed. David Grove and Rosemary Joyce, 255–299. Washington.

Grove, David, and Jorge Angulo
1987 A Catalog and Description of Chalcatzingo's Monuments. In *Ancient Chalcatzingo,* ed. David Grove, 114–131. Austin.

Guzmán, Eulalia
1934 Los relieves de las rocas del Cerro de la Cantera, Jonacatepec, Morelos. *Anales del Museo Nacional de Arqueología, Historia y Etnografía,* 5th series, 1: 237–251.

Hopkins, Nicholas
1984 Otomanguean Linguistic Prehistory. In *Essays in Otomanguean Culture History,* ed. J. Kathryn Josserand, Marcus Winter, and Nicholas Hopkins, 25–64. Nashville, Tenn.

Joralemon, Peter David
1971 *A Study of Olmec Iconography.* Washington.

1976 The Olmec Dragon: A Study in Pre-Columbian Iconography. In *Origins of Religious Art and Iconography in Preclassic Mesoamerica,* ed. Henry B. Nicholson, 27–71. Los Angeles.

1996 In Search of the Olmec Cosmos: Reconstructing the World View of Mexico's First Civilization. In *Olmec Art of Ancient Mexico,* ed. Elizabeth Benson and Beatriz de la Fuente, 51–60 [exh. cat., National Gallery of Art]. Washington.

Joyce, Rosemary
1980 Crossed Bands in Olmec, Maya, and Izapa Art. Paper presented at the Meeting of Midwestern Mesoamericanists.

Joyce, Rosemary, Richard Edging, Karl Lorenz, and Susan Gillespie
1991 Olmec Bloodletting: An Iconographic Study. In *Sixth Palenque Round Table, 1986,* ed. Virginia Fields, 143–150. Norman, Okla., and London.

Luckert, Karl
1976 *Olmec Religion: A Key to Middle America and Beyond.* Norman, Okla.

Manrique Castañeda, Leonardo
1975 Relaciones entre las áreas linguísticas y las áreas culturales. In *Balance y perspectiva de la antropología de Mesoamérica y del norte de México: Antropología física, linguística, códices,* 137–160. Mexico City.

Marcus, Joyce
1980 Zapotec Writing. *Scientific American* 242: 50–64.

1992 *Mesoamerican Writing Systems.* Princeton.

Marcus, Joyce, and Kent Flannery
1996 *Zapotec Civilization: How Urban Society*

Evolved in Mexico's Oaxaca Valley. London.

Martínez Donjuán, Guadalupe
1982 Teopantecuanitlán, Guerrero: Un sitio olmeca. *Revista Mexicana de Estudios Antropológicos* 28: 128–133.

1985 El sitio olmeca de Teopantecuanitlán en Guerrero. *Anales de Antropología* 22: 128–133. Mexico City.

1986 Teopantecuanitlán. In *Primer Coloquio de Arqueología y Etnohistoria del Estado de Guerrero,* 55–80. Guerrero, Mexico.

1995 Teopantecuanitlán. *Arqueología Mexicana* 2: 58–62.

Medellín Zenil, Alfonso
1965 La escultura de Las Limas. *Boletín del Instituto Nacional de Antropología e Historia* 21: 5–8.

Miller, Mary E.
1996 *The Art of Mesoamerica,* rev. ed. New York.

Norman, Garth
1973 *Izapa Sculpture: Album.* Papers of the New World Archaeological Foundation 30(1). Provo, Utah.

Oliveros, Arturo
1996 The Precolumbian Image of Hurricanes. In *Olmecs, Special Edition. Arqueología Mexicana,* 60–63. Mexico City.

Porter, James
1992 "Estelas Celtiformes": Un nuevo tipo de estructura olmeca y sus implicaciones para los epigrafistas. *Arqueología,* 2d series, 8: 3–13. Mexico City.

Prindiville, Mary, and David C. Grove
1987 The Settlement and Its Architecture. In *Ancient Chalcatzingo,* ed. David Grove, 63–81. Austin.

Reilly, F. Kent, III
1991 Olmec Iconographic Influences on the Symbols of Maya Rulership. In *Sixth Palenque Round Table, 1986,* ed. Virginia Fields, 151–166. Norman, Okla., and London.

1994 Cosmología, soberanismo y espacio ritual en la Mesoamérica del Formativo. In *Los olmecas en Mesoamérica,* ed. John Clark, 239–259. Mexico City and London.

Saville, Marshall
1929 Votive Axes from Ancient Mexico. *Indian Notes* 6(3): 266–299. Heye Foundation, Museum of the American Indian, New York.

Stirling, Matthew W.
1940 Great Stone Faces in the Mexican Jungle. *National Geographic Magazine* 78: 309–334.

1943 La Venta's Green Stone Tigers. *National Geographic Magazine* 80: 321–332.

Stocker, Terrence, S. Meltzoff, and S. Armsey
1980 Crocodilians and Olmecs: Further Interpretations of Formative Period Iconography. *American Antiquity* 45: 740–758.

KARL TAUBE
University of California, Riverside

Lightning Celts and Corn Fetishes: The Formative Olmec and the Development of Maize Symbolism in Mesoamerica and the American Southwest

Scepter, Middle Formative period, blackstone, from Ojoshal *ejido*, Cárdenas, Tabasco
Museo Regional de Antropología Carlos Pellicer Cámara

No other food plant had a more profound impact in the New World than corn, or *Zea mays*. As the preeminent staple since Formative times, maize played an essential role in the development of Mesoamerican civilization and also permeated its ritual and belief. Not only was agricultural abundance a central concern of ancient Mesoamerican religions, but maize also provided a means by which Mesoamericans viewed themselves and their world. In the Quiche Maya book, the *Popol Vuh*, the cosmogonic events of world creation are tantamount to fashioning the four-sided maize field. The product of this cosmic field is the present people of corn, whose flesh was formed of ground yellow and white maize obtained from Mount Paxil (Tedlock 1996: 63–64, 145–146, 220). To the Aztecs, maize was also the stuff of human substance and life, as evident in the description of the maize goddess Chicomecoatl: "indeed truly she is our flesh, our livelihood; through her we live; she is our strength" (Sahagún 1950–1982, 2: 64). Although maize symbolism constituted an essential part of the Mesoamerican worldview, there was by no means a simple dichotomy between the economic and religious roles of corn. By Middle Formative times (c. 900–500 b.c.), maize was a central component of a complex ideology involving agricultural surpluses and wealth (Taube 1996).

In this essay I explore essential and elemental aspects of maize symbolism by focusing on the Formative period Olmec imagery (c. 1150–500 b.c.). During this Formative period—the time of the first widespread appearance of maize and food production in Mesoamerica—many of the fundamental meanings and associations of maize were developed. Among the Formative themes discussed here are the identification of corn with the *axis mundi* and the cardinal directions and the comparison of corn ears to two precious materials (jadeite and quetzal plumes) and their associated artifacts (polished stone celts and feathered maize fetishes). The Olmec maize complex can be observed over much of Middle Formative Mesoamerica, including such far-flung sites as Chalchuapa, El Salvador, and Teopantecuanitlán, Guerrero, as well as the Olmec heartland. Moreover, a great deal of the maize symbolism can be traced to later cultures of Classic and Postclassic Mesoamerica. Here I document the continuity of Olmec maize symbolism in later Mesoamerica, with special focus on the Classic Maya and Postclassic Aztec. In addition, some of the most striking aspects of this early Formative complex, including the use of directional maize celts, feathered corn fetishes, and the identification of corn with items of wealth, continue in contemporary Puebloan ceremonialism of the American Southwest. I suggest that the early dissemination of maize agriculture in Mesoamerica and the American Southwest concerned more than agricultural practices and technology; it involved a complex body of ritual and belief.

1. Middle Formative Olmec maize signs and the Olmec Maize God: (a) banded maize (see fig. 1d); (b) trefoil maize, detail of La Venta incised celt (after Diehl 1990: cat. 11); (c) maize with flowing silk (after Joralemon 1971: fig. 80); (d) Olmec Maize God, detail of incised Río Pesquero celt (drawing: Linda Schele); (e) Olmec Maize God with trefoil maize sign, detail of incised Río Pesquero celt (after Medellín 1971: no. 67); (f) Olmec Maize God with trefoil maize sign with crested birds (see fig. 9d)

Maize and the Formative Olmec

Although domesticated maize is first documented for the Archaic period Coxcatlan phase in the Tehuacan Valley of Puebla, it does not appear to have been a major Mesoamerican staple until approximately 1000 b.c. (see Arnold, this volume). Thus, while corn is known for pre-Olmec, Early Formative Mokaya sites of the southern coastal region of Chiapas and neighboring Guatemala (see Clark and Pye, this volume), the cobs were relatively small and unproductive. Moreover, the analysis of Mokaya human bone collagen reveals that maize was not a major component of the local diet (Blake et al. 1992; Clark and Blake 1989). In contrast to the earlier Mokaya villages, the major Olmec occupation at San Lorenzo, Veracruz, constituted a sharp development in the accrual and manipulation of social surplus and wealth. Earthworks, long stone drains, and megalithic monuments all testify to the economic power controlled by the rulers of this great center. However, the economic base of San Lorenzo remains poorly understood. Although Michael Coe and Richard Diehl (1980, 2: 144) cite the presence of grinding stones as evidence of maize preparation, virtually no maize remains were found during their excavations. They suggest that the San Lorenzo Olmecs practiced a mixed economy with a variety of staples, including manioc and other root crops as well as corn.

Recent work in the vicinity of La Venta, Tabasco, has documented a widespread presence of corn by 1150 b.c. (Rust and Leyden 1994: 192). However, maize use increased markedly during the Middle Formative apogee of La Venta (c. 800–500 b.c.): "The maximum density of recovered maize is . . . coincident, in the La Venta period, with the greatest spread of La Venta-related settlement and ceremonial activities, including use of fine-paste ceramics . . . figurines, and polished greenstone items" (Rust and Leyden 1994: 192–194). During the roughly contemporaneous Conchas phase (c. 850–650 b.c.) in the neighboring Soconusco region of coastal Chiapas and Guatemala, both population and maize cultivation sharply increased (Blake et al. 1995: 179–180).

During the Middle Formative period, there was a florescence of maize motifs and symbolism in Olmec art. Although some of these maize elements can be traced to Early Formative San Lorenzo, depictions of corn are far more common during the Middle Formative, that is, the period when maize became much more important. David Joralemon (1971: 13) isolated and identified a number of maize motifs common in Middle Formative Olmec iconography (fig. 1a–c). Among the more important of these various motifs are "banded maize," "tripartite maize," and "maize with flowing silk." In addition, Joralemon (1971: 59–66) described and illustrated an Olmec Maize God (fig. 1d–f). I have recently provided further support for the corn deity identification and also argue that two other Olmec beings described by Joralemon, Gods IV and VI, are but aspects of the same Olmec Maize God (Taube 1996).

One of the more curious and common Olmec motifs is the V-shaped cleft, which commonly appears on the cranium of the Olmec Maize God (fig. 1d–f). In these representations, a maize cob usually emerges from the central

2. The Olmec cleft and maize foliation: (a) cleft maize ear flanked by cleft foliation (after Fields 1991: fig. 3a); (b) maize ear with cleft bracts flanked by maize leaves (after Fields 1991: fig. 2); (c) maize ear with cleft bracts, Early Classic Teotihuacán (after Berrin and Pasztory 1993: cat. 76); (d) maize in U-shaped bracts, Late Classic Maya, Copan (after Fash 1988: fig. 4); (e) maize ear in V-shaped bracts, Late Postclassic Aztec (after Nicholson and Keber 1983: cat. 53); (f) Olmec Maize God with personified cleft foliation flanking head, La Venta incised celt (after Joralemon 1971: fig. 175); (g) Olmec Maize God as personified maize foliation (after Berjonneau et al. 1985: pl. 9); (h) foliated Olmec Maize God (after Joralemon 1971: fig. 43)

cleft. With the cleft and projecting cob, the head of the Olmec Maize God represents a maize ear, with the V-shaped cleft constituting the overlapping green husks, or bracts, partly surrounding the cob (see Taube 1996). In Olmec and later Mesoamerican iconography, maize cobs are frequently enveloped in a V-shaped cleft husk (fig. 2a–e).

Aside from representing the husks containing the mature cob, V-shaped clefts can also refer to green growing maize. One linear Olmec motif identified by Joralemon (1971: 13) as "cleft-ended vegetation" commonly appears flanking maize ears and the face of the Olmec Maize God (fig. 2a, f). The late Epi-Olmec El Sitio celt reveals that these long cleft elements are green leaves of corn (fig. 2b). These leaves can also be personified as the foliated aspect of the Olmec Maize God, which corresponds to God VI in the Joralemon (1971) system of deity nomenclature. In this case, the cranium commonly turns sharply backward, resembling in this regard a modern hammer claw (fig. 2g–h). This sharp bend alludes to the pliant nature of growing corn, which is further supported by the lack of a mature cob within the cranial cleft. It subsequently will be noted that the Olmecs replicated this cranial form with headdresses fashioned of long, verdant quetzal plumes.

Maize and Greenstone Celts

The sudden appearances of both maize and greenstone items at La Venta noted by William Rust and Barbara Leyden (1994) are by no means independent, coincidental events. For the Middle Formative Olmec, jade and serpentine valuables were considered much as symbolic and rarefied forms of maize (Joralemon 1988: 38; 1996: 57; Taube 1996). In a discussion of the economics of the Inca empire, Terence D'Altroy and Timothy Earle (1985) describe the transformation of a native economy based on staples to one based on precious wealth items. With the presence of major social surpluses from taxation or tribute, wealth items have obvious advantages in terms of storage, transport, and exchange. Kent Flannery and James Schoenwetter (1970: 148–150) argue that the exchange of exotic wealth items in Formative Oaxaca was a form of agricultural risk management: "Given the erratic rainfall in semi-arid regions like Oaxaca, unusually good years—and hence maize surpluses—are unpredictable. One way of 'banking' unpredictable maize surpluses (as an alternative to storage) is to convert them into imperishable trade goods which can be used either (1) as 'wealth' in times of shortage, or (2) as part of a ritual exchange system, used to establish reciprocal relations between neighboring peoples." This scenario is notably similar to the elaborate Kula exchange of Trobriand Melanesia (Malinowski 1922). Here in a process that Paul Bohannan and George Dalton (1962: 6) term "emergency conversion," Kula valuables originally acquired from agricultural surplus could be exchanged for seed yams with distant trading partners in times of agricultural need. Although crop failure probably was not a common concern of the Middle Formative Olmecs, Bohannan and Dalton note that emergency conversion can arise from a number of causes, including warfare and disease as well as famine.

Although shell ornaments are perhaps the best-known Kula valuables, the Trobriand Massim also exchanged greenstone celts known as *beku*. Bronislaw Malinowski (1934: 195) notes that these items served as a convenient means of conserving and exchanging wealth obtained from agricultural surplus: "The production of polished axe blades was in the Central Trobriands the main process by which accumulated food was transformed into an object of condensed wealth and thus made available for purposes for which it would have been useless in the form of perishable goods." The jade and serpentine celts of the Formative Olmec may have functioned in a very similar manner. Charlotte Thomson (1975: 98) notes that greenstone celts served as blanks from which statuettes and other objects were carved: "the polished jadeite celt was the basic unit of Olmec jade exchange." Joralemon (1988: 38) suggests that these celts had a broader economic role in Olmec society: "Celts might have been a kind of currency for the Olmec, a store of wealth that could be easily traded, exchanged, and accumulated." However, rather than forms of primitive money, the greenstone celts are perhaps better regarded as primitive valuables, similar to the Massim *beku* and other items of ceremonial exchange in Melanesia. In contrast to primitive valuables, primitive monies are items of standardized value used in a commercial market context (Dalton 1977). African cowries or cacao seeds of Post-

3. Middle Formative cache of celts and earspools oriented to four directions around central bowl, Cache 11, Mound 20, San Isidro, Chiapas
Drawing: New World Archaeological Foundation

4. Celts and the bar and four dots motif in Olmec iconography: (a) Olmec Maize God between four combined celt and maize signs, Río Pesquero (drawing: Linda Schele); (b) Olmec Maize God between four combined celt and maize signs, Río Pesquero (drawing: Linda Schele); (c) the Olmec bar and four dots motif; (d) figure with four cleft celtiform heads on limbs, Las Limas Figure (drawing: Kent Reilly); (e) figure with four cleft celts marked with bar and four dots motif (after photograph courtesy of Dumbarton Oaks); (f) figure with four cleft celt signs on abdomen, La Venta (after Drucker et al. 1959: fig. 64)

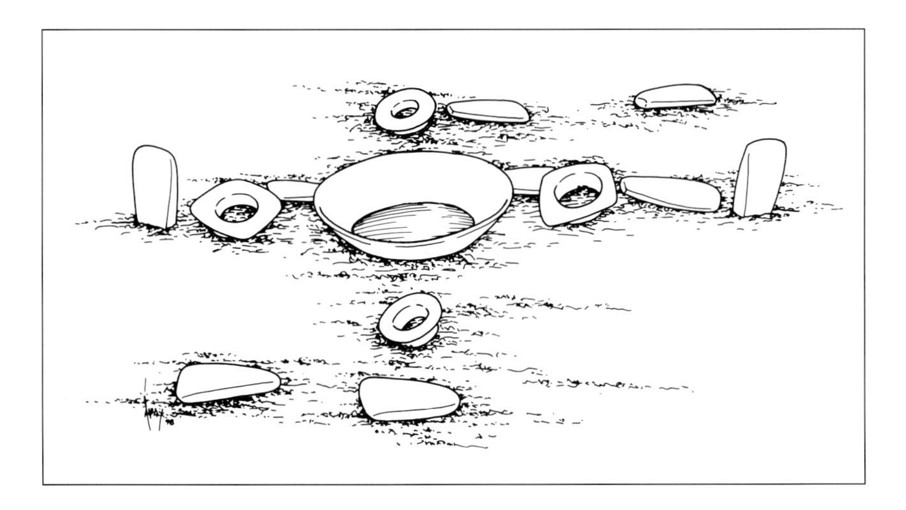

classic Mesoamerica do fit these two criteria; however, given the ritually charged meaning of the Formative greenstone celts, it is unlikely that they simply operated as primitive money in market exchange. There is little evidence of standardized value, as the quality and type of stone, size, and extent of workmanship varied widely among Olmec greenstone celts.

Marshall Saville (1929: 295–297) was the first to suggest that fine Olmec celts and effigy celts symbolized lightning, a concept known for many parts of the world (for example, Blinkenberg 1911). Among the ancient Olmecs, greenstone celts were widely used as symbols and markers of the center and four cardinal directions. In this regard, it is noteworthy that later Mesoamerican rain gods are not only identified with lightning celts and axes but also with the four directions and corn, essential attributes of Olmec ritual celts. Excavations at La Venta (Tabasco), San Isidro (Chiapas), and Seibal (Guatemala) have revealed Middle Formative caches of celts oriented to the cardinal points (Drucker 1952: fig. 10, pl. 8; Drucker et al. 1959: 185, fig. 51; Lowe 1981: 243–245; Smith 1982: 245). In the case of the San Isidro cache, celts and jade earspools are placed at the cardinal points around a central, ceramic bowl (fig. 3).

In contrast to the cited celt caches, scenes in Olmec art typically place celts at the four corners to define directional sides rather than cardinal points (fig. 4a–b). In these scenes, the four corner devices define the central image as the *axis mundi* (Reilly 1994: 22). Kent Reilly (1994: 227–228) notes that the entire composition creates the bar and four dots motif: the Olmec sign for the world in the form of the four quarters and central, pivotal axis (see also Benson 1971: 28; Marcus 1989: 172). In contrast to the later Mesoamerican quincunx sign for the center and four quarters, the Olmec symbol of centrality is expressed through bilateral rather than quadrilateral symmetry (fig. 4c). Bilateral symmetry is well suited for ceremonial architecture and linear processions, such as may have occurred in La Venta Complex A. However, the symmetry of the Olmec bar and four dots sign is also a close approximation of the human body, with the four limbs flanking the central trunk. A number of Olmec figures, including the Las Limas statuette, appear with signs placed on the four limbs or torso, thereby rendering the body as the piv-

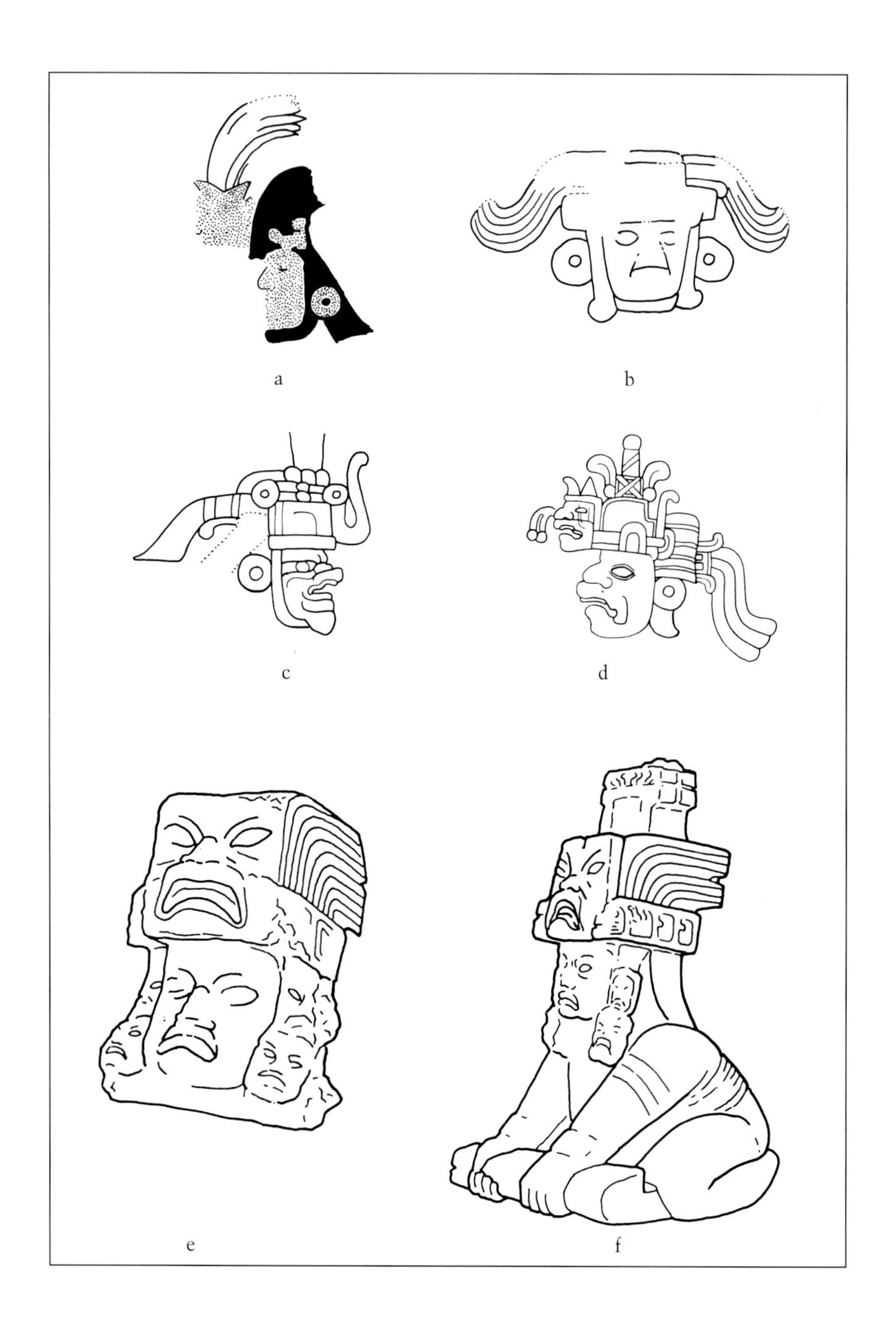

5. Quetzal plumes in Middle Formative Olmec iconography: (a) painted figure with green quetzal plumes on brow, Juxtlahuaca cave, Guerrero (after Stone 1995: pl. 1); (b) figure with quetzal plume headdress, Abaj Takalik Monument 14 (after Graham et al. 1978: pl. 6); (c) Olmec Maize God with plumed maize ear projected from back of headdress, Abaj Takalik Monument 1 (after Sharer 1994: fig. 3.1); (d) Olmec Maize God with plumed ear of corn at back of headdress, Shook Panel (after Shook and Heizer 1976: fig. 1); (e) figure wearing quetzal plume headdress with mask of Olmec Maize God, La Venta Monument 44 (drawing: Elizabeth Wahle); (f) figure with Olmec Maize God and quetzal plume headdress topped with world tree, San Martín Pajapan Monument 1 (drawing: Elizabeth Wahle)

otal, central element of the bar and four dots motif (fig. 4d–e; Taube 1996: fig. 9). Not only do these four cleft forms refer to celts, but celts can also be lashed to the limbs of Olmec figures (Taube 1996: fig. 10a–c). To the Olmecs, the human body served as a graphic model of the cosmos.

Along with marking the four quarters or cardinal points, Olmec greenstone celts also denoted the central place. Gareth Lowe (1981: 243) notes that caches of celts were placed on the central axis of San Isidro Mound 20 as well as Complex A at La Venta. One of the centerline caches of Complex A contained 213 serpentine celts, all apparently with the poll end planted in the ground and the cutting edge oriented upward (Drucker 1952: 75–76, pl. 15c; compare Rodríguez and Ortiz, this volume). The central axial celt is also represented in Olmec iconography. A number of Olmec jade statuettes portray a celt in the region of the groin, again with the blade pointing upward (see The Art Museum 1995: nos. 18, 26; Benson and de la Fuente 1996: cat. 44). For these examples, the celt assumes the central vertical form of the male loincloth, such as commonly found on Olmec greenstone statuettes (Taube 1996: 53).

For a number of incised jade celts, the central vertical element of the bar and four dots motif is the Olmec Maize God, with the four dots represented as maize ears in the form of celts (fig. 4a–b). This probably constitutes an early version of the Mesoamerican metaphor of the ordered world as a four-sided maize field, here with the corn god in the center. However, these incised celts were probably more than models of the cosmos. Instead, the bar and four dots motif and maize gods incised on these particular celts may have charged them with divine power as personified embodiments of the *axis mundi.* James Porter (1996) notes that a number of green stelae from La Venta, Monuments 25/26, 27, 58, and 66, are in the form of massive celts, here again with the curving bit oriented upward (see fig. 13d). Portrayed with images of the Olmec Maize God, these monumental celts are embodiments of the central world tree. As discussed in the next section, along with alluding to the *axis mundi,* greenstone celts, and maize, these La Venta monuments also refer to another item: a feathered maize fetish.

Maize and Quetzal Plumes

The Quetzal in Olmec Iconography. Along with jade, the long, emerald green tail feathers of the male quetzal *(Pharomachrus m. mocinno)* were among the most precious and esteemed items in ancient Mesoamerica.[1] Although depictions of long-tailed quetzals have been noted at Middle Formative La Venta and Chalcatzingo (Grove 1984: 120–121; Angulo 1987: 136, 148), there has been virtually no discussion of quetzal plumage in Olmec iconographic studies. Quetzal plumes are widely depicted in Olmec art and can be readily identified by their extreme length and pliant nature (fig. 5). Although somewhat eroded, La Venta Monument 61 portrays an Olmec figure with long quetzal plumes curving down the back of his headdress, a convention commonly found

6. Depictions of quetzals in Early and Middle Formative Olmec iconography: (a) probable quetzal with feather crest and long tail feathers, detail of Early Formative incised vessel, Tlapacoya (after Joralemon 1971: fig. 41); (b) crested bird head, design from Early Formative roller stamp (after Gay 1972: fig. 12); (c) crested bird, vessel sherd, Early Formative San Lorenzo (after Coe and Diehl 1980: fig. 140g); (d) crested bird with maize in center of brow, detail of incised serpentine celt (after Sotheby's 1990: no. 127); (e) crested bird with maize ear and double merlon sign, detail of incised celt (see fig. 11f); (f) crested bird on jade earspool, La Venta (after Diehl 1990: cat. 8)

7. Representations of quetzals in Classic and Postclassic iconography: (a) quetzal forming part of name of Early Classic Maya king, Kinich Yax Kuk Mo, Margarita platform, Copan (after Sharer 1995: fig. 1); (b) Late Classic Maya quetzal, Lintel 3, Temple 1, Tikal (after Jones and Satterthwaite 1982: fig. 70); (c) quetzal with long feather crest, Teotihuacán (after Berrin 1988: pl. 17); (d) Late Classic quetzal, Cacaxtla (after Bullé Goyri 1987: 117); (e) quetzal, Late Postclassic Maya, Codex Madrid, page 100b; (f) quetzal, Late Postclassic Central Mexico, Codex Borgia, page 53; (g) quetzal, Late Postclassic Mixtec, Codex Nuttall, page 9; (h) Aztec quetzal, Primeros Memoriales, fol. 74r

in later Classic Maya scenes (see de la Fuente 1977: illus. 72). Painting 1 from Juxtlahuaca cave, Guerrero, contains a rare color depiction of a quetzal plume bundle, here worn on the brow of the principal figure (fig. 5a). In this case, the long plumage is clearly green (see Stone 1995: pl. 1; Lombardo de Ruiz 1996: pl. 2).

Among the more common creatures of Olmec iconography is a bird displaying a feather crest, often in the form of the so-called flame-eyebrow motif (fig. 6). Because of the feather crest and frequently long, raptorlike beak, this bird has been widely identified as the great harpy eagle, *Harpia harpyja* (for example, Drucker 1952: 194–195; Joralemon 1976: 40; Furst 1995: 75). However, the prominent crest of the harpy eagle is rather conical, quite unlike the long, fanlike form of the flame-eyebrow. Instead, this feather crest is far more like that of the quetzal, a bird of great economic as well as religious importance in ancient Mesoamerica. One of the primary messages of Olmec art and ritual was the conspicuous display of social surplus and wealth, that is, economic rather than military strength. In comparison to the harpy eagle, the emerald quetzal was far better suited to express agricultural abundance and material wealth. It is noteworthy that in Olmec art the crested bird commonly appears on verdant maize growth, jade, and other greenstone items (figs. 1f, 6d–f, 9d, 10a–c, e–g). At La Venta, this creature occurs on a pair of earspools fashioned from emerald green jade, essentially the same color as quetzal plumage (fig. 6f; see Diehl 1990: cat. 8).

Although the common occurrence of the crested bird with jade and maize is well suited to the quetzal, one problem remains; the long, curving beak of the Olmec crested bird is not found with quetzals. Nonetheless, this is a trait commonly found with Mesoamerican portrayals of quetzals. Eduard Seler (1902–1923, 4: 565) early noted that in Postclassic Central Mexican manuscripts, quetzals are usually rendered with eaglelike raptor beaks (fig. 7e–h). Subsequent discoveries demonstrate that Classic period quetzals were also commonly depicted with long, curving raptor beaks (fig. 7a–d). One recently excavated Early Classic example from Copan forms part of the name of Kinich Yax Kuk Mo, the founder of the Copan dynasty (Sharer 1995). Along with the long beak, this quetzal is supplied with a feather crest notably like the flame-eyebrow of earlier Olmec iconography (fig. 7a).

Although quetzals are especially common

in Middle Formative Olmec iconography, there are few Early Formative examples. A fragmentary vessel from Tlapacoya, dating to about 900 b.c., portrays a probable pair of quetzals. For the more intact example, the crest, wing, and long tail can be readily seen (fig. 6a). Moreover, the tail is typical of the male quetzal, which has two especially long tail plumes (see Howell and Webb 1995: pl. 33). A double merlon sign may have framed the lower portion of the face, a feature also found with a Middle Formative quetzal depiction (fig. 6e). A roller stamp attributed to Las Bocas portrays a bird head with a flame-eyebrow crest, quite probably a quetzal (fig. 6b). A third example occurs on a vessel sherd from San Lorenzo, which portrays the crested bird with prominent flame-eyebrows and the raptorlike beak (fig. 6c). A major, recently discovered San Lorenzo monument may also represent a quetzal. Although this two-ton sculpture is missing its head, Ann Cyphers (1996: 64) interprets it as a macaw on the basis of its long tail. However, the curving, pliant tail plumes are not found with macaws, which have extremely stiff and straight tail feathers. Rather than a macaw, this Early Formative sculpture may well depict a quetzal.

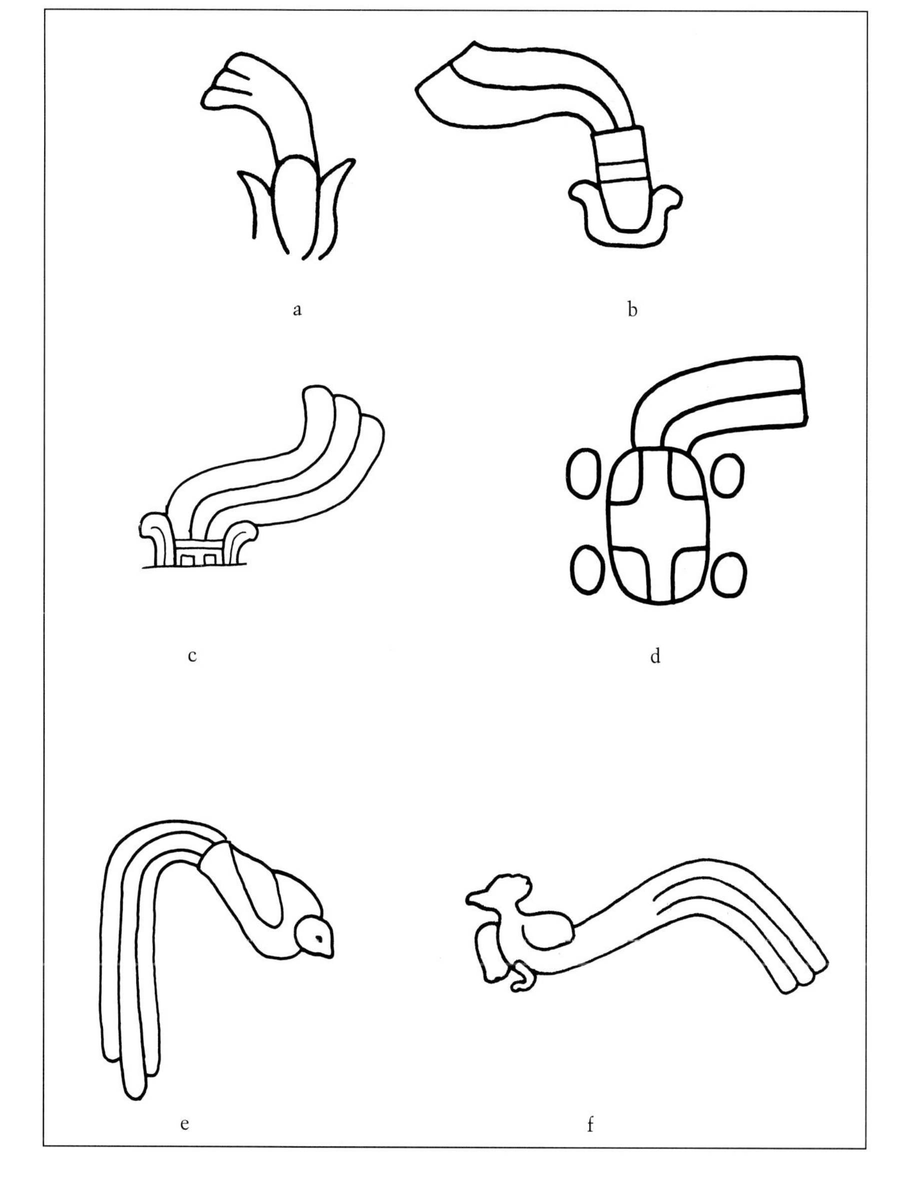

8. Olmec quetzal plumes and maize ears: (a) maize ear with plumes as silk (after Joralemon 1971: fig. 189); (b) maize ear as celt tipped with plumes, La Venta Altar 4; (c) maize ear with long plumes, Shook Panel (see fig. 4d); (d) maize ear as bar and four dots motif with plumes as silk, detail of incised celt from Tlaltenco (after Joralemon 1971: no. 34); (e) quetzal with long tail plumes, Chalcatzingo Monument 1 (detail drawing: James Porter); (f) flying quetzal, Chalcatzingo Monument 12 (see fig. 11c)

Quetzal Feathers and Maize Symbolism. Along with jade, quetzal plumes are squarely embedded in the maize symbolism of the Middle Formative Olmecs. In fact, one of the common Olmec maize motifs, described by Joralemon (1971: 33) as "maize with flowing silk," is an ear of corn with long, curving quetzal plumes as the silk (fig. 8a–c). As noted below, this is also a common motif in Classic Maya iconography. An ear of corn bedecked with quetzal plumes commonly projects behind the head of the Olmec Maize God (fig. 5c–d).

Certain quetzal-plumed headdresses were used to evoke one aspect of the Olmec Maize God, the personification of young, growing corn (see Taube 1996: 45–48). The San Martín Pajapan sculpture and the fragmentary La Venta Monument 44 portray figures wearing masks of the Olmec Maize God on their brows (fig. 5e–f). These shallow mask plaques were probably of jade, quite like the Olmec example excavated from the Aztec Templo Mayor (see Benson and de la Fuente 1996: cat. 94). For both the San Martín Pajapan and La Venta monuments, a series of long, parallel lines curve behind the mask plaque. Carl William Clewlow (1968: 40) interpreted these lines as feathers, and in view of their narrowness, length, and pliancy, they can be identified as the tail feathers of the male quetzal. The ends of these quetzal headdresses display prominent clefts, thereby labeling them as references to plant growth and the personification of growing corn, equivalent to God VI in the Joralemon system of deity classification. The cranium of this aspect of the Olmec Maize God has the same form as the quetzal plume headdress—sharply backturned and cleft at the end (figs. 2h, 9a–c). Although probably representing historical individuals rather than gods, both La Venta Mon-

9. Cleft heads and headdresses and the foliated Olmec Maize God: (a) Olmec Maize God with sharply backturned cleft cranium (after Benson 1971: fig. 45); (b) Olmec Maize God with cleft cranium, Tlapacoya (after Feuchtwanger 1989: fig. 154); (c) Olmec Maize God, detail of incised celt, Río Pesquero (after Benson and de la Fuente 1996: cat. 17); (d) two views of seated figure with sharply backturned headdress, jadeite statuette, Río Pesquero (after Taube 1996: fig. 8a); (e) figure with backturned headdress, La Venta Monument 77 (line drawing: Elizabeth Wahle)

10. Olmec crested birds displaying aspects of foliated Olmec Maize God: (a) incised celt with facial banding commonly found with foliated corn deity; note maize in center of brow (after Sotheby's 1990: no. 127); (b) crested bird with facial banding of foliated corn god, note maize ears; incised serpentine celt (after The Art Museum 1995: cat. 125); (c) paw-wing with facial attributes of crested bird and foliated Olmec Maize God (after Benson and de la Fuente 1996: cat. 101); (d) stone sculpture displaying attributes of crested bird and foliated corn deity, La Venta Monument 78 (after Ochoa and Castro-Leal 1986: 30); (e) face with attributes of crested bird and foliated maize deity, note capping maize ear; detail of incised celt (after The Art Museum 1995: cat. 195); (f) head combining attributes of foliated corn deity and crested bird, detail of incision upon the "Young Lord" statuette (after The Art Museum 1995: cat. 193); (g) head of the "Young Lord" (after The Art Museum 1995); (h) Isthmian Maize Gods with avian attributes, Late Classic Río Blanco vessel, Veracruz (after von Winning and Gutiérrez Solana 1996: 75)

ument 77 and a jade statuette in the collection of Dumbarton Oaks portray individuals with headdresses in the form of the foliated corn deity, but lacking explicit portrayal of quetzal plumes (fig. 9d–e). It would appear that these two examples constitute intermediate forms between the cleft quetzal plume headdresses and the head of the foliated Olmec Maize God.

In a number of instances, the crested quetzal bird combines with the foliated maize deity (fig. 10). Along with the avian flame-eyebrows and raptor beak, this being has the curving facial banding commonly found with God VI (see fig. 9b; Joralemon 1971: 79–81). In addition, the avian figure often appears with maize ears and cleft foliation (fig. 10a–b, d–f). The large Olmec serpentine statue now referred to as the "Young Lord" is a representation of this being, with a stylized maize sign topping his headdress (fig. 10g; see The Art Museum 1995: cat. 193). La Venta Monument 78 is an even more massive portrayal of the avian maize god. Although the sculpture is somewhat battered, the flame-eyebrows and foliated facial banding are plainly evident (fig. 10d). A jade plaque portrays an abstract form of the being, here with a cleft brow, crested quetzal eye, and facial banding atop a long paw-wing (fig. 10c).

In a number of instances, the foliated Olmec Maize God occurs in a position of flight while holding the so-called torch motif (fig. 11a–b). Often referred to as "el volador" (the flyer),

Chalcatzingo Monument 12 demonstrates that this body position denotes supernatural flight. Holding his "torch" before him, the figure is accompanied by a pair of flying quetzals and a macaw (fig. 11c). In another Olmec scene, the flying figure wears a crested bird headdress, quite probably that of the quetzal (fig. 11d). It would appear that the grasping and manipulation of the torchlike form often concerns supernatural flight.

In another essay (Taube 1996: 68), I noted that the so-called torch motif is actually a feathered, maize ear fetish. In many instances, the central cob can be seen projecting out of the feathers, much like an ear of corn emerging from its enclosing husk (fig. 11e). The upper feathered portion is often marked by the double merlon sign, the Olmec sign for "green" (Taube 1995: 89–91). In one instance, the feather-tufted region is replaced with the head of the quetzal, along with the double merlon and projecting banded ear of maize (fig. 11f). Stone effigy forms of the corn fetishes frequently appear with representations of the Olmec Maize God. One fragmentary example, fashioned from a particularly massive piece of jadeite, portrays the head of the Olmec Maize God in the central portion of the lower bound shaft (fig. 11g). A frontal bird face appears in the upper feather region above the double merlon sign, a probable allusion to the celestial realm. The feathers are delineated with diagonal crossed-lines, a convention also appearing on a maize fetish held by a serpentine statuette from Paso de Ovejas, Veracruz (see Benson and de la Fuente 1996: cat. 49).

A number of stone maize fetish effigies represent the face of the Olmec Maize God in place of the feathered region (see Navarrete 1974: 14–17). Nonetheless, one example attributed to the region of Cárdenas, Tabasco, retains the double-merlon motif in the lower region of the face (fig. 12a). A downward-facing serpent head forms the base of these stone effigy fetishes. A more anthropomorphized form of this maize fetish appears on an incised celt attributed to Río Pesquero (figs. 4b, 12b). Along with the downward-facing serpent head forming his legs, the top of his head is composed of an ear of corn projecting from an outwardly curving element marked with parallel striations. Clearly enough, this upper portion corresponds to the feathered top of the maize fetish, complete with the double-merlon sign. Personified as the Olmec Maize God, this corn fetish is framed by four maize celts, thereby delineating it as the central *axis mundi* (fig. 4b).

Maize Fetishes and Feathered Serpent Iconography. The Río Pesquero corn deity holds a long zoomorphic figure in his arms. Along with its serpentlike face, flame-eyebrows, and a broad, upturned tail, the creature is bound with the form of knot commonly appearing with the maize ear fetish (fig. 12b–c). The creature is very much like a figure appearing on an incised vessel attributed to Tabasco, which

11. Olmec flying figures and the feathered maize ear fetish: (a) figure with backturned head of foliated corn god, note fetish in hand; celts from Offering 4, La Venta (from Cervantes 1969: fig. 11); (b) figure with backturned head holding maize fetish and "knuckle duster" (after Benson and de la Fuente 1996: cat. 98); (c) figure grasping maize fetish with flying birds, Chalcatzingo Monument 12 (after Angulo 1987: fig. 10.19); (d) figure with maize fetish and crested bird headdress (after Harmer Rooke Galleries 1985: 6, no. 9); (e) feathered maize ear fetish with projecting maize cob, detail from Chalcatzingo Vase (after Gay 1972: fig. 43); (f) maize ear fetish with ear of corn projecting from crested quetzal head, incised celt (after The Art Museum 1995: cat. 125); (g) fragmentary jadeite maize ear fetish, note stylized bird and maize at top and head of Olmec Maize God (drawing by author of item in the collections of the Peabody Museum, Harvard University)

also has flame-eyebrows and the same curious tail (fig. 11d). Joralemon (1971: 84) identifies this example as God VII, which he considers as the Olmec feathered serpent. The body of the Tabasco serpent contains thin, parallel lines, recalling the handles of maize ear fetishes, which often appear to have been formed of bound sticks. Along with being personified as the Olmec Maize God, the feathered maize fetish was also compared to a snake. With the basal snake head, the tubular fetish becomes a feathered serpent, with the head of the Olmec Maize God serving as the tail (see fig. 12a–b). In both Olmec and later Mesoamerican art, plumed serpents frequently had rattlesnake tails. With its segmented form and golden color, the rattle closely resembles a small, husked ear of corn.

In Mesoamerican iconography, maize can tip the ends of serpent tails, quite probably an allusion to the tail of a rattlesnake. The well-known Olmec-style plumed serpent from Juxtlahuaca cave, Guerrero, displays the trefoil maize sign at the end of its tail, with another emerging as its tongue (fig. 12e). A similar scene occurs on a large incised serpentine statuette (see Pahl 1977). Whereas the figure is rendered in late Olmec style, the incision resembles Formative Zapotec art and may well have been made in Oaxaca (fig. 12f). The design portrays a crested serpent facing downward, an entity that I have interpreted (Taube 1995: 92) as the Avian Serpent, the early Olmec form of Quetzalcoatl. Gary Pahl (1977: 36) identifies the capping headdress of the seated human figure at the end of the serpent as a rattlesnake tail. Noting that the figure holds an ear of corn, with another emerging from the mouth of the snake, Pahl (1977: 39) suggests that it is closely related to corn: "Judging from the repetition of maize symbols in association with the seated individual, it might be safe to assume that he represents a priest of maize fertility cult." It is entirely possible, however, that the figure is the personification of corn, that is, the maize god.

The rattlesnake tail is explicitly compared to a maize ear in Aztec iconography. In one calendrical representation of Chicomecoatl, the Aztec maize goddess, the day name Coatl (Serpent) is depicted with an ear of corn substituting for the rattle (fig. 12g). The Postclassic Mixtec also compared the plumed serpent to corn. On page 3 of the Codex Selden, a green feathered serpent appears as the personification of young maize, with the quetzal plumes rendered as the long leaves of the growing plant (fig. 12h).

Greenstone celts and the feathered maize ear fetish imagery frequently merge in Olmec iconography. Many scenes portray the Olmec Maize God wearing a five-piece headband com-

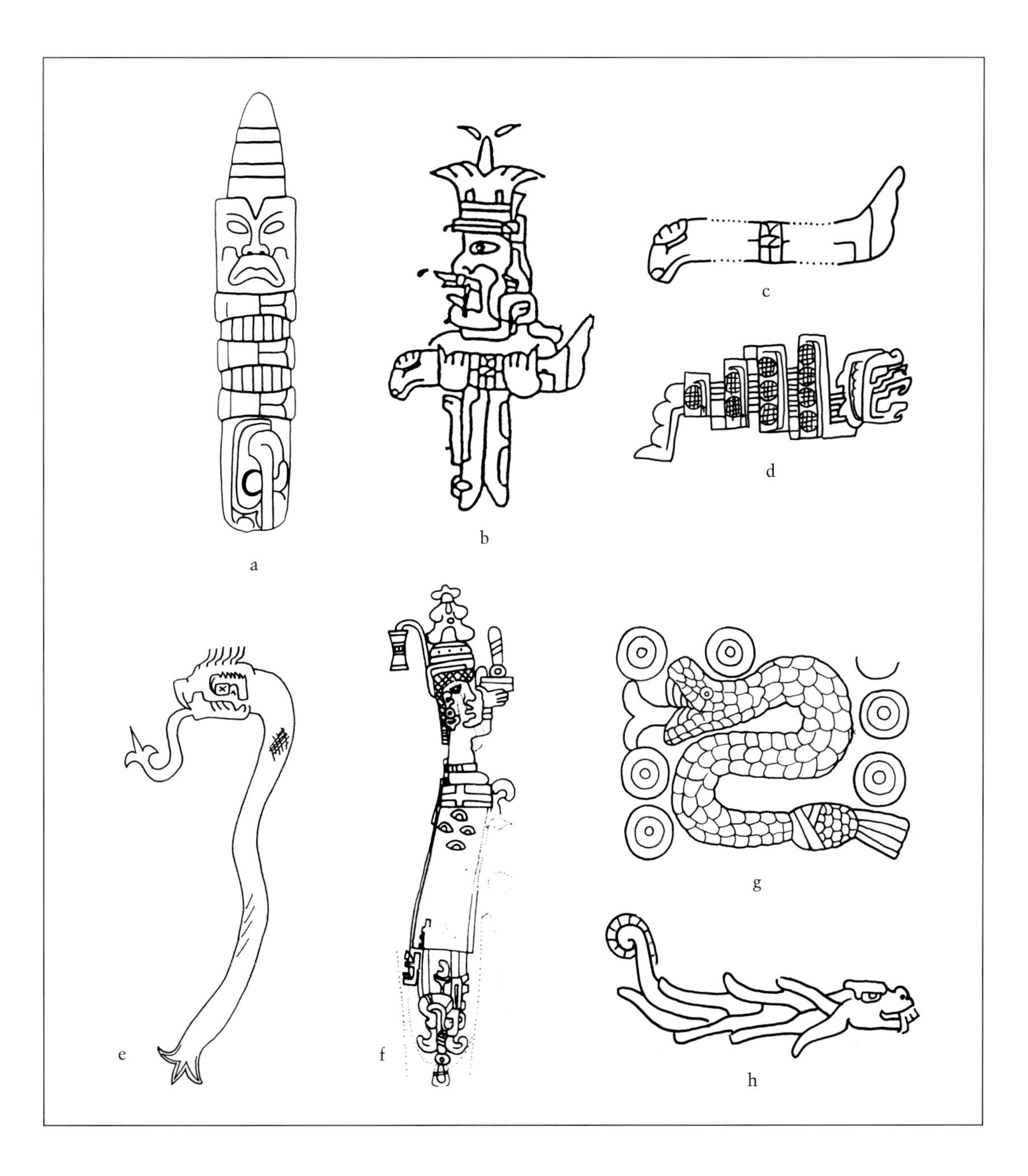

12. The Olmec maize ear fetish and serpents: (a) maize ear fetish with head of Olmec Maize God and serpent head at base (after Benson and de la Fuente 1996: cat. 104); (b) Olmec Maize God as personified maize fetish holding serpent bar (see fig. 4b); (c) detail of serpent bar held by Olmec Maize God; (d) Olmec avian serpent; compare tail to (c) (after Joralemon 1971: fig. 250); (e) Olmec avian serpent with maize sign tail, Juxtlahuaca cave (drawing: Kent Reilly); (f) crested serpent with probable maize deity in tail region, detail of incised Olmec style statuette (after Pahl 1977: fig. 2); (g) Aztec calendrical representation of Chicomecoatl; note ear of corn replacing tail rattles of serpent (after Alcina Franch et al. 1992: 55); (h) plumed serpent as green corn, Codex Selden, page 3, Late Postclassic Mixtec

13. The conflation of celts and maize ear fetishes in Olmec iconography: (a) personified cleft celt topped with feathered maize fetish (see fig. 9d); (b) celtiform Olmec Maize God with crossed-lashing and double merlon sign found with maize ear fetishes (after Coe 1965: fig. 28); (c) celtiform Olmec Maize God with double merlon on face and crossed-lashing at base; note maize ear fetishes held in arms (after Gay 1972: pl. 24); (d) celtiform stela of Olmec Maize God with crossed-lashing, double merlon, and capping feathers occurring with maize ear fetishes, La Venta Monument 25/26 (drawing: James Porter); (e) celtiform stela of Isthmian Maize God with double merlon on brow and long capping feathers, Tres Zapotes Stela C (drawing: James Porter)

posed of four celts or ears of corn flanking a central brow element (for example, fig. 1d, f). For the Río Pesquero figure, the four devices are composed of personified cleft celts topped with the upper portion of the maize ear fetish, including the double merlon and projecting cob along with a feather tuft (figs. 9d, 13a). Moreover, there are two closely related serpentine sculptures of maize ear fetishes appearing in the form of personified celts or axes (fig. 13b–c). In both cases, the figures appear as the foliated form of the Olmec Maize God, with the cranial cleft lacking the projecting maize ear. In this case, the clefts are bounded by circles forming an inverted triangle. The figures display double-merlon signs in the mouth region and the horizontal lashing of the maize ear fetish across the body. For the more elaborate example (fig. 13c), attributed to Ahuelicán, Guerrero, the lashing only appears in the area of the feet. The three maize fetishes held in the arms of this figure strongly suggest that he embodies this ritual item.

Along with alluding to celts and the Olmec Maize God, the celtiform stelae from La Venta also display traits of the maize fetish (for example, fig. 13d). With horizontal lashing in the lower portions of the stelae, each head of the Olmec Maize God is topped with feathers marked with the double-merlon sign, as if the upper portion of the maize ear fetish corresponded to the feather headdress of the corn deity. James Porter (1996) notes that Tres Zapotes Stela C is also a celtiform stela that shares many traits with La Venta Monuments 25/26, 27, 58, and 66 (fig. 13e). The entity portrayed on this monument is the Isthmian Maize God, a Late Preclassic corn deity closely related to the Olmec Maize God (see Taube 1996: 57–59). As in the case of the cited La Venta stelae, the head of the later Tres Zapotes example has a double merlon topped by long plumes, probably an allusion to the feathered maize fetishes.

The merging of greenstone celts and feathered maize fetishes probably concerns the identification of maize, jade, and quetzal plumes with centrality in Olmec thought. The previously mentioned San Martín Pajapan sculpture and La Venta Monument 44 express the identification of maize, jade, and quetzal plumes with centrality and the world tree (fig. 5e–f). Along with the quetzal plume headdress, both figures wear brow masks of the Olmec Maize God, quite like the Olmec jade masquette found in the Aztec Templo Mayor (see Benson and de la Fuente 1996: cat. 94). According to Reilly (1994: 186–187), the San Martín Pajapan figure is portrayed raising the world tree with his hands. In addition, the foliage capping the top of the more intact San Martín Pajapan sculpture qualifies both the masquette and entire sculpture as the verdant world tree.

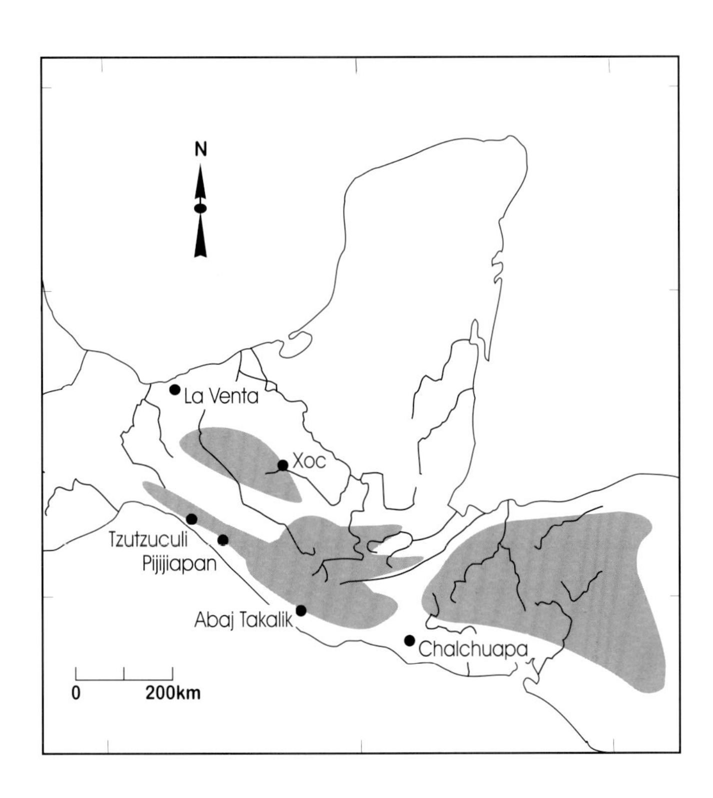

14. The distribution of the Resplendent Quetzal *(Pharomachrus m. mocinno)* in relation to sites displaying Middle Formative Olmec monumental art (map of quetzal habitat after Howell and Webb 1995: 436)

Maize, Wealth, and Fertility Cults. The close relations of jade, quetzal plumes, and maize among the Middle Formative Olmecs probably signal the development of a wealth economy from one based on staples. During the Middle Formative period, the Olmec intentionally spread a cult of agricultural fertility in distant lands as a means of securing exotic resources (Taube 1996). In the Maya region, jade and quetzal plumes were surely among the most coveted materials. It is noteworthy that the great majority of sites displaying Olmec-style art in the Maya area, including Tzutzuculi, Pijijiapan, Abaj Takalik, and Xoc, border the natural habitat of the quetzal (fig. 14). (The one major exception, Chalchuapa, El Salvador, lies between the two major habitats of the quetzal.) At these sites, there are numerous allusions to Olmec maize iconography, including depictions of the Olmec Maize God and maize ear fetishes (figs. 5c, 15a, c–e). The Middle Formative exportation of Olmec maize iconography was not limited to southeastern Mesoamerica. The same can be said for contemporaneous highland Mexican sites, including Chalcatzingo, Amuco, and Teopantecuanitlán, where there are depictions of Olmec corn fetishes and related iconography (fig. 15b, e). The ashlar masonry sunken court at Teopantecuanitlán, Guerrero, contains an especially ambitious program devoted to maize, with four depictions of the Olmec Maize God wielding feathered maize ear fetishes framing a symbolic ballcourt (Martínez Donjuán 1985) (fig. 15b). The Middle Formative images of Olmec maize symbolism outside the Olmec heartland were part of an Olmec cult of maize materially expressed through such items as precious greenstone celts and feathered corn fetishes. Many of these Formative traits constitute some of the most basic aspects of maize symbolism in Mesoamerica and the American Southwest.

15. Middle Formative Olmec maize iconography outside the Olmec heartland: (a) Olmec Maize God, Monument 1, Tzutzuculi, Chiapas (after McDonald 1983: fig. 29); (b) Olmec Maize God holding maize ear fetishes, Teopantecuanitlán, Guerrero (after Taube 1996: fig. 27c); (c, d) Olmec figures with maize ear fetishes, Monument 12, Chalchuapa, El Salvador (after Taube 1996: fig. 26c, d); (e) Olmec supernatural carrying maize fetish and probable stela marked with maize plant, Xoc, Chiapas; note maize ear at top of headdress (after Taube 1996: fig. 26e); (f) Olmec figure carrying maize ear fetish in crook of arm, note trefoil maize sign capping headdress; stela from San Miguel Amuco, Guerrero (after Taube 1995: fig. 7a)

Classic Maya Maize Symbolism

Given the fact that the Maya region was the source of quetzal plumes and jadeite, it is not surprising that a great deal of the symbolism of maize and wealth described for the Olmec also occurs among the Classic Maya.[2] In a previous study, I traced the development of the Maya corn deity from the Olmec Maize God (Taube 1996). The present discussion concerns the symbolism of celts and quetzal plumes among the Classic Maya. Like the Olmecs, the Classic Maya regarded jade and quetzal plumes as condensed agricultural wealth, that is, symbolic distillations of corn. For that reason, the Classic Maya maize god commonly appears richly bedecked in jade jewels and quetzal plumage. This is most evident with the Holmul Dancer, a very elaborately dressed form of the maize god (Taube 1985). In the same manner, rulers dressed in these items were portrayed as the controllers and providers of agricultural abundance.

As among the Olmec, jade celts had a major symbolic role in Classic Maya religion. Classic Maya rulers were commonly portrayed with jade celtiform plaques hanging from their belts, a practice that can be traced to the Formative Olmecs (Taube 1996: 42). Quite frequently the celt pendants were worn from the small of the back and the front of the loincloth, thereby marking the central axis of the body. However, in other instances, two additional sets of celts were worn on the sides of the hips, thereby ringing the body with four celt groupings (for example, Tikal Stela 16, Dos Pilas Stelae 1, 11, 14, 15). Standing within these four sets of vertical celts, the king was framed and demarcated as the central place, the *axis mundi.* Many Early Classic incised belt celts, such as the Leiden Plaque, closely resemble miniature stelae. Additionally, like the Middle Formative Olmecs, the Maya also erected celtiform stelae. Recent epigraphic research indicates that at Copan stelae were referred to as celts (Stuart 1996: 162). In this context, the logographic sign used to designate "celt" is identical in form to representations of belt celts.

16. Celts and maize in Classic Maya iconography: (a) vertical celt forming part of maize god appellative, Lintel 3 of Tikal Temple IV; (b) celt forming maize ear as the personified form of number 8, Tablet of the 96 Glyphs, Palenque; (c) maize ear represented as celt with quetzal plumes (after Kerr 1994: 623); (d) maize plant with celtiform ear, Structure 1B-2, Quirigua (after Sharer et al. 1979: fig. 6); (e) maize plant with celt as ear of corn, Tablet of the Temple of the Foliated Cross, Palenque

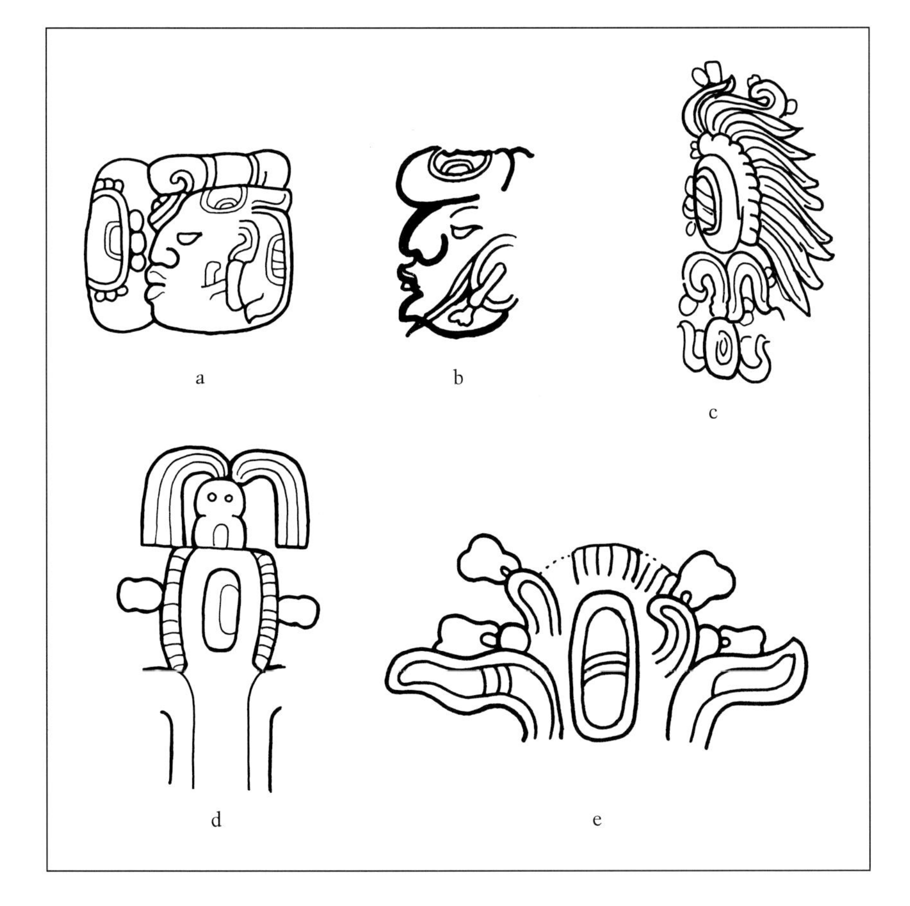

Marked with the curving or diagonal "mirror marking" band, the oval celt sign commonly represented the maize ear in Classic Maya writing and art. One form of the maize god name glyph often has a vertical celt prefix (fig. 16a). In addition, this celt sign also appeared as the ear of corn found with the foliated aspect of the maize god, the head variant of the number eight (fig. 16b). Celts often substituted for the ear of corn on maize plants (figs. 16c–e, 17b–c). In a number of instances, these celtiform cobs are also accompanied by quetzal plumes, thereby expressing the same corn, jade, and quetzal plume complex noted for the Middle Formative Olmecs (figs. 16c, 17b–c).

Among the ancient Maya, celts were closely related to lightning as well as to corn. One Protoclassic jade celt from Kendal, Belize, portrays an early incised image of Chac, the Maya god of rain and lightning (see Schele and Miller 1986: pl. 90). The head displays the smoking brow commonly found with God K, or Kauil, who is essentially a personified lightning axe closely identified with corn (Taube 1996: 69–79). Like Chac, God K is also quadripartite and appears in Classic period 819-day cycle texts describing directional day names and colors (Kelley 1976: fig. 17).

Quetzal plumes as well as celts represent corn in Classic and Postclassic Maya iconography. As in the case of Olmec examples, ears of corn are frequently tipped by quetzal plumage (fig. 17). Although this convention seems to have been generally ignored as a mere elaboration or decoration, it was a powerful economic statement: maize was the source of wealth. Although Eduard Seler (1902–1923, 4: 566) interpreted several examples from the Codex Dresden as quetzal tails, the feathered ears of corn are clearly growing out of the Kan maize glyph. Nonetheless, Seler was not far from the mark: bird tails are frequently rendered as plumed ears of corn in Maya iconography (fig. 18). In many instances the grains of the central cob are carefully indicated. James Barrio (personal communication, 1996) has pointed out a particularly early, Late Preclassic example from Abaj Takalik Altar 113 (fig. 18a). It is likely that these birds portrayed denizens

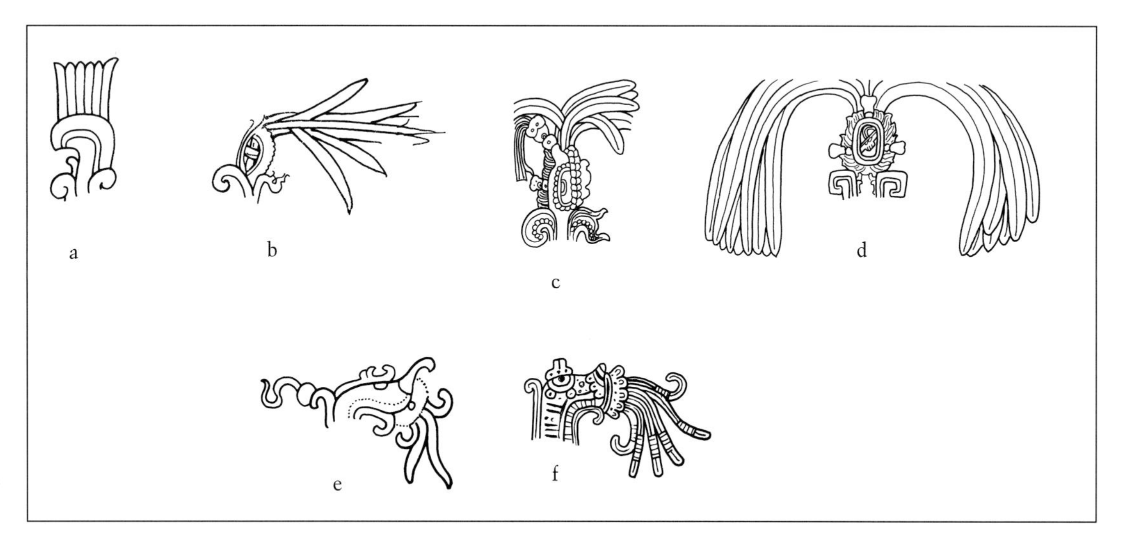

17. Quetzal plumes on growing maize ears: (a) Uaxactun Stela 3 (after Graham 1986: 137); (b) detail of Late Classic vessel (after Taube 1996: fig. 4h); (c) detail of Lintel 3 of Tikal Temple IV, Late Classic (after Jones and Satterthwaite 1982: fig. 74); (d) Stela 1, Piedras Negras (after Maler 1901: pl. 12); (e) detail of maize deity, Codex Dresden, page 9a, Postclassic period; (f) plumed maize ear, Mural 3, Tulum Structure 16 (after Miller 1982: pl. 39)

18. Bird tails as plumed maize ears in Maya iconography: (a) descending Principal Bird Deity, Abaj Takalik Altar 113, Late Preclassic period (detail of drawing courtesy of James Porter); (b) hummingbird with maize tail, detail of Early Classic incised vessel (after Berjonneau et al. 1985: pl. 329); (c) descending Principal Bird Deity with maize cob tail, Quirigua Monument 26 (after Jones 1983: figs. 13.1, 13.3); (d) Principal Bird Deity with plumed maize ear tail (after Hellmuth 1987: fig. 579); (e) descending macaw with maize tail, Copan Ballcourt (after Fash 1992: fig. 3c)

19. Quetzal plumes, jade, and the world tree in Mesoamerican iconography: (a) world tree with animate serpent necklace and Principal Bird Deity with plumed maize ear tail, Sarcophagus Lid, Palenque (drawing: Linda Schele); (b) world tree with animate serpent necklace and Principal Bird Deity with plumed maize ear tail, Tablet of the Temple of the Cross, Palenque (detail of drawing courtesy of Linda Schele); (c) Tlaloc with cruciform world tree with jade necklace and quetzal birds, detail of Early Classic Teotihuacán vessel (after Fondo Editorial de la Plástica Mexicana 1964: pl. 334); (d) doubled maize with quetzal bird and jade as central world tree, Codex Borgia, page 53, Late Postclassic period

of the world axis and, as such, were depicted with maize.

The most ambitious Maya rendering of corn as the world tree is the example mentioned from the Temple of the Foliated Cross (fig. 16e). The base of the trunk is marked with the quincunx sign, a pan-Mesoamerican symbol of the four quarters and central *axis mundi.* As mentioned, this sign was essentially identical in symbolic meaning to the bar and four dots motif so widely found with Olmec representations of maize. Although the quincunx typically contains a central dot, it can also be rendered as a cross, often referred to as the Kan Cross in Maya studies. The probable maize god from the aforementioned incised Olmec statuette sits atop such a cross (fig. 12f). In one Classic Maya scene, the Kan Cross appears in the center of a turtle shell, a Maya symbol for the earth (Freidel et al. 1993: fig. 4:27c). The maize god rises out of the cross, thereby marking him as the central world tree. Recent research indicates that, like the Olmecs, the Classic Maya also regarded corn as the central *axis mundi* (Freidel et al. 1993: 73–74).

The most complex Maya examples of world trees occur at Palenque, where they are shown as embodiments of abundance and wealth (figs. 16e, 19a–b). Mythical birds with long quetzal tail plumage perch atop the trees, and, on close inspection, it is clear that the tails are rendered as plumed ears of corn with celts as the cobs. Whereas the Temple of the Foliated Cross tree wears a conventional jade necklace, the necklaces of the Temple of the Cross and the Sarcophagus Lid are personified as bicephalic serpents. A thematically similar world tree occurs on an Early Classic Teotihuacán vessel, where the cruciform plants appear with a green jade necklace and quetzals (fig. 19c). The identification of the world tree with jade and quetzals continued in Late Postclassic Central Mexico. On page 53 of the Codex Borgia, a quetzal perches atop a maize plant marked with jade signs (fig. 19d). Seler (1963, 2: 88) noted that this tree marks the central *axis mundi* and is preceded by the trees of the four directions. As with the Middle Formative Olmecs, the world center is here marked as the place of maize, jade, and the quetzal.

Aztec Maize Symbolism

Along with the Middle Formative Olmecs and Classic Maya, jade and quetzals were closely identified with maize and agricultural abundance in Aztec thought. The Codex Chimalpopoca describes water and corn as the "true" jades and quetzal plumes of the rain gods (Bierhorst 1992: 156–157). In other words, agricultural fertility is the ultimate source of material wealth. Fray Diego Durán (1971: 155) describes the splendid riches associated with the Templo Mayor image of the rain god Tlaloc: "no other idol was more adorned or enriched with stones and splendid jewels than this, since all the foremost warriors and noblemen came to him with their gifts of magnificent stone and jewels." Durán (1971: 158) also mentions the costly offerings made by great warriors and nobility at the Tlaloc temple on Mount Tlaloc during the spring *veintena* festival of Huey Toçoztli: "everyone came in to make his offerings: one of them a mantle, another a jewel, another a

20. The double maize ear fetish and Chicomecoatl in Aztec art: (a) maize ear fetish with paper wrapping and *quetzalmiauayo* device (after Beyer 1969: fig. 3); (b) maize ear fetish with jade sign and *quetzalmiauayo,* Codex Borbonicus, page 20; (c) Chicomecoatl with double maize ears and *quetzalmiauayo* in headdress (after Nicholson 1977: fig. 6); (d) Stela of Chicomecoatl with *quetzalmiahuayo* and quetzal plume headdress, Monument 2, Castillo de Teayo, Veracruz (after Seler 1902–1923, 3: 423); (e) Chicomecoatl with double maize ear in headdress, Codex Borbonicus, page 30; see fig. 21 (after Seler 1902–1923, 3: 424)

precious stone or feathers. . . . After the offerings had been made, all went outside, leaving the chamber so rich in gold, jewels, stones, cloths, and feathers that [this wealth] might have enriched many paupers." During the late summer rites of Ochpaniztli concerning the maize goddess Chicomecoatl, the Aztec ruler redistributed other precious items to the warriors and nobles: "the sovereign of the land came in carrying splendid gifts: feathers, gems, gold, stones, arms, and insignia, shields, and other fine and precious things, such as earplugs, labrets of gold and silver, bracelets, and so forth, presenting a gift to each of the lords" (Durán 1971: 226). In the Aztec *veintena* rites of Huey Toçoztli and Ochpaniztli, the agricultural events of the spring rains and summer harvest were graphically expressed through the donation and redistribution of items of wealth.

In Late Postclassic Central Mexico, there were both male and female personifications of corn. Thus Cinteotl was the male maize god, whereas Chicomecoatl, or Xilonen, embodied the female aspect of corn. I focus on Chicomecoatl, who was specifically a maize goddess of the Aztecs, or Culhua-Mexica, and does not appear in the Borgia Group of Late Postclassic codices. Chicomecoatl, referring to the day Seven *(chicome)* Serpent *(coatl)* in the 260-day calendar, is perhaps the most commonly depicted deity in Aztec stone sculpture (see Beyer 1969; Nicholson 1977).

Among the more striking attributes of Chicomecoatl is a large, rectangular paper headdress marked with rosettes (fig. 20d–e). In addition, she commonly appears with a fetish of paired maize ears known as the *cemmaitl,* or "maize hand" (Nicholson 1977: 145). In Aztec codical depictions, this fetish often has quetzal plumes between the two ears of corn (fig. 20a–b). This feather element was known as the *quetzalmiauayo,* a term that describes the male pollen tassel of the maize plant as a quetzal plume (Seler 1902–1923, 2: 459). During the late summer Ochpaniztli *veintena* festival, the young Chicomecoatl impersonator wore this device on her head: "To the hair of the crown of this woman's head was tied a vertical green feather, which represented the tassels of the stalks of corn. It was tied with a red ribbon, indicating that at the time of this feast the maize was almost ripe but still green" (Durán 1971: 223). In Aztec art, Chicomecoatl often appears with the *quetzalmiauayo* tassel emerging from the center of the headdress (fig. 20c–e). Durán (1971: 222) mentioned that the richly dressed wooden statue of this goddess held imitation feather forms of the maize fetishes: "she held ears of corn, imitated in featherwork and garnished with gold." Moreover, in one stela portrayal of Chicomecoatl from Castillo de Teayo, Veracruz, the goddess wears a thick mass of long quetzal plumes at the top of her headdress (fig. 20d).

Along with being related to quetzal plumes, Chicomecoatl and the *cemmaitl* maize fetish often appear with jade. Quite frequently the *quetzalmiauayo* device is accompanied with a jade bead (Beyer 1969: 178). According to Durán (1971: 222), Chicomecoatl was also referred to as Chalchiuhcihuatl, meaning "jade woman," and in Aztec depictions she often appears with a prominent jade necklace (fig. 20c). Like the Olmec and later Maya corn deities, the Aztec maize goddess was solidly planted in the symbolism of precious jade and quetzal feathers.

Henry B. Nicholson (1977: 153) notes that many images of Chicomecoatl have the *cemmaitl* double maize ear topping the headdress (fig. 20c).[3] With the doubled maize ears and the central *quetzalmiauayo,* these images are essentially personified forms of the maize ear fetish. Fray Bernardino de Sahagún (1950–1982, 2: 63) mentions that during the spring ceremonies of Huey Toçoztli, young girls carried ears of corn wrapped in red paper anointed with rubber to the temple of Chicomecoatl. These ears were in groups of seven, a clear allusion to the goddess. In an Aztec song to Chicomecoatl, she is referred to as *chicomolotzin,* or seven corncob (Sahagún 1950–1982, 2: 242). In addition, both Chicomecoatl and the *cemmaitl* fetishes were frequently adorned with red-painted paper. Sahagún (1950–1982, 2: 65) describes the costume of Chicomecoatl during the Huey Toçoztli ceremony: "All her paper crown was covered completely with red ochre; her embroidered shift also was red." The ears carried by the girls represented both the heart and soul of the granary and the precious seed used for planting: "as they took them to the temple of Chicome coatl, [the ears of maize] were made hearts. They became their granary hearts. They laid them in the granary. And when the seed was sown, when it was the time for planting, this they sowed. They made seed of it, they scattered it as seed" (Sahagún 1950–1982, 2: 64).

Both Chicomecoatl and the double maize ear fetishes embodied the spirit of the maize, the fertile seed passed down through generations of planting. Double maize ear fetishes are still fashioned among contemporary Nahua of northern Veracruz, close descendants of the Postclassic Aztec: "The sacred twins, 7-Flower and 5-Flower, are represented by two or sometimes four unshucked ears of corn that are tied together and wrapped in a new red bandana. These adornments are called the eloconemej [Nahuatl for 'maize ear children']" (Sandstrom 1991: 293). The pairing of maize ears in a red bandana is markedly similar to the Aztec fetishes, which tend to be two ears wrapped in red-painted paper. Among the contemporary Nahua, 5-Flower and 7-Flower are the male and female seed spirits of corn who must be well cared for to prevent their departure from the community (Sandstrom 1991: 245).

Contemporary Mesoamerican lore is filled with warnings concerning the proper treatment of the living corn spirit. A Nahua tale recorded by Konrad Preuss (1907; English translation in Furst 1994: 137–146) from San Pedro Jícora, Durango, describes the tragic consequences of mistreating maize. A youth in search of corn finds the maize girls and brings one of the maidens to his household. The maize girl magically produces corn until she is forced to make tortillas. In cooking the maize, she blisters herself and returns to her home. Although the youth pleads for her to come back, he is only given five ears of corn for his granaries, which never produce the same amount again.

Among the Tzotzil of highland Chiapas, the maize spirit is embodied in a snake maiden, recalling the Aztec Chicomecoatl, or Seven Serpent (see Guiteras-Holmes 1961: 191–193; Gossen 1974: 267, 287, 311; Laughlin 1977: 165–170, 238–246). After leaving her underworld home with a youth, this snake girl magically produces great masses of corn for her new mate. However, after the youth stupidly beats her, she departs, leaving him and his household in abject poverty. A quite similar myth is known among the Huichol of western Mexico (Furst 1994; Shelton 1996). In the Huichol version, one of five girls of the basic colors of corn accompanies a youth as his wife. A granary marked with directional symbolism constitutes her home, where she magically creates great amounts of corn. However, her mother-in-law forces her to grind maize and, in so doing, she grinds away her arms and departs. This myth apparently constitutes a dire warning: never grind and consume the seed corn, since without it the spirit and source of future maize will be forever lost.

Peter Furst (1994: 148–149) compares elements of the Nahua and Huichol tales of the maize maiden to Chicomecoatl and the Aztec rites of Ochpaniztli. The Ochpaniztli *veintena* rites concern the purification of the community for the newly harvested corn. The term Ochpaniztli means "sweeping of the way," and as both Preuss (1907) and Furst (1994) note for the Huichol and Nahua myths, the coming of the modern maize maiden is also prepared by sweeping. The song to Chicomecoatl reveals that, like contemporary Mesoamerican peoples, the Aztecs were concerned with the departure of the corn spirit: "You are going to leave us bereft/ You are going to your home in Tlalocan" (Sahagún 1950–1982, 2: 241). Durán (1971: 425) mentions that during the spring rites of Huey Toçoztli, women pleaded for the maize goddess to hasten to the young growing corn: "the women cried out in loud voices, 'O my lady, come quickly!' They said this to the cornfields so that they would ripen soon, before the frost would fall upon them." What this spring rite appears to concern is the departure of Chicomecoatl and the rain gods from the underworld realm of Tlalocan to the Aztec fields.

Just as the granary of the Huichol maiden is filled with directional symbolism, the directions also played a prominent role in the Ochpaniztli ceremony. Sahagún (1950–1982, 2: 124) mentions scattering seed of the four colors of corn from a raised platform: "And when they had climbed up, they each flung forth, they each dispersed here, they scattered here on the people the seeds—white maize grains, yellow maize grains, black, red; and squash seeds." However, the clearest and most developed occurrence of directional symbolism with the Ochpaniztli rites occurs on pages 30 and 31 of the Aztec Codex Borbonicus. In these scenes, Chicomecoatl is surrounded by Tlalocs, the lords of clouds, rain, lightning, and the realm of Tlalocan, the home of the maize spirit.

A series of deity impersonators march across the upper portion of Borbonicus page 30. Four of the five figures have headdresses marked by two hornlike elements, and it is likely that they portray the two-horned god, a poorly known Aztec deity (see Nagao 1985). These four individuals wear costumes of the four color directions, starting with black on the left, then white, yellow, and finally red. They flank a central figure wearing a distinct green costume, here denoting the middle place. Below this scene is another set of deity impersonators (fig. 21). The four flanking figures have the same order of colors appearing in the procession immediately above, blue (rather than black), white, yellow, and red. The masks worn in the center of their headdresses identify them as Tlaloc impersonators. The central figure is the maize goddess Chicomecoatl dressed in multicolored paper to indicate the central *axis mundi*. Immediately below is a fifth Tlaloc figure dressed in the same multicolored paper to represent the fifth and central rain god.

On Borbonicus page 30, the two sets of color directional figures carry three ritual items, a bag, an ear of corn, and a celt wrapped in paper. Both the bag and the paper around the celt are the same directional color as the impersonator costume. Although at first glance each celt appears to be attached to a bag handle (Borbonicus page 5), each is clearly a separate item. The Aztec paper-wrapped celt appears to be closely related to powers of water and lightning. Thus, whereas it is wielded by the Tlalocs on Borbonicus pages 30 and 31, the water goddess Chalchiuhtlicue holds the celt on Borbonicus page 5. Moreover, in the Telleriano-Remensis

21. Chicomecoatl impersonator surrounded by four-color directional Tlalocs holding celts and maize ears; detail of Codex Borbonicus, page 30

22. Chicomecoatl impersonator in bed of maize surrounded by four-color directional Tlalocs wielding paper-wrapped celts and larger examples in the four color directions; detail of Codex Borbonicus, page 31

and Vaticanus A scenes for the *trecena* 1 Rain, Nahui Ehecatl (a deity displaying traits of Ehecatl and Tlaloc) wields both the celt and copal bag and an undulating lightning serpent. José Corona Nuñez (1964, 3: 70) suggests that the object wielded in these two scenes is a gold or copper celt. The Vaticanus A celt appears to lack the paper handle wrapping and the accompanying copal bag and, in form, is virtually identical to the large colored celts on Borbonicus page 31.

Holding celts in one hand and ears of corn in the other, the four Tlaloc figures on Borbonicus page 30 are strongly evocative of Formative Olmec maize symbolism. As in Olmec iconography, the directional celts are compared to ears of corn and are used to define a central world axis embodied as maize. The use of the four directional celts continues on Borbonicus page 31 (fig. 22). Tlaloc impersonators of the four color directions surround a central maize goddess impersonator lying on a bed of corn. In one hand, each Tlaloc figure holds a colored bag and paper-wrapped celt, and in the other hand each grasps a vertical, batonlike object colored according to the corresponding directions. The slightly flaring outlines of these objects suggest that they are massive directional celts.

Aside from the Borbonicus pages, there is a remarkable three-dimensional Aztec depiction of the four directional Tlalocs surrounding Chicomecoatl as the central world axis. A stone box from Tizapan contained a greenstone image of Chicomecoatl holding maize ear fetishes in both hands (fig. 23a). Placed atop a painting of the Aztec symbol of jade, she clearly embodies the concept of Chalchiuhcihuatl, the maize goddess as "jade woman." The painted interior of the lid contains another jade sign, here supported by four Tlalocs in the directional colors of black, yellow, white, and red (fig. 23b). When the lid is placed on the box, the four Tlalocs hover above and surround the greenstone maize goddess of the central place.[4]

American Southwest Maize Symbolism

In the American Southwest, corn first appears near the beginning of the first millennium B.C.; "directly dated Archaic *Zea mays* remains suggest that by 3,000 years ago, people in New Mexico grew maize" (Adams 1994: 278). During the next thousand years—roughly equivalent to the Middle and Late Formative of Mesoamerica—maize became widely distributed in the region. It is generally considered that the Southwestern varieties of maize derived from central and western Mesoamerican varieties (Fedick 1995: 285; Hernández Xolocotzi 1985; Sánchez González 1994: 146–149). Although the regional comparisons of Southwestern and Mesoamerican maize have primarily focused on genetic and morphological data pertaining to the plant itself, much of the attendant Puebloan imagery and ritual concerning corn also point to Mesoamerican origins. Moreover, it is particularly intriguing that much of these ancient and contemporary Puebloan data are especially similar to the incipient maize iconography of Formative Mesoamerica.

As in the case of Mesoamerica, maize is a central component of Puebloan religious thought: "Corn is the body and spirit of Pueblo life" (White 1942: 204). According to the Hopi, "people are corn," with the growth cycle of the plant being equated with human birth, maturation, and death (Black 1984). In addition, maize is also closely identified with directional symbolism (Bohrer 1994). According to Carroll Riley (1963), this great elaboration of color directional symbolism constitutes one of the most striking traits shared between Mesoamerica and the American Southwest. As in Mesoamerican thought, particular colors of maize are commonly identified with the world directions in the American Southwest. Among the Hopi, six specific colored types of corn are oriented to the four directions as well as the zenith and nadir (Geertz 1987: 18). For the four divisions of the horizontal plane, the cobs can be positioned to either the world corners or the cardinal points (fig. 24a). A ceramic canteen excavated at Gran Quivera, New Mexico, indicates that the use of corn as directional markers is an ancient tradition in the American Southwest. Dating to approximately A.D. 1650, the vessel portrays four maize plants atop stepped directional clouds. A crossed circle, delineating the world axis, lies at the center of this quadripartite arrangement (fig. 24b). It will be recalled that in ancient Mesoamerica the cross or quincunx is widely used to represent the world center and in this context commonly appears with corn (for example, figs. 12f, 16e).

Maize Ear Fetishes

Aside from representing the four directions, particular maize ears also serve as ritual embodiments of supernatural power, often as symbols of the pivotal *axis mundi.* These maize ear fetishes, occurring widely among both the Eastern and Western Pueblos, are among the most potent and cherished items of Puebloan ceremonialism: "Among different types of fetish, stones, wooden or stone images of the Spirits, or masks, the ear of corn is preeminently sacred or precious" (Parsons 1939: 319).

The most important maize ear fetishes are typically formed of an upright, perfect, and

23. The Tizapan box, Chicomecoatl surrounded by four-color directional Tlalocs: (a) greenstone image of Chicomecoatl originally placed on interior jade sign as probable reference to Chalchiuhcihuatl (after Pasztory 1983: pl. 270); (b) four Tlalocs surrounding jade sign on interior lid of Tizapan box (after Broda 1996: fig. 5)

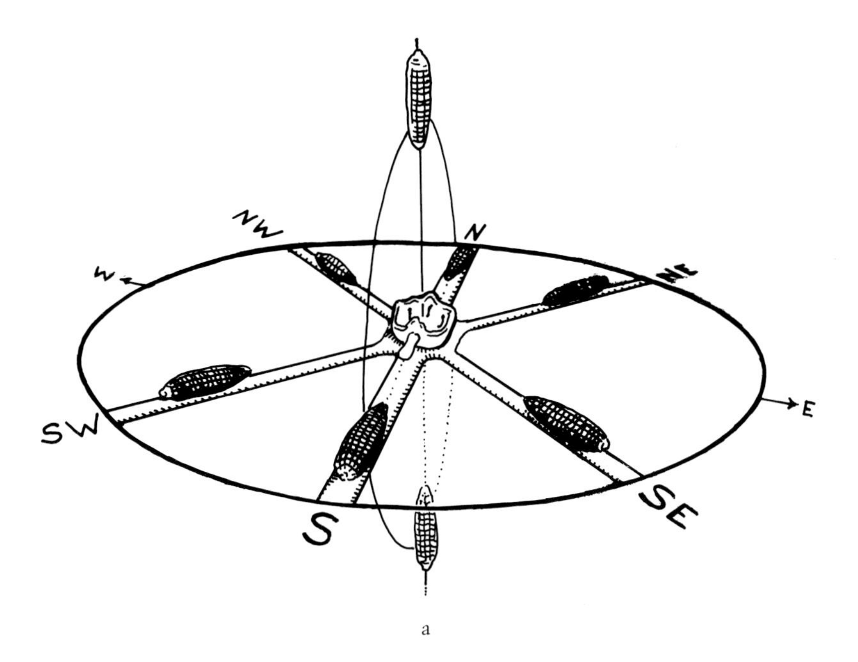

24. Maize and directional symbolism in the American Southwest: (a) maize of six directions surrounding medicine water bowl, Hopi (after Geertz 1987: fig. 1); (b) early seventeenth-century representation of directional clouds and maize surrounding central crossed circle, detail of ceramic canteen excavated at Gran Quivera (Las Humanas), New Mexico (after Hayes et al. 1981: fig. 115j)

completely kerneled ear of corn enclosed in a spray of long feathers, the whole affair being bound at the base by cotton thread, basketry, or lashed splints (Parsons 1939: 321–323; Smith 1952: 198–200). Thus, as in the case of the Olmec maize fetishes, the precious feathers serve much like a symbolic husk for the perfect ear. Like the Aztec Chicomecoatl maize fetishes, the Puebloan examples also seem to embody the concept of seed corn, the precious maize used for planting. At Isleta the specific type of fully kerneled corn used for fetishes is also saved for planting: "Such ears when found at husking are kept in their husk in the store room for planting. They are placed first in the stack—i.e., they are under the stack—and they are placed with a song" (Parsons 1932: 277). Elsie Parsons (1939: 320) notes that the Zuni also place such perfectly kerneled corn cobs in their granaries. At Sia the maize fetishes are dismantled every four years to be used at planting (Stevenson 1894: 40, note 1), while at Zuni and Cochiti, the seeds of a maize fetish are planted at the death of the owner (Parsons 1939: 322–323). It would appear that, as with the Aztec Chicomecoatl examples, the Puebloan fetishes constitute the vital source and life of corn and, by extension, humanity.

Puebloan maize fetishes are frequently bedecked with a strand of valuable beads, not only to denote their precious quality but also to portray them as animate beings wearing necklaces (figs. 25a, 26a–b; Stevenson 1904: 417; Parsons 1920: 96; 1936b: 80; 1939: 299; Stirling 1942: 32; White 1962: 309). With their projecting feathers and lower binding, these fetishes are strikingly similar to the precious feather bundles traded extensively over ancient Mesoamerica (figs. 25–27). Moreover, these contemporary maize fetishes tend to contain feathers of the Mesoamerican macaw which, in antiquity, were surely brought in similarly appearing feather bundles into the American Southwest. As feathered maize ears, these Puebloan items are especially like the Olmec torch fetishes of Formative Mesoamerica, which also could appear as personified beings (figs. 11–13, 15). In addition, it is noteworthy that, as with the Olmec examples, the Puebloan fetishes are closely identified with the world axis as conduits of divine power.

Feathered maize fetishes are of considerable antiquity in the American Southwest. Two examples of maize fetishes were discovered at Antelope House (Hall and Dennis 1986). Dating to late Pueblo III, or approximately A.D. 1300, they were supplied with feathers of the Mesoamerican macaw. Moreover, feathered maize fetishes are quite common in protohistoric Pueblo IV mural paintings, including examples at Pottery Mound, Awatovi, and Kawaika-a (see Smith 1952; Hibben 1975). These maize fetishes are typically rendered as cylindrical objects topped with a spray of feathers and, in this regard, closely resemble the probable Late Preclassic maize fetish appearing on the brow of an Isthmian Maize God from Chiapa de Corzo (fig. 27a).

Wrapped with cotton string, the heart of the Hopi feathered maize ear fetish, or *tiponi*, contains a maize ear filled with food-bearing seeds in its partly hollowed base (fig. 25a–c; Parsons 1936b: 800; Geertz 1987: 17).[5] Armin Geertz (1987: 17) notes the importance of this fetish in Hopi ritual and thought: "The central item of every ceremonial (and consequently every altar) is the *tiiponi.* Without it the society is destitute and weak, being unable to perform a vigorous ceremonial. It is owned by the clan and is used by the elder who has charge of that ceremonial. It is his symbol of authority, and those who have *tiiponis* have a special relationship with the Cloud Deities. . . . It is the mother of the people, the heart of the clan." The small wooden cup supporting the hollowed base of the Flute Society *tiponi* indicates its role as a symbolic *axis mundi.* In the nineteenth-century examples illustrated by Jesse Fewkes and Alexander Stephen, the cup sides are marked with colored maize indicating the four directions and, for the Fewkes example, stepped directional clouds as well (fig. 25b–c). The circular base of both cups displays a pair of transecting lines, which according to Parsons (1939: 322) constitute "the glyph of the directions," in other words, the *axis mundi.*[6] For the Fewkes example, the placement of the four directional ears and stepped clouds around the central circular cross is virtually identical to the previously mentioned Gran Quivera representation, much as if the ancient vessel scene were a flattened-out version of the Hopi cup (figs. 24b, 25c). In the case of the Hopi *tiponi,* the erect maize ear occupies the crossed circle demarcating the middle place. A Pueblo IV mural from Pottery Mound also portrays a feathered maize fetish with a cross placed at the base (fig. 27h).

The meaning of the *tiponi* as a symbolic world axis is also expressed by its use in Hopi ritual: "The *tiiponi* is the first thing that is set up when building an altar. It is waved *from* the six directions and is then placed on a hill of valley sand which represents the Hopi land"

a

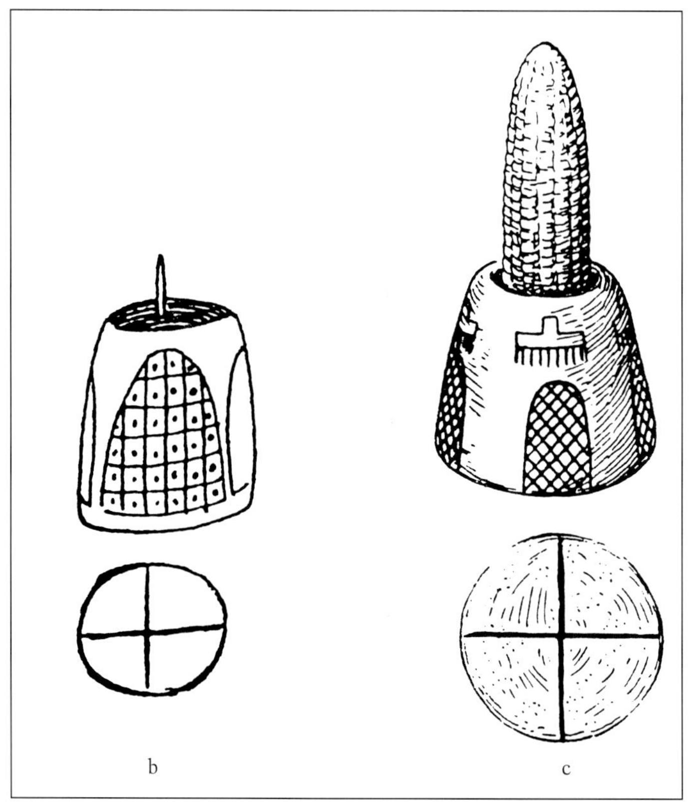

b

c

25. The Hopi *tiponi* feathered maize ear fetish: (a) two examples of *tiponi;* note bead necklaces (after Geertz 1987: pl. 1a); (b) interior cup of Flute Society *tiponi* with directional maize ears and cross on base (after Parsons 1936b: fig. 434); (c) interior cup of Flute Society *tiponi* with directional rain clouds and maize ears with cross on base; compare with fig. 24b (after Fewkes 1900: fig. 46)

26. Feathered maize ear fetishes of Zuni and Sia, New Mexico: (a) the Zuni *mili*; note basketry base with necklace and macaw feathers (after Stevenson 1904: pl. 101); (b) the Sia *iariko* fetish with necklace and macaw feathers (after Stevenson 1894: pl. 9)

(Geertz 1987: 17). The ritual waving from the six directions is an act of centering, and, as Geertz (1984: 223–224) noted, the Hopi territory is considered the middle place or world axis, as is also the *sipaapuni* place of emergence. Linking the worlds of sky, earth, and underworld, the *axis mundi* is widely considered to be a means of summoning supernatural powers into the human plane (Eliade 1964). The *tiponi* serves a very similar function in Hopi ritual: "In most ceremonials a meal path is laid from the *tiiponi* to the eastern side of the ladder and thus directly beneath the open hatchway. Upon or beneath this path is placed a *pöötavi* [symbolic road of string tipped with down feather]. It is the road travelled upon by the gods and spirits, and no human may cross that road" (Geertz 1987: 18).

In a Niman altar ceremony witnessed by Stephen (Parsons 1936b: 512), a *tiponi* was placed at the center of a set of cornmeal lines representing the six directions, clearly denoting the fetish as the world axis. This fetish was also supplied with the *pöötavi* string spirit path (Parsons 1936b: fig. 286). As an *axis mundi*, the Hopi *tiponi* serves as a conduit for life-giving supernatural forces summoned during kiva ritual.

Among the Keresan-speaking peoples of Acoma, Laguna, and the Eastern Pueblos of the Rio Grande, the feathered maize ear fetish embodies and is usually named as the great maize mother and creator goddess (fig. 26b). Generally referred to as Iariko or Iatiku, the Keresan goddess dwells at Shipap, the central place of origin and emergence (Parsons 1939: 182). This concept of Iyatiku residing in the pivotal *sipapu* recalls the Hopi god of maize and germination, Muingwu, who dwells in the central nadir in the underworld with all of the other five directional colors and animals of the zenith and horizontal plane: "Below sits Mü'inyiñwu on Sihchomo, Flower Mound. He wears a mask of clouds in all these five colors and before it flutter all the sacred birds and all the butterflies" (Parsons 1936b: 333).

Like the Hopi maize fetishes, the Keresan examples are ritual sources of life-giving power, as can be seen in the following description of the Santa Ana *iariko*: "The iarikos are placed

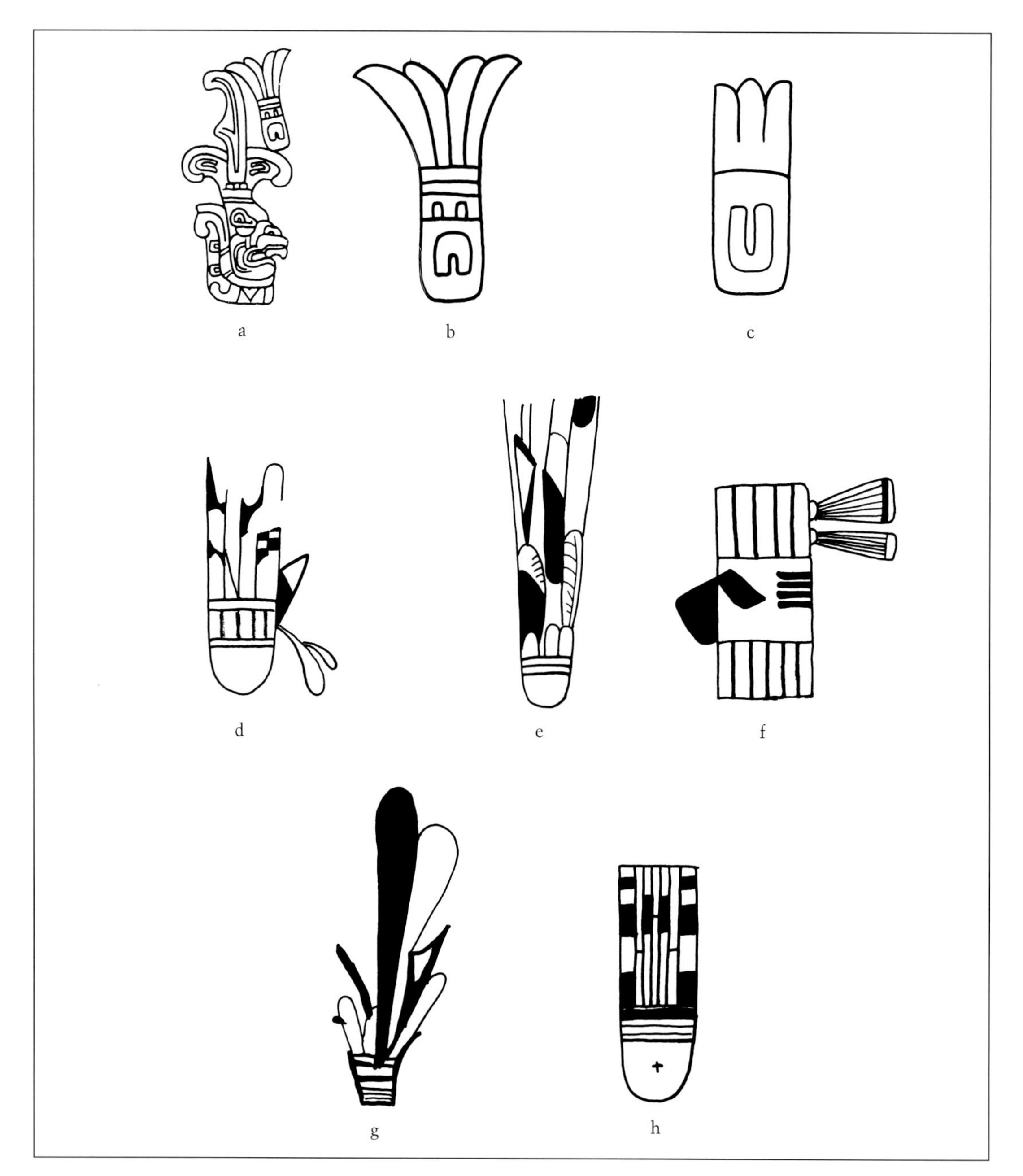

27. Comparison of probable representations of Late Preclassic maize ear fetishes of southeastern Mesoamerica with examples from Pueblo IV murals of the American Southwest: (a) probable maize fetish on brow of Isthmian Maize God, Bone 3, Chiapa de Corzo (after Taube 1996: fig. 18f); (b) detail of feathered fetish; note double merlon sign; (c) possible Late Preclassic Maya maize fetish, Abaj Takalik Stela 41 (detail after drawing courtesy of James Porter); (d–f) Pueblo IV maize fetishes from Awatovi, Arizona (after Smith 1952: fig. 14); (g, h) Pueblo IV maize fetishes from Pottery Mound, New Mexico (after Hibben 1975: figs. 88, 5)

upon the altar during ceremonies. They 'sit there' representing Iatik, the mother, and through this feather-decked ear of corn the medicinemen are able to secure ianyi [supernatural power] from naiya (mother) Iatik to bestow upon the people" (White 1942: 340). As embodiments of maize mother at Shipap, the Keresan fetishes are also replications of the sacred place of emergence, that is, the *axis mundi.* Perhaps for this reason, four arrow points are attached to sides of the Laguna maize fetish, which may allude to four directional lightnings, and by extension clouds, of the horizontal plane (see Parsons 1920: 96). At Acoma an image of Iatiku explicitly represents the world axis: "This prayer-stick is 'the centre pole, four earths down and four skies up' which holds sky and earth together . . . it is depicted as a figurine (of Iyatiku) girt with beads and downy eagle feathers" (Parsons 1939: 884). Although not a corn ear fetish, this image of maize mother is similarly dressed with the bead necklace and downy feathers commonly found with maize fetishes.

Like the Hopi *tiponi,* the Keresan corn fetish typically holds seeds of corn, melon, squash, and other food-giving plants in its hollowed base (see Parsons 1920: 96). However, honey is the content of the Acoma form, known as *honani*: "Honey was chosen because it comes from all kinds of plants and therefore symbolizes all plant food. The honey in the cob meant that there would always be food. It would be as a seed or source of all food to come" (Stirling 1942: 32). Along with representing the symbolic source of food plants, the Acoma *honani* fetish is also identified with precious valuables, namely, turquoise and shell. During the mythical creation of the first *honani* by Iatiku, a turquoise was placed under the fetish, thereby endowing this stone with value and power. As the necklace of this first maize fetish, abalone, turquoise, and shell beads also became precious, esteemed items: "All these things were to be sacred and valuable from then on" (Stirling 1942: 32). According to this Keresan account, the value of these materials ultimately derives from corn, a concept recalling the ancient Mesoamerican comparison of maize to precious jade and quetzal plumes. Moreover, as with the two Mesoamerican materials, beads of shell and turquoise are used as items of payment and wealth in the American Southwest, in other words, as primitive valuables (see Parsons 1939: 36, 299).[7] The Sia *iariko,* or *ya'ya* (mother), maize fetishes are also identified with items of wealth, in this case exotic feathers of the Mesoamerican macaw: "The ya'ya are most carefully preserved, not only on account of their sacred value, but also of their intrinsic worth, as the parrot plumes of which they are partially composed are very costly and difficult to obtain" (Stevenson 1894: 76). Along with the Olmec and Aztec examples, the Puebloan maize ear fetish embodies abundance and wealth.

Lightning Celts

Along with the use of feathered maize ear fetishes, the identification of directional celts with lightning and maize is also fully present in contemporary Hopi ritual. Commonly referred to as *chamahiya,* these thin and beautifully worked celts closely resemble ancient Mesoamerican examples and are quite unlike traditional Pueblo axeheads (fig. 28a; see Woodbury 1954: 165–169, 35; Ellis 1967). Indeed, *chamahiya* are well known from archaeological excavations, particularly from late Pueblo II and Pueblo III sites in the San Juan drainage area. According to Earl Morris (1939: 166), the lovely banded hornfels typically used for *chamahiya* derives from an area close to Four Corners. A number of authors have suggested that they served as functional tools, either as hoes (Woodbury 1954: 166–167; Judd 1954: 245) or as skinning knives (Ellis 1967). However, Arthur Rohn (1971: 248) suggests that they may never have been used for tools and notes that hornfels is poorly suited for working soil: "the brittle hornfels would probably be one of the last materials selected for heavy-duty agricultural work even if it had been readily obtainable" (Rohn 1971: 247). In addition, the discovery of *chamahiya* in excavated kivas suggests that they had an important ceremonial function in antiquity (Rinaldo 1974: 307; Wheeler 1980: 285).

Among contemporary Puebloan peoples, *chamahiya* celts are purely ceremonial and are generally considered as powerful objects of remote antiquity: "warrior spirits, anthropomorphic beings of an earlier age, turned to stone" (Parsons 1936a: 555). The Hopi term *chamahiya* derives from the Keresan word for the "ancients" (Ellis 1967: 37). Along with being revered as ancient objects, the *chamahiya* celts are identified with the four directions and lightning and constitute a prominent component of the rain and lightning symbolism of the Hopi snake dance. The following nineteenth-century account by Stephen describes the *chamahiya* used with the Hopi snake ceremonies: "The *chama'hiya,* the celts upon the altar, are from the Chiefs of the directions. . . . They are the very precious knives of these deities . . . the sacred piercers fallen from the Above. The *chama'hiya shinyümü* are originally of the Stone People, Owa'nyümü, Owa'shinyümü, of the Stone when it had speech and life, and these people were spread to the four corners of the earth" (Parsons 1936b: 707). According to Don Talayesva of Oraibi, the *katsina* are the servants of the directional chiefs, the clouds of the six directions (Geertz 1984: 228). The *chamahiya* celts are the lightning weapons of these powerful beings.

For one Hopi Powamu kiva initiation sandpainting recorded for Oraibi, directional *chamahiya* and stepped clouds frame the *sipapu,* the middle place of emergence (fig. 28b). The cruciform layout of these celts is strikingly similar to the Middle Formative Olmec cache from San Isidro, Chiapas (see fig. 3).[8] In addition, the *chamahiya* are paired with color-directional maize cobs, immediately recalling the widespread Olmec relation of celts with ears of corn. However, the identification of *chamahiya* with maize ears goes much further. A petroglyph from the Three Rivers area of southern New Mexico, dating to approximately A.D. 1000–1400, portrays a maize plant descending from a directional cloud and bird (fig. 28c). Polly Schaafsma (personal communication, 1995) has noted that the undulating maize appears to be lightning emanating from the cloud. The flaring maize ears apparently are rendered as *chamahiya*—flat-topped with no capping silk. This remarkable petroglyph seems to portray lightning as the corn of the directional cloud chiefs, with *chamahiya* celts its produce.

As emblems of lightning and maize, the *chamahiya* celts play an important role in the summer Hopi snake ceremonies. Along with mentioning the identification of *chamahiya* with the Cloud Chiefs of the directions, Stephen also notes their prominent role in the snake dance at Walpi: "The Chama'hiya were very excellent . . . they well knew all concerning Snake ceremonies, they swallowed the snakes, as the Naso'tan swallow sticks. . . . The snake went down into the stomach and was drawn up again, and rain speedily followed" (Parsons 1936b: 707). This text suggests that *chamahiya* embody the original snake dancers. This may partly explain the body paint recorded for Hopi snake dancers. Stephen describes the pattern at Shipaulovi on Second Mesa: "they lay the smear outside of calf, mid thigh, forearm, and upper arm, on each breast and on stomach" (Parsons 1936b: 754). Although the body decoration can be rapidly painted, the forms tend to be roughly triangular, narrow and pointed at the base and broad at the top. What these forms clearly resemble are *chamahiya* celts (fig. 29). The symmetrical and bit-upward placement of these painted celts on the body immediately recalls Olmec depictions of celts on the human body (figs. 4d–f, 9d; see Taube 1996: figs. 9, 10).[9]

Just as there is a convergence of celt and feathered maize fetish imagery in Olmec iconography, there is a similar merging of *chamahiya* with corn fetishes in Puebloan thought. Parsons (1920: 118, fig. 19; 1939: 194) notes that at Laguna, *chamahiya (samahiye)* are conical stones dressed with the feathers and necklace of the *iyatiku* maize fetishes. Such conical stones are well known in the archaeology and ethnology of the American Southwest, where they are frequently interpreted as images of maize deities, such as the Hopi Muingwu or the Keresan Iatiku (Fewkes 1924: 388; Hayes and Lancaster 1975: 163–164).[10] At the Village of the Great Kivas, Frank Roberts (1932: 61, pls. 10, 55) excavated a pair of these objects flanking a kiva niche. Both were supplied with hollowed bases, immediately recalling the frequently hollowed and cuplike ends of maize ear fetishes. At Acoma the *chamahiya* of the Kapina society can be substituted by a pair of maize ear fetishes (Ellis 1967: 39). In an Acoma creation myth recorded by Matthew Stirling

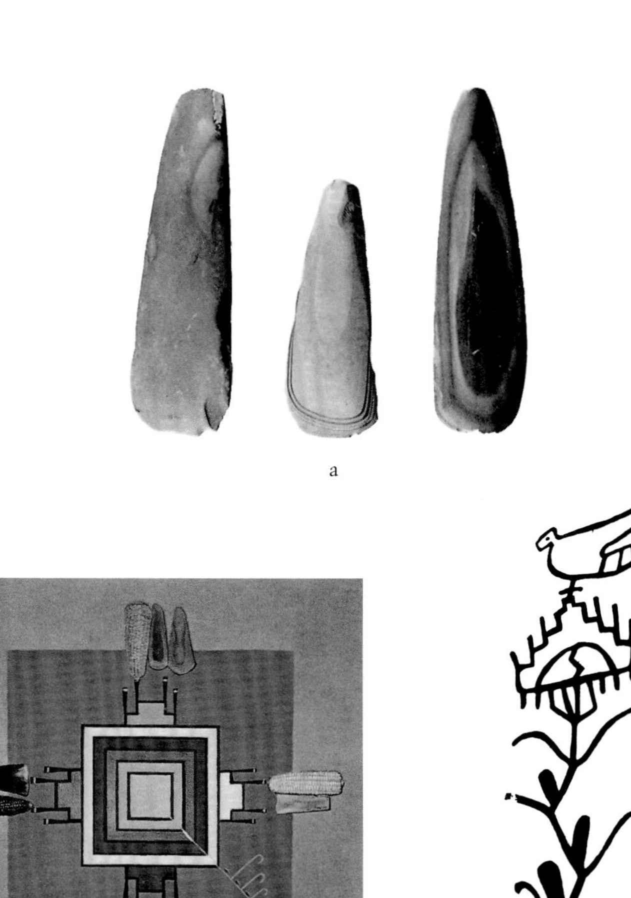

28. *Chamahiya* celts of the American Southwest: (a) three *chamahiya* from Mug House, Colorado (after Rohn 1971: fig. 296a); (b) colored *chamahiya*, maize ears, and clouds surrounding the middle place, or *sipapu*, Hopi Powamu sand painting, Oraibi (after Voth 1901: pl. 52); (c) lightning maize with *chamahiya* descending from directional cloud

29. The painting of *chamahiya* on the bodies of Hopi Snake Dance participants: (a) pair of Snake Priests with *chamahiya* body paint in Antelope Kiva, Oraibi (detail of photograph after Dorsey and Voth 1902: pl. 102); (b) Snake Priest with lightning frame; note painted *chamahiya* on limbs (detail after Dorsey and Voth 1902: pl. 109); (c) snake dancers with *chamahiya* painted on limbs and torso, community unknown (after Fewkes 1986, reproduced courtesy of Special Collections, Zimmerman Library, University of New Mexico)

a

b

c

(1942: 37), the pair of maize fetishes were termed *tsamaiya* and *umahia,* with the former being female and the latter male. According to Leslie White (1943: 309), these maize fetishes are called Tsamahi'a and Tsamai'ye. Associated with war power, the two fetishes are conceptually similar to the stone *chamahiya.*

The most striking merging of *chamahiya* and feathered maize fetishes occurs with the feathered *tiponi* used in the Hopi snake ceremonies at Oraibi and Mishongnovi, where *chamahiya* substitute for the central, vertical ear of corn (Dorsey and Voth 1902: 209–210; Voth 1903: 304). The following is a description of one of the two Mishongnovi *tiponi*: "Within the circle of eagle tail feathers and entirely concealed by them was a handsome and finely polished jasper celt, yellow in color, and about ten inches in length" (Dorsey and Voth 1902: 209–210). In a photograph of one of the two Oraibi *tiponi,* the *chamahiya* projects bit upward out of the fetish (Voth 1903: pl. 171). Henry R. Voth (1903: 304) provides a description of thc Oraibi *tiponis*: "The two tiponis are made, as far as I could ascertain, of a round piece of báhko (lit. 'water root,' meaning cottonwood root), into the upper end of which is inserted an old celt measuring three to four inches in width and probably eight inches in length. Around this are placed some old eagle wing feathers that are tied to the piece of báhko, the latter being closely wound with buckskin thong." The insertion of *chamahiya* into a hollowed piece of cottonwood may explain the secondary waisting seen on many prehistoric *chamahiya* (see Woodbury 1954: figs. 35e–f, h–j). The narrowing or waisting of the poll end would allow the *chamahiya* to be more readily set into the socket of a wood cylinder. The waisting on these ancient celts suggests that the Puebloan identification of maize *tiponi* with *chamahiya* is of considerable antiquity in the American Southwest.

As in the case of Flute Society maize *tiponi*, the bottom of the Mishongnovi *chamahiya* fetishes was marked with a cross delineating the four directional quarters, thereby identifying the item as the pivotal world axis (Dorsey and Voth 1902: 210). Similarly, in one episode of the Mishongnovi myth describing the origin of the snake ceremonies at Walpi, the first *tiponi* contained an entire snake and the rattles of three other directional snakes of the horizontal plane as well as feathers from the birds of the six directions:

> *At the first Snake Ceremony, the first Snake Chief sent his nephew to hunt snakes; the first day he sent him to the north, the second day to the west, the third day to the south, the fourth day to the east. He brought one snake from each direction. The snake priest then hollowed out a piece of bako. . . . Into this he placed one of the snakes and the rattles of the remaining three snakes, closing up the hole with a corn ear. Around this he tied small and large eagle feathers and the feathers of the six directional birds. . . . He then wrapped all this with a buckskin thong which made it very strong. After this the ceremony was celebrated.* (Dorsey and Voth 1902: 260–261)

The rattles placed in the mythical *tiponi* also recall the symbolism of certain Olmec maize fetishes, in which the corncob tip alludes to a rattlesnake tail (fig. 12a, f).

In Hopi myth, the summer snake ceremonies originated when Snake Youth went to the underworld in search of precious substances, such as shells and beads, as well as food (Fewkes 1897: 301–303; Dorsey and Voth 1902: 256–261; Voth 1903: 349–353). During his journey, he meets Snake Maiden, who returns with him as his bride. In closely related versions of this myth reported for Mishongnovi and Oraibi, the youth also returns with a miraculous sack from which precious shell and stone beads continually multiply (Dorsey and Voth 1902; Voth 1903). Of course, this concept of regenerating wealth is not a trait of precious, inanimate objects but of seeds and crops. In the Oraibi account, the sack also contains seeds of corn, melon, and other plants. For his return journey, the youth was cautioned neither to sleep with Snake Maiden nor to open the treasure-producing sack. In the Mishongnovi account, the youth opens the sack and, as the result, the people remain poor (Dorsey and Voth 1902: 259–260).

In the Oraibi version of the Hopi snake myth, the youth obeys the instructions and returns with both Snake Maiden and the precious sack: "The contents of the sack they distributed among themselves, they were very happy about the beads. The young woman [Snake Maiden] then always prepared food for the people" (Voth 1903: 352). The description of Snake Maiden feeding the people is especially intriguing in the light of the previous discussion of Chicomecoatl, or Seven Serpent, the Aztec maize goddess. Although making no mention of Mesoamerican lore, Fewkes (1897: 301) suggested that the Hopi serpent wife is but a version of Corn Maiden: "I think that Snake-maid is simply a personification of Corn-maid." Fewkes (1897: 302) also mentioned that Snake Maiden gave birth to seven snakes, immediately recalling the Aztec Chicomecoatl. The Hopi Snake Maiden is also strikingly similar to the aforementioned serpent maize girl of contemporary highland Maya lore, who also becomes the bride of a youth who journeys to the underworld. In one Tzotzil version from Zinacantan, the maize girl leaves her children a treasure chest that magically produces coins (Laughlin 1977: 244–245). It would appear that the Formative concept of maize as the producer of wealth continues to thrive in native thought of both Mesoamerica and the American Southwest.

Conclusion

Among the Formative Olmec, maize was more than mere food; it constituted a model of their world, serving as a symbol of the four corners or directions as well as the central *axis mundi*, a conduit of divine power. In Olmec iconography, maize was compared to two valued objects, these being greenstone celts and quetzal plumes. Quite frequently, Olmec celts represented the four directions or corners and the world axis. As among the Classic Maya, Postclassic Aztec, and contemporary Hopi, such celts may also have evoked the related powers of rain and lightning as well as maize. The Olmec "torch motif" is actually a feather-wrapped corn ear, evoking both the concept of precious feather bundles as well as maize. The sacred feathered maize fetishes used among pre-Hispanic and contemporary Puebloan peoples are strikingly similar to the Formative Olmec examples, despite the fact that these specific forms remain to be well documented for post-Formative Mesoamerica. Among Puebloan peoples, the feathered ear fetish also serves as an *axis mundi,* a pivotal means of summoning powers of life and fertility. The same can be said for the Puebloan *chamahiya* celts of rain and lightning. Both the form and use of these celts as directional markers and as symbolic maize strongly evoke the elaborate celt and maize iconography noted for the Formative Olmec.

In both Mesoamerica and the American Southwest, maize is closely identified with serpents. Thus the maize ear fetish of the Middle Formative Olmec can appear with a serpent head at its base. This maize fetish form may represent a plumed serpent with the rattlesnake tail replaced by an ear of corn. Similarly, in the Walpi Snake Maiden myth, the first maize *tiponi* contained a rattlesnake and rattles of three others. Quite frequently, maize is personified as a serpent being in Mesoamerican and Puebloan thought. Thus there is the Hopi Snake Maiden, a probable aspect of the Corn Maiden, who is strikingly similar to the Aztec Chicomecoatl and Snake Girl of the contemporary Tzotzil Maya. Not only is the Aztec maize goddess named Seven Serpent, but she can also appear wearing a serpent headdress (see Beyer 1969: figs. 1–10). In addition, both the Classic Zapotec and Isthmian corn deities have serpent buccal masks (see Taube 1996).

Although it is possible to note many striking details shared between the maize symbolism of Mesoamerica and the American Southwest, the larger pattern is more essential and profound. By the Middle Formative period, ears of corn and celts defined the four corners or directions and the *axis mundi.* Among the Olmec and later peoples, there is some semantic shifting and ambiguity between the corners and the cardinal points. Thus, whereas there are the four cardinal directions, humanly constructed space—whether it be maize fields or structures—has broad sides rather than points oriented to the directions. In this context, the corners have an especially prominent role as the four points. This ambiguity and tension between the cardinal points and the corners is reflected in the directional symbolism of Olmec celts. Whereas celt caches are oriented to the cardinal points, scenes in Olmec art place the celts at the corners.

Although the Olmec organization of the world with maize ears and celts to mark the four corners or directions and center was wonderfully simple and elegant, it had the ability to be replicated in myriad forms. Such a pattern could readily have spread among different peoples having their own distinct languages and religious traditions. Although such specifics as particular directional colors may vary among cultures, the overall pattern remains the same. In her discussion of maize symbolism, Vorsila Bohrer (1994) notes the widespread importance of the four corners and center in Mesoamerican and Puebloan thought. With its equidistant corners marking the middle place, the quincunx model of the cosmos is widely identified with the maize field in Mesoamerican thought. On Borgia pages 27 and 28, five directional Tlalocs and maize fields appear in a quincunx pattern, with the fifth Tlaloc representing the central point.

The identification of the quincunx with corn fields is most graphically represented in planting methods and ritual. Among the contemporary Tzeltal Maya of Tenejapa, Chiapas, corn is planted with a measuring stick in a quincunx pattern (Berlin et al. 1974: 126). In planting ceremonies recorded for the Yucatec, Chorti, and Tzotzil Maya, offerings are made to the four corners and center of the field (Redfield and Villa Rojas 1934: 115; Wisdom 1940: 439–440; Vogt 1976: 55). The following is a description of the Chorti field ceremony: "At sunrise the milpa owner goes to his cleared milpas and digs a small hole at each corner of one of them. In each he buries one fowl, preferably a turkey. . . . This is done at each of the four corners. He then digs a small hole in the center of the same milpa and throws into it an olla of unsweetened *chilate*" (Wisdom 1940: 439–440). Similar rites are known for contemporary Puebloan peoples. During the Zuni planting ceremony, there is much attention paid to the four directions and center: "The planter goes to a well-known spot near the center of the field and digs equally distant from a central point four deep holes in the four directions. By the left side of the northern hole he digs another to represent the zenith and by the right side of the southern hole still another to represent the nadir. In the center he sprinkles a cross of meal, to represent the cardinal points. . . . In each hole he plants seed corn of the proper color-direction . . . chanting a refrain at each hole as he drops the grains" (Parsons 1939: 791–792). The incised celt scenes of the Olmec Maize God standing between four celtiform maize ears indicates that the directional symbolism so widely found with maize fields was fully present among the Middle Formative Olmec.

If the Southwestern corn imagery and ritual are a reflection of ancient ceremonialism of Formative Mesoamerica, the question remains: how did it get there? It will be recalled that the spread of agriculture in Formative Mesoamerica coincides with the development of an elaborate Olmec ceremonial complex devoted to maize and agricultural fertility. Monumental portrayals of explicit maize iconography at such far-flung sites as Chalchuapa, Xoc, and Teopantecuanitlán suggest that the dissemination of this Formative cult of fertility was not casual but intentional and may have served to integrate distant lands into the Olmec economic network. Although it is unreasonable to suggest that the Olmecs ever approached the region of the American Southwest, maize fetishes and ritual celts were essential parts of the symbolic language of corn in Middle Formative Mesoamerica. The appearance of markedly similar elements in Pueblo ceremonialism suggests that the early spread of corn into the Southwest was more than a casual transmission of seed and farming methods; it also involved a rich ceremonial complex, much of which survives in contemporary ritual and symbolism of the American Southwest.

NOTES

1. Among the more striking traits of the male quetzal are its wings, which have elongated, emerald green upperwing covert feathers, which contrast dramatically with the red chest (see Howell and Webb 1995: pl. 33, no. 3). The entire effect of these feathers is much like a hand with spread and elongated fingers, like the Olmec paw-wing motif.

2. Although J. Eric Thompson (1970: 284) noted that jade was related to maize in Maya thought, he based this on an oblique passage in the Chilam Balam of Chumayel. Following Thompson's original insight, there has been little interest in the Maya identification of jade with corn, although it was subsequently noted that the jade jewelry worn by the Maya Maize God may refer to qualities of the plant (Taube 1985: 174).

3. Double maize ear fetishes may have been present at Classic Teotihuacán. Long ago, William Holmes (1915) suggested that the curious "candeleros" at Teotihuacán may have been the bases of maize ear fetishes and compared them to the cups forming the bases of Hopi maize fetishes (see fig. 25b–c). Holmes noted that the Teotihuacán ceramic items are frequently double-chambered, quite possibly to hold a pair of maize ears similar to the Aztec examples. In the collections of the Museo Nacional de Antropología in Mexico City there is a double maize ear fetish stone sculpture from Tlamacalco, Guerrero. Although of uncertain age, it is quite possibly pre-Aztec (see Díaz Oyarzábal 1990: 195).

4. On the north, or Tlaloc side, of the Templo Mayor, Chamber III contained two large polychrome urns filled with greenstone beads and other items (López Luján 1994: 322–323). The urns portray Chicomecoatl on one side and Tlaloc on the other. Within this buried chamber, these urns may refer to Chicomecoatl dwelling in her underworld home of Tlalocan.

5. It is possible that the Formative maize fetishes also held seeds of other plants. One of the Olmec fetishes depicted at Chalchuapa, El Salvador, has an eyelike item on the base that is very similar to later Zapotec depictions of bean seeds (fig. 15d). The same element also appears on the aforementioned serpentine maize form possibly from Oaxaca (fig. 12f).

6. At Jemez, New Mexico, crossed circles are considered as "hearts of the world" (see Brody 1991: fig. 115).

7. At Casas Grandes, plumed serpents are commonly rendered with bead collars marked as a series of squares containing a single dot. As early as Pueblo IV, this same convention is used to represent corn kernels on maize cobs (see Smith 1952: fig. 68).

8. In a far-ranging essay devoted to Olmec religion, Karl Luckert (1976: 153–156) previously compared Olmec celt symbolism to the Hopi use of *chamahiya*. However, rather than relating Olmec celts to either the four directions or ears of corn, Luckert (1976: 156) regarded the Olmec celts as symbolic serpent teeth.

9. A probable representation of a *chamahiya* celt oriented bit upward occurs in a seventeenth-century kiva mural from Gran Quivira, New Mexico (see Hayes et al. 1981: fig. 74).

10. The stone cones appear to embody the concept of maize hills or mountains (Smith 1952: 228). Elsie Parsons (1939: 194) notes that the Laguna conical *chamahiya* represent mountains, and, among the Hopi, conical maize ear images of stone or wood are considered as corn mountains (Parsons 1936b: 512–513).

BIBLIOGRAPHY

Adams, Karen R.
1994 A Regional Synthesis of *Zea mays* in the Prehistoric American Southwest. In *Corn and Culture in the Prehistoric New World,* ed. Sissel Johannessen and Christine Hastorf, 273–302. Boulder, Colo.

Alcina Franch, José, Miguel León-Portilla, and Eduardo Matos Moctezuma
1992 *Azteca — Mexica.* Madrid.

Angulo, Jorge
1987 The Chalcatzingo Reliefs: An Iconographic Analysis. In *Ancient Chalcatzingo,* ed. David Grove, 132–158. Austin.

The Art Museum
1995 *The Olmec World: Ritual and Rulership* [exh. cat., The Art Museum, Princeton University]. Princeton.

Benson, Elizabeth P.
1971 *An Olmec Figure at Dumbarton Oaks.* Washington.

Benson, Elizabeth P., and Beatriz de la Fuente
1996 (Editors) *Olmec Art of Ancient Mexico* [exh. cat., National Gallery of Art]. Washington.

Berjonneau, Gerald, Emile Deletaille, and Jean-Louis Sonnery
1985 *Rediscovered Masterpieces of Mesoamerica: Mexico-Guatemala-Honduras.* Boulogne.

Berlin, Brent, Dennis E. Breedlove, and Peter H. Raven
1974 *Principles of Tzeltal Plant Classification: An Introduction to the Botanical Ethnography of a Mayan-Speaking People of Highland Chiapas.* New York.

Berrin, Kathleen
1988 (Editor) *Feathered Serpents and Flowering Trees: Reconstructing the Murals of Teotihuacan* [exh. cat., Fine Arts Museums of San Francisco]. San Francisco.

Berrin, Kathleen, and Esther Pasztory
1993 (Editors) *Teotihuacan: Art from the City of the Gods* [exh. cat., Fine Arts Museums of San Francisco]. London and New York.

Beyer, Hermann
1969 Una pequeña colección de antigüedades mexicanas. *El México Antiguo* 11: 177–221. Mexico City.

Bierhorst, John
1992 *History and Mythology of the Aztecs: The Codex Chimalpopoca.* Tucson, Ariz.

Black, Mary E.
1984 Maidens and Mothers: An Analysis of Hopi Corn Metaphors. *Ethnology* 23(4): 279–288.

Blake, Michael, Brian S. Chisholm, John E. Clark, Barbara Voorhies, and Michael W. Love
1992 Prehistoric Subsistence in the Soconosco Region. *Current Anthropology* 33: 83–94.

Blake, Michael, John E. Clark, Barbara Voorhies, George Michaels, Michael W. Love, Mary E. Pye, Arthur A. Demarest, and Barbara Arroyo
1995 Radiocarbon Chronology for the Late Archaic and Formative Periods on the Pacific Coast of Southeastern Mesoamerica. *Ancient Mesoamerica* 6: 161–183.

Blinkenberg, Christopher
1911 *The Thunderweapon in Religion and Folklore: A Study in Comparative Archaeology.* Cambridge.

Bohannan, Paul, and George Dalton
1962 Introduction. In *Markets in Africa,* ed. Paul Bohannan and George Dalton, 1–26. Evanston, Ill.

Bohrer, Vorsila L.
1994 Maize in Middle American and Southwestern United States Agricultural Traditions. In *Corn and Culture in the Prehistoric New World,* ed. Sissel Johannessen and Christine Hastorf, 469–512. Boulder, Colo.

Broda, Johanna
1996 Paisajes rituales del Altiplano central. *Arqueología Mexicana* 4(20): 40–49.

Brody, J. J.
1991 *Anasazi and Pueblo Painting.* Albuquerque, N.M.

Bullé Goyri, Alfonso
1987 (Editor) *Cacaxtla.* Text by Eduardo Matos Moctezuma and photographs by Rafael Doniz. Mexico City.

Cervantes, María Antonieta
1969 Dos elementos de uso ritual en el arte olmeca. *Anales del Instituto Nacional de Antropología e Historia,* 7th series, 1: 37–51. Mexico City.

Clark, John E., and Michael Blake
1989 El origen de la civilización en Mesoamérica: Los olmecas y mokaya del Soconusco de Chiapas, México. In *El preclásico o formativo: Avances y perspectivas,* ed. Martha Carmona, 385–403. Mexico City.

Clewlow, Carl William, Jr.
1968 Comparisión de dos extraordinarios monumentos olmecas. *Boletín del Instituto de Antropología e Historia* 34: 7–41.

Coe, Michael D.
1965 Archaeological Synthesis of Southern Veracruz and Tabasco. In *Archaeology*

of Southern Mesoamerica, Part 2, ed. Gordon Willey, 679–715. Handbook of Middle American Indians, vol. 3. Austin.

Coe, Michael D., and Richard A. Diehl
1980 *In the Land of the Olmec,* 2 vols. Austin.

Corona Núñez, José
1964 *Antigüedades de México,* 4 vols. Mexico City.

Cyphers, Ann
1996 San Lorenzo, Veracruz. *Arqueología Mexicana* 4(19): 62–65.

Dalton, George
1977 Aboriginal Economies in Stateless Societies. In *Exchange Systems in Prehistory,* ed. Timothy Earle and Jonathon Ericson, 191–212. New York.

D'Altroy, Terence, and Timothy K. Earle
1985 Staple Finance, Wealth Finance, and Storage in the Inka Political Economy. *Current Anthropology* 26: 187–206.

de la Fuente, Beatriz
1977 *Los hombres de piedra: Escultura olmeca.* Mexico City.

Díaz Oyarzábal, Clara Luz
1990 *Colección de objetos de piedra, obsidiana, concha, metales y textiles del Estado de Guerrero.* Mexico City.

Diehl, Richard A.
1990 The Olmec at La Venta. In *Mexico: Splendors of Thirty Centuries,* ed. Kathleen Howard, 51–71 [exh. cat., Metropolitan Museum of Art]. New York.

di Peso, Charles
1974 (Editor) *Casas Grandes: A Fallen Trading Center of the Gran Chichimeca, Volume 4.* Dragoon and Flagstaff, Ariz.

Dorsey, George A., and Henry R. Voth
1902 The Mishongnovi Ceremonies of the Snake and Antelope Fraternities. *Field Columbian Museum Anthropological Series* 3(3): 159–261. Chicago.

Drucker, Philip
1952 *La Venta, Tabasco: A Study of Olmec Ceramics and Art,* Bureau of American Ethnology Bulletin 153. Washington.

Drucker, Philip, Robert F. Heizer, and Robert J. Squier
1959 *Excavations at La Venta, Tabasco, 1955.* Bureau of American Ethnology Bulletin 170. Washington.

Durán, Fray Diego
1971 *Book of the Gods and Rites and the Ancient Calendar,* ed. and trans. Fernando Horcasitas and Doris Heyden. Norman, Okla.

Eliade, Mircea
1964 *Shamanism: Archaic Techniques of Ecstasy.* Princeton.

Ellis, Florence Hawley
1967 Use and Significance of the Tcamahia. *El Palacio* 74: 35–43.

Fash, Barbara
1992 Late Classic Architectural Sculpture Themes in Copan. *Ancient Mesoamerica* 3: 89–104.

Fash, William L.
1988 A New Look at Maya Statecraft from Copan, Honduras. *Antiquity* 62 (234): 157–169.

Fedick, Scott L.
1995 Indigenous Agriculture in the Americas. *Journal of Archaeological Research* 3(4): 255–303.

Feuchtwanger, Franz
1989 *Cerámica olmeca.* Mexico City.

Fewkes, Jesse Walter
1897 Tusayan Snake Ceremonies. In *Sixteenth Annual Report of the Bureau of American Ethnology for the Years 1894–1895,* 267–312. Washington.

1900 Tusayan Flute and Snake Ceremonies. In *Nineteenth Annual Report of the Bureau of American Ethnology for the Years 1897–1898,* 957–1011. Washington.

1924 The Use of Idols in Hopi Worship. *Annual Report of the Smithsonian Institution, 1922.* Publication 2724: 377–398. Washington.

1986 *Hopi Snake Ceremonies.* Albuquerque, N.M.

Fields, Virginia
1991 The Iconographic Heritage of the Maya Jester God. In *Sixth Palenque Round Table, 1986,* ed. Virginia Fields, 167–174. Norman, Okla.

Flannery, Kent V., and James Schoenwetter
1970 Climate and Man in Formative Oaxaca. *Archaeology* 23: 144–152.

Fondo Editorial de la Plástica Mexicana
1964 *Flor y canto del arte prehispánico de México.* Mexico City.

Freidel, David, Linda Schele, and Joy Parker
1993 *Maya Cosmos: 3,000 Years on the Shaman's Path.* New York.

Furst, Peter T.
1994 The Maiden Who Ground Herself: Myths of the Origin of Maize from the Sierra Madre Occidental, Mexico. *Latin American Indian Literatures Journal* 10: 101–155.

1995 Shamanism, Transformation, and Olmec Art. In *The Olmec World: Ritual and*

Rulership, 69–81 [exh. cat., The Art Museum, Princeton University]. Princeton.

Gay, Carlo T. E.
1972 *Chalcacingo*. Portland, Ore.

Geertz, Armin W.
1984 A Reed Pierced the Sky: Hopi Indian Cosmography on Third Mesa, Arizona. *Numen* 31(2): 216–241.

1987 *Hopi Indian Altar Iconography*. Leiden.

Gossen, Gary
1974 *Chamulas in the World of the Sun: Time and Space in a Maya Oral Tradition*. Cambridge, Mass.

Graham, Ian
1986 *Uaxactun*. Corpus of Maya Hieroglyphic Inscriptions, vol. 5, pt. 3. Cambridge, Mass.

Graham, John A., Robert F. Heizer, and Edwin M. Shook
1978 Abaj Takalik 1976: Exploratory Investigations. *Contributions of the University of California Archaeological Research Facility* 36: 85–109. Berkeley.

Grove, David C.
1984 *Chalcatzingo: Excavations on the Olmec Frontier*. London and New York.

Guiteras-Holmes, Calixta
1961 *Perils of the Soul: The World View of a Tzotzil Indian*. New York.

Hall, Robert L., and Arthur E. Dennis
1986 Cultivated and Gathered Plant Foods. In *Archaeological Excavations at Antelope House*, ed. Donald Morris, 110–141. Washington.

Harmer Rooke Galleries
1985 *Fine Pre-Columbian Art from the Collections of Mr. and Mrs. Peter G. Wray*. New York.

Hayes, Alden C., and James Lancaster
1975 *Badger House Community*. Washington.

Hayes, Alden C., Jon Nathan Young, and A. H. Warren
1981 *Excavation of Mound 7, Grand Quivira National Monument, New Mexico*. Washington.

Hellmuth, Nicholas
1987 *Monster und Menschen in der Maya-Kunst*. Graz.

Hernández Xolocotzi, Efraim
1985 Maize and Man in the Greater Southwest. *Economic Botany* 39: 416–430.

Hibben, Frank C.
1975 *Kiva Art of the Anasazi at Pottery Mound*. Las Vegas, Nev.

Holmes, William H.
1915 Problems of the Twin Cups of San Juan Teotihuacan, Mexico. *Art and Archaeology* 1(5): 210.

Howell, Steve N. G., and Sophie Webb
1995 *A Guide to the Birds of Mexico and Northern Central America*. Oxford.

Jones, Christopher
1983 Monument 26, Quirigua, Guatemala. In *Quirigua Reports*, Robert Sharer, general editor, vol. 2, no. 13: 118–128. Philadelphia.

Jones, Christopher, and Linton Satterthwaite
1982 *The Monuments and Inscriptions of Tikal: The Carved Monuments*. Tikal Report, no. 33, pt. A. Philadelphia.

Joralemon, Peter David
1971 *A Study of Olmec Iconography*. Washington.

1976 The Olmec Dragon: A Study in Pre-Columbian Iconography. In *Origins of Religious Art and Iconography in Preclassic Mesoamerica*, ed. Henry Nicholson, 27–71. Los Angeles.

1988 The Olmec. In *The Face of Ancient Mesoamerica: The Wally and Brenda Zollman Collection of Precolumbian Art*, 9–50. Bloomington, Ind.

1996 In Search of the Olmec Cosmos: Reconstructing the World View of Mexico's First Civilization. In *Olmec Art of Ancient Mexico*, ed. Elizabeth Benson and Beatriz de la Fuente, 51–59 [exh. cat., National Gallery of Art]. Washington.

Judd, Neil M.
1954 *The Material Culture of Pueblo Bonito*. Washington.

Kelley, David Humiston
1976 *Deciphering the Maya Script*. Austin.

Kerr, Justin
1994 *The Maya Vase Book: A Corpus of Rollout Photographs of Maya Vases*, vol. 4. New York.

Laughlin, Robert
1977 *Of Cabbages and Kings: Tales from Zinacantán*. Washington.

Lombardo de Ruiz, Sonia
1996 El estilo teotihuacano en la pintura mural. In *La pintura mural prehispánica de México: Teotihuacán, Vol. 1, tomo 2*, ed. Beatriz de la Fuente, 3–64. Mexico City.

López Luján, Leonardo
1994 *The Offerings of the Templo Mayor of Tenochtitlán*. Niwot, Colo.

Lowe, Gareth W.
1981 Olmec Horizons Defined in Mound 20, San Isidro, Chiapas. In *The Olmec and*

Their Neighbors, ed. Elizabeth Benson, 231–255. Washington.

Luckert, Karl W.
1976 *Olmec Religion: A Key to Middle America and Beyond.* Norman, Okla.

McDonald, Andrew
1983 *Tzutzuculi: A Middle-Preclassic Site on the Pacific Coast of Chiapas, Mexico.* Provo, Utah.

Maler, Teobert
1901 *Researches in the Central Portion of the Usumatsintla Valley.* Cambridge, Mass.

Malinowski, Bronislaw
1922 *Argonauts of the Western Pacific: An Account of Native Enterprise and Adventure in the Archipelagos of Melanesian New Guinea.* London.

1934 Stone Implements in Eastern New Guinea. In *Essays Presented to C. G. Seligman,* ed. Edward Evans-Pritchard, Raymond Firth, Bronislaw Malinowski, and Isaac Schapera, 189–196. London.

Marcus, Joyce
1989 Zapotec Chiefdoms and the Nature of Formative Religions. In *Regional Perspectives on the Olmec,* ed. Robert Sharer and David Grove, 148–197. Cambridge.

Martínez Donjuán, Guadalupe
1985 El sitio olmeca de Teopantecuanitlán en Guerrero. *Anales de Antropología* 22: 215–226. Mexico City.

Medellín Zenil, Alfonso
1971 *Monolitos olmecas y otros en el Museo de la Universidad Veracruzana.* Mexico City.

Miller, Arthur
1982 *On the Edge of the Sea: Mural Painting at Tancah-Tulum, Quintana Roo, Mexico.* Washington.

Morris, Earl H.
1939 *Archaeological Studies in the La Plata District: Southwestern Colorado and Northwestern New Mexico.* Washington.

Nagao, Debra
1985 The Planting of Sustenance: Symbolism of the Two-Horned God in Offerings from the Templo Mayor. *Res: Anthropology and Aesthetics* 10: 5–27.

Navarrete, Carlos
1974 *The Olmec Rock Carvings at Pijijiapan, Chiapas, Mexico, and Other Pieces from Chiapas and Guatemala.* Provo, Utah.

Nicholson, Henry B.
1977 An Aztec Stone Image of a Fertility Goddess. In *Pre-Columbian Art History: Selected Readings,* ed. Alana Cordy-Collins and Jean Stern, 145–162. Palo Alto, Calif.

Nicholson, Henry B., and Eloise Quiñones Keber
1983 *Art of Aztec Mexico: Treasures of Tenochtitlan* [exh. cat., National Gallery of Art]. Washington.

Ochoa, Lorenzo, and Marcía Castro-Leal
1986 *Archaeological Guide of the Park Museum of La Venta.* Villahermosa, Tabasco, Mexico.

Pahl, Gary W.
1977 The Iconography of an Engraved Olmec Figurine. In *Pre-Columbian Art History: Selected Readings,* ed. Alana Cordy-Collins and Jean Stern, 35–42. Palo Alto, Calif.

Parsons, Elsie Clews
1920 Notes on Ceremonialism at Laguna. *Anthropological Papers of the American Museum of Natural History* 29(4): 85–131. New York.

1932 Isleta, New Mexico. In *47th Annual Report of the Bureau of American Ethnology for the Years 1929–1930,* 193–466. Washington.

1936a (Editor) Early Relations between Hopi and Keres. *American Anthropologist* 38: 554–560.

1936b (Editor) *Hopi Journal of Alexander M. Stephen,* 2 vols. New York.

1939 *Pueblo Indian Religion,* 2 vols. Chicago.

Pasztory, Esther
1983 *Aztec Art.* New York.

Porter, James B.
1996 Celtiform Stelae: A New Olmec Sculpture Type and Its Implication for Epigraphers. In *Beyond Indigenous Voices: LAILA/ALILA 11th International Symposium on Latin American Indian Literatures (1994),* ed. Mary Preus, 65–72. Lancaster, Pa.

Preuss, Konrad Theodor
1907 Die Hochzeit des Maises und andere Geschichten der Huichol-Indianer. *Globus* 91: 185–192.

Redfield, Robert, and Alfonso Villa Rojas
1934 *Chan Kom: A Maya Village.* Washington.

Reilly, Frank Kent, III
1994 Visions to Another World: Art, Shamanism, and Political Power in Middle Formative Mesoamerica. Ph.D. dissertation, Department of Art History, University of Texas, Austin.

Riley, Carroll L.
1963 Color-direction Symbolism: An Example of Mexican-Southwestern Contacts. *América Indígena* 23: 49–60.

Rinaldo, John B.
1974 Medio Period Stone Artifacts. In *Casas Grandes: A Fallen Trading Center of the*

Gran Chichimeca, Volume 7, Charles di Peso, general editor, 38–481. Dragoon and Flagstaff, Ariz.

Roberts, Frank H. H.
1932 *The Village of the Great Kivas on the Zuñi Reservation, New Mexico.* Bureau of American Ethnology Bulletin 111. Washington.

Rohn, Arthur H.
1971 *Mug House: Wetherill Mesa Excavations, Mesa Verde National Park—Colorado.* Washington.

Rust, William F., and Barbara F. Leyden
1994 Evidence of Maize Use at Early and Middle Preclassic La Venta Olmec Sites. In *Corn and Culture in the Prehistoric New World*, ed. Sissel Johannessen and Christine Hastorf, 181–201. Boulder, Colo.

Sahagún, Fray Bernardino de
1950–1982 *Florentine Codex: General History of the Things of New Spain*, trans. Arthur Anderson and Charles Dibble. Santa Fe, N.M.

Sánchez Gónzalez, José Jesús
1994 Evidence of Maize Use at Early and Middle Preclassic La Venta Olmec Sites. In *Corn and Culture in the Prehistoric New World*, ed. Sissel Johannessen and Christine Hastorf, 135–156. Boulder, Colo.

Sandstrom, Alan
1991 *Corn Is Our Blood: Culture and Ethnic Identity in a Contemporary Aztec Indian Village.* Norman, Okla.

Saville, Marshall H.
1929 Votive Axes from Ancient Mexico. *Indian Notes* 6(3): 266–299. Museum of the American Indian, Heye Foundation. New York.

Schele, Linda, and Mary Ellen Miller
1986 *The Blood of Kings: Dynasty and Ritual in Maya Art.* New York and Fort Worth.

Seler, Eduard
1902–1923 *Gesammelte Abhandlungen zur Amerikanischen Sprach- und Altertumskunde*, 5 vols. Berlin.

1963 *Comentarios al Códice Borgia*, 3 vols., trans. Mariana Frenk. Mexico City.

Sharer, Robert J.
1994 *The Ancient Maya*, 5th ed. Stanford, Calif.

1995 Excavation of Early Classic Royal Architecture at Copan, Honduras. Report submitted to the Foundation of Mesoamerican Studies, Crystal River, Fla.

Sharer, Robert J., Chistopher Jones, Wendy Ashmore, and Edward Schortman
1979 The Quirigua Project: 1976 Season. In *Quirigua Reports*, ed. Wendy Ashmore, Robert Sharer, general editor, vol. 1, no. 5: 45–73. Philadelphia.

Shelton, Anthony A.
1996 The Girl Who Ground Herself: Huichol Attitudes towards Maize. In *People of the Peyote: Huichol Indian History, Religion, and Survival*, ed. Stacy Schaefer and Peter Furst, 451–467. Albuquerque, N.M.

Shook, Edwin M., and Robert F. Heizer
1976 An Olmec Sculpture from the South (Pacific) Coast of Guatemala. *Journal of New World Archaeology* 1(3): 1–8.

Smith, A. Ledyard
1982 Major Architecture and Caches. In *Excavations at Seibal*, Gordon Willey, general editor. Memoirs of the Peabody Museum of Archaeology and Ethnology 15(1). Cambridge, Mass.

Smith, Watson
1952 *Kiva Mural Decorations at Awatovi and Kawaika-a.* Papers of the Peabody Museum of American Archaeology and Ethnology 15(1). Cambridge, Mass.

Sotheby's
1990 *Pre-Columbian Art*, 12 November 1990. Sotheby's, New York.

Stevenson, Matilda C.
1894 *The Sia.* 11th Annual Report of the Bureau of American Ethnology for the Years 1889–1890. Washington.

1904 *The Zuni Indians: Their Mythology, Esoteric Fraternities, and Ceremonies.* 23rd Annual Report of the Bureau of American Ethnology for the Years 1901–1902. Washington.

Stirling, Matthew W.
1942 *The Origin Myth of Acoma and Other Records.* Bureau of American Ethnology Bulletin 135. Washington.

Stone, Andrea
1995 *Images from the Underworld: Naj Tunich and the Tradition of Maya Cave Painting.* Austin.

Stuart, David
1996 Kings of Stone: A Consideration of Stelae in Ancient Maya Ritual and Representation. *Res: Anthropology and Aesthetics* 29–30: 148–171.

Taube, Karl
1985 The Classic Maya Maize God: A Reappraisal. In *Fifth Palenque Round Table, 1983*, ed. Merle Greene Robertson, 171–181. San Francisco.

1995 The Rainmakers: The Olmec and Their Contribution to Mesoamerican Belief and Ritual. In *The Olmec World*, 83–103 [exh. cat., The Art Museum, Princeton University]. Princeton.

1996 The Olmec Maize God: The Face of Corn in Formative Mesoamerica. *Res: Anthropology and Aesthetics* 29–30: 39–81.

Tedlock, Dennis
1996 *Popol Vuh: The Mayan Book of the Dawn of Life,* rev. ed. New York.

Thompson, J. Eric S.
1970 *Maya History and Religion.* Norman, Okla.

Thomson, Charlotte
1975 A Study of Olmec Art. Ph.D. dissertation, Department of Anthropology, Harvard University, Cambridge, Mass.

Vogt, Evon Z.
1976 *Tortillas for the Gods: A Symbolic Analysis of Zinacanteco Rituals.* Cambridge, Mass.

von Winning, Hasso, and Nelly Gutiérrez Solana
1996 *La iconografía de la cerámica de Río Blanco, Veracruz.* Mexico City.

Voth, Henry R.
1901 The Oraibi Powamu Ceremony. *Field Columbian Museum Anthropological Series* 3(2): 61–158. Chicago.

1903 The Oraibi Summer Snake Ceremony. *Field Columbian Museum Anthropological Series* 3(4): 262–358. Chicago.

Wheeler, Richard P.
1980 Stone Artifacts and Minerals. In *Long House, Mesa Verde National Park, Colorado,* George Cattanach, Jr., senior author, 243–306. Washington.

White, Leslie A.
1942 *The Pueblo of Santa Ana, New Mexico.* Menasha, Wisc.

1943 *New Material from Acoma.* Bureau of American Ethnology Bulletin 136. Washington.

1962 *The Pueblo of Sia, New Mexico.* Bureau of American Ethnology Bulletin 184. Washington.

Wisdom, Charles
1940 *The Chorti Indians of Guatemala.* Chicago.

Woodbury, Richard B.
1954 *Prehistoric Stone Implements of Northeastern Arizona.* Papers of the Peabody Museum of American Archaeology and Ethnology 34. Cambridge, Mass.

Notes on Contributors

PHILIP J. ARNOLD III is associate professor of anthropology at Loyola University Chicago. He has carried out archaeological and ethnoarchaeological fieldwork in southern Veracruz, Mexico, since 1982. His most recent book, edited with Barbara L. Stark, is *Olmec to Aztec: Settlement Patterns in the Ancient Gulf Lowlands* (1997).

JOHN E. CLARK is associate professor of anthropology at Brigham Young University and director of the New World Archaeological Foundation. He has worked in Mesoamerica for more than two decades, principally with Formative cultures and on issues of ancient lithic technology, obsidian trade, political economy, and social complexity. His most recent edited book is *Los Olmecas en Mesoamerica* (1994).

BEATRIZ DE LA FUENTE is emeritus professor and former director of the Instituto de Investigaciones Estéticas, Universidad Nacional Autónoma de México. Her work on the Olmec includes *Escultura monumental olmeca* (1973), *Las cabezas colosales olmecas* (1975), and *Los hombres de piedra* (1977). Her most recent edited books are *Olmec Art of Ancient Mexico*, with Elizabeth P. Benson, and *La pintura rural prehispánica en México: Teotihuacan* (both 1996).

RICHARD A. DIEHL is professor of anthropology and director of the Alabama Museum of Natural History at the University of Alabama, Tuscaloosa. He has directed numerous archaeological field investigations in central Mexico and southern Veracruz since 1961. He is currently finishing a book on the Olmecs.

SUSAN D. GILLESPIE is an archaeologist and ethnohistorian at the University of Illinois at Urbana-Champaign. Her excavation projects include the Olmec monument workshop at Llano del Jícaro, Veracruz, Mexico. She has published on Mesoamerican art, Maya social organization, and Aztec ethnohistory, most notably *The Aztec Kings* (1989).

DAVID C. GROVE is professor of anthropology at the University of Illinois at Urbana-Champaign. His archaeological research at Chalcatzingo, from 1966 to the present, was the subject of his two books on that site: *Chalcatzingo: Excavations on the Olmec Frontier* (1984) and *Ancient Chalcatzingo* (1987). His research interests also include Formative period art and iconography.

RICHARD G. LESURE is assistant professor of anthropology at the University of California, Los Angeles. His work focuses on ideology and social practice in early sedentary villages, and he has conducted archaeological excavations in Early Formative sites in Chiapas, Mexico. Currently he is engaged in a comparative study of anthropomorphic figurines in Formative cultures of the New World.

CHRISTINE NIEDERBERGER is an archaeologist at the Instituto Nacional de Antropología e Historia, Mexico, where she teaches paleoecology and archaeology. Her publications include *Zohapilco* (1976), "Early Sedentary Economy in the Basin of Mexico" (1979), and "Mesoamerica: Genesis and First Developments" (1996).

PONCIANO ORTIZ is a researcher at the Instituto de Antropología, Universidad Veracruzana, Mexico. He has conducted fieldwork in several areas of Veracruz and at Tres Zapotes and Laguna de los Cerros. He has received grants from the National Geographic Society and Harvard University and was codirector, with María del Carmen Rodríguez, of the Proyecto Manatí in Veracruz.

ESTHER PASZTORY is professor of art history and archaeology at Columbia University. She is the author of *Aztec Art* (1983), *Teotihuacan: An Experiment in Living* (1997), and *Pre-Columbian Art* (1998). She is currently exploring the western construction of the "primitive" and is planning an exhibit entitled "The Classical and Exotic in Mexico: J. F. Waldeck, 1766–1875."

CHRISTOPHER A. POOL is assistant professor of anthropology at the University of Kentucky. He has conducted fieldwork in southern Veracruz since 1983 and has directed the archaeological survey of Tres Zapotes since 1995. His publications include *Ceramic Production and Distribution* (1992), edited with George J. Bey III, and articles on ceramic technology and household archaeology.

MARY E. PYE received a doctorate in anthropology from Vanderbilt University in 1995. She was a Pre-Columbian fellow at Dumbarton Oaks in 1992 and a research assistant at the National Gallery of Art, Center for Advanced Study in the Visual Arts, 1995–1997. She is now working on a project examining Olmec interaction in the Pacific Coast region of Mesoamerica.

MARÍA DEL CARMEN RODRÍGUEZ is a researcher at the Instituto Nacional de Antropología e Historia, Mexico. She has conducted fieldwork in several areas of Veracruz, as well as in Chiapas and Oaxaca. She has received grants from the National Geographic Society and Harvard University and was codirector, with Ponciano Ortiz, of the Proyecto Manatí in Veracruz.

BARBARA L. STARK is a professor of anthropology at Arizona State University, Tempe, and has completed more than three decades of research in Mesoamerica. Her publications focus on ceramics and on the regional economic and social development of ancient societies in the Gulf lowlands. She has served on the executive boards of the American Anthropological Association and the Society for American Archaeology.

STACEY SYMONDS holds a doctorate in anthropology from Vanderbilt University and has been working in Mesoamerican archaeology since 1997 in both the Maya and Olmec regions. She is an adjunct professor at the Instituto de Investigaciones Antropológicas, Universidad Nacional Autónoma de México, and since 1991 has been affiliated with the San Lorenzo Regional Archaeological Project.

KARL TAUBE is professor of anthropology at the University of California, Riverside. An archaeologist specializing in the art, writing, and religious systems of ancient Mesoamerica, he has published *The Major Gods of Ancient Yucatan* (1992), *Aztec and Maya Myths* (1993), and, with Mary Ellen Miller, *Gods and Symbols of Ancient Mexico and the Maya* (1993). His *Olmec Art at Dumbarton Oaks* is in press.

Studies in the History of Art

Published by the National Gallery of Art, Washington

This series includes: Studies in the History of Art, collected papers on objects in the Gallery's collections and other art-historical studies (formerly *Report and Studies in the History of Art*); Monograph Series I, a catalogue of stained glass in the United States; Monograph Series II, on conservation topics; and Symposium Papers (formerly Symposium Series), the proceedings of symposia sponsored by the Center for Advanced Study in the Visual Arts.

[1] *Report and Studies in the History of Art,* 1967

[2] *Report and Studies in the History of Art,* 1968

[3] *Report and Studies in the History of Art,* 1969 [In 1970 the National Gallery of Art's annual report became a separate publication.]

[4] *Studies in the History of Art,* 1972

[5] *Studies in the History of Art,* 1973 [The first five volumes are unnumbered.]

6 *Studies in the History of Art,* 1974

7 *Studies in the History of Art,* 1975

8 *Studies in the History of Art,* 1978

9 *Studies in the History of Art,* 1980

10 *Macedonia and Greece in Late Classical and Early Hellenistic Times,* edited by Beryl Barr-Sharrar and Eugene N. Borza. Symposium Series I, 1982

11 *Figures of Thought: El Greco as Interpreter of History, Tradition, and Ideas,* edited by Jonathan Brown, 1982

12 *Studies in the History of Art,* 1982

13 *El Greco: Italy and Spain,* edited by Jonathan Brown and José Manuel Pita Andrade. Symposium Series II, 1984

14 *Claude Lorrain, 1600–1682: A Symposium,* edited by Pamela Askew. Symposium Series III, 1984

15 *Stained Glass before 1700 in American Collections: New England and New York (Corpus Vitrearum Checklist I),* compiled by Madeline H. Caviness et al. Monograph Series I, 1985

16 *Pictorial Narrative in Antiquity and the Middle Ages,* edited by Herbert L. Kessler and Marianna Shreve Simpson. Symposium Series IV, 1985

17 *Raphael before Rome,* edited by James Beck. Symposium Series V, 1986

18 *Studies in the History of Art,* 1985

19 *James McNeill Whistler: A Reexamination,* edited by Ruth E. Fine. Symposium Papers VI, 1987

20 *Retaining the Original: Multiple Originals, Copies, and Reproductions.* Symposium Papers VII, 1989

21 *Italian Medals,* edited by J. Graham Pollard. Symposium Papers VIII, 1987

22 *Italian Plaquettes,* edited by Alison Luchs. Symposium Papers IX, 1989

23 *Stained Glass before 1700 in American Collections: Mid-Atlantic and Southeastern Seaboard States (Corpus Vitrearum Checklist II),* compiled by Madeline H. Caviness et al. Monograph Series I, 1987

24 *Studies in the History of Art,* 1990

25 *The Fashioning and Functioning of the British Country House,* edited by Gervase Jackson-Stops et al. Symposium Papers X, 1989

26 *Winslow Homer,* edited by Nicolai Cikovsky Jr. Symposium Papers XI, 1990

27 *Cultural Differentiation and Cultural Identity in the Visual Arts,* edited by Susan J. Barnes and Walter S. Melion. Symposium Papers XII, 1989

28 *Stained Glass before 1700 in American Collections: Midwestern and Western States (Corpus Vitrearum Checklist III),* compiled by Madeline H. Caviness et al. Monograph Series I, 1989

29 *Nationalism in the Visual Arts,* edited by Richard A. Etlin. Symposium Papers XIII, 1991

30 *The Mall in Washington, 1791–1991,* edited by Richard Longstreth. Symposium Papers XIV, 1991

31 *Urban Form and Meaning in South Asia: The Shaping of Cities from Prehistoric to Precolonial Times,* edited by Howard Spodek and Doris Meth Srinivasan. Symposium Papers XV, 1993

32 *New Perspectives in Early Greek Art*, edited by Diana Buitron-Oliver. Symposium Papers XVI, 1991

33 *Michelangelo Drawings*, edited by Craig Hugh Smyth. Symposium Papers XVII, 1992

34 *Art and Power in Seventeenth-Century Sweden*, edited by Michael Conforti and Michael Metcalf. Symposium Papers XVIII (withdrawn)

35 *The Architectural Historian in America*, edited by Elisabeth Blair MacDougall. Symposium Papers XIX, 1990

36 *The Pastoral Landscape*, edited by John Dixon Hunt. Symposium Papers XX, 1992

37 *American Art around 1900*, edited by Doreen Bolger and Nicolai Cikovsky Jr. Symposium Papers XXI, 1990

38 *The Artist's Workshop*, edited by Peter M. Lukehart. Symposium Papers XXII, 1993

39 *Stained Glass before 1700 in American Collections: Silver-Stained Roundels and Unipartite Panels (Corpus Vitrearum Checklist IV)*, compiled by Timothy B. Husband. Monograph Series I, 1991

40 *The Feast of the Gods: Conservation, Examination, and Interpretation*, by David Bull and Joyce Plesters. Monograph Series II, 1990

41 *Conservation Research*. Monograph Series II, 1993

42 *Conservation Research: Studies of Fifteenth- to Nineteenth-Century Tapestry*, edited by Lotus Stack. Monograph Series II, 1993

43 *Eius Virtutis Studiosi: Classical and Postclassical Studies in Memory of Frank Edward Brown*, edited by Russell T. Scott and Ann Reynolds Scott. Symposium Papers XXIII, 1993

44 *Intellectual Life at the Court of Frederick II Hohenstaufen*, edited by William Tronzo. Symposium Papers XXIV, 1994

45 *Titian 500*, edited by Joseph Manca. Symposium Papers XXV, 1994

46 *Van Dyck 350*, edited by Susan J. Barnes and Arthur K. Wheelock Jr. Symposium Papers XXVI, 1994

47 *The Formation of National Collections of Art and Archaeology*, edited by Gwendolyn Wright. Symposium Papers XXVII, 1996

48 *Piero della Francesca and His Legacy*, edited by Marilyn Aronberg Lavin. Symposium Papers XXVIII, 1995

49 *The Interpretation of Architectural Sculpture in Greece and Rome*, edited by Diana Buitron-Oliver. Symposium Papers XXIX, 1997

50 *Federal Buildings in Context: The Role of Design Review*, edited by J. Carter Brown. Symposium Papers XXX, 1995

51 *Conservation Research 1995*. Monograph Series II, 1995

52 *Saint-Porchaire Ceramics*, edited by Daphne Barbour and Shelley Sturman. Monograph Series II, 1996

53 *Imagining Modern German Culture, 1889–1910*, edited by Françoise Forster-Hahn. Symposium Papers XXXI, 1996

54 *Engraved Gems: Survivals and Revivals*, edited by Clifford Malcolm Brown. Symposium Papers XXXII, 1997

55 *Vermeer Studies*, edited by Ivan Gaskell and Michiel Jonker. Symposium Papers XXXIII, 1998

56 *The Art of Ancient Spectacle*, edited by Bettina Bergmann and Christine Kondoleon. Symposium Papers XXXIV, 1999

57 *Conservation Research 1996/1997*. Monograph Series II, 1997

58 *Olmec Art and Archaeology in Mesoamerica*, edited by John E. Clark and Mary E. Pye. Symposium Papers XXXV, 2000

59 *Hans Holbein: Paintings, Prints, and Reception*, edited by Mark Roskill. Symposium Papers XXXVI*

* Forthcoming